CAMBRIDGE LIBRARY COLLECTION

Books of enduring scholarly value

Technology

The focus of this series is engineering, broadly construed. It covers technological innovation from a range of periods and cultures, but centres on the technological achievements of the industrial era in the West, particularly in the nineteenth century, as understood by their contemporaries. Infrastructure is one major focus, covering the building of railways and canals, bridges and tunnels, land drainage, the laying of submarine cables, and the construction of docks and lighthouses. Other key topics include developments in industrial and manufacturing fields such as mining technology, the production of iron and steel, the use of steam power, and chemical processes such as photography and textile dyes.

Historical Account of the Navigable Rivers, Canals, and Railways, of Great Britain

This account of the waterways and railways of Great Britain covers those transport routes and systems of inland navigation that had been completed or were in construction at the time of publication in 1831. Not to be confused with his polymath namesake, Joseph Priestley (1766–1852) entrenched his expertise as manager of the Aire and Calder Navigation. Here he provides alphabetical entries ranging from the Aberdare Canal in Glamorganshire to the Wyrley and Essington Canal in the Midlands. Details are given regarding location, construction, relevant Acts of Parliament, and even tonnage rates. Published to accompany a huge map of British inland navigation (a smaller version is featured here as the frontispiece), the book became a standard reference work in its day. Shedding light on the development of commercially crucial infrastructure, it remains valuable to readers and researchers interested in the history of British transport and technology.

Cambridge University Press has long been a pioneer in the reissuing of out-of-print titles from its own backlist, producing digital reprints of books that are still sought after by scholars and students but could not be reprinted economically using traditional technology. The Cambridge Library Collection extends this activity to a wider range of books which are still of importance to researchers and professionals, either for the source material they contain, or as landmarks in the history of their academic discipline.

Drawing from the world-renowned collections in the Cambridge University Library and other partner libraries, and guided by the advice of experts in each subject area, Cambridge University Press is using state-of-the-art scanning machines in its own Printing House to capture the content of each book selected for inclusion. The files are processed to give a consistently clear, crisp image, and the books finished to the high quality standard for which the Press is recognised around the world. The latest print-on-demand technology ensures that the books will remain available indefinitely, and that orders for single or multiple copies can quickly be supplied.

The Cambridge Library Collection brings back to life books of enduring scholarly value (including out-of-copyright works originally issued by other publishers) across a wide range of disciplines in the humanities and social sciences and in science and technology.

Historical Account of the Navigable Rivers, Canals, and Railways, of Great Britain

As a Reference to Nichols, Priestley & Walker's
New Map of Inland Navigation,
Derived from Original and Parliamentary Documents
in the Possession of Joseph Priestley, Esq.

JOSEPH PRIESTLEY

CAMBRIDGE
UNIVERSITY PRESS

CAMBRIDGE
UNIVERSITY PRESS

University Printing House, Cambridge, CB2 8BS, United Kingdom

Cambridge University Press is part of the University of Cambridge.

It furthers the University's mission by disseminating knowledge in the pursuit of education, learning and research at the highest international levels of excellence.

www.cambridge.org
Information on this title: www.cambridge.org/9781108069953

© in this compilation Cambridge University Press 2014

This edition first published 1831
This digitally printed version 2014

ISBN 978-1-108-06995-3 Paperback

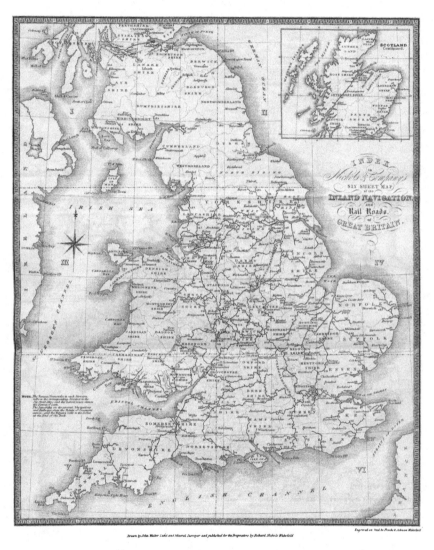

The material originally positioned here is too large for reproduction in this reissue. A PDF can be downloaded from the web address given on page iv of this book, by clicking on 'Resources Available'.

HISTORICAL ACCOUNT

OF THE

NAVIGABLE RIVERS, CANALS,

AND

RAILWAYS,

OF

GREAT BRITAIN,

AS A REFERENCE TO

NICHOLS, PRIESTLEY & WALKER'S

NEW MAP OF INLAND NAVIGATION,

DERIVED FROM ORIGINAL AND PARLIAMENTARY DOCUMENTS

IN THE POSSESSION OF

JOSEPH PRIESTLEY, Esq.

LONDON:

LONGMAN, REES, ORME, BROWN & GREEN, PATERNOSTER-ROW,

G. AND J. CARY, MAP AND GLOBE SELLERS, 86, ST. JAMES'S-STREET,

AND

RICHARD NICHOLS, WAKEFIELD.

MDCCCXXXI.

THE

LARGE SIX SHEET MAP

OF THE

INLAND NAVIGATION AND RAILWAYS,

OF

GREAT BRITAIN,

THE UNINTERRUPTED LABOUR OF SEVEN YEARS,

TO WHICH THIS VOLUME FORMS A REFERENCE,

HAVING RECEIVED THE ESPECIAL PATRONAGE OF THE

LATE KING,

IS NOW,

BY THE NATURAL COURSE OF EVENTS,

AND

WITH PERMISSION,

MOST GRATEFULLY DEDICATED TO

KING WILLIAM THE FOURTH,

BY HIS MAJESTY'S MOST OBEDIENT

AND MOST DEVOTED SUBJECTS AND SERVANTS,

NICHOLS, PRIESTLEY & WALKER.

TO

THOMAS TELFORD, Esq. F.R.S. L.&E.

PRESIDENT OF THE INSTITUTION OF CIVIL ENGINEERS,

TO THE

VICE-PRESIDENTS

AND

MEMBERS

OF THAT SCIENTIFIC AND HIGHLY TALENTED BODY,

THIS WORK,

IS

MOST RESPECTFULLY INSCRIBED,

BY THEIR OBEDIENT SERVANT,

JO. PRIESTLEY.

PREFACE.

THE ORIGIN OF INLAND NAVIGATION, like most other useful discoveries, is involved in great obscurity, and any attempt to ascertain the precise period of the invention or the name of him, who first pointed out the utility of these important adjuncts to the convenience and profit of commercial nations, would be merely to speculate on a subject, which has hitherto bid defiance to conjecture, and which will, in all human probability, for ever remain without satisfactory elucidation. Not so, however, the results to which it has given rise—as the great *Newtonian System of Gravitation* owed its existence to a trifling accident of almost daily occurrence, so the numerous canals, which intersect nearly every country of the civilized world, though they might possibly be traced to circumstances of the same trivial import, are no less remarkable for the astonishing effects they produce and the advantages · they hold out, as well to the industrious artisan as to the enterprising trader.

That the ancient inhabitants of every part of the globe, wherewith history has made us acquainted, were alive in a greater or less degree to the benefits resulting from the adoption of inland navigation, is a fact that may without difficulty be substantiated.

In *India*, particularly in that part of it known to us as the province of *Bengal*, the use of canals was early appreciated; not later than 1355 the *Emperor Ferose III.* made a canal one hundred miles long, from the *River Suttuluz* to the *River Jidger:* in the following years of his reign the same illustrious monarch completed no less than five other canals, all of which were of the greatest utility to the districts through which they passed, inasmuch as they afforded a supply of water for the fertilizing of the lands upon their banks, and an easy conveyance for the produce thus obtained. Nor should the *Ganges* and *Burrampooter* pass unnoticed, since these rivers, with many tributary streams, form a series of natural canals, which, with little aid from the art of man, add at once to the convenience and prosperity of the extensive district through which they flow; and which, we have substantial reasons for concluding, were a principal source of emolument to the people of *India* from a very early period.

In *Egypt*, the great canal, whereby a communication was made between the *Nile* and the *Red Sea*, was commenced so early as the reign of *Necos*, son of *Psammetichus*, and completed by the *Second Ptolemy*. Its breadth was such that two gallies abreast could easily be navigated thereon, and by it the riches and merchandize of the east were conveyed from the *Red Sea* to the *Nile*, from thence to the *Mediterranean*, and to all the commercial nations of that day. The *Nile* also with its numerous branches, and if we may here use the term, its collateral cuts, afforded ample means of water carriage to the people both of *Upper* and *Lower Egypt;* the result of which was an astonishing increase in the commerce, and consequently in the prosperity, of every part to which this mode of conveyance extended.

In *China*, particularly in the eastern provinces of that immense empire, multitudes of canals are every where met with; most of which furnish undeniable evidence of their antiquity and of the skill of their original constructors. The *Royal Canal* which was completed in the year 980 and occupied the labour of thirty thousand men for forty-three years, is a most stupendous monument of the enterprise, ingenuity and perseverance of the ancient *Chinese*. Its length of main line is upwards of eight hundred and twenty-five miles, and innumerable collateral branches are cut from it in every direction. Upon the surface of this canal and its subsidiaries many thousand families live in vessels, which form their travelling habitations, and which they seldom quit from their birth till their decease. And some idea may be formed of the traffic upon it, when it is stated that the Emperor alone has ten thousand vessels constantly employed upon the different parts of its line.

The utility of inland navigation was hardly likely to have escaped the notice of *Greece*, skilled as her ancient people were in every branch of art and science, we accordingly find in history, that though well supplied with rivers, many canals and aqueducts were constructed, or at least begun, in the days of her prosperity. And here it may not be out of place to offer as a conjecture, that canals were in many instances originally adapted to other purposes than those of commerce, and that this latter object was rather an adoption than an invention. Thus the canals, which *Strabo* informs us were cut in *Beotia* for drawing off and keeping at a certain level the waters of *Lake Copais*, were afterwards used for the purposes of commerce and formed a commodious line of navigation. A navigable communication between the *Ionian Sea* and the *Archipelago* was early attempted by the *Greeks*, who designed a line of canal across the *Isthmus* of *Corinth*, but failed in the execution.

Their rivals and, in most cases, successful imitators, the *Romans*, were equally alive to the advantages of inland navigation. No less than three of the Roman Emperors renewed the attempt of cutting a canal across the *Isthmus*, but were obliged to abandon the project.

Drusus, who commanded, under *Augustus*, an army which was to march into *Germany*, had a canal made from the river, now called the *Rhine* to the *Issel*, for the sole purpose of conveying his army upon it. By this canal he lessened the waters of the right branch of the *Rhine*, and in the course of his work formed a third mouth of that river into the sea, as is mentioned by *Pliny*. *Lucius Verus*, when the *Roman Army* under his command was in *Gaul*, attempted a canal between the *Moselle* and the *Rhine;* another canal twenty-three miles in length was made by the *Romans* in the reign of *Claudius*, between the *Rhine* and *Maese*, supposed to be the canal, which now commences at *Leyden* and passes by *Delft* to its junction with the *Maese* at *Sluys*. This is an instance of adoption, the canal being originally cut for the purpose of draining the country when overflowed by inundations from the sea, but subsequently applied to the purposes of navigation. The canal, which is still used for the purposes for which it was constructed, viz. that of draining *Lake Celano*, formerly the *Fucine Lake*, into the *Liris*, was executed by *Claudius*, who employed thirty thousand men thereon for no less a period than twelve years.

In *France* the history of inland navigation may be traced backward for a long succession of years. The great canal of *Burgundy,* better known as the canal of *Briare,* commencing at that town in the *River Loire,* and passing on to *Montargis,* proceeds to a junction with the canal of *Orleans,* and falls into the *Seine* at *Fontainbleau.* This work was commenced under *Henry* the *Fourth.* The famous canal of *Languedoc,* forming a junction between the *Ocean* and the *Mediterranean,* was projected in the reign of *Francis I.* in 1661, and finished in fifteen years; it is remarkable for being the first canal whereon tunnels were used, having one of considerable length under a mountain in the neighbourhood of *Belgiers.* We could easily enlarge the list of *French Canals,* but the above will be sufficient to prove the length of time, during which the utility of such modes of conveyance has been known and acted upon in that country.

In *Russia* the *Czar Peter,* ever alive to projects for the improvement of his vast empire, became soon convinced of the utility of navigable canals; in his tour of *Europe* he had means of ascertaining the extent, to which the various countries he visited were enriched by the instrumentality of these modes of conveyance; and he was not slow to profit by the example. One of his principal projected canals was that from the *Caspian Sea* to *Petersburg,* whereby he proposed to open a mercantile communication between that place and *Persia.* This project, however, he did not live to accomplish. But what he had designed was carried on by his successors with so much zeal, that there is not a country in the world, where inland navigation is more extensively employed than in *Russia.* And here, by the way, we must not omit noticing the high compliment paid by foreign countries to the talents of our English engineers, an instance of which occurred in the reign of the illustrious *Catherine,* who offered a large sum of money and many local advantages to our countryman, *Mr. Smeaton,* on condition of his accepting the office of chief engineer in her dominions.

We cannot within our present limits enumerate all the canals existing in *Russia* at the present day, it may therefore suffice to remark, that with a trifling interruption of only sixty miles, goods may be conveyed from the frontiers of *China* to *Petersburg,* being no less a distance than four thousand four hundred and seventy-two

miles; the same advantages of transit by water are experienced
by the traders between *Petersburg* and *Astracan*, whose merchandize is conveyed in that direction one thousand four hundred and
thirty-four miles.

That *England*, pre-eminent as she is in commerce, should
have promptly availed herself of this method of conveying her
manufactures from one part of the island to another, is hardly
to be wondered at. Her first canals were, however, the works
of foreigners, and amongst these, the most remarkable one on
record is the *Caerdike*, cut by the *Romans* with a view of forming
a communication between the *Rivers Nyne* or *Nene* and the
Witham; the length of this stupendous work, for such it then was,
however it has been exceeded by those of more recent date, was
forty miles from its commencement in the *Nene* near *Peterborough*
to its opening into the *Witham* three miles below *Lincoln*. For
what has been effected from that time to the present day, we
refer to the following pages, and shall now proceed to consider
the other branch of commercial transit, the rail and tramroad.

Of the first adoption of the conveyance of goods on Railways,
we have no distinct account; by whom they were originally
brought into use, and in what part they obtained their celebrity,
are facts alike unknown. To a certain degree they no doubt
have been introduced many years ago; indeed it is not too much
to suppose that the first workers of mines, not only in *Britain*
but in other countries also, were acquainted with the method of
laying a kind of tram for the sledge to run upon, afterwards
fitted with wheels and converted into small waggons; to which
we may trace the origin of our present improved mode of constructing them. But whatever may have been their origin, it
appears that they were soon generally adopted—to a trifling extent, it is true, for during a great part of the time that they have
been known, they have been limited to the conveyance of minerals
from various parts of a mine to its mouth, in places where horses
could not find room, and where the labour of propelling by manual
force would have been particularly tedious and oppressive without
their aid.

As their use became more apparent, the mode of applying
it became more extensively sought into. From their former

situation in the mine, they became a part of the machinery on
the surface, making a communication between one mine and
another, or between a series of mines and the place for depositing
the minerals dug from them ; as they became better understood,
they were made more generally useful, till at last combined with
inclined planes and other machinery connected therewith, they
formed a communication not only between the mines and their
depots, but also between these latter and the vessels, whereon the
minerals were to be embarked for the purpose of conveyance to
distant parts. Here the railway or tramroad appeared to have
reached the extreme point of application, and here for several
years it remained unaltered, except as to some trifling changes in
the materials of which it was constructed, and the form into which
those materials were shaped. But as the other branches of mechanical science became more extended, and particularly when the
application of that powerful agent, Steam, became so generally
practicable, a new era commenced with respect to railways and
tramroads.

We believe we are correct in assigning to *Mr. Treventhick*, of
Cornwall, the honour of first applying the steam engine to the
propelling of loaded waggons on railways; his scheme was improved upon by *Mr. John Blenkinsop*, manager of the collieries at
Middleton, near *Leeds*, belonging to the late *Charles Brandling*,
Esquire, of *Gosforth House*, *Northumberland*, who obtained a
patent for the construction of the railway, and the steam carriage
thereon, which he immediately put in practice on the road from
Middleton to the coal staith at *Leeds*, a distance of about four
miles, on which road the coals for supplying that town are daily
conveyed by steam. Since his application of the principle, most
of our eminent engineers have turned their attention to the subject,
and the consequence is, that in a few years we may expect travelling
in steam carriages to be of as common occurrence as the conveyance of coal by the same means is now. The late experiments,
made with the carriages of *Messrs. Gurney, Stephenson, Errickson,
Braithwaite*, and other celebrated engineers, on the *Liverpool* and
Manchester Railway, have proved with what speed the distance
between different places may be traversed, and the numerous
applications to parliament, for acts to legalize the construction of

railways in many parts of the country, sufficiently prove the interest with which the subject is taken up; whilst from the very circumstance of the rapidity wherewith carriages have been propelled on this railway, it is now probable that ere long his Majesty's mails will be conveyed on the plan introduced by *Mr. Dick.*

It is not our intention in the present work to enter into a detail of the nature and mode of construction of canals, railways, locks, aqueducts or other works connected with them. Having presented our readers with a brief account of the progress of canals and railways from their first adoption to the present day, we must refer to the following sheets for a more particular detail of proceedings in all works of either description, already executed or in course of execution in *England;* and it now only remains for us to discharge a most pleasing part of our duty, that of acknowledging, which we do with most heartfelt gratitude, the support and encouragement we have received in the progress of our arduous undertaking. The work has presented numerous difficulties, of which at the outset we had formed no adequate ideas, whilst the expenses, attendant on the whole, have been materially increased by various circumstances, over which we had no control. Cheered, however, by the gratifying list of our subscribers, amongst whom we are proud to number many of exalted rank and distinguished talent in every branch of science, we have surmounted great difficulties and feel confident of having brought our design to a successful termination. In a work of such a nature, the materials whereof were so widely scattered, it is impossible entirely to guard against error or mistake, yet this we may assert, that every care has been taken to state each particular connected with our plan, on as good authority as the most diligent attention and careful reference to original and parliamentary documents could produce, we are, therefore, willing to hope, that few mistakes of material import will be found in any of the succeeding pages.

In order to bring down the list of Canals and Railways to the time of the dissolution of the late parliament and thereby to furnish the particulars of every act at present in existence, the publication of the map has been delayed, at a great loss indeed to the proprietors, who have a large capital embarked in the undertaking, but, as they are well aware, to the advantage of their subscribers, and to the increased value of the work itself.

To many valued friends the compiler of the following pages has to express his gratitude for information and assistance in various parts within their immediate knowledge. To none of them are his thanks more justly due than to Mr. John Walker, civil engineer, one of the proprietors of the map and the surveyor by whom it has been executed. This gentleman, in the course of his survey of the kingdom, devoted a considerable portion of time to the collection of materials, which have added greatly to the value and interest of the volume now most respectfully presented to the public.

JO. PRIESTLEY.

AIRE & CALDER NAVIGATION OFFICE,
April, 1831.

HISTORICAL ACCOUNT

OF THE

NAVIGABLE RIVERS, CANALS, AND RAILWAYS,

OF

GREAT BRITAIN.

ABERDARE CANAL.

33 George III. Cap. 95, Royal Assent 28th March, 1793.

THIS canal, though limited in its extent, is amongst the first of such as may be adduced in proof of the advantages attendant upon inland navigation. The act for the formation of it is entitled, ' *An* ' *Act for making and maintaining a navigable Canal from the* ' *Glamorganshire Canal, to or near the village of Aberdare, in the* ' *county of Glamorgan, and for making and maintaining a Rail-* ' *way or Stone Road, from thence to or near Abernaut, in the parish* ' *of Cadoxtone-Juxta-Neath, in the said county.*' By this act the company were empowered to raise £22,500, in shares of £100 each, and a further sum of £11,000 was in like manner to be raised, should the expenditure on the works require it.

The Aberdare is connected with the Glamorganshire Canal, at a short distance from the aqueduct, conveying the latter over the River Taff. Its course from the Glamorganshire Canal is along the western side of the Cynon Valley, nearly parallel to the river of that name, and having passed Aberrammon it terminates at Ynys Cynon, about three quarters of a mile from Aberdare, the village from which it derives its name, being from commencement to termination about six miles and a half in length. At the head of the canal near Aberdare there is a railroad, two miles long, to the Llwydcoed Furnaces, from which branches extend to Godleys and Abernaut Furnaces.

The canal is nearly level, to the distance of four miles from its commencement; in the remaining two miles and a half, to its head or termination, there is a rise of 40 feet. The country through which it passes abounds in iron, coal and lime; numerous furnaces and mines are in its immediate vicinity, for the export of the produce of which it was originally undertaken, and which purpose it completely answers, to the evident advantage of the adjoining property.

A

TONNAGE RATES.

	d.	
For Iron, Timber, Goods, Wares, Merchandize, &c.	5 per Ton, per Mile.	
For Iron stone, Iron-ore, Coal, Coke, Charcoal, Bricks, Brick-tile and Slate .... }	2 ditto.	ditto.
For Limestone, Building-stone, Stone, Tile, Lime, Sand, Clay and all Kinds of Manure................................ }	1½ ditto.	ditto
For Cattle, Sheep, Swine and other Beasts...................	5 ditto.	ditto.

Fractions to be taken as for a Quarter of a Ton, and as for a Quarter of a Mile

TRAVELLING ON THE RAILWAYS.

	d.
For every Horse, Mule or Ass	1 per Day.
For Cows and all other Cattle	½ ditto.
For Sheep, Swine and Calves..	5 per Score.

The chief object of this navigation is the export of the produce of the iron furnaces, coal mines and limestone quarries, which abound in the immediate vicinity.

ABERDEENSHIRE CANAL.

36 George III. Cap. 68, Royal Assent 26th April, 1796.
41 George III Cap. 3, Royal Assent 24th March, 1801.
49 George III. Cap. 3, Royal Assent 13th March, 1809.

THIS navigation was executed by a company, incorporated by the name of "The Company of Proprietors of the Aberdeenshire "Canal Navigation," and was opened for the passage of vessels in June, 1805. Its commencement is in the harbour of Aberdeen, on the north bank of the Dee, and in the tideway at the mouth of that river. For a short distance it takes a northern direction, and then proceeds to the east, past the town of Aberdeen, to Wordside, at which place it approaches the southern bank of the River Don, nearly parallel to which it continues its course by Fintray to the town of Kintore: leaving that town to the west, and keeping the western side of the valley of the Don, it opens into that river at Inverurie, near its junction with the water of Urie. The length of this canal is about nineteen miles, and the fall from Inverurie, to low-water-mark in the harbour of Aberdeen, is 168 feet, by seventeen locks. The width of the canal is 23 feet, and its depth averages 3 feet 9 inches.

The first act for executing this useful work is entitled, '*An Act 'for making and maintaining a navigable Canal from the Harbour 'of Aberdeen, in the parish of Aberdeen, or St. Nicholas, into the*

' *River Don, at or near the South End of the Bridge over the same,*
' *(adjacent to the Royal Burgh of Inverurie) in the parish of Kin-*
' *tore, all within the county of Aberdeen, North-Britain.*'

By this act the company were authorized to raise £20,000 in
£50 shares, no person to be holder of less than one share, or of
more than forty; and it was further provided that in case of need
£10,000 more might be raised amongst themselves, by the admission of new subscribers or by mortgage : it appears, however,
that the original projectors of the work did not meet with the
anticipated success, for in the year 1801, an application was made
to parliament for an additional act for raising money to complete
the undertaking.

In their application the proprietors stated, that of the £20,000
which they were authorized by their former act to obtain, only
£17,800 had been subscribed, all of which had been expended,
and several debts incurred.

A second act was passed in the 41st George III. cap. 3, (24th
March, 1801), in consequence of the company being unable to
raise more than £17,800 under the former act, and had for its
title, ' *An Act for better enabling the Company of Proprietors of*
' *the Aberdeenshire Canal Navigation, to finish and complete the*
' *same,*' which was to be effected by creating one thousand new
shares of £20 each, bearing an interest of five per cent.

But the proprietors were compelled to apply for a third act,
which was granted in the 49th George III. cap. 3, (13th March,
1809), entitled, ' *An Act for better enabling the Company of Pro-*
' *prietors of the Aberdeenshire Canal Navigation to raise the neces-*
' *sary Fund to complete the same.*' By this act the company were
empowered to raise a further sum of £45,000, upon promissory
notes, under the common seal of the company, bearing interest,
with a power in the holders to become shareholders of £100, in
the ratio of the amount of their respective notes; or, at their option,
they are empowered to raise the said sum by mortgage of
the rates authorized to be collected; or by the granting of
annuities.

The tolls which were granted by the first act, (and which have
not been altered by any subsequent act), are recited in the following page :—

TONNAGE RATES.

		d.
For Hay, Straw, Dung, Peat and Peat Ashes, and for all other Ashes intended to be used for Manure, and for all Lime, Chalk, Marl, Clay, Sand, and all other Articles intended to be used for Manure, and for all Materials for the Repair of Roads..	4 per Ton, per Mile.	
For Corn, Flour, Bark, Wood Hoops, Coal, Culm, Coke, Cinders, Charcoal, Iron, Lime, (except what shall be intended to be used for Manure) Stone, Bricks, Slate and Tiles ..	5 ditto.	ditto.
For Timber and other Goods, Wares or Merchandize, not hereinbefore specified	6 ditto.	ditto.

Tolls to be taken for any greater or less Quantity than a Ton, or greater or less Distance than a Mile.

The chief article of conveyance on this canal is granite, great quantities of which are annually exported from the quarries on its banks to London and other parts of the country, by means of its communication with the harbour of Aberdeen, for the improvement of which Mr. Smeaton, and afterwards Mr. Telford, made surveys, preparatory to applications to parliament for powers to execute the same. Acts were accordingly passed in the 13th, 35th, 37th, and 50th of George III. and the harbour is now capable of receiving ships of from 18 to 20 feet draught, adding thereby considerably to the facilities of shipment and consequently increasing the traffic on the canal which opens into it.

ADUR RIVER.

47 George III. Cap. 117, Royal Assent 13th August, 1807.

The Adur River rises about four miles from Horsham, in Sussex, at a distance of thirty-six miles from the Metropolis, and takes a south-easterly course by West Grinstead, and the Baybridge Canal, to Binesbridge, to which place it was rendered navigable for barges drawing 4 feet water, by an act, entitled, '*An Act for im-* '*proving the Navigation of a certain part of the River Adur, and* '*for the better draining the Lowlands lying in the Levels above* '*Beeding-bridge, and below Mock-bridge and Bines-bridge, all in* '*the county of Sussex.*'

From the Baybridge Canal, at Binesbridge, the river takes a southerly course, passing about a mile to the east of the town of Steyning, from thence to New Shoreham; when, passing to the south of the town, it takes an easterly course running parallel with the shore of the English Channel, until it falls into the same at Shoreham Harbour, a distance of about fourteen miles from Binesbridge.

This river was a very imperfect tideway navigation, previous to the passing of this act, but it is now made navigable for barges drawing 4 feet, although the act only authorizes the trustees, for carrying the same into execution, to make it a 3 feet navigation. Seventy-nine trustees, together with the commissioners of sewers of the Rape of Bramber, were appointed to carry the act into execution. The qualification was the possession of a clear annual rental of £50, or of a personal estate of £1,000.

The funds for carrying on the works for the improvement of this navigation and drainage, were raised by an assessment of two shillings per acre on all lands lying in the level above Beeding-bridge, during the years 1807, 1808, and 1809, under the authority of an act of the 23rd of Henry VIII. and after that such sum as the trustees and commissioners shall deem necessary. They are also empowered to borrow money on security of the tolls, rates, &c.

TONNAGE RATES.

	d.
Between Shoreham Bridge and Beeding Bridge, all Goods, Wares or Merchandize	1 per Ton.
Between Shoreham Bridge and the End of the Navigation at Binesbridge, for Chalk, Dung, Mould, Soil, Compost or other Articles (except Lime) to be used for the manuring of Land...	¼ ditto, per Mile.
For all other Goods, Wares, Commodities or Merchandize	1 ditto. ditto.

The River is free of Toll from Shoreham Harbour to Shoreham Bridge.

AIRE AND CALDER NAVIGATION.

10 & 11 Wil III. C. 19, R A. 4th May, 1699   14 Geo III. C. 96, R A. 14th June, 1774.
1 Geo. IV. C. 39, R.A. 30th June, 1820.   9 Geo. IV. C. 98, R. A. 19th June, 1828.

THE rendering these rivers applicable to the purposes of commerce forms one of the most important features in the history of our inland navigation, and as they were made navigable under an act of parliament, passed above fifty years prior to the date of any enactment for a canal navigation, a brief outline of this extensive and useful undertaking may not prove unacceptable to our readers.

The source of the Aire is in Malham Tarn, a fine sheet of water belonging to Lord Ribblesdale, situate a few miles east of

Settle, in that district of the county of York which is called Craven. After running underground for near a mile from its source, it issues from the base of a perpendicular rock 286 feet high, at the centre of a romantic amphitheatre of limestone called Malham Cove. The stream is at first inconsiderable, and from the magnificent scenery of the cove, whence it emerges, would be little noticed, particularly in dry seasons; but in winter, or when the tarn above is swollen by rains, the aperture at the base of the rocks is insufficient for the stream, and the water pours over the top of the cove in a vast sheet, little if at all inferior to many of the falls of America. From Malham Cove, the Aire runs directly south, by the village of Aire Town, to Cold Coniston, thence turns easterly till it reaches Gargrave; from which place, having been considerably augmented by several lesser streams, now united with it, it pursues an easterly direction passing near to Skipton, by Kildwick, within a short distance of the town of Keighley, through Bingley and Shipley, which latter place is within three miles of Bradford; whence it proceeds, by the picturesque remains of Kirkstall Abbey, to Leeds, having given the name of Aire-dale to the beautiful valley through which it passes. Under the provisions of the act of William III. the date of which is given above, this river was made navigable to the tideway. The act is entitled, ' *An Act for the making and keeping navigable the Rivers Aire and Calder, in the county of York.'*

From Leeds the Aire continues in an easterly direction by Temple Newsam, the seat of the Marchioness of Hertford, and Swillington Hall, the seat of Sir John Lowther, Bart. to Castleford, where it unites with the Calder. The two rivers, after their junction, continue to bear the name of Aire, and passing by Fryston Hall, Ferrybridge, Knottingley, Beal, Haddlesey, Weeland, Snaith and Rawcliffe, join the Ouse a little below the village of Armin, at a short distance from the town of Howden. The authority of the first act extending only to Weeland, the subsequent continuation of the navigation to the Ouse River was under a second act, the title of which will be recited in its proper place. The Aire is not navigable above Leeds; the length of the navigation, from Leeds to the junction with the Calder, is about eleven miles and a quarter, in which distance there is a fall of 43¾ feet by six locks. From the junction of the two rivers to Weeland, the distance is eighteen miles and a quarter, with a fall of $34\frac{1}{2}$ feet by four locks, making the total length of navigation from Leeds to Weeland near thirty miles. On this part of the line of navigation are several short canals, railroads, &c. the property of individuals, who have made them for the easier conveyance of the produce of their estates to the banks of the river; as for instance, at Fairburn, a canal, the property of Lord Palmerston, a quarter of a mile long, level with the river, for the use of his lordship's extensive lime and gypsum quarries. Mr. Watson and Mr. Haxby, at Brotherton, have each one, about one furlong and one chain in length; from Mr. Haxby's canal a short railway is carried to the lime-quarries, north of Brotherton; near to the west end of Crier Cut, close to the Leeds Race Course, there is a railway and staith for conveying and shipping the coal from Lord Stourton's collieries on Rothwell Haigh; near Knowstrop there is a railway from the Marchioness of Hertford's collieries, at Waterloo, for the supply of Leeds: there are also railroads at Crier Cut and opposite the Leeds Race Course, for the delivery of coals from this colliery going eastward; near to Methley, a staith and railway from Sir John Lowther's collieries, at Astley ; and in the township of Methley, there is a railway for conveying to the river the coals from the Earl of Mexbro's works; considerable quantities of building-lime are also shipped at Weldon and Fryston. At a short distance above Leeds Bridge is the basin of the Leeds and Liverpool Canal, which locks down at this place into the River Aire, thereby connecting the two navigations.

The source of the Calder is above Todmorden, amongst the hills which constitute the grand ridge, or, as it is popularly termed, the back bone of England, in the same field where the West Calder takes its rise, which in its course westwards, joins the Ribble and enters the Irish Sea. Leaving the hills in which it rises, the Calder pursues an easterly course through the romantic valley of Todmorden, passing the populous hamlets of Hebden Bridge and Sowerby Bridge, to within two miles of Halifax; thence by Elland, Brighouse, Kirklees Park, the seat of Sir George Armytage, Bart. in the vicinity of which a considerable stream, the Colne, falls into it; proceeding thence by Mirfield, the market-town of Dewsbury, and Horbury to Wakefield; at which place this branch of the Aire and Calder Navigation commences. From the navigation warehouse, at Wakefield Bridge, the course of the Calder is by Heath, Newland Park, formerly a preceptory of Knights Templars, but now the seat of Sir Edward Dodsworth, Bart. and Methley, where the Earl of Mexborough has a seat, to its junction with the Aire near Castleford; meandering for the distance of twelve miles and a half through a fertile and delightful valley. The fall from Wakefield Bridge to the union of the two rivers is $28\frac{1}{4}$ feet by four locks, viz. at the Old Mills, Kirkthorpe, Lakes and Penbank. The total length of the navigation from Wakefield to Weeland is thirty-one miles and a half, and the total fall is $62\frac{3}{4}$ feet. A little above Wakefield Bridge are the Calder and Hebble Navigation Warehouses, and, on the opposite side of the river, the Earl of Cardigan's railway, which conveys the coal from his collieries at New Park, two miles from Wakefield. Half a mile below Wakefield the Barnsley Canal locks down into the River Calder. At Bottom Boat, about five miles and a half from Wakefield by the course of the navigation, the Lake Lock Railroad communicates with the river. This road, which was constructed about thirty years ago, by a company, without application to parliament, extends to the East Ardsley Coal-field, a distance of four miles from its junction with the navigation. When it was at first constructed, as its name imports, it joined the river at Lake Lock; it was, however, in 1804, removed to Bottom Boat, a mile lower down the river, to which place from seventy to one hundred thousand tons of coal are now annually brought down by this railroad: and another belonging to the Duke of Leeds, communicating with his collieries on Wakefield Outwood, terminates within a short distance of the former, from which forty or fifty thousand tons of coal are shipped annually.

Though the first act for making this navigation was passed in the year 1699, an attempt for the same purpose had been made long before, for on the 15th of March, 1625, the first year of Charles the First's reign, a bill was brought into the House of Commons, entitled, ' *An Act for the making and maintaining the rivers of* ' *Ayre and Cawldes, in the West Riding of the countye of Yorke,* ' *navigable and passable for Boats, Barges, and other Vessels, &c.*'

This bill was rejected, after a long debate on the question of committing and engrossing; nor does it appear that any further attempt was made for more than seventy years, when Lord Fairfax introduced a similar bill into the House of Commons, on the 18th of January, 1698. Petitions in favour of this bill were presented from the mayor, aldermen, and inhabitants of Leeds, the borough of Retford, King's Lynn, Lincoln, Manchester, the magistrates at the Quarter Sessions at Doncaster, Boroughbridge, the magistrates assembled at Wakefield Quarter Sessions, the clothiers of the town of Rochdale, Rotherham, Halifax, Kendal, clothiers of Wakefield, Bradford and Gainsbro'; and against the bill, from the lord mayor and commonalty of York, also one from Francis Nevill, of Chevet, Esq. the owner of the Soke Mills, at Wakefield.

It was not till the 3rd of April, 1699, that an act passed the House of Lords, and which received the royal assent on the 4th of May following. As some interesting particulars are contained in the petitions presented to the house in respect to the bill of 1698, they are briefly noticed below.

In the Leeds petition it is stated " that Leeds and *Wakefeild* " are the principal trading towns in the north for cloth; that they " are situated on the Rivers Ayre and Calder, which have been " viewed, and are found capable to be made navigable, which, if " effected, will very much redound to the preservation of the high- " ways, and a great improvement of trade; the petitioners having " no conveniency of water carriage within sixteen miles of them, " which not only occasions a great expense, but many times great " damage to their goods, and sometimes the roads are unpassable, " &c. &c."

The clothiers of *Ratchdale* state that they are " forty miles " from any water carriage." The clothiers of *Hallifax*, in their petition, state "that they have no water carriage within thirty " miles, and much damage happens through the badness of the " roads by the overturning of carriages."

The clothiers of Wakefield state "that the towns of Leeds and " *Wakefeild* are the principal markets in the north for woollen " cloth, &c. &c.; that it will be a great improvement of trade to " all the trading towns of the north by reason of the conveniency of " water carriage, for want of which the petitioners send their

" goods twenty-two miles by land carriage, (to Rawcliffe), the
" expense whereof is not only very chargeable, but they are
" forced to stay two months sometimes while the roads are
" passable to market, and many times the goods receive consider-
" able damage, through the badness of the roads by overturning."

The petition of the lord mayor and commonalty of the ancient
city of York, in opposition to the bill, sets forth, " that the said city
" has chiefly its support and advantage by the River Ouze and
" water of Humber, which is a passage for ships and boats from
" York to Hull, and divers parts of this realm ; and that by letters
" patent, 10th Edward IV. (1471) the said petitioners were
" appointed conservators of the River Ayre from the River Ouze
" to Knottingley Mill Dam; and have all along exercised their
" power accordingly; that if the bill pending in the house, for
" making the Rivers Ayre and Calder navigable, should pass, the
" River Ouze will be so drained by such navigation, that no boat
" or vessels will be able to pass thereon, whereby the trade of the
" city of York, carried on by the said River Ouze, will be quite
" carried into other remote parts, and the petitioners' said power
" of conservatorship destroyed, to the impoverishing the said city
" and countries adjacent, and praying that the said bill may not
" pass; the petitioners being ready to offer other reasons against
" the same." The petition of Francis Nevill, of Chevet, Esq.
against the bill, states, that " the petitioner is proprietor of several
" corn, fulling, and rape mills, and dams, upon the River Calder,
" and that by back water his mills will be inevitably stopped from
" going at all, to his great prejudice."

The tolls granted by this act were, from the 1st of May to the
1st of October, any sum not exceeding ten shillings per ton; and
from the 1st of October to the 1st of May, any sum not exceeding
sixteen shillings per ton, for the entire distance between Leeds or
Wakefield, and Weeland, or *vice versa*, and proportionably for any
greater or less weight, or for any less distance than the whole.

In order to carry into execution the powers granted by this
act for making the rivers of Aire and Calder navigable, the
undertakers immediately advanced about £12,000, to which, in
the course of a few years, other sums, to the amount of about
£16,000 were lent and advanced ; these sums, with all the money

which the tolls produced for the first twenty-four years, were laid out in completing the works of navigation. So small was the trade of the country, that in the year 1730, the whole navigation, together with all the property attached thereto, was rented at £2,000 per annum, upon condition that the *Undertakers* themselves should be at the risk of keeping all dams, on the said rivers, good against any accidents.

As the trade of the country increased, it was found expedient to avoid many impediments that took place on several parts of the navigation, some by improperly drawing off the water at the mills; but the most serious inconvenience arose on that part of the river between Weeland and Haddlesey Lock; the course of the navigation to the Ouse, at Armin, was also found very inconvenient for the trade of York, Malton, Boroughbridge, Ripon, and other places in the same direction: a project was therefore commenced in the year 1771, for making an entire new canal from Leeds to Selby, which was surveyed by Mr. Whitworth, at the request of the Leeds and Liverpool Canal Company, and a few gentlemen in Leeds; and an application was made to parliament, to carry the same into execution, by a new set of subscribers; it was, however, successfully opposed by the undertakers of the Aire and Calder Navigation.

In consequence of this application, and " of several memorials " signed by the principal merchants and traders of Leeds, " Wakefield, Halifax, Rochdale, York, Boroughbridge, Lincoln, " Gainsborough, and other places in Yorkshire, Lancashire, " Lincolnshire, and Nottinghamshire, and by many owners and " masters of vessels navigating the Rivers Aire and Calder, " complaining of the frequent and long stoppages in those rivers, " addressed to Sir William Milner and the rest of the undertakers," the undertakers of the Aire and Calder Navigation applied for and obtained a second act, to enable them to make a canal from Haddlesey to Selby, bearing date the 14th of June, 1774, entitled, ' *An Act to amend an Act passed in the Tenth and Eleventh Years* ' *of the Reign of William III. entitled, An Act for the making* ' *and keeping navigable the rivers of Aire and Calder, in the county* ' *of York; and for improving the Navigation of the said River* ' *Aire, from Weeland, to the River Ouze; and for making a*

' *navigable Canal from the said River Aire, at or near Haddlesey,*
' *to the River Ouze at the old Brick Garth at Ouzegate End,*
' *within the township of Selby, in the said county, and for other*
' *Purposes.*' The canal from Haddlesey to Selby, which was
shortly afterwards executed, has been highly advantageous, from
the great additional facilities afforded to the general trade of the
country, as well as by the shortening of the distance to York,
Malton, Boroughbridge, Ripon, and other places.   In a short time
after the passing, and by authority of the above-mentioned act, the
following improvements took place upon the Aire, viz. a cut
near Castleford, to avoid the shoals there, near the mills; a cut,
called the Methley Cut ; another cut, near Thwaite Mill ; a cut,
called Knostrop Cut; and a cut, called Leeds Cut.   The canal
from Haddlesey to Selby was opened for vessels to pass, on the
29th of April, 1778; and all the cuts mentioned above, together
with a new set of locks throughout the navigation, (except
Haddlesey Old Lock), were completed by the year 1785.   This
work, and other improvements, entailed a debt upon the concern
of above £70,000.

Since the year 1800, very considerable sums of money have
been expended in building additional locks, of larger dimensions
than the former ones, so as to admit vessels carrying eighty tons to
navigate these rivers; and within the last ten years, a serious
expenditure has been incurred by the undertakers, in the purchase
of premises at Leeds, in forming a new dock, extending the
wharfage room, and in erecting most spacious warehouses, highly
advantageous to the trade of Leeds.   On the Calder, in the same
time, Kirkthorpe-Dam has been rebuilt in the most complete and
substantial manner.

The tolls on this navigation were very materially reduced by
the second act, viz. from ten shillings per ton in summer, and
sixteen shillings per ton in winter, on all articles, for the whole
line, to the following rates :—

Scale of Tolls authorized to be taken under the Act of 1774

DESCRIPTION OF GOODS.	s.	d.	HOW CHARGED.
Dung or Stable Manure, Coals, Cinders, Slack, Culm, and Charcoal, any sum not exceeding ..	0	½	per Ton, per Mile.
Pigeon Dung and Rape Dust	0	1	ditto ditto.
Lime, if carried up the Rivers or Cuts	0	¾	ditto. ditto.
Ditto if carried down the same	0	½	ditto. ditto.
Pack, Sheet, or Bag of Wool, Pelts or Spetches, not exceeding 312lbs including Sheet..............	0	10½	
For every Quarter of Wheat, Rye, Beans, Oats, Barley and other Grain .... Of Eight Bushels Winchester Measure	0	6	
Malt, Rape, Mustard and Linseed....			
Apples, Pears, Onions and Potatoes, for every Thirty two Pecks.....................	0	9	
Chalk, Fuller's-Earth, Pig-iron, Kelp, Flints, Pipe-Clay, Calais-Sand, and other Sands, (except got in the River) Stone, Bricks, Whiting, Rags and Old Ropes, Lead, Plaister, Alum, Slate, Old Iron, Tiles, Straw, Hay, and British Timber, per Ton	3	0	
Fir, Timber, Deals, Battens, Pipe Staves, Foreign Oak, Mahogany and Beech Logs, per Ton......	3	6	
Flour, Copperas, Wood, Tallow and Ashes, per Ton..	4	0	
Bad Butter or Grease, per Ton	4	3	
Soap, per Ton	5	4	
Bar Iron, per Ton	5	6	
Cheese, per Ton	6	0	
Powder Sugar, Currants, Prunes, Brass and Copper, Argol or Tartar, per Ton.....................	4	8	
Treacle, per Ton	5	9	
Madder, per Ton	6	0	
Cloth Bales, and all other Goods, Wares and Merchandize, per Ton	7	0	

(Right-hand bracketed note:) From Leeds or Wakefield to Selby or Weeland, or *vice versa*—and so in proportion for any greater or less quantity than a Pack, Quarter, Thirty-two Pecks, or a Ton, or for any less Distance than the whole.

The length of the canal, from Haddlesey to Selby, is about five miles, and is level, there being one lock only, at the extremity, into the tideway of the River Ouse, at Selby. The distance from Leeds, by this line of canal, to the Ouse, at Selby, is about thirty miles and a half, on which there are ten locks, and from Wakefield to Selby, the distance is thirty-one miles and a half, on which there are eight locks. The length of an old lock is from 58 to 60 feet, and the width from 14 feet 6 inches to 15 feet, but adjoining to these, are new locks 18 feet wide. The depth of water admits of vessels drawing 5 feet 6 inches: and the improvements, now in execution, will enable vessels of one hundred tons burthen to navigate these rivers.

In the year 1817, and again in 1818, a project was brought forward by a few landholders in that district, for making a canal from Knottingley, down the valley of the Went, to fall into the

River Don, a little above New Bridge; and for extending a branch from the same at Norton, to Doncaster, which threatened serious injury to the trade upon the lower part of the Aire and Calder Navigation: but the hopes of the projectors were totally annihilated, by the undertakers of the Aire and Calder Navigation applying, in the year 1819, to parliament, for an act, to enable them to cut a canal from Knottingley to Goole, (now called the Goole Canal), but in consequence of the king's death, it was not obtained till the middle of June, 1820, as appears from its title, ' *An Act to enable* ' *the Undertakers of the Navigation of the Rivers Aire and Calder* ' *in the West Riding of the county of York, to make a navigable* ' *Cut or Canal from and out of the said Navigation at Knottingley,* ' *to `communicate with the River Ouze, near Goole, with two* ' *collateral Branches, all in the said Riding, and to amend the Acts* ' *relating to the said Navigation.*' This canal, projected by that eminent engineer, the late Mr. Rennie, and surveyed, laid down, and executed, by Mr. G. Leather, was opened in July, 1826. At first it commenced at the Knottingley Cut, but was subsequently extended to Ferrybridge, from which town it passes through Knottingley,·crossing the high road to Snaith, no less than three times in the short distance of three quarters of a mile. It is carried across the road in a very oblique direction, and some of the bridges exhibit that novel style of architecture (designed by Mr. G. Leather, the undertakers' engineer), popularly termed a skew-bridge. From the canal, at the end of the village of Knottingley, there is a short branch-cut to Bank Dole, with a lock of $6\frac{1}{2}$ feet fall into the river. The canal here takes a south-easterly direction, passing Egborough and Heck, (at which place, the Heck and Wentbridge Railway communicates with it), and runs to the south of Snaith, near a place called New Bridge; thence running parallel to the River Dun, or Dutch River, until it reaches its termination at Goole, where it falls into the tideway of the River Ouse.

All the works of this canal (the principal part of which have been executed by Jolliffe and Banks, under the direction of the company's engineer, Mr. G. Leather), are admirably executed; equalled by few and excelled by none in the kingdom.

The original estimate made by Mr. Rennie, for this line of

navigation, amounted to £137,000, but a far greater sum has already been expended; yet the works are not fully completed. The length of the canal from Ferrybridge to Goole is about eighteen miles and a half; the fall to low-water-mark at Goole is $28\frac{3}{4}$ feet; its width is 60 feet at top, and 40 feet at bottom ; the depth is 7 feet, and the locks 70 feet long by 19 feet wide. Goole was, when this work commenced, an obscure hamlet, containing only a few houses; but in the short period of four years, by the erection of extensive buildings, and the nature of the works, connected with the circumstance of its being admitted to all the privileges of a port of the united kingdom, it has grown into a town : it possesses a ship dock 600 feet by 200, and a barge dock of 900 feet by 150. There is also a harbour 250 feet by 200, communicating with the above-mentioned docks, and by two locks with the tideway. These docks are constructed for ships drawing 15 feet water.

The rates of tonnage on the Goole Canal are the same per ton per mile as on the old river navigation; and the accommodations of the port being so little known, from the rapidity with which it has arisen, will be best explained by the following letter :—

CUSTOM-HOUSE, LONDON, August 22nd, 1828.

WHEREAS by an act of parliament made and passed in the sixth year of the reign of his present Majesty King George the Fourth, entitled, " *An Act for the Ware-* " *housing of Goods,*" it is, amongst other things, enacted, that it shall be lawful for the Commissioners of his Majesty's Customs, subject to the authority and directions of the Commissioners of his Majesty's Treasury, by their order, from time to time, to appoint in what warehouses or places of special security, or of ordinary security, as the case may require, in certain ports in the United Kingdom, and in what different parts or divisions of such warehouses or places, and in what manner any goods, and what sort of goods, may be warehoused and kept and secured without payment of any duty upon the first entry thereof, or for exportation only, in cases wherein the same may be prohibited to be imported for home use, and it is by the same act further enacted, that every order made by the said Commissioners of the Customs, in respect of warehouses of special security, as well those of original appointment, as those of revocation, alteration or addition, shall be published in the *London Gazette*, for such as shall be appointed in Great Britain; We, the undersigned Commissioners of his Majesty's Customs, in pursuance of the powers so vested in us, have appointed at the PORT OF GOOLE, a warehouse and vaults, on the east side of the Ship Dock belonging to the AIRE AND CALDER NAVIGATION COMPANY, situate in a yard, inclosed on the north, south, and east sides, by a wall of fifteen feet high, and on the west side (being that next to the lock at the said port) by a fence, consisting of a similar wall, for about fifty-seven feet from each side towards the centre, as warehouses of special security, for the deposit of all articles except tobacco and snuff, under the provisions of the said act.

By order of the Commissioners,

T. WHITMORE, SECRETARY.

PORT OF GOOLE, 1st *September*, 1828.

" The undertakers of the Aire and Calder Navigation avail
" themselves of the promulgation of the above notice, in the *Lon-*
" *don Gazette*, to apprize the public, that the port of Goole is
" thereby placed on a footing of equality with those of London,
" Dublin, and Liverpool, and of superiority to all others in the
" United Kingdom, warehouses of special security being to be
" found in none other: the advantages derivable from bonding
" merchandize in warehouses of special security, will be best un-
" derstood by reference to the 6th of George IV. cap. 112, entitled,
" ' *An Act for the Warehousing of Goods*,' the 37th section of
" which is hereto subjoined."

Act 6. *George IV. Sec.* 37, *Cap.* 112 —"*And whereas some sorts of Goods are liable*
" *in Time to decrease—and some to increase—and some to fluctuation of Quantity*
" *—by the effect of the Atmosphere or other natural Causes, and it may be neces-*
" *sary in some cases, that the Duties should not be charged upon the Deficiency*
" *arising from such Causes ; be it therefore enacted,*

" *That it shall be lawful for the said Commissioners of His Majesty's Treasury to*
" *make Regulations for ascertaining the Amount of such Decrease or Increase of*
" *the Quantity of any particular sort of Goods—and to direct in what Proportion*
" *any Abatement of Duty payable under this Act for Deficiencies shall, upon the*
" *Exportation of any such Goods, be made, on account of any such Decrease,—*
" *Provided always, that if such Goods be lodged in WAREHOUSES declared*
" *in the Order of Appointment to be of SPECIAL SECURITY, no Duty shall be*
" *charged for any Amount whatever of Deficiency of any such Goods, on the*
" *Exportation thereof—Except in Cases where Suspicion shall arise that part of*
" *such Goods has been clandestinely conveyed away, nor shall any such Goods*
" *(unless they be Wine or Spirits) be measured, counted, weighed or gauged for*
" *Exportation, except in such Cases of Suspicion.*"

" The undertakers have the satisfaction to announce, that their
" establishments at Goole are now completed : they consist of the
" warehouse above alluded to, which comprises upwards of seven
" thousand superficial yards of vaults and floors, for the bonding
" of every description of goods and merchandize ; of another ware-
" house for the bonding of foreign grain, which comprises upwards
" of five thousand superficial yards of flooring ; of a pond for the
" reception of timber under bond, capable of receiving upwards
" of three thousand loads; of a range of deal yards, fourteen in
" number; together with spacious sheds, and every other accom-
" modation that modern ingenuity could devise, to promote, as has
" been officially reported by the highest authorities in the kingdom,
" ' the despatch of business, combined with the most ample secu-
" ' rity to the revenue and the merchant also.' "

" For the warehouses and timber pond, general bonds have
" been given, whereby a considerable saving of expense, as well
" as trouble, will accrue to the merchant."

" The undertakers will not now give themselves, or the public,
" the trouble of entering upon a formal answer to the numerous
" misstatements that have been made by interested parties."

" It is sufficient to state, that two years have now elapsed since
" the opening of Goole, and five months since it was declared a
" port for foreign trade, and during that time no accident has
" happened to any of the numerous ships or vessels which have
" been there: every shipowner has manifested the most perfect
" readiness to repeat his engagement with Goole, and the trade
" there is daily increasing."

" The approbation of the public is the best test of the security
" and advantages of the port."

" A steam towing boat, called the " Britannia," of fifty horse
" power, is provided to facilitate the navigation of the Rivers
" Humber and Ouse: her usual station is off the port of Hull,
" where vessels bound for the port of Goole are boarded by the
" boats belonging to the officers of the revenue. The master of
" the " Britannia" is at all times ready to take charge of any ves-
" sel bound to Goole."

In consequence of an application to parliament, by the projectors of another line of communication from Wakefield to Ferrybridge, the undertakers of the Aire and Calder called in Mr.
Telford, who surveyed the country and made an estimate for
shortening and improving the navigation between those two places,
and also between Leeds and Castleford; and on the 19th of June,
1828, their projected improvements were sanctioned by an act,
entitled, ' *An Act to enable the Undertakers of the Navigation of*
' *the Rivers Aire and Calder, in the West Riding of the county of*
' *York, to make certain Cuts and Canals, and to improve the said*
' *Navigation.*' The estimate for this work, including £135,350,
for extending the docks at the port of Goole, exclusive of land
there, amounted to £462,420, and parliament granted a power to
the undertakers to borrow at interest the sum of £750,000. This
work is already in execution, and when completed, the navigation
will be some miles shorter, and the depth of water will be sufficient

to admit vessels of one hundred tons burthen up to the towns of Leeds and Wakefield; and will enable vessels from Leeds and Wakefield to reach Goole in eight hours, and from Manchester within forty-five hours; these vessels are expedited by a steam tug. An elegant steam packet runs daily from Castleford to Goole for the conveyance of passengers.

ALFORD CANAL.

7 George IV. Cap 44, Royal Assent 5th May, 1826

ALFORD, whence this canal takes its name, is a market town on the Lincolnshire coast, five miles in a direct line from the German Ocean, and about equi-distant from Louth and Wainfleet. The canal was designed by Mr. William Tierney Clarke, civil engineer, and the estimated cost of completing it was £36,924, 15s. The act, which received the royal assent on the day quoted above, is entitled, ' *An Act for making and constructing a Canal,* ' *from the town of Alford, in the county of Lincoln, to the Sea, at* ' *or near the village of Anderby, in the said county, with a Basin,* ' *Harbour, and Pier.*'

The canal is 8 feet deep, and is supplied with water from Holywell Spring, and from a drain, or stream, called Boy Grift, from which are feeders communicating with the canal. It enters the sea near the village of Anderby, about a quarter of a mile from low-water-mark; it has a sea-lock, which keeps the surface of the water, in the pool next the sea, $14\frac{2}{3}$ feet above low-water at spring tides, which is equal to high-water-mark, neap tides,—the average spring tide being $18\frac{1}{2}$ feet. From the sea-lock, to another rising $7\frac{3}{4}$ feet, it is level for three miles and a half; thence it is level to the basin of the canal, which terminates half a mile south of Alford, and is rather more than a mile and a half long, making the total length of the canal to low-water-mark six miles and a half.

The subscribers to this canal were incorporated under the name and style of " The Alford Canal Company," and were empowered to raise among themselves a sum, not exceeding £38,000, of which, more than £30,000 was raised before the application to parliament. This sum was divided into seven hundred and sixty shares of £50 each. The proprietors are further empowered to raise a further sum of £15,000, on mortgage of the canal and tolls, or they may borrow the above sum, or any part of it, on promissory notes, under the common seal; or they may borrow exchequer bills of the commissioners for carrying into execution an act of George III. for authorizing the issue of exchequer bills for carrying on of public works, &c.

The management of this concern is in the hands of twelve of the company, who are chosen annually, five of whom are empowered to act.

SCHEDULE OF DUTIES OR DUES,

Payable for, or in respect of, Boats, Craft, Barges, Ships, and Vessels, passing into, or out of, or in, or along, the Harbour, Canal, or Basin.

	s.	d.	
For every Boat, Craft, Barge, Ship, or Vessel, to load or unload	0	2	per Ton, as registered.
For every Foreign Boat entering the Harbour, or Basin, for shelter, waiting for Wind, or Repairs	1	0	ditto. ditto.
For every Boat, Craft, Barge, Ship, or Vessel, belonging to the United Kingdom, entering the Harbour, for shelter, waiting for Wind, or Repairs	0	4	ditto. ditto.
For every Fishing Boat, ditto, ditto,	0	3	ditto. ditto.
For every Boat, Craft, Barge, Ship, or Vessel, remaining in the Harbour, or Basin, more than Twelve Days, unless for Repairs	0	4	per Ton, per Diem.

SCHEDULE OF RATES, TOLLS, AND DUTIES,

Payable for, or in respect of, any Goods, Wares, Merchandize, and Passengers, imported or exported by Boats, Craft, Barges, Ships, or Vessels, passing into, or out of, or in, or along, the Harbour, Canal, or Basin.

	s.	d.	
For Coal, Coke, or Cinders	4	0	per Chaldron, of 32 bushels, imp. meas.
Common or Undressed Bricks	4	0	per Thousand.
Stone, Slate, Lime, Unwrought or Cast Iron, Manure, Bones, Dressed Bricks, Pan, Ridge and Draining Tiles, Tallow, Oil Cakes, Potatoes, Sand and Gravel	4	0	per Ton.
Oak, Elm, Pine, Beech, Fir Timber, Deals, Battens, and Lath Wood	4	0	per Load.
Sugar, Salt, Soap, Candles, Clover Seed, Trefoil Seed, Raw Hides, Spirituous Liquors, Wines, Ale, Porter, Glass and Earthenware	4	6	per Ton.
Wheat, Beans and Peas	1	0	per Quarter.
Barley, Rape or Lineseed	0	10	ditto.
Malt or Oats	0	8	ditto.
Hay, Clover, Straw, Hops, Wool, Feathers, Hair, Tanned Hides, Rags, Oak Bark and Household Goods..	8	0	per Ton.
For all other Goods, Wares or Merchandize	6	0	ditto.
For every Passenger	1	0	

SCHEDULE OF WHARFAGE DUES,

For Goods laid on the Piers, Jetties, Wharf, Quays, or landing places—and of Dues on Goods deposited in Warehouses.

	Wharfage Dues for every Twenty-four Hours.	Warehouse Dues for the first Twenty-four Hours.
	d.	*d*
Coals, Cinders, Coke, Lime, Sand, Gravel, Potatoes, Wheat, Beans, Peas, Barley, Malt, Oats, Clover, Line and Rapeseed, or any other Grain or Seeds	3 per Chaldron,	3 per Chaldron, and 1*d.* per Ton for every following Twenty-four Hours.
Timber, Deals, Battens or Lath Wood......	3 per Load,	3 per Load, and ½*d* do.
Hay, Clover, Straw, Hops, Wool, Feathers, Hair, Tanned Hides, Rags, Oak Bark, and Household Goods	6 per Ton,	6 per Ton, and 1*d.* do.
For all other Goods, Wares or Merchandize	4 ditto.	4 ditto. and ½*d.* do.

This act does not extend to any of his Majesty's ships of war, or any other ship, transport, or packet of his Majesty; or any vessels employed in his Majesty's revenues of customs or excise; or in the employment of the ordnance; or to any ship, transport, or packet employed in carrying the mails of letters and expresses, under the authority of his Majesty's Post-Master General; or any vessel in, or upon, his Majesty's service; or in the conveyance of any officers or soldiers; or any horses, arms, ammunition, or baggage belonging to them; and any person who shall take the benefit of this exemption, not being entitled to it, will incur a penalty of £5.

In 1805, it was in contemplation to effect a navigable communication between Wainfleet Harbour and Alford, a distance of twelve or thirteen miles; but the scheme is now superseded by this canal.

Although this canal has not yet been executed, we may state that its projectors had for their object a more ready transmission of corn, wool, and other agricultural produce, from Alford, and its vicinity, to London and other ports on the eastern shore, and to facilitate the introduction of coals, wares, and merchandize, to Alford and its neighbourhood.

ANCHOLME RIVER NAVIGATION.

7 George III Cap. 98, Royal Assent 20th May, 1767
42 George III. Cap. 116, Royal Assent 26th June, 1802
6 George IV. Cap 165, Royal Assent 22nd June, 1825.

THE Ancholme Navigation commences from the River Humber, at Ferraby Sluice, one mile west of the village of South

Ferraby, and four miles from the market town of Barton-upon-Humber. Hence it proceeds in nearly a straight line south to Glamford Briggs (or Brigg); thence continuing this direction to Bishop Briggs, on the high road from Gainsbro' to Market Raisin. The distance from Ferraby Sluice to where the Caistor Canal falls into the Ancholme Navigation is fourteen miles and a quarter, and from thence to its termination at Bishop Briggs, five miles and a quarter, making the total length nineteen miles and a half, upon which, (with the exception of the sea-lock at Ferraby Sluice), there is only one lock, of 6 feet rise, near to the end of the Caistor Canal.

The first act for completing this navigation, was passed, as stated above, on the 20th of May, 1767; it is entitled, ' *An Act for* ' *the more effectual draining the Lands lying in the Level of* ' *Ancholme, in the county of Lincoln ; and making the River* ' *Ancholme navigable from the River Humber, at or near a place* ' *called Ferraby Sluice, in the county of Lincoln, to the town of* ' *Glamford Briggs, and for continuing the said Navigation up or* ' *near to the said Rivers, from thence to Bishop Briggs, in the said* ' *county of Lincoln.*'

A second act, for altering and enlarging the powers of this act, was passed in the 42nd George III. cap. 116, (June 26, 1802), and is entitled, ' *An Act for altering and enlarging the Powers of an* ' *Act passed in the Seventh Year of the Reign of his present Majesty,* ' *entitled, An Act for the more effectual draining the Lands lying in* ' *the Level of Ancholme, in the county of Lincoln, and making the* ' *River Ancholme navigable from the River Humber, at or near a* ' *place called Ferraby Sluice, in the county of Lincoln, to the town* ' *of Glamford Briggs, and for continuing the said Navigation up or* ' *near to the said River, from thence to Bishop Briggs, in the said* ' *county of Lincoln.*'

This act was succeeded by another, 6th George IV. cap. 165, (22nd June, 1825), entitled, ' *An Act for altering and enlarging* ' *the Powers of Two Acts of his late Majesty King George the Third,* ' *for draining Lands within the Level of Ancholme, in the county of* ' *Lincoln, and making certain parts of the River Ancholme navi-* ' *gable.*'

From the reports of the late Mr. Rennie, made in 1801 and

1802, he estimates that to improve this navigation and drainage, it would cost £63,921, but of which sum only £6,063 related to the navigation.

In the year 1825, Mr. Rennie was again employed to examine this navigation and drainage, with a view to make further improvements. He directed that the sluice at Ferraby should be lowered 3 feet, making it 4 feet above low-water-mark at spring tides; that the river for three hundred yards from the sluice should be widened to 48 feet at bottom, and from thence to Cadney, 30 feet; that a lock of 6 feet rise should be made at Thornton Beck, and the bottom of the navigation, from this lock to Bishop Briggs, to diminish from 20½ feet broad to 15 feet. He estimated those improvements at £69,200.

The navigation and drainage is under the management of commissioners, who have power to raise £5,000, on security of tolls, to be applied for the improvement of the navigation and completing it to Bishop Briggs.

By the act of 6th George IV. it is stated that the sum of £12,000 raised by virtue of the act of 42nd George III. had been expended, and that the commissioners, in addition to this sum, had also incurred a debt of £7,500. To liquidate which debt, and for the further purpose of improving the drainage and navigation, the commissioners have power of raising, by assessment, not more than £3,000 in any one year.

TONNAGE RATES BY THE FIRST ACT.

	s.	d.	
For all Goods, Wares and Merchandize .... {	2	0	per Ton for the whole Length.
Coal .... {	2	0	per Chaldron, of Forty-eight Bushels (Winchester) being estimated and taken as a Ton.
Groceries	4	0	per Ton.
Bricks or Tiles	1	8	per Thousand.
Stone .... {	0	10	per Ton for the whole Navigation, and so in proportion for any less Weight, or less Distance.
Wheat, Rye, Beans, Peas or Lentils..	0	2	per Quarter for the whole Length.
Barley, Malt, Oats and other Grain..	0	1	ditto. ditto.

By the act of 42nd George III. the new rates and dues, substituted in lieu of the above, are as follows:—

NEW RATES AND DUES.

	s.	d.	
On passing the Lock at Ferraby Sluice, for Wheat, Rye, Beans, Peas and Lentils	0	1	per Quarter, and $\frac{1}{4}d.$ per Mile additional—and if they pass through the other Lock, a further charge of $\frac{1}{2}d.$ per Quarter.
Barley, Malt, Oats and other Grain, for passing Ferraby Lock..............	0	1	per Quarter, and $\frac{1}{4}d.$ for every two Miles—and if they pass through the Second Lock, $\frac{1}{4}d.$ per Quarter in addition.
Coals, ditto. ditto.	0	3	per Chaldron, and 1$d.$ per Mile— and 2$d.$ more if they pass the Second Lock.
Lime, ditto. ditto.	0	3	per Chaldron, and 1$d.$ per Mile— and $\frac{1}{2}d.$ for the Second Lock.
Bricks and Tiles, ditto.	0	4	per Thousand, and 1$d.$ per Mile— and 2$d.$ through the Second Lock.
Timber, Iron, Lead, Slate and Plaister ..	0	4	per Ton, and 1$d.$ per Mile—and 2$d.$ through the Second Lock.
Stone	0	3	per Ton, and $\frac{1}{4}d.$ per Mile—and $\frac{1}{2}d.$ for the Second Lock.
Sand	0	$\frac{1}{2}$	per Ton per Mile through the said Navigation.
Groceries, and all other Goods, Wares and Merchandize, not before enumerated, for passing Ferraby Lock..........	0	8	per Ton, and a 1$\frac{1}{2}d.$ per Mile—and 4$d.$ per Ton for the Second Lock.
Manure (when exported) passing through Ferraby Sluice	2	0	per Ton.

The commissioners appointed for directing the affairs of this navigation and drainage are not to be less than eighty in number, whose qualification is a possession, in the level, of one hundred acres of land, or a mortgage upon the tolls, to the amount of £1,000.

The quantity of land liable to be flooded, and consequently to the assessment for drainage, is 17,197A. 3R. 10P.

It is recited in the act of 42nd George III. that the annual amount of tolls on the navigation, was £700. The spring tide at Ferraby Sluice rises 19 feet above the sill of the lock, which is placed 4 feet above low-water-mark, spring tides.

Mr. John Rennie is the engineer to this navigation appointed by the act of parliament.

ANDOVER CANAL.

29 George III. Cap. 72, Royal Assent 13th July, 1789.

THE Andover Canal commences at Barlowes Mill, near the town of Andover, and passing the village of Upper Clatford, proceeds on the western bank of the little River Anton to the

village of Fullerton; thence, after crossing the river, it takes its
direction for a short distance to the Test, which having crossed, it
proceeds on the eastern bank of that river, by the village of
Leckford, to the town of Stockbridge, thence by Compton House,
the villages of Mitchelmersh and Timsbury, to the town of
Romsey; from which latter place, its course is parallel with the
Test River, by Nutshalling to Redbridge, where it enters the
tideway of the Southampton Water. Its length is twenty-two
miles and a half, and its fall from Barlowes Mill to Redbridge is
$176\frac{1}{3}$ feet. The dues upon this canal arise chiefly from the passage
of coal and other fuel from the coast, and from the export of its
surplus agricultural produce.

The engineer employed was Mr. Robert Whitworth, and the
act for completing the same, which received the royal assent, as
stated above, is entitled, '*An Act for making and maintaining a*
'*navigable Canal from or near the borough of Andover, in the*
'*county of Southampton, to or near Redbridge, in the parish of*
'*Millbrook, in the said county.*'

The owners of this navigation are incorporated under the
name of " The Company of Proprietors of the Andover Canal
" Navigation," and they are empowered to raise and contribute
among themselves, for the execution of the work, a sum not
exceeding £35,000, in three hundred and fifty shares of £100
each, with power to raise a further sum of £30,000, if necessary,
for the purpose of carrying on and finishing the work, in the
following manner:—that is, by permitting the original shareholders
to take additional shares to the amount of £10,000, not exceeding
ten additional shares by any original subscriber, and the remaining
£20,000 by mortgage on the credit of the canal rates, tolls, &c.
with interest, not exceeding legal interest. The management of
this concern is placed in the hands of a committee of fifteen
persons annually chosen from among the proprietors.

TONNAGE RATES.

		d.
For Coal, Stone, Timber, Corn, Grain, Malt, Meal, Flour, and other Goods, Wares, Merchandize and Commodities...... }		2 per Ton, per Mile.

And so in proportion for any less Quantity than a Ton.

Vessels not to exceed Eight Feet in Breadth, and Sixty Feet in Length, and not to
draw more than Three Feet Six Inches Water. No Boat or other Vessel to pass a
Lock without paying Rates equal to Fifteen Tons.

At the termination of the canal at Redbridge, and where the same enters the river called Southampton Water, there is a wharf and quay, with warehouses, storehouses, cranes, &c. which, at the time the act was obtained, belonged to the Rev. Sir Charles Mills, Bart.; and, as it appears he was entitled to riverage, wharfage, and storehouse room, for the use of the same, certain rates, as under, were secured to him, or his tenants, by a clause in the act, for all articles conveyed or to be conveyed on the Andover Navigation.

WHARFAGE RATES, PAYABLE AT REDBRIDGE.

	s.	d.	
For Coals not landed, but taken out of, or put into, Vessels to be conveyed on the Canal	0	3	per Chaldron.
For all other Goods or Merchandize	0	1	per Ton.
For Coals landed on the Wharf	0	6	per Chaldron.
Wheat, Flour and Beans so loaded	0	3	per Ten Sacks.
Oats and Malt	0	3	per Ten Quarters.
Barley	0	½	per Quarter.
Timber (including the expense of drawing the same on Shore)	1	0	per Load of 50 Feet.
Stones, Bricks, and all other Goods landed on the Wharf, and not put into the Storehouse	0	3	per Ton.

For all Goods which are landed and warehoused for the space of One Month, the following Rates are allowed, (which includes the Wharfage above, together with the expense of Porterage of such Goods.)

	s.	d.	
Wheat, Flour and Beans	0	6	per Quarter.
Oats, Malt and Grass Seeds	0	3	ditto.
Hogsheads of Sugar, Tallow, Soap, Starch and Tobacco	0	8	per Hogshead.
Vinegar, Spirits, Beer and other Liquors	0	6	ditto.
Butter	0	1	per Firkin.
Larger Casks of Butter	0	1½	each.
Hemp	3	0	per Ton.
Paper	1	0	ditto.
Woollen Rags for Manure	0	3	ditto.
For all other Rags	1	0	ditto.

And for all other Goods in the same proportion.

N.B. Where Cranes are required for loading and unloading, an additional charge, not exceeding Three-pence per Ton.

For putting the powers of the act into execution, one hundred and thirteen commissioners, together with the bailiff and approved men of Andover, were appointed, whose qualification was a clear annual rental of £100, or personal property to the amount of £3,000, unless he be heir apparent to a peer, or be eligible to be elected as a Knight of the Shire.

ARUN RIVER NAVIGATION.

25 George III. Cap. 100, Royal Assent 13th May, 1785.

THE River Arun has its source on the eastern side of the High Downs, called Hind Head, a range of mountains, having an eleva-

tion of 923 feet above the sea, at low water, and at a short distance
north of the town of Haslemere, in the county of Surrey; when,
after taking an easterly course for some miles, it enters Sussex at
Aldfold: whence it takes a southerly direction to New Bridge,
near Billinghurst, where this navigation commences. In its course
from Aldfold, to the last mentioned place, it is crossed several times
by the Wey and Arun Canal. From New Bridge, a canal four
miles and a half long has been cut, in a parallel course with the
Arun, on its western bank, to near Haresfold, where it crosses to
the east side, and continues in that course to Pallenham Wharf,
when the river becomes navigable. From this place it pursues a
southerly direction of two miles and three quarters, to Stopham,
where the Rother, also a navigable river, falls into it: hence,
taking a circuitous route, by Pulborough and Greatham, it reaches
Greatham Bridge, to which place a canal, one mile and three
quarters long, has been cut, in nearly a direct line, from the
junction with the Rother. By this canal, the circuitous course,
above described, is avoided, and five miles saved in the distance
between Stopham and Greatham Bridge. From the latter place,
the river makes several considerable bends to Houghton Bridge,
(a distance of four miles, from the end of the canal), where this
navigation, made under the powers of an act, passed in the 25th
of George III. entitled, ' *An Act for amending and improving the*
' *Navigation of the River Arun, from Houghton Bridge, in the*
' *parish of Houghton, in the county of Sussex, to Pallenham Wharf,*
' *in the parish of Wisborough Green, in the said county ; and for*
' *continuing and extending the Navigation of the said River Arun,*
' *from the said Wharf, called Pallenham Wharf, to a certain*
' *Bridge, called New Bridge, situate in the parishes of Pulborough*
' *and Wisborough Green, in the said county of Sussex,*' ceases.
The length of the river and cuts, belonging to this navigation, is
thirteen miles; but to the sea, at Arundel Port, it is twenty-six
miles and a quarter. The lower portion of this, however, is made
navigable under other powers, and with different provisions, which
will be described under the head of Arun River.

The subscribers to this work, thirty-one in number, were
incorporated as "The Company of Proprietors of the River Arun
" Navigation," within the limits pointed out in the language of the

title of the act before recited, and were authorized to raise amongst themselves, for carrying into execution the said act, the sum of £10,000, by one hundred shares of £100 each, which shares are personal estate.

This canal is navigable for vessels drawing 3 feet 1 inch water, and the following rates of tonnage are allowed:—

TONNAGE RATES.

	s.	d.	
For Timber, Planks, Coal, Lime, Corn, Grain and all other Goods, Wares or Merchandize whatsoever (except Firewood, Chalk, Soil and Dung) from Houghton Bridge to Pallenham Wharf	0	9	per Ton.
Firewood, Chalk, Soil and Dung	0	6	ditto.
For the same Articles (with the exception as above) passing between Pallenham Wharf and the End of the Navigation at New Bridge	2	3	ditto.
The excepted Articles as above	0	6	ditto.
For every Light Barge passing through all or any of the Locks	1	0	ditto.

In clause 14, a novel mode is resorted to for preventing impositions, in regard to the quantity conveyed along this navigation; for it is there enacted, that all boatmen, &c. navigating this river, between Arundel Port and Pallenham Wharf, shall receive, for freight, including dues or rates, as follows:—

	s.	d.	
For Coals	3	6	per Chaldron.
Timber, Planks, Lime, Corn, Grain, Firewood and all other Goods, Wares and Merchandize	3	6	per Ton.
Chalk, Soil and Dung, from Houghton Chalk Pits	13	0	per Barge Load of Eight Tons.

And so in proportion for every Ton of Chalk, Soil and Dung.

A Penalty of £5 is recoverable from any Bargeman before a Justice of the Peace, should he claim any higher Sum than above specified.

No Tolls to be taken for Vessels navigating the Old River Arun between Greatham and Stopham Bridges.

Sea Gravel, brought to repair any of the Roads leading in the direction of New Bridge Wharf, to be exempted from Toll, excepting the Sum of One Shilling per Barge for any of the Locks upon the Navigation.

The affairs of this navigation are managed by a committee of three proprietors, subject to the control of a general assembly of proprietors, held twice a year.

The proprietors have a power, by public auction, to let or demise the rates and dues for any term not exceeding two years.

The original, and chief, object of this navigation was the supply of coal and fuel to the interior, and for the export of agricultural produce; but by the execution of the Wey and Arun Canal, which falls into the Wey, (and thence to the Thames), a direct communication is made with London, and when the Portsmouth and Arundel Canal is completed, a large additional revenue will doubtless be added to this concern, by the receipt of tolls upon marine stores, which, in time of war, may be safely transmitted from the Metropolis, by this conveyance, to the depot at Portsmouth.

ARUN RIVER.

6 George II. Cap. 12, Royal Assent ——— 1732.
33 George III. Cap. 100, Royal Assent 30th April, 1793.

THE navigation, to which the above acts apply, extends from Arundel Port, at the mouth of the Arun, to the town of Arundel, a distance only of five miles and three quarters: but the object of the first act, entitled, ' *An Act for erecting Piers in, and for* ' *repairing and keeping in repair, the Harbour of Littlehampton,* ' *called Arundel Port, in the county of Sussex,*' was not so much the improvement of the navigation as for the harbour, and for the protection of shipping therein.

By this act, commissioners were appointed to cut a new channel, through the sea-beach, at Littlehampton, and other works therein specified, which are here passed over as not coming within the object of the present publication. Tolls were granted for the purpose of repaying the monies which were borrowed for carrying into execution the works designed.

When this was effected, and all arrears of interest paid off, one-half of the said duties were to be taken off, and the other half to be retained, for the purpose of preserving the harbour, and navigation of the river, to the town of Arundel.

In the preamble of the second act, entitled, ' *An Act to explain* ' *and amend an Act made in the Sixth Year of the Reign of his late* ' *Majesty King George the Second, entitled, An Act for erecting* ' *Piers in, and for repairing and keeping in repair, the Harbour of* ' *Littlehampton, called Arundel Port, in the county of Sussex ; and* ' *for empowering the Commissioners, acting under the said Act, to* ' *improve the Navigation of the River Arun, from the said Harbour,* ' *to the town of Arundel, in the said county,*' it is stated that the commissioners have repaid the sums of money, and interest,

expended in constructing the harbour of Littlehampton, under the
act of 6th George II. and that half the duties, therein granted,
have consequently ceased. Under the last act, the same commissioners, as under the original act, are re-appointed to carry
into effect the provisions of the same, and have power to borrow
any sum, not exceeding £2,000, with interest, on an assignment
of the rates, tolls, or duties, authorized to be taken on the said
navigation.

In lieu of the rates granted by the first act, the following are
allowed under the act of the 33rd George III. :—

TONNAGE RATES.

	d.
For Tan or Bark, which shall be imported or exported, laid on board, landed or discharged out of any Ship or Vessel in the Port of Arundel	6 per Ton.
Spars or Ufers	4 per Dozen.
Pipe Staves..	6 per Hundred.
Hogshead Staves	4 ditto.
Barrel Staves..	2 ditto.
Flour and Meal	1½ per Quarter.

The other Duties, not being enumerated, are according to the Act of the
6th George II.

The tolls and duties, after payment of principal and interest of
money borrowed, are to be applied entirely to the keeping of the
harbour and navigation in good preservation. Vessels belonging
to the port of Arundel are exempt from toll or duties, in consideration of the inhabitants of that town and port having expended, on
the harbour, &c. the sum of £28,300. It is also worthy of remark
that they are, on this account, by the above-mentioned act, made
free of the harbours, ports, and havens of Dover, Rye, Ramsgate,
and Sandwich. There is also a clause which reserves to the
Duke of Norfolk, as water-bailiff of the River Arun, all the
privileges he before enjoyed.

Though the powers of the two preceding acts extend only to
Arundel Bridge, yet there is a good tideway navigation to
Houghton Bridge, a distance of seven miles and a half, whence the
Arun River Navigation commences. There is no act of parlia-
ment relating to this portion of the river; it is free of toll. At
Ford, about half way between Arundel Harbour and the town of
Arundel, the Portsmouth and Arundel Canal commences, the
particulars of which will be found in the proper place.

ASHBY-DE-LA-ZOUCH CANAL.

34 George III. Cap. 93, Royal Assent 9th May, 1794.

THIS canal commences from the Coventry Canal, at Marston Bridge, three miles south of the town of Nuneaton, all in the county of Warwick, and after proceeding in a north-easterly direction, for about five miles, it crosses Watling Street, at the Plough Inn, where it enters the county of Leicester. A mile further, there is a cut of two hundred yards in length, to Hinckley Wharf, one mile from the town of Hinckley. Hence the canal proceeds in a northerly direction by Shenton Hall : crossing Bosworth Field, and leaving the town of Market Bosworth a mile to the east, it continues its course to Shackerston, where it crosses the River Sence, passing, on the north of Gopsall Hall, to Snareston Tunnel; a mile beyond which it enters a detached portion of the county of Derby : passing through the village of Measham, it makes a considerable detour, and again enters Leicestershire, near Donisthorpe, and terminates at Oakthorpe Fire Engine, on Ashby Wolds, one mile north-west of the Moira Baths, in the parish of Ashby-de-la-Zouch.

This canal is twenty-six miles and a half in length, and level throughout. It was, together with several railways branching from it, constructed under the authority of an act of parliament, entitled, ' *An Act for making and maintaining a navigable Canal,* ' *from the Coventry Canal, at or near Marston Bridge, in the parish* ' *of Bedworth, in the county of Warwick, to a certain Close in the* ' *parish of Ashby-de-la-Zouch, in the county of Leicester ; and for* ' *continuing the same from thence, in one Line, to the Lime Works, at* ' *Ticknall, in the county of Derby ; and in another Line, to the Lime* ' *Works, at Cloudhill, in the said county of Leicester, with certain* ' *Cuts or Branches from the said Canal.*'

The proprietors of this canal are incorporated under the name of " The Company of Proprietors of the Ashby-de-la-Zouch " Canal," with power to raise £150,000, in fifteen hundred shares of £100 each, and a further sum of £50,000, if the proper execution of the canal and other works should require it.

TONNAGE RATES.

	d.
For Coal, Lime and Slate	1¼ per Ton, per Mile.
Iron-stone, Building-stone, Grinding-stone, Lime-stone, Bricks and Tiles, and for all Cattle, Sheep, Swine and other Beasts	¾ ditto. ditto.
For Cotton, Wool, Hops, Corn, Timber, Bark, Wrought Iron, Cheese, &c..	2 ditto. ditto.

Fractions to be paid as for Half a Mile and as for Half a Ton.

Dung, Ashes, Marl, Clay for Manure, Gravel, Sand, &c. for the purpose of making or repairing any public or private Road, are exempt from Toll.

Boats, only half the Width of the Locks, are to pay for Twenty Tons, unless Two shall pass together; then, not less than Ten Tons each.

By a Clause in the Act, the Coventry Canal Company are entitled to Five-pence per Ton for all Coals, Goods, and Merchandize, carried out of, or into, this Canal, from the Coventry, Oxford, or Grand Junction Canals.

Corn, or other Grain; Sheep, or other Cattle; Iron-stone or Wrought Iron, got or made upon the Banks of the Canal; Dung, Ashes, Marl for Manure, Gravel, Sand, and Stone for Roads, are exempt from the charge of Five-pence per Ton to the Coventry Canal Company.

It appears, that by arrangement with the Leicester Navigation Proprietors, and as an Indemnification for the great Expense they have been at in constructing Railways, &c. to the Coal Works on Thringstone Common, and to those in the parishes of Swannington and Coleorton, that they shall receive Two Shillings and Sixpence per Ton for all Coal, which shall pass a certain place in the lordship of Blackfordby, about Three Miles west of Ashby-de-la-Zouch, to be carried on the Ashby-de-la-Zouch Canal.

The estimate for the whole of the proposed works, made by Messrs. Jessop and Whitworth, February 24th, 1794, amounted to £138,238; but the estimate from Ashby Wolds, to the Coventry Canal, was only £27,316, 11s. 4½d.

The line was set out by Mr. Robert Whitworth, and the whole length was opened in May, 1805.

It is worthy of remark, that the level, from Ashby Wolds, continues uninterrupted along the whole length of this canal, the Coventry, and part of the Oxford Canal, to Hill Morton, a distance of full seventy miles. The company are under a penalty of £50,000 if they abstract any water from the Gopsall Park Estate, or in any way deteriorate the same.

The principal object of this navigation is the export of the produce of the extensive coal and lime works in the neighbourhood of Ashby-de-la-Zouch.

When authority was first obtained, for the making of this canal, it was the intention of the company to have continued the canal to the places mentioned in the title of the act, which would have made the total length of canal about fifty miles, with 252 feet of lockage. They, however, adopted railways for all the branches where lockage was necessary.

RAILWAYS CONNECTED WITH THIS CANAL.

The railway to Ticknall Lime Works, commences at the Ashby-de-la-Zouch Canal, three quarters of a mile south-west of the village of Willesley, in the county of Derby, and at the distance of two miles and a half, passes through the town of Ashby-de-la-Zouch. One mile and a half further, the railway passes under a tunnel, at the end of which the Cloudhill Branch commences; and one mile and three quarters further it enters Derbyshire: whence it is rather more than two miles and a half to Ticknall Lime Works, making the whole distance from the canal eight miles and a half.

The Cloudhill Branch Railway, commencing from the tunnel on the Ticknall Railway, runs in a westerly direction for one mile and a quarter, where a railway, more than half a mile in length, branches northwards to a colliery. A quarter of a mile further, there is another branch, running southwards, about three hundred yards, to a colliery near Park Wood. From hence it takes a northerly course, passing to the west of the village of Worthington, to the Cloudhill Lime Works, a distance of two miles and three quarters, where it terminates. The total distance of this branch is four miles and a quarter.

There is also a railway, of half a mile in length, from a colliery near Moira, to the canal, opposite the Moira Baths.

ASHTON-UNDER-LYNE CANAL.

32 Geo. III. C. 84, R. A. 11th June, 1792.   33 Geo. III. C. 21, R. A. 28th March, 1793.
38 Geo. III. C. 32, R. A. 26th May, 1798.   40 Geo. III. C. 24, R. A. 16th May, 1800.
45 Geo. III. C. 11, R. A. 18th March, 1805.

THE first act for making this canal, authorized the subscribers, who were incorporated under the name of "The Company of "Proprietors of the Canal Navigation, from Manchester to or "near Ashton-under-Lyne and Oldham," to make a canal from Manchester to Fairfield, with a branch to the town of Ashton-under-Lyne, and another branch from Fairfield, to a place called New Mill, near the town of Oldham. This act was entitled, ' *An* ' *Act for making a navigable Canal, from Manchester, to or near*

' *Ashton-under-Lyne and Oldham, in the county Palatine of*
' *Lancaster,*' and under it the company were empowered to raise
£60,000, in six hundred shares of £100 each, with further power
to raise £30,000 among themselves, should the former sum be
insufficient; or they may raise the same by mortgage of the tolls
and duties.

In the following year the company applied again to parliament, and obtained an act, entitled, ' *An Act to enable the Company*
' *of Proprietors of the Canal Navigation from Manchester, to or*
' *near Ashton-under-Lyne, and Oldham, to extend the said Canal*
' *from a place called Clayton Demesne, in the township of Droylsden,*
' *in the parish of Manchester aforesaid, to a place on the Turnpike-*
' *Road in Heaton Norris, leading between Manchester and Stockport,*
' *opposite to the House known by the Sign of the Three Boars' Heads,*
' *and from, or nearly from, a place called Taylor's Barn, in the*
' *township of Reddish, to Denton, at a place called Beat Bank,*
' *adjoining the Turnpike-Road leading between Stockport and Ashton-*
' *under-Lyne ; and also from the intended Aqueduct Bridge, at*
' *or near a place called Waterhouses, in the parish of Ashton-under-*
' *Lyne aforesaid, to a place called Stoke Leach, at Hollinwood, in*
' *the township of Oldham aforesaid ;*' under this act, they were
authorized, in addition to the main line and branches above-
mentioned, to make a branch from Clayton to near the town of
Stockport; another branch from the last-mentioned branch, to the
River Tame, near Beat Bank: and one other branch from the
aqueduct over the Medlock near Waterhouses, to Hollinwood.
Of those intended works, the branch to Beat Bank alone remains
unexecuted. By this act, the company were authorized to raise
an additional sum of £30,000, in shares, among themselves.
After having executed a considerable portion of the works, which
they were authorized to do, under the two preceding acts, and
having expended the several sums of money which they were
empowered to raise, the proprietors found it necessary again to
apply to parliament for further powers, when they obtained a
third act, entitled, ' *An Act to enable the Company of Proprietors*
' *of the Canal Navigation from Manchester, to or near Ashton-*
' *under-Lyne and Oldham, to finish and complete the same, and the*
' *several Cuts and other Works authorized to be made and done by*

c

' them, by the several Acts passed for that Purpose, and for amending
' the said Acts, and granting to the said Company further and other
' Powers.' By this act they were empowered to raise a further
sum of £30,000, by mortgage of the canal and tolls, or on
promissory notes under the common seal of the company, to be
repaid in five years, or in default, the holders of the notes were to
have the option of becoming shareholders to the same amount.

This canal commences on the eastern side of the town of
Manchester, at the end of Dale Street, and near to Piccadilly:
thence passing through the suburbs, it crosses the River Medlock;
thence to near Clayton, where the Stockport Branch commences.
From Clayton the canal proceeds to the village of Fairfield, where
the main line terminates, as described in the act, at a distance from
Manchester of three miles and three quarters, and with a rise of
162 feet 6 inches, by eighteen locks. From Fairfield there is a
branch to the Huddersfield Canal, at the Duckenfield Aqueduct,
near the town of Ashton-under-Lyne. This branch is a little more
than two miles and a half, and is level throughout. There is,
also, a branch to Waterhouses, from Fairfield, where the canal
again crosses the Medlock, by an aqueduct, after it has passed
through a tunnel of considerable extent. This branch is in length
two miles and a half, and is upon the same level as the Ashton
Branch. From the aqueduct the branch is continued to Hollinwood, and from thence by the Werneth Colliery Company, to their
extensive works near to Oldham. The length from the aqueduct,
at Waterhouses, to Hollinwood, is rather more than one mile and
three quarters; and the extension to the collieries is one mile. The
branch from the aqueduct rises 83 feet, by means of eight locks.
From the Hollinwood Branch, one-eighth of a mile from the
aqueduct, is a collateral cut to Fairbottom Colliery, of little more
than a mile in length, and level. The branch from Clayton leaves
the main line between the tenth and eleventh lock from its commencement, and passing by Garton and Reddish, terminates at
Lancashire Hill, on the high-road from Manchester to Stockport,
and but half a mile from the latter place.

In the town and suburbs of Manchester, several collateral cuts
and basins, have been made from this canal to the various wharfs,
quays, and manufactories; thus affording increased facilities to the

trade of this populous and important town and neighbourhood; amongst which, we may enumerate one, a quarter of a mile in length, which proceeds from the west side of Great Ancoats Street, across Mill Street, to Kirby Street, and from which three collateral cuts proceed. A short distance further, on the line of canal, there is another cut, nearly a quarter of a mile in length, which crosses Pollard Street, to the back of the large factories which front into Great Ancoats Street. These short cuts are all on one level.

The canal and branches are made 31 feet wide at top and 15 at the bottom, and in depth 5 feet. The locks are 70 feet long and 7 feet wide.

TONNAGE RATES ALLOWED BY THE FIRST ACT.

		d.	
For Lime, Limestone, Dung, Manure, Clay, Sand and Gravel..		½ per Ton, per Mile.	
Coals, Cannel Coal, Stone, and other Minerals, not passing through Locks .... }	1	ditto.	ditto.
On the same, passing through Locks	2½	ditto.	ditto.
On Timber, and other Goods, not passing through Locks	1	ditto.	ditto.
On the same passing through Locks.........................	1½	ditto.	ditto.

By the act of the 38th George III. cap. 32, the proprietors are allowed the following

RATES OF WHARFAGE.

	d.	
For Coal, Lime, Limestone, Clay, Iron, Iron-stone, Timber, Stone, Brick, Tile, Slate, Flag, Sand and Gravel .... }	1 per Ton.	
On all other Goods	3	ditto.
If such Goods remain more than Three Days	½	ditto.
If more than Ten Days	1	ditto.

By the act, entitled, '*An Act for amending the several Acts* '*passed for making, extending, finishing, and completing the Canal* '*Navigation from Manchester, to or near Ashton-under-Lyne and* '*Oldham, and the several Cuts and other Works authorized to be* '*made and done by the Company of Proprietors of the said Canal* '*Navigation, and for granting to the said Company further and* '*other Powers*,' the proprietors are allowed the following

ADDITIONAL RATES.

	d.
For every Boat, passing a Lock, laden with Lime or Limestone	2
For Wharfage of such Goods as shall not have paid the Company Two-pence, per Ton, Tonnage.. }	1

In the preamble of the last act, relating to this navigation, entitled, '*An Act for enabling the Company of Proprietors of the*

c 2

' *Canal Navigation from Manchester, to or near Ashton-under-Lyne*
' *and Oldham, more effectually to provide for the discharge of their*
' *Debts, and to complete the said Canal, and the Cuts and Works*
' *relating thereto,*' it is stated that the company have raised the
several sums of £60,000, and £30,000, which they were empowered
to do under the act of 32nd George III.; also the further sum of
£30,000, granted under the act of 33rd George III.; also the
sum of £29,977, 17s. in part of the sum of £30,000, which they
were empowered to raise, under the act of 38th George III.; also
the further sum of £8,677, in part of the further sum of £20,000,
granted under the powers of the act of 40th George III.   It is
further stated, that the company have expended all the monies
they have been enabled to raise, amounting to £158,654, 17s. and
that they have contracted debts to a large amount.   By this act,
they are, therefore, empowered to raise a further sum of £40,000,
over and above the several sums already granted, amounting to
£170,000, to enable them to discharge such debts and complete
their works.   The last-mentioned sum of £40,000 to be raised by
creating new and additional shares, or by calls, on original shareholders, of sums not exceeding £10 per share at each call.

This canal connects the towns of Manchester and Ashton-under-
Lyne; and by the Huddersfield Canal, it has communication with
that town, Saddleworth, and the populous clothing districts in that
part of Yorkshire, and is a portion of one of the lines of inland
navigation, which connects the Irish Sea with the German Ocean;
on the one hand through the Huddersfield and Sir John Ramsden's
Canals, the Calder and Hebble and Aire and Calder Navigations,
to the port of Goole, and from thence by the Rivers Ouse and
Humber to the port of Kingston-upon Hull; and on the other
hand, by entering the Rochdale Canal, near its junction with the
Duke of Bridgewater's Canal, and by that navigation to Runcorn,
and from thence, by the River Mersey, to Liverpool.

The town of Manchester derives considerable advantage by the
facility with which this canal and branches supply it with stone and
coal at an easy rate; an immense quantity of the latter article, in
addition to what is required for ordinary purposes, being in daily
requisition for innumerable steam engines in use in the various
manufactories.

AVON RIVER.

17 Charles II. Cap. 12, Royal Assent 2nd March, 1664.

THIS river has its source three miles east of the town of Devizes, in Wiltshire, and after passing Park Shipton, and Rushall, it takes a southerly course along the east-end of Salisbury Plain, passing Enford Priory, Syrencot House, and the town of Amesbury; and two miles to the west of Stonehenge, it proceeds by Lake House, and the ruins of Old Sarum, to New Sarum, or Salisbury, where its stream is considerably augmented, by being united with the little Rivers Wily, the Nadder, and the Bourne. From Salisbury, its course is nearly south, through a delightful country, to the town of Fording Bridge, thence to Ringwood, and to Christchurch Bay, where it falls into the sea.

This river was made navigable, from Christchurch to Salisbury, under the powers of an act of the 17th Charles II. entitled, ' *An* ' *Act for making the River Avon navigable from Christchurch to* ' *the city of New Sarum*,' but the whole of the works having been swept away by a flood, soon after its completion, it was suffered to continue in that ruinous condition until the year 1771, when the celebrated Brindley surveyed its course, and recommended a new canal to be cut parallel with the river.

Though this suggestion of Mr. Brindley's was not carried into execution, some repairs of the old works were commenced; these, however, were so inefficient, as to give rise to the scheme of a canal from Southampton to Salisbury.

When the act was obtained for the above scheme, the River Avon, as a navigation, was abandoned; and it is now navigable only as a tide river, free of toll, for very small vessels only, for the distance of two miles from the sea, with $5\frac{1}{2}$ feet water at spring tides. At other times, the bar, at the entrance of Christchurch Harbour, is an insurmountable obstacle, which may be further inferred from the circumstance that there are but four small vessels belonging to Christchurch.

The length of the original navigation, to Salisbury, was thirty-six miles, viz. from Christchurch to Ringwood, thirteen miles and a half; from thence to Fording Bridge, seven miles and a half; and from thence to Salisbury, fifteen miles.

AVON RIVER.

24 George II. Cap. 39, Royal Assent 22nd May, 1751.
33 George III. Cap. 23, Royal Assent 30th April, 1793.

THIS River Avon commences a mile west of Warwick, where the Rivers Leame and Dove (having previously received the waters of the Sow and Watergall) unite, and take the name of Avon. From the junction of these rivers, the Avon runs close to Warwick, (the county town), washing the walls of the castle, and passing through the princely grounds attached to the same, it takes a circuitous course by The Hill, Charlecote House, Alveston House, and Welcombe, to Stratford-upon-Avon, where it first becomes navigable. A mile from Stratford, it is the boundary between Gloucester and Warwick for about a mile in length; from thence its course continues through the county of Warwick, for the distance of a mile, and again becomes the boundary of Gloucester and Warwick, to Binton Bridges, to which place, from Stratford, the distance is five miles and one-eighth. From Binton Bridges, the Avon is still the county boundary, to Grange: it then passes through a portion of Warwick, to within three quarters of a mile of the junction with the Arrow River, where it again divides the counties of Warwick and Gloucester. The distance from Binton Bridges to the Arrow River is five miles and three quarters. From the Arrow Mouth, the Avon is the division for a mile and a half between Warwickshire and Worcestershire, when it enters the latter county, passing Offenham, to the bridge, at the town of Evesham. The distance from the mouth of the River Arrow, to the latter place, is six miles and a half. From Evesham Bridge, the river almost makes the circuit of the town; then proceeds, in a north-westerly direction, by the Manor-House, and Cracombe House, and by the villages of Fladbury and Wyre Piddle, to the bridge at the town of Pershore. The distance from the latter place to Evesham Bridge is eleven miles and three quarters. From Pershore, to Eckington Bridge, the river makes two or three considerable bends, so that though the distance by the river, between these places, is six miles and a half, yet, by a straight line, it is only two miles and a half. From Eckington Bridge, the river takes a southerly direction, passing Breedon, a little before which, it becomes the boundary between Gloucester and Worcester, and continues to be so to the town of Tewkesbury, where it falls into the River Severn, being in distance, from Eckington Bridge, seven miles and three quarters, and the total distance from Stratford-upon-Avon to the Severn is forty-three miles and three-eighths.

In the preamble of the first act relating to this river, we learn that, for a considerable time previous, it had been navigated, from Stratford, to its junction with the Severn; but that in consequence of frequent disputes between the proprietors of the navigation, and those using the navigation, it became necessary to apply to parliament for an act which should determine the amount of rates and duties to be paid.

The following rates have been paid ever since the river became navigable, and are still received, in addition to the rates which the proprietors of the navigation are empowered to collect, under the powers of the 24th George II.

ANCIENT TOLLS.

d.

For every Barge passing through Tewkesbury Sluice, or Lock, into the Severn .. 6
For every Boat,   ditto.   ditto.   ditto.   3
For every Boat, (except Pleasure Boats), passing through Evesham Sluice 6
For every Boat, Barge, or Vessel, passing up or down the said River—for the } 6
    setting and drawing of every Wear, and at every Wear upon the said River.. }

The following act, 24th George II. cap. 39, 22nd May, 1751, entitled, '*An Act for the better regulating the Navigation of the* '*River Avon, running through the counties of Warwick, Worcester,* '*and Gloucester, and for ascertaining the Rates of Water Carriage* '*upon the said River,*' empowers the proprietors of the navigation to demand the following rates of tonnage :—

TONNAGE RATES AND TOLLS.

Wine, Cider, or Merchants' Goods, of every Kind	Rateage per Ton, in Column marked (*)		
Wheat, Barley, Malt, Beans, Peas, Oats, Maslin, Linseed, Cutlings, Clover, Meal and Flour.....	per Wey,	ditto.	marked (†)
Cast, or Pig Iron, Brick, Stone, Lime, Coopers', Carpenters', Wheelwrights', and other Timber, Boards and Firewood ..	per Ton,	ditto.	marked (‡)
Coal, of every Kind.....	ditto.	ditto.	marked (§)
Bar Iron, Lead, Polished Stone, and all other Things, not particularly specified	ditto.	ditto.	marked (‖)

TONNAGE RATES AND TOLLS.

	(*)	(†)	(‡)	(§)	(‖)
	s. d.	s. d.	s. d.	s. d.	s. d.
From the Severn, near Tewkesbury, or any place between that and Strensham Sluice, to Stratford, or any place between that and Bidford	4 0	3 0	0 10	1 6	1 6
From the Severn, near Tewkesbury, or any place between that and Strensham Sluice, to Bidford, or any place between that and Evesham; or from Bidford, or any place between Evesham and Bidford, to or below Tewkesbury..............	3 4	2 4	0 8	1 6	1 3
From the Severn, near Tewkesbury, or any place between that and Strensham Sluice, to or below Evesham Sluice, and any place between that and Pershore........	2 4	1 8	0 6	1 6	0 10
From the Severn, near Tewkesbury, or any place between that and Strensham Sluice, to Pershore Sluice, and any place between that and Nafford Sluice	1 8	1 4	0 5	1 3	0 8
From the Severn, near Tewkesbury, or any place between that and Strensham Sluice, to Nafford Sluice, or any place between that and Strensham Sluice	1 3	1 0	0 4	0 10	0 6
From the Severn, near Tewkesbury, or any place between that and Strensham Sluice, to Breedon, or to any place between the Severn, or Strensham Sluice, provided the Vessel passes a Sluice......	0 8	0 6	0 2	0 4	0 4
From Stratford, or any place between that and Bidford, to the Severn, near Tewkesbury, or any place between that and Strensham Sluice......	4 0	3 0	0 10	1 6	1 6
From Stratford, or any place between that and Bidford, to Strensham Sluice, or any place between that and Nafford Sluice........................	3 8	2 9	0 9	1 4	1 4
From Stratford, or any place between that and Bidford, to Nafford Sluice, or any place between that and Pershore Sluice	3 4	2 6	0 8	1 3	1 3
From Stratford, or any place between that and Bidford, to Pershore Sluice, or any place between that and Chadbury Mill, or Sluice	3 0	2 3	0 7	1 1	1 0
From Stratford, or any place between that and Bidford, to Chadbury Mill, or Sluice, and any place between that and Harvington Mill............	2 0	1 8	0 6	0 10	0 9
From Stratford, or any place between that and Bidford, to Harvington Mill, and any place between that and Bidford	1 0	0 10	0 3	0 5	0 5
From Stratford, to Bidford, or any place between Bidford or Stratford	0 8	0 6	0 2	0 3	0 3
From Evesham, to Tewkesbury, or the Severn, or to Stratford, or any place between the Severn, or Tewkesbury, and Strensham Sluice; or Stratford, and Luddington Sluice	2 4	1 8	0 6	1 6	0 9
From Evesham, to Strensham Sluice, or Cleeve, or to any place between Strensham Sluice, and Pershore Sluice, or Cleeve, and Bidford........	1 8	1 4	0 4	0 8	0 6
From Evesham, to Bidford, or Pershore, and to any place between Bidford, and Harvington Mill, or Fladbury, and Pershore	1 4	1 0	0 3	0 6	0 5
From Evesham, to Harvington Mill, or Fladbury..	1 0	0 10	0 3	0 5	0 4
From Evesham, to any place between Harvington Mill, or Fladbury, provided such Vessel passes a Sluice	0 8	0 6	0 2	0 3	0 3

For all Goods taken on board at any place between Tewkesbury and Stratford, and unladen before they come to Stratford or Tewkesbury, for which no provision is herein made, the same Rates are hereby fixed from the Place where they are taken on board to Evesham, and from Evesham to the Place where the same shall be landed or unladen, and so in proportion for any greater or less Quantity.

Millers, on the Avon, in consideration of the inconvenience they occasionally sustain, by having to draw off the Water, for the purpose of repairing Sluices, &c. are exempted from Payment of Toll, upon Coals used by their Mills, or for Materials used for Repairs of the same; but if they prefer paying Tonnage, they are entitled to Twenty Shillings per Day, for drawing off Water and during such time the Water is drawn off.

Until the expenses of this act was paid, the extra toll of two shillings and sixpence, for each loaded vessel, was paid at Tewkesbury, Pershore, Evesham, or Stratford, or such other place as the vessel passed through.

This valuable property belonged, originally, to George Perrott, Esq. but it was placed in the hands of trustees, under powers of an act, entitled, ' *An Act for vesting the Navigation of the River Avon,* ' *in the counties of Warwick, Worcester, and Gloucester, &c. and* ' *certain other Estates, late the Property of George Perrott, Esq. in* ' *Trustees, &c.*' but the tolls and duties remain, as settled by the act of the 24th George II.

This river is of infinite advantage to the towns of Pershore, Evesham, and Stratford, and the country adjacent, supplying them with coal and merchandize, and serving to export their surplus agricultural produce.

AVON AND FROME RIVERS.

11 & 12 Wil. III. C. 23, R. A. 11th May, 1700.   22 Geo. II. C. 20, R. A. 26th May, 1749.
43 Geo. III. C. 140, R. A. 11th August, 1803.   46 Geo. III. C. — R. A. 23rd May, 1806.
47 Geo. III. C. 33, R. A. 1st August, 1807.   48 Geo. III. C. 3, R. A. 21st Mar. 1808.
49 Geo. III. C. 17, R. A. 28th April, 1809.

THOUGH the first act relating to the navigation of these rivers occurs in the reign of William the Third, and is entitled, '*An Act* ' *for the better preserving the Navigation of the Rivers Avon and* ' *Frome, and for cleansing, paving and enlightening the Streets of* ' *the city of Bristol,*' yet for several hundred years previous, this river, from the western end of the Avon River Navigation, at Hanham Mills, to the River Severn, King Road, has been, by ancient charters and grants from the crown, in the possession of the mayor, burgesses and commonalty of the city of Bristol, as conservators thereof, and they have, from time immemorial, received rates for wharfage, anchorage, moorage, &c. but as these have been but indifferently defined, several acts of parliament have been obtained for the determining the same, and for other purposes set forth in the respective titles, which will be briefly noticed in their place. The course of that part of the Avon under the jurisdiction of the corporation of Bristol, commencing at Hanham Mills, is in a westerly direction by Crew's Hole, thence skirting the south side of the city of Bristol, through the parish of Bedminster to Redcliffe; thence by Roundham Lodge and Abbots Leigh Park, to the River Severn at King Road. From Hanham Mills to King Road, is in length fifteen miles and a half. Its course formerly lay through the heart of the city, but a new channel for the river has been cut on the south side of Bristol, two miles in length, while the ancient course has been converted into an excellent floating-dock and harbour, which is productive of immense advantages to the commercial population of this enterprizing city.

The River Frome is but a small stream, which rising near the town of Wickwar, in Gloucestershire, passes Iron Acton, and, in its course by Stoke Gifford House, supplies a number of mills and manufactories. It enters on the north side of Bristol, and passing through the centre of the city, falls into the floating-dock, or ancient course of the Avon. The last half mile of its course is used as a dock and harbour, (no other portion being navigable,) and as it is in the very heart of the city, its value may be easily appreciated.

In the year 1749, the corporation obtained an act, entitled, ' An Act for making more effectual an Act passed in the Eleventh ' and Twelfth Years of the Reign of his late Majesty King William ' the Third, for the better preserving the Navigation of the Rivers ' Avon and Frome, &c. ;' but we forbear to enlarge upon the provisions of this act, as the rates of wharfage, anchorage, &c. were not finally ascertained and settled until 1807, when parliamentary sanction was given to an act, entitled, ' An Act for ' ascertaining and establishing the Rates of Wharfage, Cannage, ' Plankage, Anchorage and Moorage, to be received at the lawful ' Quays in the Port of Bristol; for the regulation of the Cranekeepers ' in the said Port ; and for the better regulation of Pilots and ' Pilotage of Vessels navigating the Bristol Channel.'

Under this act the powers granted to the mayor, burgesses and commonalty, by charter, grants from the crown and preceding acts of parliament, are set forth; in which it appears they have jurisdiction down the Severn and Bristol Channel, to the two small islands called the Stipe Holmes and the Flat Holmes, distant from the mouth of the Avon about twenty-three miles; and that they and their lessees are also possessed of all the lawful wharfs and quays in the city and port of Bristol.

RATES OF ANCHORAGE AND MOORAGE.

	s.	d.	
All Coasting Vessels from Ports to the Westward of the Holmes not exceeding Forty Tons Burthen,......................	0	9	each Voyage.
All Coasting Vessels, ditto, at and above Forty Tons	1	6	ditto.

	ANCHORAGE.		MOORAGE.
	s.	d.	d.
All Vessels (except Coasting Vessels) under Thirty Tons	2	6 each,	.. ½ per Ton.
All Vessels, above Thirty Tons, and under One Hundred Tons	5	0 each,	.. ½ ditto.
All Vessels above One Hundred Tons	5	0 each,	.. 1 ditto.

The rates of wharfage, cannage and plankage, are fixed and very particularly enumerated in the first schedule of this act, but as they are arranged under upwards of four hundred heads, our limits will not permit us to do more than refer our readers to the act. Also by the act separate rates are fixed for the landing or shipping, and landing and weighing of goods, wares and merchandize, which are particularly set forth in the second schedule of this act, to which we likewise refer the reader; but the charges in the latter schedule are subject to the control of the magistrates assembled in quarter sessions, who can reduce the rates.

By an act of the 43rd George III. entitled, ' *An Act for* ' *improving and rendering more commodious the Port and Harbour* ' *of Bristol*,' the mayor, burgesses and commonalty of the city of Bristol, and their successors; the master, wardens and commonalty of merchant venturers of the said city, and their successors, and several other persons were incorporated by the name and style of " The Bristol Dock Company," and were empowered to raise among themselves £250,000, in shares of £100 each; and a further sum of £50,000 to be borrowed on the credit of the rates and duties, for the purpose of improving the docks and harbour of Bristol, and for making a canal or entrance-basin in Rownham Mead, to the extent of six acres, with other works therein specified.

But in the preamble of an act which the company obtained in 1806, entitled, ' *An Act to alter and amend an Act passed in the* ' *Forty-third Year of his present Majesty, entitled, An Act for* ' *improving and rendering more commodious the Port and Harbour* ' *of Bristol, and for extending the Powers and Provisions of the* ' *said Act,*' it appears that of the £250,000 authorized to be raised among themselves, they only obtained £235,000, and were wholly unable to obtain any part of the £50,000 which they were authorized to borrow on mortgage. This act, therefore, gives power to the directors nominated for managing the affairs of the Bristol Dock Company, or any five of them, to make a call of £35 per cent. on original shares, (which would increase the capital to £317,250,) to enable them to carry into execution the works recited in the act of 43rd George III. with the alterations and improvements authorized to be made by the last recited act.

The works authorized to be done under the act of 46th George III. consist chiefly of a solid dam across the River Avon, at the Red Cliff, and another between the present course of the Avon, (now the floating-dock,) and the new intended course of the said river; also another dam over the Avon at Totterdown, and for making the westwardmost locks in the Rownham Mead Basin 33 feet wide, instead of 45 and 33 feet.

The power in the act of 43rd Geo. III. to borrow £50,000 on mortgage, is repealed by the above recited act. Persons holding ten shares in this undertaking, are qualified to serve as directors.

Two other acts have been obtained by the Bristol Dock Company, one in the 48th George III. entitled, ' *An Act for* ' *completing the Improvements of the Port of Bristol;*' and another in the following year, entitled, ' *An Act to enable the Bristol Dock* ' *Company to borrow a further Sum of Money for completing the* ' *Improvements of the Port and Harbour of Bristol;*' but as these refer to matters which are not strictly within the limits of this work, we refrain from quoting the provisions of the same.

The River Avon, by reason of the gradual contraction of the channel of the Severn, is subject to very high and rapid tides, and particularly so when the wind is from the west, or a point or two to the south. At the mouth of the Avon, where the Severn is six miles wide, the usual spring tide is 40 feet; but in November,

1813, the spring tide there was ascertained by Captain Andrew
Livingstone, of Glasgow, to be full 50 feet perpendicular rise.
At Chepstow, situate upon the mouth of the River Wye, (where
the channel of the Severn is little more than two miles wide,) the
vertical rise of the spring tide is often 60 feet.

As the River Avon is the first link of one of the chains of the
present inland communication between the ports of Bristol and
London, this circumstance alone gives to it an importance that in
former times it had no claim to; and if ever the scheme, which is
now in agitation, for making a canal between these two important
places, capable of admitting ships of upwards of four hundred tons
burthen, (the estimated expense of which is eight millions,) be
carried into execution, this river will doubtless form an interesting
portion of such a navigation.

The celebrated Smeaton reported on the proposed floating-
harbour, docks, &c. so long ago as the year 1765; but William
Jessop, Esq. was the engineer who carried into execution the
works required under the authority of the last act of parliament.

AVON RIVER.

10 Anne, Cap. 8, Royal Assent 22nd May, 1712.
47 George III. Cap. 129, Royal Assent 14th August, 1807.
51 George III. Cap. 167, Royal Assent 15th June, 1811.

THIS is a continuation of the same River Avon as mentioned
above; but was made navigable to Bath, by different parties, and
under separate authorities.   The source of the River Avon is at a
short distance west of Badminton Park, the seat of the Duke of
Beaufort, in the county of Gloucester, and after meandering through
these beautiful grounds, enters Wiltshire, taking a northerly direction close to the town of Malmsbury, and thence westward to
Dauntsey, a seat of the late Earl of Peterborough, where, changing for the south, it passes Christian Malford, winding to within
a little distance of Bowood, the seat of the Marquis of Lansdowne;
thence to the town of Chippenham, to which place, a branch of the
Wilts and Berks Canal is carried.   In its course it runs by Lack-
ham House, and Laycock Abbey, to the west of the town of
Melksham; thence to the town of Bradford, a little below which,

at Avon Cliff Aqueduct, it is crossed by the Kennet and Avon
Canal; and again, a mile north-west of Monckton Combe, by
another aqueduct, called Dundas Aqueduct; from whence, it
takes a circuitous route to Bath, at which place it becomes navigable, and continues so through Bristol, to the Severn. The Kennet and Avon Canal locks into the River Avon, at Bath, and the
proprietors, under the above acts, have jurisdiction only from the
city of Bath to Hanham Mills, the length being eleven miles, with
a fall of 30 feet, by six locks.

The river, from Bath, to the tideway at Hanham Mills, was made
navigable by certain commissioners, who were appointed by the
mayor, aldermen, and common council of the city of Bath, under
powers granted them by an act of the 10th of Anne, entitled, ' *An*
' *Act for making the River Avon, in the counties of Somerset and*
' *Gloucester, navigable, from the city of Bath, to or near Hanham*
' *Mills.*' The commissioners were thirty-three in number, and
amongst them were his Grace the Duke of Beaufort, the Marquis
of Worcester, Timothy Goodwin, Bishop of Kilmore and Ardaugh,
and Lord Noel. The deed of appointment bears date the 11th
of March, 1724.

Until 1813, the barges were towed on this navigation, by men
only, in consequence of having neglected, in the act of Anne, to
secure a horse towing-path along the banks. The proprietors, (entitled, " The Proprietors of the Tolls arising from the Navigation
" of the River Avon,") consisting of the Company of Proprietors of
the Kennet and Avon Canal Navigation, Sir C. Willoughby, Bart.
and ten other persons, found it desirable that such powers should
be obtained; they, therefore, applied to parliament, in 1807, and
obtained an act, which is entitled, ' *An Act for enabling the Pro-*
' *prietors of the Navigation of the River Avon, in the counties of*
' *Somerset and Gloucester, from the city of Bath, to or near Han-*
' *ham Mills, to make and maintain a Horse Towing-Path, for the*
' *Purpose of towing and haling, with Horses or otherwise, Boats,*
' *Lighters, or other Vessels, up and down the said River.*' Under
this act, ten commissioners were added to those appointed under
the former act, but the tolls remain unaltered.

Four years after this act of the legislature, (in 1811) a company, consisting of two hundred and eighty-three persons, many

of whom were proprietors of the Kennet and Avon Canal, obtained an act, for making a canal between the cities of Bath and Bristol, which was entitled, ' *An Act for making a navigable Canal be-* ' *tween the cities of Bath and Bristol; and also for supplying with* ' *Water the Inhabitants of the city of Bristol and its neighbourhood.*' This canal was to commence at the end of the Kennet and Avon Canal, at Bath, and to run parallel with the River Avon, on its southern bank, to the town of Keynsham, where the line crosses to the opposite bank; thence, running parallel to Crew's Hole, it leaves the river, and crosses the upper end of Pyle Marsh to Old Market Street, in the city of Bristol, and from whence there was to be a short cut, locking down into the Bristol Dock, or Floating Harbour. The length would be about thirteen miles.

The company were incorporated by the name of " The Com-" pany of Proprietors of the Bath and Bristol Canal, and Bristol " Water Works," and empowered to raise, among themselves, £500,000, to be divided into five thousand shares of £100 each, with further power to contribute, among themselves, £150,000, or to borrow the same sum by mortgage of the tolls.

The estimate for the canal and water works, which was made by John Rennie, Esq. F.R.S. amounted to £453,530, of which, £343,030 related to the canal; and it appears that £365,400 was subscribed before going to parliament.

As no portion of this canal has been executed, nor is ever likely to be, under the powers granted by the above recited act, it is unnecessary to introduce the rates that were allowed by the same. The Kennet and Avon Canal Company acted judiciously in purchasing the principal part of the shares in the River Avon; for by obtaining the management of the river, they have been enabled to secure a better navigation to the public, and to themselves ample remuneration. The parliamentary rates are as follows.

TONNAGE RATES.

The Rates allowed by the Act, 10th Anne, are Five Shillings per Ton, on all Kinds of lading, for the whole Distance, and for every Passenger, for the whole Distance, Sixpence; but the Company have considerably reduced the Rates, which vary according to the Articles of lading.

AVON AND GLOUCESTERSHIRE RAILWAY.

9 George IV. Cap. 94, Royal Assent 19th June, 1828.

THIS railway commences from the River Avon, below the town of Keynsham, whence it takes a northerly course by Willsbridge, Haul Lane Coal Works and Warmley, to the Bristol and Gloucestershire Railway, at Rodway Hill, in the parish of Mangotsfield, where it terminates.

It is in length five miles, two furlongs and four chains, with a total rise, from the level of the Avon, below the tail of Keynsham Lock, (which is 2 feet above the Bristol Floating Harbour), of 198 feet, viz. from the Avon, an inclined plane three thousand three hundred and sixty-six yards in length, rising 124 feet; another three thousand three hundred and forty-four yards in length, with a rise of 19 feet only; while the remainder of the railway, which is two thousand six hundred and eighteen yards, has a rise of 55 feet. The estimate for this undertaking was made by Mr. John Blackwell, and amounts to the sum of £20,226, 11s. 2d. The act for making it is entitled, ' *An Act for making and maintaining* ' *a Railway or Tramroad from Rodway Hill, in the parish of* ' *Mangotsfield, in the county of Gloucester, to the River Avon, in* ' *the parish of Bitton, in the same county.*'

The subscribers, at the time the act was obtained, were ten in number, together with the Proprietors of the Kennet and Avon Canal Navigation, who alone subscribed £10,000; and £12,000 were subscribed by the others. The act incorporates these parties by the name of " The Avon and Gloucestershire Railway Com- " pany," with power to raise, amongst themselves, the sum of £21,000, in two hundred and ten shares, of £100 each, and, if necessary, a further sum of £10,000 on mortgage of the undertaking.

TONNAGE RATES.

	d.
For every Description of Goods	2 per Ton, per Mile.

Fractions as for a Quarter of a Ton, and as for a Quarter of a Mile.

Owners of lands may make branches to communicate with this railway, and may erect wharfs, and demand the following rates.

WAREHOUSING AND WHARFAGE RATES.

	d.
For the Wharfage of all Coal, Culm, Lime, Lime-stone, Clay, Iron, Iron-stone, Iron-ore, Lead-ore or any other Ores, Timber, Stone, Bricks, Tiles, Slate, Gravel or other Things...........................	2 per Ton.
For the Warehousing of every Package not exceeding Fifty-six Pounds..	2
Ditto above Three Hundred Pounds, and not exceeding Six Hundred Pounds..	4
Ditto exceeding One Thousand Pounds	6

Should any Goods or other Articles remain longer than Fourteen Days, a further Sum of One Penny per Ton for Wharfage, and Two-pence per Ton for Warehousing the same for the next Three Days, and the like Sum of One Penny and Two-pence respectively, for every succeeding Three Days which the same remain on the Wharfs or Warehouses.

CRANAGE RATES.

	s.	*d.*	
For any Weight under Two Tons with one Lift of the Crane	0	6	per Ton.
Ditto of Two Tons, and less than Three Tons, ditto.	1	0	ditto.
Ditto of Three Tons, and less than Four Tons, ditto.	1	6	ditto.

And so progressively advancing Sixpence per Ton.

The object of this railway is to open more beneficially the very extensive collieries and stone quarries which abound on the line, at Coal Pit Heath, and other places in the parishes of Westerleigh, Pucklechurch, and Mangotsfield.

The coal brought down this railway to the River Avon, will find its way, by the Kennet and Avon and the Wilts and Berks Canals, through the counties of Wiltshire and Berkshire, and even down the Thames to Reading, Maidenhead and Windsor.

AXE RIVER.

42 George III. Cap. 58, Royal Assent 24th May, 1802.

THE River Axe has its rise about a mile west of the city of Wells, in Somersetshire, whence, running westward by Wookey, and across the level of Cluer, to the village of Lower Weare, two miles west of Axbridge, and thence by Loxton and Bleadon to Uphill, it falls into the Bristol Channel in Uphill Bay.

Previous to 1802, the Axe was a very indifferent navigation, as a tideway river, to the village of Lower Weare, situate on the high road leading from Bridgewater to Axbridge; but in consequence of the spring tides rising in the Bristol Channel to the height of 40 feet, and there being no locks or sluices on the course to check the advance of the tides, the low lands on its banks were

frequently overflowed and rendered useless for agricultural purposes. Application was therefore made to parliament for powers
enabling the proprietors of lands to improve the drainage of the
same, and to make the navigation more efficient; an act accordingly was obtained on the day above quoted, entitled, ' *An Act*
' *for draining, preserving from Water, and improving, certain Low*
' *Lands and Grounds, lying within the several parishes, or chapel-*
' *ries, of Wookey, Westbury, Rodney-Stoke, Wedmore, Mear,*
' *Weare, Nyland, Badgworth, Biddisham, East Brent, South*
' *Brent, Cheddar, Axbridge, Compton Bishop, Loxton, Bleadon,*
' *Brean, Berrow, and Lympsham, all in the county of Somerset;*
' *and for altering and improving the Navigation of the River Axe,*
' *within the said parishes of Bleadon, Lympsham, Loxton, East*
' *Brent, Compton Bishop, Biddisham, Badgworth, Weare, and*
' *Axbridge, some or one of them, above and from a certain place*
' *called Southern Mead Bars, situate within the said parish of*
' *Bleadon.*' By this act, the execution of the works proposed,
was entrusted to three commissioners, who were authorized to
raise £15,000, on mortgage of the rates and assessments which
they were empowered to collect, for the purposes of the act, from
owners of lands that were benefited by the drainage; and for their
trouble, in executing the trust, a salary of three guineas a-day
each was also granted them. Their power extended to four years
and six months beyond the time required for the execution of the
works, and after that, the navigation and drainage were to be
vested in the commissioners of sewers for the county of Somerset.

In the execution of the above works, the commissioners have
shortened the navigation by making two cuts, one of which, near
Loxton, is above a mile in length. They have also constructed a
lock, near Southern Mead Bars, which is the only one upon the
river. The navigation, by this act, is free of toll. It extends to the
village of Lower Weare, near Axbridge, and from its head, to its
fall into the Bristol Channel, is nine miles in length.

The line of the proposed Bristol and Taunton Canal crosses
this river, near the village of Loxton, and from whence, a branch
was laid out to extend to Cheddar, but this part of that projected
canal, together with the above-mentioned branch, is now abandoned.

BALLOCHNEY RAILWAY.

7 George IV. Cap. 48, Royal Assent 5th May, 1826.

THIS railway commences from the Kipps, or Kippbyres Colliery Branch of the Monkland and Kirkintilloch Railway, one mile and a half west of the town of Airdrie, in Lanarkshire, and proceeding by Lea-end Colliery to the north of Airdrie, it passes by Stanrig to the march or division between east and west Arbuckle, in the parish of New Monkland, where the main line terminates. The whole length of the main line is four miles, with a rise, from the Kirkintilloch Railroad, of 352 feet, to Arbuckle. At one mile and three quarters from the west end of the railway there is a branch to Brownside and Blackrig Coal Pits, near the village of Clerkston, and called the Clerkston Branch, of one mile and a quarter in length. Also from the main line another branch called the Whiterig Branch, the length of which is three quarters of a mile. At a distance of nearly a mile from Kippbyres there is a self-acting inclined plane of more than three quarters of a mile in length, and upon the remaining part of this railway the inclinations are such that locomotive machines may be employed very advantageously. The total length of the main line and branches is a little more than six miles. The original estimate was made by Mr. Thomas Grainger, civil engineer, in 1826, and amounted to £18,431, 19s.

The act for making this railway and branches is entitled, ' *An* ' *Act for making a Railway from Arbuckle and Ballochney, in* ' *the parish of New Monkland, in the county of Lanark, to or near* ' *the termination of the Monkland and Kirkintilloch Railway, at* ' *Kipps, or Kippbyres, also in the said parish of New Monkland* ' *and county of Lanark.*' The subscribers to this railway, at the time the act was obtained, consisted of fourteen persons, and were incorporated under the name and style of " The Ballochney Rail-" way Company." They were empowered to raise by subscription £18,425, to be divided into seven hundred and thirty-seven shares of £25 each.

By section 32, the company were, in addition to the sum of

£18,425, empowered to borrow any sum not exceeding £10,000, on assignment of the property of the said undertaking, and of the rates authorized to be collected, repayable with interest.

TONNAGE RATES.

	d.
For all Goods, Wares, Merchandize, Coal and other Things....	3 per Ton, per Mile.
For passing up or down any one of the Inclined Planes, or any part of one, and for every Inclined Plane .... }	6 in addition.

Tolls to be paid for a fractional part of a Mile, and for a fractional part of a Ton, and no Fractions of a Mile to be considered less than a Quarter.

The period allowed by the act for the execution of this railway is five years; after that time the power to cease, excepting on that part of the railway which may have been completed. Abundance of coal and ironstone are worked in the immediate neighbourhood of this railroad, by which, by the Monkland Canal, and the Garnkirk and Glasgow Railroad, ready communications are opened with the populous city of Glasgow, which is at the distance of only fifteen miles.

BARNSLEY CANAL.

33 George III. Cap. 110, Royal Assent 3rd June, 1793.
48 George III. Cap. 13, Royal Assent 28th March, 1808.

This canal commences from the River Calder (the Aire and Calder Navigation) three quarters of a mile below Wakefield Bridge, and about three-eighths of a mile below the junction of the Calder and Hebble Navigation, at Fall Ing Lock, with the above-mentioned navigation; from thence, proceeding in a southerly direction, it passes Walton Hall, the seat of the ancient family of the Watertons, to which place there is a rise, from the Calder, of 117 feet, by fifteen locks, in the distance of two miles and three quarters. From Walton Hall the canal is level through Haw Park Wood, where there is a feeder, communicating with Hiendley Reservoir, which reservoir was made expressly for the purpose of supplying this canal. This is situate half-a-mile to the eastward, and originally occupied eighty acres, but the head of the reservoir has since been raised 4 feet, and it now covers a surface of one hundred and twenty-seven acres, the greatest depth being 40 feet. A powerful engine is erected here for the purpose of lifting water

from the canal into the reservoir, when the long level is full, being the
principal means of supplying the reservoir with water; and in
droughty seasons it is readmitted by means of sluices. From Haw
Park Wood, the canal continues its course, on a level, by Roy-
stone, Carlton, and Burton, near which latter place, it crosses the
River Dearne by an aqueduct of stone, of five arches, of 30 feet
span each; at the south side of which, and at a distance of ten
miles from its commencement at the Calder, it forms a junction
with the Dearne and Dove Canal. From the aqueduct, the canal
takes a westwardly course, on the same level, parallel with the
Dearne, crossing the London Road within half-a-mile of the town
of Barnsley; from thence, by Gawber Hall Collieries, to near
Barugh Mill, where the long level of the canal terminates, having
extended eleven miles. From this place, to the end of the canal
at Barnby Basin, there is a rise of 40 feet, by five locks; the
water, for the supply of which lockage, is, in a time of scarcity,
lifted by a steam engine, from the long level, to which place there
is a drift, nearly a quarter of a mile in length, but this is only used
when the stream supplying Barugh Mill is very low. The length
of the canal is fiteen miles and an eighth, and the act for making
it was passed in the 33rd George III. and entitled, ' An Act for
' making and maintaining a navigable Canal, from the River Cal-
' der, in the township of Warmfield-cum-Heath, to or near the town
' of Barnsley; and from thence to Barnby Bridge, in the township
' of Cawthorne, in the West Riding of the county of York; and
' certain Railways and other Roads to communicate therewith.'

The subscribers to this work were incorporated by the name of
" The Company of Proprietors of the Barnsley Canal Naviga-
" tion," and consisted of one hundred and thirteen persons, among
whom were the Duke of Leeds, Lord Hawke, the Countess Dowager of Bute, the Earl of Wigtoun, seven baronets, and almost all
the landholders in its immediate vicinity.

They were empowered to raise among themselves £72,000,
in seven hundred and twenty shares of £100 each, with power
to raise a further sum, not exceeding £20,000, either among
themselves or by mortgage of the rates.

In this act, permission is given to the Calder and Hebble Navigation Company, and Thomas Richard Beaumont, Esq. to make a

navigable communication between the Calder, at Horbury Pasture, and the Barnsley Canal, at Barugh Mill, the length of which would be six miles, and the estimate, amounting to £72,115, was made by the late Mr. Jessop, Mr. Elias Wright, and Mr. Gott, the engineers employed on the Barnsley Canal; but no part of this canal has ever been executed.

THE RATES OF TONNAGE ALLOWED UNDER THIS ACT.

		d.	
Wheat, Shelling, Beans, Peas, Vetches and Lentils, Rape, Line, Cole and Mustard Seed, Apples, Pears, Onions and Potatoes	}	6	per Quarter for the whole Length.
Barley		5	ditto. ditto.
Oats and Malt		4	ditto. ditto.
Pack or Sheet of Wool, Dried Pelts or Spetches		6	per 312lbs. ditto.
Coal, Slack, Cinders, Culm, Charcoal and Lime		1	per Ton, per Mile.
Limestone		¾	ditto. ditto.
Stone, Iron-stone, Flag, Paving-stone and Slate		1	ditto. ditto.
Pig or Old Iron		1½	ditto. ditto.
Cast Metal Goods and Bar Iron		2	ditto. ditto.
English Oak, Timber and Planks		1½	per Forty Cubical Feet, per Mile.
Elm, Oak and other English Timber		1½	per Fifty Cubical Feet, per Mile.
Fir, and all other kinds of Foreign Timber		1½	ditto. ditto.
Deals and Battens, equal to Thirty Deals, of 12 feet long, 3 inches thick, and from 9 to 12 inches broad	}	1½	per Mile.
All other things not before enumerated		2	per Ton, per Mile.

That Ten superficial Yards of Flag Paving-stone, from One Inch to Two Inches and three-quarters in Thickness, or Sixteen Cubical Feet of Stone, to be deemed a Ton.

The only railway belonging to this company, made under the authority of the before-mentioned act, is from Barnby Basin to Norcroft Bridge, near the Silkstone Collieries, and is one mile and a quarter in length.

TONNAGE RATES ON THE RAILWAY.

d.

Coal and other Minerals .... 3 per Ton, per Mile.

From the preamble of a second act, passed in the 48th George III. and entitled, ' *An Act for amending and enlarging the Powers* ' *of an Act of his present Majesty, for making and maintaining the* ' *Barnsley Canal Navigation, and certain Railways and other* ' *Roads to communicate therewith; and for increasing the Rates,* ' *Tolls, and Duties, thereby granted,*' it appears that the company had expended the sum of £97,000, authorized to be raised under the preceding act, in the canal alone, and had incurred sundry debts; they, therefore, obtained power to raise the further sum of £43,200, by a call of £60 on every shareholder of £100 each, and they were further empowered to raise £10,000 on mortgage, if the former sum should not be sufficient. By this act the rates of tonnage are increased one half, excepting on that part of the navigation extending from the junction with the Dearne and Dove Canal at the aqueduct, to Barnby Basin, for vessels which come out of, or enter, the Dearne and Dove Canal, or on the railways connected, or that may be connected with this portion of the Barnsley Canal. An exception to the additional charge is also made on all flag, paving-stone, lime-stone, or lime, navigating on this part of the canal, which shall previously have been navigated on the Dearne and Dove Canal.

This canal was projected principally with the view of opening the very valuable and extensive coal fields in the neighbourhood of Barnsley and Silkstone, and its execution has had the effect of introducing the coal, worked in the latter place, into the London Market, where it holds a distinguished place among the Yorkshire Coals. The making of this canal has also been of incalculable advantage to the agriculturists in its vicinity, by the facility it gives to the introduction of Knottingley Lime ; but it has been more particularly experienced by those who are employed in bringing into cultivation the vast tracts of moor land lying to the north and west of its termination at Barnby Basin. The depth of this canal is 5 feet, the width of the locks 15 feet, and the length 66 feet.

When the second act was obtained, authorizing the advance of £60 for every £100 share, it was deemed so unpropitious as to induce a many original subscribers to dispose of their shares, at the rate of £5 each, after having advanced the whole amount authorized to be raised by the first act, and these shares are now (1829) valued at £325 per share.

The canal was opened on the 8th of June, 1799, but the railroad to Silkstone was not commenced until after the passing of the act of 48th George III.

BASINGSTOKE CANAL.

18 George III. Cap. 75, Royal Assent 15th May, 1778.
33 George III. Cap. 16, Royal Assent 28th March, 1793.

THIS canal commences from the navigable River Wey, one mile and three quarters south from the village of Weybridge, and about three miles from its junction with the River Thames. Its course from hence is south-west, passing Horsell, and Pirbright, to Frimley Wharf, whence it takes a southerly course to near the village of Ash, where it crosses the little River Blackwater, and enters the county of Southampton. To this point of the canal it is fifteen miles, and there is a rise, from the River Wey, of 195 feet, by twenty-nine equal locks. This part of the canal is 36 feet wide, and $4\frac{1}{2}$ feet deep, and the locks admit vessels 72 feet long, and 13 feet wide, carrying fifty tons. From this point it is level to Basingstoke, a distance of twenty-two miles.

In its course from Ash Valley, at a distance of two miles, it crosses the mail road from London to Winchester; and about a mile from hence, westward, the canal is carried across a valley of three quarters of a mile in breadth, by a very fine aqueduct; from hence it proceeds westward, passing Dogmersfield House, and close to the town of Odiham, to Grewell, where the canal enters Grewell Hill Tunnel, half-a-mile and one-eighth in length, and from which, being entirely in chalk, which yields vast quantities of water, the principal supply is obtained for lockage, &c. From hence, the canal proceeds, passing Old Basing, to the town of Basingstoke, where it terminates. The summit level of the canal, of twenty-two miles, is 38 feet wide, and $5\frac{1}{2}$ feet deep, and the total length is thirty-seven miles.

There is a reservoir, at Aldershot, for the supply of this canal, which was completed in 1796; and also a feeder from the River Lodden.

This canal was made under the authority of an act, entitled, ‘ *An Act for making a navigable Canal, from the town of Basing-* ‘ *stoke, in the county of Southampton, to communicate with the* ‘ *River Wey, in the parish of Chertsey, in the county of Surrey,* ‘ *and to the South-East Side of the Turnpike-Road, in the parish* ‘ *of Turgiss, in the said county of Southampton,*’ and the subscribers, consisting of thirty-three persons, (amongst whom were the Earl of Worthington, the Earl of Dartmouth, the Earl of Portsmouth, and Lord Rivers), were incorporated by the name of “ The Company of Proprietors of the Basingstoke Canal Naviga- “ tion.” They were empowered to raise among themselves £86,000, in eight hundred and sixty shares of £100 each, with further power to raise a further sum of £40,000, if necessary. The affairs of the company are managed by twenty proprietors, who form a committee, and who are under the control of the general meetings of the company.

TONNAGE RATES.

	d.
Lime, Lime-stone, Paving-stone, Chalk, Dung, Soil, Marl and other Manure for Land.........	1 per Ton, per Mile.
For all Goods, Wares and Merchandize, and other Things	2 ditto. ditto.

Gravel, Sand and other Materials for Roads, (except Paving-stones) are exempt from payment of Toll, when the Water is running through the Gauge, Paddle or Niche of the Lock.

Vessels not to exceed Thirteen Feet in Breadth, and Seventy-two Feet in Length; and Vessels of less Burthen than Fifteen Tons, shall not pass through any Lock without leave.

In this act, the proprietors of the navigation of the River Wey agree to receive only one shilling per ton for all descriptions of merchandize, &c. passing on the Wey River, between this canal and the Thames; and they further agree to keep their locks of the length of 81 feet, and 14 feet wide.

By an act of the 33rd George III. entitled, ' *An Act for effec-* ' *tually carrying into Execution an Act of Parliament of the* ' *Eighteenth Year of his present Majesty, for making a navigable* ' *Canal from the town of Basingstoke, in the county of Southamp-* ' *ton, to communicate with the River Wey, in the parish of* ' *Chertsey, in the county of Surrey, and to the South-East Side of* ' *the Turnpike-Road, in the parish of Turgiss, in the said county* ' *of Southampton,*' it is stated that the sum of £126,000, authorized to be raised by the preceding act, is all expended; that their works are not completed, and that they have incurred some debt: they are, therefore, empowered to raise, upon loans or annuities, on mortgage of the tolls, the further sum of £60,000, with which sum they were enabled to finish their works, which were opened in 1796.

The trade upon this canal consists chiefly of coals, deals, groceries, bale goods, &c. from London; and the exports are timber, flour, malt, bark, and earthenware.

BAYBRIDGE CANAL.

6 George IV. Cap. 164, Royal Assent 22nd June, 1825.

This canal proceeds from Binesbridge, in the parish of West-Grinstead, where the navigation of the River Arun commences, and keeps the course of the unnavigable part of the Arun, to Baybridge, where it terminates. It is in length three miles and three-eighths, with a rise of 14 feet, by two locks of 7 feet each. It is 28 feet wide at top, and 4 feet deep.

The act for making it received the royal assent in 1825, and is entitled, ' *An Act for making and maintaining a navigable Cut or* ' *Canal, from the River Adur, at or near Binesbridge, in the parish* ' *of West Grinstead, in the county of Sussex, to Baybridge, in the* ' *said parish.*'

The company of proprietors consisted of Lord Selsey, Sir Charles Merrick Burrell, Walter Burrell, William Peckham Woodward, John Wood, James Eversfield, and James Lancaster, who were incorporated by the name and style of " The Baybridge " Canal Company." They were empowered to raise among themselves £6,000, in one hundred and twenty shares of £50 each, with a power of raising a further sum of £3,000, on mortgage of the rates, &c. which are as follows.

TONNAGE RATES.

	d.
Beech, Gravel, or other Materials used in the repair of Roads, Chalk, Dung, Mould, Soil, Compost or other Articles (except Lime) to be used for the manuring of Land..........	2 per Ton, per Mile.
Goods, Wares, Articles, Commodities or Merchandize	5 ditto. ditto.

Fractions of a Ton and of a Mile, shall not be deemed less than a Quarter.

Wharfage of any Goods remaining less than Seventy-two Hours   9 per Ton.

The estimate for making this canal was made by May Upton, Esq. civil engineer, in 1824, and amounted to the sum of £5,957, 16s. 7d. The advantages arising from it are chiefly local, and consist of the increased facility by which manure may be brought into the interior, and the agricultural produce more easily disposed of.

BEDFORD LEVEL.

THE description of the several rivers, canals, and navigable drains, within the limits of this extensive level, with the several acts, under authority of which, they have been executed, will be introduced in their respective places in alphabetical order.

BERWICK AND KELSO RAILWAY.

51 George III. Cap. 133, Royal Assent 31st May, 1811.

IN the year 1811, an act was obtained to make a railway from Spittal, near Berwick, to Kelso, in Roxburgshire, entitled, ' *An* ' *Act for making and maintaining a Railway from, or from near* ' *to, Spittal, in the county of Durham, to Kelso, in the county of* ' *Roxburgh; and for erecting and maintaining a Bridge over the* ' *River Tweed, from the parish of Norham, in the county of Dur-* ' *ham, to the parish of Coldstream, in the county of Berwick.*'

The line commences at Spittal, opposite the town of Berwick, on the south bank of the River Tweed, and continues parallel to the course of that river, by Tweedmouth, and East Ord, through the parish of Norham, to near Twisell, the seat of Sir Francis Blake, where it crosses the Tweed, and enters Scotland. Passing hence, by Kersfield, and to the north of Hirsel, the seat of the Earl of Home, it crosses the Leet Water, and thence, keeps the north bank of the Tweed, to its termination at Kelso.

At the time the act was obtained, there were one hundred and thirty-two subscribers, who were incorporated under the name of " The Berwick and Kelso Railway Company." They were empowered to raise among themselves £100,000, in one thousand shares of £100 each, with a further power of raising among themselves £50,000 in addition, or by promissory notes, under the common seal of the company; or they may raise the same, or any portion of it, on mortgage of the tolls authorized to be collected under the powers of this act.

TONNAGE RATES.

	d.
Stone for the repair of Roads...............................	2 per Ton, per Mile.
Coal, Coke, Culm, Stone, Cinders, Chalk, Marl, Sand, Lime, Clay, Ashes, Peat, Lime-stone, Pitching and Paving-stone, Iron-stone or other Ore, Minerals and Bricks, and for all sorts of Manure, Grain, Flour, Meal, Potatoes, Hay and Straw	3 ditto. ditto.
For every Carriage carrying Passengers or Light Goods or Parcels, not exceeding Five Cwt.	2 per Mile.
For all other Goods, Commodities, Wares and Merchandize whatsoever	4 per Ton, per Mile.

Fractions to be taken as for a Quarter of a Ton and as for a Quarter of a Mile.

The proprietors are further empowered to collect a pontage, at the proposed bridge over the Tweed, for carriages, foot passengers, &c. but as these are without the limits of our publication, we omit them.

This railway was calculated to be of great advantage to the country through which it passed, but it has been abandoned by its original promoters, and though the act does not limit the company to any given time for the execution of the works, yet it is thought that it will never be completed under its provisions.

BEVERLEY BECK.

13 George I. Cap. 4, Royal Assent 24th March, 1726.
18 George II. Cap. 13, Royal Assent 19th March, 1744.

This canal, or creek, (called Beverley Beck), commences from the navigable River Hull, nearly opposite the village of Weel, in Holderness, and extends to the town of Beverley. Though the first act of parliament, relating to this creek, bears a very early date, yet it had long before been used as a navigation, and kept in repair by the corporation of Beverley, out of the funds of the town; but as these were insufficient for the proper maintenance of it as a navigation, an act was obtained by the mayor, aldermen, and capital burgesses of Beverley, in the 13th George I. entitled, ' *An Act for cleansing, deepening, and widening a Creek,* ' *called Beverley Beck, running into the River Hull, and for re-* ' *pairing the Staiths, near the said Beck; and for amending the* ' *Roads leading from the said River, to the town of Beverley, in* ' *the East Riding of the county of York, and for cleansing the*

' *Streets of the said Town,*' in which certain rates and duties are granted, which will be found in the first column in the schedule of rates appended hereto.

For the purpose of raising an immediate fund for carrying into execution the improvements contemplated, the corporation of Beverley obtained power to borrow the sum of money they required for this purpose, on assignment of the rates and duties granted. In consequence, however, of the very indifferent state of this navigation, and the insufficiency of the tonnage rates to keep it in proper repair, and repay the interest of the sum of money borrowed on the credit of the tolls, the corporation of Beverley applied for and obtained another act, in 1744, entitled, ' *An Act for more effec-*
' *tually cleansing, deepening, widening, and preserving, a Creek,*
' *called Beverley Beck, running into the River Hull, and for more*
' *effectually repairing the Staiths, near the said Beck, and the*
' *Roads leading from the said River, to the town of Beverley; and*
' *for cleansing the Streets of the said Town, and for regulating the*
' *Carriages to and from the said Beck, and the River Hull;*' by which they are empowered to collect rates, in addition to those granted under the 13th George I. and which are enumerated in the second column of the schedule.

SCHEDULE OF TOLLS OR DUTIES ON BEVERLEY BECK.

DESCRIPTION OF GOODS.	Rates under First Act.	Additional Rates by 2nd Act.	
	s. d.	s. d.	
Coals	0 4	0 2	per Chaldron.
Oats, Barley or Malt	0 ½	0 ¼	per Quarter.
Wheat, Rye, Mesledine and other Grain ..	0 ¾	0 ½	ditto.
Flour		0 ¼	per Cwt.
Salt		0 4	per Hogshead.
Salt in Bulk	0 4	0 2	per Ton.
Sugar, Tobacco, Molasses, or Hogsheads } packed with other Goods .... }	0 4	0 8	per every Three Hogsheads.
Wine or Rum		1 8	per Four Hogsheads.
Liquor	0 4	0 4	per Three Puncheons.
Brandy or other Spirits		0 4	per Hogshead.
Wine, Spirits or other Liquor	0 4		per every Four Hogsheads.
Soap, Raisins, Oil, Pitch, Tar, or packed } with other Dry Goods............ }	0 4	0 4	per Eight Barrels.
Currants	0 4	0 8	per Butt or Two Half Butts.
Smyrna Raisins	0 4	0 8	per Two Pipes.
Nails	0 4	0 4	per Sixteen Bags.

SCHEDULE OF TOLLS OR DUTIES CONTINUED.

DESCRIPTION OF GOODS.	Rates under First Act.	Additional Rates by 2nd Act.	
	s. d.	s. d.	
Iron or Lead	0 4	0 8	per Ton.
Butter	0 4	0 4	per Thirty-two Firkins.
Cheese	0 5	0 7	per Twenty Cwt.
Timber or Stone	0 4	0 2	per Ton.
Hops	0 4	0 8	per Two Bags.
Bricks	0 4		per Thousand.
Tiles	0 6		ditto.
Oatmeal	0 1	0 ½	per Quarter.
Deal Boards (Single)	0 1		per every Twenty.
Ditto (Double)	0 2		ditto.
Millstones	2 0		per Pair.
Laths	0 6		per every Sixty Bunches.
Faggots	0 1		per Hundred.
Pails, Barrel or Hogshead Staves	0 1		ditto.
Handspikes	0 1		ditto.
Poles	0 1		per Score.
Pipe Staves		0 1½	per Hundred.
Cinders and Charcoal	0 1	0 ½	per Dozen.
Horse, Cow, Bull or other Hide	0 ¼		each.
Sheep Skins	0 ½	0 ½	per every Twenty.
Bark	0 ½	0 ¼	per Quarter.
Wool or other Goods	0 1	0 1	per Pack.
Bottles	0 2	0 1	per Twelve Dozen.
Glass	0 2		per Case or Chest.
Firkin Staves	0 4		per Thousand.
Roots or Fruit	0 ½	0 ½	per Four Bushels.
Earthenware	0 ¼		per Dozen.
Shovels	0 ½		ditto.
Hemp, Line and Flax		0 7	per Ton.
Calf Skins	0 1		per Dozen.
Thatch	0 4		per Hundred.
Lime	0 2		per Chaldron.
Sand	0 2		per Ton.
Hoops	0 ½		per Bundle.
Chairs	0 1		per Dozen.
Fern Ashes		0 2	per Quarter.
Turfs	0 ½		per Thousand.
Liquors (not exceeding Ten Gallons)	0 ¼	0 ½	per Rundlet.
Cask, Truss, Box or Parcel	0 ¼	0 ¼	not exceeding 112lbs.

And so in proportion for any greater or less Quantity or Weights of any of the above-mentioned Goods or Ladings.

For every other sort of Goods, Wares, Merchandizes or Ladings whatsoever, not above-mentioned, according to the custom of Water Tonnage...... } 0 5 | 1 0 { and so in proportion for any greater or less Quantity.

The whole of the tolls or duties, collected under these acts of parliament, are directed to be laid out in defraying the debts incurred by the corporation, and for keeping in sufficient repair the navigation of this creek or beck, and the staiths, and the roads leading thereto, and to no other purpose whatsoever.

BIRMINGHAM CANAL NAVIGATIONS.

8 Geo. III. C. 38, R. A. 24th Feb. 1768.   9 Geo. III. C. 53, R. A. 21st April, 1769.
23 Geo. III. C. 92, R. A. 24th June, 1783. 24 Geo. III. C. 4, R. A. ——— 1784.
25 Geo. III. C. 99, R. A. 13th June, 1785. 34 Geo. III. C. 87, R. A. 17th April, 1794.
46 Geo III. C. 92, R. A. 3rd July, 1806.   51 Geo. III. C. 105, R. A. 21st May, 1811.
55 Geo. III. C. 40, R. A. 12th May, 1815.   58 Geo. III. C. 19, R. A. 17th Mar. 1818.

As some parts of these important navigations have been executed by companies, incorporated under other titles than what is now given to the whole of the canals and branches, constituting the Birmingham Canal Navigations, we shall, in the first place, recite the substance of the principal clauses in the respective acts of parliament, and in the order in which they were severally obtained.

The first act, entitled, ' *An Act for making and maintaining a* ' *navigable Cut, or Canal, from Birmingham to Bilstone, and* ' *from thence to Autherley, there to communicate with the Canal* ' *now making between the Rivers Severn and Trent, and for* ' *making collateral Cuts up to several Coal Mines,*' authorizes the original subscribers to make a canal from the town of Birmingham to Bilstone, and from thence by Wolverhampton, to join the Staffordshire and Worcestershire Canal (then in progress) at Autherley, with two collateral cuts to the coal pits, iron furnaces, and limestone quarries, in its vicinity.

The company, at the time the act was obtained, consisted of one hundred and two persons, amongst whom were the Earl of Hertford, Earl of Dartmouth, and Sir Lister Holt, Bart. who were incorporated by the name of " The Company of Proprietors of " the Birmingham Canal Navigation."

This company were empowered, under the before-mentioned act, to raise the sum of £55,000, in five hundred and fifty shares of £100 each, and a further sum of £15,000, if the proper execution of the works should require it. The duties granted under this act are as follows:—

TOLLS AND DUTIES.

	d.
Coal, Iron, Iron-stone, Stones, Timber, and other Goods, Wares and Merchandize	1½ per Ton, per Mile.
Lime and Limestone	½ ditto. ditto.

And so in proportion for any less Quantity than a Ton.

EXEMPTION FROM TOLL.

Paving-stones, Gravel, Sand, and all Materials for the making of Roads (Limestone excepted) and all Dung, Soil, Marl and all sorts of Manure, provided they do not pass a Lock but at such times as when the Water runs over the Gauge, Paddle or Niche of the Lock.

Boats of less Length than Seventy Feet, not to pass a Lock without leave.

In this act, power is given to the Staffordshire and Worcestershire Canal Company to open a communication with the Birmingham Canal, at the cost of the proprietors of the last-mentioned canal, if they do not do it within six months after it is finished to Birmingham.

The second act, entitled, ' *An Act to rectify a Mistake in an* ' *Act passed in the Eighth Year of his present Majesty, entitled,* ' *An Act for making and maintaining a navigable Cut or Canal,* ' *from Birmingham to Bilstone, and from thence to Autherley,* ' *there to communicate with the Canal now making between the* ' *Rivers Severn and Trent, and for making collateral Cuts up to* ' *several Coal Mines, and to explain and amend the said Act,*' was obtained chiefly in consequence of having neglected to introduce, in the description of the course of the intended canal, a detached part of the county of Salop, near the village of Oldbury. The company, however, took this opportunity of obtaining power to make reservoirs anywhere within three miles from that part of the canal, lying between the two extreme locks, intended to be constructed between Smethwick and Oldbury. In consequence of being enabled to raise only £50,000, instead of £55,000, they, by this act, reduce the number of shares to five hundred, instead of five hundred and fifty, retaining, however, authority to raise the additional sums of £5,000, and £15,000, granted under the former act.

In 1783, parliamentary sanction was given to a very important act, entitled, ' *An Act for making and maintaining a navigable* ' *Canal, from a place near Rider's Green, in the county of Staf-* ' *ford, to Broadwater Fire Engine, and six collateral Cuts, from* ' *the same, to several Coal Mines; and also a navigable Canal,* ' *from or near the town of Birmingham, to join the Coventry* ' *Canal, at or near Fazeley, in the parish of Tamworth, in the said* ' *county of Stafford, with a collateral Cut to the lower part of the*

' *said town of Birmingham*,' in the preamble of which, it is stated, that the canal and branches, authorized to be done under the act of 8th George III. had been some time completed.

This act, obtained by a new company, consisting of one hundred and twenty-nine persons, who were incorporated by the name of " The Company of Proprietors of the Birmingham and Fazeley " Canal Navigation," gave them power to extend the Wednesbury Branch of the Birmingham Canal, from Rider's Green, to Broadwater Engine, and to make six collateral cuts. One from Butcher's Forge Pool, to Brooke's Meadow; another from near the south end of Butcher's Forge Pool, to Wood's Engine Forge; a third from the head of Willingsworth Pool, to near the nine mile stone, on the turnpike-road leading from Ocher Hill to Wolverhampton; the fourth collateral cut extends from the Willingsworth Pool Tail, to Wednesbury Open Field; one other from the last-mentioned cut, into another part of the same field; and the sixth from out of the last-mentioned cut, to a place opposite Taylor's Engine. This act further empowers the company of proprietors to make a canal from the end of the Birmingham Canal at Farmer's Bridge, near the town of Birmingham, to join the line of the Coventry Canal, at Fazeley, in the parish of Tamworth, and county of Stafford, with a branch, called the Digbeth Branch, from the north side of the town of Birmingham, to the lower part of the said town, and where the Warwick and Birmingham Canal has since effected a junction.

The subscribers are empowered to raise among themselves the sum of £85,000, in five hundred shares of £170 each, for the purpose of executing the whole of the works above described, with further power to raise an additional £30,000, if necessary. The whole of the works to be completed in four years.

TONNAGE RATES ALLOWED UNDER THIS ACT.

		d.
Coal, Coke and Iron-stone, from Mines in the parishes of Wolverhampton, Sedgley, Tipton, Wednesbury and West Bromwich, which shall pass through the Locks, from the lower Level into the present Birmingham Canal	}	4 per Ton.
Coal, Coke and Iron-stone, from the Birmingham Canal, at Farmer's Bridge, to Fazeley	}	$\frac{1}{2}$ ditto, per Mile.
Ditto, ditto, from Farmer's Bridge to Fazeley and thence into the Coventry Canal	}	10 ditto.
Ditto, ditto, from Farmer's Bridge, to go into the Digbeth Branch	}	$\frac{3}{4}$ ditto.

E

TONNAGE RATES CONTINUED.

		d.
Timber, Stone and other Goods, Wares and Merchandize, carried on any of the Canals or collateral Cuts (except Coal and Iron-stone)	}	$\frac{1}{2}$ per Ton, per Mile.
Coal, Coke and Iron-stone, carried on any of the collateral Cuts, not entering or passing any of the Locks above-mentioned..	}	$\frac{1}{2}$ ditto. ditto.

Fifty Feet of round or Forty Feet of square Oak, Ash or Elm Timber, and Fifty Feet of Fir or Deal, Balk, Poplar, and other Wood, shall be deemed a Ton; and One Hundred and Twenty Pounds shall be deemed a Hundred Weight, for the purposes of this Act.

Lime and Limestone, one-third of the above Rates.

EXEMPTION FROM TOLL.

Paving-stones, Gravel, Sand and Road Materials, (Limestone excepted) Dung, Soil, Marl, and all sorts of Manure, for the Improvement of Lands belonging to Persons whose Land has been taken for the use of the Canal, provided the same does not pass through any Lock, but at the time when the Water is running over the Lock Weirs.

In addition to these Rates, the Company are empowered to collect the Sum of One Penny per Ton for all Coal and Coke, which shall pass through the First Lock, from Farmer's Bridge, to be erected on this Canal, in consideration of repaying a Sum of Money, not exceeding £3,600, to the Subscribers to a Canal, which had been proposed to be made between the Wednesbury Coal Fields and the town of Birmingham, and from thence to Fazeley, as a reimbursement of Expenses they had been put to in an Application to Parliament, and this Toll is to exist until the Sum and Interest is paid off.

No Boats under Twenty Tons to pass a Lock without leave, unless there is not sufficient Water for greater Tonnage.

The proprietors have power to take water, for the supply of the canal, from mines situate within one thousand yards of the canal, provided that the produce of such mines be carried along any part of the canal.

In this act is recited the substance of an agreement entered into at a meeting of delegates from the Coventry, Oxford, Grand Trunk, and Birmingham and Fazeley Canal Companies, held the year preceding the passing of this act, by which the Grand Trunk Canal Company, and the Birmingham and Fazeley Canal Company, agree to execute that part of the line of the Coventry Canal lying between Fazeley and Fradley Heath, at the joint expense of the two parties; the Birmingham and Fazeley Canal Company allowing to the Grand Trunk Canal Company £500, for superintending and directing the execution of the same; and it was further agreed, that the tolls arising upon that half part of the said canal, commencing at Fazeley, should belong to the Birmingham and Fazeley Canal Company, and the other half, terminating at Fradley, to the Grand Trunk or Trent and Mersey Canal Company.

By an act of the 24th George III. entitled, ' *An Act for incor-* ' *porating the Proprietors of a Canal Navigation, authorized by* ' *an Act, passed in the Eighth Year of his Majesty King George* ' *the Third, to be made from Birmingham to Bilstone, and Auther-* ' *ley, with the Company of Proprietors of a Canal Navigation,* ' *authorized by an Act passed in the Twenty-third Year of his* ' *present Majesty, to be made from Birmingham to Fazeley, and* ' *for consolidating their Shares, and amending the last-mentioned* ' *Act,*' " The Company of Proprietors of the Birmingham Canal " Navigation," and " The Company of Proprietors of the Bir- " mingham and Fazeley Canal Navigation," were incorporated by the name of " The Company of Proprietors of the Birmingham " and Birmingham and Fazeley Canal Navigations." By this act, these two undertakings became consolidated; the subscribers to one concern became equal proprietors of the other in the ratio of their respective ventures, though the powers of the several pre-vious acts in other respects remain unaltered.

It further directs, that there shall be no more than five hun-dred shares, the number fixed on in the original act; and that no person shall have less than one consolidated share, nor more than ten.

Power is also given in this act to borrow the £115,000 autho-rized to be raised by the act of 23rd George III. by mortgage, under the common seal of the company, instead of the mode therein prescribed: and that this sum shall be appropriated to the making of the canals and cuts enumerated in the 23rd George III. and to the paying off the proportion of the expense of making the re-quired junction from Fazeley with the Trent and Mersey, or Grand Trunk Canal, at Fradley, the act for doing which received the royal assent on the 13th June, 1785, and is entitled, ' *An Act* ' *to enable the Company of Proprietors of the Navigation from the* ' *Trent to the Mersey, and the Company of Proprietors of the Navi-* ' *gation from Birmingham to Fazeley, to make a navigable Canal* ' *from the said Trent and Mersey Navigation, on Fradley Heath,* ' *in the county of Stafford, to Fazeley, in the said county; and for* ' *confirming certain Articles of Agreement entered into between the* ' *said Trent and Mersey, the Oxford, and the Coventry Canal* ' *Navigation Companies.*'

In the preamble of an act bearing date the 17th April, 1794, and entitled, ' *An Act for extending and improving the Bir-* ' *mingham Canal Navigations,*' it is stated that all the works authorized to be done under the preceding acts, had been made and completed. By this act, power is given to make a collateral cut from Broadwater, in the parish of Wednesbury, to the town of Walsall, with three branches from the same, extending to the coal and iron-stone mines in the vicinity ; also another branch canal from Bloomfield, in the parish of Tipton, to communicate again with the original line of navigation at Deepfield, in the parish of Sedgley.

By this act the company once more change their style, being incorporated under the name of " The Company of Proprietors of " the Birmingham Canal Navigations," and three years were allowed for the due execution of the works therein described. Upon the canal and collateral cuts authorized to be made under this act, the proprietors are empowered to collect the following

TONNAGE RATES.

d.

Coal, Coke, Lime-stone, Iron-stone, and other Minerals, carried along the Branch Canal, from Broadwater to Walsall, or any of the collateral Cuts therefrom................ } 3 per Ton.

Goods, Wares, Merchandize, Lime and other Commodities.. 1¼ ditto, per Mile.

Coal, Coke, Lime-stone, Iron-stone, Lime, Goods, Wares, Merchandize, and all other things whatsoever, carried on the proposed Canal, from Bloomfield to Deepfield, the same Rates of Tonnage as are paid for other parts of the Birmingham Canal Navigation, made under the 8th George III.

By a Clause inserted in an Act of the 25th George III. entitled, ' *An Act for ex-* ' *tending the Dudley Canal to the Birmingham Canal, at or near Tipton Green,* ' *in the county of Stafford,*' it appears that the Birmingham Canal Company received 1s. 5½d. per Ton, for all Stone, Timber, Goods, Wares, Merchandize, and Commodities whatsoever, (except Coal, Coke, Iron-stone, Lime, and Limestone), which should pass between the Junction of the Dudley Canal, at Tipton Green, and the town of Birmingham; and also, the further Sum of 1½d. per Ton, per Mile; and for the same Articles, (with the same exception), between the Junction of the Dudley Canal and the western Termination of the Birmingham Canal, at Autherley, the same Rates of Tonnage as if they had been navigated along the said Canal from Autherley. By this act, however, these Tolls are reduced, in consequence of shortening the Navigation between the Junction of the Dudley Canal and Autherley, nearly Four Miles, by the proposed Canal from Bloomfield to Deepfield. Instead, therefore, of the Sum of 1s. 5½d. above-mentioned, it is reduced to 11½d. per Ton, retaining, however, the 1½d. per Ton, per Mile, granted under the Act of 25th George III. above recited.

The act of the 34th George III. empowers the proprietors of the Birmingham Canal Navigations, to borrow, on the credit of their works, the sum of £45,000, and a committee of nine are appointed to give security under the common seal of the company, upon the tolls, rates and duties arising from the same.

In the preamble of an act of the 46th George III. entitled, ' *An Act for improving the Birmingham Canal Navigations,*' it is stated, that the company have already opened a communication with the Staffordshire and Worcestershire Canal, the Coventry Canal, and the Trent and Mersey, or Grand Trunk Canal, and have completed all the collateral cuts and canals authorized under the act of 34th George III.; that they have, moreover, improved the navigation, by cutting down the summit at Smethwick, and thereby materially reducing the lockage; also by cutting off bends in the canals, and erecting steam engines for the purpose of obtaining a more regular supply of water, for the purposes of lockage; in consideration of which improvements, they obtain power to charge the same amount of tonnage and mileage as they have heretofore received upon the original circuitous line of navigation. It is also recited in this act, that the company have mortgages on these navigations to the amount of £100,000 and upwards, and for the discharging of which, they obtain power to raise that sum by granting annuities to the same amount, which annuities are to be paid half-yearly, and in preference to dividends or any other claim.

By another act, entitled, ' *An Act for enlarging the Powers of* ' *several Acts of his present Majesty, for making and maintaining* ' *the Birmingham Canal Navigations, and for further extending* ' *and improving the same,*' the five hundred consolidated shares, of which the whole of the navigation consists, are divided into one thousand shares, of which no person shall possess more than twenty, on pain of forfeiting all above the restricted number.

By the act of the 55th George III. entitled, ' *An Act for* ' *establishing a navigable Communication between the Birmingham* ' *Canal Navigations and the Worcester and Birmingham Canal,* ' *and amending certain Acts relating thereto,*' power is given to open a communication between the two above-mentioned canals, near Broadstreet in the town of Birmingham; the space between them was only 7 feet 3 inches, and the estimate for effecting this communication, with the necessary works for preventing the water from flowing either way, amounted to the sum of £2,300, and was made by Mr. John Hodgkinson, civil engineer, in 1814. By this act it is provided, that whenever the surface water, either of the Birmingham or the Worcester and Birmingham Canal, is more than 6 inches above the level of the other canal, the proprietors of such lowest canal shall pay to the other the sum of three shillings per every 4,000 cubic feet of water, expended in passing a vessel through the communication.

The Birmingham Canal Navigation Company are authorized by this act, in consideration of the amount of tolls they may be deprived of by consenting to the above communication, and the expense they will be put to in maintaining the locks at this junction, to receive the following tolls in addition to what they were before entitled to.

TONNAGE RATES.

	d.
Coals and other Minerals, Coke, Goods, Wares, Merchandize, Commodities, &c. passing out of the Birmingham Canal, and into the Worcester and Birmingham Canal, and *vice versa*	4 per Ton.
Coal or Coke, passing out of the Worcester and Birmingham Canal into the Birmingham Canal, and from thence to the termination of the Digbeth Branch of the said Birmingham Canal, or any part thereof, the further and additional Sum of	4 ditto.

And which Sum shall be in full Satisfaction for all Tolls payable between Farmer's Bridge and the said termination.

WHARFAGE RATES.

	d.
Coal or Coke, passing from the Worcester and Birmingham Canal, into the Birmingham Canal, and landed at any of the Wharfs belonging to the said Birmingham Canal Company..........................	2 per Ton.
Coal or Coke, conveyed Five Miles along this line of Canal, towards Fazeley, and passing any of the Locks between Farmer's Bridge and the termination of the Digbeth Branch......................	4 ditto.

And this Sum shall be considered as part Payment of the Rates which the said Company are entitled to collect on this part of the Navigation.

The preamble of the act of 58th George III. entitled, ' *An Act for altering, explaining and amending the several Acts of Parliament passed relating to the Birmingham Canal Navigations ; and for improving the said Canal Navigations,*' states that the whole of the works authorized by the preceding acts have been executed and found of great utility.

In this act the company are empowered to contract with the owners and occupiers of coal mines and iron furnaces, to receive a gross annual sum for the conveyance of coal, coke, iron-stone, lime-stone and other raw material along the navigation, in lieu of the tonnage rates which the act authorizes them to demand, provided that such material is for the use of the furnaces and forges of the persons claiming this mode of payment, and that they do not pass a lock.

The Old Birmingham Canal, so called from its being executed under the earliest act relating to these navigations, is twenty-two miles five-eighths in length. It commences at Farmer's Bridge, near Birmingham, and passes by Smethwick, at which place there is a side cut, with three locks, rising 19¾ feet, which materially facilitates the passage of vessels along this navigation. From the last-mentioned place the canal continues on one level by Oldbury, Tipton Green, Bilstone, and Wolverhampton, to within one mile and a half of Autherley, where it locks down 132 feet by twenty-one locks, into the Staffordshire and Worcestershire Canal. The summit level of this canal at Smethwick, was originally only one mile in length, and 18 feet higher than at present, and it was supplied with water by means of two steam engines placed at the extremities. Prior, however, to 1787, it was cut down to its present level at a cost to the company of about £30,000. It is here worthy of remark, that though two years and a half were occupied in this work, not more than fourteen days interruption took place to the passage of vessels.

There are several collateral cuts to the coal mines and iron furnaces, which are found described under the act which empowers the company to make them; the principal of which is, the branch to Wednesbury, of four miles and a half in length, which was finished in November, 1769, but as a part of it fell in, in consequence of working the coal and iron-stone underneath it, it is now of little use; there are three locks upon it, with a fall from the main line of 18 feet.

The supply of water for the lockage on this canal is chiefly derived from the Old Coal Works, from the bottom of which it is raised by steam power, at a very considerable expense. When Mr. Smeaton reported on some matters connected with this canal in October, 1782, there were eleven engines so employed. There are, also, reservoirs at Smethwick and near Oldbury. This canal communicates with the Worcester and Birmingham Canal at Birmingham; with the Dudley Canal near Tipton Green; and with the Wyrley and Essington Canal near Wolverhampton.

Under the powers of the act of 34th George III. a cut was made from Bloomfield into the original navigation again at Deepfield, of the length of one mile and three quarters, of which one thousand yards was tunnelling, by which, the circuitous course of four miles, round Tipton Hill, is avoided. Mr. Brindley was the engineer originally employed in this work, Mr. Whitworth followed him, and several others have been subsequently consulted, amongst whom was Mr. John Smeaton; but the last and greatest improvements made, were under the direction of Mr. Telford.

That part of this navigation called the Birmingham and Fazeley Canal, commences at the eastern end of the Old Birmingham Canal, near Farmer's Bridge in Birmingham, and passes through a part of the town; thence by Newhall Forge, Moxhall Hall, Middleton Hall, and Drayton Manor House, to the Coventry Canal, at Fazeley, near the town of Tamworth. The distance to this place is fifteen miles, with a fall of 248 feet. The remaining five miles and a half, to Whittington Brook, being that portion of the original line of the Coventry Canal, now forming part of the Birmingham Canal Navigations, is level. Its course from Fazeley is north-west of Hopwas, from whence, running parallel with the Tame River, it passes the villages of Tamborn and Whittington, to Whittington Brook, otherwise the Huddlesford Junction, where it communicates with the Wyrley and Essington Canal; and also, with that portion of the original part of the Coventry Canal, now forming part of the Grand Trunk, or Trent and Mersey Canal.

The Digbeth Branch is a mile and a quarter in length, with a fall of 40 feet, by six locks, to the Warwick and Birmingham Canal, on the east side of the town of Birmingham. At Salford Bridge there is an aqueduct of seven arches, each 18 feet span. There is also a short tunnel at Curdworth.

This canal, which effected an inland communication between London and Hull, was opened on the 12th of July, 1790.

The Walsall Branch was executed under authority of an act of 34th George III. It is level, and four miles and a half in length, and was opened in June, 1799.

By an act of the 32nd George III. (cap. 81, royal assent 30th April, 1792), entitled, ' *An Act for making and maintaining a* ' *navigable Canal from or from near Wyrley Bank, in the county*

' *of Stafford, to communicate with the Birmingham and Birming-*
' *ham and Fazeley Canal, at or near the town of Wolverhampton,*
' *in the said county ; and also, certain collateral Cuts therein*
' *described, from the said Canal,*' the following tonnage rates are
secured to the proprietors of the Birmingham Canal.

TONNAGE RATES.

d.

For all Goods landed within One Mile of the First Lock at Wolverhampton 2 per Ton.
And if passing through any one or more of the Wolverhampton Locks .... 6 ditto.

The Warwick and Birmingham Canal Act, of 33rd George
III. enables the proprietors to connect their navigation with the
Digbeth Branch of the Birmingham and Fazeley Canal, upon
payment to the latter company of the following tonnage rates, in
lieu of dues, between Farmer's Bridge and the said communication.

TONNAGE RATES.

d.

On all Goods passing from the Warwick and Birmingham Canal, into } 6 per Ton.
    the Birmingham and Fazeley Canal, for a limited time .... }
At the end of the period .... 5 ditto.
Also, on all Goods out of the Warwick and Birmingham Canal, into the } 3 ditto.
    Birmingham Canal .... }

The Birmingham Canal Navigations, connected as they are
with the Coventry, the Grand Trunk, the Worcester and Birmingham, the Dudley, the Warwick and Birmingham, the Wyrley
and Essington, the Staffordshire and Worcestershire, and the Birmingham and Liverpool Junction Canals, present a very important
feature in the map of inland navigation, as by these, a communication is opened with the most important towns in England and
Wales.

The populous towns of Birmingham, Wolverhampton, Bilstone, Wednesbury and Walsall, are on its banks, and it affords the
greatest facilities to the transit of the produce of the most valuable
mineral district in the world. Some estimate of the trade upon
this navigation may be formed by the following amount of tonnage
received by the company from the years 1818 to 1823, inclusive.

Amount of Tonnage, in 1818, £84,295   Amount of Tonnage, in 1821, £85,675
......................1819, 83,442   ....1822, 79,733
......................1820, 83,303   ....1823, 88,805

BIRMINGHAM AND LIVERPOOL JUNCTION CANAL.

7 George IV. Cap. 95, Royal Assent 26th May, 1826.
7 & 8 George IV. Cap. 2, Royal Assent 21st March, 1827.

THIS line of canal, which is now in the course of execution, commences in the summit level of the Staffordshire and Worcestershire Canal, near Tettenhall, about one mile from Autherley, the place where the Birmingham Canal communicates with the Staffordshire and Worcestershire Canal. Its course is to the northwest, upon a level with the last-mentioned canal, by Chillington Part, Stretton Hall, and Little Onn Hall, where there is a lock, with a fall of 7 feet 3 inches, and which is the summit level, at a distance of eleven miles and a quarter from the commencement. From thence it continues, by the village of Cowley, for the distance of four miles and a half, on the same level, to near the village of Norbury, where the Newport Branch commences: from thence it continues for the further distance of nine miles and a half to the second lock, so that this canal is extended through the country a distance of twenty-five miles and a half, with only one lock. From the second lock, the canal is continued, in a northerly course, by Cheswardine Hill, to the town of Drayton, crossing the River Tarn; hence by the Brine Spring, near Adderley Hall, to the town of Audlem, in Cheshire; then, crossing the River Weaver, it proceeds by the Salt Springs, and by the town of Nantwich, to the United Navigation of the Ellesmere and Chester Canals, near Dorfold Hall, about three quarters of a mile north-west of the last-mentioned town.

The length from the second lock, to its termination at the above-mentioned navigation, is thirteen miles and a half, with a fall of 167½ feet, by twenty-six locks, thus disposed—from the second to the fifth lock, is a distance of half a mile; between the fifth and the sixth, it is nearly four miles; in the next half mile are five locks; then a pool of one mile and a quarter; in the following mile are eleven locks; in the next four miles are four locks; then a pool, of nearly three miles; and within one-tenth of a mile further, two locks; the remaining distance to the Chester

Canal is two miles and three quarters, on a level. The total length of the navigation is thirty-nine miles, with a fall of 174¾ feet, by twenty-seven locks.

The act for making this canal, which received the royal assent the 26th of May, 1826, is entitled, ' *An Act for making a navigable* ' *Canal from the Staffordshire and Worcestershire Canal, in the* ' *parish of Tettenhall, in the county of Stafford, to the United* ' *Navigation of the Ellesmere and Chester Canals, in the parish of* ' *Acton, in the county palatine of Chester.*' The subscribers to this canal, at the time the act was obtained, were three hundred and twenty-three in number, amongst whom were the Earl and Countess of Surrey, Earl Gower, Lord Levison Gower, Lord Crewe, and many other distinguished individuals, who were incorporated by the name of " The Company of Proprietors of the " Birmingham and Liverpool Junction Canal Navigation." They are empowered to raise among themselves the sum of £400,000, in four thousand shares of £100 each, and the act directs that the whole shall be subscribed before the work is commenced, of which, £325,000 was raised before going to parliament. They were further empowered to raise an additional sum of £100,000, on mortgage of the rates and duties, the interest of which is made payable in preference to any other claim.

TONNAGE AND WHARFAGE RATES.

	d.
For Coal or other Minerals, (except Lime,) Coke, Goods, Wares, Merchandize, Commodities and Things whatsoever	1½ per Ton, per Mile.
Lime	½ ditto. ditto.

Fractions to be taken as for a Quarter of a Ton, and as for a Quarter of a Mile.

EXEMPTION FROM TOLL.

Paving-stones, Gravel, Sand, and all other Materials for making or repairing of Roads, (Limestone excepted) all Dung, Soil, Marl, and all sorts of Manure for the Improvement only of any Lands or Grounds lying within any Parish or Place through which this Canal will be carried, and belonging to the Owners or Occupiers of such Lands as may be required for the purposes of the Act.

Boats of less Burthen than Twenty Tons not to pass without leave, unless there is not Water for a greater Burthen.

Five years are allowed for the execution of the works authorized to be done under this act, and the powers are to cease at the expiration of that period, excepting as to such part as shall have been completed.

In consideration of the lockage water, which is derived from the Staffordshire and Worcestershire Canal, by locking down from it, the proprietors of that canal are authorized to collect the following

TONNAGE RATES.

	s.
For Coal or other Minerals, Coke, Goods, Wares or Merchandize, Commodities and Things whatsoever, which shall pass out of the Staffordshire and Worcestershire Canal into the Birmingham and Liverpool Junction Canal, or out of the last-mentioned Canal into the former...	2 per Ton.

The last-mentioned rates are to be collected by the Birmingham and Liverpool Junction Canal Company, at the expense of the Staffordshire and Worcestershire Canal Proprietors; and in order that no unnecessary waste of water may be made, the Birmingham and Liverpool Junction Canal Company are required to construct on the sumit level, a regulation lock, consisting of four pairs of gates. The locks upon this navigation are 7 feet 6 inches in width, and 80 feet long.

The company had originally intended to make a branch from near the village of Cowley, to join the Donnington Wood, or Marquis of Stafford's Canal, at Pave Lane, which was subsequently abandoned. Its length was seven miles and three quarters, and level. The estimate for making it was made by Mr. W. A. Provis, under the direction of Mr. T. Telford, and amounted to the sum of £55,466, 17s. 1d. The estimate for the main line was also made by the same parties, and which amounted to the sum of £388,454, 1s. 6d.

In 1827, the company applied to parliament, and obtained another act, entitled, ' *An Act to enable the Company of Proprietors* ' *of the Birmingham and Liverpool Junction Canal Navigation, to* ' *alter the Line of the said Navigation, and to make certain Branches* ' *therefrom, in the counties of Stafford and Salop.*'

The deviations in the original line here contemplated are of little importance, as they consist merely of three alterations in the line between Connery Pool and Plardiwick, amounting, in length, to one mile and one thousand eight hundred and nineteen yards, while the parts abandoned are three hundred and forty-one yards longer; but this act gives power to make two branches from the main line, one of which, called the Newport Branch, commences near the village of Norbury, from whence it passes close to the town of Newport, and from thence to the Shrewsbury Canal, at Wappinshall Bridge, in the parish of Wellington. Its length is ten miles and a quarter, with a fall, from the main line, of 139 feet, by twenty-three locks; the last four miles and a half to the Shrewsbury Canal, being level. From this branch there is a collateral cut to a place called The Buttery, in the parish of Edgmond, which is nearly half a mile in length, the estimate for which is £2,421, 18s. 10d. and for the Newport Branch, £72,629, 13s. 2d. The company had it in contemplation to make a second collateral cut, from the Newport Branch, to Lime Kiln Bridge, but it was abandoned. The length was two miles and three quarters, and the estimate for making it amounted to the sum of £17,652, 14s. 6d.; in lieu, however, of which, the company are required to make a cut or railway from the Newport Branch to the limestone works, at Donnington Wood, and Lilleshall, belonging to the Right Honourable George Granville Lord Gower, whenever he shall require it to be done.

All these estimates were made by Mr. Thomas Telford, in 1826.

On the above branches, the company are empowered to collect the same tonnage rates as are allowed on the main line by the act of 7th George IV.

In this act, the company are restricted from using the water in Aqualate Mere, Wyn's Well Pool, and the Moss Pool, belonging to Sir T. F. Fenton Boughey, Bart. or the streams of water supplying and passing through the same.

The chief advantages arising from the execution of this canal is a shorter navigation between the ports of Chester, Liverpool, and the district of North Wales, and the important towns of Shrewsbury, Wolverhampton, Birmingham, the mineral districts of Staffordshire and Shropshire, and the Metropolis. The agricultural districts in the south of Cheshire, the western parts of Staffordshire, and the north-eastern parts of Salop, through which this canal is now being constructed, will also be greatly benefited.

BLYTH RIVER.

30 George II. Cap. 47, Royal Assent 1st April, 1757.

THIS river rises near Laxfield, in the north-eastern parts of Suffolk, whence it takes an easterly course, by Ubbeston Hall, Hevingham Hall, and Walpole, to near the market town of Halesworth, from which place to the sea, at Southwould, it was made navigable under the authority of an act, entitled, '*An Act* '*for making the River Blyth navigable from Halesworth Bridge,* '*in the county of Suffolk, into the Haven of Southwould.*'

It is in length nine miles, and there are four locks upon it, and although it is in a part of the kingdom where there are neither minerals or manufactures, it is of considerable advantage to the district lying between the navigable Rivers Waveney and Gipping, by the facility it gives for the export of its agricultural productions, and the import of lime, coal, and merchandize in general.

BLYTH RIVER.

THIS river rises a few miles west of Belsay Castle, in Northumberland, the seat of Sir Charles Miles Lambert Monck, Bart. whence, taking a westerly course, by Kirkley Hall, and about a mile to the north of Blagdon Park, it pursues a circuitous route by Bedlington, and falls into the harbour of Blyth, near a village bearing that name, which is situate on its southern bank.

It is navigable only for a short distance, as a tideway river, and consequently free of toll. On its northern bank, at about a mile above the village of Coopen, are the Bedlington Iron Works, and a short distance west of the last-mentioned place, a railway of considerable length extends to the collieries near Willow Bridge, five miles east of Morpeth. At Blyth there are also private railways from the collieries situate three quarters of a mile to the west of the village, upon which coal is conveyed to the harbour, to be shipped for London, and the towns on the eastern coast.

BOLTON AND LEIGH RAILWAY.

6 George IV. Cap. 18, Royal Assent 31st March, 1825.
9 George IV. Cap. 8, Royal Assent 26th March, 1828.

This railway commences at the Manchester, Bolton, and Bury Canal, in the township of Haulgh, near the town of Bolton-le-Moors, and proceeds in a south-westerly direction through the extensive collieries in the neighbourhood of Hulton Hall, thence by Atherton Hall, to that branch of the Leeds and Liverpool Canal which communicates with the Duke of Bridgewater's Canal, at the town of Leigh. It is in length seven miles and three quarters, and there is a rise of 119 feet, in the first two thousand three hundred and sixty yards from Bolton; and from this point to the highway adjoining the canal, at Leigh, is a fall of 337 feet. There is an inclined plane of one inch per yard, in the township of Great Bolton, one thousand three hundred and eighty-six yards in length; and by the parliamentary plan it appears that another is intended to be made in the townships of Over Hulton and Atherton, of the length of four thousand six hundred and twenty yards, with a fall of 303 feet.

The act for making this railway, received the royal assent on the 31st March, 1825, and is entitled, '*An Act for making and* '*maintaining a Railway or Tramroad from or from near the Man-* '*chester, Bolton, and Bury Canal, in the parish of Bolton-le-Moors,* '*to or near the Leeds and Liverpool Canal, in the parish of Leigh,* '*all in the county palatine of Lancaster.*'

The subscribers to this scheme, at the time the act was obtained, consisted of fifty persons, who were incorporated by the name of "The Bolton and Leigh Railway Company," and they obtained power to raise among themselves, by subscription, the sum of £44,000, in four hundred and forty shares of £100 each; and if any part of the said sum of £44,000 remains unsubscribed, the company have power to borrow such part upon promissory notes under the common seal, or they may raise the same by mortgage, on security of the rates, the interest of which is to be paid in preference to dividends.

TONNAGE RATES.

	d.	
Limestone, Dung, Compost and all sorts of Manure, all Materials for the repair of Roads, which shall be drawn, propelled, and carried, by and at the expense of the Company	3	per Ton, per Mile.
Ditto, drawn or propelled only by the Engines of the Company	2	ditto. ditto.
Ditto, drawn or propelled by the Engines, or other Power, and carried in the Waggons belonging to other Persons than the said Company	2	ditto. ditto.
Coal, Culm, Coke, Charcoal, Cinders, Stone, Marl, Sand, Clay, Building, Pitching and Paving-stones, Flags, Bricks, Tiles, Slate, Lime, Earth, Staves, Deals, Lead and Iron in Pigs, or other Metals which shall be drawn, or propelled, and carried by and at the expense of the Company	3½	ditto. _ ditto.
Ditto, drawn or propelled only by the Engines of the Company	3	ditto. ditto.
Ditto, drawn or propelled by the Engines, or other Power, and carried in the Waggons belonging to other Persons than the said Company	2½	ditto. ditto.
Timber, Cotton, Wool, Hides, Drugs, Dye-woods, Sugar, Corn, Grain, Flour, Manufactured Goods, Lead in Sheets, or Iron in Bars, and all other Wares and Merchandize, drawn, or propelled, and carried, by and at the expense of the Company.......	4½	ditto. ditto.
Ditto, drawn or propelled only by the Engines of the Company	4	ditto. ditto.
Ditto, drawn or propelled by the Engines, or other Power, and carried in Waggons belonging to other Persons than the said Company.......	3½	ditto. ditto.
All Articles ascending on each of the Inclined Planes where permanent Engines are used.............	8	per Ton in addition.
Ditto, descending on each of the Inclined Planes where permanent Engines are kept.............	3	ditto, per Mile, in addition.

Fractions to be taken as for a Quarter of a Ton, and as for a Quarter of a Mile.

Two branches to this railway are contemplated, both commencing near a place called The Lecturer's Closes, one of which will terminate in Great Moor Street, and the other in Deansgate, both in the town of Bolton.

The estimate for the whole work was made by Mr. James Stevenson, and amounted to the sum of £43,000, of which, £36,000 was subscribed before the act was obtained; it is said, however, that to finish it according to the present designs of the company, it will cost £75,000.

Soon after the passing of the act, Mr. Daglish, civil engineer, was employed upon this railway, but it has been subsequently under the direction of Mr. Stevenson. Stationary engines will be placed on the inclined planes, and locomotive engines on the other parts. Both are to burn their own smoke.

Seven years are allowed for the execution of the works, and if not then finished, the company's power is to cease, excepting as to such parts as may have been completed.

On the 26th March, 1828, another act, entitled, ' *An Act for* ' *amending and enlarging the Powers and Provisions of an Act* ' *relating to the Bolton and Leigh Railway,*' received the royal assent, but does not contain any thing in which the public have an interest.

The principal object of this railway, is the facilitating the conveyance of coal, slate, stone, and other commodities, from the interior of the country to the port of Liverpool, by the Leeds and Liverpool Canal from Leigh; and the return of corn, iron, lime, and merchandize from the above port, and from Warrington and other places, to Bolton, Bury, and their populous environs.

An act received the royal assent on the 14th May, 1829, for making a railway from Leigh to the Liverpool and Manchester Railroad, in the township of Kenyon, which, when completed, will greatly improve the value and add to the importance of the line above described.

BORROWSTOWNESS CANAL.

8 George III. Cap. 63, Royal Assent 8th March, 1768.
24 George III. Cap. 5, Royal Assent 24th December, 1783.

THIS canal was originally intended as a branch or collateral cut to the Forth and Clyde Canal, and the necessary powers for making it are contained in an act of 8th George III. entitled, ' *An* ' *Act for making and maintaining a navigable Cut or Canal from* ' *the Firth or River of Forth, at or near the mouth of the River of* ' *Carron, in the county of Sterling, to the Firth or River of Clyde,* ' *at or near a place called Dalmuir Burnfoot, in the county of* ' *Dumbarton; and also a collateral Cut from the same to the city* ' *of Glasgow; and for making a navigable Cut or Canal of Com-* ' *munication from the Port and Harbour of Borrowstowness, to join* ' *the said Canal, at or near the place where it will fall into the* ' *Firth of Forth.*'

Though it is thus embodied in the first act relating to the Forth and Clyde Canal, yet a separate company, consisting of one hundred and fifteen persons, (amongst whom were the Dukes of Hamilton and Brandon, Buccleugh, Argyle, and Duchess of

Argyle, Earls of Buchan, Home, Roseberry, Hopetoun, and Countess of Hopetoun, and many other distinguished individuals,) were incorporated by the name of " The Company of Proprieto:s " of the Borrowstowness Canal Navigation." They were authorized to raise £5,000, in one hundred shares of £50 each, and a further sum of £3,000, if the former sum should be found·insufficient.

The line of canal stretches along the south shore of the Firth of Forth, from th₃ port and harbour of Borrowstowness; it crosses the water of Avon, and thence proceeds to the Forth and Clyde Canal, at Grangemouth, near the mouth of the Carron River. Its length is about seven miles, and level throughout; the depth is 7 feet.

Considerable progress had been made in this canal previous to 1783, and the £8,000 which the company were empowered to raise under the act already recited, was expended, when they were under the necessity of again applying to parliament for a second, entitled, ' *An Act to enable the Company of Proprietors of* ' *the Borrowstowness navigable Cut or Canal more effectually to* ' *complete and maintain the same.*' By this act, the proprietors are empowered to raise among themselves the additional sum of £12,000, to be divided into shares of £50 each, and a further sum of £4,000 should it be deemed necessary; or they may obain the same by mortgage of the tolls, or by granting annuities on lives.

TONNAGE AND WHARFAGE

Granted by the Act of 8th George III. which have not been altered by the subsequent Act.

	d.
Iron, Coal, Stones, Timber and all other Goods, Wares and Merchandize, and Commodities whatsoever............	3 per Ton, per Mile.
Lime, Lime-stone and Iron-stone	1 ditto. ditto.

EXEMPTION FROM TONNAGE RATES.

Paving-stones, Gravel, and all Materials for the repairing of Roads, (Limestone excepted,) Dung, Marl and all sorts of Manure.

As Borrowstowness is (with the exception of Leith) the principal trading town on the Forth, and where there is depth of water for vessels of three hundred tons, at neap-tides, it was the original intention of the promoters of the Forth and Clyde Canal to terminate it at this port; but they were subsequently induced by the force of private interests, to abandon this intention, and adopt this canal as a collateral branch.

The principal object of the Borrowstowness Canal was to avoid the difficult navigation of the Forth, and for improving the estates through which it passed; and though considerable sums of money have been expended on this work, it appears now to be entirely abandoned.

BOURN EAU RIVER.

21 George III. Cap. 22, Royal Assent 29th March, 1781.

THIS river proceeds from the navigable River Glen, in Deeping Fen, in a north-western direction to the town of Bourn. It is three miles and a half in length, and nearly straight.

It appears by the preamble of the only act relating to this navigation, entitled, ' *An Act for improving the Navigation of the* ' *River called Bourn Eau, from the town of Bourn to its Junction* ' *with the River Glen, at a place called Tongue End, in the county* ' *of Lincoln*,' that it had been previously used as a navigation, but that it had become of little use, in consequence of being nearly choked up by mud, and other obstructions; the above recited act, therefore, gives authority to trustees therein named, to make good the navigation by scouring, cleansing, and making the same 5 feet deep and 30 feet wide, where its present banks will admit of it.

TONNAGE RATES.

	s.	d.
For all Goods, Wares, Merchandize or Commodities whatsoever	2	6 per Ton.

And so in proportion for any greater or less Weight than a Ton.

The trustees, in whom this navigation is vested, are the lord of the manor of Bourn, with the members for the time being; the owner of Bourn South Fen Pastures; the lord of the manor of Bourn Abbots, with its members, and nine other persons, three to be chosen annually by each of the parties above-mentioned; also all other persons who shall be holders of £100 stock, to be raised for the purposes of this act. The sum of £60 per annum is paid to the trustees by the owners of an estate of eight hundred and sixty acres, situate on the banks of the river, and which, at the time the act was obtained, belonged to Sir Gilbert Heathcote, Bart. in quittance of the obligation he was under of keeping in repair a considerable portion of the north-west bank of this navigation, and which, in consequence, devolved upon the trustees. The Marquis of Exeter also pays to the trustees the sum of forty shillings annually on a similar account.

The principal use to which this navigation is put, is to facilitate the conveyance of the surplus agricultural produce of the fens, to the port of Boston, (to which it has communication by the River Glen) and to supply Bourn and its environs with groceries and other articles.

BRADFORD CANAL.

11 George III. Cap. 89, Royal Assent 29th April, 1771.
42 George III. Cap. 93, Royal Assent 22nd June, 1802.

THIS canal commences in the Leeds and Liverpool Canal, near the manufacturing village of Shipley, and extends along the eastern side of the valley, in which runs the rivulet called Bradford Brook, and terminates at Hoppy Bridge, situate in the lower part of the town of Bradford. It is in length three miles, with a rise from the Leeds and Liverpool Canal of $86\frac{1}{4}$ feet by ten locks. The locks are 66 feet in length, and in width 15 feet 2 inches, being the same in dimension as those on the Leeds and Liverpool Canal. The depth of water is 5 feet.

The act under which this canal was executed, is entitled, ' *An* ' *Act for making a navigable Cut or Canal from Bradford, to join* ' *the Leeds and Liverpool Canal, at Windhill, in the township of* ' *Idle, in the county of York.*' The subscribers to this canal, at the time the act was obtained, consisted of twenty-eight persons, who were incorporated by the name of " The Company of Pro- " prietors of the Bradford Navigation." They were empowered to raise among themselves £6,000, in sixty shares of £100 each, but the works were not to commence until the whole sum was raised; and if the above sum was insufficient, they were empowered to raise an additional sum of £3,000, by the admission of new subscribers.

TONNAGE RATES.

		d.
Clay, Bricks, Stones, Coal, Lime, Dung and Manure....................	6	per Ton.
Timber, Goods, Wares, Merchandize or other Commodities	9	ditto.

And so in proportion for a greater or less Quantity than a Ton.

If Goods remain upon the Company's Wharfs more than Twenty-four Hours, they are entitled to Wharfage, the Amount of which to be agreed on between the Parties.

That Fifty Feet of round, or Forty Feet of square Oak, Ash, or Elm Timber, or Fifty Feet of Fir, or Deal, Balk, Poplar, and other Timber Wood, shall be estimated as One Ton; and that Lime, Stone, Coal, and other Goods, shall consist of Twenty-two Hundred Weight of One Hundred and Twelve Pounds each.

No Boat of less than Twenty Tons Burthen to pass a Lock without leave, unless Tonnage is paid to that Amount.

The canal was finished in 1774.

For the purpose of giving a better supply of water to this canal, the proprietors were under the necessity of purchasing mills and lands contiguous to its banks, by which the shares were increased, by additional calls, to £250 per share; and in order to secure this part of their property from the operations of the statute of mortmain, they applied to parliament, and obtained an act, entitled, ' *An Act for vesting divers Estates in the parishes of* ' *Bradford and Calverley, in the West Riding of the county of* ' *York, purchased for the benefit of the Proprietors of the Brad-* ' *ford Canal Navigation, in Trustees, upon certain Trusts, dis-* ' *charged from all Claims of the Crown, in respect of any* ' *Forfeiture incurred under or by virtue of the Laws or Statutes* ' *of Mortmain.*'

As the neighbourhood of Bradford abounds in flag paving-stone, coal, and valuable beds of iron-stone, this canal has been of infinite advantage in conveying them to various parts of the country. The extensive iron works at Bowling, and Wibsey Low Moor, with others of inferior note in the vicinity, may, in a great measure, be said to have been founded, or at least greatly enlarged, in consequence of the facility which this canal afforded, by its connection with the Leeds and Liverpool Canal, for the conveyance of their castings to all parts of the kingdom.

From these foundries, iron railways approach the town of Bradford, but though they do not extend to the head of the canal, yet they have the effect of materially reducing the price of the carriage of the heavy articles from these works. Flag, stone and slate from the eastern bank of this canal, and also near its head, (where it is very extensively worked) finds its way to the London

Market, and to the towns on the eastern coast; and coal, and the first-mentioned articles, are sent by this and the Leeds and Liverpool Canal, into the extensive district of Craven. Since Bradford became the centre of the stuff manufacture and principal market for it, wool is also become a considerable article of traffic upon this navigation.

BRANDLING'S RAILROAD.

31 George II. Cap. 22, Royal Assent 9th June, 1758.

THIS railroad proceeds from the extensive collieries, situate at Middleton, (belonging to the Rev. R. H. Brandling,) about three miles south of the town of Leeds, and terminates at convenient staiths, near Meadow-Lane in the above town. It is three miles in length, and was constructed under the powers of an act, entitled, ' An Act for establishing Agreements made between Charles Brand- ' ling, Esq. and other Persons, Proprietors of Lands, for laying ' down a Waggon Way, in order for the better supplying the town ' and neighbourhood of Leeds, in the county of York, with Coals.'

There are upon this railway two inclined planes, one at the southern corner of Hunslet Carr, and the other at Belleisle, near Middleton, upon which the full descending waggons, regulated by a brake, draw up the empty ones. It is here worthy of remark, that it was upon this railway that the powers of the locomotive engine were first applied in this part of the country, by the ingenious inventor, Mr. John Blenkinsop, the manager of the Middleton Collieries.

BRECKNOCK AND ABERGAVENNY CANAL.

33 George III. Cap. 96, Royal Assent 28th March, 1793.
44 George III. Cap. 29, Royal Assent 3rd May, 1804.

THIS canal commences in the Monmouthshire Canal, about one mile south of the town of Pontypool, and crossing the River Avon by an aqueduct, enters a tunnel of two hundred and twenty yards in length; thence, in a northerly direction, by Mamhilad, Great House, Blaenavon Iron Works, and the town of Abergavenny, to Govilon; where, taking a north-easterly course, and keeping parallel with the Usk River, it proceeds by Daney Park, Llanelly Iron Works, Crickhowel, Peterstone Court, and Tyn Maur, to Brecon, near which town it communicates with the Hay Railway. At Buckland House, it communicates with the Brynoer Tramroad, from the Blaen Rumney Iron Works; and near Crickhowel, several railways extend from it to the extensively worked limestone quarries, collieries and iron works, which abound in that immediate neighbourhood. At the village of Govilon, the Llanfihangel Railroad, passing by the town of Abergavenny, connects with this navigation; and three miles north of Pontypool, it is also joined by the Mamhilad Railway. There is also a railway of one mile and a quarter in length, proceeding from it, across the River Usk, to Llangroiney.

From the junction with the Monmouthshire Navigation, this canal is continued on a level with its summit to Abergavenny, a distance of eleven miles, and maintains the same level three miles and a half further; from thence to its termination at Brecon, is eighteen miles and a half, with a rise of 68 feet; the total length being thirty-three miles.

Mr. T. Dadford, Jun. was the engineer employed on this work, which was executed under the powers of an act, entitled, ' *An Act for making and maintaining a navigable Canal from the* ' *town of Brecknock to the Monmouthshire Canal, near the town of* ' *Pontypool, in the county of Monmouth; and for making and* ' *maintaining Railways and Stone Roads to several Iron Works and* ' *Mines in the counties of Brecknock and Monmouth.*' By this act the subscribers were incorporated by the name of " The Company " of Proprietors of the Brecknock and Abergavenny Canal Navi- " gation," with power to raise among themselves the sum of £100,000, in one thousand shares of £100 each, and the additional sum of £50,000, if necessary.

TONNAGE RATES ON THE CANAL.

		d.	
Iron-stone, Iron-ore, Lead-ore, Coals, Culm, Coaks, Cinders and Charcoal...	}	2 per Ton, per Mile.	
Lime, Lime-stone, Tiles, Slate, Bricks, Flag-stones, and other Stones, Clay, Sand, Hay, Straw, and Corn in the Straw, and all Material for the repairing of Roads, and all kinds of Manure	}	1 ditto.	ditto.
Cattle, Sheep, Swine and other Beasts........................		4 ditto.	ditto.

TONNAGE RATES CONTINUED.

	d.
Iron and Lead	3 per Ton, per Mile.
Timber, Goods, Wares and Merchandize	4 ditto. ditto.

Fractions to be taken as for a Quarter of a Ton, and as for Half a Mile.
Boats under Twenty Tons lading not to pass any Lock without leave, or without paying for that Tonnage.

RAILROAD DUES.

	d.
Every Horse, Mule or Ass	1 each.
Cows and other Cattle..	½ each.
Sheep, Swine and Calves	5 per Score.

As the making of this canal would materially increase the value of the shares in the Monmouthshire Canal Navigation, that company agreed to give the Brecknock and Abergavenny Canal Proprietors the sum of £3,000; also to take the same tonnage upon their navigation, on all articles conveyed along any part of the Brecknock and Abergavenny Canal, as that company were empowered to collect.

In 1804, this company, having expended the money authorized to be raised under the preceding act, applied to parliament and obtained an act to enable them to raise an additional fund to complete their works, entitled, ' *An Act for enabling the Company of* ' *Proprietors of the Brecknock and Abergavenny Canal to raise a* ' *further Sum of Money for completing the said Canal, and the* ' *Works thereto belonging ; and for altering and enlarging the* ' *Powers of an Act made in the Thirty-third Year of his present* ' *Majesty, for making the said Canal.*'

As this canal skirts the rich mineral districts of Monmouth and Glamorgan, and has a direct communication with the Bristol Channel, by means of the Monmouthshire Canal, every facility is afforded for the export of its valuable productions, which was the ostensible object of its promoters.

BRIDGEWATER'S (THE DUKE OF) CANAL.

10 Geo. II. C. 22, R. A. 22nd Apr. 1737.   32 Geo. II. C. 2, R. A. 23rd Mar. 1759.
33 Geo. II. C. 2, R. A. 24th Mar. 1760.   2 Geo. III. C. 11, R. A. 24th Mar. 1762.
6 Geo. III. C. 17, R. A. 18th Mar. 1766.   35 Geo. III. C. 44, R. A. 28th Apr. 1795.

The 32nd George II. is the first act of parliament, under power of which the execution of this navigation was commenced,

and it is entitled, ' *An Act to enable the Most Noble Francis Duke*
' *of Bridgewater, to make a navigable Cut or Canal from a certain*
' *place in the township of Salford, to or near Worsley Mill, and*
' *Middlewood, in the manor of Worsley, and to or near a place*
' *called Hollin Ferry, in the county palatine of Lancaster.*'   In this
act it is . recited, that certain persons had obtained an act in the
10th George II. entitled, ' *An Act for making navigable the River*
' *or Brook called Worsley Brook, from Worsley Mill, in the town-*
' *ship of Worsley, in the county palatine of Lancaster, to the River*
' *Irwell, in the said county,*' but that they had hitherto neglected
to carry any of the powers of this act into execution.   This, then,
was the first step taken towards making this very early and useful
navigation; but the degree of supineness exhibited by the original
undertakers, in having so long neglected the execution of a work
which has been and is yet the source of immense wealth to its
noble owner, is most strikingly contrasted by the enterprising
spirit and astonishing perseverance of the Duke of Bridgewater,
who, unassisted, except by the natural genius of Brindley, carried
into execution a series of difficult and expensive works, which are,
even at this time, unexampled.

The primary object of " The Father of British Inland Navi-
" gation," as the Duke of Bridgewater has been justly styled, was
to open his valuable collieries at Worsley, and to supply the town
of Manchester with coal, at a much cheaper rate than could be
done by the imperfect navigation of the Mersey and Irwell.   The
works were commenced immediately on the royal assent being
given to the act, under the powers of which, a considerable portion
of that part of the canal, between Worsley Mill and Manchester,
was executed; but the proposed line from Worsley to Hollin Ferry,
on the Mersey and Irwell Navigation, was abandoned.   In the
year subsequent to the obtaining of the first act, the Duke again
applied to parliament and obtained a second, entitled, ' *An Act to*
' *enable the Most Noble Francis Duke of Bridgewater, to make a*
' *navigable Cut or Canal from or near Worsley Mill, over the*
' *River Irwell, to the town of Manchester, in the county palatine of*
' *Lancaster, and to or near Longford Bridge, in the township of*
' *Stretford, in the said county.*'

Under this act the whole of the canal from Worsley to Manchester, together with the extensive subterranean works, at his coal mines, in Worsley, were executed. The aqueduct over the Mersey and Irwell Navigation at Barton, was opened on the 17th July, 1761, and shortly afterwards the line of canal to Manchester. The underground canals and tunnels at Worsley are said to be eighteen miles in length, and to have cost £168,960. From Worsley, a branch of one mile and a half in length extends to Chat Moss, across which, the line to Hollin Ferry, near Glazebrook, was intended to pass.

In 1762 this spirited and patriotic nobleman applied to parliament, and obtained the necessary powers to enable him to extend his navigation, so as to open a better navigable communication with Liverpool. This act is entitled, ' *An Act to enable the Most* ' *Noble Francis Duke of Bridgewater, to make a navigable Cut or* ' *Canal from Longford Bridge, in the township of Stretford, in the* ' *county palatine of Lancaster, to the River Mersey, at a place* ' *called the Hempstones, in the township of Halton, in the county of* ' *Chester.*' It is here recited that the canal from the Duke's coal mines to Longford Bridge, whence the proposed extension was to proceed, together with a considerable portion of the remainder of the line to Manchester, was finished.

The original line to Hempstones takes a south-westerly course from Longford Bridge, crossing the Mersey by an aqueduct; by the town of Altringham, and Dunham Massey, (the seat of the Earl of Stamford and Warrington) near which place it passes over the River Bollin by an aqueduct, thence by Lymm, Groppenhall, crossing the London Road two miles south of Warrington, to the River Mersey, at Hempstones; but before the latter portion could be executed, an act of the 6th George III. was obtained by a company, to enable them to make a canal to connect the Rivers Trent and Mersey, which is entitled, ' *An Act for making a navi-* ' *gable Cut or Canal from the River Trent, at or near Wilden* ' *Ferry, in the county of Derby, to the River Mersey, at or near* ' *Runcorn Gap.*' This act contains a clause, whereby the Duke of Bridgewater engages to form a junction with the above line of the Trent and Mersey Canal at Preston Brook, instead of opening into the Mersey at Hempstones, which is nearly one mile and a half higher up the river than the place where the Trent and

Mersey Canal proposed to enter it; also to execute that part of
the line of the Trent and Mersey Canal, from the junction above-
mentioned, at Preston Brook, to its termination at Runcorn; for
which the Duke should receive the following rates upon that part
of the Trent and Mersey Line of Canal, which, commencing from
Preston Brook, takes a circuitous route through the beautiful
grounds of Norton Priory, the seat of Sir R. Brooke, Bart. and
thence by Lower Runcorn to the Mersey. On the 31st of December, 1772, the ten locks at Runcorn were opened, and the whole
of the canal and other works were completed to Manchester, on
the 21st of March, 1776.

TONNAGE RATES.

For all Coal, Stone, Timber, and other Goods, Wares, Merchan- } 1 per Ton, per Mile.
dize and Commodities .... } *d.*

And so in proportion for any greater or less Distance than a Mile, or less Weight than
a Ton; but if any Boat shall pass the whole of the Locks, to be erected at Runcorn, then the same Tonnage to be paid as if the Vessel had passed along the
whole Distance between Runcorn and Preston Brook. Also, the Duke has power
to charge, upon this part of the Navigation, such additional Tonnage to the
Penny Rate above-mentioned, so that the total Amount does not exceed the Rate
which the Duke is empowered to collect upon the other parts of his Navigation.

On the 18th of March, 1766, the royal assent was given to an
act, entitled, ' *An Act to enable the Most Noble Francis Duke of*
' *Bridgewater, to extend a Branch of his Navigation, Cut, or*
' *Canal, upon Sale Moor, in the county of Chester, to the Market*
' *Town of Stockport, in the said county,*' but no portion of this pro-
posed canal was ever executed. It was in length seven miles and a
half, with a rise of 68 feet. By another act obtained in the 35th
George III. entitled, ' *An Act to enable the Most Noble Francis*
' *Duke of Bridgewater, to make a navigable Cut from his present*
' *Navigation, in the township of Worsley, in the county palatine of*
' *Lancaster, to the township of Pennington, near the town of Leigh,*
' *in the said county,*' the Duke of Bridgewater was enabled to
extend his navigation to the town of Leigh, to which place the
Leeds and Liverpool Canal Company have subsequently extended
a branch of their navigation, so that now another navigable communication is made through the heart of Lancashire, connecting
the towns of Wigan, Chorley, Blackburn, Preston, and those two
important places, Liverpool and Manchester.

The length of the Duke's Canal from Castle Field, in Manchester, to near Longford Bridge, where the main line leaves the Worsley Branch, is three miles and a quarter ; and from the last-mentioned place to Preston Brook, where it joins the Trent and Mersey, is eighteen miles and a half; and from thence to Runcorn, is five miles and a quarter, all on the same level, at which place it has a fall into the tideway of the Mersey, at low water, of 82½ feet, by ten locks.   The branch to Worsley is five miles, and from thence to Leigh is six miles, and are both upon the same level with the main line.

TONNAGE RATES.

	s.	d.	
For all Coal, Stone, Timber, and other Goods, Wares, Merchandize, and Commodities whatsoever, passing on any part of, or on all his Navigations, (with the exception of that part between Runcorn and Preston Brook)	2	6	per Ton.
For passing by the New Locks and Basin at Runcorn..	0	8	ditto, in addition.
For every description of Articles (except Paving-stones) passing to or from the Rochdale Canal, into or out of the Duke's Canal, at Manchester................	1	2	per Ton.
Paving-stones	0	4	ditto.

All kinds of Manure, and Stones for repairing the Roads, are exempt from the Payment of Toll.

For the purpose of continuing this justly celebrated canal on one level from Manchester to Runcorn, and from Longford Bridge, by Worsley, to Leigh, great embankments became necessary, in consequence of the numerous vallies which intercept its course ; amongst them is one over Stretford Meadows, nine hundred yards in length, 17 feet high, and 112 feet at the base; that made at Barton Aqueduct, where it is 39 feet above the Mersey and Irwell Navigation, is two hundred yards in length.   There is also a stupendous embankment between Dunham Massey and Oughtrington Hall.   The whole of these canals and branches, with the exception of the cut to Leigh, were executed in five years, under the direction of Mr. Brindley, and at an expense to his noble patron of upwards of £220,000 ; but, as it all issued from his private purse, the public have no means of arriving at the exact amount, nor have they much better means of ascertaining the annual income, though it was estimated, some years ago, at £130,000.

This valuable concern is now the property of the Most Noble the Marquis of Stafford, and it is said to have increased his annual income to the enormous amount of £260,000.

These navigations, although made at the private expense of the Noble Duke, and valuable as they have proved to his successors, are of much greater importance to the town of Manchester and the surrounding country, from the facilities they have afforded for the transit of merchandize, and in reducing the price of minerals, which, before the execution of these works, could only be obtained at nearly double their present value.

BRIDGEWATER AND TAUNTON CANAL.

51 George III. Cap. 60, Royal Assent 14th May, 1811.
5 George IV. Cap. 120, Royal Assent 17th June, 1824.

THE line of this proposed canal, commencing at Morgan's Pill, on the River Avon, about six miles below the port of Bristol, proceeds in a straight line, and in a south-easterly direction, to near Clevdon Court; from which place, taking a southerly course, it crosses the River Yeo ; thence, west of the village of Puxton, crossing the eastern termination of the Mendip Hills, on the south side of which, an aqueduct is to be thrown over the navigable River Axe; hence, its course is continued in a straight line to near Huntspill Court, passing over the River Brue or Glastonbury Canal; thence, to the Tone and Parrett Navigation, near the village of Puriton, where it crosses the River Carey, at its junction with the Tone River, along the eastern bank of which, it continues its way two miles above the town of Bridgewater, where there is another aqueduct over the river. From the last-mentioned place it takes the course of the English and Bristol Channels' Ship Canal for two miles, when, diverging to the west, it passes the village of St. Michael's, running parallel with the last-mentioned canal, until it approaches the Tone, on the north bank of which it continues to its termination at Fire Pool Mills ; there forming a junction with the intended Grand Western Canal, near the town of Taunton. The length is forty-two miles and a half.

From the main line, there is a branch of two miles and a

quarter, to the coal and other works at Nailsea; and another, of four miles and three quarters, on the north bank of the Axe, by the town of Axbridge, to Cheddar. At Clevdon Hill there is a proposed tunnel of six hundred yards in length; and another at Banwell, the eastern edge of the Mendip Hills, the length of which is one thousand and fifty yards.

The subscribers to this canal were, at the time the act was obtained, three hundred and twenty-six in number, amongst whom were Sir James Dubberley, Sir Richard Graves, Sir John Kennaway, Sir William Rawlins, and the Right Honourable Sir George Yonge, Baronets. They were incorporated, in the first act, by the name of "The Company of Proprietors of the Bristol " and Taunton Canal Navigation," with power to raise among themselves the sum of £420,000, in four thousand two hundred shares of £100 each, with further power to raise among themselves, in proportion to the first subscription, if necessary, an additional sum of £150,000; or they may raise the same on mortgage of the tolls and duties hereby granted, the interest of which to be paid in preference to dividends or any other claim. In addition to the line of canal, the company obtained power to make railways or stone roads from the Nailsea Branch to the collieries and other works in that neighbourhood.

In the aqueducts over the navigable River Brue, or Glastonbury Canal, and the Axe River Navigation, the company are bound to specified areas; that for the first-mentioned river to be 360 square feet, and for the Axe 240; they are also required to make, on each of those rivers, near their respective aqueducts, two locks sufficient for passing vessels of ten tons burthen; and in order that these, and other things therein mentioned, should be properly executed, the company are directed to invest, in the public funds, the sum of £10,000, to be under the control of the commissioners of sewers acting for the county of Somerset.

The company are prohibited from taking the water from Lox Yeo, and from Banwell Hill Spring, and if injury be done to the latter, which is in the estate of the Bishop of Bath and Wells, the fund of £10,000 above-mentioned is to be answerable for damages. They are also restricted from cutting any portion of the canal between the parish of Clevdon and the Parrett, until it is finished between the first-mentioned place and the Avon; and if the former portion be not done in four years after the passing of this act, the power to cease. The affairs of the company are under the direction of a committee of fifteen persons, to be called " The " Committee of Management."

TONNAGE RATES.

	d.
Hay, Straw, Dung, Peat and Peat Ashes, and all other Ashes intended to be used for Manure; Chalk, Marl, Clay and Sand, and for all Lime and other Articles intended for Manure, and Material for repairing Roads	1½ per Ton, per Mile.
Coal, Culm, Coke, Cinders, Charcoal, Iron-stone, Pig-iron, Iron-ore, Lead-ore, Copper-ore, Lime, (except what shall be used for Manure,) Lime-stone, and other Stone, Bricks, Tiles, Paving-stones and Pipe Clay......................	2 ditto. ditto.
Corn and other Grain, Flour, Malt, Meal, Cyder, Timber, Ochre, Calamine, Bar Iron, Lead, Kelp, Sand, (except what shall be used for Manure,) Pitch, Tar, Turpentine and Resin	2½ ditto. ditto.
Passengers...	1¼ per Mile each.
Cattle, Sheep, Swine and other Beasts	1½ per Head, per Mile.
All other Goods, Wares, Merchandize and Commodities......	3 per Ton, per Mile.

Tolls to be paid for a full Half Mile, and for a Quarter of a Ton.

TOLLS ON THE RAILWAYS.

	d.
For every Horse, Mare, Gelding, Mule or Ass, passing along the Railways, (except such as are employed in drawing any Goods, for which any of the Rates will be paid)	2 each.
Cows, Horned or Neat Cattle..	1 each.
Sheep, Swine and Calves	3 per Score.

To pay but once a Day.

Boats under Twenty Tons not to pass Locks without leave, or without paying for that Amount of Tonnage.

There are many clauses in this act for protecting the property of individuals on the line of navigation ; but which, having a local interest only, it is unnecessary further to notice than by a reference to the act of parliament. In this act are recited three others, 10th and 11th William III. 6th Anne, and 44th George III. relating to the navigation of the Tone from Bridgewater to Taunton, in which it appears that certain persons are appointed conservators of that river, and certain tolls are thereby directed to be collected, and that the surplus of such rates, after doing that which is necessary for the maintenance of the navigation, shall be employed for the benefit of the poor of Taunton, and the parishes of Taunton St. Mary Magdalene, and Taunton St. James ; and as the making of this canal will materially injure the above interests, the company are directed to purchase them, and afterwards to maintain the

River Tone out of the tolls received from that navigation under the acts above-mentioned. The estimates for this canal and branches were made by Mr. Rennie, and are as follow :—

For the Main Line................................ £404,314
      Nailsea Branch........................ 6,582
      Cheddar Branch 19,094

              Total................ £429,990

So confident were the subscribers of the ultimate success of this measure, and so eager were they to possess shares in the undertaking, that the sum of £571,800 was actually subscribed before the application to parliament; and yet, thirteen years afterwards, the following act was obtained by the same company, to enable them to abandon a great part of the line and branches.

The act of 5th George IV. is entitled, ' *An Act to abridge,* ' *vary, extend and improve the Bristol and Taunton Canal Navi-* ' *gation, and to alter the Powers of an Act of the Fifty-first Year* ' *of his late Majesty, for making the said Canal.*' This act, therefore, repeals so much of the former as relates to the line of the proposed canal, between Morgan's Pill, on the Avon, and the parish of Clevdon, with the branch to Nailsea; and the company had already forfeited all right to make that part between Clevdon and the Parrett, with the Cheddar Branch, by having neglected to execute them within the prescribed period of four years from the passing of the former act.

Instead, therefore, of a navigation from the River Avon, the company determined to make it only from the River Parrett, a little above Bridgewater, to the town of Taunton, with some alterations in the original line between those places; they, consequently, have abandoned their original title, and are incorporated in this act by the name of " The Company of Proprietors of the " Bridgewater and Taunton Canal Navigation." The deviation in the original line was from Mansell, through the parish of North Petherton and chapelry of North Newton, to the Parrett, a distance of five miles and a quarter, with a fall of 35 feet, by five locks. There is also a branch, with a dock or basin, and locks to communicate with the Parrett Navigation, in the parishes of Bridgewater and North Petherton, and chapelry of North Newton.

The estimate of the work (which was made by Mr.
James Hillinsworth, civil engineer, in 1824,) from
Firepool Weir to the commencement of the vari-
ation at Mansell was .... } £15,291

And the variation line to the River Parrett 18,854

Total £34,145

This act enables the company to take any water within four
hundred yards of the line of the canal, and three years are allowed
for the execution of these works, if not then done, the powers to
cease, excepting as to such parts as may have been completed.
The tonnage rates remain as in the former act.

The object of this canal was to facilitate the communication
between the ports of London, Bristol, Bridgewater and Exeter,
and to afford a better mode of conveyance for the produce of the
agricultural and mineral districts through which it passes ; the
utility whereof can only be appreciated by that portion of the
public which partakes of such important benefits.

BRIDGEND RAILWAY.

9 George IV. Cap. 92, Royal Assent 19th June, 1828.

THIS line of railway commences at the Duffryn Llynvi and
Pwll Cawl Railway, near the village of Ceffn Gribbwr, in the
parish of Laleston, and proceeds in an eastwardly course to the River
Ogmore, over which it crosses at a short distance south of the
church of St. Bride's Minor, and thence proceeds, in the same
direction, on the east bank of the same river, to the town of
Bridgend, where it terminates.

The act for making this railway, is entitled, '*An Act for making
' and maintaining a Railway or Tramroad from the Duffryn
' Llynvi and Pwll Cawl, otherwise Porth Cawl Railway, to com-
' mence at a certain point therein, in the parish of Laleston, in the
' county of Glamorgan, and to terminate near to the town of Bridg-
' end, in the same county.*' The subscribers, at the time the act
was obtained, were thirty-three in number, amongst whom were

Sir J. Nicoll and Sir D. Mackworth. They were incorporated by the name of " The Bridgend Railway Company,"; with power to raise £6,000, in shares of £20 each, (of which £4,380 was subscribed before going to parliament,) and an additional sum of £4,000 on mortgage of the railroad and the rates authorized to be collected, should such sum be necessary to complete the same. Five years are allowed by the act for its completion. The concern is to be managed by a committee of five proprietors, who are subject to the control of general meetings.

The railway is four miles and a half in length, and is on one inclined plane to Bridgend, to which place there is a fall of 190 feet. The estimate for completing it amounts to £6,000, and was made by Mr. John Hodgkinson, civil engineer.

TONNAGE RATES.

		d.
Limestone, Lime, Materials for the repair of Roads, Dung, Compost and Manure......................................	}	1 per Ton, per Mile.
Coal, Coke, Culm, Cinders, Stone, Marl, Sand, Clay, Iron-stone, and other Minerals, Building-stone, Pitching and Paving-stone, Bricks, Tiles, Slate and all gross and unmanufactured Articles...	}	2 ditto. ditto.
Iron, Lead, Timber, Staves, Deals and all other Goods, Commodities, Wares and Merchandize	}	5 ditto. ditto.

Fractions to be taken as for a Quarter of a Ton, and as for a Quarter of a Mile.

For the purposes of this Act, One Hundred and Twelve Pounds is to be considered a Hundred Weight, and Twenty-one Hundred Weight to be a Ton.

Owners of Lands may make Wharfs, with Cranes and Weighing Machines, the Rates for which are regulated by this Act.

The principal object of this railroad is to facilitate the transmission of coal from the extensive collieries on the line of the Duffryn Llynvi and Pwll or Porth Cawl Railroad, to the town of Bridgend and its vicinity. It will also open a communication with the harbour of Pwll or Porth Cawl, which will be attended with considerable advantages to the trade of the above-mentioned town.

BRISTOL AND GLOUCESTERSHIRE RAILWAY.

9 George IV. Cap. 93, Royal Assent 19th June, 1828.

THE line of this railway commences at Cuckold's Pill, near the harbour or floating-dock on the east side of the city of Bristol, and takes a north-easterly course by Upper Easton, Staple Hill,

and Rodway Hill, about half a mile south of the village of Mangotsfield ; from thence it pursues a more northerly course through
the collieries which abound in the parishes of Pucklechurch and
Mangotsfield, to Coalpit Heath, in the parish of Westerleigh,
where it terminates.

The act for making this railway received the royal assent on
the 19th of June, 1828, and is entitled, ' *An Act for making and*
' *maintaining a Railroad or Tramroad, from or near the city of*
' *Bristol, to Coalpit Heath, in the parish of Westerleigh, in the*
' *county of Gloucester.*' The length is nine miles; in the first two
miles and three quarters of which there is an inclined plane rising
185 feet; in the next mile, another plane of 12 feet rise to the
summit ; at Staple Hill it enters a tunnel, which is eight hundred
and eighty yards in length, and continues, on the same level, for a
further distance of nearly one mile and three quarters ; from
which, to its termination, there is another plane declining 24 feet.
The estimate for this work was made by Mr. W. H. Townsend,
and amounted to the sum of £41,819, 14s. 2d.   Near Rodway
Hill, this railway is intended to be joined by the Avon and Gloucestershire Railway, for the making of which, an act was obtained
at the same time as for this, and the royal assent was given on the
same day.

The subscribers to this work, when application was made to
parliament, were eighty-five in number, amongst whom were Sir
John Smyth, Bart. and Sir Henry Nicoll, Bart. K.C.B.   They
were incorporated by the name of " The Bristol and Gloucester-
" shire Railway Company," with power to raise among themselves
the sum of £45,000, in shares of £50 each; and with further
power to raise among themselves, or to borrow on mortgage of
the rates, the additional sum of £12,000 ; or any part of this last-
mentioned sum may be borrowed of the Exchequer Bill Commissioners, appointed under the act of the 3rd George IV.; but in
this case the commissioners have priority over all other claims
whatsoever.

The concern is to be under the management of a committee of fifteen persons, possessed of at least five shares each,
who are subject to the control of the general meetings of the proprietors.

TONNAGE RATES.

	d.	
Coal, Culm, Coke, Building Lime, Sand, Clay, Brick, Tile and Slate, Building, Pitching and Paving-stone and Flags ..	3 per Ton, per Mile.	
Lime-stone, Lead-ore, Iron-ore and other Minerals in their raw state, Manure and Lime for Husbandry purposes, Stone and other Material for the repair of Roads	2 ditto.	ditto.
Timber, Deals, Corn, Grain, Flour, Hay, Straw, Corn in the Straw, Green Fodder and Vegetables, and all other Commodities not before specified	4 ditto.	ditto.
Coal, Culm and Coke to be afterwards conveyed to the River Avon, in the parish of Bitton, by any Railroad branching from the said Railway	5 ditto.	ditto.
For every Person passing in any Carriage upon this Railroad..	2½ per Mile.	
For every Horse, Mule, Ass, Ox, Cow, Bull or other Cattle	1½ ditto.	
For every Calf, Sheep, Lamb or Pig	¼ ditto.	

Fractions as for a Quarter of a Ton, and as for a Quarter of a Mile.

Carriages of Four Wheels not to carry more than Four Tons, including the Weight of such Carriage; and those of Six Wheels may carry Six Tons.

WHARFAGE RATES.

	d.	
For Goods loaded, landed, or placed, in, or upon, any of the Wharfs or Warehouses, and which shall not remain there more than Seventy-two Hours	1 per Ton.	
If more than Seventy-two Hours, the further Sum of	1 ditto.	
And for the Warehousing for the succeeding Week	6 ditto.	

And the like additional Sum of One Penny and Sixpence for every subsequent Week.

CRANAGE RATES.

	s.	d.	
Any Weight under Two Tons at one lift of the Crane	0	6	per Ton.
Of Two Tons and less than Three	1	0	ditto.
Of Three Tons and less than Four	1	6	ditto.
And for every additional Ton	0	6	

The act allows six years for the execution of the railroad, and if not then done, the powers so granted are to cease, excepting as to such parts as may have been completed.

The chief object of this railway is the making a cheaper and more expeditious conveyance for coal and stone to the city of Bristol, and for the return of merchandize in general, to the populous mining districts on its line.

BRITTON CANAL.

THIS canal, the property of the gentleman through whose estate it is made, commences in the River Neath, about half a mile above Britton Ferry, three miles below the town of Neath, and directly opposite the end of the Neath Canal. Its course is in a westerly direction north of Coed-y-yarll, and across the Morass, called Crymlin Burrows, in a direction parallel with the north shore of Swansea Bay. It terminates in the pool called Swansea Harbour, in the River Tawe, a short distance below Swansea and close to Salthouse Point, and is four miles and a quarter in length.

As the principal object of the proprietor was the improvement and drainage of his own estate, it was made without having recourse to any parliamentary enactment.

BUDE HARBOUR AND CANAL.

14 George III. Cap. 53, Royal Assent 24th May, 1774.
59 George III. Cap. 55, Royal Assent 14th June, 1819.

THE original design for this navigation was made by Mr. Edmund Leach, (the Author of " A Treatise on Inland Naviga- " tion,") and an act was obtained in the 14th George III. for that purpose, entitled, ' *An Act for making a navigable Cut or Canal* ' *from the Port or Harbour of Bude, in the hundred of Stratton, in* ' *the county of Cornwall, to the River Tamar, in the parish of* ' *Calstoke, in the said county.*' It was intended to commence in the tideway of Bude Haven, in the Bristol Channel, and thence, by the course of the Tamar, by Launceston, to the tideway of the Tamar River and Navigation, in the parish of Calstoke. From the sea at Bude Haven there was to be an inclined plane of 54 feet rise; then, a level pool of six miles and a half; another plane of 120 feet rise, and a level pool at the end of it four miles in length; from this, a third plane rising 66 feet, to the summit level, being a total of 240 feet above the level of the sea. This summit level was maintained for the distance of sixty-eight miles, by a very circuitous course, occasioned by the necessity they were under of continuing on the level of the natural face of the country, by a clause in the act, which prohibits them from cutting more than 39 inches in depth on the lower side of the canal. From the end of the summit, only two miles and a half from the termination of the proposed canal, there was to be a plane of 120 feet fall; then a level pool of two miles and a half in length, with a fifth plane, at Kelly Rock, of 120 feet fall. The total length of the canal was eighty-one miles, though the direct distance, between the two extremes, was only twenty-eight miles. The canal was to be 21 feet wide at top and 12 feet at bottom, and of depth sufficient for boats of ten tons. The estimated expense was £81,000, but as there was a provision in the act that the powers should cease in ten years from the passing of it, and as this period was suffered to elapse without any further steps being taken, it was accordingly abandoned ; though in 1785 Mr. Leach endeavoured to revive the project, and to shorten the course to forty miles and three quarters, by cutting down the summit level 18 feet, 'and making a tunnel of one hundred yards in length, with other works, the estimated cost of which was £53,200 ; but as no act was obtained for this purpose, his project fell to the ground.

In the year 1819, however, a new company, consisting of three hundred and thirty persons, amongst whom were the Right Honourable P. H. Earl Stanhope, Countess Stanhope, Sir Arscott Ourry Molesworth, Sir William P. Call, and Sir Thomas Dyke Ackland, Baronets, obtained an act, entitled, ' *An Act for im-* ' *proving the Harbour of Bude, in the county of Cornwall, and for* ' *making and maintaining a navigable Canal from the said Har-* ' *bour of Bude, to or near the village of Thornbury, in the county of* ' *Devon, and divers Branches therefrom, all in the said counties of* ' *Cornwall and Devon.*' The subscribers are incorporated by the name of·" The Bude Harbour and Canal Company," and have power to raise among themselves the sum of £95,000, in nineteen hundred shares of £50 each, with power to raise an additional sum of £20,000 if necessary, either among themselves or by the admission of new subscribers, or on mortgage of the undertaking and the rates and duties herein granted.

The main line of this canal commences in Bude Haven, within the port of Padstow, and pursues a southerly course along the western bank of the little River Bude, to Hele Bridge, where it turns suddenly eastward to near Marhamchurch. Here is an inclined plane, and hence it takes a circuitous course by Camorchard, a little beyond which is another inclined plane, to Red Post, in the parish of Launcells, where the Launceston Branch commences. From Red Post, the canal takes a northerly direction on the western bank of the Tamar, which it crosses near Burmsdon. Thence, ascending an inclined plane, and proceeding to Veala, where the branch to Virworthy commences, it passes, in a very circuitous course, by Pancrasweek and Holsworthy, a mile and a half beyond which place, it enters a tunnel of considerable length, and is continued thence, by Ford and North Week to Thornbury, where it terminates.

The Launceston Branch proceeds from Red Post, by a very serpentine course, on the west bank of the Tamar, through the several parishes of Launcells, Bridgerule, Marhamchurch, Whitstone, Week Saint Mary, North Tamerton, Tetcot, Boyton, Werrington, North Petherwin, and St. Giles' in the Heath, to Druxton Bridge, about three miles north of the town of Launceston. From Burmsdon there is a branch up the west bank of the Tamar to Moreton Mill, where the feeder from Langford Moor Reservoir communicates with it. The feeder from Moreton Mill to the reservoir on Langford Moor is two miles and a half in length.

	M.	F.	C.	M.	F.	C.
The length of the Main Line from Bude Haven to the Launceston Branch at the Red Post is...............	5	6	5			
From thence to the Moreton Mill Branch is.....................	3	0	3			
From thence to the Virworthy Branch is	1	1	8			
Thence to the termination at Thornbury	11	3	1			
Total length of the Main Line....				21	3	7
The Branch to Druxton Bridge or Launceston Branch				19	0	7
The Moreton Mill Branch is....................				1	3	8
The Virworthy Branch is				3	7	2
Total Main Line and Branches				45	7	4

TONNAGE AND WHARFAGE DUES.

	d.	
Coal, Coke and Freestone...................................	4 per Ton, per Mile.	
Lime, Dung and Manure, Sand, Limestone and Slates, Stones and Clay	3 ditto.	ditto.
Cattle, Calves, Sheep, Swine and other Beasts, Bricks, Tiles, Rough Timber, Bark, Faggots, Tin, Iron-stone, Iron and Lead..	4 ditto.	ditto.
Wheat and Potatoes	2 ditto.	ditto.
Barley, Beans, Peas, Vetches, Seeds and Oats	3 ditto.	ditto.
All other Goods, Wares and Merchandize whatsoever	4 ditto.	ditto.

And so in proportion for any greater or less Quantity than a Ton, or greater or less Distance than a Mile.

Boats of less than Twenty Tons Burthen not to pass Locks without leave, unless Two Boats, containing together that Weight, are ready to pass at the same Time.

HARBOUR DUTIES.

	d.
Ships belonging to Great Britain or Ireland, or the British Plantations, (unless carrying Coal or Limestone) importing into, or exporting from, the Harbour of Bude, (according to their Measure)	4 per Ton.
Foreign Ships	6 ditto.
Vessels putting in from stress of Weather, or otherwise, when they neither land or take in Cargo ..˙....................................	2 ditto.

All Vessels belonging to his Majesty, or employed in his Majesty's Service, and such as are under Seven Tons, laden with Fish, are exempt.

WHARF AND BASIN DUES.

	d.
For every Vessel entering or using any Dock, Basin, Wharf, &c..........	2 per Ton.

Goods, Wares and Merchandize ....Wharf and Basin Dues, per Ton in Column (*)
Timber and Pig and Bar Iron............	ditto,	ditto,	ditto,	(+)
Coal, Culm, Stone, Iron-stone, Slate, Flint, Clay and Sand	ditto,	ditto,	ditto,	(‡)
Lime or Limestone, Bricks, Tiles or Plaister	ditto,	ditto,	ditto,	(₰)
Corn, Grain, Pulse, Seeds, Apples and Potatoes......................	ditto,	per Qr.	ditto,	(‖)

	(*)	(+)	(‡)	(₰)	(‖)
	s. d.	s. d.	s. d.	s. d.	s. d.
Remaining on such Wharf or Quay more than Twenty-four Hours, and less than Six Days..	0 6	0 3	0 0½	0 1	0 0½
If remaining Six Days, and less than One Month ..	0 9	0 6	0 1	0 2	0 1
If remaining One Month, and less than Six Weeks..	1 0	0 9	0 1½	0 3	0 1½
If remaining Six Weeks, and less than Two Months	1 3	1 0	0 2	0 4	0 2
And if remaining Two Months, and less than Ten Weeks.....................	1 6	1 3	0 2½	0 5	0 2½

And so in proportion for any longer Time the said Articles shall remain in or upon such Wharf or Quay.

WAREHOUSE DUES.

	s. d.
For every Cask, Case, Bundle, Bale, or other Package, containing Articles of Merchandize, being of the Weight of 224lbs. or upwards	5 0
Ditto, being under the Weight of 224lbs	2 6
For any Article of Merchandize brought loose, and subject to any Duty of Customs, chargeable according to the Weight of every 112lbs............	1 0
For any Article of Merchandize brought loose, and subject to any Duty of Customs, per every 112lbs...	1 0

Which Rates shall be paid for every calendar Month such Goods are warehoused.

The estimate was made by Mr. James Green, civil engineer, in 1818, and amounted to the sum of £91,617; of which sum, £4,618 was for the improvement of the harbour of Bude. The company have occasionally called in Mr. Whitworth, to inspect the works. The whole of the sum of £95,000, authorized to be raised by the act, was subscribed before the application to parliament. The management of this work is vested in a committee of eighteen persons.

Besides the authority which the act gives the company to make the canal, they are empowered to improve the harbour of Bude, by erecting a breakwater, together with a dock, basin, or inner harbour, warehouses, piers, quays, wharfs, and jetties, mooring chains, lighthouses, buoys, and what other works may be necessary for the convenient accommodation of such ships and vessels as resort to the same. They are restricted from taking any water from the Tamar, or the brooks which flow into it, except when the water flows 3 inches over the weir at Aldfordisworthy Mill.

The chief object of this canal, is to facilitate the introduction of Welsh Coal, and the carrying of Shelly Sand from the coast, to be used in the interior as manure.

BULLO PILL OR FOREST OF DEAN RAILWAY.

49 George III. Cap. 158, Royal Assent 10th June, 1809.
7 George IV. Cap. 47, Royal Assent 5th May, 1826.

PRIOR to the act of 49th George III. a railroad had been nearly completed, without the authority of parliament, from the Severn at Bullo Pill, near the town of Newnham, to Cinderford Bridge, in his Majesty's Forest of Dean, by Roynon Jones, Esq. Margaret Roberts, William Fendall and James Jelf, Esquires, the owners, but who, being desirous of obtaining power to extend their railway, and to make branches therefrom, applied to parliament and obtained an act, entitled, ' An Act for making and ' maintaining a Railway or Tramroad, from the summit of the ' Hill above Churchway Engine, in the Forest of Dean, in the ' county of Gloucester, to a certain place in the said Forest, called ' Cinderford Bridge,' by which the above parties are incorporated by the name of " The Bullo Pill Railway Company."

The line of extension which the above company are empowered to make, proceeds from the above-mentioned private railway, at Cinderford Bridge, in a northwardly direction, up a valley in the forest, to the summit of the hill above Churchway Engine, and the place where the Severn and Wye Railroad Company have subsequently formed a junction ; its length is about three miles. There is also a branch from a place called the Dam, to the Upper and Lower Bilson Works; another from the same place to Kelmsley Green, and one from Nofold Engine, to the Old Engine and Nofold Green. These collateral and very short branches extend to several coal and other mines in the forest.

The Forest of Dean, through which this railway passes, belongs to the King; but after the passing of this act, the ground occupied by the railroad and branches is vested in the company, on payment of the yearly rent of £100, and one guinea per week towards the cost and charges of his Majesty's Inspectors. The railway not to exceed seven yards in breadth, except in passing places, embankments, deep cuttings, or where warehouses or wharfs may be erected.

TONNAGE RATES.

	s.	d.	
Coal, Coke, Culm, Stone, Coal Cinders, Chalk, Marl, Sand, Lime, Clay, Ashes, Peat, Lime-stone, Iron-stone, Iron or other Ore, and other Minerals and Bricks, the produce of the said Forest, to be conveyed from any place on the said Forest, to or near Cinderford Bridge..........	1	6	per Ton.
Ditto, conveyed from one place to another within the said Forest...	0	6	per Ton, per Mile.
Timber, Goods, Commodities, Wares and Merchandize, whether the produce of the Forest or not	0	6	ditto. ditto.

Fractions to be taken as for a Quarter of a Ton, and as for Half a Mile.
One Hundred and Twenty Pounds to be deemed a Hundred Weight, for the purposes of this Act.

RATES UPON THE PRIVATE RAILWAY FROM CINDERFORD BRIDGE TO THE SEVERN AT BULLO PILL.

	s.	d.	
For Bark stripped within the Forest, Coal, Timber and Wood for the use of the Coal Pits, Mines and Quarries within the Forest	4	6	per Ton.
For Timber felled in the Forest under the direction of his Majesty's Surveyor General, and conveyed along the private Railway....	0	2	per Foot.

None but Free Miners of the Forest, and his Majesty's Surveyor General, have power to use this private Railway, without consent of the Proprietors.

The private railway is nearly four miles and a half long, with a tunnel upwards of five hundred yards in length, situate about a mile and a half from Bullo Pill, at which place are convenient wharfs for goods intended for shipment on the Severn.

On the 5th of May 1826, the royal assent was given to another act, entitled, '*An Act for maintaining an existing public Railway* '*from the summit of the Hill above Churchway Engine, in the* '*Forest of Dean, to Cinderford Bridge, and for making public a* '*private Railway from thence to the River Severn, at or near Bullo* '*Pill, all in the county of Gloucester; and for amending an Act of* '*his late Majesty relating to the said Railways*,' by which a company, consisting of eighteen persons, agree to purchase the interest of the Bullo Pill Railway Company, and make the whole public, and they are by this act incorporated by the name of "The "Forest of Dean Railway Company," with power to raise among themselves for these purposes, the sum of £125,000, to be divided into two thousand five hundred shares, of £50 each. Edward Protheroe, Esq. was the principal proprietor of this concern. The rents and payments due to his Majesty and inspectors, are by this act reserved, with the many other privileges which the King enjoys as owner of the Forest of Dean; so much of the former act as related to the tonnage is repealed, and the following are now the

TONNAGE RATES.

	s.	d.	
Coal, Coke, Culm, Stone, Coal Cinders, Chalk, Marl, Sand, Lime, Clay, Ashes, Peat, Lime-stone, Iron-stone, Iron or other Ore, and other Minerals and Bricks, the produce of the said Forest, to be conveyed from any place on the said Forest, to or near Cinderford Bridge	1	6	per Ton.
Ditto, conveyed from one place to another within the said Forest	0	6	per Ton, per Mile.
Timber, Goods, Commodities, Wares and Merchandize, whether the produce of the Forest or not..............	0	6	ditto. ditto.
Coal, Coke, Culm, Stone, Coal Cinders, Marl, Sand, Lime, Clay, Ashes, Peat, Lime-stone, Iron-stone, Iron or other Ore, and other Minerals and Bricks, carried downwards from Cinderford Bridge to Bullo Pill, or any part thereof, which Sum shall include all Tonnage chargeable upon the Railway, from Churchway Engine to Cinderford Bridge	3	0	per Ton.
Timber and Wood, felled in the Forest under the direction of his Majesty's Surveyor General, conveyed from Cinderford Bridge to Bullo Pill	0	2	per Foot.
All other Timber, Goods, Commodities, Wares and Merchandize, from Cinderford Bridge to Bullo Pill........	0	6	per Ton, per Mile.

WHARFAGE RATES.

	d.	
Goods, Wares, Merchandize and other Things remaining on the Wharf at Bullo Pill, any Time less than Two Months	3	per Ton.
For Two Months and not exceeding Three	6	ditto.
For a longer Time than Three Months	6	ditto, per Month, in addition.

His Majesty's Timber is exempt from Payment of Wharfage Rates.
Fractions to be taken as for a Quarter of a Ton, and as for a Quarter of a Mile.

The object of this railway and branches, is to convey, with facility, for shipment on the Severn, the timber, coal, iron-ore, and other minerals, with which the Forest of Dean abounds, thus enabling the owners to transport their superabundant produce to distant markets.

BURE OR NORTH RIVER.

13 George III. Cap. 37, Royal Assent 7th April, 1773.

THE River Bure rises a few miles north of the town of Foulsham; it thence pursues an easterly course by Thurningbeck Hall, Blickling Park, to the town of Aylsham, to which place, from the head of the Bure Navigation at Coltishall, it was made navigable under the authority of an act of 13th George III. entitled, ' *An Act for making and extending the Navigation of the* ' *River Bure, commonly called the North River, by and from* ' *Coltishall, to Aylsham Bridge, in the county of Norfolk.*' The length of this portion of the navigation is nine miles, with six locks, and it is in the natural course of the stream, with the exception of a few short cuts, made for the purpose of cutting off some bends of the river, or for passing the mills upon it.

This navigation is under the management of commissioners, whose qualification is the possession of freehold or copyhold estates in the hundreds of North and South Erpingham, Taverham, Eynsford, and Tunstead, in the county of Norfolk, of the annual value of £100, or a personal estate of £3,000; any seven of whom, whose usual place of residence is in any of the hundreds above-named, are empowered to act. They are authorized to borrow £5,000, for the purpose of carrying the powers of this act into execution, on security of the tolls therein granted.

TONNAGE RATES.

	s.	d.	
Coals, Cinders, Bricks, Pavements, Tiles, Lime and Terras..........	1	0	per Ton.
Corn, Grain, Meal, Flour, Timber, Goods, Wares, Merchandize or Commodities whatsoever......................................	1	6	ditto.

And so in proportion for any greater or less Weight than a Ton.

From Skeyton Brook, and for passing through the Two Locks at Buxton and Horstead only, Two-thirds of the above Rate.

EXEMPTION FROM TOLL.

Straw, Muck, Marl, Clay, or other Manure, and Materials for the repair of the Mills upon the River.

As the navigable part of the North River and River Bure, from the head of this navigation, at Aylsham, to the sea at Yarmouth, is, by its course, forty-two miles, and as it passes through one of the finest agricultural districts of which this kingdom can boast, the advantages arising from the facilities it affords for the export of the natural productions of its vicinity are incalculable. The towns of Aylsham, Cawsham, Reepham, and the immediate neighbourhood, participate, perhaps, more directly in the advantages thus derived.

BURE, YARE AND WAVENEY RIVERS, AND YARMOUTH HAVEN.

22 Charles II. C. 16, R. A. 11th Apr. 1670.   9 Geo. I. C. 10, R. A. 22nd Mar. 1722.
20 Geo.   II. C. 40, R. A. 17th June, 1747. 23 Geo. II. C. 6, R. A. 14th Mar. 1749.
12 Geo. III. C. 14, R. A. 1st April, 1772.

As these rivers and the harbour of Yarmouth are under one description of management, and the principal legislative enactments relating to them are, with only one exception, combined, the description of them will be given under the above title. The first act of parliament relating to a part of these navigations, occurs in the 22nd Charles II. and is entitled, '*An Act for making navi-* '*gable the Rivers Brandon and Waveney*,' in which commissioners were appointed to carry the act into execution, and to ascertain the damage done to the banks of the said rivers, by the haling of vessels thereon; so that it clearly appears that the River Waveney was navigable previous to this early date; but as this river became subsequently under the control of commissioners appointed by the corporations of Yarmouth, Norwich, and the magistrates of the counties of Norfolk and Suffolk, it is not necessary to enter into the earlier provisions of the above recited act. The first act, therefore, in which is embodied the necessary power for rendering the whole of the above-mentioned rivers navigable, is the 9th George I. which is entitled, '*An Act for clearing, depthening,* '*repairing, extending, maintaining and improving the Haven and*

' *Piers of Great Yarmouth; and for depthening and making more*
' *navigable the several Rivers emptying themselves at the said town;*
' *and also for preserving Ships, wintering in the said Haven, from*
' *accidents by Fire;*' whereby several duties were granted for the
above recited purposes, and for depthening the channel of that part
of the River Yare called Braydon, and for making more navigable
the Rivers Yare, Waveney and Bure, &c.; but as the time to
which this act limited the receipt of these duties had expired
previous to 1747, another act was obtained in the 20th George II.
to revive the duties granted under the 9th George I. and make
them payable for two years from the above date, and from thence
to the end of the session of parliament immediately following.
This act is therefore entitled, ' *An Act to revive, continue and*
' *amend an Act made in the Ninth Year of the Reign of his late*
' *Majesty King George the First, entitled, An Act for clearing,*
' *depthening, repairing, extending, maintaining and improving the*
' *Haven and Piers of Great Yarmouth; and for depthening and*
' *making more navigable the several Rivers emptying themselves at*
' *the said town; and also for preserving Ships, wintering in the*
' *said Haven, from accidents by Fire.*' Twelve commissioners were
appointed to carry into effect the purposes of this act; three of
whom were appointed by the corporation of Yarmouth, other
three by the mayor, sheriff, citizens and commonalty of Norwich,
and the remainder by the magistrates of Norfolk and Suffolk,
assembled at quarter sessions; which said commissioners, or any
seven of them, (five being of the counties of Norfolk and Suffolk,)
are empowered to act.

In the preamble of the act of 23rd George II. entitled, ' *An*
' *Act for repairing, improving, and maintaining, the Haven and*
' *Piers of Great Yarmouth; and for depthening and making*
' *more navigable the several Rivers emptying themselves into the*
' *said Haven; and also for preserving Ships, wintering therein,*
' *from accidents by Fire,*' we learn, that the duties heretofore
granted were insufficient for the maintenance of the several navigations connected with the haven of Yarmouth; the corporation of
Great Yarmouth are, therefore, by this act, empowered to collect
new duties for the term of twenty-one years, from the 25th March,
1750; but as these are repealed, and give place to others granted

by the 12th George III. it is unnecessary here to recite them. The act of 12th George III. is entitled, ' *An Act for clearing,* ' *depthening, repairing, maintaining and improving the Haven and* ' *Piers of Great Yarmouth ; and for depthening and making more* ' *navigable the several Rivers emptying themselves into the said* ' *Haven; and for preserving Ships, wintering therein, from accidents* ' *by Fire ;*' in the preamble of which it is recited, that the duties granted under the former act of 23rd George II. ceased on the 25th March, 1772, and the following are granted in lieu of them.

RATES AND DUTIES.

d.

For every Chaldron of Coals, (Winchester Measure) Last of Wheat, Rye, Barley, Malt, or other Grain, and for every Weigh of Salt, and every Ton of other Goods or Merchandize, (except Fish) which shall be unladen or imported into the Haven of Yarmouth, or on that part of the Sea called Yarmouth Road, extending from Scratby to Corton..................................   10

Or such other greater Sum, not exceeding Twelve-pence, which the Commissioners appointed by this Act, or any Seven of them, may order and direct; which Commissioners are to be chosen as directed in the Act of 22nd Charles II.

The Duties on all Goods imported, to be repaid on Exportation.

The Master of each Vessel to pay to the Pier Master One Shilling on entering the Haven.

The duties are to be disposed of, for the several purposes recited in the act, in the following proportions;—three-twentieths to the chamberlain of the city of Norwich, to be applied for the purposes of depthening and otherwise improving that part of the River Yare, or Wensom, which lies between the New Mills at Norwich and Hardly Cross; one-twentieth to the magistrates of Norfolk, for the purpose of clearing and depthening the River Bure, the River Ant from St. Bennett's Abbey, to Dilham, and the Thurne River from Bastwick Bridge to Hickling; one-twentieth to the magistrates of Suffolk, for the improvement of the navigation of the Waveney; one-twentieth to be applied to the purpose of repairing the bridge and public quays of Yarmouth; one-twentieth to be applied, by the Norfolk Magistrates, for the further clearing of the River Bure, and other branches above-mentioned; five-twentieths to the corporation of Yarmouth, for the improvement of the River Yare from Yarmouth to Hardly Cross, in such manner as the commissioners may appoint; and the remaining eight-twentieths is to be appropriated to the purpose of improving the haven of Yarmouth, and maintaining the piers and jetties, &c. &c.; and if the last-mentioned sum is insufficient, the commissioners have power to collect the twelve-penny duty for this purpose. The act to be in force for twenty-one years only, but its cessation is not to extinguish, or in any way to affect, the port duties which have been, by immemorial custom, paid to the corporation of Great Yarmouth.

That portion of the Bure River to which the above-recited acts relate, commences at Coltishall, where the Bure or North River Navigation terminates. Its course is very circuitous, in an eastwardly direction, by Wroxham Bridge, to the Ant River at Horning Marsh; from thence, by Weybridge and Runham Hall, to the town of Yarmouth, where it falls into the Yare. The distance from Coltishall to the mouth of the River Ant, is fifteen miles; from thence to the Thurne is two miles and a quarter; and from thence to the Yare is thirteen miles and a quarter. The Ant River Branch commences at the North Walsham and Dilham Canal, at Wayford Bridge, and takes a southwardly course, passing the Barton Broad, and the villages of Irstead, Ludham Bridge, to Horning Marsh, where it enters the Bure. Its length is nearly eight miles, and without locks. The Thurne River Branch commences at Hickling Broad, whence, passing through Heigham Sound, it takes a south-westwardly course by Heigham Bridge, to the River Bure, into which it falls near the village of Thurne. Its length is about seven miles, and level. In the township of Tunstall, about eight miles from Yarmouth, there is a navigable drain, of one mile in length, from the Bure to Tunstall Staith; and a little above Weybridge there is another, of half a mile in length, across Upton Marsh.

The Yare, or Wensom, has its source between the towns of Fakenham and Litcham, in Norfolk; whence, pursuing a southeasterly course by Sennowe Lodge, Westfield Park and Taverham Hall, to the city of Norwich, it there becomes navigable. From this place it continues, in a circuitous course, through low marshy grounds, by Hardly Cross, to near the village of Burgh, where it is joined by the Waveney; from thence its course is through Braydon Water, to Yarmouth, where the Bure falls into it; and from thence it takes a southerly course, running parallel with the coast, by South Town and Gorleston, to Yarmouth Roads. From

Norwich to Hardly Cross, is eighteen miles and a half; from thence, to the Waveney, is six miles and a half; from thence, to the Bure at Yarmouth, is three miles and three quarters; and, to the sea, a further distance of three miles and a quarter.

The River Waveney has its source near Finningham Hall, a few miles north of the town of Mendlesham, in Suffolk; it takes an easterly course, and afterwards a northerly, by the town of Eye; thence, by Harlaston to Bungay, where it becomes navigable. From this place its course is east, by Barsham Hall and the town of Beccles, to within three miles of Lowestoft, whence it takes a northerly course by St. Olave's Bridge, to Burgh Flatt, where it falls into the Yare. From Bungay to Beccles Bridge, the distance is seven miles and a half; from thence, to St. Olave's Bridge, is twelve miles and a half; and to the place where it joins the Yare, five miles and a quarter. Two miles above Beccles there is a navigable cut, from the river to Geldestone Staith, of three quarters of a mile in length, and level.

To any one who will take a cursory glance at the position of these rivers on the accompanying map of inland navigation, the great advantages which must accrue to above one half of the county of Norfolk, is so strikingly manifest, as to render it quite unnecessary that we should further expatiate on them.

It may not be amiss here to state, that the royal assent was given to an act on the 28th of May, 1827, for making a navigable communication for ships, between the city of Norwich and the sea at Lowestoft, which follows the course of a considerable portion of the Yare, with a part of the Waveney, but which is not to injure the navigation of those rivers.

Further particulars of the Norwich and Lowestoft Navigation, as it is to be called, will be found in the proper place.

BURY, LOUGHOR AND LLIEDI RIVERS.

53 George III. Cap. 183, Royal Assent 2nd July, 1813.

THE River Bury is a very wide estuary, situate between a promontory of Glamorganshire, terminating at Worms Head, and the

H

southern coast of Carmarthenshire. Its length, from the bar at the entrance of the harbour of Bury, near Holmes Island, to where the River Loughor falls into it, is (taking the course of the channel,) about twelve miles. Over the bar, which changes frequently, there is about six feet at low water, with from three to five fathoms within the harbour.

The River Loughor rises in the mountains of Carmarthenshire, south of the town of Llangadoc, thence, proceeding in a southerly direction by Glynheir, Bettus, Penclear Castle, Llandilo Talybont, to Llangennech Ford, to which place it is navigable. From the ford to the estuary of the Bury, opposite the village of Loughor, is about two miles.

The Lliedi is a very inconsiderable stream, which falls into the River Bury, a short distance below the dock belonging to the Carmarthenshire Railway Company, which terminates near the town of Llanelly ; and it is navigable only to this place.

The only act relating to these rivers is entitled, ' *An Act for* ' *the Improvement of the Navigation of the Rivers Bury, Loughor,* ' *and Lliedi, in the counties of Carmarthen and Glamorgan;*' by which certain commissioners are appointed to cleanse, scour, enlarge, and deepen the same; and to make and erect buoys, beacons, and lights; and to establish and regulate the pilotage, anchorage, and mooring of ships and vessels in the said rivers. The qualification of a commissioner, is the possession of a freehold estate of the clear annual value of £80, and which must be situate within seven miles of some one of the rivers above-named ; or a capital to the amount of £2,500, engaged in any mine or manufactory, within the prescribed distance above-mentioned ; or have the same amount vested in ships, or other vessels, trading to the above rivers ; or unless he be principal or managing clerk to any concern within seven miles, where £8,000 capital is employed ; or a proprietor of the Carmarthenshire Railroad, the Penclawdd Canal, or Kidwelly and Llanelly Canal and Tramroad, to the amount of £500.

A committee of five are annually appointed to conduct the business of the commissioners, who are empowered to raise the sum of £2,000 on mortgage of the duties hereby authorized to be collected, or by granting annuities.

TONNAGE RATES.

d.

For every Ship or other Vessel passing over the Bar into any of these Rivers 1 per Ton.

The Duties received in the Port of Llanelly, to be entirely applied to the Purposes of improving the Lliedi.

EXEMPTION FROM DUTIES.

All Vessels employed in his Majesty's Service; or in conveying Limestone or Fish; and all Vessels for Pleasure, or such as are under Fifteen Tons.

There is a clause, reserving to the Duke of Beaufort the rights and privileges of water-bailiff for the seigniories of Gower and Cilrey, in the county of Glamorgan; also the rights of the Lords of Kidwelly, the layer and keelage of the Carmarthenshire side of the Loughor; or the rights of the portreeve and burgesses of Llanelly; the Carmarthenshire Railroad Company; the Kidwelly and Llanelly Canal and Tramroad Company; the Borough of Loughor; the Penclawdd Canal and Tramroad Company; and the corporation of Trinity House of Deptford Strond.

These rivers, together with the canals and railroads connected with them, give great facility for the export of the produce of the valuable collieries, iron-stone mines, and limestone quarries in the immediate vicinity.

BUTE SHIP CANAL.

1 William IV. Cap. 133, Royal Assent 16th July, 1830.

THIS canal commences in Cardiff Harbour, at a place called The Eastern Hollows, near the mouth of the River Taff, in the county of Glamorgan. Its course is in a straight line northwards to Cardiff Moors, and thence in a parallel course with the Glamorganshire Canal to near Whitmoor Lane, on the south side of the town of Cardiff, where it terminates. The length of that part lying between the Eastern Hollows and Cardiff Moors, (called The Entrance Ship Canal) is one mile, three furlongs and eight chains in length; the surface water of which is to be maintained at an elevation of 41 feet above the level of low-water-mark, spring tides, in Cardiff Harbour, which here averages 39 feet, by means of a sea lock and flood gates to be erected at its southern extremity; the depth of water in the canal is to be 33 feet. The upper portion of this navigation, called The Basin, is to be nearly one thousand five hundred yards in length, and 20 feet deep; from which are two communications by short cuts to the Glamorganshire Canal; one of which proceeding at right angles westwards from the inner lock at the northern extremity of the Entrance Canal, is three hundred and twenty yards in length; the other proceeds in the same direction from the upper end of the basin next to the town of Cardiff, and is two hundred and seventy yards in length.

The canal and basin is to be supplied with water by means of a feeder extending from a place in the River Taff, about half a mile north of Cardiff Castle; it is in length one mile and a half, and in its course will pass along some of the streets of Cardiff.

The whole of these works are to be executed at the sole expense of The Most Honorable John Crichton Stuart, Marquis of Bute and Earl of Dumfries, under the authority of an act which received the sanction of his Majesty King William IV. on the 16th July, 1830, entitled, ' *An Act for empowering the Marquis of* ' *Bute to make and maintain a Ship Canal, commencing near the* ' *Mouth of the River Taff, in the county of Glamorgan, and termi-* ' *nating near the town of Cardiff, with other Works to communicate* ' *therewith.*'

Mr. James Green, civil engineer, designed the above works, and estimated the cost at £76,669.

For the security of the water belonging to the proprietors of the Glamorganshire Canal, the Marquis is bound to maintain, by means of stop locks, his basin and the two collateral cuts extending therefrom at an elevation of 3 inches above the level of the top-water-mark of the above-mentioned canal; and the proprietors of that navigation are in return required, upon one month's notice being given in writing, to let off their water to enable the Marquis to execute his works; but upon payment to them, on these occasions, the sum of £50 per diem, during the time their navigation is so obstructed.

The act empowers the Marquis of Bute to demand the following tonnage rates :—

TONNAGE RATES.

FIRST CLASS.

Vessels entering or departing with Cargoes.

	s.	d.	
For every Ship, Boat, Barge, Craft, Lighter or other Vessel laden, which shall enter from or depart to any Part of Great Britain, Ireland or the Isle of Man	0	4	per Ton, Measurement.
From or to any other Part of Europe, the Islands of Guernsey, Jersey, Alderney, Sark, The Faro Isles or Iceland........	0	8	ditto.
From or to any Part of Asia, Africa or America, to the Northward of the River La Plata inclusive, and to the Northward of the Cape of Good Hope, the Islands of St. Helena, Ascension, Cape de Verd Islands, Madeira Azores, Newfoundland, Greenland and Davies Straits..............................	1	0	ditto.
From or to any Part of South America, to the Southward of the River La Plata, from or to any Part or Place in the Pacific Ocean, from or to any Part of Africa and Asia, to the Eastward of the Cape of Good Hope...........................	1	2	ditto.

SECOND CLASS.

Vessels entering or departing in Ballast.

	s.	d.	
For every Ship, &c. which shall enter into or depart from the said Ship Canal or Basin in Ballast, from or to any Part of Great Britain, Ireland or the Isle of Man....................	0	2	ditto.
For ditto from or to any other Part of the World	0	4	ditto.

THIRD CLASS.

	s.	d.	
For every Ship, Boat, Barge, Craft, Lighter or other Vessel laden, which shall enter from the Bristol Channel and depart therefrom without breaking Bulk, or which shall discharge and depart with the same Cargo....................	0	6	ditto.
For ditto which shall enter and depart in Ballast................	0	3	ditto.
For every Boat, Barge or other Craft, which shall enter from the Glamorganshire Canal and pass through the Basin and Ship Canal..	0	6	ditto.

For every Ship, &c. which shall enter the Canal or Basin for the purpose of unloading from or discharging Goods, &c. on board of any Ship, Boat, Barge, Craft, Lighter or other Vessel being within the Ship Canal or Basin, such and the like Rates and Duties upon the Goods so discharged or loaded, as are allowed for Wharfage Rates on Goods, as per the after-mentioned Schedule.

	s.	d.	
And upon every Ship, &c. which shall continue in the Ship Canal or Basin for any Space of Time exceeding Twenty-one Days, for every Week and fractional Part of a Week over and above the said Twenty-one Days.................	0	½	ditto.
For every Ship or Vessel which shall not enter the said Ship Canal, but shall either land or receive Passengers or Goods upon any of the Piers or Jetties constructed under the provisions of this Act	0	3	ditto.

WHARFAGE RATES,

To be levied on all Minerals, Goods, Wares, Merchandize, &c. brought upon any Pier, Jetty, Wharf, Quays or Landing Places, or deposited in any Warehouse belonging to the Marquis of Bute—over and above the preceding Duties.

	s.	d.
For Bar, Bolt or Pig-iron, Cast Iron, Wrought Iron, Guns, Gun Carriages or Shot, Iron Wire, Lead, Lead Shot and Tallow, per Ton..................	1	0
For Broken or Bushel Iron, Ballast Iron, Iron-ore, Lead-ore, Salt and Slates, per Ton	0	6
For Copper-ore, per Ton	0	8
For Copper or Brass, (or Battery) per Ton	1	3

WHARFAGE RATES CONTINUED.

	s.	d.
For Wrought Copper or Brass and Nails, per Ton	1	8
For Brass Wire, and Red and White Lead, per Ton	1	6
For Tin, per Block or Barrel	0	2
For Tin Plates, per Box	0	1
For Coal, Culm or Stone Coal, per Ton	0	9
For Oak Bark, per Ton	2	0
For Oak, Ash, Elm, Fir, or other Timber, per Load	1	3
For Deal Ends, per 120	0	4
For Deals, per 120	1	0
For large Oak Knees, each	0	2
For small ditto, each	0	1
For Oak, Ash, Elm and Fir Plank, per 100 Superficial Feet	0	6
For Quarter Oak, per 100 Feet in length	0	6
For Mast, Yard or Bow-sprit, Six Inches and under Eight in Diameter	0	3
For ditto, Eight Inches in Diameter and under Twelve	0	6
For ditto, if Twelve and upwards	1	0
For Wheat, Barley, Oats, Peas and Beans, per Quarter	0	2
For Flour, or Meal, per Twenty Barrels or Bags	2	0
For Tar, per Barrel	0	1
For Gunpowder, per Barrel	0	2
For Bricks or Pantiles, per Thousand	1	0
For Paving Bricks and Malt Kiln Tiles, per Hundred	0	6
For Fire Bricks, per Thousand	2	0
For Limestone, per Ton	0	3
For Manure, per Ton	0	1

And so in proportion for any greater or less Quantity than a Ton.

For any other Article or Merchandize whatsoever, which shall be shipped from or landed or deposited upon any of the Wharfs, such reasonable Rate, Rent or Sum, not exceeding the Rates then usually paid in the Port of Bristol.

Goods not to remain on the Quays or Landing Places more than Three Days, without consent of the Marquis of Bute, or his Agents.

His Majesty's Vessels are exempt from payment of any of the above Rates or Duties.

The object of this canal is to avoid the dangers and difficulties of the present intricate navigation from the sea to the Glamorgan-shire Canal; and by affording additional accommodation to the shipping interest it will have the effect of increasing and improving the trade of Cardiff and its vicinity; and by facilitating the exportation of the mineral productions of this rich district, and providing a safe and convenient place for the loading and unloading afloat ships, and other vessels of greater burthen than can be at present accommodated, a general advantage will of necessity accrue to the public, and too much praise cannot be given to the noble Marquis for his spirited undertaking.

CAISTOR CANAL.

33 George III. Cap. 114, Royal Assent 3rd June, 1793.

This canal commences on the New River Ancholme Navigation, near Creampoke, in Kesley Carrs, and proceeds in an easterly direction by the village of South Kelsey, to its termination at Moortown, three miles and a half west of the town of Caistor. It is four miles in length, with six locks, and it was made under the authority of an act, entitled, ' *An Act for making and maintaining* ' *a navigable Canal, from the River Ancholme, in the parish of* ' *South Kelsey, in the county of Lincoln, into the parish of Caistor,* ' *in the said county,*' by which the subscribers are incorporated by the name of " The Company of Proprietors of the Caistor Canal " Navigation," with power to raise £15,000, in one hundred and fifty shares of £100 each, with further authority for raising an additional sum of £10,000, if necessary.

TONNAGE RATES.

	d.		
Wheat, Rye, Shelling, Beans, Peas, Vetches, Lentils, Apples, Pears, Onions and Potatoes	$1\frac{1}{2}$	per Quarter, per Mile.	
Barley, Malt, and Oats	1	ditto.	ditto.
Wool, Dried Pelts or Spetches	$1\frac{1}{2}$	per Pack, per Mile,	
Coal, Slack, Cinders, Culm, and Charcoal	4	per Ton, per Mile.	
Lime	3	ditto.	ditto.
Bricks and Tiles	2	ditto.	ditto.
Stone-flag, Paving-stone and Slate	3	ditto.	ditto.
Cast Metal Goods, Bar and other Iron	6	ditto.	ditto.
Timber (English or Foreign) and Deals	4	ditto.	ditto.
Groceries, Linen and Woollen Yarn, Cotton, Flax, Hemp, Manufactured Goods, and all Wares and Merchandize	8	ditto.	ditto.

Fractions to be taken as for a Mile, and as for a Quarter of a Ton.

EXEMPTION FROM RATES.

Timber and Stone for the use of his Majesty; Gravel and Sand for the repair of Roads; Dung, Marl, and Soil for the purpose of Manuring Lands belonging to Owners of adjoining Lands; though these last-mentioned Articles are not permitted to pass a Lock free, unless the Water shall flow over the Waste Weir. Vessels under Twenty Tons, not to pass without leave, or without paying for that Tonnage.

By this canal, and the Ancholme Navigation, the surplus agricultural produce of the north of Lincolnshire is exported; and coal, agricultural lime, and general merchandize, is the return to Caistor and its neighbourhood.

There was some attempt made, in 1801, to make a canal from this, along the foot of the Wolds, to near Market Raisin, but as no act was obtained for the purpose, it seems now to be abandoned.

CALDER AND HEBBLE NAVIGATION.

31 George II. Cap. 72, Royal Assent 9th June, 1758.
9 George III. Cap. 71, Royal Assent 21st April, 1769.
6 George IV. Cap. 17, Royal Assent 31st March, 1825.

THE River Calder rises in the mountainous district north of the
town of Todmorden, running along a most romantic and deep valley, called The Vale of Todmorden, where in many places the
river, the turnpike road, and the Rochdale Canal, are within a few
yards of each other; having passed Todmorden, it runs by My-
tholme and Hebden Bridge, to Sowerby Wharf, about two miles
from Halifax, where the Calder and Hebble Navigation commences.   The Hebble is a small but rapid stream, which, rising
above Ovenden, passes round the north and east sides of the town
of Halifax, and falls into the Calder below Salterhebble.   The
course of the Calder, from the commencement of this navigation,
is in an easterly direction, by Elland, Kirklees Park, near which
place it is joined by the Colne, and Sir John Ramsden's Canal;
from hence it passes by Dewsbury and Horbury Bridge, to
Wakefield; at a quarter of a mile below Wakefield Bridge it terminates, on entering the Aire and Calder Navigation at a place
called Fall Ing.

This river was rendered navigable by making cuts and locks
for the purpose of passing mill weirs, &c. under the authority of an
act of the 31st George II. entitled, ' *An Act for extending the*
' *Navigation of the River Calder, to or near to Sowerby Bridge, in*
' *the parish of Halifax ; and for making navigable the River Heb-*
' *ble, Halig, or Halifax Brook, from Brooksmouth to Salterhebble*
' *Bridge, in the county of York.*'   Mr. Smeaton surveyed the proposed line in 1757, and it was carried into execution, under his
superintendence, by commissioners appointed in the act, whose
qualification was a landed estate of the annual value of £100, or
a personalty to the amount of £3,000; any nine of whom were
empowered to act.

Authority is given to raise money, for the purpose of carrying
this act into execution, at five per cent. interest, on security of the
tolls granted, which were as follow.

TONNAGE RATES.

	s.	d.	
Stones, Slate, Flags, Lime, Limestone, and Coal	1	1½	per Ton, for the whole Distance.
All other Goods, Merchandize, and Commodities	8	0	ditto. ditto. ditto.

And so in proportion for any shorter Distance.

EXEMPTION FROM TOLL.

Stones, Timber, Gravel, Sand, or other Materials, for the use of the Mills within the Limits of this Line of Navigation.

Soaper's Waste, Dung, and all Sorts of Manure, except Lime or Limestone.

Coal, under this Act, is prohibited from being carried down the Stream towards Wakefield, (except for the Use of the Vessels navigating the same) under the Penalty of £50, one-half to the King, the other Moiety to the Person who sues for the same.

Considerable damage having been done to this navigation by a great flood, which occurred in the night between the 7th and 8th October, 1767, and a total stop being put to the navigation, application was made in the following year to parliament, by the parties who had furnished the funds for constructing the navigation, and they obtained an act, entitled, ' *An Act for extending the* ' *Navigation of the River Calder to Salterhebble Bridge, and to* ' *Sowerby Bridge, in the county of York, and for repealing an Act* ' *for that Purpose ;*' in the preamble of which, after reciting the title of the original act, is the following statement of the reason for this measure ;—

" And whereas the commissioners appointed for carrying the " said act into execution, have borrowed of several persons consi- " derable sums of money, which they have laid out for the purposes " aforesaid, and great advantages arising therefrom have been " already experienced : and whereas, before such navigation was " completed, and all the necessary works for the defence and " security of the cuts, locks and other works were perfected, such " of the works as were then made, were, by the violence of re- " peated floods, destroyed or very greatly damaged, and the na- " vigation is ruined so far as to be no longer passable for any kind " of vessels from Wakefield to Brooksmouth, or from Brooksmouth " to Salterhebble Bridge : and, whereas, the said commissioners " cannot raise money to make the same good again, no person " being willing to lend any, under the present circumstances, " upon such security as they are empowered to give by virtue of

" the said act, so that all those who have already advanced money
" for making the said navigation, are likely to lose their money so
" advanced, to the great discouragement of all persons willing to
" engage in such useful undertakings; and the public is in danger
" of losing the benefit of such navigation, unless some further pro-
" vision be made by law for restoring, completing, and main-
" taining the same : may it therefore please your Majesty,
" &c. &c."

The proprietors, or original mortgagees, were eighty-one in
number, amongst whom was Sir George Savile, Bart. and they
were, by this act, incorporated by the name of " The Company of
" Proprietors of the Calder and Hebble Navigation," with power
to raise among themselves, and by the admission of new subscribers, such sums of money, for the purposes of this act, as the
company, at any general meeting, shall direct to be raised; and
that this, together with the money already advanced, with interest
due thereon, shall be divided into £100 shares. The company
are also authorized to borrow, on security of the tolls, the sum of
£20,000. The concern is under the direction of a committee of
five, or more, who are under the control of the general meetings.
As this act repeals the act of 31st George II. the following tonnage
rates were substituted.

TONNAGE RATES

	s.	d.	
Stones, Slate, Flags, Lime, Limestone, and Coal......................................	4	2	per Ton, for the whole Distance.
All other Goods, Wares, Merchandize, and Commodities	9	0	ditto.　　ditto.　　ditto.

And so in proportion for any less Distance or Weight.

EXEMPTION FROM TOLL.

Materials for the repairs of any of the Mills on this Line of Navigation, Soaper's
Waste, Dung, or any Kind of Manure, except Lime and Limestone, provided such
Articles pass through the Locks at the time when Water is flowing over the Dam
of such Locks.

Boats under Fifteen Tons, not to pass without leave.

Owners of Wharfs may charge Three-pence per Ton for any Article which may
remain less than Six Days, if more, a Half-penny per Day in Addition.

The act contains this condition as regards dividends, viz. that
whenever more than ten per cent. shall be paid in any one year,
on the original sums expended on the navigation, then a reduction

shall take place in the rates, in the year following the payment of more than ten per cent. in the proportion of two shillings and sixpence in the pound upon all such surplus.

Millers are required to stop their mills, when the water is reduced 18 inches below the crown of the dam.

Mr. Smeaton was again directed to view the Calder, by the new proprietors, with reference to the repairing and perfecting the navigation; and he accordingly reported on it in December, 1770, the year after the obtaining of the act. In February, 1779, he again examined the river and suggested several improvements, which were carried into immediate execution.

The Calder and Hebble Navigation, from its junction with the Aire and Calder Navigation at Fall Ing Lock, to the basin at Sowerby Wharf, where it communicates with the Rochdale Canal, is twenty-two miles in length, with a fall of 192 feet 6 inches, by twenty-eight locks.

A considerable portion of the line of this navigation occupies the original course of the river, and the remainder consists of cuts, to avoid the circuitous course of the river, and for the purpose of passing the mill weirs. It was first projected with the sole object of giving greater facilities to the populous manufacturing district situate westward of the town of Wakefield; but it has subsequently, by its connection with the Rochdale and Huddersfield Canals, become a very important part of the line of inland navigation between the ports of Liverpool, Goole and Hull, thus connecting the German Ocean and the Irish Sea.

For many years a considerable portion of the manufactures of Manchester and Rochdale were brought, by land carriage, across the grand ridge, to this navigation at Sowerby Bridge Wharf; but when the Rochdale and the Huddersfield Canals were opened, the increase to the revenues of this navigation was such, as to enable the proprietors to divide fourteen per cent. notwithstanding the prohibitory clause in the act of 9th George III. besides accumulating a considerable fund for any exigency. The country through which it passes has also partaken of the great advantages arising from a well regulated navigation. Agricultural lime has, by its means, been carried to fertilize a sterile and mountainous district; stone and flag quarries have been opened in its vicinity,

which have furnished inexhaustible supplies for the London
Market, and other parts of the kingdom; we allude, in particular,
to the celebrated flag quarries of Cromwell Bottom and Elland
Edge, at the former of which there is an extensive wharf. Iron-
stone and coal works have been, and continue to be, extensively
worked on its banks; and from the collieries at Flockton, a railway extends to the river at Horbury Bridge; from the Storr's
Hill Colliery there is also a railway, terminating at the Calder, a
little above the same bridge; within a few years there was a
railway from the White Lee Colliery, above Heckmondwike,
which terminated at this navigation, a short distance above Dewsbury, but the colliery is now worked out, and the railway taken
up. At Kirklees a railway is laid to this navigation, from Sir
George Armytage's Collieries; and the Earl of Cardigan has also
a railway from his valuable collieries at New Park, to the Calder,
at Wakefield, where are convenient staiths for shipment. Many
other collieries, stone quarries, &c. have been opened on its banks,
in consequence of the facility it gives for exporting their heavy
produce, but they are too numerous to be all introduced within
our pages.

In 1825 the company of proprietors applied for an act to
enable them to extend a branch of their navigation to the town of
Halifax, which will be attended with considerable advantage to
that populous and important manufacturing town; it is entitled,
' *An Act to enable the Company of Proprietors of the Calder and*
' *Hebble Navigation, to make a navigable Cut or Canal from*
' *Salterhebble Bridge, to Bailey Hall, near to the town of Halifax,*
' *in the West Riding of the county of York ; and to amend the Act*
' *relating to the said Navigation.*' By this act the company are
empowered to raise among themselves, or by the admission of new
proprietors, the sum of £40,000 for carrying into execution (only
one mile and three-eighths of canal,) the works proposed; with
further power to raise, by way of loan, or by creating new shares,
an additional sum of £10,000; but which sums of £40,000 and
£10,000 may be raised upon promissory notes, or on mortgage of
the tolls and duties authorized to be collected.

The clause in the former act relating to the limitation of the
dividends, is in this act repealed, so that the proprietors may here-

after divide the whole of their profits: the tonnage rates are also altered, and the following are what the proprietors are now empowered to collect.

TONNAGE RATES.

	s.	d.	
Stones, Slate, Flags, Lime or Limestone, and Coal	2	0½	per Ton, for the whole Distance.
All other Goods, Wares, Merchandize, and Commodities	4	1½	ditto. ditto. ditto.

And so in proportion for any less Weight or Distance.
Fractions to be taken as for a Quarter of a Mile, and as for a Quarter of a Ton.

The new tonnage rates above-recited came into operation for the whole line of navigation on the 1st day of June, 1825. The gross receipts of this work amount to about £40,000 per annum.

The cut authorized to be made by the last act, is nearly one mile and three-eighths in length, with a rise of $100\frac{1}{2}$ feet. It commences in the Salterhebble Basin, and proceeds up the valley to the east side of the town of Halifax, where there are convenient wharfs and basins for the accommodation of the trade. The water for supplying it is procured by means of a drift eleven hundred and seventy yards in length, from the basin of the canal, at Salterhebble, to a pit beyond the uppermost lock, from which it is raised by a powerful steam engine, into the head level. This novel and expensive mode of procuring the lockage water was resorted to by Mr. Bradley, the company's engineer, for the purpose of avoiding disputes with the numerous mill owners on the line of the Hebble Brook, below Halifax.

CALEDONIAN CANAL.

43 George III. Cap. 102, Royal Assent 27th July, 1803.
44 George III. Cap. 62, Royal Assent 29th June, 1804.
6 George IV. Cap. 15, Royal Assent 31st March, 1825.

This canal, or rather series of canals and navigable lochs, forms one of the most magnificent inland navigations in the world; and its execution has been justly accounted one of the brightest examples of what the skill and perseverance of our engineers can accomplish. It commences at the Corpach Basin, in the tideway of Loch Eil, at the north end of Linnhe Loch, near Fort William, and

at the foot of that celebrated Mountain Ben Nevis, which rises
4,370 feet above the level of the sea. From hence its course is
nearly in a straight direction, north-eastwardly, through Lochs
Lochy, Ness, Doughfour, to Clacknacarry Basin in Loch Beauly,
where it enters the Murray Firth, on the west side of the town of
Inverness. Its total length is sixty miles and a half, and the following are the particulars of the lengths of the several cuts and
lochs, extracted from a document ordered by the Honourable the
House of Commons, on the 1st of June, 1821.

	M.	F.	C.
Canal, from the sea lock at Clacknacarry to Muir Town......	1	1	0
From Muir Town through Loch Doughfour to Loch Ness	6	5	5
Length of Loch Ness	23	5	6
From the south-west end of Loch Ness to Loch Oich	5	3	5
Length of Loch Oich	3	5	6
From the south-west end of Loch Oich to Loch Lochy......	1	6	5
Length of the Loch Lochy....................	10	0	0
From the south-west end of Loch Lochy to Cor- pach Sea Lock........................	8	0	3
Total length of the navigation....	60	4	0

Of this, twenty-three miles and eight chains are artificially formed,
and the remaining thirty-seven miles, three furlongs and two
chains, are natural lochs or lakes, which have been made navigable.

There are twenty-eight locks upon this navigation, viz:—from
Loch Eil to Loch Lochy, twelve locks ; and two more to the
summit level at Loch Oich; from hence are seven locks to Fort
Augustus, at the west end of Loch Ness; and seven from the
end of the last-mentioned loch to the sea, at Loch Beauly, above
low water of which, the summit level is only 91 feet.

The first act relating to this grand national undertaking occurs
in the 43rd George III. and is entitled, ' An Act for granting to
' his Majesty the Sum of £20,000, towards defraying the Expense of

' making an Inland Navigation from the western to the eastern Sea,
' by Inverness and Fort William ; and for taking the necessary steps
' towards executing the same,' by which, commissioners were appointed to carry the act into execution; some progress was, in
consequence, made, but in the following session, another act was
passed, entitled, ' An Act for making further provision for making
' and maintaining an Inland Navigation, commonly called " The
' Caledonian Canal," from the eastern to the western Sea, by Inver-
' ness and Fort William, in Scotland.' By this legislative enactment,
the commissioners, appointed in the first act, are authorized to
receive, at his Majesty's Exchequer, the sum of £50,000, in two
half yearly instalments, for the purposes set forth in the preamble.

Though this line of navigation was commenced by government,
yet the last-recited act contains a clause securing a proportionate
dividend to all who may be disposed to become shareholders in the
undertaking for any sum above £50 ; ten per cent. to be paid at
the time of subscribing, the other at such times, and by such
instalments as the commissioners may determine. For the purpose
of securing a supply of water for the lockage in this navigation,
the act empowers the commissioners to embank Loch Garry, Loch
Quoich or Quich, and Loch Arkeg, so that they may more effectually act as reservoirs.

THE RATES OF TONNAGE ALLOWED UNDER THIS ACT.

	d.
Goods, Wares, Merchandize and Commodities	2 per Ton, per Mile.

And so in proportion for any greater or less Quantity than a Ton; and payment shall
    be made for a full Mile, if any Portion of such Mile shall have been passed.
Vessels entering a Loch or Lake shall pay for the whole Length of such Loch or Lake.
Thirty-six cubic Feet of Oak, Ash, Elm, Beech, Poplar, or Birch Timber, and Forty
    five cubic Feet of Fir, or Deal Balk, shall be deemed a Ton.
All Vessels in his Majesty's Service are exempt from Toll.

The act of 6th George IV. entitled, ' An Act to explain and
' amend two Acts passed in the Forty-third and Forty-fourth Years
' of the Reign of His late Majesty King George the Third, for
' making and maintaining an Inland Navigation, commonly called
' " The Caledonian Canal," by establishing further Checks upon the
' Expenditure of the Public Money for that Purpose, in certain
' cases,' was passed chiefly with the view of better regulating the

payment of compensation claims, in respect of consequential damage, wherein it is required that all such claims should be made on or before the 1st of February, 1826.

This canal, which was projected and commenced chiefly with the view of giving facilities to the Baltic Timber Trade, was opened in October, 1822. Its depth is 15 feet, although it was proposed, originally, to be 5 feet deeper; but as the estimate for giving this increased depth was £41,000, and, as the Baltic Timber Trade has been in a great measure destroyed, by the new scale of duties having directed the trade to Canada, the commissioners have, at present, decided, not to add this cost to the enormous sum of £977,524, which had been expended on the canal up to the 1st of January, 1828.

Though this is a capital navigation for ships drawing 15 feet water, in addition to the advantages gained by avoiding the circuitous and dangerous navigation through Pentland Frith, and the Western Hebrides, it has not hitherto attracted the attention of seafaring adventurers so much as might have been expected; for it appears from the twenty-fourth report of the commissioners in July, 1828, that the total number of ships which availed themselves of this passage, in 1826, was nine hundred and forty-four; in 1827, seven hundred and sixty-six; and in 1828, eight hundred and eighty-two; and the total produce of the rates for the year ending May, 1828, was only £2,870, whilst the expense incurred in keeping up the canal amounted to £4,173, leaving a deficiency of £1,303, which has been borrowed.

Since January 1st, 1828, the tonnage rates have been reduced to the original rate of one farthing per ton per mile, which may have the effect of attracting the shipping interest to the more frequent use of this canal.

Nearly thirty years previous to the passing of the first act relating to this canal, Mr. Watt surveyed the line, and estimated that a canal of 12 feet water would cost £164,031, exclusive of land. Two years, however, previous to the date of the first act, Mr. Telford, along with Mr. Murdoch Downie, being directed by government to examine the line, recommended a canal of the width of 110 feet at the surface, and 50 feet at the bottom, with 20 feet water, and the locks 162 feet by 38; and the estimate formed by Mr. W.

Jessop, according to these dimensions, amounted to £497,531, including the land required, and the necessary mooring chains. It was afterwards directed that the locks should be 172 feet by 38 to 40 feet; and, with the view of giving greater facility to the passage of small vessels, it was in contemplation to construct side locks for vessels of two hundred tons, but as this appendage was estimated to cost £75,200, and the advantage appearing very uncertain, the idea was abandoned.

The whole of the works on this line of canal are of the first order, and exhibit the combined skill of the excellent engineers, who were entrusted with its execution, in the most favourable point of view; and whoever views the celebrated chain of eight locks, called " Neptune's Staircase," situate at the eastern end of this navigation, which alone cost upwards of £50,000, and the sea lock at Clacknacarry, extending upwards of four hundred yards into the sea, will not hesitate to confirm the opinion we have thus expressed.

CAM OR GRANT RIVER.

1 Anne, Cap. 11, Royal Assent 27th February, 1702.
53 George III. Cap. 214, Royal Assent 21st July, 1813.

THIS river rises on the confines of Hertfordshire, between Biggleswade and Royston, from whence it pursues a north-easterly course, on the south side of Orwell Hill, to the Queen's Mill, at Cambridge, to which place it is navigable. From hence its course is by Fen Ditton to Clayhithe Ferry, the place where the London and Cambridge Junction Canal was intended to communicate with this river, and where the navigation, as comprehended under the foregoing acts, terminate. The remaining portion of the Cam River being in Bedford Level, and consequently under the jurisdiction of the Bedford Level Corporation, will be described under the head of Ouze River, as all the legislative enactments relating to the lower end of the Cam are introduced into acts of parliament, obtained by the above body, the titles of some of which terminate in the following manner, viz :—' and for improving the Naviga- ' tion of the River Ouze, in the county of Norfolk, and of the ' several Rivers communicating therewith.' The first act, therefore,

relating to the upper portion of the Cam, was passed in the first
year of the reign of Anne, and is entitled, ' *An Act for making the*
' *River Cham, alias Grant, in the county of Cambridge, more navi-*
' *gable from Clayhithe Ferry to the Queen's Mill, in the University*
' *and Town of Cambridge,*' from which it would appear that it was
navigable previous to this early date, but from what period we
cannot learn.

The navigation, which is only about seven miles in length, is
managed by conservators appointed under the authority of the
above-mentioned act.

Another act of parliament was obtained in 1813, entitled, ' *An*
' *Act for extending and amending an Act of Queen Anne, for*
' *making the River Cham more navigable from Clayhithe Ferry to the*
' *Queen's Mill, in the county of Cambridge,*' but it does not contain
any clauses wherein the public are generally interested.

The principal uses to which this navigation is put, is to export
the surplus agricultural produce of the country through which
it passes, and to facilitate the import of coal and general merchandize.

CAMEL RIVER.

THIS river rises three miles north of Camelford, in Cornwall,
on the east side of which town it passes; thence by Tredethy and
Penhargate, to Dunmeer Bridge, where it changes to a north-
eastwardly course, by Guinea Port, to Wade Bridge, where it
enters an estuary which falls into the sea at Stepper Point, three
miles east from Padstow.

It is navigable, as a tideway river, from Guinea Port, near
Wade Bridge, to the sea, a distance (by the low water channel)
of eight miles and a half. An act was obtained in 1797 to extend
this navigation, by means of the Polbrook Canal, but it has not yet
been carried into execution. It was entitled, ' *An Act for making*
' *and maintaining a navigable Canal, from Guinea Port, in the*
' *parish of St. Breock, in the county of Cornwall, to Dunmeer*
' *Bridge, in the parish of Bodmin, in the said county; and also*
' *a certain collateral Cut, from Cood, to, or near to, Ruthern*
' *Bridge, in the said parish of Bodmin.*'

There is no act relating to the river, and being in the tideway, it is consequently free of toll.

The chief uses to which this navigable estuary is put, is to export the produce of the tin and copper mines in its immediate vicinity, and the import of coal and general merchandize. Slate, also, forms an article of exportation from the port of Padstow, a considerable town on its banks.

CANTERBURY NAVIGATION OR RIVER STOUR.

6 Henry VIII. Cap. 17, Royal Assent —— —— 1514.
6 George IV. Cap. 166, Royal Assent 22nd June, 1825.

THE River Stour rises on the south side of the Chalk Hills, near Lenham, whence, taking a south-eastwardly course by Surrenden Dering, Hothfield Place the seat of the Earl of Thanet, to the town of Ashford, where it is joined by another considerable stream, which also bears the name of Stour, and which rises on the Downs, eastward of Mount Morris; hence it pursues a north-westwardly course through a portion of the Weald of Kent, and south of Mersham Hatch, the seat of Sir E. Knatchbull, to the junction at Ashford. From hence the united streams pursue a northerly course through one of the most fertile vallies of this delightful county, by Godmersham Park, Chilham Castle, and Chartham, to the city of Canterbury, where the river becomes navigable. From this place its course is north-eastwardly, by Fordwich, to near Sarr, below which place the Little Stour or Seaton Navigation falls into it; hence pursuing a course nearly east, until within three quarters of a mile of the sea at Sandwich Haven, from which point, however, by the line of the river, it is upwards of seven miles, in consequence of the circuitous course it takes by Sandwich to the above haven, in Pegwell Bay. To obviate this, however, a cut, called Stonar Cut, has been made between the channels, which takes off a considerable portion of this circuitous route by Sandwich.

The Stour is a very ancient navigation, as we find an act in the 6th year of the reign of Henry VIII. entitled, ' *An Act concerning*

' *the River at Canterbury*,' but whether it was the one under which the river was originally made navigable, is a question we have not the means of deciding upon. The act above-recited is, however, the act under which the navigation has been managed, until the early part of the present reign, though the royal assent was given to an act, on the 10th of June, 1811, (51 George III.) for the purpose of superseding the upper portion of this navigation, which is entitled, ' *An Act for making a Harbour and Wet Dock,* ' *at or near St. Nicholas' Bay, in the parish of St. Nicholas, and* ' *all Saints, in the Isle of Thanet, in the county of Kent, and for* ' *making a navigable Canal, from the said Harbour, to the City of* ' *Canterbury*,' but, of these proposed works, no portion has ever been carried into execution.

As this river, in its present state, and the haven of Sandwich, had become very inadequate to the trade of Canterbury and Sandwich, a company, consisting of four hundred and forty-nine persons, amongst whom were the Earl of Darnley, Lord Viscount Teynham, and Sir E. W. Campbell Rich Owen, Sir Gerard Noel, Sir William Kay, Admiral Sir John Knight, and Sir Robert Farquhar, obtained an act, entitled, ' *An Act for improving the Navi-* ' *gation of the River Stour, and Sandwich Haven, from the City of* ' *Canterbury to the Town and Port of Sandwich, in the county of Kent;* ' *and for making and maintaining a New Haven from the said Town* ' *and Port of Sandwich to the Sea, and a Harbour on the Sea Shore;*' by which the above persons were incorporated under the name of " The Canterbury Navigation and Sandwich Harbour Company."

The improvements contemplated under this act consist chiefly of a canal or harbour, 8 feet deep, from the Small Downs, commencing between the Batteries, Nos. 1 and 2, to the River Stour, at Sandwich, which is in length, from the end of the proposed jetty, two miles, four furlongs and five chains; from thence the navigation is continued in the old course of the river, sixteen miles and five chains, to Fordwich, where there is a lock rising 6 feet; from hence to the tail of Abbott's Mill, Canterbury, the length is two miles and a quarter, including three short cuts, together amounting in length, to one mile, one furlong and seven chains; half a mile from Canterbury there is another lock of 6 feet rise.

At the end of the canal, in the Downs, where the spring

tide rises 18 feet, there is to be a jetty 1000 feet in length. Basins
are to be constructed at Sandwich, and Abbott's Mill, Canterbury.
At the latter place the surface of the navigation will be 27 feet
above low water spring tides, and 9 feet above high water.

The total length of the navigation, when improved, will be
twenty miles, six furlongs and eight chains; the estimate for
which was made by Mr. James Morgan, civil engineer, and
amounted to the sum of £70,657, 13s. 7d.

The company have power to raise among themselves, for the
above purposes, the sum of £100,000, in four thousand shares of
£25 each, and in case the above sum is insufficient, power is
given to raise an additional sum of £40,000, by mortgage of the
undertaking; half of which sum may be raised by way of annuity,
or they may borrow, at their option, the above sum of £40,000
of the Exchequer Bill Commissioners.

The improved navigation is to be under the management
of directors, who have power to appoint a governor and deputy.
The present navigation, however, is not to be interfered with until
the harbour and the cuts from Fordwich to Canterbury are finished.

The new harbour and haven of Sandwich to be considered as
within the liberties of the town and port of Sandwich and the Cinque Ports; and that the lord warden of the Cinque Ports, the con-
stable of Dover Castle, and the mayor, jurats, and commonalty of
Sandwich, &c. are to have jurisdiction in the same manner as before
exercised by them over the old haven and harbour of Sandwich.

By an act of 32nd George III. entitled, ' *An Act for the Main-*
' *tenance and Improvement of the Harbour of Ramsgate, in the*
' *county of Kent, and for cleansing, amending, and preserving the*
' *Haven of Sandwich, in the said county,*' the corporation of Sandwich are entitled to the annual sum of £200, for the purpose of
preserving Sandwich Haven, and which is by the act of the 6th of
his present Majesty directed to be applied, with the same object,
on the works of the new haven.

The company of proprietors are directed to invest £5,000 in
the three per cents. as a security for the due execution of the
works hereby authorized, and this sum, and the dividends arising
from it, is to remain until it accumulate to £20,000.

HARBOUR DUES ON THE TONNAGE OF VESSELS FREQUENTING THE
PORT AND RIVER.

	£.	s.	d.	
Foreign Vessels to load or unload	0	1	6	per Ton.
British Vessels from Foreign Countries	0	1	3	ditto.
Ditto, Coastwise	0	0	9	ditto.
Ditto, Colliers laden ditto	0	0	9	ditto.
Ditto, Vessels laden with Lime-stone, Lime-chalk, Sand, Manure, Ballast, or any Description of Compost for the Land	0	0	3	ditto.
Passage Vessels, Keels, and Boats	0	0	6	ditto.
Pleasure Yachts under Thirty Tons, and Boats in the Harbour or on the River, belonging to the Port and River	1	0	0	per Annum.
The same Description of Vessels or Yachts, exceeding Thirty Tons Burthen, either belonging to the Port or entering the Harbour or River from any other Port	0	0	9	per Ton.
Every Foreign Fishing Boat	0	0	4	ditto.
Every English ditto	0	0	3	ditto.
Every Vessel entering and using the Harbour, Basin, or Wet Dock, from Stress of Weather, or Outward Bound, waiting for a Wind, or for repairs	0	0	6	ditto.
Every Vessel remaining in the Harbour or Basin more than Twelve Days after the Weather abates, or the Wind permits, unless for Repairs	0	0	2	per Ton, per Diem.

There is an exemption in favour of vessels belonging to the
port of Arundel, in Sussex, which are made free of the harbours,
ports, and havens of Dover, Rye, Ramsgate and Sandwich, by authority of an act of 33rd George III. (see page 29, under the head
of Arun River.)   The ships and vessels in his Majesty's service
are also exempt from payment of these duties.

There is, also, a special clause relating to the rates to be paid
by the owner or occupier of the corn mill, wharfs, and warehouses,
situate on the Little Stour or Seaton Navigation, at Seaton, in the
parish of Ickham, directing the harbour duties to be paid in full;
but for the period of twenty-one years from the commencement of
such rates, one-half only of the river rates are to be demanded for
and in respect of all cargoes belonging to them, conveyed in
barges drawing 3 feet 6 inches only, and loaded or discharged in
the Little Stour or Seaton Navigation.   The navigation here referred to has been made without application to parliament, and
extends from Seaton to the Canterbury Navigation, into which it
enters a little below Stourmouth. Its length is little more than six
miles, and no part of it is more than 15 feet above low water
spring tides.

Ships receiving or unlading goods upon any part of the sea
coast, between Cliffs End, in the parish of St. Lawrence, in the
Isle of Thanet, and Sandown Castle, are liable to the aforesaid tonnage duties.

When the works, contemplated under the last act, are carried into execution, they will tend greatly to improve the city of Canterbury and port of Sandwich, as hitherto, the haven of Sandwich, by reason of the shifting of the channel of the Stour, through the sands in Pegwell Bay, has been very unsafe for vessels of considerable burthen.

The importance of a harbour in the Downs was felt so early as the time of Edward VI. in which reign an attempt was made to form one near Sandwich; again in Elizabeth's reign; and, in 1744, an estimate for this purpose was laid before the Honourable the House of Commons, which amounted to the sum of £389,168, 13s. 2d. exclusive of land.

This scheme, however, was abandoned, and ultimately the excellent harbour at Ramsgate was proposed.

This is situate three miles to the northward of Sandwich Haven, and is the only secure harbour, in case of storm, on this part of the coast.

The celebrated piers which form it were begun in 1749, and are built entirely of Portland and Purbeck Stone.

The east pier extends, southerly, 800 feet into the sea; it then turns to the west, exhibiting a front, to the Downs, of a polygonal form of five sides, each 450 feet in length.

From the end of this an advanced pier, of 400 feet in length, was added to it by Mr. Smeaton, and at right angles with this, is the termination of the west pier, of nearly similar form and dimensions, leaving an entrance into the harbour of 200 feet in width.

The area enclosed from the sea is forty-six acres, and a basin has been subsequently formed, under the direction of the last-mentioned engineer, at the upper end, by which the tide water can be so penned up, that when at low water the sluices are drawn, it has the effect of scouring out the silt which collects in the outer harbour.

THE FOLLOWING SCHEDULE OF HARBOUR AND RIVER RATES,

On Cargoes, Wharfage, and Charges on Goods warehoused in the Harbour or on the Line of Navigation, are granted by this Act.

DESCRIPTION OF GOODS.	Harbour and River Rates.	Wharfage Rates.	Rates on Goods Warehous'd	HOW CHARGED.
	s. d.	*s. d.*	*s. d.*	
Wheat, Barley, Malt, Beans, Peas, Tares, Canary, Mustard, and other Seeds	0 3	0 ½	0 ½	per Quarter, (W. M.)
Oats	0 2	0 ½	0 ½	ditto. ditto.
Flour	0 2	0 ½	0 ½	per Sack of Five Bushels.
Meal, Middlings, Sharps, Pollard and Bran	0 2	0 ½	0 ½	per Quarter.
Clover, Trefoil, and other heavy Seeds	0 3	0 ½	0 ½	per Sack.
Potatoes and Onions	0 1	0 ½	0 ½	ditto.
Apples, Pears, &c.................	0 1	0 ½	0 ½	per Bushel.
Hops	0 6	0 1	0 1	per Bag.
Ditto.............................	0 3	0 ½	0 ½	per Pocket.
Oil Cakes.........................	2 0	0 6	0 6	per Thousand.
Wool, Cotton, &c..................	0 4	0 1	0 1	per Pack of 240lbs.
Tanned Hides and Calf Skins	0 2	0 ½	0 ½	per Cwt.
Raw Hides........................	0 1	0 ½	0 ½	each.
Pelts.............................	0 9	0 2	0 2	per Hundred.
Sugar, Fruits, Bacon, Cheese, Butter, Pork, Ham, Tongues, Salt, Salted Fish, Tallow, Soap, Candles, and all heavy Grocery Goods not here specified, and Tan or Bark...................	1 8	0 4	0 4	per Ton.
Tea, Coffee, and Spices	0 3	0 ½	0 ½	per Cwt.
Oranges, Lemons, &c..............	0 2	0 1	0 1	per Chest.
Molasses	1 0	0 3	0 3	per Puncheon,
Ale, Porter, Cyder, Perry, Vinegar, and Oil.....................	1·0	0 3	0 3	per Butt.
Ditto. ditto.	0 9	0 2	0 2	per Puncheon.
Ditto. ditto.	0 6	0 1½	0 1½	per Hogshead.
Ditto. ditto.	0 4	0 1	0 1	per Barrel.
Ditto. ditto.	0 2	0 ½	0 ½	per Kilderkin or Runlet.
Ditto. ditto.	0 2	0 ½	0 ¼	per Dozen, in Hampers.
Madder	0 2	0 ½	0 ¼	per Cask, per Cwt.
Pipe Clay	1 6	0 4	0 4	per Ton.
Spirits and Wine	3 6	0 6	0 6	per Pipe, or Butt.
Ditto. ditto.	2 6	0 4	0 4	per Hogshead.
Ditto. ditto.	1 6	0 3	0 3	per Half Hogshead.
Ditto. ditto.	1 0	0 2	0 2	per Quarter ditto.
Ditto. ditto.	0 1	0 ½	0 ½	under 20 Gals. at per Gal.
Ditto. ditto.	0 3	0 ½	0 2	per Dozen, in Hampers.
Passengers	0 6			
Every Four Wheeled Carriage....	7 0			
Every Two Wheeled ditto.	3 6			
Horse, Mare, or Gelding	7 0			
For every other Beast..............	3 0			
Coal, Coke, Culm, Cinders or Breeze	2 0	0 ౿		per Chal. (36 Bus. W. M.)
Hay, Cinquefoil, Clover or Straw..	2 0	0 6	0 2	per Ton.
Oak, Elm, Pine, Beech, and Fir Timber	2 0	0 6	0 2	per Load.

THE SCHEDULE OF HARBOUR AND RIVER RATES CONTINUED.

DESCRIPTION OF GOODS.	Harbour and River Rates.	Wharfage Rates.	Rates on Goods Ware-hous'd	HOW CHARGED.
	s. d.	s. d.	s. d.	
Deals, Battens, and Lathwood......	2 0	0 6	0 6	per Load.
Mahogany, Teak, or other valuable Woods........................	0 1	0 ½	0 2	per Cubic Foot.
Hemp, Cordage, and Yarn........	2 0	0 6	0 2	per Ton.
Pitch, Tar, Grease, Resin, &c......	0 3	0 1	0 2	per Barrel.
Stone, Slate, Plaster of Paris, and Alum........................	2 0	0 6	0 3	per Ton.
Unwrought Iron, Bar Iron, Lead, &c.	2 0	0 6	0 3	ditto.
Marble...........................	0 3	0 1	0 ½	per Cubic Foot.
Gutter, Pan, Mathematical and Plain Tiles......................	3 0	0 9	0 3	per Thousand.
Bricks and Paving Tiles............	4 0	1 0	1 0	ditto.
Glass or Earthenware.	0 9	0 3	0 3	per Crate.
Vitriol or Oil......................	0 3	0 1	0 1	per Carboy.
Corpse............................	21 0	5 0	5 0	
Organ............................	20 0	5 0	5 0	
Piano-forte, Harpsichord, Harp, or Bass Viol......................	5 0	1 0	1 0	
Pipe Staves.......	2 0	0 6		per Hundred.
Copper, Pewter, Brass or Metals (except Lead and Iron)........	2 0	0 6	0 6	per Ton.
Ballast,...........................	1 0			ditto.
Bale Goods, and all other Articles, Wares, or Merchandize not before specified, according to the Amount of the Freight........	0 2	1 6	1 6	per Cwt.

The Rates for Wharfage, as per annexed Schedule, are to be paid for any Time not exceeding the First Twenty-four Hours, and an additional Rate or Duty, to the same Amount, for every Forty-eight Hours beyond the First Twenty-four Hours, or for any shorter Period of Time after the first Twenty-four Hours, or after any one complete Term of Forty-eight Hours.

The warehousing Rates are to be paid for any Time not exceeding the First Twenty-four Hours, and at the same Rate per Week after that Term.

Vessels of less Burthen than Twenty-five Tons, or with less Burthen of Goods than Twenty Tons, not to pass Locks without leave.

CANTERBURY AND WHITSTABLE RAILWAY.

6 George IV. Cap. 120, Royal Assent 10th June, 1825.
7 & 8 George IV. Cap. 11, Royal Assent 2nd April, 1827.
9 George IV. Cap. 29, Royal Assent 9th May, 1828.

THIS railway commences in Whitstable Bay, directly opposite the eastern point of the isle of Sheppey; from whence it pursues a southerly course through Clowes Wood, and by the village of Blean; thence parallel with the west side of the park at Hales

Place, (the seat of Sir Edward Hales, Bart.) by the village of St. Stephen's, to St. Dunstan's, near the city of Canterbury. The length of the original line was six miles, one furlong and three chains, and the estimate for making it was made by Mr. John Dixon, and amounted to the sum of £29,400.

A company, consisting of twenty-four persons, (amongst whom were Sir Henry Montresor, K.C.B. and General Ramsay,) obtained an act in 1825, entitled, ' *An Act for making and main-* ' *taining a Railway or Tramroad from the Sea Shore at or near* ' *Whitstable, in the county of Kent, to, or near to, the city of Can-* ' *terbury, in the said county*,' by which they were incorporated by the name of " The Canterbury and Whitstable Railway Com- " pany," with power to raise among themselves the sum of £31,000, in shares of £50 each, (of which £25,000 was subscribed before going to parliament,) with unlimited power, under the act, for borrowing any additional sum on mortgage of the undertaking.

TONNAGE GRANTED BY THIS ACT.

	s.	d.	
Limestone, Materials for the repair of Roads, Dung, Compost, and all Sorts of Manure, except Chalk and Lime	0	3	per Ton, per Mile.
Coal, Coke, Culm, Charcoal, Cinders, Stone, Marl, Sand, Lime, Clay, Iron-stone, and other Minerals, Building-stone, Pitching and Paving-stone, Bricks, Tiles, Slate, Chalk, Timber, Staves, Deals, Lead, Iron, and other Metals, and all Gross and Unmanufactured Articles, and Building Materials	0	4	ditto. ditto.
Cotton, Wool, Hides, Drugs, Drywoods, Sugar, Corn, Grain, Flour, Manufactured Goods, Agricultural Produce, and all other Goods, Commodities, Wares, and Merchandize	0	6	ditto. ditto.
For every Person carried in any Carriage upon this Railway for any Distance not exceeding Two Miles	0	4	
Two Miles and not exceeding Four Miles	0	8	
Any Distance exceeding Four Miles	1	6	
For every Ton of Goods drawn or propelled by the Engines of the Company	0	2	per Ton, per Mile.
For every Person carried in each Carriage for any Distance not exceeding Three Miles	0	6	
Exceeding Three Miles and not exceeding Five Miles	0	10	
Exceeding Five Miles	1	0	

Fractions to be taken as for a Quarter of a Mile, and as for a Quarter of a Ton.

WHARFAGE RATES.

	d.	
For every Description of Goods which does not lay on the Quay or Wharf, or remain in the Warehouses more than Six Days	1	per Ton.

WAREHOUSING RATES.

		d.	
For every Package not exceeding 56lbs. Weight	}	2 per Ton.	} Which does not lay on the Quay or Wharf, or remain in the Warehouses more than Six Days.
Ditto, above 300lbs. and not exceeding 600lbs.	}	4 ditto.	
Ditto exceeding 1000lbs:		6 ditto.	
If longer than the above Time, then for Wharfage	}	1 ditto.	} For the next Seven Days.
And for Warehousing		2 ditto.	

And the like Sum of One Penny and Two-pence, respectively, per Ton, for every further Seven Days so remaining on Wharf or in Warehouse.

In 1827, the company again applied to parliament and obtained an act, entitled, ' *An Act to authorize the Company of* ' *Proprietors of the Canterbury and Whitstable Railway, to vary* ' *the Line of the Railway, to raise a further Sum of Money for* ' *completing their Works, and to alter and enlarge the Powers of* ' *the Act passed for making and maintaining the said Railway,*' in the preamble of which it is stated, that this measure was necessary in consequence of the unexpected cost of a tunnel, and the insufficiency of the sum appropriated by the original estimate for the purchase of the land required. By this act power is given to alter the line of the railway, so that instead of terminating at St. Dunstan's, nearly three quarters of a mile from Canterbury, it now comes directly to the North Lane, adjoining the River Stour, on the north side of the city. The deviation line is three quarters of a mile in length, on one inclined plane, with 92 feet fall, and the estimate for making it amounts to £5,000. It is fifteen chains longer than the part abandoned, so that the total length of the line will be now six miles, two furlongs and eight chains. The company also obtained power to make two short branch railways or cart roads; one to St. Dunstan's Street, and the other across the Stour, to Pond Lane and St. Peter's Lane, in the city.

ADDITIONAL RATES,

To be taken for the Use of the Quays, &c. are granted by this Act, as follows :—

	s.	d.	
For all Goods, Wares and Merchandize, imported or exported from the Piers, Wharfs, Landing Places, Quays, and other Works.... }	0	1	per Cwt.
For any Parcel less than One Hundred Weight	0	½	
For every Person landed upon or embarked from the said Piers	1	0	

The Commissioners for Paving and Lighting the City of Canterbury have, under the Powers of an Act of the 27th George III. a Claim of One Shilling per Chaldron or Ton on all Coke, Coal, or Cinders brought into or within Three Miles of the said City; a Clause is, therefore, inserted in this Act, securing to them the same Tonnage on all the above-mentioned Articles brought by means of this Railroad, to cease, however, when the Sum of £4,000, which was borrowed to carry the Act of the 27th George III. into Execution, is paid off.

For the purpose of carrying into effect these extra works, the proprietors are empowered to raise among themselves, or by the admission of new subscribers, the further sum of £19,000, or they may borrow the same of the Exchequer Bill Commissioners, on the credit of the undertaking. Seven years are allowed for making the railway.

In the year following the passing of the last-recited act, the company had again recourse to parliament, and on the 9th May, 1828, the royal assent was given to an act, entitled, ' *An Act to* ' *authorize the Company of Proprietors of the Canterbury and* ' *Whitstable Railway, to raise a further Sum of Money for com-* ' *pleting the Undertaking; and for enlarging and amending the* ' *Powers of the Acts passed for making and maintaining the said* ' *Railway and Works connected therewith,*' in the preamble of which it is stated, that no part of the £19,000 they were authorized to raise under the last-recited act, has been obtained; the clause authorizing this is therefore repealed, and power is given to raise £40,000 among themselves, or by the admission of new subscribers, or they may borrow it on mortgage of the rates and duties.

The object of this railroad is to facilitate the conveyance of merchandize in general between London, and other places on the Thames, and Canterbury, which will, doubtless, improve the trade of the last-mentioned place, and beneficially affect the commercial and agricultural interests of its vicinity; and as the proprietors have power to construct piers at Whitstable, (though restricted to 900 feet in length,) it will have the effect of rendering that hitherto exposed bay, a safe and commodious haven ; than which, nothing will more directly tend to the advancement of trade in its vicinity.

CARLISLE CANAL.

59 George III. Cap. 13, Royal Assent 6th April, 1819.

THIS canal commences on the eastern side of the city of Carlisle ; from thence, taking a north-westwardly course, it twice crosses the site of the ancient Picts Wall; whence, continuing by Kirkandrews, to Wormanby, it takes a westerly direction, running parallel with, and on the south side of, the Picts Wall, by Burgh; thence across the marshes bordering the Solway Firth, by Drumburgh Castle and Glasson, to the Firth, into which it falls at Fisher's Cross, near Bowness. The length is eleven miles and a quarter, with a rise of 70 feet by nine locks. From Carlisle, where there is a commodious basin, the canal continues on one level four miles; in the next mile and a quarter there is a fall of 46 feet by six locks; thence to Fisher's Cross is level, and into the sea there is a fall of 24 feet by three equal locks of 8 feet each, with basins between them, called the Upper and Lower Solway Basins. The first basin from the sea is on a level with high water at lowest neaps; and the long pool, or level, of the third lock is 6 inches above an extraordinary tide (15 feet 6 inches above high water at lowest neaps) which occurred in January, 1796.

The estimate for this canal and basins was made by Mr. W. Chapman, of Newcastle-upon-Tyne, and amounted to the sum of £73,392. The act for making it is entitled, ' *An Act for making* ' *and maintaining a navigable Canal from, or from near, the city* ' *of Carlisle, to the Solway Firth, at or near Fisher's Cross, in the* ' *parish of Bowness, in the county of Cumberland,*' by which the proprietors, consisting of three hundred and four persons, amongst whom were the Earl of Lonsdale, Lord Viscount Lowther, Sir James Graham, Sir William Musgrave, Sir Hew Dalrymple Ross, and Sir Joseph Dacre Appleby Gilpin, were incorporated by the name of " The Carlisle Canal Company." The canal is supplied with water from the Rivers Eden and Caldew, and from a reservoir on the south side of the canal, in the parishes of Grinsdale and Kirkandrews-upon-Eden ; and the company were authorized to raise £80,000 among themselves, in sixteen hundred shares of £50 each, with an additional sum of £40,000 among themselves, or by the admission of new subscribers, or on mortgage of the undertaking, or upon promissory notes under the common seal of the company. The work is under the management of a committee of nine proprietors, possessed of at least ten shares each, who are chosen annually.

The object of this canal was to form a communication between the sea and the city of Carlisle, shorter and safer than the navigation of the Solway Firth and the River Eden afforded, and to facilitate the conveyance of lime, coal and general merchandize to and from the said city. Having been now some time finished, its advantages are duly felt; and when the railway, proposed between Newcastle and Carlisle, (for the making of which an act received the royal assent during the last session of parliament,) is effected, it will materially increase the revenues derived from this undertaking.

TONNAGE RATES.

	d.
Dung, or Ashes for Manure......................................	1 per Ton, per Mile.
Coal, Cinders, Culm, Lime, Slate, Stone, Alabaster, Potatoes, Pig-iron, Bricks, Peats, Gravel, Sand, Clay, and Marl .... }	2 ditto. ditto.
Timber, Malleable and Wrought or Manufactured Iron, Lead, and other Unwrought Metals .... }	2½ ditto. ditto.
Corn, Grain, Malt, Peas, and Beans .... {	½ per Mile, per Qr. of Eight Bushels W. M.
Wool, Cotton Wool, Cotton Yarn, Cotton, Linen and Woollen Manufactured Goods, Hemp, Flax, Groceries, and all other Goods, Wares, and Merchandize .... }	3½ per Ton, per Mile.

Fractions to be taken as for a Quarter of a Mile, and as for a Quarter of a Ton.

Vessels passing through Locks to pay for Forty Tons, whether they have as much or not, provided there is sufficient Water for such a Weight.

WHARFAGE RATES.

	d.
For all Goods loaded from or landed upon any of the Wharfs and Staiths, and which shall remain thereupon not more than Forty-eight Hours... }	3 per Ton.
For every Day or Part of a Day after this Period.....................	1 ditto.

Forty Cubic Feet of Light Goods to be deemed a Ton.

CARDIFF CANAL.

(SEE GLAMORGANSHIRE CANAL.)

CARMARTHENSHIRE RAILWAY.

42 George III. Cap. 80, Royal Assent 3rd June, 1802.

THIS railway commences from the River Bury, near a place called The Flats, in the parish of Llanelly, and takes a northerly direction by Stradey Furnace, and up the valley of the Lliedi or Morfa Bach River, by Pandyback and Gynhydre Farm; thence, in an easterly course, crossing the Gwendraeth Faur River, 'to Castell-y-Garreg Limestone Quarries, in the parish of Llanfihangel-Aberbythich. It is in length sixteen miles; and upon the line, for the purpose of carrying the same on a more gradual inclination, are many deep cuttings and embankments; among the latter is one near Munydd Maur, composed of upwards of forty thousand cubic yards of earth, &c. At its termination, in Bury River, there is a dock for the reception of shipping. These works were projected and laid out by Messrs. Barnes and Morris, civil engineers, in 1801.

The act, under authority of which this railroad was executed, received the royal assent on the 3rd June, 1802, and is entitled, ' *An Act for making and maintaining a Railway or Tramroad,* ' *from, or from near, a certain place called The Flats, in the parish* ' *of Llanelly, in the county of Carmarthen, to, or near to, certain* ' *Lime Works called Castell-y-Garreg, in the parish of Llanfihan-* ' *gel-Aberbythich, in the said county; and for making and main-* ' *taining a Dock or Basin at the termination of the said Railway* ' *or Tramroad, at or near the said place called The Flats.'* The subscribers, at the time the act was obtained, were fifty-seven in number, who were incorporated by the name of " The Carmar- " thenshire Railway or Tramroad Company," and authorized to raise among themselves, for the purposes of this act, the sum of £25,000, in two hundred and fifty shares of £100 each; and if this is insufficient, a further sum of £10,000 may be raised among themselves, or by the admission of new subscribers, or by mort- gage of the rates.

RATES OF TONNAGE ON THIS RAILWAY.

d.

Dung, Limestone, Chalk, Lime, and all other Manure, Clay, Breeze, Ashes, Sand, and Bricks, Tin, Copper, Lead, Iron, Stone, Flints, Coal, Charcoal, Coke, Culm, Fuller's Earth, Corn, and Seeds, Flour, Malt, and all other Goods, Wares, and Merchandize .... } $1\frac{1}{2}$ per Ton, per Mile.

Fractions to be taken as for a Quarter of a Mile, and as for a Quarter of a Ton.

DOCK DUES.

d.

On every Ship or other Vessel entering the Dock or Basin .... } 1 per Ton, Register Measure.

For all Goods exported and imported .... 1 per Ton, in addition.

Goods shipped in this Dock, which have not paid One Penny per Ton, on the Railroad, to make good this Deficiency, in addition to the usual Charge of Dock Dues.

TOLLS FOR HORSES OR CATTLE PASSING ON THE RAILWAY.

d.

For every Horse, Mare, Gelding, Mule, or Ass, (excepting such as are used on the Railway, or which are going to the Farms or Common) .... } 2

Cows and other neat Cattle .... 1 each.

Sheep, Swine, and Calves .... 8 per Score.

One Hundred and Twenty Pounds to be deemed a Hundred Weight for the Purposes of this Act.

The work to be managed by a committee, under the control of the general meetings.

The chief object of this railway, is to convey for shipment the produce of the several lime-stone quarries, collieries, and iron-stone mines, which abound in its immediate vicinity.

CARRON RIVER.

THE source of this river is among the Campsie Hills, whence it takes an easterly direction by the villages of Denny, Larbert, and Carron Shore, to the River Forth, into which it falls near the termination of the Forth and Clyde Canal. As this river is in the tideway, and no act has ever been passed relating to it, and there-fore free of toll, it is noticed chiefly on account of the celebrated Carron Iron Works, situate in its vicinity, the supply of which with coal and iron-stone, and the export of the manufactured article, constitute the principal trade on this navigation, which is only three miles in length. Vessels drawing 7 to 8 feet may get up at neap tides.

CART RIVER.

26 George II. Cap. 96, Royal Assent 7th June, 1753.
27 George III. Cap. 56, Royal Assent 21st May, 1787.

THIS river, (which is sometimes called the White Cart,) has its source on the north side of the mountains which separate the counties of Renfrew and Ayr, from Lanarkshire ; from whence it takes a northerly course by Eaglesham and Cathcart, to which place it forms the division between the last-mentioned county and Renfrewshire. From Cathcart it proceeds directly to Paisley, from thence, northward, by Inchinnan, to the Clyde. From the Clyde to Paisley the length is about five english miles, and as this river was navigable to the latter place only at high water, spring tides, an act was obtained in 1753, for the purpose of improving it, which act is entitled, ' *An Act for laying a Duty of Two Pen-* ' *nies Scots, or One Sixth Part of a Penny Sterling, on every Scots* ' *Pint of Ale and Beer, which shall be brewed for Sale, brought*

' *into, tapped, or sold, within the town of Paisley and liberties there-*
' *of, in the county of Renfrew, for improving the Navigation of*
' *the River Cart, and for other Purposes.*' The magistrates and
town council of the burgh of Paisley, are appointed trustees for
carrying this act into execution, with power to borrow any sum of
money, for this purpose, on security of the duties hereby authorized to be collected. In the 27th of the reign of his late Majesty,
another act was obtained, entitled, ' *An Act for enabling the*
' *Magistrates and Town Council of Paisley, to improve the Naviga-*
' *tion of the River Cart, and to make a navigable Cut or Canal*
' *across the Turnpike Road, leading from Glasgow to Greenock,*'
in the preamble of which it is stated to be impassable, excepting
for small boats, in spring tides. By this act, power is given to
the parties mentioned in the title, to deepen the river from Snedda
Bridge, and make a side cut for the purpose of passing Inchinnan
Bridge, so that vessels drawing 7 feet, may, in ordinary spring
tides, navigate the whole length. The canal not to be more than
nine hundred yards in length; to be 7 feet deep, and 54 feet in
width.

TONNAGE RATES.

d.

Goods, Wares, Merchandize, or other Things, (except Coal) .... 8 per Ton.
Coal .... 5 ditto.

For any Article carried no higher than Knockford, half Toll only to be paid.

EXEMPTION FROM TOLL.

All Goods not brought into the navigable Cut, or past the Mouth of the Black Cart
River, which falls into this Navigation, near Inchinnan.

Dung, Lime, Marl, or other Manure, belonging to any Owner or Occupier of Lands,
within Five Miles of the River, is also free of Toll.

Commissioners are appointed to carry the act into execution,
and are empowered to lessen the duties; and particularly that on
coals, so soon as the money is borrowed for the purposes of this
act; the power for which is vested in the magistrates and town
council, who may take up the sum of £3,000 on the security of
the tolls and duties granted by the act.

As the burgh of Paisley, by its successful manufactures, has
become a place of considerable population, the navigation of the
Cart, from the tideway of the Clyde, is of the first importance;

and, from the facility with which coal can be brought up, and merchandize exported, has been one of the principal means in bringing this place to its present flourishing condition.

CHELMER AND BLACKWATER NAVIGATION.

6 George III. Cap. 101, Royal Assent 6th June, 1766.
33 George III. Cap. 93, Royal Assent 17th June, 1793.

THE River Chelmer has its source near Thaxsted, in Essex, from whence it pursues a southerly course, by Dunmow, to Chelmsford, where the navigation commences. Its course from Chelmsford is directly east, to near Maldon, where it joins the Blackwater, by which name the wide estuary, opening into the sea at Sales Point, is designated.

When the design was first promulgated for making the Chelmer navigable, Mr. Smeaton was directed to examine its course, and he accordingly reported upon it in June, 1762. He recommended a canal of thirteen miles in length, instead of rendering the channel of the river the site of the navigation, and his estimate for this amounted to £16,697.

Four years after Smeaton had viewed and reported as above, an act was obtained, entitled, ' *An Act for making the River* ' *Chelmer navigable from the Port of Maldon, to the town of* ' *Chelmsford, in the county of Essex,*' by which, commissioners, consisting of the principal inhabitants of the country through which it passed, or any seven of them, were appointed to carry the powers of the act into execution. Twelve years were allowed for finishing the necessary works, but no portion was to be commenced until an advance of twenty-five per cent. had been made upon the sum of £13,000, which the commissioners were authorized to borrow. Under this act, however, it appears that little or nothing was done; but a new company, (twenty-seven years after the date of the former act,) consisting of one hundred and forty-seven persons, (amongst whom were Lord Petre, the Hon. R. E. Petre, the Hon. G. Petre, Sir John Jervis, K.B. and Sir John Henniker, Baronets,) obtained an act in the year 1793, entitled, ' *An Act* ' *for making and maintaining a navigable Communication between*

' *the town of Chelmsford, or some part of the parish of Springfield,*
' *in the county of Essex, and a place called Colliers' Reach, in or*
' *near the River Blackwater, in the said county.*' They were incorporated under the name of " The Company of Proprietors of
" the Chelmer and Blackwater Navigation," and empowered to
raise among themselves the sum of £40,000, in four hundred
shares of £100 each, and in case that sum be insufficient, they
may raise an additional £20,000, either among themselves, or by
the admission of new subscribers, or by mortgage of the undertaking, or by granting annuities. Under this company, the
Chelmer and Blackwater Navigation, as it now is, was completed.
The total length, from the basin at Chelmsford to the tideway at
Colliers' Reach, is a little more than thirteen miles and a half, viz.
from the head of the navigation to Beleigh Mill, above Maldon, is
ten miles and seven furlongs, with a fall of 59 feet 5 inches; from
Beleigh Mill, by a cut, to the Blackwater, and by the course of
that river, to Heybridge, is one mile and one furlong, with a fall
of 7 feet $3\frac{1}{2}$ inches; and from thence, by canal, to the basin at
Colliers' Reach, opposite Northey Isle, one mile and five furlongs,
with a fall, to low-water-mark, in the basin, of 12 feet $8\frac{1}{2}$ inches.
From Colliers' Reach, the length of the estuary of Blackwater
River, where it falls into the sea opposite Sales Point, is nearly
eleven miles. The spring tides flow 8 feet at Maldon Bridge, so
that vessels of considerable burthen can enter that port at those
times; but at neaps it only flows 1 foot. The basin at Colliers'
Reach was executed under the direction of Mr. John Rennie, and
was opened in the early part of 1796.

TONNAGE RATES.

	d.	
Coal....................................	2 per Chaldron, per Mile.	
Stone	1 per Ton,	ditto.
Lime for Manure, Chalk, Dung, and other } Manures............................ }	1 ditto.	ditto.
Wheat, Barley, Rye, Peas, Beans, and Tares	$\frac{1}{2}$ per Quarter,	dttto.
Oats, Malt, and other Grain or Seeds......	$\frac{1}{4}$ ditto.	ditto.
Meal or Flour	$\frac{1}{4}$ per Sack, of Five Bushels, per Mile.	
All other Goods, Wares, and Merchandize	$2\frac{1}{4}$ per Ton, per Mile.	

EXEMPTION FROM TOLL.

Stone, Gravel, and Sand, for the repair of Roads, (not being Turnpike), in any Township through which this Navigation passes, and which shall not be carried more
than Five Miles, provided they do not pass a Lock, except at such Times as when
the Water flows over the Gauge, Paddle, or Waste Weir of the Lock.

For the Purposes of this Act, Sixteen Cubic Feet of Stone, Ten Yards Square of Flag-stone (from One Inch and a Half to Three Inches Thick,) Ten Yards of Lineal Curb Stone (from Eleven to Thirteen Inches Wide and from Five to Seven Inches Thick,) Fifty Cubic Feet of Round, or Forty Cubic Feet of Square Oak, Ash or Elm Timber, or Fifty Cubic Feet of Fir, or Deal, Balk, Poplar, or other Timber Wood, shall be deemed One Ton Weight.

Millers upon this Navigation are restrained from drawing their Mill Ponds more than Twenty-one Inches below the Height of a full Pond.

Vessels under Twenty Tons not to pass Locks without leave, or without paying for Tonnage to that Amount.

WHARFAGE RATES.

	s.	d.	
Chalk, Lime, or other Manure, when it does not remain more than Six Days	0	3	per Ton.
All other Goods or Merchandize for the same Term	1	0	ditto.
And if any of the above-mentioned Articles remain longer than Six Days	0	6	ditto, per Week, in addition.

Goods or Merchandize remaining on the Quays or Wharfs, not more than Twenty-four Hours, are exempt.

Coal is likewise exempt from Wharfage Rates.

The chief object of this navigation is the supply of Chelmsford, and the interior of Essex, with coal, deals, timber, and groceries, and for the export of corn and other articles which this agricultural district produces.

CHESTER CANAL.

(SEE ELLESMERE AND CHESTER CANAL NAVIGATION)

CHESTERFIELD CANAL.

11 George III. Cap. 75, Royal Assent 28th March, 1771.

THIS canal commences in the tideway of the Trent, at Stock-with, in Nottinghamshire, near to the place where the navigable River Idle falls into it, about four miles below Gainsborough. Its course is nearly west for six miles, passing round to the north of Gringley Beacon, whence it pursues a southerly course, to East Retford; thence, westward, by Worksop, to Shire Oaks, where it enters the county of York; when passing south of the village of Wales, and entering Derbyshire, it proceeds, in a southerly course, along the east bank of the River Rother, through a country abounding in coal, to Chesterfield, where it terminates. Its length is forty-six miles. From the Trent to Worksop it is twenty-four miles, with a rise of 250 feet; from thence, to the summit, at the tunnel near Harthill, nine miles, with a rise of 85 feet, being a total rise of 335 feet. From the summit to Chesterfield, the distance is thirteen miles, with a fall of 45 feet. The number of locks is sixty-five. Between Wales and Harthill there is a tunnel two thousand eight hundred and fifty yards in length; it is in width $9\frac{1}{4}$ feet, and 12 feet high. Near Gringley Beacon is another tunnel one hundred and fifty-three yards in length. Between the long tunnel and Chesterfield, many individuals have laid down private railways, for the purpose of transporting the production of the mines and iron-works in that district.

This navigation was projected by Mr. Brindley, in 1769, but before any application was made to parliament for authority to carry it into execution, Mr. Grundy was directed to view the intended line of canal, upon which he reported in August, 1770. His proposal was to carry the line of canal from Stockwith, in nearly a straight course, to Bawtry, and from thence, by Scrooby, Blyth, and Carlton, and to join Brindley's line at the Shire Oaks.

Mr. Brindley's estimate was £94,908, 17s. and the length, according to the original plan made by Mr. Varley, is forty-four miles, six furlongs and eight chains and a half, and Grundy's estimate, by his proposed alteration, is £71,479, 6s. $9\frac{1}{2}d.$ being less by £23,429, 10s. $2\frac{1}{2}d.$ and shorter by nearly five miles and a half; yet, notwithstanding the apparent advantages of Grundy's line, such confidence had the proposed company in Brindley's designs, that they applied to parliament and obtained an act to enable them to carry his scheme into execution ; it is entitled, ' *An Act* ' *for making a navigable Cut or Canal from Chesterfield, in the* ' *county of Derby, through or near Worksop and Retford, to join* ' *the River Trent, at or near Stockwith, in the county of Nottingham.*'

The proprietors, at the time the act was obtained, consisted of one hundred and seventy-four persons, amongst whom were the Most Noble the Dukes of Devonshire and Newcastle, Lord Scarsdale, the Dean of York, and Sir Cecil Wray, Bart. who were incorporated by the name of " The Company of Proprietors of the Canal " Navigation from Chesterfield to the River Trent," and empowered to raise among themselves the sum of £100,000, in one thousand shares of £100 each, for the purpose of carrying the same into execution, but the canal was not to be begun until the whole sum was raised; and in case the above sum was insufficient, they might raise among themselves, or by the admission of new subscribers, or by mortgage of the rates and duties, the additional sum of £50,000. The work to be managed by a committee, under the control of the general assembly. The act, which is very long, contains many clauses for the protection of private property; particularly such as belong to the Dukes of Norfolk and Leeds, and Lord Byron. Immediately on the passing of the act, the works were commenced, under the direction of Mr. Brindley, and so continued until his death, in September, 1772, when they were conducted and finished by Mr. Henshall, his brother-in-law, in 1776. From the Trent to Retford, the canal is constructed for vessels of fifty to sixty tons burthen; the remaining portion is for such as carry about twenty tons only.

RATES OF TONNAGE AND WHARFAGE.

	d.	
Lime	1	per Ton, per Mile.
Coal, Lead, Timber, Stone, and all other Goods, Wares and Merchandize	1½ ditto.	ditto.
Soap, Ashes, Salt, Salt-scrow, Foul Salt, and Grey Salt, Soot, Bone-dust, Pigeons' Dung, Rape or Cole Seed Dust, to be used for the manuring of Lands of any Persons, whose Lands shall be cut through by this Canal, such Lands being in any Township through which it passes, and Rags or Tanners' Bark	½ ditto.	ditto.

EXEMPTION FROM TOLL.

Hay, and Corn in the Straw, not sold, but to be laid up in the Outhouses of the Owner; Small Rubbish or Waste Stones, Gravel and Sand for the repair of Roads, (not being Turnpike) in any Township through which the Canal passes, and which shall not be carried more than Five Miles.

Dung, Soil, Marl, Ashes of Coal and Turf, for the Improvement of Lands lying in any Township through which the Canal will pass, and belonging to Persons whose Lands may be taken for the Canal, provided these excepted Articles do not pass a Lock, except when the Water is running over the Gauge or Niche of the Lock.

If any Iron, Iron-stone, Coals, Lime for the Improvement of Lands, or other Goods whatsoever, remain on the Wharfs longer than Twenty-four Hours, then such additional Rate to be paid as may be agreed upon.

Fifty Feet of Round, or Forty Feet of Square Oak, Ash, or Elm Timber, or Fifty Feet of Fir, or Deal, Balk, Poplar, and other Timber Wood, shall be deemed One Ton.

A Ton of Coal or Limestone to be Twenty-two Hundred Weight of One Hundred and Twelve Pounds each.

Vessels under Twenty Tons not to pass Locks without leave unless they pay for that Weight.

RATE,

To be received by any Lord of the Manor or Owner of Land who may erect Wharfs.

	d.
For every description of Goods or Merchandize for a period less than Six Days	3 per Ton.

Up to the year 1789, the whole of the works had cost about £152,400, and the following is a statement of the income and expenditure of that year:—

INCOME AND EXPENDITURE.

	£.	s.	d.
The Gross Income in that Year, was..................................	8,320	9	6
Expenditure, which included Interest to the Amount of £2,670, exclusive of Arrears .... }	5,540	9	3
Nett Income	2,780	0	3

Upon which a Dividend of One per Cent. only was paid, amounting to £990.

A tolerable idea of the traffic upon this canal, at that period, (forty years ago) may be formed, from the following return of tonnage made by the proprietors, in 1789.

RETURN OF TONNAGE.

	Tons.
Coal	42,379½
Lead	3,862¼
Lime..	3,955¼
Corn	4,366¼
Stone..	7,569¾
Iron	1,554½
Timber..	3,444¼
Sundries	7,180¼
	74,312

	£.	s.	d.
Upon which the Duties and Wharfage amounted to	8,303	9	6

Sixteen years after this period the proprietors divided six per cent. and the undertaking has been gradually improving.

The chief objects of this canal are the export of coal, lime, and lead from Derbyshire, and, of the produce of the iron furnaces in the neighbourhood of Chesterfield; and corn, deals, timber, groceries, &c. on the other hand, are conveyed into the county of Derby.

CLARENCE RAILWAY.

9 George IV. Cap. 61, Royal Assent 23rd May, 1828.
10 George IV. Cap. 106, Royal Assent 1st June, 1829.

The line of railway contemplated by the act of 9th George IV. commenced at the River Tees, near Haverton Hill, about four miles north-east of Stockton, and proceeded in a westerly direction, crossing the Sunderland Road three miles north of Stockton; thence, by the village of Carlton, and across the Little River Skern, to Sim Pasture, where it was intended to join the Stockton and Darlington Railway, at the point between the 17¼ mile post and the 17½ post from Stockton. A branch was intended from Sim Pasture to the Deanery Estate, near Bishop Auckland; but this was not to be made without the consent of the Earl of Eldon; another from How Hills, by Great Chilton, to Broom Hill; and one other branch from Harrowgate House to Brown's Bridge, near Stockton.

	M.	F.	C.
The length of the first projected Main Line, from the Tees to the Stockton and Darlington Railway at Sim Pasture, was	14	0	4
The Deanery Estate Branch	3	4	6
The Broom Hill Branch.....................	7	2	6
Brown's Bridge Branch	1	7	7
Total length of Main Line and Branches....	26	7	3

The line was laid out by Mr. Edward Steel; and he estimated the cost (including an inclined plane upon the Deanery Branch, and a steam engine for the Broom Hill Branch) at £98,113. The data for the estimate was a single railway, with one-sixth for passing places.

To carry these railways into execution, a company, consisting of fifty-eight persons, amongst whom was Sir William Foulis, Bart. applied to parliament, and obtained an act, in 1828, entitled, ' *An Act for making and maintaining a Railway from the River* ' *Tees, near Haverton Hill, in the parish of Billingham, to a place* ' *called Sim Pasture Farm, in the parish of Heighington, all in the* ' *county of Durham, with certain Branches therefrom,*' by which they were incorporated as " The Company of Proprietors of the " Clarence Railway." They were empowered to raise among themselves the sum of £100,000, (of which £80,000 was raised before the act was obtained) in one thousand shares of £100 each; the whole of which was to be subscribed before the work was commenced. An additional sum of £60,000 may be raised, on mortgage of the rates, if necessary.

TONNAGE RATES ALLOWED BY THIS ACT.

			$d.$	
Coal, Culm, Coke and Cinders, for Exportation.............			$\frac{3}{4}$ per Ton, per Mile.	
Ditto, ditto, for Home Consumption			$1\frac{1}{2}$ ditto.	ditto.
Lime			$\frac{3}{4}$ ditto.	ditto.
Alluvial Soil, SeaWeed, Dung, Compost and all Sorts of Manure, Material for the repair of Roads, Stone, Marl, Sand and Clay			$\frac{1}{2}$ ditto.	ditto.
Lead, Iron, Timber, Staves, and Deals, and all other Goods, Wares, and Merchandize			3 ditto.	ditto
Coal, Culm, Coke, and Cinders, passing an Inclined Plane....			3 per Ton.	
All other Articles			6 ditto.	

Fractions to be taken as for a Quarter of a Mile, and as for a Quarter of a Ton.

Six years were allowed for the execution of the works; but upon its being ascertained that the line might be materially improved, an application was made in the following session of parliament for an act to enable the company to make the alterations contemplated, which act is entitled, ' *An Act to enable the Clarence Railway Company to vary and alter the Line of their Railway, to abandon some of the Branches thereof, and to make other Branches therefrom; and for altering, amending, and enlarging the Powers of the Act passed for making and maintaining the said Railway.*' Under the powers of this act, the company are authorized to commence with the main line from Samphire Beacon, in the parish of Billingham, instead of Haverton Hill, and continue it to Sim Pasture, with some deviations from the original line. The Broom Hill Branch, and that to Brown's Bridge, near Stockton, are abandoned, and in lieu, one is to proceed from near Stillington, to the city of Durham; another from the main line at the Old Durham and Yarm Road, to the River Tees, at Stockton; another out of the City of Durham Branch, at Ferryhill, to the lime and coal works at Sherburn; and another to Byer's Green, from the same point of the City of Durham Branch from whence the Sherburn Branch proceeds. There is another from the City of Durham Branch, which is very short, called the Chilton Branch. The power given in the first act to make the Deanery Branch remains unrepealed.

The total rise of the main line, from high water in the Tees to Sim Pasture, is 306 feet. The City of Durham Branch leaves the main line at a distance of little more than ten miles from its commencement, and at an elevation of 208 feet.

To its summit, within two miles of Durham, it attains an elevation, from high water, of 278 feet; from thence, to the River Wear, there is a fall of 163 feet; thence, to Durham, it is level. At the distance of five miles and three quarters from the commencement of the last-mentioned branch, the Chilton Branch leaves it, at an elevation of 262 feet, and rises 40 feet; upon the same level, at the distance of about seven miles and a half, the Sherburn and Byer's Green Branches proceed from it; the first of which rises 72 feet, and the latter 115 feet.

	M.	F.	C.
The length of the Main Line from Samphire Batts Beacon, to the Stockton and Darlington Railroad, at Sim Pasture, is	15	4	2
The Deanery Branch	3	4	6
The City of Durham Branch..................	13	0	0
The Sherburn Branch	5	6	3
The Chilton Branch.........................	0	3	4
The Stockton Branch	2	3	2
The Byer's Green Branch....................	5	0	0
Total length of Main Line and Branches....	45	5	7

On the line of the City of Durham Branch, where it crosses the River Wear, a cast iron bridge is intended, of one arch, of 100 feet span, and 35 feet above the surface of the river.

The estimates, under the last act, for this railway and branches, were made by Mr. Leather, of Leeds, civil engineer, in February, 1829, and are as follow:—

ESTIMATES FOR THE RAILWAY AND BRANCHES.

Main Line..	£94,411
Stockton Branch	14,402
Deanery Estate Branch	13,686
City of Durham Branch ....'	70,777
Sherburn Branch	24,754
Byer's Green Branch	23,767
Chilton Branch	1,206
	£243,003

The company are empowered to raise the sum of £100,000, in addition to the sums of £100,000 and £60,000, authorized in the preceding act; which two latter sums may be borrowed on bonds under the common seal, or by mortgage of the undertaking, on security of the rates and duties. They are further empowered to purchase sixty acres of land, in such place as the company shall deem most eligible, for the erecting and constructing of yards, staiths, wharfs, quays, landing places, and other conveniences for the loading and unloading of vessels.

RATE,

In addition to the Tolls allowed by the former Act.

d.

For every Coach or other Carriage used for the Conveyance of Passengers or Small Packages.. } 6 per Mile.

Fractions to be taken as for a Quarter of a Mile, and as for a Quarter of a Ton.

Clauses are introduced in the act to restrain the company from the use of locomotive engines, on that part of the City of Durham Branch which passes through the townships of Mainforth and Chilton, or on the Byer's Green Branch, passing through the township of Whitworth, without the consent of the respective land owners, which clauses, if enforced, may act prejudicially to the interests of the company should locomotive engines come into general use.

This railway (which, with its branches, is the longest for which parliamentary sanction has ever been obtained, with the exception of the Newcastle-upon-Tyne and Carlisle Railway) is directed to be carried into execution, by a committee of eighteen proprietors, who are allowed six years, from the date of the last-recited act, for this purpose. The Deanery Branch is not subject to this limitation, as it may be made any time after the consent of the Earl of Eldon is obtained.

Previous to the second application to parliament, it appears the company had it in contemplation to extend the Deanery Branch to the Stockton and Darlington Railroad at Bishop Auckland, and another branch, of nearly ten miles in length, from the City of Durham Branch to the Hagger Leazes Branch of the last-mentioned railroad, near St. Helen's Auckland, but these were subsequently abandoned.

The object of this undertaking is to open, more effectually, the valuable coal fields and limestone quarries to which the railway and branches severally extend; and to afford a cheaper mode of conveyance to a place where the minerals can be conveniently shipped for exportation.

CLYDE RIVER.

32 Geo. II. C. 62, R. A. 2nd June, 1759.   8 Geo. III. C. 16, R. A. 24th Feb. 1768.
10 Geo. III. C. 104, R. A. 12th April, 1770.   14 Geo. III. C. 103, R. A. 5th May, 1774.
49 Geo. III. C. 74, R. A. 20th May, 1809.   6 Geo. IV. C. 117, R. A. 10th June, 1825.

THIS noble river has its source on the northern side of Queensberry Hill, situate among that lofty range of mountains which separate the southerly point of the county of Lanark from Dumfrieshire. Its course is northerly, and very circuitous, passing Crawford and between the mountains of Tinto and Culter Fell, to near Pettinain, where, after changing to a south-westerly course for a few miles, it pursues a north-westerly course by Lanark and Hamilton, its stream being considerably augmented by the water of Avon, which here falls into it. Its course, which is now very crooked, continues by Bothwell and Rutherglen, to the city of Glasgow, where it becomes navigable ; and hence by Govan and Renfrew, a little below which town it joins the navigable River Cart. From this point it gradually widens, and becomes a noble estuary, which at Port Glasgow is above two miles in width. From Gorbells Bridge, in Glasgow, the course of the Clyde to the Cart River is about seven miles; from thence to Port Dundas, where the Forth and Clyde Canal communicates with it, is nearly four miles and a half; from that place to Dumbarton Harbour, three miles; and thence, to Port Glasgow, five miles. The total length of the navigable part of this river, to where it falls into the Firth of Clyde, opposite the point of land on which is situate Roseneath, (the beautiful seat of the Duke of Argyle) is about twenty-five miles. This river was, originally, navigable at high water, spring tides, as far as Glasgow, but when trade and manufactures increased, the necessity of having a better navigation became so manifest, that the magistrates and city council of Glasgow, in 1759, obtained an act to enable them to improve it, which is entitled, ' *An Act for improving the Navigation of the River Clyde* ' *to the city of Glasgow; and for building a Bridge cross the said*

' *River, from the said city to the village of Gorbells.*' The improvements contemplated, were between Dumbuck Ford and the bridge at Glasgow; and consisted, chiefly, of a dam and lock at Merlin Ford, to deepen the water over the shallows toward the city; to carry which into execution, the act empowered them to borrow £20,000, on security of the following

TONNAGE AND KEELAGE DUTIES.

		d.		
For every British, Irish, or Plantation-built Ship, coming into or going out of the Port of Glasgow, (which comprehends Port Glasgow and Greenock), from any Foreign Country or the British Plantations	}	1½	per Ton, which such Ship shall Measure.	
For every Foreign Ship or Vessel coming in or out........		3	ditto.	ditto.
And from the Owners of any Vessel trading to or from Glasgow to any Part of Great Britain or Ireland......	}	½	per Ton.	

EXEMPTION FROM TONNAGE AND KEELAGE DUTIES.

Any Vessel laden with Fish or other Provisions, Corn, Grain, Meal, Stones, Slate, or Coal, discharged at any of the Quays or Creeks within the Port of Glasgow, and open Boats under Fifteen Tons.

ADDITIONAL TONNAGE AT MERLIN FORD.

		s.	*d.*	
Goods, Wares, and Merchandize of every Description, (except Coal), passing through the Lock to be erected at Merlin Ford	}	1	0	per Ton.
Coal..		0	8	ditto.

EXEMPTION.

Dung, Lime, Marl, and other Manure, carried in any Boat belonging to the Owner or Occupier of any Lands within Five Miles of the River; Sand, Clay, or Wood for the Use of any Delph Manufactory; Brick, Kelp, Soapers' Waste, or Broken Glass for the Use of any Glass Works in Glasgow; Wood, Iron-stone, or Iron-ore, Clay, Bricks and Lime-stone for the Use of any Company for making Pig or Bar Iron.

Vessels from Foreign Parts discharging or loading at the Quay of Glasgow, are liable only to the last-mentioned Duties.

The act of 8th George III. is entitled, ' *An Act for making* ' *and widening a Passage or Street, from the Salt Market Street,* ' *in the city of Glasgow, to St. Andrew's Church, in the said city:* ' *and for enlarging and completing the Church Yard of the said* ' *Church; and for making and building a convenient Exchange, or* ' *Square, in the said city; and also for explaining and amending* ' *an Act passed in the Thirty-second Year of his late Majesty, for* ' *improving the Navigation of the River Clyde, to the city of Glas-* ' *gow; and for building a Bridge cross the said River, from the* ' *said city to the village of Gorbells;*' but it does not contain any clause relating to the navigation.

In the preamble of the act of the 10th George III. it is stated, that instead of a lock and dam at Merlin Ford, a more efficient navigation may be effected, by contracting the channel of the river and dredging; and that, being apprehensive that the high tonnage and keelage duties would be prejudicial to trade, they are therefore repealed. The other tonnage rates are to be paid on all articles, as above, passing between Dumbuck Ford and Glasgow.

The river to be made with 7 feet water, at neap tides; and the quay to be repaired and enlarged, and the following quay duties are allowed to be taken.

THE BROOMIELAW QUAY DUTIES.

d.

All Vessels brought to these Quays to load or unload.................. 1 per Ton.

But these Duties are not to be applied to the Purpose of improving the Navigation.

For the Purpose of a more equitable payment of the Tonnage Duties, this Act divides the Clyde into Three Stages; the First terminates at Renfrew Ferry, the Second at Dalmuir Burn Foot, and the last at Dumbuck Ford. For the First Stage or any Part of it Four-sixths of the above Rate, and for the other Stages One-sixth each.

Fifty Feet of Round, or Forty Feet of Square Oak, Ash, or Elm Timber, or Fifty Feet of Fir, or Deal, Balk, Poplar, or other Wood, to be deemed a Ton.

The act of the 14th George III. entitled, '*An Act for explain-* '*ing and amending an Act made in the Thirty-second Year of his* '*late Majesty, for improving the Navigation of the River Clyde,* '*to the city of Glasgow; and for building a Bridge cross the said* '*River, from the said city to the village of Gorbells; and part of* '*another Act, made in the Eighth Year of his present Majesty,* '*for amending the said Act; and for repairing, widening, and* '*enlarging the old Bridge cross the River of Clyde, from the city* '*of Glasgow to the village of Gorbells,*' relates, chiefly, to the imposition of additional tolls and portages for the passage near the new bridge.

The act of the 49th George III. is entitled, '*An Act for ex-* '*plaining and amending Two Acts for improving the Navigation of* '*the River Clyde to the city of Glasgow,*' in the preamble of which it is stated, that in consequence of some doubts which had arisen respecting the proper interpretation of such parts of the preceding acts as relates to the tonnage upon coal, some further explanation was necessary.

TONNAGE RATES.

The Toll of Eight-pence per Ton on Coal to be paid until the 8th of July, 1810, and from that Period until the 8th of July, 1817, the Tonnage shall be Four-pence, when they shall entirely cease.

The Tonnage Rates upon Bricks, Lime, Limestone, and Pantiles, shall from and after the 8th of July, 1810, be diminished from One Shilling per Ton, to Sixpence, and so to continue until the 8th of July, 1817, when the Duty is to cease.

In addition to the Old Quay Duty of One Penny per Ton, a Rate of One Penny per Ton is to be levied on all Ships and other Vessels loading or unloading Coal, Bricks, Lime, Limestone, and Pantiles, at the Harbour of The Broomielaw.

This act, however, authorizes the lord provost, magistrates and city council of Glasgow, to make the Clyde 9 feet deep at neap tides, in every part of it between the bridge of Glasgow and the castle of Dumbarton. They are further empowered by this act to borrow £30,000, for the purpose of enlarging the harbour of Broomielaw, on security of the new rates and duties, the former sum having been paid off.

The last act relating to this navigation received the royal assent on the 10th of June, 1825, and it is entitled, ' *An Act for amending* ' *Three Acts for enlarging the Harbour of Glasgow, and improving* ' *the Navigation of the River Clyde, to the said city ; and for other* ' *Purposes therein mentioned*,' by which, power is given to make the navigation 13 feet deep, at neap tides, throughout its length; to enlarge the harbour of Broomielaw, and to extend the navigation to the south-east extremity of the public green of Glasgow. For the purpose of raising a fund for carrying these works into execution and discharging a debt of £54,350, 17*s*. 9*d*. contracted under the authority of the recited acts, they are empowered to collect the following additional rates and duties, and to borrow the sum of £100,000, on the credit of the undertaking.

RATES AND DUTIES.

The One Shilling Rate upon all Goods, Wares, and other Commodities, (with the Exception of the exempted Articles in the last-recited Act), to be increased One-third, if necessary, according to the Stages of the River.

Coal, Bricks, Pantiles, Freestone, Whinstone, and other Articles, a River Rate of Two-pence per Ton.

Lime and Limestone, Dung, Marl, and other Manure, as also Brick, Kelp, Sand, Soapers' Waste, or Broken Glass, for the Use of any Glass Works, in Glasgow, are exempt from the above Rate.

NEW HARBOUR AND QUAY DUTIES.

For every Ship or other Vessel loading or unloading at the Quays, Two-pence per Ton.

Steam Vessels, for the Conveyance of Passengers, to pay only Half of the Duties for each Time beyond the First Arrival on the same Day.

NEW HARBOUR AND QUAY DUTIES CONTINUED.

The Shed Duties for every Article are particularly specified, but as the enumeration of them would far exceed the Limits of our Publication, we refer the Reader to the Act. The highest Rates are Two-pence per Ton, and the lowest One Penny; and if those Duties shall, on an Average of Three Years, exceed fifteen per Cent. of the Cost of Erection, the Duties to be reduced until the Annual Revenue be fifteen per Cent.

For the Navigation of the River above The Broomielaw, a River Duty of Two-pence per Ton upon all Articles; but when the Annual Revenue, thus derived, exceeds £600, then the Duty to be reduced to One Penny per Ton; and, again raised to Two-pence per Ton if the Revenue should be below £600, or, the Proprietors may, at their option, take the full Produce of the One Penny Rate.

For the further Purpose of improving the Clyde Navigation, above the Harbour of Broomielaw, from and after the opening of the Communication, they are entitled to a further Duty of from Three-pence to One Shilling per Ton, as the Trustees shall determine, on all Wares and Merchandize whatever, navigating the said proposed Extension.

Coal brought downwards and unshipped at the Harbour of Broomielaw are exempt from the above Duty if not re-shipped.

Vessels and Goods passing up the River to the Quays of Glasgow are not liable to the Charges on the Extension to the East of the City.

For the more equitable Payment of the River Duties, the Clyde is again divided into Three Stages. The First Stage comprehends the space between the Harbour of Broomielaw and the Old Ferry of Renfrew; the Second Stage is between the last-mentioned Place and the Mouth of Dalmuir Burn; and the last extends to the Castle of Dumbarton; and the Rates and River Duties are to be paid on these Stages in the Proportion recited in the preceding Act.

None of the New or Additional Duties shall be paid on any Goods, Wares, or Merchandize, which shall pass from the Forth and Clyde Canal into any Part of the River lying Westward of Dalmuir Burn, (except Coal, which shall pay a Duty of One Farthing per Ton); and at the Expiration of Nine Years from the Date of this Act, the present Duty of Two-pence per Ton on all Goods (except Coal) conveyed on the lowermost Stage, on entering the Forth and Clyde, or *vice versa*, shall be reduced to One Penny per Ton; and if after the Expiration of the above Term of Nine Years, an Annual Revenue, exceeding One-third of the Annual Expenditure on these Works, below Dalmuir Burn, the Duties of One Penny and One Farthing per Ton shall be so reduced until the Revenue from this Stage be no more than One-third of the Expenditure on this part of the Navigation.

All Vessels (including those propelled by Steam, going direct between Glasgow and Dumbarton) belonging to the Royal Burgh of Dumbarton, are, by Virtue of a Contract, entered into with the Corporation of Glasgow, in the Year 1700, exempt from River and Harbour Dues upon the Clyde. If Steam Vessels make any Voyages, except direct from Dumbarton and Glasgow, they are liable to the River and Harbour Duties; so are Coals not *bona fide* for the Use of the Burgesses of Dumbarton. This Exemption does not extend to the Navigation beyond the Harbour of Broomielaw.

The Burgesses of Glasgow are likewise exempted, by Virtue of the original Contract above-mentioned, from the Payment of any Duties on entering the Harbour of Dumbarton.

Ships or Vessels in His Majesty's Service are exempt from any Rates or Duties by Virtue of this Act.

In addition to the great advantages which the city of Glasgow experiences, from the facilities which this excellent navigation gives for importing colonial and other produce, and for exporting the vast quantity of manufactured cotton goods, which a population of one hundred and fifty thousand souls continues to produce, it is connected with the Great Lanarkshire Coal Field, by means of the Monkland Canal and the Garnkirk Railway, which connect with the Ballochney and the Garturk and Cariongill Railways, by means of which, coal is supplied at a comparatively low rate; besides these, considerable advantages arise from a branch of the Forth and Clyde Canal, terminating on the east side of the city, which gives certain communication with the Forth, and city of Edinburgh.

Some idea may be formed of the traffic to the Clyde, from a return to parliament, by which it appears, that three hundred and ten British, and thirty-seven Foreign Ships, entered it in the year 1824.

Before the American War, the import of tobacco from Maryland and Virginia, into this river, was from 35 to 45,000 hogsheads, and the year immediately preceding that event, the amount was 57,143 hogsheads. From the West Indies, 540,198 hogsheads of sugar, 1,251,900 gallons of rum, and 6,530,177 lbs. of cotton were imported. Of the exports, which consist chiefly of their own manufactures, we need not do more than state, that in 1815, there were 52 cotton mills, containing 511,200 spindles; 18 works for weaving by steam power, which weekly produced 8,400 pieces; 39 calenders, which worked off, daily, 118,000 yards; besides dressing 116,000, and glazing 30,000.

COLNE RIVER.

21 James I. C. 34, R. A. —— —— 1623. 9 & 10 Wil. III. C. 19, R. A. 16th May, 1698.
5 Geo. I. C. 31, R. A. 18th Apr. 1718. 13 Geo. II. C. 30, R. A. 29th Apr. 1740.
23 Geo. II. C. 19, R. A. 12th Apr. 1750. 21 Geo. III. C. 30, R. A. 18th May, 1781.

This river rises a few miles north-west of Castle Hedingham, in the hundred of Hinckford, Essex, by which places it runs to the town of Halstead; from whence, it takes a more eastwardly course by Earls Colne Priory, to The Hythe, near the town of Colchester, from which place to the sea, into which it falls at Mersea Island, it is navigable. From The Hythe to Wivenhoe, the distance is three miles and a half, and from thence the river opens into an estuary, terminating in the sea opposite the eastern end of Mersea Island, at the distance of four miles and a half. It is one of the earliest navigations, as appears by an act of the 21st James I.

entitled, ' *An Act for the repairing and maintaining of the Haven,*
' *River, and Channel running unto the Borough and Town of*
' *Colchester, in the County of Essex, and also for the paving of the*
' *said Town.*' The succeeding acts relate only to the river above
Wivenhoe, for to that place the navigation has always been of
sufficient depth, and where now there is a dock-yard for building
frigates and merchant-men.

By the act of the 9th and 10th William III. entitled, ' *An Act*
' *for cleansing and making navigable the Channel from The Hythe,*
' *at Colchester, to Wivenhoe,*' certain duties were granted to the
corporation of Colchester, on all goods navigated between Wivenhoe
and The Hythe, for the term of twenty-one years, and the powers
of which said act was, by another of the 5th of George I. entitled,
' *An Act for enlarging the Term granted by an Act of the Ninth*
' *and Tenth of William III. for cleansing and making navigable*
' *the Channel from The Hythe, at Colchester, to Wivenhoe, and for*
' *making the said Act more effectual,*' extended to the 1st of May,
1740.

By another act, dated the 29th of April, 1740, entitled, ' *An*
' *Act for further enlarging the Term granted by an Act of the*
' *Ninth and Tenth Years of the Reign of King William III. for*
' *cleansing and making navigable the Channel from The Hythe, at*
' *Colchester, to Wivenhoe, and for making the said Act, and another*
' *Act of the Fifth Year of the Reign of his late Majesty King*
' *George the First, for enlarging the Term granted by the said Act*
' *of the Ninth and Tenth Years of the Reign of King William the*
' *Third more effectual,*' the powers of the former acts, together
with the additional powers, should be in force for ever.

DUTY ON SEA COAL.

That the Duty on Sea Coal should be Three-pence per Chaldron, to be levied for
Forty Years, from the 1st of May, 1740, and that no other Duty should be raised
upon any other Goods, Wares, or Merchandize.

In the preamble, however, of the 23rd of George II. it appears,
that in consequence of the powers of the mayor and commonalty
to collect a large amount of arrears of rates, due under the former
acts, having ceased, together with the loss of a considerable sum of
money, then laying in the hands of the representatives of the late

receiver general of these duties, and for the payment of which no
legal discharges could be given, that the only lock upon this navigation, together with other of the works, had necessarily fallen
into decay ; fresh powers are, therefore, indispensable ; accordingly,
an act received the royal assent on the 12th of April, 1750,
entitled, ' *An Act for making more effectual several Acts of Parlia-*
' *ment passed for cleansing and making more navigable the Channel*
' *from The Hythe, at Colchester, to Wivenhoe, in the County of*
' *Essex, and for repairing and cleansing the Streets and Lanes of*
' *the Town of Colchester.*' By this act an additional duty of three-
pence per chaldron is levied on sea coal for thirty years, from the
1st of May, 1750, the collection of which is placed in the hands of
a number of gentlemen, who are entitled, " The Commissioners
" for putting in Execution the several Acts of Parliament made
" for cleansing and making navigable the Channel from The
" Hythe, at Colchester, to Wivenhoe."

The last act relating to this navigation was passed in 1781, and
is entitled, ' *An Act for continuing, and making more effectual,*
' *several Acts of Parliament passed for cleansing and making navi-*
' *gable the Channel from The Hythe, at Colchester, to Wivenhoe, in*
' *the County of Essex ; and for repairing and cleansing the Streets*
' *of the Town of Colchester ; and also for lighting the Streets and*
' *Lanes, and for preventing Annoyances in the said Town,*' by
which the powers of the above-recited acts are extended to the
further term of forty years, and from thence to the end of the then
next session of parliament. Commissioners are appointed for
putting the acts in execution, who are directed to apply for and
dispose of the sum of £2,000, which was vested in the fund called
The South Sea Annuities, for the purpose of keeping this navigation in sufficient repair.

The chief objects of this navigable river are the import of coal,
deals, and groceries, and the export of farming produce, and
Colchester Oysters from the banks below Wivenhoe.

CONWAY RIVER.

THIS river has its source in that mountainous tract which separates the counties of Denbigh and Carnarvon from Merionethshire ; from whence it takes a northerly course by the village of Yspytty Efan, near which place it is crossed by the Holyhead Mail Road; having in its way received the waters of the Llygwy, it pursues a north-easterly route to Llanrwst, whence, at high water, it continues navigable to its fall into the sea, about a mile below the Conway Suspension Bridge. Conway Harbour, situated at the mouth of this river, is well protected from the north and east, by the promontory called Great Orme's Head, but is fit only for vessels of small burthen, and the channel is very difficult to navigate.

The length of this navigation is about thirteen miles and a half. Being a tideway river, and not being the subject of any parliamentary enactment, it is toll free ; and is chiefly used for the trade of Conway and Llanrwst.

COOMBE HILL CANAL.

32 George III. Cap. 83, Royal Assent 11th June, 1792.

THIS canal proceeds from the River Severn at Fletcher's Leap, in the parish of Deerhurst, in nearly a straight course, to Coombe Hill, a village situate about seven miles from Gloucester, on the road to Tewkesbury. It is three miles and a half in length, with a rise of 15 feet, and was made under the authority of an act, entitled, ' *An Act for making and maintaining a navi-* ' *gable Canal from the foot of Coombe Hill, in the parish of Leigh,* ' *in the county of Gloucester, to join the River Severn, at or near a* ' *place called Fisher's otherwise Fletcher's Leap, in the parish of* ' *Deerhurst, in the said county,*' at the sole expense of T. Burges and W. Miller, Esquires, and Mrs. Sarah Mumford.

The principal object proposed was the shortening and rendering more cheap, the communication between the River Severn and the town of Cheltenham, which is about five miles distant from

Coombe Hill; but since the Gloucester and Cheltenham Railway has been constructed, the business on this canal has been materially reduced.

TONNAGE RATES.

s. d.

Coal, Iron, Iron-stone, Timber, and all other Goods, Wares, and Merchandize } 2 6 per Ton, for the whole Distance

COVENTRY CANAL.

8 George III. Cap. 36, Royal Assent 29th January, 1768.
26 George III. Cap. 30, Royal Assent 22nd May, 1786.
59 George III. Cap. 62, Royal Assent 14th June, 1819.

THE original line, for which the act of 8th George III. was obtained, commences at the Trent and Mersey or Grand Trunk Canal, on Fradley Heath, from whence it takes a southerly direction to Huddlesford, where it is joined by the Wyrley and Essington Canal; afterwards by Hopwas to Fazeley, near Tamworth, where the Birmingham and Fazeley Canal locks down into it. From this place its course is across the River Tame, in a north-eastwardly direction by Amlington, where it approaches the banks of the Little River Anker; thence, it takes a south-easterly direction, and runs in nearly a parallel course with the river above mentioned; then by Polesworth, to the west side of the town of Atherstone; by Hartshill, the town of Nuneaton, and the villages of Bedworth and Longford, to the city of Coventry, where it terminates.

The original subscribers to this canal were one hundred and thirteen in number, amongst whom were Lord Archer, Lady Mary Greatheed, and Sir Roger Newdigate, Bart. who were incorporated by the name of " The Company of Proprietors of the " Coventry Canal Navigation." The act of 8th George III. so incorporating them, is entitled, ' *An Act for making and main-* ' *taining a navigable Canal from the city of Coventry, to communi-* ' *cate, upon Fradley Heath, in the county of Stafford, with a Canal* ' *now making between the Rivers Trent and Mersey,*' and it empowered the subscribers to raise, among themselves, for the purposes of this act, the sum of £50,000, in five hundred shares of £100 each, and an additional sum of £30,000, if necessary, by creating new shares.

TONNAGE RATES.

		d.	
Coal, Timber, Stone, and all other Goods, Wares, and Merchandize .... }		1½	per Ton, per Mile.
Lime and Limestone.....................................		¼	ditto. ditto.

EXEMPTION FROM TOLL.

Paving-stones, Sand, Gravel, and all other Material for the repair of Roads; Dung, Soil, Marl, and all sorts of Manure, provided they do not pass a Lock, except at such Times as the Water flows over it.

Vessels under Fifteen Tons not to pass Locks without leave.

Wharfage to be paid for all Goods remaining more than Twenty-four Hours on the Wharfs, but no Charge to be made for the Use of the Crane, which the Company are required to erect on the Bank of the Canal, near Támworth.

Proprietors of Lands may erect Wharfs, but that no more than Three-pence per Ton shall be charged for Goods which shall not remain more than Six Days.

Mr. James Brindley was the original engineer to this canal, and made the estimate for constructing it; but it appears that the amount of subscriptions was expended in executing between sixteen and seventeen miles of the line, viz. from Coventry to Atherstone; and as the company failed to raise any portion of the £30,000, which the act of 8th George III. authorized them to do, an end was put to the further prosecution of the remaining twenty-one miles of canal, until 1782, when a meeting of delegates from the Coventry, Oxford, and Trent and Mersey Canal Companies, and the subscribers to a proposed canal from the Wednesbury Collieries, to join the Coventry Canal, at Fazeley, took place at Coleshill, on the 20th of June in that year, where it was agreed that the Trent and Mersey Canal Company and the subscribers to the proposed canal, should execute the line from Fradley to Fazeley, (which is eleven miles in length and level,) and divide it equally between the last-mentioned company and the Birmingham and Fazeley Canal Company.

In an act passed on the 24th of June, 1783, authorizing the making of the Birmingham and Fazeley Canal, the agreement above referred to is confirmed, and that half lying between Fazeley and Whittington Brook, is declared to belong to the last mentioned company, and the other half, terminating at Fradley, to the Trent and Mersey Canal Company; and, it was further agreed, that the tonnage upon all coal navigated from Birmingham to Fazeley, and upon all or any part of the Coventry and Oxford Canals, should not exceed one penny per ton, per mile.

The act embodying this agreement, and authorizing the several parties to carry the works into execution, was passed on the 13th June, 1785, (25th George III. cap. 98,) and is entitled, ' *An Act to enable the Company of Proprietors of the Navigation* ' *from the Trent to the Mersey, and the Company of Proprietors of* ' *the Navigation from Birmingham to Fazeley, to make a navigable* ' *Canal from the said Trent and Mersey Navigation on Fradley* ' *Heath, in the county of Stafford, to Fazeley, in the said county ;* ' *and for confirming certain Articles of Agreement entered into* ' *between the said Trent and Mersey, the Oxford, and the Coventry* ' *Canal Navigation Companies.*' The act also confirms an agreement between the Coventry and Trent and Mersey Canal Companies, to this effect, viz. that within two months after notice had been given to the Coventry Canal Company that the part between Whittington Brook and Fradley Heath was completed, such company should be at liberty to purchase this portion at the original cost, with interest, from the time of advancing the several sums expended thereon.

In the preamble of the act of the 26th George III. entitled, ' *An Act to enable the Company of Proprietors of the Coventry* ' *Canal Navigation, to complete the said Canal to Fradley Heath,* ' *in the county of Stafford, and for other Purposes therein men-* ' *tioned,*' it is stated, that the sum of £50,000 had been expended in making the canal from Coventry to Atherstone, and that they had not been able to raise any portion of the additional sum of £30,000, which the act of 8th George III. authorized them to do. For the purpose, therefore, of enabling the company to execute the remaining part of the canal, between Atherstone and Fazeley, and to purchase that half-part of the canal between Fazeley and Fradley, belonging to the Trent and Mersey Canal Company, authority is given to raise, on mortgage of the undertaking, the sum of £40,000. This act limited the dividends, on that part of the navigation already executed, to three per cent. until the whole was completed ; it also repeals that part of the original act limiting the number of shares to be held by one person, to ten, unless

they came by will or act in law; instead of which, it enacts that
any person may have any number of shares not exceeding thirty.
The line of canal from Fazeley to Fradley being completed, and
notice given to the Coventry Canal Company, in January, 1787,
they agreed to purchase the half-part above-mentioned, and it was
accordingly conveyed to them in October, 1787. The whole line
of canal was completed and opened in July, 1790. The length of
this canal, from Fradley Heath to Coventry, was thirty-seven
miles and three-quarters, including the portion of the original line
now belonging to the Birmingham Canal Company. The first
eleven miles, to Fazeley, is level; there is then a rise, to Glascote,
near Tamworth, of 14$\frac{1}{2}$ feet, by two locks; thence, to Grendon,
six miles and a half, is level; from Grendon to Atherstone, a distance of two miles and a half, there is a rise of 81$\frac{1}{2}$ feet; from
which place, to its termination at Coventry, it is level. At
Marston Bridge, near Bedworth, the Ashby-de-la-Zouch Canal
joins it, and at Longford, the Oxford Canal communicates with it.
Between Nuneaton and the junction with the Ashby-de-la-Zouch
Canal, there is a short branch of three-quarters of a mile in length,
to some collieries; and at Griff, near Marston Bridge, there is
another branch. It is here worthy of remark, that these three
canals conjointly preserve the longest canal level in England,
being upwards of seventy miles, exclusive of branches.

TONNAGE RATES.

By an Act of the 9th George III. for making the Oxford Canal, it is stipulated that the
    Coventry Canal Proprietors shall receive all the Rates, arising from Coal, on the
    Oxford Canal, on the Two Miles nearest the Coventry Canal; and, that the
    Oxford Canal Company shall have all the Rates, arising from all Articles except
    Coal, which shall be navigated upon any Part or Parts of the Oxford Canal, and
    afterwards upon the Coventry Canal, within Three Miles and a Half from the
    Junction of the Two Canals towards Coventry; and by the Act of 34th George
    III. for making the Ashby-de-la-Zouch Canal, the Coventry Canal Company are
    authorized to collect Five-pence per Ton upon all Coal, Goods, and Merchandize
    whatsoever, which shall be navigated upon the Ashby-de-la-Zouch, and after-
    wards upon the Coventry, Oxford, or Grand Junction Canals, or upon any of the
    above-mentioned Canals, and afterwards upon the Ashby Canal.

EXEMPTION.

An Exemption to this Toll is extended to Corn or Grain; Sheep or other Cattle; Iron,
    Stone, Wrought Iron, got or made upon the Banks of the Ashby-de-la-Zouch
    Canal; Dung, Ashes, and Marl, for Manure; and Gravel, Sand, and Stone, for the
    repair of Roads.

The last act relating to the Coventry Canal Navigation, received the royal assent on the 14th of June, 1819, and is entitled,

' *An Act for amending several Acts of his present Majesty, rela-*
' *ting to the Coventry Canal Navigation,*' and was obtained chiefly
for the purpose of enabling proprietors of shares to transfer a portion equal to one or more tenths, and for enabling the company to
create a fund for repairs, but which is not to exceed £25,000.

This canal was a part of Mr. Brindley's scheme for completing
an inland navigation between the ports of London, Liverpool, and
Hull, and now that that object is effected, its revenue is derived
chiefly from cargoes passing between those places, as will appear
from the circumstance, that shortly after the completion of the
Oxford Canal, the original shares were quadrupled in value, and
have, since that period, considerably advanced.

CREE RIVER OR WATER OF CREE.

THIS river has its source in Loch Moan, situate among the
hills which separate the counties of Kirkcudbright and Ayr ;
from whence its course is southerly, by Newton Stewart, to
Carty, to which place it is navigable for small vessels. From
hence its course is very crooked to Creetown, where it empties
itself into Wigton Bay. The navigable part of it is nearly eight
miles in length, and is free of toll.

There is no proper harbour in Wigton Bay, although there
are several places where vessels may stop in moderate weather, or
with off-shore winds.

The channel to the water of Cree lies on the east side of the
bay, but as there is neither buoy or perch, it is difficult to find;
however, a vessel drawing 9 to 10 feet, at four hours flood, may
get up a considerable distance.

This river is chiefly useful for facilitating the importation of
coal from Ayr, Troon, and Irvine, to Newton Stewart and its
vicinity.

CRINAN CANAL.

33 George III. Cap. 104, Royal Assent 8th May, 1793.
39 George III. Cap. 27, Royal Assent 10th May, 1799.

THIS canal was made across an isthmus in Argyleshire, lying
between Lochs Crinan and Gilp, under the authority of an act,

entitled, ' *An Act for making and maintaining a navigable Canal*
' *from Loch Gilp to Loch Crinan, in the shire of Argyll.*' It
commences at the point of Ardreshaig, in Loch Gilp; thence, by
Oakfield, Craiglass, Auchinshellach and Leikachluan, to Loch
Crinan, into which it falls near Duntroon Castle. It is nine miles
and a half in length, and 12 to 15 feet deep; there are fifteen
locks upon it, with a rise of 58 feet from Loch Gilp, and a fall of
59 feet to Loch Crinan. Mr. Watt surveyed the line, in the first
instance, but Mr. John Rennie was afterwards appointed engineer,
and we believe it was carried into execution under his direction.

The subscribers, at the time the act was obtained, consisted of
two hundred and eighty-eight persons, amongst whom were the
Duke of Argyle, the Marquesses of Tweedale and Lorne, Earl of
Breadalbane, Lord Frederick and Lord J. Campbell, Lord Mac-
donald, Sir A. Edmonstone, Sir J. Sinclair, Sir A. Campbell, and
Sir James Riddell, Baronets, and Sir J. Campbell, Knight, besides
nearly fifty other gentlemen bearing the last-mentioned name of
Campbell. They were incorporated by the name of " The Com-
" pany of Proprietors of the Crinan Canal," and empowered to
raise among themselves the sum of £120,000, in two thousand
four hundred shares of £50 each, and an additional sum of
£30,000, should the former sum prove insufficient, or they may
borrow the last-mentioned sum on mortgage of the undertaking,
or by granting annuities on lives. The work is under the management of a director and fourteen other persons, who are called,
" The Governor and Directors of the Company of Proprietors of
" the Crinan Canal." The width of the canal and towing path is
not to exceed 450 feet, except where the canal is raised higher or
cut deeper than 16 feet from the surface of the ground.

TONNAGE RATES.

	s.	d.	
All Goods, Wares, Merchandize, and Commodities whatsoever	0	3	per Ton, per Mile.
Coal, Salt (Outward-bound), Lime, Limestone, Shell-sand, Marl, and all Sorts of Manure	0	2	ditto. ditto.
Open Boats, not exceeding Seven Tons Burthen	1	2	per Mile each.
Empty or Light Vessels (for every Ton Burthen)	0	1	per Mile.

HARBOUR DUES.

	s.	d.	
Goods landed or loaded in the Harbour or Basins	0	1	per Ton.
Vessels entering the said Harbour or Basins without unload-ing or passing upon the Canal	0	2	ditto.

Fractions to be taken as for a Quarter of a Ton, and as for a Quarter of a Mile.
No Wharfage to be taken for any Goods unless they have been upon the Wharfs or
Quays more than Twenty-four Hours.
The Wharfage Rates are fixed by the Bye-Laws of the Company.

By an act of 39th George III. entitled, ' *An Act for amending*
' *and rendering more effectual an Act passed in the Thirty-third*
' *Year of the Reign of his present Majesty, entitled, An Act for*
' *making and maintaining a navigable Canal from Loch Gilp to*
' *Loch Crinan, in the shire of Argyll,*' the company are authorized to raise or borrow the sum of £30,000, (although the whole
of the sum of £150,000, allowed to be raised by the above-recited
act, may not have been raised,) on mortgage of the undertaking,
by granting annuities, or by creating new shares, or by bonds, or
promissory notes under the common seal of the company ; but as
there afterwards appeared little probability of raising the above
sum, in consequence of many of the subscribers being unable to
make good their engagements, the lord chief baron and other the
barons of the court of exchequer, of Scotland, were directed, under
authority of an act of 39th George III. cap. 71, entitled, ' *An Act*
' *for empowering the Company of Proprietors of the Forth and*
' *Clyde Navigation to repay into the Court of Exchequer, in*
' *Scotland, the Sum advanced to them for the Purpose of completing*
' *the said Navigation; for repealing so much of an Act of the*
' *Twenty-fourth Year of his present Majesty as relates to the said*
' *Company, and for enabling the Barons of the said Court of Ex-*
' *chequer to advance Part of the Sum, so to be received, to the Com-*
' *pany of Proprietors of the Crinan Canal, on certain Conditions,*'
to pay to the Crinan Canal Company, on security of the rates and
duties, the sum of £25,000 : the interest of which sum, and the
other moiety of the sum of £50,000, to be paid by the Forth and
Clyde Navigation Company, is by the same act directed to be laid
out in the repair of the roads and bridges in the highlands of
Scotland.

The chief object of this ship canal is the shortening of the passage between the ports in the highlands, or the Caledonian Canal
and the River Clyde, by avoiding the circuitous route round the
peninsula of Cantire. The distance thus saved is more than
seventy miles, and when we take into consideration the difficulty

of this circuitous navigation, the islands and rocks to be avoided, the tacks and evolutions necessarily occasioned by contrary winds and lee-shores, and the certainty that the wind which favours vessels to the Mull of Cantire must be directly opposed when the point is doubled, the advantages arising to the navigation from the execution of this canal, and the safety and certainty with which the voyage through it can at all times be accomplished, must be much more largely appreciated, than from the mere consideration of the saving of time and distance.

CROMFORD CANAL.

29 George III. Cap. 74, Royal Assent 31st July, 1789.
30 George III. Cap. 56, Royal Assent 1st April, 1790.

This canal commences in the Erewash Canal, near Langley Bridge, in the county of Nottingham, and near its junction with the Nottingham Canal, from whence it pursues a northerly course, following the line of the River Erewash, which it crosses, but still proceeds along its banks to Codnor Park Iron Works, when it takes a westwardly course to Butterley Park, where it enters a tunnel of two thousand nine hundred and sixty-six yards in length, terminating a short distance west of Butterley Iron Works, under which it passes. From hence its course is by Buckland Bottom to Bull Bridge, where it crosses the River Amber by an aqueduct two hundred yards in length and 50 feet high. Near this place it enters a short tunnel, and from thence takes a north-westwardly direction, following the course of the Derwent, by Hepstandell Bridge, a mile beyond which, at Lea Hurst, it enters another short tunnel, and at a little distance further crosses the last-mentioned river by an aqueduct two hundred yards long and 30 feet high.

The span of the principal arch of the Derwent Aqueduct, through which the river flows, is 80 feet. From this place it is about a mile and three-quarters to the wharf at Cromford, where the canal terminates. Within half a mile of Cromford it is joined by the Cromford and High Peak Railway, now in execution. Near the Derwent Aqueduct there is a branch a quarter of a mile in length, extending towards Lea Bridge; and at the Bull Bridge Aqueduct it is joined by a railway a mile and a quarter in length, from the Crich Limestone Quarries. Near Codnor Park Iron Works, a branch from the Mansfield and Pinxton Railway communicates with this canal; and about half a mile north-west of this junction, a cut called the Pinxton Branch of this canal, proceeds from the main line to Pinxton; and at the basin, at its termination, the main line of the Mansfield and Pinxton Railway commences. At the place where the canal crosses the River Erewash, a short railway is laid from it to the collieries lying east of the village of Codnor, and at Langley Bridge, communicating with another railway from the coal works near the village of Heanor.

This canal is eighteen miles in length; in the first four miles of which, to Codnor Park Iron Works, it rises 80 feet; the remaining fourteen miles, and the Pinxton Branch of nearly three miles, are level. It is, in a great measure, supplied with water from a stream taken in by means of a feeder at the Cromford End, assisted by reservoirs; one of which, near the tunnel at Butterley Iron Works, is fifty acres, and, when full, will contain two thousand eight hundred locks of water; besides this, there are other reservoirs of smaller capacity; one of which is situated at the eastern end of the Great Tunnel, and another where the Pinxton Branch commences. The head level of the canal of fourteen miles in length, acts also as a reservoir, in consequence of being made 1 foot extra depth of water.

Mr. William Jessop designed this canal for narrow boats drawing $2\frac{1}{2}$ feet only, the tunnels being 9 feet wide at the surface of the water.

The act authorizing the execution of this canal, is entitled, ' *An Act for making and maintaining a navigable Canal from, or* ' *from near to, Cromford Bridge, in the county of Derby, to join* ' *and communicate with the Erewash Canal, at or near Langley* ' *Bridge; and also a collateral Cut from the said intended Canal,* ' *at or near Codnor Park Mill, to or near Pinxton Mill, in the said* ' *county.*'

The original subscribers were seventy-eight in number, amongst whom were the Duke of Newcastle and Sir Richard Arkwright, who were incorporated by the name of "The Cromford Canal "Company," with power to raise among themselves the sum of

£46,000, in four hundred and sixty shares, of £100 each, and an additional sum of £20,000, if necessary, either among themselves, or on mortgage of the undertaking.

TONNAGE RATES.

	s.	d.	
Coal, Coke, Lime, and Limestone, intended to be burnt into Lime...	0	1	per Ton, per Mile.
Iron, Iron-stone, Lead, and other Minerals, Marble, and Alabaster, and other Stone, Timber, and all other Articles not before specified, and which shall not have passed from the Erewash Canal	0	1½	ditto. ditto.
For every Article which shall have passed from the Erewash Canal...	0	2	per Mile.
Coal, or Coke conveyed towards Cromford upon any part of this Canal, from the Aqueduct over the River Amber, or from any place within Two Miles of it	1	0	per Ton, in addition.
For all Goods (except Lime and Limestone intended to be burnt into Lime) passing out of the Erewash Canal or going into it	0	3	ditto. ditto.

Fractions to be paid as for a full Mile, and as for a Quarter of a Ton.

EXEMPTION FROM RATES.

Small Rubbish or Waste Stones, Paving or other Stones, Gravel and Sand for the repairs of Roads, in any Township through which the Canal passes; Dung, Soil, Marl, Ashes of Coal and Turf, and all other Manure, (except Lime used for the Improvement of Lands, in any Township through which the Canal is made, and carried only at such Times as when the Water is running over the Lock Weirs.)

By a Clause in 29th George III. the Erewash Canal Company agree to take only One-half of the Rates they were authorized to take by the 17th George III. for all Goods (except Coke or Coal) which shall pass along the said Canal out of the Cromford Canal.

The Cromford Canal Company are entitled to Wharfage for any Article laying longer than Six Months.

For the Purposes of this Act Fifty Cubic Feet of Round, or Forty Feet of Square Oak, Ash, Elm, or Beech Timber, or Fifty Feet of Fir, or Deal, Balk, Poplar, or other Timber Wood, shall be deemed One Ton.

Nine Score Pounds Avoirdupois of Limestone; and Six Score Pounds of Unwrought Stone, Coal, and other Articles, shall be deemed a Hundred Weight.

Proprietors of estates may make railways and cuts to communicate with this canal, on payment of damages done by crossing the lands of other persons; they may also erect warehouses and wharfs, but the charges for the latter are limited by the act as follows.

RATES ON PRIVATE WHARFS.

	d.	
Coal, Lime-stone, Lime, Clay, Iron, Iron-stone, Timber, Stone, Bricks, Tiles, Slate, or Gravel	1	per Ton.
All other Goods and Things	3	ditto.

Provided that they do not remain more than Six Days (except Coal, Iron, and Iron-stone which may remain Six Months,) and Timber, Clay, Lime, Iron-stone, Stone, Brick, Tile, Slate, or Gravel, may remain Thirty Days   If any Articles remain for the Space of Ten Days over the several Periods as above, One Penny per Ton per Day for every Day such Ten Days, as above-mentioned, are exceeded.

In the year following the passing of the original act, another was obtained for the purpose of amending the provisions relating to the supply of water; it is entitled, ' *An Act to alter and amend* ' *an Act passed in the last Session of Parliament, for making and* ' *maintaining a navigable Canal from, or from near to, Cromford* ' *Bridge, in the county of Derby, to join and communicate with the* ' *Erewash Canal, at or near Langley Bridge; and also a collateral* ' *Cut from the said intended Canal at or near Codnor Park Mill, to* ' *or near Pinxton Mill, in the said county.*' It enacts, that for the supply of the canal, not more shall be taken than one-twentieth of the water of the River Derwent at Cromford Bridge, and that only between the hours of eight o'clock on every Saturday afternoon, and eight o'clock on Sunday afternoon; but at all times when less than five hundred and seventy tons per minute shall be passing Cromford Bridge, then the company are restrained from taking any water from the Derwent, or from any of the streams which flow into it.

The chief object of the promoters of this canal, was to open a better communication with the valuable and extensive mineral districts on its line; but it has partaken amply of the advantage arising from an extended trade, by becoming a part of the line of communication between London and the northern counties.

CROMFORD AND HIGH PEAK RAILWAY.

6 George IV. Cap. 30, Royal Assent 2nd May, 1825.

This railway commences from the Cromford Canal, about half a mile from its termination at Cromford Wharf; from whence it takes an eastwardly course by the village of Middleton, and within a mile of the town of Wirksworth; thence, by a circuitous course, by Carsington Pasture, Brassington, and over the high grounds of the parish of Hartington, by Hurdlow, and Church Sterndale, to the north side of the range of hills called Axedge, where the line makes a considerable detour, for the purpose of passing a valley; from this place its course lies within little more than a mile of Buxton, passing Goyts Bridge, to the Peak Forest Canal, at Whaley Bridge, where it terminates. It is in length thirty-three miles and seven furlongs, and it attains an elevation of 990 feet above the head level of the Cromford Canal, and 1271 feet above the level of the sea at low water, by means of six inclined planes, which are thus disposed—the first inclined plane, from Cromford, is four hundred and sixty yards in length, rising 240 feet; another at its termination, two hundred and forty yards, rising 225 feet; from thence, it is level one mile, three furlongs and four chains; next then is another inclined plane of five hundred and fifty yards in length, with a rise of 265 feet; then a level for the distance of one mile, six furlongs and seven chains; next a plane of three hundred and thirty yards in length, rising 70 feet; from the end of this inclined plane, it continues level for six miles, one furlong and seven chains; then a rise of 45 feet only in the next three miles and three furlongs; it is afterwards level three miles and six chains to the foot of the last inclined plane at Hurdlow, which is four hundred and eighty-four yards in length, with a rise, to the summit, of 145 feet. The summit level is maintained for the distance of twelve miles, three furlongs and eight chains, and in its course passes under a hill 150 feet below the summit, by means of a tunnel six hundred and thirty-eight yards in length. From the end of this elevated stretch of railway, there is a fall of 740 feet to the Peak Forest Canal, by three inclined planes; the first is nine hundred yards in length, with a fall of 460 feet, at the foot of which, the line of railroad crosses into Staffordshire, near Goyts Bridge; it then runs level two miles, four furlongs and two chains, to an inclined plane of seven hundred yards, with a fall of 237 feet; it is then level five furlongs and two chains; and the last inclined plane descends 43 feet in one hundred and ten yards, from the foot of which it is level to the Peak Forest Canal, a distance of one furlong and two chains.

Mr. Josias Jessop was the engineer employed to lay out this railroad, and he estimated the cost (including £20,000 for stationary engines to work the inclined planes,) at the sum of £155,079, 16s. 8d. The act for making it received the royal assent on the 2nd May, 1825, and is entitled, ' *An Act for making and maintain-*
' *ing a Railway or Tramroad, from the Cromford Canal, at or near*
' *to Cromford, in the parish of Wirksworth, in the county of*
' *Derby, to the Peak Forest Canal, at or near to Whaley, (otherwise*

' *Yardsley-cum-Whaley,)* in the county palatine of Chester.' It was obtained by a company consisting of one hundred and sixteen persons, amongst whom were the Dowager Viscountess Anson, the Honourable Edward Curzon, Sir Charles H. Colville, and Admiral Digby, who were incorporated by the name of "The "Cromford and High Peak Railway Company," and empowered to raise among themselves the sum of £164,000, in sixteen hundred and forty shares of £100 each, (which sum was subscribed before going to parliament,) and, if necessary, the further sum of £32,880, by mortgage of the undertaking.

TONNAGE RATES.

d.

Dung, Compost, and Manure, Lime-stone, Free-stone, Paving-stone, and all other Stone, Mineral, and Metallic Ores, Pig-iron, Bricks, Tiles, Slate, Clay, and Sand....................................	1	per Ton, per Mile.
Coal, Coke, Lime, Bar and Plate Iron, and Iron Castings, Lead, and other Metals, and Timber........	1½	ditto. ditto.
Corn, Malt, Flour, and Meal	2½	ditto. ditto.
All other Goods, Wares, and Merchandize	3	ditto. ditto.
All Articles (except Lime and Limestone) which do not pass the whole Length of Railway	6	per Ton, in addition.
All Goods, Wares, and Merchandize, conveyed on any of the Inclined Planes	1½	per Ton, at each of them, in addition.

Fractions to be taken as for Half a Mile, and as for a Quarter of a Ton.

Forty Cubic Feet of Oak, Mahogany, Beech and Ash, and Fifty Cubic Feet of all other Wood, shall, for the Purposes of this Act, be deemed a Ton.

Waggons of Four Wheels not to be allowed to carry more than Six Tons, including the Weight of such Carriages, and Waggons of Six Wheels to be allowed Nine Tons.

WHARFAGE RATES.

d.

Coals, Culm, Lime, Lime-stone, Clay, Iron, Iron-stone, Copper-ore, or any other Ores; Timber, Stone, Bricks, Tiles, Slate, Gravel, or other Things, remaining on the Wharfs any Time less than Ten Days....	1	per Ton.

If longer than Ten Days, One Penny per Ton, in Addition; and Sixpence per Ton for the Warehousing the same for the succeeding Week; and the like Sum of One Penny and Sixpence for every subsequent Week.

CRANAGE RATES.

s. d.

For any Weight to be raised by One Lift, being less than Two Tons	0 6	per Ton.
Ditto, being Two Tons, and less than Three.......................	1 0	ditto.
Ditto, being Three Tons, and less than Four......................	1 6	ditto.

And so progressively, advancing Sixpence per Ton for greater Weights.

The chief object of this railway, is to open a nearer and more convenient communication between the counties of Derby, Nottingham and Leicester, with the port of Liverpool, and the towns of Manchester and Stockport. A glance at the accompanying map will shew, in less time than words can express it, the great advantages which cannot fail to attend the execution of this grand scheme, for passing such a mountainous tract of country.

CROUCH RIVER.

This river has its source about three miles east of the magnificent seat of Lord Petre, called Thorndon Hall, in Essex; whence, its course is easterly, passing to the south of the town of Billericay, and Wickford, to Hull Bridge, to which place it is navigable for barges at high water. From hence its course is directly east, by Cricksey and Burnham, to Foulness, where it falls into the Thames. It is sixteen miles in length, and being a tideway river, is consequently free of toll.

As a navigation, it is chiefly used for the importation of fuel and groceries, and for the export of agricultural produce.

CROYDON CANAL.

41 George III. Cap. 127, Royal Assent 27th June, 1801.
48 George III. Cap. 18, Royal Assent 14th April, 1808.
51 George III. Cap. 11, Royal Assent 4th April, 1811.

This canal commences in the Grand Surrey Canal, about three quarters of a mile west from Deptford Dock Yard; from whence its course is southerly, crossing the London and Greenwich Road near New Cross, and shortly afterwards enters Kent, whence it passes Brockley, Sydenham, and re-enters Surrey, on the east side of Penge Common, over which it passes in a direct course, to its termination at Croydon, where there is a convenient wharf and basin. Its length is nine miles and a half; in the first of which it rises 70 feet, by twelve locks; from whence, it continues level something more than three quarters of a mile, where another series of locks, terminating at the entrance into Forest Wood, and rising 79½ feet in the space of three quarters of a mile, conducts to its summit level, which is seven miles in length. The act for making it was obtained in 1801, by a company consisting of two hundred and four persons, (amongst whom were the Duke of Norfolk, Lord Gwydir, Sir Francis Baring, Sir C. W. Blunt, Sir John Bridger, Admiral Pigot, Sir Thomas Turton, and Sir Benjamin Hammett and Company,) who were incorporated by the name of " The " Company of Proprietors of the Croydon Canal." It is entitled, ' An Act for making and maintaining a navigable Canal from, or ' from near, the town of Croydon, in the county of Surrey, into the ' Grand Surrey Canal, in the parish of St. Paul, Deptford, in the ' county of Surrey ; and for supplying the towns of Croydon, ' Streatham, and Dulwich, and the district called Norwood, in the ' parish of Croydon, in the said county of Surrey, and the town of ' Sydenham, in the county of Kent, with Water from the said Canal.' Many clauses are introduced in the act for the protection of the mill owners on the Rivers Wandle and Ravensbourne, or any streams running into them, and as the company are prohibited from taking water from any of these, they are, with this view, required to maintain the surface of the summit pool of the canal 2 feet above the highest part of Croydon Common. To carry this canal into execution, the company were empowered to raise among themselves the sum of £50,000, in five hundred shares of £100 each, and, if necessary, a further sum of £30,000, or by mortgage of the undertaking.

This canal is 5 feet deep, and the locks are 60 feet long and 9 feet wide, and it is supplied with water by small reservoirs, (one of which is situate on the edge of Penge Common,) and by drains cut in the adjoining lands, though the act gives authority to raise water for this purpose from the Grand Surrey, which is on a level with high water in the Thames; but at that time it seems to have been the intention to use inclined planes instead of locks; and the steam engines to be used in raising the water, to replace the loss by leakage and evaporation, were also intended to draw the boats up the inclined planes.

TONNAGE RATES.

	d.
Timber, Stone, Coal, Bricks, Tiles, and all other Goods and Commodities, except as herein-after mentioned	3 per Ton, per Mile.
Dung, Chalk, Marl, Clay, Lime, Compost, and other Manure..	1½ ditto. ditto.

Fractions to be taken as for a Quarter of a Ton, and as for a Quarter of a Mile.

TOLLS FOR PASSING ON THE TOWING PATHS.

		s.	d.	
For every Horse, Mare, Gelding, Mule, or Ass, except such as are drawing any Boat or Vessel	}	0	2	each.
Drove of Oxen or Neat Cattle		1	8	per Score.
Swine, Sheep, or Lambs		0	10	ditto.

And so in proportion for any greater or less Number.

Forty Cubic Feet of Round, and Fifty Cubic Feet of Square Oak, Ash, Elm, or Beech Timber, and Forty Feet of Fir or Deal, Balk, Poplar, Birch, or other Timber or Wood, not cut into Scantlings, shall be deemed a Ton.

Boats under Twenty Tons, not to pass any Lock without leave, unless Tonnage is paid for that Weight.

A clause is introduced in this act, securing to the corporation of London, as conservators of the Thames, the annual sum of £40, as a compensation for any diminution which may arise in the tolls and duties made payable by an act of the 17th of George III. for particulars of which, see article, 'Thames River.'

Mr. John Rennie and Mr. Ralph Dodd were the engineers originally employed upon this canal.

In 1808 the company found it necessary to apply again to parliament for an act to enable them to raise more money, which is entitled, ' *An Act for enabling the Company of Proprietors of the* ' *Croydon Canal, to complete the same,*' by which it appears, that of the £50,000 and £30,000 authorized to be raised by the former act, they had obtained, by subscription, £47,508, and borrowed the sum of £20,357, and from rents of land and sale of timber and clay, £195, 16s. 6d. making, together, £68,060, 16s. 6d. the whole of which had been expended on the works, with the exception of a balance of £449, 19s. 1d.; and that to complete the works and repay the money borrowed, the sum of £30,000 will be required, which sum the act of 48th George III. enables them to raise, by creating new shares, or by promissory notes under the common seal of the company, or by mortgage.

Three years after the passing of the last act, an application was again made to parliament, when another was obtained, entitled, ' *An Act for enabling the Company of Proprietors of the* ' *Croydon Canal, to raise Money to complete the said Canal and* ' *Works; and for amending the former Acts relative thereto,*' in the preamble of which it is stated, that the company have raised the sum of £30,000, authorized by the last-recited act, by creating new shares of the value of £19,900, and by borrowing, on mortgage, the sum of £10,100; and they have, by virtue of the powers of the act of 41st George III. (since the last-recited act,) raised, by shares, £9,647, which said sums have all been expended on the canal and works, except the sum of £2,658, 9s. 7d.; but in consequence of the high prices of the land required for the canal and reservoirs, and the expenditure in the necessary erection of wharfs, warehouses, &c. the company have incurred a debt of £25,700. It further states, that for the purpose of constructing the reservoirs, bridges, and other additional works, they will require the sum of £27,343; and for the discharging of their debts and completing the canal and works, the further sum of £50,385. This act, therefore, authorizes them to raise these by granting annuities, with benefit of survivorship, if required, for the works abovementioned, and to pay off the mortgage debt of £29,615. The work is directed to be put under the management of a committee of from fifteen to twenty-one persons, who are severally possessed of five shares at the least.

The principal object of this canal is the supply of Croydon and its vicinity with coal, deals, and general merchandize, and the export of agricultural produce, chalk, fire-stone, fuller's-earth, &c. to London.

CROYDON, MERSTHAM AND GODSTONE RAILWAY.

43 George III. Cap. 35, Royal Assent 17th May, 1803.
46 George III. Cap. 93, Royal Assent 3rd July, 1806.

THIS railway commences at the south end of the Surrey Iron Railway, on the west side of the town of Croydon, from whence it proceeds, in a southerly direction, running parallel with the Brighton Road, to the village of Merstham, from whence, the act gives authority to continue it by Gatton Park, the residence of Sir Mark Wood, Bart. to the town of Reigate. The Godstone Green Branch commences at Merstham, whence it takes a south-eastwardly course by Pendhill and Chevington, and terminates at Godstone Green, on the high road between Croydon and East Grinstead. From Croydon to Merstham the length is nearly eight miles and three quarters, and from thence to Reigate, three miles and three quarters; and the Godstone Branch is in length three miles and a quarter. The estimate for the whole was made by Mr. William Jessop, and amounted to the sum of £52,347, of which, £35,800 was subscribed before going to parliament, and the act, authorizing its execution, is entitled, ' *An Act for making* ' *and maintaining a Railway from, or from near, a place called* ' *Pitlake Meadow, in the town of Croydon, to, or near to, the town* ' *of Reigate, in the county of Surrey, with a collateral Branch from* ' *the said Railway, at or near a place called Merstham, in the* ' *parish of Merstham, to, or near to, a place called Godstone* ' *Green, in the parish of Godstone, all in the said county of Surrey.*' It was obtained by a company consisting of seventy-three persons, amongst whom were Sir R. Barclay and Sir J. Lade, Baronets, who were incorporated by the name of " The Croydon, Merstham " and Godstone Iron Railway Company," who are empowered to raise among themselves the sum of £60,000, in six hundred shares of £100 each; and if this is found insufficient, they may raise an additional sum of £30,000, or by mortgage of the rates which are as follows.

TONNAGE RATES.

	d.	
Dung	2 per Ton, per Mile.	
Limestone, Chalk, Lime, and all other Manure, (except Dung) Clay, Breeze, Ashes, Sand, and Bricks	3 ditto.	ditto.
Timber, Copper, Tin, Lead, Iron, Stone, Flints, Coal, Charcoal, Coke, Culm, Fuller's Earth, Corn and Seeds, Flour, Malt and Potatoes	4 ditto.	ditto.
All other Goods, Wares, and Merchandize	6 ditto.	ditto.

Fractions of a Mile to be paid for as for a full Mile, but Fractions of a Ton as for a Quarter.

One Hundred and Twenty Pounds Avoirdupois, to be deemed a Hundred Weight.

Owners of Lands may erect Wharfs, but if they refuse, the Company may do it and charge a reasonable Sum for all Goods remaining longer than Twenty-four Hours.

In the preamble of an act of the 46th George III. entitled, ' *An* ' *Act for better enabling the Company of Proprietors of the Croydon,* ' *Merstham and Godstone Iron Railway, to complete the same,*' it is stated, that the company had been enabled only to raise the sum of £45,500, instead of £90,000; the act, therefore, empowers them to raise the remaining sum of £45,500 among themselves, or by creating new shares, or by promissory notes under the common seal of the company, or by mortgage or annuities secured on the rates.

By the first recited act, two years only were allowed to make that part of the line towards Reigate, which passes through Gatton Park Estate, and as this was not done within the time, the power to make it has consequently ceased. The railway is double throughout, and is, with the carriage driver's path on each side, 24 feet in width.

The principal object is to facilitate the transit to London, of the heavy minerals and other produce, found in the vicinity of its southern end, which is effected by its connection with the Surrey Iron Railway, and the Croydon Canal; and, in return, to bring sea-borne coal and other general merchandize, for the supply of this district of country.

DANE RIVER.

7 George I. Cap. 17, Royal Assent 7th June, 1720.

This river rises on the west side of Axedge, a mountain in Derbyshire, from whence it pursues a south-eastwardly course, forming, for several miles, the division between the counties of Derby and Chester, and afterwards of Stafford and Chester; from whence it flows past the town of Congleton, and by the beautiful seats of Somerford Park, Swettenham Hall, and Davenport Park; thence, by Holmes Chapel, and within a mile of Middlewich, where it is crossed by the Trent and Mersey or Grand Trunk Canal; from which place it pursues a north-eastwardly and very serpentine course, by Bostock Hall and Whatcroft, to the town of Northwich, where it falls into the Weaver Navigation, a little above the bridge.

As no portion of this river is navigable, we introduce it merely because an act was passed for making it so, in the early part of the reign of George I. which is entitled, ' *An Act for making* ' *navigable the River Dane, from Northwich, where it joins the* ' *River Weaver, to the falling of Wheelock Brook, in the county of* ' *Chester.*' The stream here mentioned, enters the River Dane at the place where the Grand Trunk Navigation crosses it, in its course to Northwich, so that whatever object the original projectors had in view, it is presumed that it will now be much more effectually answered.

DARENT RIVER.

This river rises in Surrey, two miles from Westerham, from whence it takes an eastwardly course down one of the most beautiful vales in Kent, passing Hill Park, Brasted Place, and Chipsted, to River Head, where it takes a northerly course by Lullingstone Castle, (the seat of Sir Thomas Dike, Bart.) Farningham and Darent, to the town of Dartford. From this place to the Thames, into which it falls in Longreach, it is navigable for barges at high water. The navigable part is in length about four miles, all tideway and free of toll; and it is chiefly used for the trade of Dartford. The celebrated Dartford Gunpowder Mills are situate on its banks, besides other manufactures in the vicinity, which reap the benefit necessarily resulting from this navigation.

DART RIVER.

This river rises on the south side of Cut Hill, on Dartmoor Forest, in the county of Devon; from whence it pursues a southerly direction to Two Bridges, and thence, south-eastwardly, by New Bridge and Buckfastleigh, to a mill weir about a mile above the town of Totness, to which place it is navigable. Its course, to the sea, is very crooked, by the above-mentioned town, Stoke Gabriel, and the port of Dartmouth, a mile below which place it falls into the English Channel, in Dartmouth Harbour. The navigable part, by the low water channel, is twelve miles and a half in length; the tide flows throughout, and it is free of toll. The entrance to the river forms an excellent harbour, and as Dartmouth is a port, into which, in the year 1824, seventy-three English and six Foreign ships entered, some estimate may be formed of its importance.

As a navigation, the chief uses to which it is put, are the conveyance of coal and shell-sand manure from Totness and vicinity; and to export the produce of the tin, lead and copper mines, which are worked to a considerable extent on the borders of Dartmoor Forest.

DEARNE AND DOVE CANAL.

33 George III. Cap. 115, Royal Assent 3rd June, 1793.
39 & 40 George III. Cap. 37, Royal Assent 30th May, 1800.

THIS canal commences in a side cut belonging to the River
Dunn Navigation, near to the Dunn Pottery, in the township of
Swinton; from whence, it takes a north-westwardly course through
a short tunnel, about a mile from the Dunn; thence, by Wath,
Brampton, Wombwell and Ardsley, to its termination at the aqueduct conducting the Barnsley Canal over the River Dearne, near
Barnsley. The length is nine miles and a quarter, with a total
rise, at the above-mentioned point of junction with the Barnsley
Canal, of 127 feet. In little more than half a mile from its commencement, there are six locks, rising 36 feet 9 inches; from thence,
to within a quarter of a mile of the Cob Car Ing, or Elsiker
Branch, it is three miles and a half, and level; to the above-mentioned branch it rises 30 feet 3 inches, by four locks, and from
thence, to within less than half a mile of the Worsbrough Bridge
Branch, it is level; in the next half mile, to the last-mentioned
branch, there are eight locks, rising 60 feet; from thence, to the
Barnsley Canal, it is level. The branch to Worsbrough is two
miles in length, and level; and the branch to Elsiker Iron Works,
(belonging to Earl Fitzwilliam,) is two miles and a half, rising 48
feet, by six locks. This canal is chiefly supplied with water from
reservoirs situate at Elsiker, and in the vale of Stainbro', called the
Worsbrough Reservoir. From some extensive collieries situate
to the south of Stainbro' Hall, there is a railway extending to the
basin at Worsbrough Bridge, which, together with the produce of
the iron furnace working there, furnishes considerable tonnage
upon this branch.

The first act relating to this navigation, received parliamentary
sanction in 1793, and is entitled, ' *An Act for making and main-*
' *taining a navigable Canal from the River Dunn Navigation Cut,*
' *in the township of Swinton, to or near, the town of Barnsley, in*
' *the parish of Silkstone, in the West Riding of the county of York;*
' *and certain collateral Cuts branching out of the said Canal.*'

It was obtained by a company of two hundred and eleven persons, amongst whom were the Duke of Leeds, Earl Fitzwilliam, Sir L. Copley, Sir G. Wombwell, and Sir F. Wood, Baronets, who were incorporated by the name of " The Dearne and Dove " Canal Company," and authorized to raise among themselves, for the purposes of this act, the sum of £60,000, in six hundred shares of £100 each, and, if necessary, a further sum of £30,000, or by mortgage, on assignment of the undertaking as a security.

TONNAGE RATES.

	d.	
Wheat, Shelling, Beans, Peas, Vetches, and Lentils, Rape, Line, Coal, and Mustard Seed; Apples, Pears, Onions, and Potatoes	4 per Quarter of Eight Winchester Bushels.	
Barley	3 ditto. ditto.	
Oats and Malt	2½ ditto. ditto.	
Wool, Dried Pelts, or Spetches	4 per Pack, or Sheet, of 312lbs. Avoirdupois.	
Coal, Slack, Cinders, Culm, Charcoal, and Lime ..	1 per Ton, per Mile.	
Limestone	¾ ditto. ditto.	
If any Boat, carrying up Lime, or Limestone, return with Coal or any other Article to the Amount of Thirty Tons, the Tonnage on the Lime shall be only	¾ ditto. ditto.	
And on the Limestone	½ ditto. ditto.	
Stone, Iron-stone, Flag Paving-stone, and Slate	1 ditto. ditto.	
If any Boats, carrying up the last-mentioned Articles, shall return laden with any other Article to the Amount of Thirty Tons, then they shall be charged only	¾ ditto. ditto.	
Cast Metal Goods and Bar-iron	2 ditto. ditto.	
Old or Pig-iron	1 per Ton.	
English Oak, Timber, and Plank	1½ per Ton of 40 Cubic Feet, per Mile.	
Elm, Ash, and other English Timber	1 per Ton of 50 Cubic Feet.	
Fir, and other Kinds of Foreign Timber	½ per Ton of 50 Cubic Feet, per Mile.	
Deals and Battens, equal to Thirty Deals of Twelve Feet in Length, Three Inches Thick, and from Nine to Twelve Inches Broad	1¼ per Ton, per Mile.	
Groceries, Linen and Woollen Yarn, Cotton, Flax, Hemp, Manufactured Goods, and any other Wares and Merchandize	2 ditto. ditto.	

And so in Proportion for any shorter Distance than One Mile.

Vessels passing any one of the Locks of this Navigation shall pay for Six Miles, and the lading shall be charged as not less than Thirty Tons; and in case the lading be of Articles charged of various Rates, any Quantity that it is wanting of Thirty Tons shall be charged at the highest Rates; but if such Boat be going up, and return with Coal or other Matters, and shall pay the Rates for Thirty Tons or upwards in coming down, then such lading shall be charged Rates according to the Quantity and Distance carried.

Fractions of a Mile to be charged as a whole Mile, and Fractions of a Ton, according to the Number of Quarters.

As it was apprehended that the Barnsley Canal would be made to communicate with this Navigation, it was enacted that any light Vessel going up from Swinton, and through a Junction Lock, (directed to be made within One Hundred and Fifty Yards,) into the proposed Barnsley Canal, and not return loaded the same Way, shall pay the full Rates of Three-halfpence per Ton, per Mile, upon Thirty Tons; and if down the Canal light, and return loaded, the same Rates as before specified.

CRANAGE AND PORTERAGE RATES.

For every Ton of Goods, Wares, or other Merchandize, loaded or landed from, or on to any Wharf belonging to the Company .... } *d.* 6 per Ton.

WHARFAGE RATES.

DESCRIPTION OF GOODS.	(*)	(†)	(‡)	(§)	(‖)	And so in proportion, for any Time such Goods shall lay upon or within any such intended Wharfs, Staiths, or Warehouses; but for any Time under Twenty-four Hours they are not liable to pay any Wharfage.
	s. d.	*s. d.*	*s. d.*	*s. d.*	*s. d.*	
For every Ton of Goods, Wares, Merchandize, and Commodities, and other Things, (except what are hereinafter enumerated)................	0 6	0 9	1 0	1 3	1 6	
For every Ton of English Timber of all Kinds, and Pig and Bar-iron........	0 3	0 6	0 9	1 0	1 3	
For every Ton of Coals, Stone, Iron-stone, Flint, Limestone, Clay and Sand....	0 ½	0 1	0 1½	0 2	0 2½	
For every Ton of Lime, Bricks, Tiles, Plaster, and Soapers' Ashes	0 1	0 2	0 3	0 4	0 5	
For every Quarter of Corn of all Kinds, Cole, Rape, Line, and Mustard Seed, Apples, Pears, Onions, and Potatoes	0 ½	0 1	0 1½	0 2	0 2½	

* More than 24 Hours, and not more than Six Days. + Six Days, but less than One Month. ‡ One Month, but less than Six Weeks. ₹ Six Weeks, but less than Two Months. ‖ Two Months, but less than Ten Weeks.

Sixteen Cubic Feet of Stone, Ten Superficial Yards of Flag Paving-stone, (from One to Two Inches and Three Quarters Thick,) Ten Yards of Lineal Curb Stone, (from Eleven to Thirteen Inches Wide and from Five to Seven Inches Thick,) Forty Cubic Feet of English Oak Timber, Fifty Cubic Feet of Elm, Ash, and other English Timber, Fifty Cubic Feet of Fir, and all other Foreign Timber, Thirty Deals of Battens, (Twelve Feet Long, Three Inches Thick, and from Nine to Twelve Inches Broad,) shall be respectively deemed One Ton for the Purposes of this Act.

EXEMPTION FROM TONNAGE RATES.

Dung, Soil, Marl, Ashes of Coal and Turf, and all other Manure, except Lime, for the Improvement of Lands through which the Canal is intended to pass; all Materials for the repairs of Roads, (except Flag, Curb, and Paving-stones,) provided they do not pass a Lock, except at such Times as when the Water flows over the Waste Weir.

Vessels of less Burthen than Thirty Tons not to pass through Locks without leave, unless they pay Tonnage for the same as for a Boat of Thirty Tons, laden with Coal.

The company are restricted from taking, for the supply of the canals and branches, any water from Blacker Brook or Hollin Well Spring, in the township of Worsbrough; or from the River Dove or Dodworth Brook, except for the purpose of filling the reservoir in Stainbro' Valley, at a time of flood water.

This act authorizes proprietors of lands to make railways to any mines within one thousand yards of the canal; but in the parish of Wath, they may extend them two thousand yards. The canal is 4 feet 6 inches deep, and the locks are 53 feet in length, and 14 feet 4 inches wide; admitting such vessels as usually navigate the Dun, and Aire and Calder Navigation.

Seven years subsequent to the date of the first act, the company were, after having completed a considerable portion of the canal, under the necessity of applying to parliament for another act, to enable them to borrow more money and to increase the rates; which act received the royal assent on the 30th May, 1800, and is entitled, ' *An Act to enable the Dearne and Dove Canal* ' *Company to finish and complete the said Canal, and the several* ' *collateral Cuts branching therefrom ; and for explaining, amend-* ' *ing and enlarging the Powers of an Act, passed in the Thirty-third* ' *Year of the Reign of his present Majesty, for making and main-* ' *taining the said Canal and collateral Cuts ; and for increasing* ' *the Tolls thereby granted.*' This act empowers the company to raise among themselves, or by the admission of new subscribers, or by calls upon the original shareholders, the sum of £30,000, instead of by mortgage, as prescribed by the former act; if by a new subscription, the act directs it to be raised by dividing the same into six hundred half shares of £50 each; and if this sum be insufficient, they may borrow an additional £10,000, on mortgage of the undertaking.

Power is also given to demand one-half, or fifty per cent. additional tonnage, and the same advance upon cranage, porterage, warehouse and wharfage rates, upon every article, except flag paving-stone, limestone or lime, which shall have been previously navigated up the Barnsley Canal from Wakefield.

Mr. Whitworth, who projected and laid out this canal, continued to be the engineer till the time of his death. The works were finished and the opening took place in 1804.

The chief object of the undertaking was to open a cheaper communication with the mining districts towards its western termination, in order that their rich and various productions should find a more advantageous market; and to give greater facilities for the transit of the manufactures of Barnsley to the port of Hull.

DEBEN RIVER.

THIS river has its source near the town of Debenham, in Suffolk, from whence it takes a south-eastwardly course by Nonewden Hall, Easton, and by Campsey Meer and Abbey, to near Beverets, whence it pursues a south-westwardly course by Ufford and Bromswell, to Wilford Bridge, about a mile above the town of Woodbridge, to which place it is navigable. The course from Woodbridge is nearly south, passing Waldringfield and Hemley, to within a mile and a half of Felixstow, where it falls into the sea about four miles north-west of the port of Harwich. From Woodbridge, the river, at high water, has the appearance of a considerable estuary, being in some parts, and in particular opposite the village of Waldringfield, above half a mile in width.

The length of the navigation is about nine miles and a half, and at Woodbridge there are docks for the building of ships and other vessels, besides commodious wharfs and quays; there is also a dock for ship building near Ramsholt, situate about six miles down the river. The tide flows its whole length, and it is free of toll, the principal trade upon it being the import of coal and deals, and the export of the surplus agricultural produce of this part of Suffolk.

DEE RIVER.

11 & 12 Wil. III. C. 24, R. A. 11th Apr. 1700.   6 Geo. II. C. 30, R. A. 13th June, 1734.
14 Geo. II. C. 8, R. A. 21st Mar. 1740. 17 Geo. II. C. 28, R. A. 12th May, 1744.
26 Geo. II. C. 35, R. A. 15th May, 1753. 31 Geo. III. C. 88, R. A. 10th June, 1791.

THIS river has its source on the north side of a mountain in Merioneth, North Wales, called Arennig; from whence it flows by the town of Bala, and from thence, north-eastwardly, by Corwen, to Llantysilio, to which place, from Bala Lake, it is used as feeder to the Ellesmere Canal. From Llantysilio it runs by Llangollen, and thence to the place where the famous Pont-y-Cysylty Aqueduct has been thrown across it; it then proceeds within a short distance of Wynnstay, (the seat of Sir Watkin Williams

Wynn, Bart.) from whence it pursues a northerly and serpentine course, passing Eaton Hall, the splendid mansion of Earl Grosvenor, to the city of Chester, from which place, to the sea, it is navigable. The length of the present navigation, from Hand Bridge to the end of the new channel, where it opens into the estuary of the Dee, is little more than eight miles; and from thence, by the low water channel, passing Park Gate, to the opening into the Irish Sea, off Great Helbre Island and Light-House, the distance is fifteen miles and a half.

The first act of parliament relating to this river occurs in the 11th and 12th years of the reign of William III. entitled, ' *An* ' *Act to enable the Mayor and Citizens of Chester to recover and* ' *preserve the Navigation of the River Dee,*' in which it is stated, that the Dee was anciently navigable to Chester for ships and vessels of considerable burthen, but by neglect of the said river, and for want of sufficient protection against the flux and reflux of the sea, the channel had become so uncertain, that the navigation was nearly destroyed. It was upon this River Dee, as history relates, that Edgar the Peaceable was rowed by eight tributary princes.

By the act of William, however, the mayor and citizens of Chester were authorized to make the Dee navigable, between Chester and the sea, for ships of one hundred tons burthen or upwards; and for which certain rates on coal, lime, and limestone, were allowed to be collected for the term of twenty-one years; in which time, however, the river was not made navigable, although considerable sums of money were spent in endeavouring to attain this desirable end.

Another act was therefore obtained in 1734, entitled, ' *An* ' *Act to recover and preserve the Navigation of the River Dee, in* ' *the county palatine of Chester,*' by which Nathaniel Kinderley, his heirs and assigns, were appointed undertakers of the navigation, and authorized to make the river navigable to Wilcox Point, with 16 feet water in moderate spring tides.

Seven years were allowed for the execution of the necessary works, and certain rates were allowed to be collected; but it appears that Kinderley was in trust for Thomas Watts and Richard Manley, Esquires, who afterwards nominated forty persons as the undertakers.

By an instrument dated 9th of April, 1734, these last-mentioned gentlemen, together with Joseph Davis and William Parsons, of London, and ninety others, agree to raise a joint stock of £40,000, in four hundred shares of £100 each, for the purpose of carrying the act into execution; but, as more money was wanted, it was agreed by deed-poll, on the 17th of August, 1736, to advance ten per cent. on the original subscription, and in a little time afterwards twenty per cent. ; and it further appears, that the sum of £47,830 was expended in making a new channel for the Dee, and vesting £10,000 in South Sea Annuities, to answer any claim for damages in making the navigation.

The new channel was opened in April, 1737, and the whole of the works completed before the 25th of March, 1740; and on the 11th of December in the same year, it was agreed that the joint stock should be increased to £52,000, and that the company should be incorporated. Accordingly an act was obtained in the 14th George II. entitled, ' *An Act for incorporating the Under-* ' *takers of the Navigation of the River Dee,*' by which they were incorporated by the name of " The Company of Proprietors of the " Undertaking for recovering and preserving the Navigation of " the River Dee," and empowered to do what Nathaniel Kinderley was authorized to do in the preceding act; but as the high rates granted under the 6th of George II. were injurious to the trade of Chester, it was again agreed to reduce them. An act was in consequence obtained in the 17th of George II. entitled, ' *An Act for explaining and amending an Act passed in the Sixth* ' *Year of his present Majesty's Reign, entitled, An Act to recover* ' *and preserve the Navigation of the River Dee in the county pala-* ' *tine of Chester; and another Act passed in the Fourteenth Year* ' *of his present Majesty's Reign, entitled, An Act for incorporating* ' *the Undertakers of the Navigation of the River Dee; and for* ' *repealing the Tonnage Rates payable to the said Undertakers;* ' *and for granting to them other Tonnage or Keelage Rates in lieu* ' *thereof; and for other Purposes therein mentioned;*' by which the rates allowed in the former acts are repealed, and the following substituted.

TONNAGE RATES.

	s.	d.	
For every Vessel conveying any description of Goods, Wares, or Merchandize, (except Lead, Oysters, Slates and Paving-stones, which are exempted from payment of Toll,) to or from Chester, or to or from any Place between the said City and Park Gate, on the North Side of the Dee, or to or from any Place between Chester and the Town of Flint, on the South Side of the Dee, and to or from any of the said Places, to or from any Place between St. David's Head, or Carlisle	0	2	per Ton.
For any Vessel coming or going from any Place between St. David's Head and the Land's End, or beyond Carlisle, to or from any Part South of the Shetlands, or to or from the Isle of Man	0	3	ditto
Ditto, from or to any Part of Ireland	0	4	ditto.
Ditto, from or to any Place up the King's Channel, beyond the Land's End or the Shetlands	0	4	ditto.
Ditto, from or to any Part of Norway, Denmark, Holstein, Holland, Hamburgh, Flanders, or any Part of France, without the Straits of Gibraltar, or the Islands of Jersey or Guernsey	0	8	ditto.
Ditto, to or from Newfoundland, Greenland, Russia, and within the Baltic, Portugal and Spain, without the Straits, Canaries, Madeiras, Western Isles, or the Azores	1	0	ditto.
Ditto, to or from the West Indies, or any other Part of America, Africa, Europe or Asia, within the Straits, or not named before, or any Part of Africa without the Straits, or Cape de Verd Isles	1	6	ditto.
And for every Vessel carrying Goods from, or bringing Goods to Chester, to be put on board or discharged from any Ship or Vessel lying at Park Gate, Flint, or any other Place within the Port of Chester	0	2	ditto.

And so in proportion for any greater or less Quantity than a Ton, and to pay but once a Voyage, notwithstanding they may have lading both inward and outward.

	s.	d.	
Cheese conveyed in Barges to any Ship lying at Park Gate or Flint, employed by the Cheesemongers of London....................	0	2	per Ton.

For the Purposes of this Act the Tonnage of Vessels is directed to be ascertained in the following Manner—the Length of the Keel to be multiplied by the Breadth between Planks on the Midship Beam, and that Product again by Half the Breadth for the Depth, and the Whole divided by 94 ; the Quotient, under this Operation, to be deemed the Number of Tons Burthen of such Ship. Skins or Wool to be charged by Weight, and not by the Burthen of the Ship. Vessels loaded within any Dock, to pay, according to the Burthen of the Ship, Sixpence per Ton.

Of the Sum of £10,000, invested in the South Sea Annuity Stock, the Sum remaining, amounting to £7,180, 3s. 6d. was, by the Act, transferred to the Company ; and it is also enacted, that unless the River Dee is maintained a Fifteen Feet Navigation at moderate springs, that the Rates and Duties are entirely to cease, until it is restored to that Depth.

By an act of the 26th George II. entitled, ' *An Act for con-* ' *firming an Agreement entered into between the Company of Pro-* ' *prietors of the Undertaking for recovering and preserving the* ' *Navigation of the River Dee, and Sir John Glynne, Bart.* Lord ' *of the Manor of Hawarden, and several Freeholders and Occu-* ' *piers of Land within the said Manor ; and for explaining and* ' *amending Three several Acts of Parliament of the Sixth, Four-* ' *teenth, and Seventeenth Years of his present Majesty's Reign, for* ' *recovering and preserving the Navigation of the River Dee,*' we learn that the works belonging to the navigation had cost the company £60,000 over and above what had been paid out of the rates; and as more money was wanted for repairs of dams, &c. the company are hereby empowered to make a call of twenty per cent. upon the capital stock, besides eight and a half per cent. which remained uncollected of the previous per centages.

The last act relating to this navigation, was obtained principally with a view of confirming certain arrangements relating to the waste and salt marshes adjoining the Dee, and is totally void of any thing of public interest; it is dated 10th June, 1791, and entitled, ' *An Act for confirming an Agreement entered into between* ' *the Company of Proprietors of the Undertaking for recovering* ' *and preserving the Navigation of the River Dee, and certain* ' *Lords of Manors and other Persons entitled to Right of Common* ' *upon the Wastes and Commons, and the Old Common Salt* ' *Marshes, lying on the South Side of the said River, below or to* ' *the North-East of Greenfield Gate, in the county of Flint, and an* ' *Award made in consequence thereof.'*

Though Chester is a port into which, in the year 1824, twenty-four English and four Foreign ships entered, yet it falls into perfect insignificance, when placed in comparison with the neighbouring port of Liverpool, into which one thousand five hundred and fifty-four English and five hundred and ten Foreign ships entered its capacious docks in the year above-mentioned. And, as a proof of the small revenue derived from this navigation, we need only to observe, that when the act was passed for making the Ellesmere Canal in 1793, a protecting clause was introduced by the Dee Navigation Company, stipulating that if their annual income should ever fall short of £210, the Ellesmere Canal Company should make up the deficiency.

The objects of this navigation are of a general nature, as may be inferred from the tonnage rates.

DERBY CANAL.

33 George III. Cap. 102, Royal Assent 7th May, 1793.

THIS canal commences on the northern bank of the River Trent, near the village of Swarkstone, and enters the Trent and

N

Mersey or Grand Trunk Canal at the distance of three furlongs to the northward. The main line proceeds from the last-mentioned canal, a quarter of a mile to the eastward of the junction above-named, whence it takes a northwardly course by Osmaston Hall to Derby, on the east side of which town it crosses the River Derwent, thence, by Little Chester and Breadsall, to Little Eaton, where it terminates. The branch to join the Erewash Canal commences from the main line, on the north side of the Derwent, near Derby, whence, taking an eastwardly course, by Chaddesden, Spondon, Borrowash, and Breaston, it terminates in the Erewash Canal, about three quarters of a mile south of the village of Sandiacre. The length of the main line, from the Grand Trunk Canal to Derby, is five miles and a quarter, with a rise of 12 feet; and, to its termination at Little Eaton, it is three miles and a quarter, with a further rise of 17 feet. The branch to the Erewash is eight miles and a half, with a fall of 29 feet. From the northern end of the main line at Eaton, a railway proceeds by Horsley and Kilbourn, to Smithy House, which is nearly four miles and three quarters in length. From Smithy House there is a branch one mile and three quarters in length, to the collieries at Henmoor, situated one mile and a half east of the town of Belper; another one mile and a half in length, by the potteries, to the extensive coal works near Denby Hall; with a collateral branch out of the last-mentioned branch, three quarters of a mile in length, to other collieries north of Salterswood.

The canal is 44 feet wide at top, 24 feet at the bottom, and 5 feet deep; but the head level of the canal, which is two miles in length, and terminates at Little Eaton, is made 1 foot deeper, that it may act as a reservoir. The locks are 90 feet in length, and 15 feet wide.

This canal and railways were made under the authority of an act of the 33rd George III. entitled, ' *An Act for making and*
' *maintaining a navigable Canal from the River Trent, at or near*
' *Swarkstone Bridge, to and through the borough of Derby, to Little*
' *Eaton, with a Cut out of the said Canal in or near the said bo-*
' *rough, to join the Erewash Canal near Sandiacre, and for making*
' *Railways from such Canal to several Collieries in the parishes or*
' *liberties of Denby, Horsley, and Smalley, all in the county of*

'*Derby.*' The proprietors of this canal and railways were incorporated by the name of "The Derby Canal Company," with power to raise among themselves the sum of £60,000, in six hundred shares of £100 each, and a further sum of £30,000, if necessary. The dividends of this concern are not to exceed eight per cent.; and after the sum of £4,000 is accumulated for the purpose of meeting any emergency, the rates are to be reduced, so that the profits may be no more, in future, than eight per cent.

TONNAGE RATES UNDER THIS ACT.

	s.	*d.*	
Lime, Lime-stone and other Stone, Coal and Coke, navigated only on that part of the Canal between the River Trent and the Grand Trunk Canal	0	3	per Ton.
Lime, Lime-stone and other Stone, Coal, Coke, and all other Goods and Merchandize, carried between the River Trent and the Town of Derby	0	9	ditto.
Lime and Lime-stone carried between Derby and Little Eaton, and upon the Railways	0	4	ditto.
Coal, Coke, and other Goods, ditto	1	5	ditto.
Bricks, Grit-stone, or Free-stone, for Building, ditto	0	3	ditto.
Coal, Coke, Lime, Lime-stone, and other Goods, Wares, or Merchandize, carried between Derby and the Erewash Canal	0	10	ditto.

TOLL ON THE RAILWAYS.

	d.
For every Horse, Mare, Gelding, Mule or Ass, (not carrying or drawing) which shall pass along the Railways	1
For all Cows and Horned or Neat Cattle	½

Boats laden with Straw, Corn in the Straw, or Hay, or any Kind of Manure, shall not pass a Lock without consent, unless the Water be running over the Waste Weir.

	d.	
In Consideration of the great Advantage which the Erewash Canal Company would, in all probability derive from this connexion with the Derby Canal, it is enacted, that for Coal or Coke navigated on the Erewash and passing thence into the Derby Canal, the Erewash Canal Company's Toll shall be no more than	5	per Ton.
And Mercantile Goods which shall pass on the Erewash, between the Derby Canal and the River Trent	3	ditto.

Lime and all other Articles navigated on the Erewash, and afterwards brought on the Derby Canal, One-half only of the Rates and Duties which they are empowered to charge under the Act of the 17th George III. but, should the Derby Canal Company ever permit any other Canal or Railway to be made between the Erewash Canal and the Town of Derby, in such Case, the Erewash Canal Company will be entitled to demand the full Toll granted by the above-mentioned Act. The Tonnage Rates on the Trent Navigation are also reduced in the same Proportion, upon all Goods which shall not have been carried on the Trent for a greater Distance than Three Miles, and which shall be carried on the Derby Canal, on the North Side of the Grand Trunk Canal.

EXEMPTION FROM TOLL.

Gravel and Sand for making and repairing any public Roads (Turnpike Roads excepted,) in any Township through which the Canal or Railways shall pass; also Dung, Soil, Marl, Ashes of Coal or Turf, and all other Manure (except Lime,) to be used only on the Lands in any Township through which the Canal or Railways pass; also Puncheons, Clogs, or other Wood to be used under ground in any of the Collieries on the Line of Canal, &c. provided Three Hours Notice be given, and that they do not pass a Lock, except at such Times as when the Water flows over the Waste Weir.

WHARFAGE.

For any Goods which shall remain more than One Month on the Wharf, a reasonable Satisfaction to be made.

For Goods which shall be carried into or out of the Grand Trunk or Trent or Mersey Canal, and navigated along that part of the Derby Canal which connects the River Trent and the Grand Trunk, the last-mentioned Company are entitled to One Shilling per Ton.

EXEMPTION FROM THE ABOVE TOLL.

Coal, Coke, Lime, Lime-stone, and Unwrought Stone, brought along the Derby Canal from its Northern Extremity, or from any of the Villages on the Line ; or gotten in any of the Parishes of Melborne, Stanton-by-Bridge, and Castle Donnington; and such Goods, Wares, and Merchandize to be used by Persons residing between the Trent and Mersey Canal and the River Trent, within the Parish of Swark-stone.

The Trent and Mersey Canal Company are also authorized to charge, for all Goods carried along or crossing the Canal, the same Amount of Toll as though they had navigated a full Mile; also for all Goods (except Bricks manufactured in the Parishes of Barrow, Twyford, Stenson, Findern, and Willington, and not passing any Lock of this Canal,) which shall be carried from the Westward of Swarkstone, and along the Derby Canal, and down the Derby Canal to Swarkstone, and from thence Westward on the Trent and Mersey Canal, such Tonnage Rates as the said Trent and Mersey Canal Company would have been entitled to, had such Goods been conveyed along their Canal from Swarkstone to Shardlow.

The Derby Canal Company are bound by this Act to make a Cut at Weston Cliff, to join the River Trent with the Grand Trunk Canal, (which is close on its Northern Bank,) whenever the Proprietors of Breedon Lime-stone Quarries shall require it, but not until a Canal or Railway be made between the Trent, at Weston Cliff, and the Works above-mentioned.

The Company have also engaged to make good to the Trustees of the Mansfield Road any Reduction on the Toll on Coal, which the making of their Canal may have occasioned ; that is, if such Reduction is below Four per Cent.

As this canal would greatly injure the revenue derived from the navigation of the River Derwent, which runs through Derby, this company were required to purchase it, which they did for the sum of £3,996.

For the use of the poor of Derby, five thousand tons of coal are annually permitted to pass, toll free, on this navigation, the distribution of which is under a committee of three members of the corporation of Derby, and the same number of proprietors of this undertaking.

This canal was finished in 1794, and it was made chiefly with the view of better supplying the populous town of Derby with coal, by means of its connection with the Erewash and Cromford Canals, and by the railways which extend to the collieries north of the town.

DERWENT RIVER.

6 George I. Cap. 27, Royal Assent 7th April, 1720.

THIS river has its source on the western side of that well
known mountainous tract, in the northern part of Derbyshire,
called the High Peak; whence, it pursues a south-eastwardly
course, forming, for some miles, the division between the counties
of Derby and York; thence, to Dinbank, where its stream is
considerably augmented by its junction with the mountain stream,
called the Ashop. From this place its course is southerly, by
Mytham Bridge, through a romantic country, by Baslow, and
through the princely grounds of Chatsworth, the seat of the Duke
of Devonshire; thence, to Rowsley, where the Wye falls into it.
Its course hence is by Matlock, Cromford, and Belper, to Derby.
From the last-mentioned place, its course is more eastwardly and
very circuitous, until it falls into the Trent, at Wilden Ferry,
below Shardlow, and at the place where the Trent and Mersey or
Grand Trunk Canal forms a junction with that river.

This river, from the Trent to the town of Derby, was made
navigable under powers granted by an act of 6th George I. entitled ' *An Act for making the River Derwent, in the county of*
' *Derby, navigable;*' but, as by the making of the Derby Canal
and branches, its use would be nearly superseded, all interest in it,
as a navigation, was disposed of to the Derby Canal Company,
for the sum of £3,996. The navigable part is thirteen miles in
length, and it was used chiefly for the supply of Derby and its
vicinity with coal.

DERWENT RIVER.

1 Anne, Cap. 20, Royal Assent 6th May, 1701.

THIS river has its source on the moors, near the Flask Inn,
about twelve miles north-west of Scarborough, and three miles
south-west of Robin Hood's Bay. It pursues a southerly course
through Harwood Dale, and by Hackness, the seat of Sir John
Vanden Bempdè Johnstone, Bart. thence, by East Ayton, to near

Ganton, whence it runs due east to Yedingham Bridge, to which place it is navigable for small barges. From Yedingham it pursues a sluggish course through the low marshy grounds north of Scamston Hall, to near Wycomb, where it is greatly augmented by the united waters of the Rye and Costa, which here fall into it. Hence, its course is by the town of New Malton, to which place, from the Ouze at Barmby-on-the-Marsh, it was made navigable under the powers of an act of the 1st of Anne, entitled, ' *An Act for making the River Derwent, in the county of York,* ' *navigable.*'

The course of the Derwent from Malton, lies through a beautifully diversified district, passing by Welham House, Mennithorpe, the ruins of Kirkham Abbey, Howsham Hall, Aldby Park, Stamford Bridge, and Kexby, to East Cottingwith, where the Pocklington Canal locks down into it. Thence, its course lies directly south, by Bubwith and Wressel Castle, to Barmby, where it falls into the tideway of the River Ouze, about seven miles below Selby.

The length of the original navigation to New Malton, is thirty-eight miles, viz. from the Ouze to the first lock, between Sutton-upon-Derwent and Elvington, is fifteen miles and a half; from thence, to Stamford Bridge Lock, six miles and a half; to Buttercrambe Lock, it is two miles and three quarters further; from whence, to the fourth lock, near Howsham Hall, it is three miles and a half; thence, to the last lock at Kirkham Abbey, it is two miles and a half; and to New Malton, it is seven miles. From the last-mentioned town, the river was made navigable, in 1805, to Yedingham Bridge, a distance of nearly eleven miles and a half, making a total navigation of forty-nine miles and a half in length.

This river, as a navigation, is the private property of Earl Fitzwilliam, and was, by his ancestor, the Marquis of Rockingham, let on lease to Mr. William Fenton, for the term of twenty-one years, commencing on the 20th of October, 1755; and subsequently, by the present noble owner, to Thomas and James Fenton, who quitted possession of it on the 25th March, 1805; since that period, we believe, it has been in the occupation of the proprietor, and is used chiefly for the supply of Malton, and the country through which it passes, with coal, deals, and general merchandize ; and for the export of the surplus agricultural produce, to the populous manufacturing districts of the West Riding.

DEVON RIVER.

This river rises on the south side of the Ochil Hills, in the county of Perth, from whence it takes an eastwardly course by Glendovan, whence it pursues a south-eastwardly direction by Muckhart to Fossaway, from whence it changes to a westwardly course by Dollar, Tillicouterie, and Sauchie, and falls into the River Forth about two miles and a half west of Alloa. As a tideway river it is navigable for some distance ; and at Cambus Quay, about one furlong from the mouth of the river, there is 12 feet water at neap tides, and a rise at spring tides of 20 feet. In 1765, and again in 1768, Mr. Smeaton examined the river, at the request of Lord Cathcart and the proprietors of the extensive collieries on its banks, with a view to extend the navigation to Mellock Glen Foot, either by deepening the river or making a canal along side of it. The estimate for the latter mode was £9,357, 1s. ; but, as no act was obtained for improving this navigation, it does not appear to have ever been carried into execution.

For the purpose of avoiding the difficult and circuitous course of the Forth between Alloa and the mouth of the Cambus, a cut was proposed between the last-mentioned town and the Devon, near Menstrie Bridge ; but it has not been executed. The object of these projected improvements was to facilitate the conveyance of coal to the Forth to be shipped.

DORSET AND SOMERSET CANAL.

36 George III. Cap. 47, Royal Assent 24th March, 1796.
43 George III. Cap. 108, Royal Assent 4th July, 1803.

The line of this projected canal commences from the navigable River Stour, at Gains Cross, in the parish of Shillingston Okeford, and county of Dorset, whence it proceeds in a north-westwardly direction by the towns of Sturminster Newton, Stalbridge, and within a mile of Wincaunton, whence it takes a northerly course, crossing the River Frome two miles north-west of Bruton; thence, along its western bank, and by Marston House to Frome, where it again crosses the river, and follows its course by the village of Road to the Kennet and Avon Canal at Widbrook, near the town of Bradford. A branch proceeds from Frome, by a very circuitous course, to the collieries at Nettle Bridge, situate near the eastern termination of the Mendip Hills.

The royal assent was given to an act for making this canal on the 24th of March, 1796, which is entitled, '*An Act for making a* '*navigable Canal from or near Gains Cross, in the parish of* '*Shillingston Okeford, in the county of Dorset, to communicate* '*with the Kennet and Avon Canal at or near Widbrook, in the* '*county of Wilts; and also a certain navigable Branch from the* '*intended Canal.*' The subscribers to this undertaking were incorporated by the name of " The Company of Proprietors of the " Dorset and Somerset Navigation," and empowered to raise among themselves the sum of £150,000, in fifteen hundred shares of £100 each, and an additional sum of £75,000, either by the admission of new subscribers, or on mortgage of the undertaking. Although another act was obtained in 1803, entitled, '*An Act for* '*enabling the Company of Proprietors of the Dorset and Somerset* '*Canal Navigation to raise a further Sum of Money towards* '*completing the said Canal, and for altering and amending an Act* '*passed in the Thirty-sixth Year of the Reign of his present* '*Majesty, for making and maintaining the said Navigation,*' yet it does not appear that any portion of the main line of canal was ever executed. A portion of the Nettle Bridge Branch was excavated; and upon a fall of 21 feet at Mells, near Frome, one of Fusell's balance locks was erected, and publicly tried on the 6th of September and 13th of October, with vessels of ten tons burthen; but, in consequence of the abandonment of the works generally, it never came into useful operation. The parliamentary line of this canal was forty miles in length, and the branch nine miles.

The chief object proposed by the projectors of this scheme, was to open an inland communication between the mining and manufacturing districts of Somerset, Gloucester, and Wilts, with the English Channel and the agricultural counties of Dorset and Hants.

DOUGLAS NAVIGATION.

(SEE LEEDS AND LIVERPOOL CANAL.)

DRIFFIELD NAVIGATION.

7 George III. Cap. 97, Royal Assent 20th May, 1767.
41 George III. Cap. 134, Royal Assent 2nd July, 1801.
57 George III. Cap. 64, Royal Assent 7th July, 1817.

THIS navigation commences at Aike Beck Mouth, in the River Hull, about four miles and a half north of Beverley, and half a mile above the place where the Leven Canal falls into that river. Its course is northwardly, passing Baswick Steer and Emmotland, to Fisholme Clough, to which place the navigation is continued along the original course of the Hull River, excepting in one instance, where a cut of three quarters of a mile in length is made near Hempholme, for the purpose of avoiding a circuitous part of the river. From Fisholme Clough, the remainder of the navigation to Great Driffield, is by an entire canal of nearly five miles and a half in length. The river part of this navigation, to Fisholme Clough, is five miles and three quarters; but the navigation is extended up Frodingham Beck, to the bridge, a distance of nearly a mile. From thence there is a private navigable cut made to Foston Mills, by the proprietor thereof, which is about three quarters of a mile in length.

The first act relating to this navigation was passed in the 7th of George III. and is entitled, ' *An Act for improving the Navi-* ' *gation of the River Hull and Frodingham Beck, from Aike Beck* ' *Mouth to the Clough, on the East Corner of Fisholme, and for* ' *extending the said Navigation, from the said Clough, into or near* ' *the town of Great Driffield, in the East Riding of the county of* ' *York;*' in the preamble of which it is stated, that it was then navigable to Fisholme, but might be greatly improved. Accordingly commissioners were appointed by this act to carry the necessary measures into effect, and to cut the canal to Driffield; for which purpose, they are empowered to borrow any sum of money, on security of the rates and duties, and, for the repayment of which, and legal interest, the act empowered them to demand the following tonnage rates.

TONNAGE RATES.

	s.	d.	
Wheat, Rye, Beans, Peas, or Rapeseed	0	6	per Quarter.
Malt, Oats, Barley, or any other Sort of Grain	0	4	ditto.
Meal or Flour	0	6	per Sack.
Coal, Culm, or Cinders .... {	3	6	per Chaldron of 48 Bushels.
Brick, Stone, Tile, or Lime, for Building...................	3	6	per Ton.
All other Goods, Wares, or Merchandize whatsoever	4	0	ditto.

And so in proportion for any greater or less Weight.

For any Goods, Wares, or Merchandize carried to or from the Village of Brigham, (which is situate Three Quarters of a Mile from Fisholme Clough,) a Moiety only of the above Tolls is to be demanded.

Pleasure Boats to pay for passing through each Lock the Sum of Sixpence.

A Public Wharf with Cranes is directed to be made at Great Driffield; the Rates and Duties payable thereat, to be settled by the Commissioners, or any Seven of them.

In the preamble of another act, passed in the 41st of George III. entitled, ' *An Act to amend an Act, passed in the Seventh Year* ' *of the Reign of his present Majesty, entitled, An Act for improving* ' *the Navigation of the River Hull and Frodingham Beck, from* ' *Aike Beck Mouth to the Clough, on the East Corner of Fisholme,* ' *and for extending the said Navigation, from the said Clough, into* ' *or near the town of Great Driffield, in the East Riding of the* ' *county of York, and to extend and improve the said Navigation,*' it is stated, that the commissioners had made considerable improvements in the navigation, but it was still very imperfect; they, therefore, obtain power to make cuts for avoiding considerable bends, particularly one from opposite Goodall Clough to Seven Hills; another from Emmotland to Corps Landing, situate on the West Beck; and to widen and make navigable the beck to Frodingham Bridge; also to take down and rebuild, within six years, Hull Bridge, near Beverley, and to maintain a towing path from that bridge to Fisholme.

In addition to the tolls granted by the preceding act, the following may be demanded for every article passing on any of the cuts.

ADDITIONAL RATES.

	s.	d.	
Wheat, Rye, Beans, Peas, or Rapeseed....................	0	3	per Quarter.
Malt, Oats, Barley, or any other Grain	0	2	ditto.
Meal or Flour .... {	0	3	per Sack of Five Bushels.
Coal, Culm, or Cinders .... {	1	9	per Chaldron of 48 Bushels.
Brick, Stone, Tile, or Lime, for Building	1	9	per Ton.
All other Goods, Wares or Merchandize....................	2	0	ditto.

TOWING PATH RATE.

		s.	d.
For every Description of Merchandize towed along the River by the Haling Paths from Hull Bridge to Fisholme, Corps-landing, and Frodingham..........	}	0	0¼ per Ton, per Mile.

After Hull Bridge is rebuilt, a Pontage Rate of Two Shillings and Sixpence will be levied on every Vessel passing under it, in lieu of the present Charge of Fourpence, which has hitherto been paid to the Corporation of the Town of Beverley, to whom the Bridge belonged.

For the Purpose of determining what Rates the Owners or Occupiers of Foston Mills (to which there is a private Navigation from Frodingham Bridge,) shall pay, an Arbitrator is appointed, whose Award is to be final.

The last act relating to this navigation received the royal assent on the 7th of July, 1817, and is entitled, ' *An Act to amend and* ' *enlarge the Powers of Two Acts of his present Majesty, for im-* ' *proving the Navigation of the River Hull and Frodingham Beck,* ' *and extending the same to the town of Great Driffield, in the* ' *county of York,*' in the preamble of which it is stated, that the commissioners borrowed, under authority of the act of 7th George III. the sum of £15,175, which sum was yet owing when the act was passed, together with an arrear of interest, amounting to £8,194, 10s.; and for carrying on the works directed to be done under the act of 41st George III. the sum of £6,143, 8s. was raised by subscription, of which sum, £4,300, 7s. 9d. was repaid, leaving due £1,843, 0s. 3d.; this act, therefore, directs that so soon as the principal and interest due to the mortgagees is paid off, the tolls are to be reduced, so that no greater income be derived from this navigation than is necessary to keep it in proper repair, and pay other incidental expenses.

To prevent the water in the river at Frodingham Bridge from being raised so as to injure the drainage of the adjacent lands, a mark was made in a stone on the steeple of Frodingham Church, on the 15th of September, 1815, which is 15 feet 11 inches above the level of the surface water; and by which the height of the water is to be hereafter regulated.

This navigation is chiefly used for the import of coal from the West Riding, and timber, deals, and groceries from Hull; and to export wool, corn, and other farming produce from the East Riding.

DROITWICH CANAL.

8 George III. Cap. 37, Royal Assent 29th January, 1768.

This canal commences at Chapel Bridge, in the town of Droitwich, whence it takes a south-eastwardly course, running parallel
with, and on the south bank of the Salwarp River, by the village
of that name, and at a short distance from Westwood, the seat of
Sir John Packington, Bart.; hence its course is continued by
Woods Mill, and it terminates half a mile west of Hawford Lodge,
and where the above-mentioned river falls into the Severn.

It is five miles and three quarters in length, with a fall, to the
Severn, of 56 feet 6 inches, by eight locks; and it was made under
the authority of an act of 8th George III. entitled, ' *An Act for*
' *making and maintaining a navigable Cut or Canal from the*
' *River Severn, at or near a place called Hawford, in the parish of*
' *Claines, in the county of Worcester, to or near a place called*
' *Chapel Bridge, within the borough of Droitwich, in the said*
' *county.*' The subscribers to this undertaking were incorporated
by the name of " The Company of Proprietors of the Droitwich
" Canal Navigation," with power to raise among themselves the
sum of £33,400, in three hundred and thirty-four shares of £100
each; and a further sum of £20,000, either among themselves or
by the admission of new subscribers. The original proprietors are
restricted to seven shares each; unless new ones be taken, for the
purpose of raising the additional £20,000, in which case they may
have five in addition.

TONNAGE RATES.

	s.	d.	
Salt, Coal, Stone, Slate or Flags	1	6	per Ton.
Wheat, Rye, Beans, Peas, Malt, Barley, Oats, or other Grain	0	2	per Quarter.
Meal	0	2	per Six Bushels.
All other Goods, Wares, or Merchandize	1	6	per Ton.

A clause is inserted in an act of the 31st George III. cap. 59,
for making the Worcester and Birmingham Canal, by which that
company are bound to make compensation to the Droitwich Canal
Company for any diminution which may be made in the profits of
their concern below five per cent. on every share, each being

reckoned at £160 at the least. This navigation was carried into execution by Mr. Brindley, and for the excellency of the works, is thought to be his *chef d'ouvre*.

The principal object the proprietors of this concern had in view, was to bring coal up to Droitwich, and to export salt, which is made from the brine springs abounding in the vicinity of that town, and which have so strongly impregnated the water of this canal, that the common fresh-water fish cannot live in it.

DUDLEY CANAL.

16 Geo. III. C. 66, R. A. 2nd Apr. 1776.　25 Geo. III. C. 87, R A. 4th July, 1785.
30 Geo. III. C. 60, R. A. 7th May, 1790.　33 Geo. III. C. 121, R. A. 17th June, 1793.
37 Geo. III. C. 13, R. A. 23rd Dec. 1796.

This canal commences from the Worcester and Birmingham Canal, near Selly Oak, in Worcestershire, and proceeds in a westwardly course to near Stone House, where it enters the Lapal Tunnel, which is three thousand seven hundred and seventy-six yards in length. From the west end of the tunnel at Lapal Lane (which is in a detached part of Shropshire,) the canal pursues a northerly course by the Leasowes, and within half a mile of the town of Hales Owen; a short distance beyond which, it enters another tunnel six hundred and twenty-three yards long, and egresses into the county of Stafford, near Gosty Hill, whence it continues a north-westwardly course to near Netherton; and after taking a circuit round the base of a hill to Dudley Woodside, enters a third tunnel two thousand nine hundred and twenty-six yards in length, and emerges near Tipton Green, within a short distance of which, it communicates with the Birmingham Canal. From near Dudley Woodside, a branch proceeds to join the Stourbridge Canal at Black Delph, about a mile north of the town of Stourbridge.

The main line of canal is thirteen miles in length, ten miles and a half of which, from Selly Oak, is level; thence, to the entrance of the Dudley Tunnel, there are five locks, rising 31 feet, and in the last furlong, before entering the Birmingham Canal, there is a fall of 13 feet, by two locks. The Black Delph Branch is two miles in length, with a fall, to the Stourbridge Canal, of 85 feet, by nine locks; the lockage water of which is chiefly supplied from Cradley Pool Reservoir.

The first act relating to this navigation was obtained in the
16th of George III. and entitled, ' *An Act for making and main-*
' *taining a navigable Canal, within and from certain Lands*
' *belonging to Thomas Talbot Foley, Esq. in the parish of Dudley,*
' *in the county of Worcester, to join and communicate with the*
' *Stourbridge Navigation, at a place called Black Delph, upon*
' *Pensnet Chace, in the parish of Kingswinford, in the county of*
' *Stafford.*' The original subscribers to this canal were only
twenty-one in number; amongst whom, however, was the Right
Honourable John Lord Dudley and Ward. They were incorporated by the name of " The Company of Proprietors of the
" Dudley Canal Navigation," with power to raise among themselves the sum of £7,000, in seventy shares of £100 each; and an
additional sum of £5,000, either among themselves, or by the
admission of new subscribers. By this act were also granted the
following

TONNAGE RATES.

	d.
Iron, Iron-stone, Coal, Timber, Stone, and all other Goods, Wares, and Merchandize, (for the whole Length, or any part of it)	6 per Ton.

Wharfage to be charged for any Goods lying more than Twenty-four Hours.

EXEMPTION.

Lime and Lime-stone to pay only One-third of the above Rates; but Paving-stones, Gravel, Sand, and other Materials for the repair of Roads, (except Lime-stone) Dung, Soil, Marl, and all Sorts of Manure for the Improvement only of Lands belonging to Persons whose Lands may be taken for this Canal is exempt, provided they do not pass a Lock, except at such times as when the Water flows over the Lock Weir.

Forty Feet of Round, or Fifty Feet of Square Oak, Ash, or Elm Timber, and Fifty Feet of Fir, or Deal, Balk, Poplar, and other Wood, shall be deemed a Ton; and Six Score Pounds Avoirdupois shall be deemed a Hundred Weight for the Purposes of this Act.

Boats under Fifteen Tons not to pass Locks without leave.

Owners of lands may erect wharfs, and are allowed the following rates.

RATES OF WHARFAGE.

	d.
For Coal, Lime, Lime-stone, Clay, Iron, Gravel, Timber, Stone, Brick, Tile, or Slate, which shall lie on the Wharfs more than Six Hours during the Day	1½ per Ton.
Any other Goods or Merchandize which shall not continue more than Six Days	3 ditto.

The second act was obtained in 1785, for the purpose of
opening a communication with the Birmingham Canal, which they
were prohibited from doing by a clause in the former act. It is

entitled, ' *An Act for extending the Dudley Canal to the Birming-*
' *ham Canal, at or near Tipton Green, in the county of Stafford;*'
and by which the Dudley Canal Company are empowered to
incorporate a certain number of new subscribers, to enable them
to raise the sum of £22,000, and an additional £5,000, if necessary,
for the purpose of carrying into execution the works proposed;
and the following are the additional rates allowed to be taken on
this canal.

ADDITIONAL TONNAGE RATES.

		d.
Coal, Coke, and Iron-stone, which shall have paid Tonnage to the Birmingham Canal......	3	per Ton.
For the same Articles, for which no Rates shall have been paid to the said Canal, and which shall pass through any part of the Dudley Tunnel......	3	ditto.
For the same Articles which pass between the South End of the Tunnel and the present Dudley Canal	3	ditto.
For the same Goods got or raised within a Mile of the Birmingham and Fazeley Canal, and which shall pass into the said Birmingham Canal......	½	ditto.
Lime and Lime-stone which shall pass out of the South End of the Tunnel	4½	ditto.
For the same which shall pass into the Birmingham Canal	½	ditto.
For all Stone, Timber, and other Goods......	6	ditto.

The original shares in the Dudley Canal were sixty-five; and
they may, by this act, be increased to one hundred and thirty.

In consideration of the permission granted to the Dudley Canal
to connect with the Birmingham Canal, the proprietors of the
last-mentioned navigation have had secured to them certain tonnage rates; for particulars of which, see Birmingham Canal
Navigation, p. 68.

By another act which received the royal sanction on the 7th of
May, 1790, entitled, ' *An Act for effectually carrying into Execution*
' *Two Acts passed in the Sixteenth and Twenty-fifth Years of the*
' *Reign of his present Majesty, for making and maintaining a*
' *navigable Canal from the Stourbridge Navigation to the Birming-*
' *ham and Birmingham and Fazeley Canal Navigation, in the*
' *counties of Worcester and Stafford,*' the company are authorized
to raise among themselves, for the purposes set forth in the title of
the act, the sum of £10,100, to be divided into new shares. They
may also, if necessary, borrow the further sum of £10,000, on
mortgage of the undertaking.

The act of the 33rd George III. enabling the Dudley Canal
Company to connect their navigation with the Worcester and

Birmingham Canal, received the royal assent on the 17th June, 1793; it is entitled, ' *An Act for making and maintaining a navi-* ' *gable Canal from the Dudley Canal, in the county of Worcester,* ' *to the Worcester and Birmingham Canal, now making at or near* ' *Selly Oak, in the said county ; and also certain collateral Cuts to* ' *communicate therewith.*' The new subscribers to this extension are incorporated and made part of the Dudley Canal Company, who are hereby empowered to raise £90,000, in nine hundred shares of £100 each, and an additional sum of £40,000, if necessary.

TONNAGE RATES.

	s.	d.	
Coal or Coke passing through the Lapal Tunnel, towards the Birmingham and Worcester Canal, but which shall not pass along the last-mentioned Canal, towards Birmingham, nor have paid any of the Rates or Duties payable to them under the Act of the 25th of his present Majesty	2	0	per Ton.
For the same Articles which shall have passed in the Direction above-mentioned, and which have paid any of the Rates and Dues under the said Act of 25th George III.	1	9	ditto.
For all Coal and Coke conveyed in the Direction above-described, and which shall have passed towards the Town of Birmingham, along that part of the Worcester and Birmingham Canal, and none other, nor have paid any of the Duties under the Act above-recited	2	0	ditto.
For the same Articles passing in the above Direction towards Birmingham, and which shall have paid the Dues authorized to be demanded under the Act above-mentioned	1	9	ditto.
Coal, Coke, and Iron-stone carried between the present Dudley Canal and the Lapal Tunnel, and which shall not pass into or through the Tunnel, or into the present Dudley Canal	0	2	per Ton, per Mile.
The above Articles carried between the Lapal Tunnel, and which shall pass out of this Canal, and into the present Dudley Canal, without having passed into or out of the said Tunnel	0	6	per Ton.
For all Goods, Wares, and Merchandize, (except Coal, Coke, Lime, and Lime-stone,) which shall pass into or through Lapal Tunnel, and which shall not have paid any of the Duties liable under the Act of 25th George III....	2	0	ditto.
For the above Articles which shall pass into or through the Tunnel above-mentioned, and which shall have paid the Charges under the above-recited Act........	1	6	ditto.
For all Goods, Wares, and other Merchandize (except Coal, Coke, Iron-stone, Lime and Lime-stone,) carried between the present Dudley Canal and Lapal Tunnel, without passing into or through such Tunnel	0	2	per Ton, per Mile.
For all Goods, Wares, Merchandize, Lime, Lime-stone, and other Commodities, carried between the Worcester and Birmingham Canal, and the East End of Lapal Tunnel, and which shall not have passed through such Tunnel	0	3	per Ton.
Lime and Lime-stone, which shall have paid the Tonnage imposed by the Act of 25th George III. upon Lime and Lime-stone, passing out of the South End of the Dudley Tunnel, and which shall not pass through the Gosty Hill Tunnel	0	1	per Ton, per Mile.

TONNAGE RATES CONTINUED.

	s.	d.	
Lime and Lime-stone, which shall have paid the Tonnage as above directed, and which shall pass through the Gosty Hill Tunnel	0	4½	per Ton.
Lime and Lime-stone, which has not paid the Duties under the Act of 25th George III. upon Lime and Lime-stone, passing out of the South End of Dudley Tunnel, and for which no other Rate is imposed by this present Act	0	9	ditto.
For all Goods, Wares, Merchandize, and Commodities, navigated on that part of the Dudley Canal made under the Powers of an Act of the 16th George III. and which shall not be liable to any other Rates in the 16th and 25th of George III. or this present Act	0	2	per Ton, per Mile.

There is a clause in this act which restrains the Dudley Canal Company from reducing the rates on any goods passing out of the Stourbridge Canal into this navigation, without first obtaining consent from the Worcester and Birmingham Canal Company, which company have, in return, agreed that when any reduction of the customary rates for navigating their canal shall take place, a similar reduction shall be made on all goods passing from the Dudley Canal, except such as go towards Birmingham ; and they further agree to take such rates only as will be found particularly described under the head, ' Worcester and Birmingham Canal.'

A stop lock is, by this act, directed to be made within five hundred yards of the Worcester and Birmingham Canal, to prevent loss of water; and if the two canals are not kept on one level, the passage may be stopped. It is also enacted, that if by reason of making this canal, the profits of the Stourbridge Navigation shall be reduced below £12 on each share, the Dudley Canal Company shall make up the deficiency, provided it does not amount to more than £3 per share, and provided the last-mentioned company shall, in the same year, have received by their rates £5 on each share.

The Worcester and Birmingham Canal Company are also, by this act, exonerated from the operations of that clause which rendered them liable to make up deficiencies to the Dudley Canal Company.

The last parliamentary enactment relating to this canal, occurs in the 37th of George III. and is entitled, ' *An Act to enable the* ' *Company of Proprietors of the Dudley Canal Navigation, to raise* ' *a further Sum of Money for completing the said Navigation ; and* ' *for amending the several Acts relating thereto ;*' in the preamble

o

of which we learn, that a considerable portion of the work, authorized by the preceding act of the 33rd George III. had been done, but that the sums they were empowered to raise by the above act being insufficient, the proprietors obtained power to raise among themselves, in proportion to their respective shares, (which amount to the sum of £175,325, deducting the sum of £6,000, which was directed to be raised by mortgage of the undertaking, or by the admission of new subscribers,) the sum of £40,000, which shall be raised and be made payable in the same way as if the whole sum of £40,000, authorized to be raised by the last-recited act, had been paid. The calls to be made in respect of the last-mentioned sum, is not to exceed, at any one time, the sum of £3 per cent. on the sum of £175,325, deducting the sum of £6,000 borrowed, or to be borrowed on mortgage, save and except two calls of £6 per cent. each on the above sum, to be made in March and September next ensuing the passing of this act. The proprietors have power to raise the above sum of £40,000, by mortgage of the undertaking, should they prefer it to the mode above-recited ; or the company's committee may borrow the above sum on their bond.

The depth of this canal is 5 feet, and width of the locks 7 feet; and the principal articles carried upon it are coal, iron-stone, lime, lime-stone, and manufactured iron goods; but in consequence of the communication which is effected with the Severn, by means of the Stourbridge Navigation, and by the Worcester and Birmingham Canal to the town of Birmingham, and thence, by numerous canals, to all parts of the midland counties and the eastern ports, a general and very extensive trade has been established upon this truly useful and improving navigation.

DUFFRYN LLYNVI AND PORTH CAWL RAILWAY.

6 George IV. Cap. 104, Royal Assent 10th June, 1825.
10 George IV. Cap. 38, Royal Assent 14th May, 1829.

THIS railway commences at the harbour of Pwll, or Porth Cawl, near Newton Nottage, in Glamorganshire, whence it proceeds by the above-named village, South Corneley and North Corneley, to Pyle, then taking an eastwardly course by the iron

works near Cefn Gribbwr, at which place the Bridgend Railway
communicates with it.   Hence, its course is by the collieries west
of St. Brides Minor; it then changes to a northerly direction,
running parallel with, and on the west side of the Little River
Llynvi, by Cavenydan, the village of Llangonoyd, and round the
east side of Troedrhwy Garth; and at about a mile north of this
place, it crosses the river, near Typhylly Chwyth, to Duffryn
Llynvi, where it terminates.   Its length is sixteen miles and three
quarters; the first seven of which, from the sea, is one inclined
plane, rising 200 feet; in the next seven miles and a quarter, it
rises 180 feet; it then rises 110 feet in the following two miles and
seven chains; from whence, to its termination at Duffryn Llynvi,
it is level.   The estimate for this work was made by Mr. John
Hodgkinson, and amounted to the sum of £40,000.   The act for
making it received the royal assent on the 10th of June, 1825, and
is entitled, ' *An Act for making and maintaining a Railway or*
' *Tramroad from, or from near to, a certain place called Duffryn*
' *Llynvi, in the parish of Llangonoyd, in the county of Glamorgan,*
' *to, or near to, a certain Bay, called Pwll Cawl, otherwise Porth*
' *Cawl, in the parish of Newton Nottage, in the same county ; and*
' *for extending and improving the said Bay, by the Erection of a*
' *Pier and other suitable Works for that Purpose.*'   The subscribers
consisted of fifty-seven persons, amongst whom were the Earl of
Dunraven, Sir John Nicholl and Sir Digby Mackworth, Baronets,
who were incorporated by the name of " The Duffryn Llynvi and
" Porth Cawl Railway Company," with power to raise among
themselves the sum of £40,000, in four hundred shares of £100
each, for the purposes of this act, (and which had already been
subscribed before application was made to parliament,) and a
further sum of £20,000, on mortgage of the undertaking.

TONNAGE RATES.

	d.
Lime-stone, Lime, Materials for the repair of Turnpike Roads or Highways, Dung, Compost, and all Sorts of Manure ..	$\frac{1}{2}$ per Ton, per Mile.
Coal, Culm, Coke, Cinders, Stone, Marl, Sand, Clay, Iron-stone, Iron-ore, and other Minerals, Building-stone, Pitching and Paving-stone, Bricks, Tiles, Slates, and all Gross and Unmanufactured Articles........................	1 ditto. ditto.
Iron, Lead, Timber, Staves, and Deals, and all other Goods, Wares, and Merchandize...............................	$2\frac{1}{2}$ ditto. ditto.

Fractions to be taken as for a Quarter of a Mile and as for a Quarter of a Ton.
For the Purposes of this Act, Twenty-one Hundred Weight shall be deemed a Ton.

HARBOUR DUES.

	d.
For every Ship or Vessel (except his Majesty's Vessels, and such as shall by Stress of Weather, be driven into, or in consequence of Accident at Sea, enter the said Bay, and shall not unload her Cargo for the Purpose of Sale)	2 per Ton.

The Burthen to be ascertained and charged according to the Custom-House Register.

Lords of manors or owners of lands may erect wharfs, but they are restricted to the following

WHARFAGE RATES.

	d.
Coal, Culm, Lime, Lime-stone, Clay, Iron, Iron-stone, Iron-ore, Lead-ore, or any other Ores, Timber, Stone, Brick, Tiles, Slate, Gravel, or other Things	1 per Ton.
For any Package not exceeding Fifty-six Pounds Weight	2
For any Package above Three Hundred Pounds Weight and not exceeding Six...	4
For any Package exceeding One Thousand Pounds Weight	6

The above Rates to be paid if the Goods remain on the Wharfs more than Two Calendar Months; but should such Articles continue above that Time, there shall be paid the further Sum of One Penny per Ton for Wharfage and Two-pence per Ton for the Warehousing for the next Seven Days; and the like Sum of One Penny and Two-pence respectively, per Ton, for every further Seven Days which such Articles shall remain upon such Quays, Wharfs, or Warehouses.

In 1829 the proprietors again applied for another act, entitled, ' *An Act to alter, amend, and enlarge the Powers of an Act passed* ' *in the Sixth Year of the Reign of his present Majesty, for making* ' *and maintaining the Duffryn Llynvi and Porth Cawl Railway,* ' *and other Works connected therewith,*' in the preamble of which we learn, that the sum of £40,000 (being the amount of the estimate,) had been expended, and also the sum of £8,000, which last sum was all the money the company were enabled to raise of the £20,000 which the act of 6th George IV. empowered them to borrow by way of mortgage.

This last act is, therefore, chiefly obtained for the purpose of raising the remainder of the last-mentioned sum of £20,000, and to enable the company to admit mortgagees to become proprietors, to the amount of their respective claims upon the company.

The object of this railway is to open the extensive limestone and freestone quarries, and the numerous mines of iron-ore and coal, which abound in the immediate vicinity of its course.

DULAIS RAILWAY.

7 George IV. Cap. 102, Royal Assent 26th May, 1826.

THIS railway, commencing at Aber Dulais, near the canal which crosses the River Neath at its junction with the Dulais River, runs parallel with the latter on the western bank, for nearly five miles, to Ynis-y-bout; at this place it crosses the river and keeps the eastern bank till it reaches the lime works of Cwm-Dulais. It is on one inclined plane of eight miles, five furlongs and five chains, from Aber Dulais to its termination, in which distance there is a rise of 426 feet. The survey and estimate, amounting to £8,730, were made by Mr. William Brough, civil engineer.

The act for executing this work is entitled, '*An Act for making*
'*and maintaining a Railway, or Tramroad, from or from near a*
'*certain place called Aber Dulais to or near to a certain other place*
'*called Cwm Dulais, both in the parish of Cadoxtone-Juxta-Neath,*
'*in the county of Glamorgan.*'

The company, which consisted of fifteen persons, at the time the act was obtained, were incorporated under the name and style of " The Dulais Railway Company." They subscribed the sum of £10,000 which was divided into two hundred shares of £50 each, and power was granted to raise a further sum of £4,000, by way of mortgage of the rates. It is provided by the act that no more than three tons, including the weight of the carriage, shall be conveyed on this road in a waggon having two wheels, nor more than four tons, also including the weight of the carriage, in waggons having four wheels.

TONNAGE RATES.

	d.	
For all Iron-stone, Iron-ore, Charcoal, Coal, Culm, Stone Coal, Coke, Cinders, Timber, Stone, Tiles, Bricks, Clay, Lime-stone, Lime and Manures	1½ per Ton, per Mile.	
For all Pig-iron...	2½ ditto.	ditto.
For all Iron Castings	3 ditto.	ditto.
For all other Goods, Wares, Merchandize and other Things not before enumerated	4 ditto.	ditto.

Tolls to be taken for fractional Parts of a Ton or Mile.

DUNDEE AND NEWTYLE RAILWAY.

7 George IV. Cap. 101, Royal Assent 26th May, 1826.
11 George IV. Cap. 60, Royal Assent 29th May, 1830.

THIS railway commences on the north side of the royal burgh and port of Dundee, whence it takes a northwardly course, through Stirlings Park, the parish of Mains, and across Bakers Brig Burn; thence, through the parish of Strathmartin, and over the water of Dighty, to within a short distance of Auchterhouse Castle; from whence it passes over a low part of the Sadley Hills, to the mill at Newtyle, where it terminates. It is in length eleven miles and a half; in the first six furlongs of which, from Dundee, it rises 84 feet 5 inches from the level of low water, spring tides; there is then an inclined plane seven hundred and three yards in length, rising 244 feet 4 inches, from the end of which it is continued level for the space of nearly four miles and three quarters; from whence another inclined plane extends sixteen hundred and ninety yards, and rises 200 feet; from the engine, placed on the top of this plane, it continues, for the distance of four miles and a furlong, with a rise of only 3 feet 9 inches; at this point another stationary engine is to be erected, and from whence, to its termination at Newtyle, there is another inclined plane one thousand and twenty-five yards in length, descending 244 feet 7 inches. Mr. C. Langdale designed and laid out this railway, and estimated the cost, including three steam engines of sufficient power to work the inclined planes, at the sum of £27,600. The first act for making it received the royal sanction on the 26th of May, 1826, and is entitled, ' *An Act for making a Railway from the Royal Burgh* ' *and Port of Dundee, in the county of Forfar, to Newtyle, in the* ' *said county;*' and by which the subscribers, eighteen in number, together with the magistrates and town council of Dundee, were incorporated by the name of " The Dundee and Newtyle Railway " Company," and empowered to raise among themselves the sum of £30,000, in six hundred shares of £50 each; and, if necessary, a further sum of £10,000, on the credit of the undertaking.

TONNAGE RATES.

		d.
For every Description of Goods, Wares, Merchandize, or other Things	}	6 per Ton, per Mile.
For each Passenger travelling in any Carriage upon the Railway		3 per Mile.

Fractions to be taken as for a Quarter of a Mile, and as for a Quarter of a Ton.

Land-owners may construct wharfs and erect warehouses, for which the following rates are allowed.

WHARFAGE RATES.

	d.
Coal, Culm, Lime, Lime-stone, Clay, Iron-stone, Stone, Bricks, Gravel, Hay, Straw, Corn in the Straw, or Manure (remaining less than Six Months)	} ½ per Ton.
Iron, Lead-ore, or other Ore, Tin, Timber, Tiles, and Slates (ditto)	½ ditto.
For any other Goods, Wares, or Merchandize (ditto)	2 ditto.

ADDITIONAL WHARFAGE RATES,

To be paid by the Month, for such Articles as remain more than Six Days beyond the Period of Six Months, and so in Proportion for any less Time than a Month.

	d.
For the First Series of Articles as above enumerated	¼ per Ton, per Month.
For the Second List of enumerated Articles	½ ditto. ditto.
And for the Last	1 per Ton.

Seven years are allowed by the above-named act for the due execution of its provisions; and if the railway is not then finished, the power to do so will cease, except as to such part of it as may then be completed.

But the company of proprietors of this railway having raised and nearly expended all the money authorized to be raised under the authority of the 7th George IV. and their works being yet incomplete, applied to parliament last session for power to raise an additional sum; accordingly the royal assent was given on the 29th May last to an act, entitled, ' *An Act to amend an Act for* ' *making a Railway from Dundee to Newtyle.*' By this last act they are empowered to raise amongst themselves, or by the admission of new subscribers, in addition to the sum authorized by and under the act of 7th George IV. the further sum of £10,000, to be applied in the first place to paying the expense of obtaining this act, then in paying the sums borrowed under the former act, and afterwards in completing the necessary works; and such further sum is directed to be divided into shares of £50 each, to be consolidated with the original shares. The proprietors may also borrow the further sum of £20,000 over and above the sum of £10,000

which the first recited act enables them to raise, and to pay off
and again borrow, when necessary, any portion of the above sums;
but the company are restrained from ever increasing their debt to
more than £30,000 at one time.

For the purpose of facilitating the communication between the
railway and the port of Dundee, the proprietors have authority to
treat with the owners of property for a branch railway, upon
which, this act empowers them to demand the same tonnage rates
as upon the original line.

This railway will be very important to the mountainous district of country through which it passes, affording access to the
port of Dundee, which heretofore seemed quite impracticable..

DUN RIVER NAVIGATION.

12 Geo. I. C. 38, R A. 24th May, 1726.　13 Geo. I. C. 20, R. A. 24th Apr. 1727.
6 Geo. II. C. 9, R. A. 21st Mar. 1732.　13 Geo. II C. 11, R. A. 19th Mar. 1739.
2 Geo. IV. C. 46, R. A. 7th May, 1821.　7 Geo. IV. C. 97, R. A. 26th May, 1826.

THE River Dun has its source near Saltersbrook, in the high
moorlands which separate the counties of York and Chester, and
pursues an eastwardly course by Thurlstone and Peniston, whence
it takes a south-eastwardly direction by Huthwaite, and near
to Wortley Hall, the residence of Lord Wharncliffe; its line from
hence is through a deep and romantic dale, overhung by extensive
woods; thence it passes the villages of Oughtibridge and Wadsley,
to the town of Sheffield, on the north-east side of which it is joined
by the River Sheaf. Its course hence is north-eastwardly by the
village of Attercliff to Tinsley, where this navigation commences.

In describing the line of this navigation, we shall introduce the
numerous cuts and improvements which the act of 7th George IV.
enables the company to make, and which are now in progress.

This navigation begins in the Dun River, near the village of
Tinsley, thence by the Tinsley Cut, which was made to avoid a bend
in the river, under powers of the act of 12th George I.; and, at the
distance of five furlongs it locks down into the river. The Dun is
here the course of the navigation to the Ickles Cut, constructed
under the powers of the above-recited act, upon the north side of
the river, and which is something more than three furlongs in
length. The river again becomes navigable to the Rotherham

Cut, which cut runs parallel with the old river, and on its northern bank, for the length of a mile, where it locks down into the river at Eastwood; but, instead of this, a new canal is to be continued from Eastwood, along the north side of the river, to near Aldwark Mill, which is in length twelve hundred and twenty yards; the river from hence becomes the course of the navigation for a short distance, where another cut, of three hundred and seventy yards in length, is intended to be made, for the twofold purpose of avoiding a considerable bend in the river, and passing the mill; the Old Aldwark Cut will consequently be abandoned. From the east end of the intended cut at Aldwark, the navigation is continued for two miles in the old bed of the Dun; it then enters the Kilnhurst Cut, along which, and through Swinton and Mexbrough Cuts, it continues on the north side of the river, to near Mexbrough Church, where it again locks down into the Dun; but the canal is to be extended to the river, near the west end of the Denaby Cut, where the navigation is to be continued along the old line of the river as a canal, while a new channel, three hundred and sixty yards in length, is to be excavated for the river, between the present course and Denaby Cut. From the Dun, at Bull Green, a little above the east end of the last-mentioned old cut, a new canal is intended to be made along the north bank of the river, to a bend about a furlong west of the place where the Dearne River falls into the Dun. The length of the new cuts, from Mexbrough Church to the last-mentioned place, are two thousand two hundred and twenty yards. Hence the navigation is continued along the river, about half a furlong beyond the junction with the Dearne, to a place in the river called the Devil's Elbow, where a new river channel, one hundred and thirty yards in length, is to be opened. Hence the river is continued as the navigation to within half a furlong of Conisbrough Cut, which is to be abandoned, and a new canal, in lieu thereof, four hundred and forty yards in length, is intended to be made on the north side of the river and cut; from the end of which, the navigation continues in the river to near Sprotbrough Mills; but to pass which there is an old cut three furlongs in length. From Sprotbrough Cut, the navigation makes a considerable detour by Sprotbrough Hall, (the seat of Sir John Copley, Bart.) towards Balby, and by Hexthorpe and Newton, to Doncaster.

The length of the navigation from Tinsley to Doncaster, by the old course, is twenty-one miles, and by the course as it is intended to be improved, it will be eighteen miles only, with a fall of 67 feet 6 inches, by eleven locks. From Doncaster Mill the course of the navigation is very circuitous to Milethorne, or Redcliffe Lock, where there is a short cut; thence passing by Wheatley (the residence of Sir W. B. Cooke, Bart.) in a crooked course to about midway between Wheatley and Long Sandall, where a new channel for the river, nearly three furlongs in length, is directed to be made on the west side of the river, which shortens it considerably. The river is again the navigation to Long Sandall Cut, where it will be diverted to the west side of its present line, and the old bed of the river will become the continuation of the Kirk Sandall Cut, from Long Sandall Lock to the cut last-mentioned; thence taking a direct course to Barmby Dun, and across the low grounds to South Bramwith and Stainforth, a distance of five miles, where it locks down into the river, and also communicates with the Stainforth and Keadby Canal. From this point the river proceeds to Fishlake Ferry, from which place the navigation company have the power to charge dues. The navigation hence proceeds in an eastwardly course to Thorne Quay, whence it runs directly north, to New Bridge; it then proceeds eastwardly, and in nearly a straight line, until it enters the Ouze, at the port of Goole. From New Bridge, the original course of the Dun was by Turnbridge, to the River Aire, into which it entered about three quarters of a mile west of Rawcliffe; but, since its waters have been directed into the Dutch River, the ancient course has been suffered to silt up. The present line of the navigation, from New Bridge to Goole, was formerly two parallel drains, cut by Sir Cornelius Vermueden, a Dutchman, in the beginning of the reign of Charles the First, for the purpose of draining the low lands in the vicinity of Hatfield Chase; and his successors, now called the participants, levy an acre-age rent upon the lands so benefited. A great flood happening about the year 1688, the sluices at Goole were carried away, and the tides having free access to these drains, they had the effect of destroying the division between them; so that as nothing but the outward banks remain, it assumes the appearance of a very wide canal, which, at high water, in spring tides, is navigable for brigs of three hundred tons burthen. There are three draw bridges over this part of the River Dun or Dutch River, which are kept in repair by the Dun Navigation Company, to whom a certain pontage is paid for every vessel passing through the same. The length of the navigation, from Doncaster Mills to Fishlake Ferry, which formerly was above twelve miles, is now reduced to ten miles and a quarter; and from thence to New Bridge, five miles and a half; from New Bridge to Goole, by the Dutch River, is five miles and a quarter. When the tide flows 15 feet at Goole, it will flow only 7 feet at Fishlake, and but $3\frac{1}{2}$ at Barmby Dun Ford.

The total length of the navigation, from the River Ouze to Tinsley, when the improvements are completed, will only be thirty-nine miles, and the total rise, by sixteen locks, from low water mark in the Dutch River, is $92\frac{1}{4}$ feet; viz. from low water mark to the crown of Doncaster Mill Weir, $24\frac{3}{4}$ feet, by five locks; and from thence to the highest level on the navigation $67\frac{1}{2}$ feet, by eleven locks.

This navigation is joined by the Sheffield Canal in Tinsley Cut; and, from the west end of the Ickles Cut on this navigation, a private canal, called the Holmes Goit, proceeds from it to Masbrough Iron Works. From the west end of the Old Rotherham Cut, there is another private canal, extending to the Greasborough Coal and Iron Works. In the side cut of the Dun, near Swinton Pottery, the Dearne and Dove Canal forms a junction with this navigation; and, at Stainforth, the Stainforth and Keadby Canal proceeds from it.

The first parliamentary enactment relating to this navigation was in the 12th George I. and entitled, ' *An Act for making the* ' *River Dun, in the West Riding of the county of York, navigable* ' *from Holmstile in Doncaster, up to the utmost extent of Tinsley,* ' *westward, a township within two miles of Sheffield;*' by which the masters, wardens, searchers, assistants, and commonalty of the company of cutlers in Hallamshire, in the county of York, were appointed undertakers of the navigation, with power to make it navigable at their own expense, within the limits prescribed by the title of the act; by which also the following tonnage rates were allowed.

TONNAGE RATES OF 12 GEORGE I.

	s.	d.	
Lead or Lead-ore	2	6	per Fodder.
Iron, Steel, Horns, Hoofs, Bones and Box-wood	3	0	per Ton.
Deals, Boards, or Foreign Timber, Cheese, Salt, Corn, Cutlery Wares, Iron Wares, Groceries or other Merchandize	3	6	ditto.
Lime or Lime-stone brought up to Rotherham or Aldwark Wash	0	6	ditto.
Lime or Lime-stone brought up to Tinsley	0	9	ditto.
Ditto carried up or down the said River, to Doncaster Wash, or any other Place between Aldwark Wash and Doncaster	0	3	ditto.
Coal, Stone, Iron, Sough, Metal, and Foreign Timber, from Tinsley down to Holmstile or Doncaster, or *vice versa*	2	6	ditto.
Wood and English Timber from Tinsley to Doncaster, and *vice versa*	1	6	ditto.
Ditto, from Rotherham to Holmstile	1	0	ditto.
Coal, Stone, Iron, Sough, Metal, and Foreign Timber, from Rotherham to Holmstile	2	0	ditto.
Ditto, from any Place between Rotherham and Kilnhurst Works; and from thence to Denaby, Mexbrough, and Conisbrough	1	6	ditto.
Or on any part of the Navigation between Conisbrough and Holmstile	1	0	ditto.

In addition to these, is a Toll of One Penny for every customary Ton of Goods carried upwards or downwards through the Township of Tinsley, to be applied to the making and repairing of the Road between Tinsley and Sheffield.

There is also another Toll of One Penny for every customary Ton of Twenty-five Hundred Weight, which shall be brought to, or carried from, any Wharf at or near Tinsley, to be carried up or down the said River.

The year following the passing of the above-recited act, the mayor, aldermen, and burgesses of the borough of Doncaster, obtained an act, entitled, ' *An Act for improving the Navigation of* ' *the River Dun, from a place called Holmstile, in the township of* ' *Doncaster, in the county of York, to Wilsick House, in the* ' *township of Barmby Dun, in the said county,*' by which they are appointed undertakers of this part of the navigation.

In addition to the tonnage rates granted for the lower part of this navigation, certain duties are directed to be paid to the corporation of Doncaster, as a remuneration for the expenses they are at in maintaining three draw bridges over the Dutch River, which are by this act granted to them, besides the annual sum of £20, payable by the participants and owners of lands in the level of Hatfield Chase.

Under the powers of the above-recited acts, the two navigation companies together expended, in the necessary works, the sum of £17,250, but on finding it would be to their common advantage to unite into one company, an act was obtained in the 6th George II. for this purpose, which is entitled, ' *An Act to explain and* ' *amend Two Acts of Parliament, one made in the Twelfth and the* ' *other in the Thirteenth Years of his late Majesty's Reign, for*

' making navigable the River Dun, in the county of York, and for
' the better perfecting and maintaining the said Navigation, and for
' uniting the several Proprietors thereof into one Company.'

It was accordingly divided into one hundred and fifty shares, being at the rate of £115 per share on the amount expended. The proprietors of the upper part consisted of forty-nine persons, besides the cutlers' company; and the ownership of the lower part was vested in the corporation of Doncaster, and twenty other persons. These several parties are therefore incorporated in one company, by the name of " The Company of Proprietors of the " Navigation of the River Dun;" and the several tonnage rates, and other duties, hitherto received by either party, is hereafter to form one fund, (except the duty of one penny a fodder for lead, and two-pence a ton for other goods and merchandize, except lime and limestone to be converted into lime,) which the mayor, aldermen, and burgesses of the borough of Doncaster, are empowered to take, by virtue of the act of 12th of George I. in lieu of an ancient toll. Of the one hundred and fifty shares of which the navigation consists, ten are, by this act, appropriated to the corporation of Doncaster, six to the cutlers' company, ten to seven persons as trustees to the town of Sheffield, and the remainder among private individuals.

ADDITIONAL TONNAGE RATES.

d.

For any Goods or Merchandize which shall be landed or loaded from off or upon any Wharf or Place on the South Side of the River Dun, or Cheswould, between Holmstile and Fryers Bridge, which shall not pass, or shall not have passed, the Lock at Doncaster Mill .... } 2 per Ton, of 2,500 lbs.

The navigation is directed to be made to the farthest part of the township of Tinsley, westward, for vessels of twenty tons burthen; and if not done within the space of two years from the passing of this act, the cutlers' company are authorized to do it at their own expense, and to collect, for their own use, all the duties which may arise upon any part of the river between Mexbrough and Tinsley. The navigation company have, by this act, jurisdiction only as far down the river as Wilsick House; below that place to New Bridge it is subject to the commissioners of the level of Hatfield Chase; and the New or Dutch River, to the mayor and commonalty of the city of York, as conservators of the Ouze.

In 1739 a fourth act was obtained, entitled, '*An Act for the*
'*more effectual improving the Navigation of the River Dun, from*
'*a place called Wilsick House, in the parish of Barmby Dun, in*
'*the county of York, to Fishlock Ferry, in the same county,*' in
consequence of the imperfect state of the river between the
above-mentioned places, which, in dry seasons and neap tides, was
impassable. The improvements, authorized by this act, have been
carried into effect, by making a canal from Bramwith to Stainforth,
and by deepening the channel from the west end of this cut to
Wilsick House.

ADDITIONAL RATES ALLOWED BY THIS ACT.

	d.	
Coal and Bark, Lime, Stone, Wood and Timber of English Growth, passing up or down the River Dun, through the lower End of the Cut at Barmby Dun, and by the new proposed Stainforth Cut................................	2	per Customary Ton of 25 Cwt.
All other Goods, Wares, or Merchandize..................	4	ditto.

EXEMPTION.

All Goods and Commodities whatsoever, the Produce of the Neighbourhood between
Goole and the lower End of the Cut at Barmby, which shall be shipped between
these Places, and which shall be carried above the lower End of the Barmby Cut.

Any Goods passing down the Dun, and landed anywhere between the Barmby Cut
and Goole, and not shipped again, are also exempted from the above Toll. Grain
put on board below Doncaster Mill Dam, to go down the River, is also free of the
Duties chargeable under this Act.

	d.	
All Goods belonging to the Inhabitants of Doncaster, or any Inhabitant of the Country between that Place and Goole, passing through the Stainforth Cut...	2	per Ton.
And, under the Act of the 13th George I. the further Toll only of......	2	ditto.

For the purpose of repairing the Roads between Sheffield and Tinsley, a Toll of One
Penny per Ton is to be levied on all Goods brought to the Wharf at Tinsley to be
shipped on this Navigation.

From the date of the last-recited act, a period of eighty-two
years elapsed before any additional parliamentary enactment was
passed relative to this navigation; but, in consequence of the
delays to which the increasing trade of the country were subjected
by the shallows in the river below Sandall Lock, an act was passed
to enable the company to avoid them, by making a new canal
from Sandall to the west end of the Stainforth Cut; which act is
entitled, '*An Act for improving the River Dun, and for altering*
'*the Course thereof, by making certain new Cuts or Canals from*
'*the same, and for amending, altering, and enlarging the Powers*
'*granted to the River Dun Company, by several Acts relating to*
'*the said Navigation.*' The proprietors are further authorized to

make two short cuts, or a new river channel, four hundred and
seventy-three yards in length, in Arksey Ings, for the purpose of
cutting off two considerable bends in the river; also a new channel
for the river at Sandall, six hundred and sixty yards in length.
To carry these into execution, the proprietors of the navigation
are empowered to borrow the sum of £40,000, on the credit of
the undertaking.

ADDITIONAL RATES ALLOWED BY THIS ACT.

		d.
Lead, Iron, Iron-castings, and Steel, Horns, Hoofs, Bones, Box-wood, Timber, Broken and Unbroken Deals, Boards, Cheese, Salt, Cutler's Wares, Iron Wares, and all other Merchandize, conveyed along all or any of these proposed Cuts	}	10 per Ton.
Metal Iron for Ballast..		6 ditto.
English Pig-iron		8 ditto.
Corn, Grain, or Malt (per Eight Bushels Winchester)...........		1 per Quarter.
Lime or Lime-stone (except from Conisbrough, Warmsworth, Sprotbrough, Cadeby, and Newton)........................	}	2 per Ton.
Stone	{	6 per Ton, of 18 Cubic Feet.
Ditto, put on Board between Barmby Dun and South Bramwith, and going down the River..................................	}	3 ditto.

Coal is exempted from any additional Toll; but the Act determines that the customary Ton thereof shall not in future exceed Forty-five Hundred Weight, or
Five Thousand and Forty Pounds.

The last act relating to this navigation, received the royal
assent on the 26th of May, 1826, and is entitled, ' *An Act for*
' *improving the Navigation of the River Dun, and for altering the*
' *Course thereof, by making certain new Cuts or Canals from the*
' *same ; and for amending, altering, and enlarging the Powers*
' *granted to the Company of Proprietors, by several Acts now in*
' *force.*'

The improvements here contemplated, were designed by
Mr. G. Leather, and consist chiefly of five new cuts, which
considerably shorten, and otherwise improve this important navigation.   They are two miles and a half in length, and are particularly described at the beginning of this article.   The estimated
cost is £64,000.

To carry these alterations into effect, the act empowers the
company of proprietors to borrow the amount of the estimate, on
mortgage of the rates and duties arising on this navigation.   Ten
years are allowed for the completion of the works hereby authorized to be made.

ADDITIONAL RATES GRANTED BY THIS ACT.

d.

For every Vessel, either empty or containing less than Four Tons of⎫
   Twenty-five Hundred Weight, and passing through the Mex-⎬ 3
   brough New Cut ....⎭

For every Vessel loaded solely with Coal, Stone, or Lime-stone......   7½

For all other Goods, Wares, or Merchandize (but not exceeding Two⎫ ¾ per Ton, of
   Shillings per Vessel)...⎭   25 Cwt.

The same Rates for all Vessels, empty or loaded, as above, which pass the New Cut or
     Canal to be made at Eastwood.

Note.—That if empty Vessels, which have paid the above Rate, should return laden
   with Lime-stone from the Parishes of Doncaster, Warmsworth, Conisbrough, or
   Sprotbrough, the Rate so levied shall be returned.

The two tolls of one penny each, which were levied for the purpose of keeping in repair the road from Tinsley to Sheffield, is, by an act of the 55th George III. entitled, ' *An Act for making* ' *and maintaining a navigable Canal from Sheffield to Tinsley, in* ' *the West Riding of the county of York,*' vested in the company of proprietors of the Sheffield Canal.

By an act of 33rd George III. cap. 117, for making the Stainforth and Keadby Canal, it is enacted, that all vessels which turn out of the Dun Navigation Cut, and pass down this canal, shall pay to the Dun Company the same rates as though the vessel passed through the lock near the junction.

The Dun Navigation is of the utmost importance for exporting the produce of the extensive coal and iron works which abound at its western extremity; also the vast quantity of manufactured iron goods and cutlery which is annually produced in the populous town and neighbourhood of Sheffield. The trade of Rotherham, the limestone and plaster at Sprotbrough, and other places in the line, together with the agricultural produce of the neighbourhood of Doncaster, constitute a considerable branch of traffic on this navigation. The imports consist of every article requisite for the supply of an extensive, populous, and manufacturing district.

EDEN RIVER.

8 George I. Cap. 14, Royal Assent 12th February, 1721.

THIS river rises near Pendragon Castle, in Westmoreland, and among that range of hills on which Shunnor Fell stands conspicuous, at an elevation of 2,329 feet above the level of the sea. Its course is northerly, by the town of Kirkby Stephen, and near to the town of Brough, and thence, in a north-westwardly direction by Appleby to Edenhall Hall, near which it is joined by the River Eamont, which flows from the beautiful lake of Ulles Water, and by Penrith, and at the same time, forms the division between the counties of Westmoreland and Cumberland. From the junction above-mentioned, it winds through a fine country, by the town of Kirkoswald, Armathwaite, and Corby Castle, to Warwick Hall, where it receives the waters of the Little River Irthing. From this place it runs westward, by a winding course, to the city of Carlisle, at the bridge of which place the navigation commences. From Carlisle its course is very circuitous, passing Grinsdale, Kirkandrews, Beaumont, and Rockcliff, to Burgh Marsh Point, where it falls into the Solway Firth. Its length is ten miles and a quarter; the tide flows the whole distance, and it was made navigable under authority of an act of 8th George I. entitled, ' *An Act for making the River Eden navigable to Bank End,* ' *in the county of Cumberland.*'

This river was chiefly used for importing supplies to the city of Carlisle, and to export its various manufactures; but since the opening of the Carlisle Canal, the transit of merchandize has been principally through the latter channel ; and, consequently, the navigation of the river has been nearly superseded.

EDINBURGH AND DALKEITH RAILWAY.

7 George IV. Cap. 98, Royal Assent 26th May, 1826.
10 George IV. Cap. 122, Royal Assent 4th June, 1829.

This railway commences on the south side of the city of Edinburgh, near Salisbury Craigs, from whence it proceeds in an eastwardly direction, skirting the King's Park ; thence, on the south side of Duddingston House, and by the village of Hunters Hall, to Redrow, where it communicates with the Edmonstone Railway. It afterwards takes a southerly course by Miller Hill Row, to within half a mile of the west side of the town of Dalkeith, where it crosses the North Esk River ; thence, to the banks of South Esk River, at Dalhousie Mains, near Newbattle Abbey, from whence, the last act enables the company to extend it to Newton Grange.

There is a branch from Wanton Walls to Fisher Row Harbour, in the Firth of Forth; another from Cairney to the collieries situate on the east side of the Esk, at Cowpits, near Musselburgh; and another by a subsequent act, which extends to Leith Harbour. The main line of this railroad, with the extension to Newton Grange, to be made under powers of the act of 10th George IV. is ten miles and three quarters; the first three furlongs of which, from the depôt at Edinburgh, is level; it then descends 130 feet, by an inclined plane five furlongs in length, in which distance it passes through a tunnel of six hundred yards. From the end of the inclined plane, it continues level for three miles; when there is a rise of 150 feet to its termination, which is at an elevation of 280 feet above the level of the sea.

The branch to Cowpits is one mile and a half in length, and that to Fisher Row Harbour one mile and a quarter. Other branches to Duddingston, Salt Pans, and Portobello, were in contemplation before the first application to parliament, but were subsequently abandoned. Mr. James Jardine, of Edinburgh, projected this railway, and estimated the cost at £70,125; of which sum, £56,150 was subscribed at the time the act was obtained.

The first act relating to this railway received the royal assent on the 26th of May, 1826; it is entitled, ' *An Act for making and* ' *maintaining a Railway from Edinburgh to the South Side of the* ' *River North Esk, near Dalkeith and Newbattle, with Branches* ' *therefrom, all in the county of Edinburgh.*' The subscribers to this undertaking, at the time the above act was obtained, were eighty-seven in number, amongst whom were the Duke of Buccleugh and Queensberry, Marquis of Lothian, Earl of Wemyss and March, Earl of Roseberry, Viscount Melville, Sir J. H. Dalrymple, Sir John Hope, Sir Hugh Innes, Sir Robert Keith Dick, Admiral Sir P. C. H. Durham, Baronets, the Lord Provost and Corporation of the city of Edinburgh, and the Magistrates of the town of Musselburgh. They were incorporated by the name of " The Edinburgh and Dalkeith Railway Company," with power to raise among themselves the amount of the estimate, in shares of

£50 each; and they may borrow the additional sum of £20,000, if necessary, on the credit of the undertaking. The concerns of this company are to be managed by a committee of nine or more persons, possessed of ten shares each at the least, and of whom three is at all meetings to be a quorum.

TONNAGE RATES.

<table>
<tr><td></td><td align="right">d.</td></tr>
<tr><td>Stone for the repairs of any Roads or Bridges, (not being in the Dalkeith District) Coal, Coke, Culm, and for all Stone, (except Stone for the repair of the Roads in the Dalkeith District,) Cinders, Chalk, Marl, Sand, Lime, Clay, Ashes, Peat, Lime-stone, Pitching and Paving-stone, (not being for the repair of Public Roads,) Iron-stone, or other Ore or Minerals, Bricks, Tiles, Slates, and all Gross and Unmanufactured Articles, Building Materials, and for all sorts of Manure and Grain, Flour, Meal, Potatoes, Hay, and Straw ....</td><td>4 per Ton, per Mile.</td></tr>
<tr><td>For every Carriage conveying Passengers, or Goods or Parcels not exceeding Five Hundred Weight ....</td><td>6 ditto.   ditto.</td></tr>
<tr><td>For the Carriage of Small Parcels (not exceeding Five Hundred Weight) ....</td><td>1 per Mile, per Cwt.</td></tr>
<tr><td>For all other Goods, Wares, or Commodities ....</td><td>1 ditto.   ditto.</td></tr>
</table>

ADDITIONAL RATES ON THE INCLINED PLANES.

<table>
<tr><td></td><td align="right">s. d.</td></tr>
<tr><td>For every Article which shall pass the Inclined Planes, by means of Stationary or Locomotive Engines (provided that not more than Two Inclined Planes be constructed between Edinburgh and the village of Hunters Hall) ....</td><td>1 0 per Ton, for each Plane.</td></tr>
</table>

Fractions to be paid as for a Quarter of a Mile, and as for a Quarter of a Ton.

PONTAGE RATES IN ADDITION.

<table>
<tr><td></td><td align="right">d.</td></tr>
<tr><td>For every Article carried across the Railway Bridge, to be erected over the North Esk River at Eskbank...................................</td><td>4 per Ton.</td></tr>
</table>

Which Rate is to be levied only for the Purpose of repaying the original Cost, with Interest; and for the future Maintenance of the same.

For the Bridge to be erected over the Railway Branch, which crosses the Esk near Cowpits, the same Rate is to be levied as on that over the North Esk as above, and with the same Object.

WHARFAGE RATES.

<table>
<tr><td></td><td align="right">d.</td></tr>
<tr><td>For all Coal carried to Fisher Row ....</td><td>1 per Ton.</td></tr>
</table>

Private wharfs may be erected by owners of lands, or by the company if they neglect to do so, and for which the following rates are allowed.

<table>
<tr><td></td><td align="right">d.</td></tr>
<tr><td>Coal, Culm, Lime, Lime-stone, Clay, Iron, Tin Plates, Iron-stone, Lead or other Ore, Timber, Stone, Bricks, Tiles, Slate, Gravel, Hay, Straw, Corn in the Straw, or Manure, which does not remain more than One Calendar Month ....</td><td>¼ per Ton.</td></tr>
<tr><td>For any other Goods, Wares, or Merchandize, if they do not remain more than Six Days ....</td><td>½ ditto.</td></tr>
<tr><td>For any Articles which may remain for the Space of Six Days over and above the time hereby limited for the same respectively</td><td>1 ditto for such Six Days.</td></tr>
</table>

And One Half-penny per Ton for every further Day.

Six years are allowed for the execution of this railway and branches, and if not then made, the power granted under this act will cease, except as to such part as may have been completed.

Among the clauses relative to private property, is one which compels the company to execute that part of the railway which is intended to pass over the estate of Sir Robert Keith Dick, Bart. within eighteen months from the commencement of the works on the estate, or suffer a penalty of £20 for every succeeding month which it may remain unfinished. And as a way-leave, an annual payment is to be made, (over and above the value of the land) of a sum not exceeding £990, nor less than £490, which payments are to be regulated by the average daily amount of tonnage passing along the railway through his estate.

If the Average be Nine Hundred Tons daily, the Annual Payment to be...... £990
If less than Nine Hundred, and not less than Eight Hundred Tons............ 890
If less than Eight Hundred, and not less than Seven Hundred Tons.......... 790
If less than Seven Hundred, and not less than Six Hundred Tons 690
If less than Six Hundred, and not less than Five Hundred Tons 590
If less than Five Hundred, the Annual Payment to be not less than 490

And should the Company ever abandon the Railway through Sir Robert Keith Dick's Estate, they shall be quit of the above Obligation, on Payment of the Sum of £1,830.

For Compensation to Andrew Wauchope, of Niddrie Marischall, Esq. for passing through his Estate, (in addition to the Value of the Land so to be occupied,) the Company agree to pay One Half-penny per Ton for every Article passing over his Estate, except the Produce thereof; with the Privilege of enjoying the use of the Railway which passes over his Estate, free of Toll, for the Produce of his Estate, or for any other Articles intended for his own use, or that of his Tenants.

To John Wauchope, of Edmonstone, Esq. the Sum of £670 is directed to be paid (in addition to the Value of his Land,) for the Privilege of carrying the Railway across his Estate, together with the Rate of One Half-penny per Ton, under the Provisions and with the same Privileges as are enjoyed by Andrew Wauchope, Esq.

On the 4th of June, 1829, the royal assent was given to another act, entitled, ' *An Act to enable the Edinburgh and Dalkeith Rail-* ' *way Company, to raise a further Sum of Money to make a Branch* ' *from the said Railway to Leith, and for other Purposes relating* ' *thereto.*' The extension here contemplated is from Niddrie North Mains, by Portobello, to Leith Harbour, the length being three miles, six furlongs and four chains, with a fall, to the Forth, of 130 feet.

The main line is also to be extended five furlongs, from Dalhousie Mains to Newton Grange.

Mr. Jardine also made the estimates for the Leith Branch and Extension. For the branch, if a double road, £29,628; but if

single, £22,260; and for the extension of the main line to Newton Grange, £7,815; towards which, the Marquis of Lothian
subscribed £1,000.

By the second act, the branch to Fisher Row Harbour is, in
future, to be accounted a portion of the main line; for the purpose
of completing which, power is given to raise, in addition to the
several sums of £57,695 and £4,136, which had already been
expended, any sum not exceeding £54,875, which is directed to
be raised by creating new shares of £50 each; and an additional
sum of £10,000, over and above the £20,000 which they were
empowered to borrow by the last-recited act. For the Leith
Branch, a new list of subscriptions is to be raised by a company
who may act independently of the shareholders on the main
line, by appointing their own committee of management, as well
as possessing the power to make separate dividends of the proceeds of this branch.

The subscribers are empowered to raise among themselves the
sum of £25,700, in one thousand and twenty-eight shares of £25
each, (of which sum, £19,600 was subscribed before this act was
obtained) and a further sum of £10,000, on assignment of the
rates as a security.

This branch crosses the estate of the Marquis of Abercorn, who
has the privilege of a way-leave for himself and tenants free of
charge, and is entitled to make branch railways to connect with
this.

William Miller, Esq. another considerable landed proprietor,
has obtained the same power and privileges as the above-named
nobleman, by obtaining the introduction of a similar clause.

With respect to the extension of the main line to Newton
Grange, it is enacted, that, should the Marquis of Lothian think
proper to do it at his own expense, the pontage rates which the
company are authorized to demand for all articles crossing the
North Esk Bridge, shall not be collected.

The principal object of this railway and branches, is to open
more effectually, a better and cheaper communication between
the city of Edinburgh and the port of Leith, with the valuable
collieries and limestone quarries that abound in the rich mineral
district to which they extend.

EDINBURGH AND GLASGOW UNION CANAL.

57 Geo. III. C. 56, R. A. 27th June, 1817.   59 Geo. III. C. 29, R. A. 19th May, 1819.
1 & 2 Geo. IV. C. 122, R. A. 23rd June, 1821.   4 Geo. IV. C. 18, R. A. 12th May, 1823.
7 Geo. IV. C. 45, R. A. 5th May, 1826.

THE Edinburgh and Glasgow Union Canal commences from
the sixteenth lock of the Forth and Clyde Navigation, about two
miles west of Falkirk, in the county of Sterling, whence it takes
an eastwardly course on the south side of the above-mentioned
town, by some collieries; thence, through Black Hill Tunnel, and
across the Glen Water, on which stream, at a short distance to the
southward, is constructed a considerable reservoir. Its line hence
is by Brighton Freestone Quarries, and about a mile north from
Park Hill Colliery, to the Avon River, over which there is an
aqueduct conveying the canal at an elevation of 80 feet above the
surface of the river. The canal here enters the county of Linlithgow, and passes within a mile and a half on the south side of its
capital, to Craighton House, where its course is more southerly
and circuitous, to the River Almond, near Clifton House, where it
crosses into Edinburghshire, by means of an aqueduct. Its course
hence is by Ratho House, and across Leith River, to the city of
Edinburgh, where it terminates by a basin at the Lothian Road,
about half a mile south-west of the castle. The length of the
canal is thirty miles, the depth of water 5 feet, and is on one level
from Edinburgh to its western extremity, where it falls 110 feet,
in one series of locks, into the Forth and Clyde Canal.

This navigation is supplied by feeders from all the streams it
crosses, and from reservoirs constructed for that purpose; one of
which is at Barbauchlay, in the parishes of Torphichan and Shotts,
and in the counties of Linlithgow and Lanark; another at Loch
Coat, in the parish of Torphichan, and another at Cobbinshaw, in
the parish of West Calder. There is a feeder of more than three
miles in length, taken from below the junction of the Linhouse
and Almond Rivers, which crosses the latter river by a suspension
aqueduct; and between which and the aqueduct over the Almond
River there are three tunnels, one of which is more than half a
mile in length; there is also another feeder from the Avon River.

There are two other canal aqueducts besides those above-mentioned; one over the Gogar Burn, and another over the Murray Burn.

This undertaking was designed by Mr. Thomas Telford and Mr. Baird, who estimated the cost at £240,468, 17s. 2d.; of which sum £198,650 was subscribed before going to parliament. The first act of parliament, relative to this canal, passed in the 57th George III. and is entitled, ' *An Act for making and maintaining* ' *a navigable Canal from the Lothian Road, near the city of* ' *Edinburgh, to join the Forth and Clyde Navigation near Falkirk,* ' *in the county of Stirling.*' The company of proprietors consisted, at the time the first act was obtained, of three hundred and eighty-four persons, amongst whom were the Lord Provost of Edinburgh, Sir William Forbes, Sir John Hay, and Sir John Marjoribanks, who were incorporated by the name of " The Edinburgh and " Glasgow Union Canal Company," with power to raise £240,500, in four thousand eight hundred and ten shares, of £50 each, and a further sum of £50,000, either among themselves, by the admission of new subscribers, or on mortgage of the undertaking.

TONNAGE RATES.

	d.		
Lime-stone, Iron-stone, Stone for Building, Paving-stone, Flags, Coal, Coke, Culm, Lime, Bricks, Tiles, Slates, Ores, Dung, Earth, Sand, Clay, Peat Moss, Marl and Manure	2	per Ton, per Mile.	
Timber, Deals, Bark, and Wood of every Kind	3	ditto.	ditto.
Corn, and all other Goods, Wares, and Merchandize	4	ditto.	ditto.
For Empty Vessels, or in Ballast, or with less than Fifteen Tons...	4	ditto. on 15 Tons.	ditto.

But if such Vessel return loaded within less than Fourteen Days, deduction will be made from the above Charge, in Proportion to the Distance they have carried the new lading.

Boats under Fifteen Tons not to pass Locks without consent, unless Tonnage to that Amount be paid.

Fractions to be taken as for a Quarter of a Mile, and as for a Quarter of a Ton.

WHARF AND BASIN DUES.

	d.	
For every Vessel loading or unloading at any of the Wharfs or Basins belonging to the Company	2	per Ton.

If Goods remain on the Wharfs more than Twenty-four Hours, such additional Rates to be paid as the Committee may deem reasonable.

The Company are directed to indemnify the Magistrates and Town Council of the Royal Burgh of Linlithgow for any Diminution of the Customs upon Cattle, Carriages, or Goods carried over the Avon at Torphichan Mill; also to secure to the Magistrates and Town Council of the City of Edinburgh the Rate of One Penny per Ton on all Goods, Wares, or other Things (except Manure,) shipped or unloaded at any of the Wharfs and Basins, in lieu of certain Rates, Dues, Causeway, Mail, and Petty Customs, which they are now entitled to; as it appears that, by a Charter or Gift of Charles the First, dated 17th May, 1636, the

Ministers of Edinburgh are entitled to a Duty or Custom of Thirteen Shillings and Four-pence Scots, upon each Ton or Pack of Goods imported to Edinburgh, Leith, or Newhaven. The Company are therefore directed to pay the same on all Goods which may be imported by this Navigation. They are also bound to indemnify the Edinburgh Road Trustees, the Bathgate, and another Trust, in any Diminution of Tolls arising from these Turnpike Roads, which may be affected by their Canal.

The act of the 59th George III. entitled, ' *An Act for altering* ' *and amending an Act for making and maintaining a navigable* ' *Canal from the Lothian Road, near the city of Edinburgh, to join* ' *the Forth and Clyde Navigation near Falkirk, in the county of* ' *Stirling*,' was obtained chiefly for the purpose of making some alterations in the line in the parishes of Ratho, Kirkliston, and Falkirk. The company are, however, by this act enabled to anticipate two calls of ten per cent. each, by borrowing the sum, which amounts to £48,100, and which was rendered necessary by the works proceeding with greater rapidity than they were calculated to do at the outset.

The royal assent was given to a third act on the 23rd June, 1821, which is entitled, ' *An Act for amending certain Acts for* ' *making and maintaining a navigable Canal from the Lothian* ' *Road, near the city of Edinburgh, to join the Forth and Clyde* ' *Navigation near Falkirk, in the county of Stirling, and giving* ' *Power to borrow a further Sum of Money on the Credit of the* ' *Tolls granted by the said Acts*;' by which power is given to raise the further sum of £50,000, either by the creation of new shares, or on the credit of the undertaking. In the preamble it is stated, that the whole of the monies they were authorized to raise under the preceding acts, had been expended, besides the sum of £50,000, which the Commissioners for issuing Exchequer Bills, under the authority of two acts of the 57th George III. and 1st George IV. had advanced to this company on the 1st of June, 1820.

In the preamble of an act of the 12th of May, 1823, entitled, ' *An Act to enable the Edinburgh and Glasgow Union Canal Com-* ' *pany to borrow a further Sum of Money*,' after reciting the previous acts, and stating that the whole of the sums granted had been expended on the works, it is stated, that a further sum was required in consequence of claims for extra work and awards of arbitrators, &c.; they are, therefore, empowered to raise a further sum of £60,000, either by the creation of new shares, or by borrowing the same on security of the works. In this act power is given to the Exchequer Bill Commissioners to advance the further sum of £50,000, in part of the sum of £60,000 the company is authorized to borrow by this act.

The last act relating to this navigation received his Majesty's assent on the 5th of May, 1826; and it is entitled, ' *An Act to alter* ' *and amend the Edinburgh and Glasgow Union Canal Acts, and* ' *to enable the Company to borrow a further Sum of Money ;*' in the preamble of which it is stated, that they have opened the canal, but as the reservoirs, authorized by the first-recited act, are not yet entirely completed, and the restricted time for executing the above works being nearly expired, the acts are in consequence directed to be continued in force.

The power which was given in the act of 57th George III. to make a reservoir at Fannyside Loch, is hereby repealed, and authority given to make one in lieu of it, in the parishes of Torphichan and Slamanan ; and the proprietors are allowed to raise the further sum of £60,000, either by the creation of new shares, or by borrowing on the credit of the funds and property of the company, who have power to allocate the whole debts of the company, by burthening each original share with its proportion of the debt; or they may divide the whole debt into new shares of £50 each; and it is enacted that no dividends shall be made until the debt be reduced to £100,000.

The primary object of this navigation was to effect an inland communication between the cities of Edinburgh and Glasgow; to the former of which it must be essentially serviceable, in consequence of the increased facilities afforded to the transit of lime, coal, stone, &c. which abound in its course.

ELLESMERE AND CHESTER CANAL.

12 Geo. III. C. 75, R. A. 1st Apr. 1772.   17 Geo. III. C. 67, R. A. 2nd June, 1777.
18 Geo. III. C. 21, R. A. 27th Mar. 1778.   33 Geo. III. C. 91, R. A. 30th Apr. 1793.
36 Geo. III. C. 71, R. A. 26th Apr. 1796.   36 Geo. III. C. 96, R. A. 14th May, 1796.
41 Geo. III. C. 70, R. A. 20th June, 1801. 42 Geo. III. C. 20, R. A. 15th Apr. 1802.
44 Geo. III. C. 54, R. A. 29th June, 1804. 50 Geo. III. C. 24, R. A. 6th Apr. 1810.
53 Geo. III. C. 80, R. A. 21st May, 1813. 7 & 8 Geo. IV. C. 102, R. A. 21st June, 1827.
11 Geo. IV. C. 51, R. A. 29th May, 1830.

THIS canal commences from the tideway of the River Mersey, at Ellesmere Port, about two miles east of Hooton Hall, the seat

of Sir Thomas S. Massey Stanley, Bart. and ten miles south-east
of the port of Liverpool. Its course is south by Stoke, Wervin,
and between Moston and Mollington Hall, to Chester, where there
is a short branch which locks down into the River Dee. Hence its
course is eastwardly, skirting the north wall of the city, by the shot
manufactories; thence more southerly, passing Christleton, Waver-
ton, Beeston Castle, to Wardle Green, from whence a branch
proceeds to join a branch of the Trent and Mersey or Grand Trunk
Canal at Middlewich. The main line proceeds for about one
mile and a half from Wardle Green to near Hurleston, where
another branch proceeds to near Darfold Hall, about three quarters
of a mile west of Nantwich, where it connects with the Birmingham and Liverpool Junction Canal, now in course of execution.
From Hurleston the main line proceeds southward by Burland to
Woodcot, and thence westward by Wrenbury and Tushingham,
near Whitchurch, where the canal enters the county of Salop.
Hence its course lies on the west side of the town of Whitchurch,
to which there is a short branch; thence it skirts the boundary of a
detached portion of the county of Flint to The Cottage, where
there is a branch to a wharf near Edstaston. The main line
proceeds in a westwardly direction, crossing a point of Flintshire,
and by Welsh Hampton to the south side of Ellesmere, to which
town there is a short branch; hence its course is more southerly, by
Tetchill to Francton Common, where the Llanymynech Branch
proceeds from it. The main line continues from the last-mentioned
point in a westwardly direction, by Halston Hall and Belmont,
and across the River Ceiriog, by a fine stone aqueduct; thence
through Chirk Tunnel to the River Dee, over which it is carried
by means of the famous cast iron aqueduct at Pont-y-Cysylte.
From this aqueduct a navigable feeder is made along the north
bank of the Dee to Llantysilio. There is also a railway from the
same place to Ruabon Brook Collieries, which also belongs to the
proprietors of this navigation.

The Llanymynech Branch takes a south-westerly course
from Francton Common by Wood House and Crickheath Hall,
to near Llanymynech, where it forms a junction with the Montgomeryshire Canal, in the township of Careghofa, in the county
of Salop.

Out of the last-mentioned branch, near the village of Hordley, a collateral cut proceeds by Bagley and Shire Oak, to Weston Wharf, near Weston Lullingfield, where it terminates. The total length of the main line from Ellesmere Port to the Montgomery-shire Canal, is sixty-one miles; viz. from the first-mentioned place, to the cut which connects with the Dee at the city of Chester, is eight miles and three quarters, with a rise, from low water mark in the Mersey at Liverpool, of 46 feet, which rise takes place at its commencement, from whence it is level to Chester. From Chester to the Hurleston Locks, and where the Nantwich Branch proceeds from it, is fifteen miles and three quarters, with a rise of 131 feet, by means of eleven locks, five of which are within a mile of Chester. The branch to meet the Birmingham and Liverpool Junction Canal is two miles in length, and level. The main line from the Hurleston Locks to Francton Common is twenty-five miles, with a rise of 115 feet. The branch to Edstaston Wharf from The Cottage, upon this part of the main line, is nearly three miles in length. The branch towards the town of Ellesmere is about a furlong in length only. From Francton Common it is eleven miles and a half to its termination in the Montgomeryshire Canal, with a fall of 52 feet. The branch to the Ruabon Brook Railway, near the Pont-y-Cysylte Aqueduct is little more than eleven miles, with a rise of 13 feet.

The railway which proceeds from the end of the canal at Cysylte, through an extensive coal field to Ruabon Brook, in the county of Denbigh, is three miles and a quarter; and the navigable feeder, which comes from the Dee at Llantysilio, and falls into this canal at the aqueduct above-mentioned, is nearly six miles in length; and the branch from near Hordley to Weston Wharf, is five miles and a half in length. The branch from Wardle Green to join the Grand Trunk Canal at Middlewich, takes a westwardly course by Cholmondeston Hall, and across the River Weaver, near Wades Green; thence northwardly, and runs in a parallel course on the east side of that river, by Minshull Vernon and Lea Hall; thence eastwardly to the south side of the town of Middlewich, where it forms the junction above-mentioned. Its length is nearly ten miles, with a fall to the Grand Trunk of 44 feet 4 inches, by four locks.

The necessary powers for making and perfecting this navigation are contained in thirteen acts of parliament, but as by the act of 7th and 8th George IV. all the former ones are repealed, we shall but briefly notice the chief provisions. The first act occurs in the 12th George III. and is entitled, ' *An Act for making a naviga-* ' *ble Cut or Canal from the River Dee, within the liberties of the* ' *city of Chester, to or near Middlewich and Nantwich, in the county* ' *of Chester,*' by which one hundred and nineteen subscribers, (amongst whom were the Honourable Wilbraham Tollemache,) are incorporated by the name of " The Company of Proprietors of " the Chester Canal Navigation," with power to raise among themselves the sum of £42,000, in four hundred and twenty shares of £100 each; and an additional sum of £20,000, if necessary.

In the preamble of the act of 17th George III. entitled, ' *An* ' *Act for varying and enlarging the Powers of an Act made in the* ' *Twelfth Year of the Reign of his present Majesty, for making a* ' *navigable Cut or Canal from the River Dee, within the liberties* ' *of the city of Chester, to or near Middlewich and Nantwich, in the* ' *county of Chester,*' it is stated, that considerable progress had been made in the works, and that the sums of £42,000, and £19,000 of the £20,000 authorized by the preceding act, had been expended; and as more money was required, the act enabled the company to raise the further sum of £25,200, by a call of sixty per cent. on the original stock of £42,000; and an additional sum of £30,000, on security of the rates and duties. This act enables the company to change the course of the Middlewich Branch; but, by a clause which is here introduced for the purpose of protecting the interests of the Duke of Bridgewater and the Grand Trunk Canal Company, they are restricted from approaching nearer than one hundred yards to the last-mentioned canal.

The third act, which was obtained in the year following the preceding act, was to enable the company to make a call of eighty per cent. on the original stock of £42,000, in consequence of having failed to raise the sums wanted, in the manner prescribed by the preceding act; it is entitled, ' *An Act for the more effec-* ' *tually carrying into Execution the Powers contained in two several* ' *Acts of Parliament, the one made in the Twelfth Year of his* ' *present Majesty's Reign, for making a navigable Cut or Canal*

' *from the River Dee, within the liberties of the city of Chester, to*
' *or near Middlewich and Nantwich, in the county of Chester; and*
' *the other made in the Seventeenth Year of his said Majesty's*
' *Reign, for varying and enlarging the Powers of the said former*
' *Act.*'

If the sum of £33,600, hereby authorized to be raised by
the call above-recited, be insufficient for the purposes required,
the company may borrow, on security of the tolls, the further sum
of £10,000.

Under these several acts the canal from Chester to Nantwich
was completed about 1780; but the branch to Middlewich, in
consequence chiefly of the restrictive clause contained in the act
of 17th George III. remained unexecuted until the present time,
when the united companies of the Chester and Ellesmere Canals
have, under new powers lately granted, commenced the undertaking under the skilful direction of Mr. Telford; and it is
expected shortly to be opened. Mr. James Brindley was employed
upon this canal as well as other engineers. So much was this concern depressed at the time it had no communication with other
navigations, that it is said that shares were sold for one per cent.
of their original value.

About fifteen years subsequent to the passing of the last-recited
act, an act was obtained by a company consisting of twelve hundred and thirty-eight persons, (amongst whom were Sir Foster
Cunliffe, Sir Richard Hill, and Sir Thomas Hanmer,) entitled,
' *An Act for making and maintaining a navigable Canal from the*
' *River Severn, at Shrewsbury, in the county of Salop, to the River*
' *Mersey, at or near Netherpool, in the county of Chester; and*
' *also for making and maintaining certain collateral Cuts from the*
' *said intended Canal,*' by which they were incorporated by the
name of " The Company of Proprietors of the Ellesmere Canal,"
and empowered to raise among themselves the sum of £400,000,
and an additional sum of £50,000, if necessary; and, by mortgage
of the tolls, the further sum of £50,000.

The line of this proposed navigation was from the Mersey
along its present course to Chester, where it crosses the Dee, and
thence by Wrexham and Poolmouth to the Pont-y-Cysylte Aqueduct, and thence along the present executed line by Francton Com-

mon, Hordley, and as far as Weston Wharf; thence through a
tunnel to Shrewsbury, where it was intended to lock down into the
Severn.

The length of the main line was fifty-six miles and three
quarters, with a rise to Poolmouth of about 380 feet, and a fall to
the Severn of 226 feet. The branches were to Llanymynech as
at present; one to Brumbo, in the county of Denbigh, and another
to Holt, in the same county; with one to Prees, in the county of
Salop. Power is also given by this act to extend the Prees Collateral Cut from Fenshall to the Chester Canal, near Tattenhall,
provided the land-owners' consent could be obtained; and another
branch from the Llanymynech Branch to Morda Bridge, under the
same conditions. Mr. William Jessop and Mr. Dadford were
appointed the engineers to carry into execution the necessary
operations.

In the preamble of an act of the 36th George III. cap. 71,
entitled, ' *An Act to explain and amend an Act, passed in the*
' *Thirty-third Year of the Reign of his present Majesty, entitled,*
' *An Act for making and maintaining a navigable Canal from the*
' *River Severn, at Shrewsbury, in the county of Salop, to the River*
' *Mersey, at or near Netherpool, in the county of Chester; and also*
' *for making and maintaining certain collateral Cuts from the said*
' *intended Canal; and for varying and altering certain Parts of*
' *the Whitchurch Line of the said Canal and collateral Cuts, and*
' *for extending the same from Francton Common to Sherryman's*
' *Bridge, in the parish of Whitchurch, in the said county of Salop;*
' *and for making and maintaining several other Branches and col-*
' *lateral Cuts to communicate therewith,*' it is stated, that a part of
the canal has been already executed, but that it would be more
beneficial to the public, if the company were authorized to abandon the Whitchurch Line; and, instead of it, to make a branch
from Francton to Sherryman's Bridge, near Whitchurch; and out
of this last-mentioned line of canal at Whixall Moss, a collateral
cut to Prees Higher Heath; also a short cut to Blackwater's Barn,
near Ellesmere; which is accordingly granted.

By this act the Ellesmere Company were required, within
two years, to apply for an act to effect a junction with the Chester Canal; and directions were therefore given to Mr. J. Fletcher,

as engineer to the Chester Canal Company, and Mr. J. Duncombe for the Ellesmere Canal Company, to examine the country between the Whitchurch Branch of the Ellesmere Canal and the Chester Canal at Stoke, and report upon the practicability of forming a junction; they did so; and their estimate for this purpose amounted to £36,478.

Eighteen days after the passing of the last-recited act, another received the royal assent, on the 14th May, 1796, entitled, ' *An* ' *Act to explain and amend an Act, entitled, An Act to explain and* ' *amend an Act, passed in the Thirty-third Year of the Reign of his* ' *present Majesty, entitled, An Act for making and maintaining a* ' *navigable Canal from the River Severn, at Shrewsbury, in the* ' *county of Salop, to the River Mersey, at or near Netherpool, in* ' *the county of Chester ; and also for making and maintaining cer-* ' *tain collateral Cuts from the said intended Canal; and for varying* ' *and altering certain Parts of the Course of the said Canal and* ' *collateral Cuts; between Ruabon and Chester, and for making* ' *and maintaining several other Branches and collateral Cuts, to* ' *communicate therewith,*' by which, power is given to vary the original line, and make a new branch from near Pont-y-Cysylte, in the parish of Ruabon, to the parish of St. Mary on the Hill, in the city of Chester, with a collateral cut from the same on Cefn Common, to near Acrefair Coal Works, in the county of Denbigh ; and another from the same branch, in the township of Gwersyllt, to Talwern Coal Works, in the parish of Mold and county of Flint ; and one other collateral branch from the Broad Oak in the township of Burton, into the township of Allington.

It is by this act that the canal company are bound to make good any deficiency which may arise in the amount of tolls payable to the Dee Navigation Company, by reason of the Ellesmere Canal being made, in case the annual amount be less than £235. The discrepancy between the amount here stated and what appears in the account of the Dee Navigation, (page 193,) arose in consequence of the Dee Company having neglected to take into consideration the toll for and in respect of coal, which on the average amounted to £25 annually.

The act of the 41st George III. is entitled, ' *An Act to autho-* ' *rize the Company of Proprietors of the Ellesmere Canal, to extend*

' the said Canal from the Whitchurch Branch thereof, at or near
' certain Water Corn Mills, called the New Mills, in the parish of
' Whitchurch, in the county of Salop, to, and to communicate with,
' the Chester Canal, in the township of Stoke, in the parish of
' Acton, in the county of Chester, and for altering and amending
' the several Acts passed for making and maintaining the said
' Ellesmere Canal;' and under authority of which, this extension
of the Whitchurch Branch, which is now part of the main line,
was carried into execution.

In the year following the passing of the last-recited act, application was again made to parliament, when another was obtained,
entitled, ' An Act for repealing so much of an Act passed in the
' Thirty-third Year of his present Majesty, entitled, An Act for
' making and maintaining a navigable Canal from the River
' Severn, at Shrewsbury, in the county of Salop, to the River Mer-
' sey, at or near Netherpool, in the county of Chester ; and also for
' making and maintaining certain collateral Cuts from the said in-
' tended Canal, as restrains the Company of Proprietors of the said
' Canal from taking Tonnage on Coals, Coke, Culm, Lime, or
' Limestone, upon any Part of the said Canal ; and for authorizing
' the said Company of Proprietors to raise a Sum of Money to
' make up the Amount of their original Subscriptions, and for fur-
' ther amending the several Acts passed relative to the making of the
' said Canal;' in the preamble of which it is stated, that as a considerable portion of the shares which had been apportioned to the
landholders had not been taken, and that as the present stock of
the company was only £333,000, instead of £400,000, the proprietors were desirous of raising the deficiency among themselves,
without having recourse to the powers contained in the 33rd
George III. for raising two several sums of £50,000, which the
company are permitted to do by the admission of new subscribers;
or they may raise it on promissory notes under the common seal.

The act of the 44th George III. was obtained chiefly for the
purpose of enabling the company to make the Ruabon Brook
Railway, and the feeders from the Dee, at Llantysilio, and Bala
Pool, in Merionethshire ; it is entitled, ' An Act to enable the
' Company of Proprietors of the Ellesmere Canal, to make a Rail-
' way from Ruabon Brook, to the Ellesmere Canal, at or near the

' *Aqueduct at Pont-y-Cysylte, in the parish of Llangollen, in the*
' *county of Denbigh; and also to make several Cuts or Feeders for*
' *better supplying the said Canal with Water;*' and by which the
company are restrained from taking more water from the Dee, by
the feeder, than they can replace from Bala Pool. On the 6th of
April, 1810, the royal assent was given to another act, for the purpose of making a short branch to the town of Whitchurch; it is
entitled, ' *An Act to enable the Company of Proprietors of the*
' *Ellesmere Canal, to extend the Whitchurch Line of the said Canal*
' *from Sherryman's Bridge to Castle Well, in the town of Whit-*
' *church, in the county of Salop; and for amending the several Acts*
' *for making the said Canal.*' This branch, (which is very short)
and the basin and quays at its termination, were designed by Mr.
Telford, whose estimate amounted to the sum of £2,284.

The act of the 53rd George III. was obtained for the purpose
of uniting and consolidating the interests of the Ellesmere with
the Chester Canal Company; it is therefore entitled, ' *An Act for*
' *uniting the Interests and Concerns of the Proprietors of the Ches-*
' *ter Canal and Ellesmere Canal; and for amending the several*
' *Acts of his present Majesty, relating to the said Canals,*' in the
preamble of which, after reciting the several acts relating to the
two navigations, and another act of the 47th George III. cap. 3,
entitled, ' *An Act for continuing the Term and altering and enlarg-*
' *ing the Powers of an Act of the Twenty-sixth Year of his present*
' *Majesty, for amending the Road from Flookersbrook Bridge to*
' *the South End of Wilderspool Causeway, and from the town of*
' *Frodsham to Ashton Lane End, in the county of Chester, so far*
' *as respects the Chester District of the said Roads; and for extend-*
' *ding the same from the present Termination thereof at Flookers-*
' *brook Bridge aforesaid, to the North End of Cow Lane Bridge,*
' *in the city of Chester, and for making a new Road from*
' *such proposed Extension of the said Road, to the North End of*
' *Queen Street in the same city,*' the two canal companies are incorporated by the name of " The United Company of Proprietors
" of the Ellesmere and Chester Canals." By this act the proprietors of each share of the Chester Canal were, after the 30th of
June in this year, admitted to one fourth of a share in the united
navigation, making in the whole fifty of such shares.

The act of the 7th and 8th George IV. entitled, ' *An Act to* ' *amend and enlarge the Provisions of the several Acts relating to* ' *the Ellesmere and Chester Canal Navigations;*' after reciting the works executed in the several acts of parliament relating to this navigation, states, that the branch from Wardle Green to Middlewich, which the acts of the 12th and 17th George III. empowered the Chester Canal Company to make, has not been done ; this act, therefore, enables the united company to execute this branch with some deviations from the original line ; and to form a junction with a short branch of one hundred yards in length, which the Trent and Mersey or Grand Trunk Canal Company are required to make, by virtue of an act passed this session of parliament, from their canal at or near the Brick Kiln Field Bridge, or Brooks Lane Bridge, situate on the south side of the town of Middlewich. The deviation on this branch occurs near the Middlewich end, and is fifteen hundred and sixty yards in length, which does not materially alter the length of the line. The estimate for this deviation line was made by Messrs. Telford and W. A. Provis, and amounts to £14,009, 3*s.* 1*d.* The locks upon this branch are directed to be 77 feet in length, 8 feet 4 inches in width at the top, and 7 feet 1 inch at the level of the bottom sill, and the rise of each 10 feet 4 inches.

Although this act repeals all the previous acts relating to the united navigation, yet the original contracts remain in force, and the present committee are to be continued in the same way as though the acts had not been repealed.

There are clauses for the protection of Tilstone Mills, Darnhall Mills, Tattenhall Mills, Stoke Mills, and the mills belonging to Earl Kilmorey, in the county of Chester. The water of the River Perrey above Platt Mill, situate in the township of Ruytun of the Eleven Towns, and some other streams, are not to be taken.

Upon all the canals, branches, and railroads, belonging to the united company of the Ellesmere and Chester Canal, the following tonnage rates are allowed.

TONNAGE RATES.

	d.	
Coke, Culm, Lime-stone, and Rock Salt	1½	per Ton, per Mile.
Freestone, Timber, Slate, Pig and Bar Iron, Iron-stone, Pig Lead, and Lead-ore .... }	2	ditto. ditto.
All other Goods, Wares, and Merchandize whatsoever	3	ditto. ditto.

In addition to the above Rates, the Company are empowered to charge the Sum of Two Shillings per Ton upon the Cargo of any Boat which shall not have passed along the Canal the Distance of Twelve Miles, but which shall have passed through any Lock or Locks (except on Lime, Lime-stone, or Coal.)

For the Purposes of this Act, One Hundred and Twenty Pounds Avoirdupois, of Coal, Coke, Culm, Lime, Freestone, and Lime-stone—and One Hundred and Twelve Pounds of any other Commodity shall be deemed a Hundred Weight.

If any Vessel pass through a Lock with less than Thirty Tons, to pay for that Amount at the highest Rates; unless such Vessel be returning after having passed with more than Thirty Tons, or unless the Water be running over the Waste Weirs of the Locks;—if there is not sufficient Water for Thirty Tons of Lading, then the Rates are to be paid upon the Quantity carried.

Empty Vessels, or such as have less than Eighteen Tons lading, passing the Locks which are only adapted for Vessels of Seven Feet Beam, and have not passed through a Fourteen Feet Lock, shall pay a Tonnage equal to the highest Rates on Eighteen Tons, unless such Boat be returning after having passed with more than Eighteen Tons, or unless the Water is running over the Waste Weirs of every Lock such Boat passes through.

Fractions to be taken as for a Mile and as for a Quarter of a Ton.

EXEMPTION.

Paving-stones, Gravel, Sand, and all other Materials for Roads, also Dung, Soil, Marl, and Ashes to be used as Manure for the Improvement only of the Lands and Grounds through which the Canals or Railway passes.

Lords of manors and owners of lands may erect wharfs; but if they refuse, the company may do it, and charge the following

WHARFAGE RATES.

	d.
Coal, Culm, Lime, Lime-stone, Clay, Iron, Iron-stone, Lead-ore, or any other Ores, Timber, Stone, Brick, Tiles, Slates, Gravel, or other Things..	1 per Ton.
For the Warehousing of any Package not exceeding Fifty-six Pounds Weight..	2
Above Three Hundred Pounds Weight, and not exceeding Six Hundred Pounds Weight...	4
Exceeding One Thousand Pounds Weight..........................	6 per Ton.

The above Rates to be paid if the Articles do not remain more than Twenty-four Hours on the Wharf.

	d.
Should any of the above Articles remain Seven Days above the Time specified (for Wharfage)	1½ per Ton, in addition.
Ditto, (for Warehousing)	2 ditto.

And the like Sum of Three Half-pence or Two-pence, respectively, per Ton, for every further Seven Days which such Articles shall remain on Wharf or in Warehouse after the Expiration of the first Seven Days.

For the purpose of carrying into execution the Middlewich Branch of this canal, (which is estimated to cost £68,837, 18s. 3d.) the company are authorized to borrow the sum of £80,000 of the Exchequer Bill Commissioners, upon mortgage, or assignment of the rates and duties; or they may borrow the same of other persons; or by creating new or additional shares; but not more than four hundred and twenty-five, so that the total number of shares in this navigation may not be more than four thousand.

This act also declares, that unless new shares are created, the consolidated stock of this navigation shall consist of the sum of £475,568, 15s. divided into three thousand five hundred and seventy-five shares, and three quarters of a share of £133 each; and the management is to be under the direction of a committee of twenty-five persons, possessing at least five shares each; and a sub-committee of six for the management of the Wirral Branch of this navigation, extending from Chester to the Mersey.

A fund for repairs may be created to the extent of £20,000, after all debts are paid, by deducting not more than one tenth of the dividends in each year. For the purpose of preventing injury to the navigation of the River Dee, by abstracting water from this river into the collateral cut or feeder at Llantysilio, it is enacted, that the united company shall, from their canal, supply the River Dee, at Chester, with as much water as is taken from it by the feeder, and which shall not have been previously restored to the Dee.

Of the canals and collateral branches authorized to be made, by powers granted under the respective acts of parliament relating to this navigation, the following have not been executed, and as the acts are repealed, they cannot now be done. That part of the original main line from the basin at Chester to the aqueduct at Pont-y-Cysylte being twenty miles in length, with 455 feet of lockage; another portion between Weston Wharf and the Severn at Shrewsbury, which was nine miles and a half in length, with 107 feet of lockage; together with a proposed tunnel at Weston Lullingfield, of four hundred and eighty-seven yards in length. A branch to Holt, of four miles in length; another to the Talwern Collieries; another from Gresford to Allington; and another from Pont-y-Cysylte to the collieries at Acrefair; a branch of seven miles to Prees Heath; and a collateral cut from that part of the main line formerly called the Llanymynech Branch, to the Montgomeryshire Canal, at Portywain Lime Works; and another to Morda Bridge, near Oswestry.

The objects contemplated by the proprietors of these navigations, in their recent application to parliament, are chiefly to enable them to establish a carrying trade from the port of Ellesmere, on the banks of the River Mersey, across that river to the different towns and navigations with which it communicates, and to construct a reservoir of about twenty-four acres near the Hurlestone Locks, between the canal and the turnpike-road leading from Chester to Nantwich, for the purpose of catching the surplus water of the Upper Pound Locks, and supplying the Lower Locks in time of scarcity. They had further intended to make a short extension of their canal of a mile in length, from Pont-y-Cysylte Basin to the road leading to Plas-Kynaston Hall, in the county of Denbigh; this, however, they ultimately abandoned, and their act is in consequence entitled, ' *An Act to enable the united Company* ' *of Proprietors of the Ellesmere and Chester Canals to make a* ' *Reservoir, and to establish Vessels for the conveyance of Goods* ' *from Ellesmere Port across the River Mersey; and also to amend* ' *and enlarge the Powers of the said Act relating to the said Canal.*'

The estimate for the several works contemplated, including £4,000 for the cut subsequently abandoned, was made by Mr. Thomas Stanton, amounting to £55,200, of which, the reservoir was calculated to cost £31,200; and for purchase of proper vessels for the carrying trade, an additional sum of £20,000 would be required; the company are, therefore, empowered to raise for these purposes, and for completing their branch canal from Wardle Green to Middlewich, a further sum of £70,000, by all or any of the means by which the said company are authorized to collect any sum of money by virtue of the preceding acts.

This act also enables the united proprietors to purchase Dee Mills, in the city of Chester, for the purpose of avoiding any dispute which might arise respecting the use of the water of the River Dee, which supplies both the canal and mills.

For the carriage of goods and merchandize across the Mersey, the company are empowered to collect the following

TONNAGE RATES.

	s.	d.	
For Pig-iron	3	0	per Ton
For Bar and Rod Iron......	3	6	ditto.
For Sheet, Hoop and other Iron, Lead and other Metals	4	0	ditto.
For Timber	4	0	ditto.
For Corn, Grain, Malt and Flour	5	6	ditto.
For Sugar, Groceries, Drugs, Hides and Manufactured Goods	6	6	ditto.
For Wine, Spirits, Vitriol, Glass and other Goods and Merchandize..	8	0	ditto.

Fractions to be taken as for a Quarter of a Ton.

On some parts of this navigation some astonishing works have been constructed, but the limits to which our work is prescribed, precludes the possibility of enumerating them; however we must not omit to notice the well known aqueduct over the Dee at Pont-y-Cysylte. This stupendous work is carried over the river, at an elevation of 125 feet above its bed, on nineteen pairs of stone pillars, 52 feet asunder. The trough through which the vessels pass is 320 feet long, 20 feet wide, and 6 feet deep, and it is entirely composed of cast iron plates. There is also another very large aqueduct over the River Ceiriog, which is built of stone; it is two hundred yards in length, and is supported on ten arches, at an elevation of 65 feet above the river.

This navigation, from the immediate connection it has with the Rivers Mersey and Dee, and with the Montgomeryshire Canal, and the communication it has, by means of collateral cuts and the Ruabon Branch Railway, with the mineral districts to which they severally extend, and the fertile agricultural parts of North Salop and the county palatine of Chester, through which it winds its way, is of first rate importance; and it will doubtless increase in value when the desirable junction with the Grand Trunk Canal has been effected.

ENGLISH AND BRISTOL CHANNELS SHIP CANAL.

6 George IV. Cap. 199, Royal Assent 6th July, 1825.

The parliamentary line of this intended ship canal, commences in the English Channel at Beer Roads, Seaton Bay, whence it takes a north-eastwardly course, skirting the shore, to the village of Seaton; thence, running parallel with the Axe River, to Colyford, where it crosses the River Coly, a mile south of the town of Colyton; thence continuing in the vale of the Axe, by Whitford, to the River Yarty, which it crosses by an aqueduct; thence half a mile west of the town of Axminster, and across the Little River Kilbridge to Hurtham, where it quits the valley and proceeds northwards a mile east of Chard, to its summit level. Hence its course is over a flat and uninteresting country for the space of twelve miles and a half, without a lock; thence it passes Thorpe Falcon, and across the navigable River Tone by an aqueduct, about five miles east of Taunton. The line from the Tone runs parallel, for some miles, with the intended Bridgewater and Taunton Canal, and along the line of a part of it by St. Michael's and Huntworth, to the town of Bridgewater, which it passes on its west side, and thence north-westwardly by Wembdon, to the River Parrett, along the shore of which it continues to Combwich, where it leaves the river, and running direct to Stolford, locks down into Bridgewater Bay, in the Bristol Channel.

The canal will be forty-four miles and five furlongs in length; in the first eleven miles and three quarters, from Seaton Bay, it rises 245 feet, by twenty-nine locks, from low water in the English Channel; thence for twelve miles and a half it is level; and for the remaining twenty miles and three furlongs there is a fall of 267 feet 7 inches, by twenty-nine locks, to low water in the Bristol Channel. By the section here described, it would seem as though the levels had been mis-stated by us, or that an error had been committed in taking them; but the apparent discrepancy is to be accounted for by the different rise of the tides in the two channels. At Bridgewater Bay in the Bristol Channel, the ordinary spring tides are 36 feet 6 inches, and the high spring tides rise 40 feet; while in Seaton Bay, in the English Channel, the ordinary spring tides are but 12 feet, and the high spring tides seldom exceed 15 feet 6 inches, so that the latter in the Bristol Channel are higher by 2 feet than in the English Channel; whilst the low water line is 22 feet 7 inches below it.

This canal is to be made 15 feet deep, 90 feet wide, and capable of being navigated by ships of two hundred tons register. It is to be supplied with water from reservoirs; viz. one in the Axe Valley, near Seaborough, covering a surface of two hundred and seventeen acres and three roods; and another in the same valley, in the parish of Winshem. The third is at the upper end of the valley of the Yarty, near Hilhaven Bridge, in the parishes of Yarcombe and Membury; and the other at Ridge, on the Kilbridge River, in the parish of Chardstock, in the county of Dorset. The Hilhaven Bridge Reservoir is to be to the extent of one hundred and five acres, and that at Ridge sixteen and a half.

Between the two last-mentioned reservoirs there is a cut of communication six miles and a half in length; and from the Ridge
Reservoir to the canal, the feeder is three miles and a half.

The feeder from the Seaborough Reservoir follows the north
bank of the Axe by Ford Abbey, thence it turns northward, and
enters the canal near Chard, being eight miles and a half in
length. Mr. Telford's estimate for this magnificent undertaking
was made in 1824, and amounted to the sum of £1,712,844.

The act for carrying this great work into execution, was
obtained in 1825. It is entitled, ' *An Act for making and main-*
' *taining a Canal for Ships and other Vessels, to commence at or*
' *near Seaton Bay, in the county of Devon, and terminating in the*
' *Bristol Channel, at or near Stolford or Bridgewater Bay, in the*
' *county of Somerset, with several collateral Branches to communi-*
' *cate therewith.*' The subscribers, consisting of two hundred and
seventy-one persons, (amongst whom were the Earl of Cork and
Orrery, the Dean of York, and Major-General Sir James Kempt,)
were incorporated by the name of " The Company of Proprietors
" of the English and Bristol Channels Ship Canal," with power to
contribute among themselves the sum of £1,750,000, in seventeen
thousand five hundred shares of £100 each, the whole of which is
to be subscribed before the work is commenced. The company
may also borrow the further sum of £750,000 on mortgage of the
rates, or by granting annuities, or on promissory notes under the
common seal. In obtaining supplies of lockage water for this canal,
the company are prohibited from taking any from the Rivers Parrett or Tone, or any streams which flow into them; they are also
restricted from taking any but the flood waters arising on the Rivers
Axe and Yarty, and Wambrook. In this act is recited a very important agreement, bearing date 28th March, 1825, between this
company and the Bridgewater and Taunton Navigation Company,
by which the former company agree to give the latter, for their
interest in the new canal, between Bridgewater and Taunton, together with the machines and materials used in carrying on the
work, the sum of £90,000, together with the sum of £7,307,
1s. 10d. owing to the Bridgewater and Taunton Canal Company,
by virtue of the purchases made from the proprietors of shares in
the debt due on the River Tone.

The Bridgewater and Taunton Canal Company are to continue their works, but the expenses are to be reimbursed by the English and Bristol Channels Ship Canal Company. The purchase money to be paid by three equal instalments; the last of which is to be paid at the end of nine months from the passing of the above-recited act, or within three months afterwards; in default of which, the agreement to be void. And, in case it is paid, the monies are to be applied to carrying into execution what remains to be executed of the Bridgewater and Taunton Canal; and after the residue, if any, is distributed among the shareholders, they are to be dissolved, and be no longer a corporate body ; and are henceforward released from all obligation to maintain the said canal, which is by this act transferred to the English and Bristol Channels Ship Canal Company.

TONNAGE RATES.

	d.
Hay, Straw, Dung, Peats, and Peat Ashes, Chalk, Marl, Clay, Sand, Lime, Lime-stone to be used for Manure, and all other Articles intended to be used as Manure, and all Materials for the repair of Roads. Coal, Culm, Coke, Cinders, Charcoal, Iron, Stone, Bricks, and Tiles............	1 per Ton, per Mile.
All other Goods, Wares, or Merchandize	3 ditto. ditto.

Fractions to be taken as for a Quarter of a Mile, and as for a Quarter of a Ton.

For the Purposes of this Act Forty Cubic Feet of Oak, Ash, Elm, Beech. Larch, Mahogany, and other heavy Timber or Wood; and Fifty Cubic Feet of Pine, Fir, Deal, Poplar, and other light Wood; and Forty Cubic Feet of Goods which shall not weigh Twenty Hundred Weight, of One Hundred and Twelve Pounds each, shall be deemed a Ton.

If any Vessel pass along this Canal for any less Distance than Ten Miles, and shall pass through any Lock, shall pay, in Addition to the above Rates, One Penny per Ton upon One Hundred and Fifty Tons at the least, upon passing the first Lock upon the Canal, and One-half of such Amount at every succeeding Lock.

For every Vessel, whether Laden, Unladen, or in Ballast, passing the Tide Locks at either Extremity, and which shall not have passed the whole Length of the Canal, there shall be paid Two-pence per Ton upon the Registered Tonnage of such Ship; and in no case shall less be paid than for One Hundred and Fifty Tons.

For Vessels Unladen or in Ballast, (except such as are used for Agricultural Purposes,) which shall navigate a Distance of Ten Miles or upwards, One Penny per Ton per Mile, as upon One Hundred and Fifty Tons at the least; if less than Ten Miles, and shall pass any Lock, (except the Tide Locks,) One Penny per Ton per Mile; and also a Rate of One Penny per Ton for passing such Lock, upon One Hundred and Fifty Tons at the least, and One-half of such Amount for every succeeding Lock.

As the canal company intend to construct harbours, or ports, with piers, jetties, lights, and other works at the two extremities of the navigation, it is enacted, that they shall be entitled to the following harbour dues, to be paid by all ships or other vessels which may use the said harbours, &c. without navigating the said canal.

HARBOUR DUES.

For every Vessel entering either of the Harbours of Beer, or Seaton, or ⎱
Stolford, of Twenty Tons Burthen and upwards, according to the ⎬ 3 per Ton.
Registered Tonnage of such Ship or Vessel .... ⎰

d.

From the last-mentioned Rate all Vessels in his Majesty's Service are exempt.

TOWING PATH RATE.

d.

For every Horse or other Beast passing on any of the Towing Paths (except such ⎱ 3
as are used in Haling any Ship or other Vessel) .... ⎰

Such Toll to be taken but once a Day.

Vessels (not being a Ship or Sea Vessel,) laden with Hay, Straw, or Corn in the Straw,
or with any Material for the repair of Roads, or with any Kind of Manure, shall
not pass through any Lock; but upon Payment of One Penny per Ton as upon
One Hundred Tons at the first Lock they shall pass, and Half the Amount at every
succeeding Lock. As many Barges as the Lock will receive, are to pass upon Payment together of the Rates above-mentioned.

Lords of manors, or land-owners, may make or erect wharfs
or warehouses; but if they refuse, the company may do it, and
charge the following rates.

WHARFAGE RATES.

d.

For any Goods lying on the Wharfs not more than Twenty- ⎱ ½ per Ton.
four Hours .... ⎰
More than Twenty-four Hours, and less than Seven Days...... 1 ditto.
Except Coal, Iron, and Iron-stone, which may remain Two ⎱ ¼ per Ton, per Day.
Months, and after such Time............................ ⎰

There are many clauses in this act relating to private property,
but more especially with regard to estates belonging to Lord Sid-
mouth, Sir William Oglander, Bart. and William Manning, Esq.
situate where the reservoirs are intended to be made, by which
the company are required to purchase the whole of these several
estates, if any portion is taken under the authority of this act.

The chief object and advantages to be derived from the execution of this ship canal, is the shortening and rendering more
certain and expeditious the passage of all vessels trading from the
Bristol Channel, the ports of Ireland, and the western ports of
England, to the English Channel. Indeed, if we take into consideration the danger and difficulty, at all times, of the navigation
round the Land's End, and the detention, frequently amounting to
six weeks, arising from the prevalence of south-westerly winds,
the importance of having a passage in the line above described,
cannot but be seen by every one who will for a moment consult
the accompanying map. The distance saved, by means of this

canal, between Bridgewater Bay or the ports eastward of it, and any ports eastward of Beer Harbour, is upwards of two hundred and twenty miles.

In addition to the great advantage which must necessarily accrue to the shipping interest, the prospects held out to the speculator in this work, are sufficient to tempt the cupidity of the most sceptical, if reliance may be placed in the accuracy of the data from whence the projectors have derived the probable sources of revenue. In a prospectus, published by the committee on this navigation, it is stated, that the clear annual income applicable to a dividend among the proprietors, is calculated, by very low estimates, to amount to twelve per cent. or £210,846, 12s. 4d. But the reader must bear in mind that the latter end of 1824 was a time of high expectations. When this article was drawn up (1830) the work had not commenced.

EREWASH CANAL.

17 George III. Cap. 69, Royal Assent 30th April, 1777.

The Erewash Canal commences in the River Trent, about a mile east of the village of Sawley, and nearly opposite the Soar River, or Loughborough Navigation; whence it takes a northerly course on the east side of Long Eaton, a mile and a half beyond which the Derby Canal Branch locks down into it. From this junction it runs parallel with and on the west side of the River Erewash, by Sandiacre, and across Nutbrook, by an aqueduct, at which place it is also joined by the Nutbrook Canal, about a mile and a half north of the last-mentioned village; hence it continues its course up the Erewash Vale, by Ilkeston and the Cotman Hay Collieries, to Newmanleys Mill, where it crosses the river into Nottinghamshire, and at about a mile beyond, it terminates in the Cromford Canal, near Langley Bridge. It is in length eleven miles and three quarters, viz. from the Trent to the Derby Canal, three miles and a quarter; from thence to the Nutbrook Canal, two miles and a half; and from thence to the Cromford Canal, six miles, to which there is a total rise, from the Trent, of nearly 109 feet. The canal was made under the authority of an act of the 17th George III. which is entitled, ' *An Act for making and* ' *maintaining a navigable Cut or Canal from the River Trent, in* ' *the lordships of Sawley and Long Eaton, in the county of Derby,* ' *to or near Langley Bridge, in the counties of Derby and Not-* ' *tingham.*' The proprietors, at the time the act was obtained, consisted of seventy-four persons, (amongst whom was the Duke of Rutland,) who were incorporated by the name of " The Com- " pany of Proprietors of the Erewash Canal, in the counties of " Derby and Nottingham," with power to raise among themselves the sum of £15,400, in one hundred and fifty-four shares of £100 each; and a further sum of £7,700, if necessary, either among themselves, or by the admission of new subscribers, or they may borrow the same on assignment of the rates as a security.

TONNAGE RATES.

	s.	d.	
Wheat, Rye, Beans, or Peas	0	6	per Quarter.
Malt	0	4	ditto.
Barley, or other Grain not before enumerated	0	5	ditto.
Coal and Coke	1	6	per Ton.
Slate	0	6	ditto.
All other Goods, Wares, or Merchandize (except Gravel, Stone, or other Materials for the repair of Roads)	2	0	ditto.
Lime or Lime-stone	0	1	per Ton, per Mile.

And so in Proportion for any greater or less Weight than a Ton.
One Hundred and Twenty Pounds Avoirdupois to be deemed a Hundred Weight.

	s.	d.	
Coal from the Hallam and Shipley Collieries, coming down the Nutbrook Canal, and passing along this Canal....	0	9	per Ton.
For all other Goods, Wares, or Merchandize	1	0	ditto.

Lords of manors or owners of lands may make wharfs or erect warehouses, and may charge the following rates.

WHARFAGE RATES.

	d.	
For any Description of Goods remaining for the Space of Ten Days....	6	per Ton.
For every Day after the Expiration of the above Time	½	ditto.

In the Act of the 33rd George III. cap. 102, for making the Derby Canal, a Clause is introduced, whereby the Erewash Canal Company have agreed, in consideration of the Advantages they will derive from a Connection with the Derby Canal, to reduce the Rates upon all Coal or Coke navigated on the Erewash, and passing thence into the Derby Canal, to Five-pence per Ton.

	d.	
Mercantile Goods which shall pass on the Erewash, between the Derby Canal and the River Trent, shall be charged only	3	per Ton.

And upon Lime, and all other Articles navigated on the Erewash, and afterwards on the Derby Canal, One-half only of the Rates they were previously entitled to.
The original Rates are however to be collected in case any other Canal or Railway be made between Derby and the Erewash.

By the 34th George III. cap. 95, for improving the Trent Navigation, it is enacted, that the Annual Rent of £5, paid by the Erewash Canal Company, shall cease, and in Lieu of it, every Boat laden, and crossing the River between the Loughborough Navigation and the Erewash Canal, shall pay Sixpence.

This canal was designed and executed chiefly by the owners of the extensive collieries and other mines situate on its line and at its northern extremity, with a view of obtaining a more certain mode of transporting their heavy produce to distant markets; but it has, subsequently, by its connection with the Derby, Cromford and Nottingham Canals, and by the great improvements which have taken place in the Trent Navigation, become a part of the line of communication for general commercial purposes; and when the Cromford and Peak Forest Railway is completed, it will derive some additional revenue incident to a position on the line of communication between London and the northern manufacturing districts.

EXE RIVER AND EXETER CANAL.

31 Henry VIII Cap. 4, Royal Assent ————— 1539.
10 Geo. IV. Cap. 47, Royal Assent 14th May, 1829.

This river has its source on Exmoor, at the westwardly termination of the Dunkerry Hills, in the county of Somerset, whence it pursues a south-eastwardly course, to within a mile of the town of Dulverton, and by Pixton Park, the seat of the Earl of Caernarvon, near which place it enters Devonshire. Its course, hence, is by Stuckbridge to Tiverton, to which place a branch of the intended Grand Western Canal extends; it then follows a southerly course, by Thorverton and Pynes, to the city of Exeter, near which place it is joined by the Creedy. From Exeter, the ancient course of the river is by Countess Wear Bridge, to the town of Topsham, where the river navigation commences. From the last-mentioned town to the sea, (into which it falls at Exmouth,) it is a considerable estuary, being in some places a mile and a half in width; and its length, by the low water channel, is nearly eight miles.

From the west side of the river, a little above the town of Topsham, a canal, above three miles in length, and running

parallel with the river, was made by the corporation of Exeter, to
that city, so early as the reign of Henry VIII. under powers of an
act granted in the thirty-first year of that reign, entitled, ' *An Act*
' *concerning the amending of the River and Port of Exeter,*' but
as this work was but very imperfectly constructed, and subject
to the ebb and flow of the tide, which, at its entrance, rises 13
feet at the springs, the mayor, bailiffs and commonalty stopped
up the entrance of this old canal, at the lower sluice, and extended
it lower down, into a deeper part of the tideway, to a place called
The Turf; considerable sums had been borrowed for carrying these
works into execution and improving the old cut, and as more
money was required for the purpose of completing the same and
the additional works contemplated, an act was obtained during the
last session, to enable the corporation to borrow a competent sum,
on mortgage of the undertaking, or by granting annuities on lives,
or by tontine.

This act is entitled, ' *An Act for altering, extending, and im-*
' *proving the Exeter Canal ;*' and when all is done which the act
authorizes, the canal will be, by the extension from the old lower
sluice to the estuary of the Exe, (two miles lower down,) five
miles in length, with a basin and entrance tide lock at The Turf,
and another commodious basin near the King's Arms Sluice, in the
city, where there is a public wharf 500 feet in length.   Another
entrance into this canal, with a lock, will also be placed above the
old sluice, near the town of Topsham, to facilitate the communication between that town and Exeter. The depth of the canal will be
15 feet.   Within a mile and a half from Exeter, there is a double
lock, with a fall of 6 feet; and at The Turf, a tide lock, with a fall
of 4 feet to high water, spring tides, which here rise 14 feet.
Mr. James Green projected these improvements in 1829, and
estimated the cost at £10,000, the whole of which sum is to be
advanced by the corporation of Exeter.

TONNAGE DUTIES.

		s.	*d.*	
For every Ship or other Vessel passing along any Part of this Canal, according to the Registered Tonnage of such Vessel, (if such Ship or Vessel shall be above Ten Tons, and under One Hundred and Ten)		0	6	per Ton.
If more than One Hundred and Ten Tons		0	9	ditto.
If less than Ten Tons		5	0	for such Vessel.

In ascertaining the admeasurement of ships entering this port, the party whose duty it is, shall be guided by the directions contained in an act of the 6th of George IV. cap. 110, entitled, ' *An* ' *Act for the Registering of British Vessels.*'

This act is not to prejudice the right which Edward and Robert Trood, as proprietors and occupiers of Matford Limekilns, have heretofore exercised, of passing along the canal to and from the lower sluice and the above works, at all times, free of toll; nor is it to affect the persons who have hitherto enjoyed, (in right of their estates,) the privilege of landing articles for their private use; nor any rights, privileges, tolls, petty customs, duties, powers, or authorities of the mayor, bailiff, and commonalty of the city of Exeter, or any of their accustomed rights and privileges.

In addition to the duties before-mentioned, the following tonnage rates are payable for wares and merchandize, &c.

SCHEDULE OR TABLE OF TOLLS.

Description of Goods.	Amount of Duty.		Quantity.
	s.	*d.*	
Alum	2	1	per Ton.
Almonds	2	6	Ditto.
Anchovies	0	1	per Barrel.
Anvils	2	6	per Ton.
Archel	2	6	Ditto.
Argoll	2	6	Ditto.
Ashes	0	6	per Barrel.
Bacon	2	6	per Ton.
Bales and Boxes by Measurement of 40 solid Feet	2	6	Ditto.
Bales of Woollens returned	0	4	20 Pieces.
Barilla	2	6	per Ton.
Ditto	0	7½	per Seron.
Bark	2	6	per Ton.
Barley	0	3	per Quarter.
Baulk Timber	1	4	per Load of 50 Feet.
Beans	0	4	per Quarter.
Bells and Bell Metal	2	6	per Ton.
Beer and Porter	1	6	per Butt.
Ditto	0	9	per Hogshead.
Ditto	0	6	per Barrel.
Ditto	0	3	per Kilderkin.
Bones	1	3	per 1,000.
Bottles (Quarts)	0	1	per Dozen.
Bones and Hoofs	1	0	per Hogshead.
Bran	0	3	per Quarter.
Brass and Iron Pots	2	6	per Ton.
Bricks (Stourbridge)	3	0	per 1,000.
Ditto (Scouring)	2	6	Ditto.
Ditto (Building)	2	6	Ditto.

SCHEDULE OR TABLE OF TOLLS CONTINUED.

Description of Goods.	Amount of Toll.		Quantity.
	s.	*d.*	
Brimstone...............................	2	6	per Ton.
Bristles.................................	2	6	Ditto.
Brooms	0	1	per Dozen.
Brush or Mop Sticks......................	0	1	per Bundle.
Brush Heads	0	1	per Six Dozen.
Brush Covers............................	0	0½	per Twelve Dozen.
Bullocks	1	6	each.
Burrs	6	3	per 100.
Butter..................................	2	6	per Ton.
Butts (empty)...........................	0	2	each.
Casks (empty)...........................	0	1	each.
Candles.................................	0	2½	per Box, Six Dozen.
Candy	2	6	per Ton.
Ditto..................................	0	2	per Box.
Carboys (full)	0	3	each.
Ditto (empty)	0	1	each.
Carraway Seeds	0	4	per Sack.
Cement	0	4	per Barrel.
Ditto..................................	0	2	Half ditto.
Ditto..................................	0	1	Quarter ditto.
Chariot or Chaise	6	3	
Chalk..................................	1	0	per Ton.
Chairs	0	2	each.
Cheese	2	6	per Ton.
Chimney Pots...........................	0	1	each.
Ditto Caps	0	1	per Dozen.
Ditto Hoods	0	1½	Ditto.
China..................................	1	6	per Hogshead.
Cider	1	6	per Pipe.
Ditto..................................	0	9	per Hogshead.
Clay (Pipe)	1	0	per Ton.
Clover Seed	0	1½	per Cwt.
Ditto..................................	0	4	per Sack.
Coach (Four Wheels)	7	6	
Coals (..................................	1	0	per Quarter.
Ditto (Canal)............................	2	6	per Ton.
Cochineal...............................	3	1½	Ditto.
Coffee..................................	2	6	Ditto.
Ditto..................................	0	6	Half Chest.
Ditto...	0	2	per Bag of One Cwt.
Coke..................................	1	3	per Ton.
Copper in Cases	2	6	per Ton of 40 Feet.
Ditto in Bolts and Plates	2	6	per Ton.
Copperas	2	6	Ditto.
Cork	5	0	Ditto.
Ditto..................................	0	3	per Bag of One Cwt.
Cordage................................	2	6	per Ton.
Crates of Earthenware....................	1	0	each.
Ditto Vial Bottles	2	6	per 40 Feet.
Ditto Glass	2	6	Ditto.
Currants................................	2	6	per Butt of Twenty Cwt.
Ditto..................................	1	3	per Pipe of Ten Cwt.
Ditto in Sacks	0	1½	per Cwt.
Deals 12 Feet 9 Inches...................	7	3	per 120.
Dye Stuff	2	6	per Ton.
Dye Woods in general	2	6	Ditto.

SCHEDULE OR TABLE OF TOLLS CONTINUED.

Description of Goods.	Amount of Duty.		Quantity.
	s.	d.	
Drain Pipes	2	6	per 1,000.
Earthenware (loose)	2	6	per Load.
Ends of Serges	0	2	Ten Pieces.
Bales of Ditto	0	4	Twenty Pieces.
Feathers	0	9	per Sack, Three Cwt.
Fellies of Wheels	0	2	per Dozen.
Fender Plate	2	6	per Ton.
Figs	1	3	per Twenty Frails.
Ditto	0	9	per Twenty Drums.
Fish (Newfoundland)	2	6	per Ton.
Fish (fresh) subject to a Toll of Six Dozen	Free.		
Fire Wood	1	0	per Fathom.
Flax	3	1½	per Ton.
Flocks	2	6	Ditto.
Flour	0	3	per Sack.
Ditto	0	2½	per Barrel.
Frying Pans	0	1½	per Bundle.
Furniture	2	6	per Forty Feet.
Ginger	2	6	per Ton.
Glass	0	6	per Side.
Ditto (White) broken	2	6	per Ton.
Ditto (Green) Ditto	1	3	Ditto.
Glue, in Bags	2	6	Ditto.
Ditto, Pieces	1	0	per Hogshead.
Ditto, ditto, in Bundles	2	6	per Ton.
Grinding Stones	2	6	per Chald. Thirty-six Feet
Gunpowder	0	3	per Barrel.
Gunstocks	0	2	per Dozen.
Hair, in Bales	2	6	per Forty Feet.
Hampers (full)	2	6	
Ditto, empty Bottles, Three or Four Dozen	0	4	each.
Handspikes	1	0	per Hundred.
Hemp	3	1½	per Ton.
Herrings (Red)	0	4	per Barrel.
Hides (Raw)	3	6	per Fifty.
Ditto (Dry)	3	6	Ditto.
Ditto (Horse)	1	6	Ditto.
Ditto (Kips)	0	3	per Dozen.
Horns and Bones (loose)	1	3	per 1,000.
Hops	0	6	per Bag.
Ditto	0	3	per Pocket.
Hoops Wood (broad)	0	1	per Dozen.
Ditto Wood (small)	2	6	Fifty Bundles.
Ditto Iron	2	6	per Ton.
Hurdles, Wood and Iron	2	6	per Thirty.
Jars (Quart)	0	0½	per Dozen.
Indigo	0	1½	per Cwt.
Iron (Bar and Bolt)	2	6	per Ton.
Iron Pots, Kettles, and Weights	2	6	Ditto.
Iron in Pigs	2	0	Ditto.
Ironmongery, in Packages	2	6	per Forty Feet.
Iron (Scrap)	1	3	per Ton.
Junk	2	6	Ditto.
Ladder Poles	12	0	per 120
Laths	0	4	per 1,000.
Lath Wood	4	0	per Fathom.

SCHEDULE OR TABLE OF TOLLS CONTINUED

Description of Goods.	Amount of Duty.		Quantity.
	s.	*d.*	
Lancewood Poles	6	0	per 120.
Lead, in Sheets	2	6	per Ton.
Ditto in Pigs	2	6	Ditto.
Ditto in Pipe	2	6	Ditto.
Ditto in White Ground	2	6	Ditto.
Leather	2	6	Ditto.
Lignum Vitæ	2	6	Ditto.
Lime	1	3	Ditto.
Lime-stone	0	6	Ditto.
Litharge	2	6	Ditto.
Logwood	2	6	Ditto.
Madder	2	6	per Ton.
Mahogany	2	6	per Forty Feet
Malt	0	3	per Quarter.
Manganese	1	6	per Ton.
Manure	0	10	Ditto.
Marble	2	6	per Ton of Twelve Feet.
Ditto in Cases	2	6	Ditto of Twenty Feet.
Mats (Gardeners)	0	4	per Bundle of 50.
Ditto (Door)	2	6	per Forty Feet.
Metal (Brass or Bell)	2	6	per Ton.
Millstones	1	9	each.
Molasses	1	3	per Puncheon.
Mops	0	1	per Dozen.
Mopsticks	0	1	per Bundle.
Mustard	0	2	per Barrel, Seventy-two lbs.
Nails, in Bags	0	1½	per Cwt.
Nail Rods	2	6	per Ton.
Naive Stocks	0	2	per Pair.
Nuts	0	3	per Bag.
Oakum	2	6	per Ton.
Oak Timber	2	6	per Forty Feet.
Oats and Oatmeal	0	3	per Quarter.
Ochre	2	6	per Ton.
Oil (not exceeding 120 Gallons)	1	6	per Pipe.
Oil	0	2¼	per Half Chest.
Ditto, Olive	0	7½	per Jar.
Oilcake	2	6	per Ton.
Oranges and Lemons	0	4	per Chest.
Ditto	0	2	per Box.
Ox Bows	0	1	per Dozen.
Paints	2	6	per Ton.
Paper in Bales	2	6	per Forty Feet.
Ditto (Writing)	0	0½	per Ream.
Ditto (Whited Brown)	0	0½	Ditto.
Patten Rings	2	6	per Ton.
Pepper	3	1½	Ditto.
Ditto, per Mat of Three Cwt.	0	6	Ditto.
Peas	0	4	per Quarter.
Pipes (Tobacco) in Boxes	2	6	per Forty Feet.
Pipe Clay	1	0	per Ton.
Pitch	0	4	per Barrel.
Plaister Paris	2	0	per Ton.
Potatoes	1	0	Ditto.
Ditto	0	1	per Bag.
Rags	2	6	per Ton.

SCHEDULE OR TABLE OF TOLLS CONTINUED.

Description of Goods.	Amount of Duty.		Quantity.
	s.	*d.*	
Raisins......................................	0	6	per Barrel.
Ditto......................................	0	1	per Box of Half Cwt.
Ditto......................................	0	0½	per Half Box.
Rice......................................	0	9	per Barrel.
Ditto......................................	0	2	per Bag of One Cwt.
Rosin	0	4	per Barrel.
Ditto in Cakes	2	6	per Ton.
Salt......................................	2	1	Ditto.
Salt and Ashes for Manure	0	10	Ditto.
Saltpetre	0	2	per Barrel.
Salting Pans (large)	0	6	per Dozen.
Ditto (middle)	0	4	Ditto.
Ditto (small)	0	2	Ditto.
Sand	0	9	per Ton.
Scythe Stones	0	2½	per Basket.
Seeds in general	0	4	per Sack.
Sharemoulds................................	2	6	per Ton.
Shreds.....................................	2	6	Ditto.
Ditto.....................................	1	0	per Hogshead.
Shot.......................................	2	6	per Ton.
Shumac	2	6	Ditto.
Skins, Calves (wet)	0	1	per Dozen.
Ditto, ditto (dry)	0	1	Ditto.
Ditto, Deer	2	6	per Hundred.
Ditto, ditto (in Hair)	2	6	Ditto.
Ditto, Goat	0	0½	per Dozen.
Ditto, Pelts	1	0	per Hogshead.
Ditto, Pelts (loose).........................	0	0½	per Dozen.
Ditto, Seal	0	1	Ditto.
Ditto, Roan...............................	2	6	per Ton.
Ditto, Sheep (dressed)	0	2	per Dozen.
Ditto, Lamb (ditto)........................	0	0½	Ditto.
Ditto, Lamb Pelts..........................	0	3	per Ten Dozen.
Ditto, Lamb Split Pelts	0	2	Ditto.
Ditto, Indian Deer	0	1½	per 100.
Ditto, Beaver	0	1½	Ditto.
Ditto, Kid	0	3	per 120.
Ditto, Bazil...............................	0	1	per Dozen.
Slate, Duchesses...........................	3	6	per 1,200.
Ditto, ditto (small)	3	0	Ditto.
Ditto, ditto, Countesses	2	6	Ditto.
Ditto, ditto (small)	2	0	Ditto.
Ditto, Ladies	1	6	Ditto.
Ditto, ditto (small)	1	1½	Ditto.
Ditto, Doubles	1	0	Ditto.
Ditto, Scantile	1	0	Ditto.
Ditto, common or small	0	6	Ditto.
Ditto, Unsized Rag	0	2	per Dozen.
Ditto, ditto, Half ditto	0	1	Ditto.
Ditto, Queen or Sized Rag	2	0	per Ton.
Ditto, Slab	2	0	Ditto.
Ditto, Block	2	3	Ditto.
Ditto, Westmoreland Rag....................	2	3	Ditto.
Ditto, Imperial or Milled	2	4½	Ditto
Ditto, Welsh and Rag Square	1	8	Ditto.
Smalts.....................................	0	1½	per Cwt.

SCHEDULE OR TABLE OF TOLLS CONTINUED.

Description of Goods.	Amount of Duty.		Quantity.
	s.	*d.*	
Soap in Chests	2	6	per Forty Feet.
Ditto, Foreign	2	6	per Ton.
Spars	12	0	per 120.
Staves, Pipe...........................	1	0	Ditto.
Ditto, Puncheon........................	0	8	Ditto.
Ditto, Hogshead	0	6	Ditto.
Ditto, Barrel	0	5	Ditto.
Ditto, Quebec Logs.....................	1	6	Ditto.
Starch in Chests.......................	2	6	per Forty Feet.
Steel	2	6	per Ton.
Stone Ware (loose)	0	0½	per Three Gallons.
Stone, Portland.......................	1	6	per Ton of Sixteen Feet.
Ditto, Bath	1	6	per Twenty Feet.
Ditto, Paving	1	6	per Sixty Feet.
Ditto, Beer...........................	1	6	per Eighteen Feet.
Ditto, Granite	1	6	per Twenty-seven Feet.
Ditto, Free	1	6	per Eighteen Feet.
Ditto, Grave and Gutter	1	6	per Thirty Feet.
Ditto, Step	1	6	Ditto.
Ditto, Rolling........................	1	6	per Sixteen Feet.
Ditto, Trough	1	6	per Sixty Feet.
Ditto, Moor...........................	1	6	per Twenty-seven Feet.
Ditto, Pebble.........................	1	3	per Ton of Twenty Cwt.
Sugar, Solid	1	3	per Hhd. of Fifteen Cwt.
Ditto, packed.........................	1	3	per Hogshead.
Ditto, in Lumps and Loaves	2	6	per Ton.
Ditto, in Bags	0	1¼	per Cwt.
Ditto, in Mats	0	1½	Ditto.
Tallow................................	2	6	per Ton.
Tar	0	4	per Barrel.
Tea	1	0	per Chest.
Ditto.................................	0	6	per Half ditto.
Ditto.................................	0	3	per Quarter ditto.
Tiles	2	6	per 1,000.
Timber in general	2	6	per Ton of Forty Feet.
(If shipped from the Quay, 4*d.* per Ton Quayage.)			
Tin	0	2	per Box.
Tobacco...............................	3	1½	per Ton.
Trees and Shrubs, in Mats	2	6	per Forty Feet.
Valonia	2	6	per Ton.
Veneers	2	6	per Forty Feet.
Vinegar	1	6	per Pipe.
Vitriol	0	3	per Carboy.
Vetches and Tares.....................	0	4	per Quarter.
Wainscot Logs	2	6	per Forty Feet.
Wax	2	6	per Ton.
Withies	2	6	per Forty Bundles.
Whalebone	2	6	per Ton.
Wheat.................................	0	4	per Quarter.
Wheels (Coach)	1	3	per Set.
Whitng...............................	1	0	per Ton.
Wire.................................	0	2	per Bundle of One Cwt.
Wine and Spirits......................	1	6	per Pipe.
Ditto, ditto, cased	1	8	Ditto.
Wine and Spirits......................	0	9	per Hogshead.

SCHEDULE OR TABLE OF TOLLS CONTINUED.

Description of Goods.	Amount of Duty.		Quantity.
	s.	d.	
Wine and Spirits, cased......................	0	10	per Hogshead.
Wine in Hampers	2	6	per Forty Feet.
Woad	1	6	per Hogshead.
Wool...	0	6	per Pack of Three Cwt.
Yarn...	2	6	per Ton.
Yarn Wick...................................	0	6	per Bag of Twelve Dozen.

All Goods not herein specified to pay Two Shillings and Sixpence per Ton of Twenty Hundred Weight, or Measurement of Forty solid Feet. All empty Packages to pay One Penny each. No single Package, full or empty, to pay less than Two-pence.

It is to be understood, that the payment of the above tolls does not free the owners of vessels from the petty customs and town dues payable to the corporation, in respect of all goods entering the port of Exeter.

Some idea may be formed of the traffic on this navigation, by stating, that in the year 1824, sixty-nine British and five Foreign vessels entered the port of Exeter.

It may here be remarked, that several attempts have been made to extend the navigation from Exeter; one in 1769, when Mr. John Brindley designed a canal to commence at that city, thence by the towns of Tiverton, Wellington, Taunton, and Glastonbury, to the Bristol Channel at Uphill Bay. It was to be called the Exeter and Uphill Canal; but the act was never obtained.

Another attempt was made by a company of twenty-two persons (amongst whom was Sir Lawrence Palk, Bart.) to form a navigation from the Exeter Canal to the town of Crediton, by widening and deepening the Rivers Exe and Creedy, and making cuts for the purpose of passing the mill weirs, &c.; an act was obtained for this purpose on the 20th June, 1801, entitled, ' *An* ' *Act for improving and extending the Navigation of the River* ' *Exe, from the public Quay at Exeter, to the public Road ad-* ' *joining Four Mills, near Crediton, in the county of Devon, by* ' *making a navigable Canal or Cuts, and deepening and widening* ' *such Parts of the Rivers Exe and Credy, as shall be necessary* ' *for that Purpose.*' The subscribers were incorporated by the

name of " The Company of Proprietors of the Exeter and Cre-
" diton Navigation," with power to raise £21,400, in two hundred
and fourteen shares of £100 each, and an additional sum of
£10,700, if necessary.

At the two extremities of this proposed navigation, basins were
to be made, with the necessary accommodation of warehouses,
wharfs, weighing beams, cranes, &c. Very heavy rates were allowed by this act, viz. for timber, 1s. per ton per mile, and all
other articles, except manure and lime for manure, 6d. per ton
per mile. An additional rate of 2d. per ton was also to be paid for
entering any basin belonging to this navigation.

Notwithstanding these demonstrations, and the encouragement
given by the legislature to the projectors by this favourable act,
no further steps appear to have been taken for carrying its powers
into execution; nor is there now much prospect of it.

FAL OR VALE RIVER.

30 Charles II. Cap. 11, Royal Assent 15th July, 1678.

THIS river has its source on the high grounds three miles east
of the town of St. Columb Major, in Cornwall, whence it flows
southwardly by the stream works on Tregoss Moor, and by other
tin mines, to Grampound; thence through Golden Vale, and by
Tregony to Trewarthenick, where it becomes of considerable
width; and, after winding through the extensive woods and plan-
tations belonging to Tregothnan, the elegant seat of the Earl of
Falmouth, it opens into a considerable estuary, sometimes called
the Mopus, which conducts through Garreg Roads to Falmouth
Harbour, and thence into the sea at Falmouth Bay.

This is a tideway river; and an act was obtained in the reign
of Charles the Second to improve it; but, in consequence of Tregony declining in the exact ratio with the growing importance of
Truro, (which may be said to be the capital of Cornwall,) this
navigation seems now to be of little consequence. The act is entitled, ' An Act for making navigable the River Fale or Vale, in
' the county of Cornwall.'

Truro is one of the principal markets for the sale of the produce of the Cornish Mines; and, from its being situate on a navigable branch of the Fal, called the River Mopus, and about eleven miles north from Falmouth, it possesses all the advantages required for the shipment of the vast quantity of copper and other valuable ores, which this rich mineral district continues to produce.

Falmouth, situate at the mouth of this river, is a sea-port, into which, in 1824, twenty-nine British and eight Foreign vessels entered. It possesses an excellent harbour, and a fine and spacious roadstead; but it derives its chief importance from being the regular station of the packet boats, which carry Foreign mails into all parts of the world.

FORTH RIVER.

THIS noble river has its source about two miles north of Ben Lomond, (that celebrated mountain in Scotland, which rears its giant form 3,262 feet above the level of the sea,) and proceeds south-easterly, passing the Clachan of Aberfoil by a very serpentine course, through a comparatively level district, (which in Scotland is denominated Carse Lands,) to a short distance above Stirling, where it is joined by the River Teth, which flows from the Lochs Catrine, Achray, Venacher, and others situate in the wild district of the Grampians.

About midway between the above junction and Stirling, it is joined by the River Allan. From Stirling the windings of the river are singularly intricate; and, in its meanderings to Alloa, (which is but six miles in a straight line,) it takes such strange peninsulating sweeps, that its course measures nearly twenty miles. However beautiful this part may appear, it is exceedingly troublesome to the navigator; for, though vessels of from sixty to seventy tons burthen have sufficient water to Stirling, yet if they trusted to sails alone, they would require wind from every point of the compass to bring them to their destination, and that more than once; on which account, this part of the river is little used as a navigation.

About three miles west of Alloa, the navigable River Devon falls into the Forth; but between it and the town above-mentioned, a stratum of rock occupies the bed of the river, which constitutes a kind of bar, over which vessels of more than seventy tons seldom venture. This place is a little above the largest island in the river, and is designated the Thrask Shallows. From the Devon, the Forth gradually opens into an estuary, which, opposite the mouth of the Carron, is two miles in width; and a few miles further down, between Borrowstounness and Culross, it is full three miles; but again contracts to little more than one mile a short distance below Queen's Ferry. At Leith, which is seven miles and a half below the last-mentioned place, it is nearly six miles in width; and between Preston Pans and Kirkaldy, it is above twelve miles.

The length of this magnificent river and estuary, from Stirling to the Isle of May, where it may be said to enter the German Ocean, is about seventy English miles, viz. from Stirling to opposite the River Carron and Forth and Clyde Canal, twenty-four miles; thence to Leith twenty miles; and to the Isle of May it is twenty-six miles. Within the limits above described are five ports, viz. Leith, Alloa, Anstruther, Grangemouth and Preston Pans.

The tide flows up this river to Craigforth Mill, a short distance beyond Stirling; and at Cambus Quay, at the mouth of the Devon, (though above fifty miles from the sea,) it is frequently known to rise 20 feet at spring tides. Several attempts have been made to improve the navigation beyond Alloa; and in particular by Messrs. Watt and Morrison, in 1767. These gentlemen proposed to extend the navigation from Stirling to the lime and slate quarries at Aberfoil, and, by four cuts, to shorten the course from Stirling to Alloa seven miles. Mr. Smeaton's opinion was taken on these proposed improvements, and also as to the removal or avoiding the Thrask Shallows; and though all was proved quite practicable, they have been suffered, either from the want of spirit in the parties most interested, or from one cause or other, to remain in *statu quo*, with all their imperfections.

The River Forth is a free navigation; the only tolls paid on it being for the use, and towards the support of several ferries, for which an act was obtained in the 32nd of George III. cap. 93, entitled, ' *An Act for improving the Communication between the* ' *county of Edinburgh and the county of Fife, by the Passages or* ' *Ferries across the Firth of Forth, between Leith and Newhaven, in* ' *the county of Edinburgh, and Kinghorn and Bruntisland, in the* ' *county of Fife; and for rendering the Harbours and Landing* ' *Places more commodious.*'

It appears, by an act made in the parliament of Scotland in 1669, entitled, ' *Act for repairing Highways and Bridges,*' and another in 1686, entitled, ' *Additional Act anent Highways and* ' *Bridges,*' that justices of the peace, assisted by the commissioners of supply in the several shires, are empowered to manage and regulate the ferries of the Forth.

By the act of 32nd George III. above-recited, additional powers are granted for maintaining the ferries between Kinghorn and Newhaven, and Bruntisland and Leith and Newhaven, and the following tolls and duties are payable.

FERRY TOLLS.

	s.	d.	
For every Person	0	1	
For every Horse and Cart Load of Goods	0	2	each.
Carriages with Two Wheels (not subject to a higher Duty)	0	3	ditto.
Ditto, ditto, (liable to pay Duty)	0	6	ditto.
Ditto, Four Wheels	1	6	ditto.
Oxen and other Cattle	1	8	per Score.
Calves, Hogs, Sheep or Lambs	0	10	ditto.
Grain or Meal	0	$\frac{1}{2}$	per Boll.

These Duties are over and above what is paid to the Skipper or Boat's Crew.

Vessels entering the Harbours of Kinghorn or Bruntisland, according to their Admeasurement............ } 0 $\frac{1}{4}$ per Ton.

The trustees for the management of these ferries may borrow £3,000 on the credit of the duties; of which £600 was to be spent in improving the basin at Kinghorn, otherwise Pettycur; and an equal sum in improving the communication to this harbour from the east; £900 in building an inn at Pettycur, (of which £600 is to be repaid by the burgh of Kinghorn;) £50 towards keeping a light at Pettycur Harbour, and the like sum for another at Bruntisland; £500 in improving the communication between the turnpike road and the harbour of Bruntisland; and £1,000 in erecting a pier and landing at Newhaven.

On the River Forth a very extensive general trade is constantly maintained; for, independently of the vast quantity of merchandize which must necessarily pass along it, to supply the richest and most populous parts of Scotland, it has, by means of the Forth and Clyde Canal, a communication with the extensive manufacturing districts around Glasgow and Paisley, and with the western parts of England and Scotland, and with Ireland. On its banks are eighteen market towns; and it washes the shores of eight of its counties.

Leith being the port of. Edinburgh, and the principal rendezvous for shipping, considerable cost has been incurred in rendering the harbour proportionably commodious. In 1777 a new quay was constructed on the north side of the harbour. In 1806 a beautiful basin, 750 feet in length, and 300 in breadth, was opened, capable of containing forty ships of two hundred tons burthen. A second was finished in 1817; and these, together with three graving docks, occupy a site of eight acres, and have cost £250,000. Ships of very large burthen cannot enter this port; there being but 16 feet at spring tides, and 9 only at neaps.

A tolerable estimate of the extent of the trade which is carried on at this port, may be formed from parliamentary documents, by which it appears that custom duties were paid, in the year 1824, upon two hundred and twenty-two British, and one hundred and forty-six Foreign ships.

FORTH AND CLYDE CANAL.

8 Geo. III. C. 63, R. A. 8th Mar. 1768.   11 Geo. III. C. 62, R. A. 8th Mar. 1771.
13 Geo. III. C. 104, R. A. 10th May, 1773.   24 Geo. III. C. 59, R. A. 19th Aug. 1784.
27 Geo. III. C. 20, R. A. 21st May, 1787.   27 Geo. III. C. 35, R. A. 28th May, 1787.
30 Geo. III. C. 73, R. A. 9th June, 1790.   39 Geo. III. C. 71, R. A. 12th July, 1799.
46 Geo. III. C. 120, R. A. 12th July, 1806.   54 Geo. III. C. 195, R. A. 14th July, 1814.
1 Geo. IV. C. 48, R. A. 8th July, 1820.

This magnificent canal commences in the River Forth, in Grangemouth Harbour, and near to where the Carron empties itself into that river. Its course is parallel with the Carron, and in nearly a westwardly direction, passing to the north of the town of Falkirk, and thence to Red Bridge, where it quits the county of Stirling, and enters a detached portion of the shire of Dumbarton. Hence it passes to the south of Kilsyth, and runs along the south bank of the River Kelvin, and over the Logie Water, by a fine stone aqueduct, at Kirkintilloch; it then approaches within little more than two miles of the north-west quarter of the city of Glasgow, to which there is a branch communicating with the Monkland Canal at Port Dundas, near that city. The remaining part of the line is in a westwardly direction, crossing the Kelvin River by a noble aqueduct, and thence to the Clyde, into which, after running parallel with it for some distance, it locks down at Bowling's Bay, near Dalmuir Burnfoot.

The canal is thirty-five miles in length, viz. from Grangemouth to the east end of the summit pool, is ten miles and three quarters, with a rise, from low water in the Forth, of 155 feet, by twenty locks. The summit level is sixteen miles in length, and in the remainder of its course, there is a fall to low water, in the Clyde, at Bowling's Bay, of 156 feet, by nineteen locks.

The branch to the Monkland Canal at Glasgow is two miles and three quarters; and there is another cut into the Carron River, at Carron Shore, in order to communicate with the Carron Iron Works.

Though this canal was originally constructed for vessels drawing 7 feet, yet by recent improvements, sea-borne craft of 10 feet draught may now pass through it, from the Irish Sea to the German Ocean. The locks are 74 feet long and 20 wide; and upon its course are thirty-three draw-bridges, ten large aqueducts and thirty-three smaller ones; that over the Kelvin being 429 feet long and 65 feet above the surface of the stream. It is supplied with water from reservoirs; one of which, at Kilmananmuir, is seventy acres, and 22 feet deep at the sluice; and that at Kilsyth is fifty acres in extent, with 24 feet water at its head.

The first act of parliament relating to this canal, received the royal assent on the 8th of March, 1768, and it is entitled, ' *An Act* ' *for making and maintaining a navigable Canal from the Firth or* ' *River of Forth, at or near the mouth of the River Carron, in* ' *the county of Stirling, to the Firth or River of Clyde, at or near a* ' *place called Dalmuir Burnfoot, in the county of Dumbarton; and* ' *also a collateral Cut from the same to the city of Glasgow; and* ' *for making a navigable Cut or Canal of Communication from the* ' *Port or Harbour of Borrowstounness, to join the said Canal at or* ' *near the place where it will fall into the Firth of Forth.*'

The subscribers were incorporated by the name of " The " Company of Proprietors of the Forth and Clyde Navigation," with power to raise among themselves the sum of £150,000, in fifteen hundred shares of £100 each, and an additional sum of £50,000, if necessary.

Although it was not until after the passing of the above act that this great work was commenced, yet the project of forming a communication between the eastern and western seas had been agitated a long time previous; and, even as early as the reign of Charles the Second, the design was thought to be one of so much utility, that that monarch took measures for cutting a canal, through which, not only ordinary vessels, but also small ships of war might pass between sea and sea, without the danger of coasting.

The estimated cost of this early project was £500,000; but a variety of circumstances, and particularly the difficulty of raising such a sum, caused the prosecution of the design to be neglected, and no further steps were taken till 1723. In that year a survey and estimate were made by Mr. Gordon, an engineer of repute; but his calculation of the expenses deterred the projectors, and nothing was done. Thirty-six years after, Lord Napier employed Mr. Machell to lay down the plan of a canal, which should begin at the Clyde, about four miles below Glasgow, and end in the Forth, near the mouth of the River Carron. Mr. Machell's report in 1764 placed the utility of the undertaking in so striking a point of view, that " The Honourable the Board of Trustees for " encouraging Fisheries, Manufactures, and Improvements in " Scotland," immediately employed Mr. Smeaton to make the necessary surveys, and to estimate thereon. This eminent engineer produced a design, which at first deterred the parties by whom he was employed, as well by the apparent difficulties to be encountered, as by the immense sum he deemed necessary for its completion; but, on the projection of a smaller canal, opening a communication between Glasgow and the Forth, Mr. Smeaton's plan was reconsidered; and, after he had convinced all parties of the practicability of it, and completely refuted the objections of Mr. Brindley and other engineers, the act above-recited was obtained, and the execution of the canal immediately commenced under his direction.

Estimates were made by Mr. Smeaton, of the several lines and various dimensions proposed for this canal; but the one under which the work was commenced amounted to £147,337, but augmented to £149,244, 8s. by the additional expense incident to a change in the line, which was effected under powers of an act of 11th George III. entitled, '*An Act to explain, amend, and render*
'*more effectual, an Act made in the Eighth Year of his present*
'*Majesty's Reign, entitled, An Act for making and maintaining a*
'*navigable Cut or Canal from the Firth or River of Forth, at or*
'*near the mouth of the River of Carron, in the county of Stirling,*
'*to the Firth or River of Clyde, at or near a place called Dalmuir*
'*Burnfoot, in the county of Dumbarton; and also a collateral Cut*
'*from the same to the city of Glasgow; and for making a navigable*
'*Cut or Canal of Communication from the Port and Harbour of*
'*Borrowstounness, to join the said Canal at or near the place*
'*where it will fall into the River of Forth.*' Several other acts became necessary as the works proceeded; but as they have relation chiefly to the supply of the requisite funds for prosecuting the undertaking, we shall but briefly notice them.

The third act received the royal assent on the 10th May, 1773, and is entitled, '*An Act to enlarge the Powers of two Acts,*
'*made in the Eighth and Eleventh Years of the Reign of his pre-*
'*sent Majesty, for making and maintaining a navigable Cut or*
'*Canal from the Firth or River of Forth, at or near the mouth of*
'*the River of Carron, in the county of Stirling, to the Firth or*
'*River of Clyde, at or near a place called Dalmuir Burnfoot, in*
'*the county of Dumbarton; and also a collateral Cut from the*
'*same to the city of Glasgow; and for making a navigable Cut or*
'*Canal of Communication from the Port and Harbour of Borrow-*
'*stounness, to join the said Canal, at or near the place where it*
'*will fall into the Firth of Forth;*' by which the company are authorized to borrow, on assignment of the tolls as a security, the sum of £70,000.

The execution of this canal proceeded with such rapidity, under the direction of Mr. Smeaton, that in two years and three quarters from the date of the first act, one half of the work was finished; when, in consequence of some misunderstanding between him and the proprietors, he declined any further connection with the work, which was shortly afterwards let to contractors, who however failed, and the canal was again placed under the direction of its original projector, who brought it to within six miles of its proposed junction with the Clyde, when the work was stopped in 1775 for want of funds, and it continued at a stand for several years.

For the purpose, however, of opening a communication between the part already executed and the city of Glasgow, a subscription was entered into by the inhabitants of that place, to make a branch, so that by effecting a junction with the Forth, the part excavated might immediately be brought into useful operation.

After the lapse of nine years from the stoppage above alluded to, an act was obtained, entitled, ' *An Act for extending, amending* ' *and altering the Powers of an Act made in the Eighth Year of* ' *his present Majesty, entitled, An Act for making and maintaining* ' *a navigable Canal from the Firth or River of Forth, at or near* ' *the mouth of the River Carron, in the county of Stirling, to the* ' *Firth or River of Clyde, at or near a place called Dalmuir Burnfoot,* ' *in the county of Dumbarton; and also a collateral Cut from the* ' *same to the city of Glasgow; and for making a navigable Cut or* ' *Canal of Communication from the Port or Harbour of Borrow-* ' *stounness, to join the said Canal at or near the place where it will* ' *fall into the Firth of Forth,*' by which the Barons of the Court of Exchequer in Scotland, are, out of the money arising from the sale of forfeited estates, directed to lend the Forth and Clyde Navigation Company the sum of £50,000, by which they were enabled to resume their labours, under the direction of Mr. Robert Whitworth, an engineer possessing a well earned reputation, and by whom it was finished and opened on the 28th July, 1790. Previous, however, to this period, three other acts of parliament relating to this canal received the royal sanction; of which, one was on the 21st of May, in the 27th of George III. and another the week following, and the last on the 9th of June, in the 30th of that reign.

The first which passed into a law is entitled, ' *An Act for* ' *varying and extending the Powers of the Company of Proprietors* ' *of the Forth and Clyde Navigation;*' and the other, ' *An Act for* ' *altering and extending the Line of the Cut or Canal, authorized*

' to be made and maintained by so much of several Acts made in the
' Eighth, Eleventh, Thirteenth and Twenty-fourth Years of the
' Reign of his present Majesty, as authorizes the making and main-
' taining a navigable Cut or Canal from the Firth or River of
' Forth, at or near the mouth of the River of Carron, in the county
' of Stirling, to the Firth or River of Clyde, at or near a place
' called Dalmuir Burnfoot, in the county of Dumbarton; and also
' a collateral Cut from the same to the city of Glasgow; for
' deepening the said Cut or Canal; and for explaining and amending
' so much of the said Acts, as relates to the making and maintaining
' the said Cut or Canal.' The 30th George III. is entitled, ' An
' Act for forming a Junction between the Forth and Clyde Naviga-
' tion, and the Monkland Navigation; and for altering, enlarging
' and explaining several former Acts passed for making and main-
' taining the said Navigation.'

On the 12th of July, 1799, an act was passed to enable the
company to repay the sum of £50,000, borrowed of the Court of
Exchequer in Scotland, and to declare the capital stock of the
company to amount to £421,525, notwithstanding that the company were restrained, by the act of 8th George III. from dividing
more than ten per cent. on the original stock of £150,000. This,
however, was permitted, in consequence of the proprietors having
never received any dividend. This act is entitled, ' An Act for
' empowering the Company of Proprietors of the Forth and Clyde
' Navigation to repay into the Court of Exchequer in Scotland, the
' Sum advanced to them for the Purpose of completing the said
' Navigation; for repealing so much of an Act of the Twenty-fourth
' of his present Majesty as relates to the said Company; and for
' enabling the Barons of the said Court of Exchequer to advance
' Part of the Sum so to be received, to the Company of Proprietors
' of the Crinan Canal, on certain Conditions.'

By the act of 46th George III. a very material change is
effected in the constitution of the company, and of the rates which
they have hitherto received. It is entitled, ' An Act to alter and
' amend the several Acts passed for making and maintaining the
' Forth and Clyde Navigation;' by which it is enacted that the
management of this concern shall be in future vested in a governor
and seven other persons, who shall be called "The Governor and

" Council of the Company of Proprietors of the Forth and Clyde
" Navigation," who have power to appoint a committee of three.
The schedule of tolls granted in the former acts are hereby
repealed ; and the following tonnage rates are allowed in lieu
thereof.

TONNAGE RATES.

	d.
All Goods and Commodities whatsoever	4 per Ton, per Mile.
Light Boats or other Vessels, without lading or in Ballast only, (according to their respective Register or Admeasurement)	2 ditto. ditto.
British or Irish Vessels lying in any of the Harbours or Basins	2 per Ton.
Foreign ditto, ditto, ...	4 ditto.
Timber lying in any of the Basins	4 per Ton, per Month.

And so in Proportion for any greater or less Time than a Month.

WHARFAGE RATES.

	d.
Goods and Commodities, remaining above Twenty-four Hours upon any of the Quays, Wharfs, or Landing Places, or at any Place on the Line of Navigation	2 per Ton, per Day.

And so in Proportion.

Goods landed or put into Lighters from, and on all Goods loaded into, Vessels lying in the said Canal or Basins....	2 per Ton.
Every Vessel lying in any of the Basins for a longer Time than Twenty-four Days.................................	1 per Ton, per Day.

Every Vessel coming into any of the said Harbours or Basins, a Duty of Sixpence
sterling, on every Fifty Tons of the Burthen thereof, for Lighting the said Harbours
and Basins.

The act of 54th George III. is entitled, ' *An Act to enlarge,*
' *alter, and amend the Powers of the several Acts for making and*
' *maintaining the Forth and Clyde Navigation ;*' and by which the
company of proprietors are empowered to purchase ground for
extending the basin, and to make new wharfs at Port Dundas, near
Glasgow, and to make the canal 10 feet deep. This act further
directs that Lord Dundas shall be entitled to receive, for all vessels
lying on the south side of the outer basin at Grangemouth, the
same rates of wharfage which the company are empowered to
collect under power of the 46th George III. In the act which
authorizes the company to carry the above works into execution,
a power is given to borrow the sum of £40,000, on security of the
rates and duties.

In consideration of the expense the company will incur by
maintaining a bank and towing paths from the harbour of Grangemouth to the mouth of the Carron River, they are empowered to
demand, from all ships and other vessels coming from Grange-

mouth Harbour, or using the towing path in navigating the river of Carron, the sum of 4*d*. per ton, according to the registered admeasurement of such vessel.

The last act relating to this navigation received the royal assent on the 8th of July, 1820. It is entitled, ' *An Act for altering and* ' *amending several Acts for making and maintaining the Forth and* ' *Clyde Navigation ;*' wherein it appears, that since the passing of the act of 39th George III. the company have, by enlarging the canal, and increasing its depth to 9 feet, and by other works, expended the further sum of £98,315, including the £40,000, borrowed under authority of the last-recited act; by which their stock has accumulated to, and is hereafter to be considered as £519,840.

Power is given to borrow £80,000, on assignment of the rates, for the purpose of making the canal 1 foot deeper, so that the navigation may be 10 feet deep throughout.

The original object proposed by this canal was to open a communication between those important rivers, the Forth and Clyde, and between the northern metropolis and the manufacturing towns of Glasgow and Paisley; and whether as respects the utility of the work, the magnitude of the undertaking, or the skill and ingenuity with which it was designed and executed, the Forth and Clyde Canal will ever hold a distinguished place amongst the most important branches of our inland navigation.

Besides the fine rivers above-mentioned, it is joined by the Edinburgh and Glasgow Union Canal, near Falkirk; with the Monkland and Kirkintilloch Railway at its summit, near the last-mentioned village; and with the Monkland Canal and the Garnkirk and Glasgow Railway, at Port Dundas, near the city of Glasgow.

FOSS NAVIGATION.

33 George III. Cap. 99, Royal Assent 30th April, 1793.
41 George III. Cap. 115, Royal Assent 23rd June, 1801.

THE river which gives a name to this navigation, has its source near Newburgh Hall, about four miles north of Easingwold, whence it crosses Oulstone Moor, where a reservoir is constructed, for the purpose of supplying the navigation in dry seasons. Its

course hence is through a detached part of the Bishopric of Durham by Stillington Mill, and to Sheriff Hutton Bridge, where the
navigation commences. From the New Inn, near the bridge last-
mentioned, a canal, two miles in length, is made, which cuts off a
considerable bend, and enters the river near Duncombe House ;
thence the old course of the river is the line of navigation by
Strensall, Towthorpe, Earswick, and Huntington, to the city of
York, through the east quarter of which it flows, and falls into the
Ouze on the south side of the castle. The length of the navigation is twelve miles and a half, with a total rise of 47 feet 8 inches
from the surface of the Ouze in its ordinary summer state.

Mr. William Jessop designed this navigation in 1791, and estimated the cost at £16,274 ; but the first act was not obtained
until the 30th April, 1793. It is entitled, ' *An Act for making*
' *and maintaining a navigable Communication from the Junction*
' *of the River Foss with the River Ouze, at or near the city of*
' *York, to Stillington Mill, in the parish of Stillington, in the*
' *North Riding of the county of York; and for draining and im-*
' *proving certain Low Lands lying on each side of the said River*
' *Foss.'* The subscribers, at the time the act was obtained, were
one hundred and six in number; amongst whom were Viscountess
Irwin, Sir William M. Milner, and the Lord Mayor and Commonalty of the city of York, who were incorporated by the name
of " The Foss Navigation Company," with power to raise among
themselves the sum of £25,400, in two hundred and fifty-four
shares of £100 each ; and, if necessary, they may borrow the further sum of £10,000 on the credit of the undertaking.

TONNAGE RATES ALLOWED BY THIS ACT.

	d.
Lime, Coal, Slack, Cinders or Culm, per Chaldron of Thirty-two Winchester Bushels .... }	2 per Mile.
Dung, Soot, Rape-Dust, or other Manure, Wheat, Rye, Oats, Barley, Beans, Malt, Hay Seeds, Rapeseed, Mustard-seed, Linseed, and other Grain and Seeds of all Sorts, Oatmeal, Flour, Oat Shelling, Stock and Common Bricks, Square Paving Bricks or Tiles, Oak, Ash, Elm, Beech, Fir, or other Timber, or Logs of Mahogany, Oak Bark, Deals of all Kinds, Wainscot Boards, Pipe Staves, or other Articles of Wood, Stone, Flags, Slate, Bar Iron, or Manufactured Iron, Butter, Bacon, Cheese, Salt, Hay, Straw, and Wool...... }	2 per Ton, per Mile.
For every other Sort of Goods, Wares or Merchandize	3 ditto.　　ditto.

For the Purposes of this Act, Forty Feet of Oak, Ash, Elm, or Beech Timber; and
Fifty Feet of Fir, or Deal, Balk, Poplar, or other Wood, shall be deemed a Ton.

For all Articles conveyed between the River Ouze and Monkbridge only, double Rates may be demanded.

If Goods remain on the Wharfs belonging to the Company a longer Time than Twenty-four Hours, an Allowance to be made for the same.

Vessels under Twenty-five Tons not to pass Locks without leave, or without paying for that Amount.

Land-owners may make Wharfs and charge Two-pence per Ton for all Goods remaining on them for any Period under Six Days.

The act of the 41st George III. is entitled, ' *An Act to explain* ' *and amend an Act passed in the Thirty-third Year of the Reign* ' *of his present Majesty, entitled, An Act for making and maintain-* ' *ing a navigable Communication from the Junction of the River* ' *Foss with the River Ouze, at or near the city of York, to Stilling-* ' *ton Mill, in the parish of Stillington, in the North Riding of the* ' *county of York; and for draining and improving certain Low* ' *Lands lying on each side of the said River Foss, so far as the said* ' *Act relates to the said Navigation; and for enabling the Company* ' *of Proprietors of the said Navigation to complete the same.*' It was obtained chiefly for the purpose of raising money to complete the navigation, the company having failed in their endeavour to borrow the sum of £10,000, which the former act authorized them to do. This act therefore directs that the above-mentioned sum shall be raised by the admission of new subscribers, or by calls on the proprietors in proportion to their respective shares; and if £10,000 is not sufficient, they may borrow, on mortgage of the rates, the further sum of £10,000; and if the funds are insufficient to complete the navigation to Stillington Mill, the company are authorized to terminate this navigation at Sheriff Hutton Bridge.

This act further empowers the company to demand an additional tonnage rate, equal to half the former rate, whenever the nett profits of the navigation are below four per cent. upon the outlay.

The object of this navigation is the conveyance of coal and general merchandize into the interior of the county north of York; and to export the surplus agricultural produce. It serves, also, to drain the low grounds in the immediate vicinity of York, for which a drainage tax is annually levied upon the adjoining land.

FOSSDIKE NAVIGATION.

THIS very ancient canal commences in the River Trent, at Torksey, about ten miles south of Gainsborough; from whence its course lies south-eastwardly, through a very flat and monotonous district to Brayford Mere, about a quarter of a mile west of Lincoln High Bridge. It is there joined by the Witham River, and at about five miles west of Lincoln the River Till falls into it, and these, together, supply the necessary lockage water.

This navigation is eleven miles in length, and level throughout. At Torksey there is a double lock, with gates pointed both ways, so that it equally prevents the entrance of the flood waters of the Trent, and pens up the water in the canal for navigation purposes; and, at its other extremity, is another lock into the Witham, for keeping up the water in the canal at a greater height than heretofore, and for preventing the flood waters of the Witham from entering it, which formerly did great damage to the banks.

As we are much in the dark respecting the time at which, or by whom this canal was excavated, it has afforded considerable scope for ingenuity and research. The celebrated antiquary and ingenious author of ' Itinerarium Curiosum,' Dr. Stukeley, in a letter addressed to Mr. Gale, August 2nd, 1735, states his belief that it was executed by the Romans as a continuation of Caerdike, a deep excavation, apparently made for the purposes of navigation, extending from the navigable River Nene, near Peterborough, in Northamptonshire, to the Witham, into which it enters at Washenburgh, a short distance below the city of Lincoln. He further states that the village of ' Torksey was a Roman town, ' built at the entrance of the Foss into the Trent, to secure the ' navigation of those parts, and as a storehouse for corn, and was ' walled about.'

The Doctor is borne out in this opinion from the account given in Domesday Book, wherein it appears, that before the coming of the Normans, Torksey was a place of considerable consequence, with two hundred burgesses, who possessed many privileges on condition that they should carry the King's Ambassadors, as often as they came that way, down the Trent in their own barges, and conduct them to York; and their original charter is still preserved, and occasionally acted upon.

Leland observes, ' The Fosse-Diche begynnith a quarter of a ' mile above Lincoln, and so goeth to Torksey a 7 mile strait in ' length. Bishop Atwater began to cleanse Fosse-Diche and did ' so half its length from Torksey in hope to bring vessels to ' Lincoln—but on his death it was neglected.' But this by no means leads to the conclusion that it had been previously navigated; nor does it disprove the contrary opinion; as, by its connection with the Till and Witham, it was liable to be silted up by the mud and sand introduced by flood waters.

Camden will have it that the Fossdike was cut by Henry I.; but as he quotes Hovedon, and the latter historian has almost literally copied Simeon Dunelmensis, it seems more than doubtful that he has truly interpreted his author. Simeon's passage is this,—' Eodem anno (1121,) Henricus rex facto longa terræ in- ' tercessione fossato à Torkseie usque Lincolniam per derivationem ' Trentæ fluminis fecit iter navium.' Now, as the surface of the water in the Fossdike is 4 or 5 feet above the level of the Trent, it is matter of impossibility that the waters of the Trent should have been diverted through this channel, unless the surface of the Fossdike has been raised to the difference which now exists in the level between the Trent and this navigation. But, as neither Hovedon or Simeon Dunelmensis ever saw the Fossdike, we ought not to be surprized that they have been led into this opinion.

It seems very probable, and it is the opinion of Dr. Stukeley, that King Henry only scoured out the canal, and rendered it a better navigation; and, as a proof, if proof it may be called, that he did not execute the canal, we have it on record that, in the time of Domesday Book, it was said that the King's Monnetari at Nottingham, had, in the days of Edward the Confessor, the care of the River Trent, and of the Fossdike, and of the navigation therein. Now, as this King died in 1066, before the Norman Conquest, it is clear that the supposition of Camden is not supported.

The proprietors employed Messrs. Smeaton and Grundy, in

1762, to suggest a mode of improving this navigation, which they did by recommending a lock at Brayford Head, and to raise the water 10 inches higher, so as to make the canal 3 feet 6 inches in depth. Their estimate for this and other necessary works amounted to £3,816, 18s. 8d. Twenty years afterwards, Mr. Smeaton again reported on this navigation, by which it appears that the previous designs of this eminent engineer and his colleague had not been carried into execution. But, as these reports relate more particularly to the drainage of the adjacent lands, we shall not further advert to them.

The original object of this canal, adopting the opinion that it is a monument of Roman ingenuity and greatness, was to convey the corn produced in the rich provinces of Lincolnshire, Northamptonshire, &c. direct to their favourite station of Eboracum (York,) by means of a canal, rather than trust to the uncertain circuitous navigation seaward. It is still used for the export of the surplus agricultural produce, but more particularly to import coal to Lincoln and its vicinity.

Those who desire further information respecting these Roman works, we refer to a letter addressed by the Rev. Dr. Stukeley, in 1735, to Francis Drake, F.R.S. at the time the latter gentleman was engaged in writing his Eboracum, and which will be found at full length, at page 38 of that excellent History of the Antiquities of the City of York.

GARNKIRK AND GLASGOW RAILWAY.

7 George IV. Cap. 103, Royal Assent 26th May, 1826.
7 & 8 George IV. Cap. 88, Royal Assent 14th June, 1827.
11 George IV. Cap. 125, Royal Assent 17th June, 1830.

THIS railway commences from the Monkland and Kirkintilloch Railway at Cargill Colliery, near Gartsherrie Bridge, in the county of Lanark, whence it proceeds in a westwardly direction by Gartcloss, Gartcosh, Garnkirk, Robroyston, Milton, Broomfield, Gernuston, Rosebank, and Pinkston, to the north end of the bridge across the cut of junction between the Forth and Clyde and Monkland Canals, on the road between Glasgow Field and Keppoch. It is in length eight miles, one furlong and four chains;

in the first five thousand one hundred and forty-eight yards from its western termination near Glasgow, it is on one inclined plane, rising 116 feet 9 inches; the remaining five miles and a quarter is a dead level. The railway was designed by Mr. Thomas Grainger, who estimated the cost, according to the first design, at £28,497, 17s. 4d.; but subsequently, when it was determined to alter it to the line above-described, at £37,847, 17s. 4d. The subscribers to this undertaking, at the time the first act was obtained, were twelve persons only, who were incorporated by the name of "The Garnkirk and Glasgow Railway Company," and empowered to raise the amount of the original estimate of £28,497, 17s. 4d. in fifty shares; and if this sum is insufficient, they may borrow the additional sum of £10,000, on the credit of the undertaking. The act is entitled, ' An Act for making a ' Railway from the Monkland and Kirkintilloch Railway, by ' Garnkirk to Glasgow;' and by it the following tonnage rates are allowed.

TONNAGE RATES.

	s.	d.		
Lime-stone, Dung, Compost, and all Sorts of Manure, and Materials for the repair of Roads	0	2	per Ton, per Mile.	
Coal, Coke, Culm, Charcoal, Cinders, Stone, Sand, Bricks, Slates, Lime, Earth, Iron, Lead or other Metals or Minerals Unmanufactured	0	3	ditto.	ditto.
Timber, Corn, Flour, Goods, Lead in Sheets, Iron in Bars and all other Wares and Merchandize	0	6	ditto.	ditto.

For the use of any Waggon, Machinery, Engine, or Power belonging to the Company, One-half of the above Rates in Addition.

For every Description of Goods which shall pass the Inclined Plane...	1	0	per Ton.

Fractions to be charged according to the Number of Hundred Weights, and Fractions of a Mile not less than a Quarter.

Passengers carried in any Carriage belonging to the Company　0　2 per Mile.

Owners of lands may erect wharfs; but if they neglect, the company may make them, and demand the following rates.

WHARFAGE RATES.

	d.	
Coal, Culm, Lime, Lime-stone, Clay, Iron-stone, Stone, Bricks, Gravel, Hay, Straw, Corn in the Straw or Manure	½	per Ton.
Iron, Lead-ore, or any other Ore, Tin, Timber, Tiles and Slate	1	ditto.
Any other Goods or Merchandize	2	ditto.

Goods may remain Six Months, on Payment of the above Rates, but if they continue Six Days beyond that Period, One-half of the above Rates in Addition may be demanded, for every Month such Period is exceeded; and so in Proportion for any less Time than a Month.

The Company are restricted from receiving more than Ten Pounds per Cent. on their Capital Stock, until they have reduced their Tonnage, on Distances not exceeding Three Miles, to Three-fourths, and on Distances exceeding Three Miles, to One-half the Rate they are empowered to collect; provided that, for Distances exceeding Three Miles, the Rates shall not be less than Four-pence Halfpenny.

The act of 7th and 8th George IV. entitled, '*An Act for 'altering and amending the Garnkirk and Glasgow Railway Act,'* was obtained for the purpose of altering the line to the course described at the commencement of this article; which alteration was estimated by Mr. Grainger to cost the additional sum of £9,350. The company are therefore authorized to raise this sum in £50 shares; and, should they determine to make a double railway, they may raise an additional sum of £11,000 for that purpose, in £50 shares; all which sums shall be deemed the capital stock of the company. Five years, from the passing of this act, is allowed for the execution of the necessary works.

The act of 11th George IV. entitled, '*An Act for amending 'certain Acts for making the Glasgow and Garnkirk Railway, and 'for raising a further Sum of Money,'* is simply to enable the company of proprietors to raise a sufficient fund for completing the works; the act, therefore, empowers them to raise the further sum of £21,150, either by creating new shares to that amount, or by borrowing upon credit of the undertaking the sum of £10,000, and creating new shares to the extent of £11,150.

The object of this railway is to convey to Glasgow, and for exportation, the valuable minerals at its eastern termination, and such as is brought down the Ballochney and the Wishaw and Coltness Railways, which extend further into the Lanarkshire Coal Field.

GARTURK.

(SEE WISHAW AND COLTNESS RAILWAY.)

GIPPEN OR GIPPING RIVER.

30 George III. Cap. 57, Royal Assent 1st April, 1790.
33 George III. Cap. 20, Royal Assent 28th March, 1793.

THIS river rises near Gipping Hall, situate two miles south-west of the town of Mendlesham, in Suffolk, whence it flows by Stow Market to Stowupland Bridge, near the said town, where the navigation commences. Its course from hence is south-easterly, by the town of Needham, and Shrubland Hall, the seat of Sir W. F. Middleton, Bart. to the south side of the town of Ipswich, where it falls into the tideway of the Orwell, near Stoke Bridge.

Its length is about sixteen miles; and the necessary works for making it navigable, were commenced under the authority of an act of the 30th George III. entitled, ' *An Act for making and* ' *maintaining a navigable Communication between Stowmarket and* ' *Ipswich, in the county of Suffolk.*'

Six gentlemen, resident in the vicinity, were appointed trustees for carrying the act into execution, with power to borrow the sum of £14,300 on the credit of the undertaking, and a further sum of £6,000, if necessary, either on mortgage or by granting annuities.

Power is also given to extend the navigation three quarters of a mile from Stowupland Bridge towards the Bury St. Edmund's Road, if it shall be deemed desirable.

TONNAGE RATES.

	d.
Corn and other Grain, Hops, Stone, Timber, Goods, Wares, Merchandize, and other Things, (except Coal)............ }	1 per Ton, per Mile.
Coal	½ ditto. ditto.

And so in Proportion for any Weight or Quantity less than a Ton, or for any Distance less than a Mile.

If these Rates are insufficient for the Purposes of this Act, power is given to double them for such Time only as may be required; but not until Three Months' Notice has been given. Vessels of less than Thirty-five Tons lading, to be charged for Thirty-five Tons.

The Trustees can also, for all Goods deposited in their Wharfs, and which shall continue for a longer Period than Six Months, charge such additional Sums as they may think fit; provided Notice to such Purpose be deposited with the Clerk of the Peace.

Manure is exempt from Rates, unless the Commissioners shall determine to the contrary; in that case the same Rate is to be paid as for Coal.

The act of the 33rd George III. entitled, ' *An Act for effectu-* ' *ally carrying into Execution an Act of Parliament of the Thir-* ' *tieth Year of his present Majesty, for making and maintaining* ' *a navigable Communication between Stowmarket and Ipswich, in* ' *the county of Suffolk,*' is obtained solely for the purpose of enabling the trustees to borrow the sum of £15,000 over and above the sums authorized by the last-recited act, which had already been expended.

This navigation is chiefly used for exporting the surplus farming produce of the country, and for importing coal, lime, timber, deals, groceries, and other commodities generally required in an agricultural district.

GLAMORGANSHIRE CANAL.

30 George III. Cap. 82, Royal Assent 9th June, 1790.
36 George III. Cap. 69, Royal Assent 26th April, 1796.

THIS navigation, which is sometimes called the Cardiff Canal, commences at a place called The Lower Layer, a mile and a half below the town of Cardiff, on the east side of the River Taff, and near its entrance into Penarth Harbour. Its course is directly north, passing on the east side of the town of Cardiff, and thence in a north-westwardly direction, parallel with the Taff, and by the city of Llandaff, to near the junction of the Taff and Cynon. It crosses the Taff by an aqueduct, and within a short distance is joined by the Aberdare Canal. From hence its course is round the base of the Twyn Maur Hills, still keeping in the vale, but on the western side of the Taff, to its termination at the town of Merthyr Tidvile. The length is about twenty-five miles, with a total rise of about 611 feet. At its termination in the tideway of the River Taff, at Lower Layer, there is a sea-lock, with a floating-dock 16 feet deep, and capable of admitting ships of three hundred tons burthen. The line from Merthyr to Cardiff was opened in February, 1794.

Many railways extend from the several iron-works, mines and collieries which abound in this rich mineral district. The Cardiff and Merthyr Tidvile Railway takes a parallel course with the canal from Merthyr to the aqueduct, but on the opposite side of the river. There is also a railway from the mines near Glancayach, to this canal, a little below the above-mentioned aqueduct; and there is another railway of considerable extent, which commences at the collieries at Dinas Ucha, on the west bank of the River Rhondda Vawr, along which it continues to below its junction with the River Taff, near Forest Bridge.

The act of the 30th George III. is entitled, ' *An Act for* ' *making and maintaining a navigable Canal from Merthyr Tidvile,*

' to and through a place called The Bank, near the town of Cardiff,
' in the county of Glamorgan.' The subscribers to this canal, at
the time the above act was obtained, were seventy-seven in number,
(amongst whom were Lord Cardiff and Count de Redin,) who
were incorporated by the name of " The Company of Proprietors
" of the Glamorganshire Canal Navigation," with power to raise
among themselves the sum of £60,000, in six hundred shares of
£100 each, and a further sum of £30,000, should it be deemed
necessary, by mortgage of the undertaking.

TONNAGE RATES.

	d.
Iron-stone, Iron-ore, Coal, Lime-stone, Lime, and all Kinds of Manure.. }	2 per Ton, per Mile.
Stone, Iron, Timber, Goods, Wares, Merchandize, or other Things	5 ditto. ditto.

Fractions as for a Quarter of a Mile, and as for a Quarter of a Ton.

Ships or other Vessels, whether laden or unladen, passing through the Lock at the Bank into or out of the Dock or Basin, shall be subject to the Payment of One Penny per Ton, according to the registered Admeasurement of such Ship or Vessel.

The company are restricted to divide no more than eight per
cent. Proprietors of any mines lying within four miles of any
part of this canal, may make collateral cuts or railways across the
grounds of other persons, on payment of damages. Owners of
lands may make wharfs and charge the following rates.

WHARFAGE RATES.

	d.
Coal, Lime, Lime-stone, Clay, Iron, Iron-stone, Timber, Stone, Brick, Tile, Slate, or Gravel .... }	1 per Ton.
Any other Goods...	3 ditto.

The above Rates are payable if they remain upon the Wharfs for the Space of Six Days, except for Coal, Iron and Lime-stone, which may continue at the above Rate Six Calendar Months ; and Timber, Clay, Lime, Iron-stone, Stone, Brick, Tile, Slate, or Gravel, may remain Thirty Days. If any Goods lie on the Wharfs or Quays for the Space of Ten Days beyond the respective Periods above prescribed, One Penny per Ton shall be paid for such Ten Days; and One Penny per Ton per Day for every Day beyond such Period. It is further enacted, that all Ships or other Vessels, passing from the Sea or the River into any Dock or Basin belonging to this Company, shall pay the same Duties, in Addition to the Rates which the Bailiffs, Aldermen, and Burgesses of the Town of Cardiff, have hitherto received as Port Dues.

The act of 36th George III. which received the royal assent
on the 26th April, 1796, and is entitled, ' An Act to amend an
' Act of the Thirtieth Year of his present Majesty, for making and
' maintaining a navigable Canal from Merthyr Tidvile, to and
' through a place called The Bank, near the town of Cardiff, in the
' county of Glamorgan, and for extending the said Canal to a place

' *called The Lower Layer, below the said town,*' was obtained chiefly for the purpose expressed in the title, viz. the extension to a point nearer the sea, and to obtain power to raise the additional sum of £10,000 among themselves, in proportion to their respective shares, for the completion of the line of extension, and for no other purpose whatsoever. But if this last-mentioned sum is insufficient, £10,000 more may be contributed; but upon this no more profit than five per cent. per annum shall be received. Two years only, from the date of the last act, are allowed for the completion of the whole of the works.

On consideration of the Marquis and Marchioness of Bute giving consent to the making of the extension, they and their tenants of the ground on the west side of the extension, have the privilege of using the canal and towing path below the south gate of the town of Cardiff, without payment of rates.

The chief object of this navigation and the railways with which it is connected, is to facilitate the export of the vast quantity of coal, iron-stone, and other ores and minerals which are worked in great abundance on its line, and in particular at Merthyr Tidvile and its immediate vicinity.

GLASGOW, PAISLEY, AND ARDROSSAN CANAL AND RAILWAY.

46 George III. Cap. 75, Royal Assent 20th June, 1806.
7 & 8 George IV. Cap. 87, Royal Assent 14th June, 1827.

THE canal commences from Tradestown, or Port Eglinton, on the west side of the city of Glasgow, whence it takes a western course, approaching the northern bank of the White Cart River, along which it continues to near the town of Paisley, where it crosses the above-mentioned river, and passes on the south of that town, to Johnstone, where it terminates.

The railway commences at the canal wharf at Johnstone, and takes a south-westerly course, running parallel with, and on the east side of the Black Cart, and by Lochs Swinnock and Tanker, and along the eastern bank of the River Rye, which it crosses near Blair House, and continues along the course of that river to near the village of Kilwinning, whence it takes a westward course through the collieries, by Kerrylaw, and thence northward of the town of Saltcoats, to the harbour of Ardrossan, where, at an elevation of 9 feet 6 inches above high water mark, it terminates. The railway is twenty-two miles and three furlongs in length, and the canal eleven miles.

From the harbour above-mentioned, there is an inclined plane one mile and five chains in length, rising 11 feet 6 inches, and another one mile and a chain in length, which descends 8 feet. It is then level for the space of one mile, seven furlongs and four chains. Then another plane one mile, three furlongs and seven chains in length, rising 46 feet; then a further rise, to the summit level, of 45 feet, in one mile, five furlongs and nine chains. The next twelve miles, three furlongs and two chains are level; from the end of which it descends 20 feet in the next two miles, one furlong and two chains; and, in the remaining distance of five furlongs, there is a further fall of 44 feet to the level of the quay of the canal at Johnstone, which is 40 feet above the level of high water at Ardrossan. A branch of half a mile in length extends from the main line to Saltcoats Harbour, which descends 3 feet in that distance to a point 10 feet above high water mark.

It was originally intended by the proprietors of these works to have constructed an entire canal from near Glasgow to Ardrossan, and for which purpose their first act was obtained; but circumstances, which are explained below, prevented this. The estimate for making the whole canal was £140,000; but when it was found desirable to make the railway above described, instead of continuing the canal, a separate estimate for it was made by Mr. James Jardine, which, for the Main Line, amounted to £92,568

And for the Saltcoats Branch...............   1,525
                                                    _____
Making a total of....................   £94,093

The first act relating to this undertaking, is entitled, ' *An Act* ' *for making and maintaining a navigable Canal from the Harbour* ' *of Ardrossan, in the county of Ayr, to Tradestown, near Glasgow,* ' *in the county of Lanark; and a collateral Cut from the said* ' *Canal to the Coal Works at Hurlet, in the county of Renfrew;*' by which the subscribers, two hundred and twenty-six in number, (amongst whom were the Earl of Eglinton, Lord Montgomerie,

and Lady Jane Montgomerie,) were incorporated by the name of
" The Company of Proprietors of the Glasgow, Paisley, and
" Ardrossan Canal," with power to raise among themselves the
sum of £140,000, in two thousand eight hundred shares of £50
each; and an additional sum of £30,000 if necessary, either
among themselves, or they may borrow the same on assignment
of the rates, as a security.

TONNAGE RATES.

	d.	
Lime-stone, Iron-stone, Stone for Building, Dung, Earth, Sand and Clay	2 per Ton, per Mile.	
Coal, Coke, Culm and Lime	3 ditto.	ditto.
Bricks, Tiles, Slates, Ores, Iron and Metals	4 ditto.	ditto.
Timber, Bark, Corn and Grain	5 ditto.	ditto.
All other Goods, Wares or Merchandize......................	6 ditto.	ditto.

Fractions to be paid as for a Mile, and as for a Quarter of a Ton.

BASIN DUES.

	d.	
For every Vessel loading or unloading in any Basin belonging to this Company, in addition to the before-mentioned Rates	2 per Ton.	

Vessels under Twenty Tons Burthen not to pass Locks without leave, or without
paying Tonnage to that Amount.

Owners of lands may erect wharfs; but if they do not within
six months after notice has been given them for that purpose, the
company may do it, and charge a rate to be agreed on between
the company and the owners of any goods which may remain
more than twenty-four hours upon such wharfs.

In carrying into execution that part of the original line of
canal from near Glasgow to Johnstone, the proprietors expended
of the original stock, authorized to be raised by power of the act
of 46th George III. the sum of £44,342, besides contracting a
debt of £57,860, 10s.; also old subscription loans from various
proprietors of canal stock, amounting to £2,398, 3s.; and new
subscription loans, amounting to £10,950, 4s. 6d. making a total
of £115,550, 17s. 6d.

After the lapse of twenty years from the date of the act above-
recited, it was found impossible to raise the necessary funds for
completing the remaining portion of the line from Johnstone to
Ardrossan, without complying with this condition, that the debts
incurred in executing the canal from Johnstone to Glasgow,
amounting (as above-recited) to £71,208, 17s. 6d. should be

alone entailed upon that part of the canal. With this understanding, an act received the royal sanction on the 14th June, 1827, entitled, ' *An Act to amend an Act of the Forty-sixth Year of the* ' *Reign of his late Majesty, incorporating the Glasgow, Paisley,* ' *and Ardrossan Canal Company ; and to empower the said Com-* ' *pany to form a Railway from Johnstone, in the county of Ren-* ' *frew, to Ardrossan, in the county of Ayr, and certain Branch* ' *Railways communicating therewith ;*' by which the company are authorized to employ the remainder of the original capital stock (of £140,000,) amounting to £95,658, in the formation of a railway to Ardrossan; and that this railway stock should not be liable to the above-recited debts, but that separate accounts shall be kept of the expenditure and proceeds of the canal and of the railway.

By means of this canal and railway, great facilities will be given for exporting coal, from the extensive mines in the line, for the supply of the north and eastern coasts of Ireland, and to receive, in return, supplies of corn for the consumption of the populous places of Glasgow, Paisley, &c. Moreover, it will have the effect of shortening considerably the distance, and rendering more safe the transit of exported manufactured goods from the above-mentioned towns, by avoiding the circuitous route by the River and Firth of Clyde.

GLASTONBURY NAVIGATION.

7 & 8 George IV. Cap. 41, Royal Assent 28th May, 1827.

THIS navigation commences from the confluence of the Rivers Brue and Parrett, in Bridgewater Bay, Bristol Channel, whence it takes a south-eastwardly direction along the course of the River Brue, to Highbridge Lower Floodgates. From this point a canal is to be made in the bed of the river, by Newbridge, to about ten miles beyond Basin Bridge, where it then follows the course of the south drain, over Westhay and Meare Heaths, and through a very flat country to the west side of the town of Glastonbury, where it terminates. The total length of the navigation is fourteen miles, one furlong and seven chains, viz. from low water mark on the shore of the Bristol Channel, to the proposed tide lock near High

Bridge, is seven furlongs and six chains. This tide lock will be so constructed, that the top of the gates will be on a level with the highest known smooth tide, which rose 40 feet. The surface of the canal will be 10 feet below the top of the gates, and the canal will be 10 feet deep from the lock to the junction with the South Brue Drain, a length of ten miles, three furlongs and three chains. At the end of this fine pool there is another lock, with a rise of 3 feet 2 inches, and thence, the remainder of the canal to Glastonbury will be only 6 feet deep. The estimate for this navigation was made by Mr. John Beauchamp, and amounts (exclusive of application to parliament, plans, &c.) to the sum of £15,234.

The act for making this navigation is entitled, ' *An Act for* ' *improving and supporting the Navigation of the River Brue from* ' *the mouth thereof, at its Junction with the River Parrett, to* ' *Cripp's House, and for making and constructing a Canal from* ' *thence to the town of Glastonbury, in the county of Somerset.*'

The party who undertook to execute this navigation consisted of thirty-six persons, (amongst whom was Sir Alexander Hood, Bart.) and was incorporated by the name of " The Glastonbury " Navigation and Canal Company," and who are empowered to raise among themselves the sum of £18,000, in three hundred and sixty shares of £50 each, and a further sum of £5,000 on mortgage of the undertaking; and they may borrow any part of the original sum of £18,000 on promissory notes under the common seal, or of the Exchequer Bill Commissioners.

TONNAGE RATES.

	s.	d.
Coal, Culm, Coke, Cinders, Charcoal, Timber, Iron, Bricks, Tiles, Stone, Slate, Turf and Manure....................................	1	6 per Ton.
Cheese, Timber, and other Goods, Wares and Merchandize..........	3	0 ditto.

And so in Proportion for any greater or less Weight than a Ton.

WHARFAGE RATES.

For any Goods remaining on any of the Wharfs or Quays beyond the Period of Twenty-four Hours, such additional Rates as may be fixed by the Company; but that not more than Three-pence per Ton shall be paid for any Goods which do not remain on the Wharfs, or Warehoused, more than Six Days.

As the drainage of the low lands on the banks of the Brue is under the management of the Commissioners of Sewers, the company are bound to invest £1,000 in the Three per Cent. Consolidated Bank Annuities, to be at the disposal of the commissioners, to be applied in repairing or making any alteration in the necessary drainage works, which may be required in consequence of the making and completing this navigation.

The object of this navigation is to open a short and more ready communication between Glastonbury and the sea, and to facilitate the exportation of the agricultural produce of that part of Somerset, and to import fuel and other general merchandize.

GLENKENNS CANAL.

42 George III. Cap. 114, Royal Assent 26th June, 1802.

THIS navigation commences in the tideway of the River Dee, close to the north side of the town of Kirkcudbright, whence it takes a northerly course, running parallel with and on the east bank of the Dee, by Kelton House, to Loch Ken, into which it enters a short distance south of Glenlochar Bridge. This part of the navigation is ten miles and a quarter, and has fourteen locks upon it, besides a stop lock and weir at its entrance into Loch Ken. This navigation is continued for the space of twelve miles and a half through Loch Ken, by Kenmore Castle and the town of New Galloway, a little beyond which place a canal of three miles in length extends to the Boat Pool at Dalry, where the navigation terminates. The total length is twenty-five miles and three quarters. Mr. John Rennie projected the navigation, and made the estimate, which amounted to the sum of £33,382.

The act for making it received the royal assent on the 26th June, 1802, and is entitled, ' *An Act for making and maintaining* ' *a navigable Canal from the Boat Pool of Dalry, in the Glenkenns,* ' *to the port and town of Kirkcudbright, in the stewartry of Kirk-* ' *cudbright.*' The subscribers for carrying the work into execution, consisted of twenty-eight persons, (amongst whom were the Hon. John Gordon, the Hon. Montgomerie Granville Stewart, Sir William Douglas, and Sir Alexander Gordon,) who were incorporated by the name of " The Company of Proprietors of the " Glenkenns Canal Navigation," and empowered to raise among themselves the sum of £30,000, in three hundred shares of £100 each; and a further sum of £15,000, if necessary, by equal calls

T

upon the holders of the three hundred shares ; or they may obtain the last-mentioned sum by mortgage of the undertaking; but if £20,000 ¡be found sufficient to make that part of the navigation extending from Loch Ken to the tideway of the Dee, the company may, in preference, complete that part, and suspend, until funds can be raised, the further prosecution of the remainder of the original design.

TONNAGE RATES.

	d.
Coal, Lime, Sand, Stone, Lime-stone, and all Kinds of Manure, (upon the Canal)...............	3 per Ton, per Mile.
Grain, Potatoes, Slate, Iron-stone, Iron, Timber, and other Goods, Wares and Merchandize, (upon the Canal)........	6 ditto. ditto.

For all Goods carried upon the navigable part of the River Dee, or Loch of Ken, half only of the above Rates.

Fractions to be taken for Half a Mile and Quarter of a Ton.

For every Ship, whether laden or unladen, passing through the Tide Lock into the Dee, and into or out of the Basin at Kirkcudbright, an additional Charge of Sixpence per Ton for every Ton upon the Burthen of such Ship.

WHARFAGE RATES.

If any Goods remain on the Wharfs for above the Space of Two Calendar Months, an Allowance to be made to the Proprietors, to be adjusted by Commissioners appointed by the Act.

For the purposes of this Act, One Hundred and Twenty Pounds Avoirdupois to be deemed a Hundred Weight.

Owners of land may also erect warehouses and construct wharfs, and charge the following rates.

RATES FOR PRIVATE WHARFS.

	d.
Coal, Lime, Lime-stone, Clay, Iron, Iron-stone, Timber, Stone, Brick, Tile, Slate or Gravel	2 per Ton.
For any other Goods..	3 ditto.

Provided the same does not continue more than Twenty Days, except the enumerated Articles as above, which may remain Two Calendar Months, on payment of Fourpence per Ton. But should any of the above-mentioned Articles remain on the Wharf or Quays for the Space of Twenty Days over and above the Time specified, then Three-pence per Ton shall be paid for such Twenty Days, and One Penny per Ton per Week afterwards.

The object of this navigation is to give facilities for the conveyance of coal, lime, manure and general merchandize, into the interior of the stewartry or county of Kirkcudbright, and for the improvement of the estates which border upon it.

GLOUCESTER AND BERKELEY CANAL.

33 Geo. III. C. 97, R. A. 28th March, 1793. 37 Geo. III. C. 54, R. A. 9th May, 1797.
45 Geo. III. C. 104, R. A. 27th June, 1805. 58 Geo. III. C. 17, R. A. 17th March, 1818.
3 Geo. IV. C. 53, R. A. 24th May, 1822. 6 Geo. IV. C. 113, R. A. 10th June, 1825.

This admirable ship canal commences from the River Severn, at Sharpness Point, about three miles north of the town of Berkeley, whence it runs along the shore for the space of two miles; thence by Slimbridge, Frampton-on-the-Severn, Saul and Wheatenhurst, between which last-mentioned places it crosses the Stroud Canal; thence, west of Hardwick Court, Quedgeley House and Hempstead House, to near the county gaol on the south side of the city of Gloucester, where it terminates in a spacious basin, out of which there is a lock into the River Severn. Its length is sixteen miles and a half; it is 70 feet wide, and in depth 18 feet, and level throughout; and therefore capable of receiving Indiamen of four hundred tons burthen. It was originally intended to have made the canal from Berkeley Pill, and only 15 feet deep; the length of which would have been eighteen miles and a quarter. A branch is also to be made from near Saul to the River Severn at Hock Cribb, in the parish of Arlington, of nearly one mile and a quarter in length.

The first act relating to this navigation received his late Majesty's assent on the 28th of March, 1793, and is entitled, ' *An Act for making and maintaining a navigable Canal from the River Severn, at or near the city of Gloucester, into a place called Berkeley Pill, in the parish of Berkeley; and also a Cut to or near the town of Berkeley, in the county of Gloucester;*' and by which the original subscribers were incorporated by the name of " The " Gloucester and Berkeley Canal Company," with power to raise among themselves for the purposes of this act, the sum of £140,000, in fourteen hundred shares of £100 each, and a further sum of £60,000, if necessary.

The tolls which the company were permitted to take, under the authority of this act, are expressed at great length; but, as they are repealed by the act of 6th George IV. and new rates allowed, it is unnecessary to introduce them here.

T 2

The act of the 37th George III. was obtained chiefly for the purpose of enabling the company to make some deviations from the original line, through the parishes of Slimbridge, Frampton-upon-Severn, Fretherne, Saul, Wheatenhurst, Moreton, Valence, and Standish. It is entitled, '*An Act for authorizing the Company* ' *of Proprietors of the Gloucester and Berkeley Canal Navigation* ' *to vary the Line of a certain part of the said Canal, so as to render* ' *the Execution thereof more easy, expeditious and less expensive;* ' *and for altering and amending the Act passed in the Thirty-third* ' *Year of the Reign of his present Majesty, for making the said* ' *Canal.*' Power, however, is given in this act to raise £40,000, part of the £140,000, besides the £60,000 authorized by the last act, either by the admission of new subscribers for shares, half shares, or quarters; or by way of mortgage, or on bond. The company are required by the act to pay the Stroudwater Navigation Company, for every day which the making of this canal shall obstruct the passage on their canal, the sum of five guineas.

Eight years after the date of the last-recited act, the proprietors being desirous of making a branch from the main line, near Saul, to the Severn, at Hock Cribb, application was made to parliament for the necessary powers; and an act was accordingly obtained on the 10th July, 1805, entitled, ' *An Act to enable the Company of* ' *Proprietors of the Gloucester and Berkeley Canal, to vary and* ' *alter the Line of a certain part of the said Canal, and to enable the* ' *said Company to raise a further Sum of Money for carrying into* ' *Execution the several Acts for making the said Canal.*' This branch is one mile, one furlong and five chains in length; and the estimate for making it was made by Mr. John Wheeler, which amounted to the sum of £28,765, 12s. 4d.; and, for this purpose, and for completing the main line of the canal, they are empowered to raise the additional sum of £80,000, by creating new shares of not less than £60 each.

Twenty-five years after the passing of the first act, the company of proprietors again applied to parliament for an act to enable them to alter the line, and make the canal terminate at Sharpness Point, as described in the early part of this article, instead of at Berkeley Pill.

The act was passed on the 17th March, 1818, in the 58th George III. and is entitled, ' *An Act to enable the Gloucester and* ' *Berkeley Canal Company to vary and alter the Line of their Canal;* ' *and for altering and enlarging the Powers of several Acts passed* ' *for making and maintaining the said Canal.*' This variation of the main line had the effect of shortening it one mile and three quarters. The estimate for this deviation, commencing in Sir Samuel Wathen's land, near Branwood, which was one mile, six furlongs and eight chains in length, was made by Mr. John Upton, and amounted to the sum of £49,230.

Although the preceding acts authorized the company to raise £280,000 for making the canal, yet, at the passing of this act, they had only raised and expended £112,000; and, from the great difficulty they had already experienced in obtaining the above sum, the company was apprehensive that, without additional powers, they could not raise the remaining £168,000; this act enables them to raise that sum by the creation of new shares, which shall not be granted at less than £60 per share.   But they are also further empowered to raise any part of the above sum of £168,000 on mortgage, bond, or by granting annuities.   By this act the company are authorized to charge for all goods, which shall remain upon any of the wharfs belonging to this company above forty-eight hours, the sum of sixpence per ton per diem.

In the prosecution of the work it was found desirable to construct the canal so as to admit vessels drawing 18 feet water, instead of the original proposition of limiting it to 15 feet; it was also found expedient to erect a breakwater in the Severn, near the outer harbour of the canal, in order to facilitate the entrance of vessels.   These alterations made a considerable addition to the expenditure, an act was therefore obtained in the 3rd George IV. to enable them to borrow the additional sum of £150,000, either by the admission of new subscribers, or in any way authorized by the preceding acts.   This act is entitled, ' *An Act for enabling the* ' *Gloucester and Berkeley Canal Company to raise a further Sum* ' *of Money to discharge their Debts, and to complete the said Canal;* ' *and for amending the several Acts passed for making the said* ' *Canal.*'   Here it may be remarked, that the Exchequer Bill Commissioners advanced to this company, on security of the rates, the sum of £65,000, by four instalments of £16,250 each, viz. on the 24th July, 1818, the 2nd August and 7th December, 1819, and 11th of August, 1820; and the last-recited act gives authority to the commissioners above-mentioned, to advance the further sum of £60,000, in part of the £150,000 which the act empowered them to raise. It is further enacted by the 3rd George IV. that the management shall be vested in a committee of fifteen proprietors instead of nine.

The last act relating to this canal received the royal assent on the 10th June, 1825, and is entitled, ' *An Act for enabling the* ' *Gloucester and Berkeley Canal Company to raise a further Sum* ' *of Money; and for altering, amending, and enlarging the Powers* ' *and Provisions contained in the several Acts for making the said* ' *Canal;*' in the preamble of which it is stated, that the sum of £430,000, which the several preceding acts enabled them to raise, had been expended on the work relating to this canal, but that the further sum of £50,000 would be required; this act, therefore, enables the company to borrow this sum upon the same securities as is prescribed by the preceding acts. For the purpose, however, of paying off simple contract debts, the company may issue £15,000 of the £50,000, in transferable promissory notes of £100 each, payable in ten years. Of the £150,000 which the company were empowered to raise under the act of 3rd George IV. the Commissioners for the issuing of Exchequer Bills, advanced the further sum of £60,000, by two instalments of £30,000 each; and the last-recited act authorizes the commissioners above-named to advance the further sum of £35,000, as part of the sum of £50,000, which the last act authorized the company to borrow.

As the tonnage rates granted by the act of 33rd George III. are repealed by the last-recited act, the following are the rates now allowed to be collected.

TONNAGE RATES.

	s.	d.	
Coal conveyed upon all or any part of the Canal	1	0	per Ton.
All other Goods, Wares and Merchandize	5	0	ditto.
Ditto, not passing through either of the Locks upon this Canal	0	3	per Ton, per Mile.

Vessels entering or going out of either End of this Canal, empty or in ballast, One Penny per Ton for Lockage.
Fractions to be charged as for a Quarter of a Ton.

EXEMPTIONS.

Stone, Gravel or Sand to be used in the repair of any Road in any Township through
which this Canal shall pass, and which shall pass from one part of the Canal to
another; also all Dung, Soil, Marl, Ashes of Coal and Turf and Lime for Manure,
for the Improvement of Lands only within Three Miles of the Canal; but should
any of the above Articles pass through either of the Locks at the two Extremities
of this Canal, Rates shall be paid as above.

Among the many advantages derived from the execution of
this magnificent canal, the avoiding of the dangerous and very
difficult navigation of a circuitous part of the Severn, is not the
least. The distance, by the river, from Sharpness Point to Gloucester, is twenty-eight miles, while by the canal it is only sixteen
miles and a half, consequently there is a saving of more than
eleven miles.

The difference in time cannot exactly be calculated; one is
subject to all the inconveniences of the worst part of the Severn,
the other is easy, smooth and certain. The completion of this
canal is likely to make Gloucester a powerful rival of the port of
Bristol; and its further important uses will be much better deve-
loped by an inspection of the accompanying map, than by any
observations we can add.

GLOUCESTER AND CHELTENHAM RAILWAY.

49 George III. Cap. 23, Royal Assent 28th April, 1809.
55 George III. Cap. 41, Royal Assent 12th May, 1815.

This railway commences at the basin of the Gloucester and
Berkeley Canal, within the city of Gloucester; from whence,
skirting the south side of the town, it passes the village of Wotton,
and thence, in a north-easterly direction, by the side of the Mail-
Road between Gloucester and Cheltenham, and terminates at the
Knapp Toll Gate, at the latter place. A branch is proposed to
be extended to the Limestone Quarries at Leckhampton Hill; but
this is not yet executed. The length of the main line from the
basin is rather more than eight miles and three quarters; but,
including the length of the quay, it is nine miles.

The proposed branch is two miles and three quarters.
The estimates for this railway and branch were made by Mr.
John Hodgkinson, which amounted to £25,261, 14s. viz. for the

main line, £19,005, 14s. and for the branch, £6,256. The calculation was made upon a single road, with passing places at every quarter of a mile.

The subscribers to this undertaking, at the time the act was obtained, were twenty-six in number, amongst whom were the Earl of Suffolk, Lord Sherborne, and Sir William Hicks, Bart. who were incorporated by the name of " The Gloucester and " Cheltenham Railway Company," and authorized to raise among themselves the sum of £25,000, in two hundred and fifty shares of £100 each, and a further sum of £10,000, if necessary, on mortgage. The act is entitled, ' *An Act for making and* ' *maintaining a Railway or Tramroad from the River Severn, at* ' *the Quay, in the city of Gloucester, to or near to a certain Gate in* ' *or near the town of Cheltenham, in the county of Gloucester,* ' *called the Knapp Toll Gate, with a collateral Branch to the top* ' *of Leckhampton Hill, in the parish of Leckhampton, in the said* ' *county.*'

TONNAGE RATES.

	d.	
Stone for the repair of Roads, (except the present Turnpike Road from Gloucester to Cheltenham)	1 per Ton, per Mile.	
Coal, Coke, Culm, Stone, Cinders, Chalk, Marl, Sand, Lime, Clay, Ashes, Peat, Lime-stone, Iron-stone and other Minerals, Building-stone, Pitching and Paving-stone, Bricks, Tiles, Slates, Timber, Lead in Pigs or Sheets, Bar-iron, Waggon-tire, and all Gross and Unmanufactured Articles and Building Materials..	3 ditto.	ditto.
All other Goods, Commodities, Wares or Merchandize	6 ditto.	ditto.

EXEMPTION.

All Stone for the repairs of the Turnpike-Road between the City of Gloucester and Cheltenham.

Fractions to be taken as for a Quarter of a Ton and Half a Mile ; but Tonnage is not to be taken for more than Eight Miles and a Half on the Main Line, and upon Ten Miles and Three Quarters, including the Branch.

Owners of land may erect wharfs ; but if they refuse, the company may do it, and charge the following

WHARFAGE RATES.

	d.
Coal, Culm, Lime-stone, Clay, Iron, Iron-stone, Lead Ore or any other Ores, Timber, Stone, Brick, Tiles, Slates or Gravel	1 per Ton.
All other Goods, Wares and Commodities	2 ditto.

Provided they do not remain more than Twenty-one Days ; but should they continue for the Space of Ten Days over and above that Period, an additional One Penny per Ton shall be paid for such Ten Days, and One Penny per Ton for every further Day.

WHARFAGE AND WAREHOUSING RATES AT CHELTENHAM.

		d.
For every Package not exceeding Fifty-six Pounds......................		1
Ditto,	above Fifty-six Pounds and under Five Hundred	2
Ditto,	exceeding Five Hundred Pounds	6 per Ton.

The act of the 55th George III. was obtained for the purpose of enabling the proprietors to borrow the further sum of £15,000, to enable them to complete the railway, and to pay off the debt which had been incurred. It is entitled, ' *An Act for enabling* ' *the Gloucester and Cheltenham Railway Company to raise a fur-* ' *ther Sum of Money for the completion of their Works.*' The sum above-mentioned may be obtained by the creation of new shares, or in the mode prescribed by the preceding act.

This railway was originally projected with the two-fold purpose of relieving the roads between Gloucester and Cheltenham from the carriage of heavy articles, and for bringing coal to the highly celebrated and improving town of Cheltenham; the importance of which to the inhabitants of that place has been abundantly felt by the great reduction in the price of coal that immediately took place on completing the railway.

GRAND JUNCTION CANAL.

33 Geo. III. C. 80, R. A. 30th Apr. 1793.	34 Geo. III. C. 24, R. A. 28th Mar. 1794.
35 Geo. III. C. 8, R. A. 5th Mar. 1795.	35 Geo. III. C. 43, R. A. 28th Apr. 1795.
35 Geo. III. C. 85, R. A. 2nd June, 1795.	36 Geo. III. C. 25, R. A. 24th Dec. 1795.
38 Geo. III. C. 33, R. A. 26th May, 1798.	41 Geo. III. C. 71, R. A. 20th June, 1801.
43 Geo. III. C. 8, R. A. 24th Mar. 1803.	45 Geo. III. C. 68, R. A. 27th June, 1805.
52 Geo. III. C. 140, R. A. 9th June, 1812.	58 Geo. III. C. 16, R. A. 17th Mar. 1818.
59 Geo. III. C. 111, R. A. 22nd June, 1819.	

THIS stupendous and most useful line of navigation begins at Braunston, in the county of Northampton, where it unites with the Oxford Canal, bordering upon the county of Warwick.. Its course from Braunston is between Welton and Daventry, with a cut one mile and a half to the latter place; leaving Long Breckby to the left, it proceeds to Gayton, where a cut goes off five miles to Northampton. From Gayton it passes Blisworth, and through a tunnel to Stoke, Grafton and Cosgrove, near which last place there is a branch to Stoney-Stratford; below this, the canal joins the River Ouse, which it crosses; thence, passing

Great Dinford, Little and Great Wolston, Woughton, &c. to
King's Langley, and from that place through a short tunnel, by
Grove Park to Rickmansworth, at a little distance from which
town a branch of two miles extends to Watford; from Rickmansworth, as far as Uxbridge, in a parallel line with the River Colne,
which it crosses several times; from Uxbridge it proceeds to
Norwood and Osterley Park, where, intersecting the River Brent,
it falls into the Thames, between Brentford and Sion House, completing a course of above ninety miles.

It was in the year 1792 that this undertaking first had its
origin. In the beginning of that year the Marquis of Buckingham
instructed Mr. Barnes, the eminent engineer, to make a survey of
the country between Braunston, in Northamptonshire, the place
where the Oxford Canal has its junction with the present canal,
and the Thames near London, in order to mark out a line of
canal, whereby the circuitous course by the Thames Navigation
from Oxford might be avoided, and the transit of goods to the
metropolis accelerated. Mr. Barnes's survey was laid before a
public meeting at Stoney-Stratford, in June of the above year,
when his plan was approved, and a committee formed for carrying
on the scheme. The first act was consequently obtained, and
received the royal assent on the 30th April, 1793. It is entitled,
' *An Act for making and maintaining a navigable Canal from the*
' *Oxford Canal Navigation at Braunston, in the county of North-*
' *ampton, to join the River Thames at or near Brentford, in the*
' *county of Middlesex ; and also certain collateral Cuts from the*
' *said intended Canal.*' By this act the shareholders, who were
incorporated under the title of " The Company of Proprietors of
" the Grand Junction Canal," are empowered to raise £500,000,
in shares of £100 each, to be deemed personal estate; and should
that sum be insufficient to carry the powers of the act into effect,
they may raise £100,000 more, either amongst themselves, or by
the admission of new subscribers, or by mortgage of the tolls of
the canal. By this act it is provided that the canal shall unite
with the Thames, at the place where that river receives the
eastern branch of the River Brent, near Sion House; and it is
also enacted that a collateral cut for the navigation of boats,
barges, and other vessels, shall branch from it at the north-east

end of the town of Daventry, and another, for the same purposes, to branch therefrom in the parish of Gayton, in the county of Northampton, to join the navigation of the River Nen, at Northampton; a third cut from the parish of Cosgrove, to join the turnpike road leading to London, at Old Stratford, in the same county; and a fourth branch, extending from Rickmansworth to Watford, both in Hertfordshire. It is provided, by one of the clauses of this act, that, in passing through Osterley Park, the estates of J. Robinson, Esq. the Duke of Northumberland, and James Clitheroe, Esq. the towing-paths shall be on the north, north-east, and east side of the canal, and that no water shall be taken from those domains to the use of the canal. Reservoirs are also to be provided for supplying the Rivers Gade, Colne, and Bulbourne, with as much water as may be taken from them for its use, and the same provision is made for the River Brent. From the Thames to Bax's Mill, the owners of wharfs, warehouses, &c. are not to pay any rates or tolls of this canal, not even the duty of one half-penny per ton, which, it will be seen below, is granted to the city of London; and it is further enacted, that waste water from this canal shall be so carried from the summit at Marsworth, as neither to impede the navigation of the Brent, nor inconvenience the owners of wharfs, &c. on it. By this act the following are allowed as

TONNAGE RATES.

		d.		
Lime and Limestone		¼	per Ton, per Mile.	
Cattle, Sheep, Swine and other Beasts, Flint and other Stone, Bricks, Tiles, Slate, Sand, Fuller's-earth, Iron-stone, Pig-iron, Pig-lead, and all Kinds of Manure, (except Lime)..		½	ditto.	ditto.
Coke and Coal		¾	ditto.	ditto.
All other Goods, Wares and Merchandize whatsoever		1	ditto.	ditto.
For all Goods, Wares and Merchandize, passing from the Canal into the Thames, or *vice versa*		¼	per Ton.	
All Barges and other Vessels whatsoever, navigated on the Thames, or any part thereof Westward of London Bridge to Strand-on-the-Green, or Brentford, by an Act of the 17th George III. pay to the Lord Mayor, Aldermen and Commons of the City of London		½	ditto.	

Fractions to be considered as One Mile, and all Fractions of a Ton to be taken according to the Quarters of a Ton contained therein.

Forty Cubic Feet of Oak, Ash, or Elm, and Fifty Cubic Feet of Fir, Deal, Plank, Poplar, Beech or Birch, to be rated as One Ton; One Hundred and Twenty Pounds, Avoirdupois, of Coal or Coke, as One Hundred Weight; and One Hundred and Twelve Pounds of any other Article.

Proprietors may fix the Price of Carriage for any Parcel not exceeding Five Hundred Weight, affixing the same on every Wharf of the said Canal.

EXEMPTIONS.

Officers and Soldiers on march, their Horses, Arms and Baggage, Timber for his Majesty's Service, and the Persons having Care thereof; Stores for ditto, on Production of Certificate from the Navy Board or Ordnance. Also Gravel, Sand, and other Materials for making or repairing any Public Roads, and Manure for Land, if the same do not pass any Lock.

Lords of manors and land-owners may erect warehouses and wharfs in their own lands adjoining the canal; but if not done after due notice from the company, the said company may themselves build the same.

No Rates to be taken by the Owners of Wharfs for Wharfage of Minerals, Timber or other Goods, unless the same shall lie on the Wharfs or Quays more than Six Hours, and no more than One Penny per Ton shall be taken for Wharfage of Coal, Lime-stone, Iron-stone, Brick, Tile, Slate, Flint, or other Stone or Sand; nor more than Twopence per Ton for any other Goods, where the same shall remain more than Six Hours, but shall not continue longer than Six Days, except Coal, Iron and Lime-stone, which may remain for Six Months, on Payment of One Penny per Ton; and after that Time One Half-penny per Ton per Day shall be paid for Wharfage; no Money being taken for the Conveyance of Materials for repairing or making of Roads.

The navigation of this canal is open, on payment of the rates, as above, for vessels, between the hours of seven and five in November, December, January, and February; between the hours of five and seven in March, April, September, and October, and between the hours of four and nine in May, June, July, and August; but no boat of less than 60 feet in length, and 12 in breadth, or of less than thirty tons burthen, can pass any lock without special consent, or paying tonnage for thirty tons, unless the water runs over at the weir; but when there is a want of water in the locks, vessels only pay for such tonnage as the water allows them to carry. But to parties who constantly travel by night, the company grant licenses at certain rates per annum for that permission.

When this canal was projected, it was thought that it might injure the Oxford Canal Company, it was therefore provided by the present act, that the following rates should be paid to that company.

TONNAGE RATES.

	s.	d.
For all Coals passing from the said Oxford Canal into or upon the intended Grand Junction, without any regard to the Distance the same shall pass on the said Oxford Canal..................	2	9 per Ton.

TONNAGE RATES CONTINUED.

	s.	d.
For all other Wares, Merchandize and Goods, passing from any navigable Canal into the Oxford, and thence into the intended Canal, and *vice versa*, except Lime, Limestone, and such other Articles as are exempt from Payment of Rates or Duties by the Oxford Canal Act, without any regard to the Distance passed on the said Oxford Canal	4	4 per Ton.

Proportionate Charges to be made for less than a Ton.

If, after the completion of the canal, from its junction with the Oxford Canal to Old Stratford, the tolls to the Oxford do not amount to £5,000 a year, the deficiency shall be made good by the Grand Junction Company; and if, after the communication is opened between the Oxford Canal and the Thames, or after the 1st January, 1804, the rates shall not secure to the Oxford Canal Company the sum of £10,000 a year, the deficiency shall be made good by this company within three months; it being understood that the Oxford Canal is kept in good condition.

We have mentioned above, the toll of one half-penny per ton, to be paid for goods going in or out of this canal from the Thames, and the toll of equal amount due to the municipal authorities of London; if these rates do not amount annually to £200 from 30th April to Midsummer, 1795, and to £500 for the year ending Midsummer, 1796; £600 for the year 1797, and so on, increasing by £100 each year, till 1801, when the sum of £1,000 is to be paid to the said Mayor, Aldermen and Commons, or those whom they shall appoint, the deficiency shall be made up by the company; and if the said tolls exceed the said sums, then the said Mayor, Aldermen and Commons shall pay to the said company the surplus for the purposes of the act; but after 1801, the excess above £1,000 per annum shall belong to the said Mayor, Aldermen and Commons of London. A penalty of £50 is to be levied, if coals, culm, or cinders are brought by this canal, nearer to London than the mouth of the tunnel at Langley Bar.

In 1794, about a year after the granting of the first act, a second was obtained, entitled, ' *An Act for making certain navi-* ' *gable Cuts from the towns of Buckingham, Aylesbury, and* ' *Wendover, in the county of Buckingham, to communicate with the* ' *Grand Junction Navigation authorized to be made by an Act of* ' *the last Session of Parliament, and for amending the said Act.*'

The cuts made under the powers of this act are, one from the town of Buckingham, to join the branch canal at Old Stratford; a second from Aylesbury, to unite with the canal at Marsworth, two miles above Tring; and a third from Wendover, meeting the canal at Bulbourne, at the summit level. This last is a feeder rendered navigable.

The original line of canal authorized by the first act obtained by the company, having been found capable of improvement in the parishes of Abbot's Langley, &c. in Hertfordshire, another act received the royal assent in March, 1795, entitled, ' *An Act for* ' *authorizing the Company of the Grand Junction Canal to vary* ' *the Course of a certain Part of the said Canal, in the county of* ' *Hertford, so as to render the Navigation thereof more safe and* ' *convenient, and for making some other Amendments and Altera-* ' *tions in an Act made in the Thirty-third Year of the Reign of his* ' *present Majesty, for making the said Canal.*' The rates of tonnage payable on the old line are hereby made payable on the new; but it is enacted that no articles, the respective rates of tonnage and wharfage whereof were, by the first act, fixed at a less sum than one penny per ton per mile, should be permitted to pass any lock when the water does not flow over the waste weir above such lock, without consent, unless the person conducting such articles shall pay the company an additional rate; which rate, together with the rates made payable on the said articles by the first act, shall not amount to more than one penny per ton per mile; and, in consequence of the safer and speedier conveyance by the projected deviation, the company are empowered to receive, over and above the former rates of tonnage and wharfage, the following

RATE.

	d.
For all Goods, Wares, Merchandize and Things whatsoever, carried and conveyed on any Part of the Line of said Deviation of the Canal....	2 per Ton.

By this act, the clause of 33rd George III. restraining persons from conveying coal, culm, or cinders nearer to the city of London than Langley Bar, is repealed, and these articles are now to be conveyed not nearer to London than the north-west end of Grove Park, under forfeiture of vessel and cargo.

By another act passed in April, 1795, and entitled, ' *An Act*
' *for making a navigable Cut from the Grand Junction Canal, in*
' *the precinct of Norwood, in the county of Middlesex, to Padding-*
' *ton, in the said county,*' the company are empowered to make
and maintain a navigable cut from the canal in Norwood aforesaid,
through several parishes, &c. therein enumerated, to Paddington,
with a towing-path on each side of the same; and it is also provided that the following should be allowed as

TONNAGE RATES.

For all Lime and Ashes, passing Westward on the said Cut, to
be used for Manure, and for all other Manure whatsoever
passing Westward on the said Cut .... } 1 per Ton, per Mile. *d.*

For all Goods, Wares, Merchandize and Things whatsoever .. 1½ ditto.   ditto.

For all separate Packages, Parcels and other Articles, not exceeding Two Hundred Weight each, and belonging and
consigned to different Persons................... .... } 1½ per Mile.

And the Company are empowered to receive, over and above the Rates now quoted,
such Rates or Allowances as may be fixed by them, for all Minerals, Wares, Timber or Goods carried on the said Cut, which shall remain on any Wharf or Quay
belonging to the Company, above Three Hours.

No Vessel of less Burthen than Twenty Tons, nor any Boat or Vessel used for carrying
Passengers or any Persons not employed in navigating such Boats or Vessels,
shall be used on the said Cut without the Company's Consent, under a Fine to
them of Ten Pounds for every Offence.

A further act passed in the same year (1795,) entitled, ' *An*
' *Act for making and extending a navigable Cut from the town of*
' *Watford, in the county of Hertford, to the town of St. Alban, in*
' *the same county,*' authorizes the company to receive, over and
above the rates already secured to them by the former acts, for
goods, &c. conveyed on the canal or cuts therefrom, the further
rate of two-pence per ton for all goods, &c. conveyed by them the
whole length of the intended cut, and so in proportion for any less
distance.

A fourth act was obtained in December, 1795, bearing for its
title, ' *An Act to enable the Company of Proprietors of the Grand*
' *Junction Canal to finish and complete the same, and the several*
' *Cuts and other Works authorized to be made and done by them, by*
' *virtue of several Acts of Parliament.*' By this act the company
had authority to raise, in addition to their former capital, a sum not
exceeding £225,000, for carrying on the works; and they are also
empowered to take, on all parts of the said canal, or its various
cuts, except that from Norwood to Paddington, the following rates.

ADDITIONAL RATES.

For all Lime, Lime-stone, Iron-stone, Flint, and other Stone; all Bricks, Tiles, Slate, Coal and Manure .... } ¼ per Ton, per Mile.

All other Goods, Wares, Merchandize and Things whatsoever ½ ditto. ditto.

The proprietors of the Warwick and Braunston Canal having obtained legal sanction for varying the course of a certain part of that canal, to unite with the Oxford Canal at Napton instead of Braunston, which might injure the Oxford Canal Company, it was inserted in a clause of their act that the Oxford Company should claim the following

TONNAGE RATES.

For all Coal navigated out of the said intended Canal into the said Oxford Canal, and along the same into the Grand Junction Canal .... } 2 9 per Ton.

For all Goods, Wares and Merchandize, except Coals, Lime, Limestone and Manure, which shall be *bona fide* navigated out of said intended Canal into said Oxford Canal, and along the same into the said Grand Junction Canal, or *vice versa* .... } 4 4 ditto.

And in proportion for a less Quantity than One Ton.

Inasmuch as, by the first act for making the Grand Junction Canal, certain rates were secured and granted to the Oxford Canal, of which, if the annual receipts did not amount respectively to £5,000 and £10,000, the Grand Junction were to make good the deficiency, it is by this act provided, that the rates or dues then granted to the Oxford Canal Company, shall now be deemed part of the aforesaid sums, and the Company of the Oxford Canal may lessen their rates, but not so as to lessen the said sums, without consent of the Grand Junction Company; and in case the reduction should lessen the said sums, then the said Oxford Canal Company shall again advance the same, if requested by the Grand Junction Canal Company.

And the Grand Junction Canal Company, to obviate any injury from the intended deviation, are empowered to collect, on coal and all other goods and things except lime and limestone, passing from or out of said Warwick and Napton Canal, as it is now called, into the Oxford Canal, and navigated on the same, and *vice versa*, an additional rate of sixpence per ton, and so on, in proportion, for less quantities. And for collecting the same, and preventing evasion, the Grand Junction are authorized to cause a bar or stop-gate, with a toll-house, to be placed upon or across the said

Warwick and Napton Canal at any place they chuse, within one hundred yards of the junction of the said Warwick and Napton with the Oxford Canal.

The next act obtained by the Grand Junction Canal Company was passed in 1798; and is entitled, ' *An Act for confirming and* ' *carrying into Execution certain Articles of Agreement made and* ' *entered into between Beilby, Lord Bishop of London, Thomas* ' *Wood, Esq. Sir John Frederick, Bart. and Arthur Stanhope, Esq.* ' *Sir John Morshead, Bart. and Dame Elizabeth his wife, and* ' *Robert Thistlethwaite, Esq. and Selina his wife, and the Company* ' *of Proprietors of the Grand Junction Canal; and for other* ' *Purposes therein-mentioned.*'

This act may be considered as the foundation of the Grand Junction Water Works, of which it is not necessary in this work to speak particularly.

The immense undertaking, in which the proprietors of the Grand Junction Canal had now, for some years, been engaged, demanded a greater supply of funds than they were able to provide; they therefore were obliged to go to parliament for its authority, to enable them to raise the sums required for the completion of their plans; and obtained another act in 1801, entitled, ' *An Act for enabling the Company of Proprietors of the Grand* ' *Junction Canal more effectually to provide for the Discharge of* ' *their Debts, and to complete the whole of the Works to be executed* ' *by them, in pursuance of the several Acts of the Thirty-third,* ' *Thirty-fourth, Thirty-fifth, Thirty-sixth, and Thirty-eighth Years* ' *of the Reign of his present Majesty; and for altering and en-* ' *larging the Powers and Provisions of the said Acts.*' They were hereby empowered to raise an additional sum of £150,000; and, to this end, it was thought advisable, that the parts of £100 shares, already or hereafter to be created, instead of being called half, quarter, and eighth parts, should in future be reduced into shares of £12, 10s. each; and that every possessor of one £100 share should, henceforth, be considered as the holder of eight shares at £12, 10s.; and that each holder of one or more such shares of £12, 10s. should have a proportionate part of the profits of the said undertaking, according to his number of shares; but no proprietor can vote who has less than eight such shares, nor give more

U

than *one* vote for every eight shares he possesses, as far as *ten* votes; and no proprietor can be elected on the committee who has not at least *forty* such shares.

At the time of passing this act, it appears that an adjustment of accounts took place between the company and the corporation of London, and a balance of £1,562 being due from the former to the latter, an arrangement was made for liquidating this claim; and, in future, the company agreed to pay the corporation £600 per annum, in lieu of any deficiencies in the tolls due to the corporation, as recited in the first act; the said sum of £600 per annum to be paid clear of all parochial rates, or other deductions whatsoever.

Though so considerable a sum of money had been already raised, it was still found insufficient, and accordingly another act was obtained in 1803, designated, ' *An Act for empowering* ' *the Company of Proprietors of the Grand Junction Canal, to* ' *raise a further Sum of Money to enable them to complete the* ' *Works authorized to be executed, in pursuance of the several Acts* ' *passed in the Thirty-third, Thirty-fourth, Thirty-fifth, Thirty-* ' *sixth, Thirty-eighth, and Forty-first Years of the Reign of his* ' *present Majesty; and for amending, altering, and enlarging the* ' *Powers and Provisions of the said Acts.*' By this the proprietors are enabled to raise a further sum of £400,000, or such parts thereof as they should deem necessary for completing the works; and to provide for the extra cost of making a tunnel at Blisworth, and an aqueduct over the Ouse at Wolverton, and for completing other works yet unfinished, they have power given them to collect the following additional rates.

TONNAGE RATES.

	s.	d.	
For all Coal, Coke, Lime, Lime-stone, Flint and other Stones, Bricks, Tiles, Slate, Sand, Fuller's-earth, Iron-stone, Pig-iron, Pig-lead, and all Kinds of Manure, carried and conveyed on the said Canal, or through the said Tunnel, or the Deep Cutting at the two Mouths or Entrances of the same	0	8	per Ton.
For all other Goods, Wares, Merchandize, and Things whatsoever ..	1	4	ditto.
For all Coal, Coke, Lime, Lime-stone, Flint and other Stone, Bricks, Tiles, Slate, Sand, Fuller's-earth, Iron-stone, Pig-iron, Pig-lead, and all Kinds of Manure, carried and conveyed on or over any Part of the said Aqueduct	0	4	ditto.
For all other Goods, Wares, Merchandize, and Things whatsoever ..	0	8	ditto.

As the Rules established by the first Act for ascertaining the Weight of Timber and other Articles conveyed on the said Canal, had been found very uncertain, it is provided by this Act that the Tonnage for Timber and all other Goods whatever, should be charged according to their *real* Weight. One Hundred and Twelve Pounds Avoirdupois, being deemed and taken for One Hundred Weight with respect to all Timber and other Goods whatever.

By this act it is provided, that a certain part of the money to be raised by its authority shall be appropriated *solely* to the making and completing of a collateral branch from the canal at Gayton, to join the Nen Navigation at Northampton, and that such collateral branch should be completed on or before the 25th March, 1805, for all purposes stated in the act.

Parliamentary assistance was again sought in the year 1805, when another act was obtained, entitled, ' *An Act for altering,* ' *amending, and enlarging the Powers of certain Acts for making* ' *and maintaining the Grand Junction Canal.*' By this act the company, in addition to their other charges, are enabled to demand the following

TONNAGE RATES.

	d.
For all Goods, Wares, Merchandize, and Things navigated and conveyed on or through the said Canal and collateral Cuts, or any Part of them, excepting Timber, Coal, Coke, Lime, Lime-stone, Flints, Ashes, Breeze, Manure, Clay, Bricks, Tiles, Slate, Stone, Fuller's-earth, Iron-stone, Pig-iron, Bar, Rolled and Rod Iron, Nails, all Articles of Cast Iron, Pig-lead, and every Article of Wrought Iron, not before specified, provided such Wrought Iron Articles shall exceed the Weight of Fifty-six Pounds	$\frac{1}{4}$ per Ton, per Mile.

No Tonnage, however, is to be charged in Addition for any Goods, Merchandize, or Things conveyed along or over the Railroad or collateral Communication, or any Part thereof, leading from the said Canal to join the River *Nine* or *Nen*, at or near the Town of Northampton, so long as the said Railroad or any Part of the same, should be made use of as a collateral Communication for the Conveyance of Goods, until the said Company shall have completed the Water Communication for the whole Length.

This Act further allows an additional Rate of Sixpence per Ton on all Goods, &c. conveyed through any Lock on the Canal and its collateral Cuts, or any of them, except any Lock between Brentford Bridge and the Thames, a less Distance than Eight Miles, or paying for a Distance of Eight Miles; and it is further provided, that the additional Rate of Sixpence per Ton shall not be paid by Owners and Occupiers of certain Brick Fields in the Parish of Isleworth, on the side of the Canal and Towing-path there, for Bricks or Tiles manufactured there, or for the Coals, Ashes, and Breeze, Sand, &c. used in making them.

The Clause of the first Act, regarding the Conveyance of Timber and Stores for his Majesty's Service is repealed; and the Company are empowered to demand Rates for these as for all other Goods, subject, however, to a drawback of the whole Amount of each Year, provided the Tonnage does not exceed One Thousand Tons; but if more, the drawback shall only be demanded for such Articles, amounting to One Thousand Tons, as shall have been first navigated on the Canal in the preceding Year. By another Act of the same Year, 1805, Fifty Thousand Tons of Coal are allowed to be conveyed for One Year, from 1st August, 1805, on the said Canal to London, paying a Rate of 10*s*. 9$\frac{3}{4}$*d*. per Ton.

In 1812 another act was passed, entitled, ' *An Act to explain,* ' *amend, and enlarge the Powers of certain Acts passed for making* ' *and maintaining the Grand Junction Canal,*' by which the proprietors were enabled to complete their truly arduous undertaking, and, agreeably to the provisions of the said act, to make a sufficient reservoir for supplying the mills situated on the River Colne; they were also pledged by this act to make similar reservoirs for the mills upon the Berkhampstead or Bulbourne River, and on the united Rivers Bulbourne and Gade; which however they did not do; but, in lieu thereof, erected a steam engine near Nash Mill, on the Bulbourne and Gade, and also made and worked sideponds at four locks, situate near Nash Mill aforesaid, in order to diminish the consumption of water. Disputes having arisen between the company and the owners of the various mills, through the ponds of which, by some great error, the line of canal passes, and great delays having occurred in passing the above-noticed locks, the company applied for and obtained another act, bearing date 17th March, 1818, entitled, ' *An Act to enable the Grand* ' *Junction Canal Company to vary the Line of Part of their Canal* ' *in the county of Hertford, and for altering and enlarging the* ' *Powers of several Acts relating to the said Canal.*'

By this act that part of the canal between Frogmoor Swing Bridge, in the parish of Hemel-Hempstead, and its junction with the Tail Water of Nash Mill, was abandoned, and the line of canal carried into the united Rivers Bulbourne and Gade, as far as Nash Mill aforesaid, thereby preventing waste of water and loss of time in navigating. The company are also enabled to borrow a further sum of £30,000 for the purposes of the act; for completing the said deviation; and for making any other improvements on the same.

The next act was obtained in June, 1819, and entitled, ' *An* ' *Act to vary and alter certain Acts of his present Majesty, relating* ' *to the Grand Junction Canal, the Grand Junction Water Works,* ' *and the Regent's Canal, in order to effect an Exchange of Water,* ' *for the better Supply of the Regent's Canal Navigation and* ' *Grand Junction Water Works.*'

It will be now necessary to state the different levels on which the canal is constructed, from its junction with the Oxford Canal at Braunston to its termination at Brentford. There are two summit levels; one at Braunston, the other, and most considerable, at Tring. From the junction of the two canals, by Braunston Tunnel, which is two thousand and forty-five yards long, there is a rise of 40 feet, in a distance of five miles and a quarter, to Norton; from Norton to Blisworth Tunnel, (which is three thousand and eighty yards in length,) the distance is fourteen miles and a quarter, with a fall of 60 feet; from Blisworth Tunnel to the Stratford Branch, six miles, with a fall of 80 feet; from Stratford Branch to Fenny Stratford, ten miles and a half, with a fall of 10 feet; from Fenny Stratford to the Wendover Branch, in a distance of thirteen miles and a half, there is a rise towards the summit level in Tring parish, of 100 feet; from Wendover Branch to the principal summit at Tring aforesaid, a rise of 50 feet; the summit level here is nearly three miles and a half in length; the descent is then continued with little intermission by Hemel-Hempstead, Rickmansworth, and other places, to Harefield Park, a distance of twenty-one miles, with 300 feet fall; thence to Uxbridge, four miles, with 16 feet fall; from Uxbridge to its termination at Brentford, there is a level of seven miles, the elevation of the summit level at Tring being 380 feet above low-water-mark in the Thames at Limehouse. The Paddington Branch of fourteen miles, is 90 feet above low water.

The main line of the canal, as before stated, is upwards of ninety miles in length; its depth averages 5 feet, and its width 43; the Paddington Branch, which may in fact be considered a continuation of the main line, is of the same dimensions, and it is remarkable that for nearly twenty miles, reckoning from the wharf at Paddington to Uxbridge, the direction of the canal is so level, as to require only one lock. The branch to Old Stratford is also of the same depth as above, and has no lock in a distance of one mile and a half. The continuation of this branch to Buckingham has two locks in a distance of nine miles and a half, with a depth of 4 feet, and width of 28. The Bulbourne Branch is nearly seven miles long, without lock, 4½ feet deep, and 32 feet wide. The whole number of locks from the junction with the Oxford Canal at Braunston, to the termination of the Paddington Branch, is ninety-eight; their dimensions on the main line are, width 14½

feet; length, from upper to lower gates, 82 feet. On the Buckingham Branch, at the junction with the Old Stratford Branch, the
locks are 7 feet wide, with a rise of 13 feet; the rise of the other
locks averages about 7 feet each, and require nearly two hundred
and fifty tons of water to fill them. The communication with
Northampton and the River Nen is by a double railway, allowing
carriages, going different ways, to pass without interruption. The
two tunnels average a width of 15 feet, and a height of 19 feet;
that at Blisworth is 60 feet below the summit of the hill, through
which it is excavated. There is a line of deep cutting through the
great chalk-hills between Cow-Roost and Bulbourne, which is
three miles long, and, in some parts, 30 feet deep; near Blisworth
Tunnel, and at Dawley, there are also great lengths of cutting of
considerable depth; and, between Wolverton and Cosgrove, there
is a very lofty embankment, with three aqueduct arches, at the
crossing of the Ouse River: by means of this embankment nine
locks are avoided, and a length of twelve miles of level pound on
the north side of the embankment is held up by a single lock of 18
inches rise. The embankment is half a mile long, and, at the
crossing of the Ouse, 30 feet high. An unfortunate mistake
occurred in taking the levels near Fenny Stratford, for rectifying
which it was necessary to place another lock of 18 inches rise, in
order to hold up a pound of some miles, which otherwise would
have been united to a level pound of ten miles near the same town.
There are various embankments at Weedon Beck, Bugbrook and
other places, which it would be superfluous to notice particularly,
though several of them are of considerable size. Some extensive
pieces of water are on the canal in different places; the largest
being at Harefield Moor, Great Berkhampstead, Halton Park, and
Wendover. In a line which passes through the ponds of so many
mills as this does, it is necessary to have a more than ordinary
number of reservoirs to supply the consumption of water in these,
as well as in the canal itself; the Grand Junction has five; one at
Daventry, another at Weston Turville, and a third at Braunston;
these are all of large size. There is also one at Wilston, covering
forty acres of ground; but the largest is at Aldenham, covering
above sixty acres.

Several feeders are connected with this navigation on different parts of the line; that for the southern summit is near Wendover; and there are three others near Tring and Miswell, the last of which is arched over to the length of a quarter of a mile. The northern summit's feeder is from Watford, near Daventry; and this level has also its banks considerably raised for the purpose of accumulating extra water during wet weather. The water let down from this summit by lockage is again pumped up out of the level of the Oxford Canal by a powerful steam engine. The water out of the Wilston Reservoir is also pumped into the Wendover Branch of the southern level by an engine erected in 1803; and a little below Two-Waters, in the Colne Valley, the lockage-water of four locks there is returned by another engine. A great saving of water is also effected on the north and south sides of the Tring Summit Level, by the addition of side-ponds to the locks, and there are many considerable tumbling bays or weirs throughout the line, the most remarkable of which are near Great Berkhampstead, Uxbridge, and the passage of the Tove or Towcester River; the necessity for which has been occasioned by the peculiar direction of the line, which, as we have before stated, passes through an immense number of mill-ponds: besides these, there are overfalls, stop-gates and trunks, culverts and bridges, in great numbers. The navigation of this canal is used by barges, square at head and stern, and having flat bottoms, of sixty tons burthen, and smaller vessels of twenty-five tons burthen, with sharp heads and sterns. The canal was opened from its junction with the Oxford Canal to the embankment at Weedon Beck, in 1796, and, before the end of 1797, extended to the tunnel at Blisworth; a communication between Two-Waters and the Thames was effected in 1798; in the ensuing year the canal was completed as far as Bulbourne, together with the Wendover Branch; in 1800 the canal, commencing at the Thames, had reached the south end of the projected tunnel at Blisworth; and, till this was completed, a communication between this part and the one from the Oxford Canal, which, as is seen above, was opened as far as the north end of the same tunnel, was made by a temporary railroad three miles and upwards in length, over Blisworth Hill. In 1801 the Buckingham Branch was completed, and the whole of this magnificent line opened in 1805, when the Blisworth Tunnel was finished.

It will be seen, from the title of one of the acts quoted above, that the company had powers granted for supplying part of Paddington with water; they have also immense warehouses and covered docks at White Friars, which afford stowage to the boats and barges of Mr. Pickford's establishment. At Paddington there is a basin four hundred yards long, and thirty broad, with ranges of wharfs, warehouses, and immense sheds for stowing goods in all directions around it; in addition to which, there are all necessary accommodations for persons attending the Paddington Market (established in 1802,) with cattle, hay, corn, vegetables, &c.

Packet-boats regularly ply on the canal between London and Uxbridge, for the conveyance of passengers and parcels; and Mr. Pickford has a succession of barges day and night, conveying goods on this canal and those connected with it. Mr. Barnes, Mr. Telford, Mr. Holland, Mr. Jessop, and Mr. Bevan, all of them engineers of first rate abilities, have been consulted and employed on this canal, and the expectation of the original projectors, as far as regards public utility, have been fully realized. The design of making a communication between the Grand Junction and the various docks at London, has been effected by the Regent's Canal, out of which this company have now the privilege of taking the water, which they before were authorized to take from the Thames.

The advantages which the metropolis, and indeed all places on the main line and branches, derive from this grand undertaking, are incalculable. The staple goods of Manchester, Stourbridge, Birmingham, and Wolverhampton; cheese, salt, lime, stone, timber, corn, paper, bricks, &c. &c. are conveyed by it to London, whilst in return, groceries, tallow, cotton, tin, manure, and raw materials for the manufacturing districts, are constantly passing upon it. The immense trade on this concern is briefly stated, by observing that the tonnage amounts to near £160,000 per annum.

GRAND SURREY CANAL.

41 Geo. III. C. 31, R. A. 21st May, 1801.   47 Geo. III. C. 80, R. A. 8th Aug. 1807.
48 Geo. III. C. 99, R. A. 3rd June, 1808.   51 Geo. III. C. 170, R. A. 15th June, 1811.

The first act obtained for the execution of the Grand Surrey Canal is entitled, ' *An Act for making and maintaining a navigable*

' *Canal from the River Thames, at or near a place called Wilkin-*
' *son's Gun Wharf, in the parish of St.* Mary, *at Rotherhithe, in*
' *the county of Surrey, to the town of Mitcham, in the parish of*
' *Mitcham, in the said county; and also divers collateral Cuts or*
' *Branches communicating from the same to certain parishes and*
' *places within the counties of Surrey and Kent.*' By this act the
proprietors are made a corporate body, under the title of " The
" Company of Proprietors of the Grand Surrey Canal," and are
empowered to raise the sum of £60,000 in shares of £100 each,
or by loan on bond, or mortgage, with a further sum of £30,000,
if necessary.

The canal commences at Wilkinson's Gun Wharf, on the south
banks of the River Thames, in Rotherhithe, a quarter of a mile
below the Thames Tunnel, and directly opposite Shadwell Dock.
It almost immediately enters the docks belonging to the navigation,
along which it continues upwards of twelve hundred yards, running
parallel with the Commercial Docks. Hence its course is southward, entering Kent and approaching, at Bridge Place, within
two hundred and fifty yards of the King's Dock Yard at Deptford.
Its course from this point is directly west by Peckham New Town,
crossing the Kent Road, and thence in a straight course to the
north side of Adlington Square, Camberwell Road, where it terminates. Its total length, including the docks, is four miles and six
chains. Within seven furlongs of its western termination, there is
a branch of half a mile in length proceeding southwardly to Peckham ; and near its junction with the Thames, there is a capacious
outer dock on the west side of the main dock, five hundred and
seventy yards in length.

By the act it is provided that the intended canal and cuts shall
be supplied with water from the Thames, and all other rivers,
streams, or brooks found in digging the said canal, except the
River Wandle and streams, within two thousand yards thereof,
running into the same. The company may also cut collateral
branches to any place within fifteen hundred yards thereof, with
consent of the owners, on purchasing the ground. Aqueducts are
to be made, if necessary, over the Wandle, at least 15 feet from
mark-stake high in that river, to the surface of the water in the
canal, and proper aqueducts over an intended railway from

Wandsworth to Croydon, so that loaded waggons may pass under the same; the span of the arch under such aqueducts to be full 16 feet wide. The company may make rollers, inclined planes, railways, waggon-ways, and cranes, if the conveyance of goods over any part of the projected line should require it; such rollers, &c. to be considered as part or parts of the said canal or branches. If the cut into Greenland Dock should be made, the proprietors are to pay certain sums to be agreed upon by them and the proprietors of the dock, for the use thereof for vessels on this canal. This act also provides that the company shall receive the following

TONNAGE RATES.

	d.	
For Free-stone, Lime-stone, Chalk, Bricks, Slates, Tiles, Corn in the Straw, Hay, Straw, Faggots, Dung, Manure, Stones and Clay........................	2 per Ton, per Mile.	
For all Cattle, Calves, Sheep, Swine, and other Beasts; Lime, Rough Timber, Hemp, Tin, Bark, Iron-stone, Pig-iron and Pig-lead	3 ditto.	ditto.
For all Coal, Charcoal, Coke, Culm, Flour, Wheat, Barley, Oats, Beans, Peas, Malt, and Potatoes..................	4 ditto.	ditto.
For all Hops, Fruit, Goods, Wares, Merchandize, and other Things whatsoever	6 ditto.	ditto.

And in Proportion for more or less than a Ton, and more or less than a Mile.

Vessels passing in or out of any Outlet or Lock communicating with the Thames, to pay according to their Tonnage as for One Mile; which Charge shall never be calculated for less than Five Tons. The same Quantum of Rate to be paid for every Vessel passing up or down any Inclined Plane.

Vessels entering any other company's basins, and landing or taking in goods, shall pay the following rates.

RATES.

	d.
For all Goods, Wares, Merchandize, and other Things whatsoever	3 per Ton.
For every Barge or Vessel which has not passed One Mile along the Canal or Cuts	3 ditto.

This last Rate is to be deducted from the gross Amount of Toll, provided the Vessel so charged shall afterwards proceed along the whole Line or collateral Cut.

Fractions of a Quarter of a Ton or a Quarter of a Mile to be reckoned as a Quarter of a Ton and a Quarter of a Mile. Fifty Cubic Feet of Fir, Balk, Poplar, Deal or Birch; Fifty Cubic Feet of Round, and Forty Cubic Feet of Square Oak, Ash, Elm, Beech, or other Timber not cut into Scantlings, to be estimated as One Ton; One Hundred and Twelve Pounds Avoirdupois of all other Goods, Wares, Merchandize, or Things whatsoever, to be considered One Hundred Weight; and Two Thousand Two Hundred and Forty Pounds Weight of the same, One Ton. Rates for conveying small Parcels to be fixed by the Proprietors; and Goods remaining on the Wharfs above Twenty-four Hours to be paid for according to Bargain between said Company and the Owners.

The act further provides that £2, 2s. shall be paid as a fine or acknowledgment to the mayor and commonalty of London, for the liberty of opening a communication between the canal and the

Thames, together with an annual rent of £60, as a compensation for the diminution of tolls, secured to the said mayor and commonalty under an act of 17th George III.

The second act obtained by the company in 1807, and entitled, ' *An Act to enable the Company of Proprietors of the Grand Sur-* ' *rey Canal to complete the same,*' after reciting the previous act, and showing that the money thereby authorized to be raised, had already been expended in cutting part of the said canal, and excavating a basin at Rotherhithe, enables the proprietors to raise a further sum of £60,000, for completing the same, by creating new shares, or by promissory notes, or by mortgage, or annuities, as shall seem most advisable.

In June, 1808, a third act was obtained by the proprietors, entitled, ' *An Act to enable the Company of Proprietors of the* ' *Grand Surrey Canal to supply with Water the several Towns,* ' *Districts, and Places therein mentioned, and to amend the several* ' *Acts relative to the said Canal.*' The parishes and hamlets which the company is by this act authorized to supply with water, are St. Mary Rotherhithe, New Cross, St. John and St. Mary Magdalen Bermondsey, St. Giles Camberwell, Walworth, Peckham, and places adjacent in Surrey and Kent, for the accomplishment of which, £14,000 is to be raised by creating additional shares of £100 each, or by mortgage; and the proprietors are authorized to pay from the 29th September, 1807, interest at five per cent. per annum on all monies already advanced, and hereafter to be advanced, for shares in this undertaking.

Though considerable sums, as appears from the acts already recited, had been raised for the carrying on of this work, so many alterations had been made, and such a variety of additional expenses had been incurred, that the proprietors were obliged again to go to parliament ; and, accordingly, a further act was obtained in the year 1811, entitled, ' *An Act to enable the Company of* ' *Proprietors of the Grand Surrey Canal to make a collateral Cut* ' *communicating therewith, in the parish of St. Mary Rotherhithe,* ' *in the county of Surrey, and to enable the said Company to com-* ' *plete the said Canal, and for amending the several Acts relating* ' *thereto.*' After stating that the company had already completed a basin and entrance into the Thames at Rotherhithe, with a line of four miles of canal from the said basin to the Camberwell Road, and that they had paid off part of the mortgage debt due from them, the act empowers them to make a collateral cut, from the canal opposite the Commercial Docks in Rotherhithe, along the eåst side of the canal, and parallel thereto, to communicate with the basin aforesaid, at the lower end thereof, near the Thames; whereby vessels, using the canal or its cuts, might go into the Thames without passing through the basin; for this purpose, and that of liquidating their debts, they are empowered to raise no less a sum than £150,000, in addition to the money already subscribed, in shares of £100 each, or by promissory notes, or by mortgage, or by annuities. By this act also, certain privileges are secured to the Croydon Canal Company, the Commercial Dock Company, the Kent Water Works' Company, and the city of London. Some of the former tolls are repealed, and the following is declared to be the scale of the future tonnage and dockage rates.

TONNAGE AND DOCKAGE RATES.

Description of Goods, &c.	£. s. d.	Rent per Quarter. £. s. d.
Dockage on all light Vessels on entering the Basin, per Register Ton	0 0 6	
Ditto, for the Privilege of receiving or discharging a Cargo additional, per Register Ton	0 0 6	
For which Charges, Vessels may continue in the Basin as follows, viz.		
Vessels of from Thirty Tons to One Hundred Tons, Ten Days.		
Ditto, from One Hundred Tons to One Hundred and Fifty Tons, Fourteen Days.		
Ditto, from One Hundred and Fifty Tons to Two Hundred Tons, Eighteen Days.		
Ditto, from Two Hundred Tons to Two Hundred and Fifty Tons, Twenty-one Days.		
Ditto, from Two Hundred and Fifty Tons to Three Hundred Tons, Twenty-four Days.		
Ditto, from Three Hundred Tons to Three Hundred and Fifty Tons, Twenty-seven Days.		
Ditto, from Three Hundred and Fifty Tons to Four Hundred Tons, Thirty Days.		
After which Time all Vessels may be charged a Weekly Rate as follows, viz.		
From Thirty Tons to One Hundred Tons	0 8 0	
From One Hundred ditto to One Hundred and Fifty ditto	0 10 0	
From One Hundred and Fifty ditto to Two Hundred ditto	0 12 0	
From Two Hundred ditto to Two Hundred and Fifty ditto	0 14 0	
From Two Hundred and Fifty ditto to Three Hundred ditto	0 16 0	
From Three Hundred ditto to Three Hundred and Fifty ditto	0 18 0	

TONNAGE AND DOCKAGE RATES CONTINUED.

Description of Goods, &c.	£.	s.	d.	£.	s.	d.
				Rent per Quarter.		
From Three Hundred and Fifty Tons to Four Hundred Tons	1	0	0			
From Four Hundred ditto to Five Hundred ditto.................	1	3	0			
Docking each Vessel	0	10	6			
Undocking ditto..	0	10	6			
Wharfage on Oak and other heavy Timber, per Load	0	6	0	0	3	0
Ditto on ditto, and other heavy Planks ditto	0	6	0.	0	3	0
Ditto on large Timber and Masts ditto				0	2	0
Ditto on small Timber ditto				0	3	0
Ditto on Deals from the Baltic, per reduced Standard of One } Hundred and Twenty ditto................................. }	0	5	0	0	5	0
Ditto on ditto from America, ditto	0	5	0	0	5	0
Ditto on Quebec Pipe Logs of Three and Four Inches, per Thousand				0	15	0
Ditto on Staves of Two and Two and a Half ditto.................				0	15	0
Ditto on ditto of One and One and a Half ditto ditto				0	15	0
Ditto on Hogshead Logs of Three and Four ditto ditto				0	15	0
Ditto on ditto Staves of Two and Two and a Half ditto ditto				0	15	0
Ditto on ditto of One and One and a Half ditto ditto				0	15	0
Ditto on Barrel Logs of Three and Four ditto ditto				0	10	0
Ditto on Barrel Staves of Two and Two and a Half Inches, per } Thousand .... }				0	10	0
Ditto on ditto of One and One and a Half ditto ditto				0	10	0
Ditto on Heading Logs of Three and Four ditto ditto				0	10	0
Ditto on ditto Staves of Two and Two and a Half ditto ditto.......				0	10	0
Ditto on ditto of One and One and a Half ditto ditto				0	10	0
Ditto on Flax and Hemp per Ton.................................	0	2	6	0	1	0
Ditto on Iron ditto..	0	1	6			
				Rent per Week.		
Ditto on Mats per Bundle of One Hundred	0	1	3	0	0	6
Ditto on Russia Ashes per Ton...................................	0	1	3	0	0	2
Ditto on Tallow ditto	0	1	6	0	0	6
Ditto on Oil per Ton of Two Hundred and Fifty-two Gallons	0	2	6	0	1	0
Ditto on Bristles per Cask	0	0	8	0	0	3
Ditto on Brimstone per Ton	0	1	6	0	1	0
Ditto on Pitch, Tar, and Turpentine per Barrel	0	3	0	0	0	2

The last Column is the Rent to be paid while stored on the Company's Premises.

Mr. Ralph Dodd was the engineer for this undertaking, and his estimate amounted to £80,220, 3s. 7d. The sum originally subscribed by the shareholders was £45,200; but by the different acts the company have had authority to raise above £300,000. The work has not yet remunerated the proprietors for their outlay, not more than two and a half per cent. annual interest having yet been received on each £100 share. The loan of course has had regular interest paid upon it, according to the provisions of the act. But as the profits of this concern, as originally intended, would partly depend upon dockage, this source of expected revenue will be greatly diminished by the extensive accommodation provided by St. Catherine's Docks, and the further extension of the London Docks.

GRAND UNION CANAL.

50 George III. Cap. 122, Royal Assent 24th May, 1810.

THIS canal was commenced under the authority of an act of parliament, bearing date as above, and entitled, ' *An Act for* ' *making and maintaining a navigable Canal from the Union Canal,* ' *in the parish of Gumley, in the county of Leicester, to join the* ' *Grand Junction Canal near Long Buckby, in the county of North-* ' *ampton; and for making a collateral Cut from the said intended* ' *Canal.*'

This canal unites with the Leicester Union Canal near Gumley Hall and Foxton, about four miles from Market Harborough; to which latter place there is a collateral cut; from the junction it proceeds in a southern direction to the turnpike-road between Lutterworth and Northampton, which it crosses, and near to which there are reservoirs for supplying it with water, at the eastern extremity of a branch forming the communication with Welford; leaving the Welford Branch on the east, it proceeds in the same direction as before, by Elkington and Guilsbrough to Crick, where there is a considerable reservoir; leaving Watford on the east, it continues its course to its termination in the Grand Junction Canal at Long Buckby, in the parish of Norton, having traversed a distance of nearly forty-five miles. On this line there are two tunnels; one near the crossing of the turnpike-road to Northampton, the other at Crick.

By the act the proprietors are incorporated under the name of " The Company of Proprietors of the Grand Union Canal," and are empowered to raise a sum not exceeding £200,000, for the purposes of the said act, in shares of £100, or half shares of £50 each, as shall seem best to the subscribers at their first general meeting: and, in case such sum shall not be found sufficient for completing the work, the proprietors may raise a further sum not exceeding £50,000, either amongst themselves, or by the creation of fresh shares, or by mortgage, or by promissory notes. And, for reimbursing themselves, they are empowered to claim the following

TONNAGE RATES.

	s.	d.	
For all Coal and Coke passing from the Grand Junction Canal into the Grand Union, but not carried thereon more than Twelve Miles...	2	6	per Ton.
For Coal and Coke conveyed on the said Canal to a greater Distance than Twelve Miles, and not afterwards conveyed on the Leicestershire and Northamptonshire Canal, for every Mile beyond the said Twelve Miles, in addition	0	2½	ditto
For all Coal and Coke passing from the Leicestershire and Northamptonshire Canal into the Grand Union, and not carried thereon more than Eighteen Miles	2	6	ditto.
For all Coal and Coke conveyed above Eighteen Miles, a further Rate, so that the whole Tonnage does not exceed Two Shillings and Eleven-pence per Ton	0	2½	ditto.
For all Coal and Coke passing from the Leicestershire and Northamptonshire Canal, along said Grand Union into the Oxford Canal, in addtion to the said Rate of Two Shillings and Eleven-pence	2	9	ditto.
For all Lime, Dung, Manure and Limestone, passing through a Lock or Locks at either End of said Canal	1	3	ditto.
For all Cattle, Sheep, Calves, Swine and other Beasts; and for all Stone, Bricks, Tiles, Slates and Sand, Iron-stone, Pig-iron and Pig-lead, passing a Lock or Locks	2	6	ditto.
All other Goods, Merchandize, Wares and Things whatsoever, passing through a Lock or Locks	3	0	ditto.

Fractions to be taken as a Quarter of a Mile and a Quarter of a Ton; and Vessels passing Locks with less than Twenty Tons of heavy Goods, to pay for Twenty Tons.

The Proprietors have the Power of reducing the Rates, and of again advancing them to the Sums specified above, as Circumstances may allow; but they are not to reduce the Sums of Two Shillings and Sixpence and Two Shillings and Ninepence per Ton, on Coal and Coke conveyed on the Leicestershire and Northamptonshire, and Oxford Canals, respectively, without Consent from those Companies; and no other Reductions are to be made without Consent of the Companies interested therein.

The Grand Union Canal Company may erect wharfs and warehouses for receiving goods, and make charges for wharfage, &c. in addition to their tonnage rates; and owners of lands, lords of manors, and others, having property on the line of navigation, may erect wharfs on the canal or collateral cuts; they may also erect bridges, stiles, &c. at their own cost, the consent of the company being first obtained.

The plans and estimate of the Grand Union Canal were made by Mr. B. Bevan, in the year 1810. The cost of making the said canal, with the branch or collateral cut to Welford, was estimated at £219,000, including the expenses of tunnels and twenty-one locks. The subscription list contained names for two thousand two hundred and fifty-six shares and a half, or £225,650, and, consequently, the work was immediately undertaken.

Though not so extensive as many other parts of our inland navigation, the utility of the Grand Union Canal is commensurate with most. By means of its communication with the Grand Junction, the Oxford, and the Leicestershire and Northamptonshire Canals, it affords the means of conveying goods to and from many populous manufacturing districts and commercial towns, and secures a ready transit for their various productions along the above-named canals, the Grand Trunk, the Trent and Thames Rivers, and most of the navigations of Derbyshire, Yorkshire, and Lancashire.

GRAND WESTERN CANAL.

36 George III. Cap. 46, Royal Assent 24th March, 1796.
51 George III. Cap. 168, Royal Assent 15th June, 1811.
52 George III. Cap. 16, Royal Assent 20th March, 1812.

This canal, which is designed to open a communication between the Severn and the Bristol Channel, thereby facilitating the supply of the country on its line with coals, timber, &c. as well as the export of farming produce, was sanctioned by the legislature in 1796, under an act, entitled, ' *An Act for making a navigable* ' *Canal from the River Exe, near the town of Topsham, in the* ' *county of Devon, to the River Tone, near the town of Taunton,* ' *in the county of Somerset; and for cleansing and making naviga-* ' *ble a certain Part of the said River Tone; and for making certain* ' *Cuts from the said Canal.*'

By this act the company were incorporated under the title of " Proprietors of the Grand Western Canal," and were authorized to make a line of navigation from the tideway in the River Exe, near Topsham, into the Tone River, in the parish of Bishop's Hull, in Somersetshire. They had also the power of making three collateral cuts or branches, viz. one in the parish of Cullompton; a second from the parish of Burlescombe to the parish of Tiverton; and a third in the parish of Wellington. They also were empowered to make two reservoirs in the valley of the River Culme, and two others in the valley of the Tone; from both which rivers they may take supplies of water. That part of the Tone which lies between Bishop's Hull and Taunton Bridge is, by this act, considered part of the canal, and vested in the proprietors thereof.

By this act the proprietors were authorized to collect certain rates, which it is not necessary to mention here, as they were repealed by a subsequent act, and another table substituted in place thereof. The sum of £220,000 is directed to be raised in shares of £100 each, and they might raise £110,000 in addition, if necessary, either amongst themselves, or by new subscribers, or on interest. The provisions of the act above-recited, were put into immediate execution, and the proprietors proceeded to complete their undertaking without delay; but it having been found necessary to vary the line prescribed by the above act, a second was obtained for that purpose in 1811, entitled, ' An Act to vary and alter the ' Line of a Cut authorized to be made by an Act of the Thirty-sixth ' Year of his present Majesty, for making a Canal from the River ' Exe, near Topsham, in the county of Devon, to the River Tone, ' near Taunton, in the county of Somerset, and to amend the said ' Act.' In consequence of this second act, the line was varied, but some difficulties still remained; to remedy which, parliament was again applied to, and in the following year a third was granted, entitled, ' An Act to alter and increase the Rates of Tonnage au- ' thorized to be taken by the Company of Proprietors of the Grand ' Western Canal; and to amend the several Acts passed for making ' the said Canal;' whereby the former rates, as we before stated, were repealed; and, for securing to them a fair remuneration for the money expended on the works, and to be hereafter laid out in completing them, the proprietors were empowered to demand the following

TONNAGE RATES.

		d.	
For all Coals, Culm, Cinders, Coke, Lime, Lime-stone, Iron-stone, Iron-ore, Lead-ore, and all other Ores, Stones, Tiles, Slates, Bricks, Flag-stones, Clay and Sand, and all Articles used for Manure, and for repairing Roads............		3	per Ton, per Mile.
For all Rough Timber, Pig-iron, Bar-iron, Pig-lead, Sheet-lead, Tin in Lumps and Bars, Charcoal, Salt, Corn, Hay, and Straw		4	ditto. ditto.
For all Wrought Metals, Oils, Wines, Liquors, Groceries, Cheese, Earthenware, and all other Goods, Wares and Merchandize, not specified before, carried on the Canal and Cuts, or any Part thereof........................		6	ditto. ditto.

Fractions in Distance to be taken as a whole Mile, and in Weight as a Quarter of a Ton.

The Company may charge Rates, to be determined by themselves, for the Carriage of small Parcels, and for the Wharfage of such Goods as shall remain more than Twenty-four Hours on their Wharfs. Tables of such Rates to be put up in some conspicuous Part of the Wharfs.

The direction of the canal is nearly north-east; the length about thirty-five miles, crossing the south-west branch of the Grand Ridge.

When it is considered, that by its means, particularly if connected with the projected Bristol Ship Canal, those populous places, Exeter, Wellington, Tiverton, Taunton, &c. will be enabled to import and export articles of commerce and produce, it will be evident that the completion of this undertaking must be of general utility.

GRANTHAM CANAL.

33 George III. Cap. 94, Royal Assent 30th April, 1793.
37 George III. Cap. 30, Royal Assent 3rd March, 1797.

THIS canal was executed in consequence of an act of parliament, bearing date 30th April, 1793, and entitled, ' *An Act for* ' *making and maintaining a navigable Canal from or nearly from* ' *the town of Grantham, in the county of Lincoln, to the River* ' *Trent, near Nottingham Trent Bridge; and also a collateral Cut* ' *from the said intended Canal, at or near Cropwell Butler, to the* ' *town of Bingham, both in the county of Nottingham.*'

According to the tenor of the above-recited act, the canal commences on the east side of the town of Grantham, in Lincolnshire, from which place it pursues its course nearly due east, though in a very circuitous direction, to its termination at the Trent Bridge at Nottingham, having completed a distance of above thirty miles. After leaving Grantham, it passes by Harloxton to Woolsthorp Point, a distance of five miles on the summit level, $197\frac{1}{2}$ feet above low water; from Woolsthorp Point to Stainwith Close, a distance of less than two miles, there is a fall of 59 feet nearly; from Stainwith to Cropwell Butler, the distance is twenty miles, and level; from this place to the termination at Trent Bridge, in Holme Pierpoint, a distance of four miles, there is a fall to the Trent of $88\frac{1}{2}$ feet. The canal is cut through a clay soil, and has its water entirely supplied by reservoirs, of which there are two; one at the summit level near Denton, of twenty acres, 9 feet deep; the other at Knipton, made for the purpose of receiving the flood waters of the River Devon, and covering sixty acres; when first made, this reservoir was 9 feet deep, but the head has since been raised 4 feet higher. The act authorized the proprietors to raise amongst themselves the sum of £75,000, and an additional sum of £30,000, whereof £20,000 should be raised by shares of £100 each, amongst the said proprietors, and £10,000 by mortgage of the tolls and rates.

The money originally directed to be raised having been expended on the works, and some misunderstanding having arisen amongst the shareholders as to their liability to raise the additional £20,000 mentioned above, application was made to parliament for a second act, to set the matter at rest, which was obtained in 1797, and bears for title, ' *An Act for enabling the Company of Proprie-* ' *tors of the Grantham Canal Navigation, to finish and complete* ' *the same, and the collateral Cuts to communicate therewith ; and* ' *for amending the Act of Parliament, passed in the Thirty-third* ' *Year of the Reign of his present Majesty, for making and main-* ' *taining the said Canal and collateral Cut.*'

By this act, such proprietors as had not paid the two calls of £10 each, over and above the original £75,000, already made under the first act, were required to pay the same forthwith, and the said calls were consolidated, with their original subscriptions, into shares of £120 each; and the company were empowered to raise £24,000 more, by creating additional shares of £120 each.

By the first act it was determined, that the proprietors should not divide a profit of more than eight per cent. per annum; and that after a fund of £3,000 had been collected, the tolls were to be reduced; but, by the subsequent act, these clauses were repealed; and they are now at liberty to divide the nett receipts, and to raise or lower their tolls, as may seem expedient to the committee.

TONNAGE RATES.

		d.
For all Goods, Wares, Merchandize and Things, passing on this Canal to or from the Trent River	}	2½ per Ton.
For the same navigating on this Canal		1½ ditto, per Mile.
Limestone		¾ ditto. ditto.

Manure, Materials for Roads, and Goods for the sole Use of Charles Pierpoint and John Musters, Esquires, and of the other Proprietors and Tenants of Estates through which the Canal passes, are exempt from the Toll of Two-pence Half-penny per Ton, on passing in or out of the Trent.

x 2

The proprietors of the Trent Navigation are compelled to make the bed of that river 30 inches deep of water at Trent Bridge in the driest seasons.

The navigation is now complete, with the exception of the collateral cut to Bingham, and the advantages to the town of Grantham are very great; corn, timber, coals, lime, and many other articles both of import and export, by the communication opened through this canal, with those of Nottingham and Cromford, are now transferred at a comparatively easy cost, giving, amongst other things, to the inhabitants of this district, the comforts of fuel at a much less expense than heretofore.

GRESLEY CANAL.

15 George III. Cap. 16, Royal Assent 13th April, 1775.

THIS canal, which pursues a north-west direction, and is level throughout, was made at the expense of Sir Nigel Gresley, Bart. and Nigel Bowyer Gresley, Esq. his son and heir-apparent, for the purpose of conveying the produce of their extensive coal mines in Apedale, in Staffordshire, to the town of Newcastle-under-Lyne, in the same county, and of facilitating their transit to other parts of the country by means of the Newcastle-under-Lyne Junction, and other navigations.

The act obtained as above, is entitled, ‘ *An Act to enable Sir* ‘ *Nigel Gresley, Bart. and Nigel Bowyer Gresley, Esq. his Son, to* ‘ *make and maintain a navigable Cut or Canal from certain Coal* ‘ *Mines in Apedale, to Newcastle-under-Lyne, in the county of* ‘ *Stafford.*’ This act, after making the usual provisions, binds the proprietors for twenty-one years from and after the date thereof, to furnish the inhabitants of Newcastle with coals at 5s. per ton of twenty hundred weight, weighing one hundred and twenty pounds each hundred weight, and in like proportion for a single hundred weight.   At the expiration of the first twenty-one years the proprietors, or their heirs, are to furnish coals at 5s. 6d. per ton for an additional term of twenty-one years; which last quoted price may, under certain conditions, be raised to 6s. per ton; the proprietors, in either case, binding themselves, under the penalty of £40 for each offence, to keep a supply of coals sufficient for the consumption of the town, at a wharf in or near the same.

There are few private works of more real utility to the public than Sir Nigel Gresley's Canal, which has added considerably to the interests of the inhabitants of Newcastle, by the regularity wherewith they are supplied with coal at a moderate charge.

GRIMSBY PORT OR HAVEN.

36 George III. Cap. 98, Royal Assent 14th May, 1796.
39 George III. Cap. 70, Royal Assent 12th July, 1799.

THE wet docks in Grimsby Harbour or Haven are connected with the mouth of the Humber, in the tideway of that river, by one of the largest cuts in the kingdom, being calculated to admit ships of as much as one thousand tons burthen. The length of the canal is inconsiderable, being only one mile and a half, with one lock 126 feet long, 36 feet wide, and 27 feet high within the walls; which lock, independent of the charge for piling and foundations, cost upwards of £14,000. Mr. Rennie was the engineer employed upon this useful undertaking; the first act for which was put in execution soon after the royal assent thereto had been obtained. The wet docks at Grimsby having proved insufficient, an addition thereto of three acres was made and completed in 1804, under the powers of the second act obtained in 1799. The direction of the canal is south-west, and the depth of water in it 20 feet.

When Grimsby obtained the privilege of becoming (independent of Hull) a port for the purpose of Foreign imports and exports, the extent of the port was precisely defined by his Majesty's commissioners; and, by the act of parliament, and the powers and privileges granted to the port, certain dues can be charged upon all shipping which enter the same. But the enumeration of such charges could answer no purpose, except to lengthen this article; we therefore think it better to refer parties immediately interested in the port dues, to the act of parliament under which they are imposed.

GROSMONT RAILWAY OR TRAMROAD.

52 George III. Cap. 107, Royal Assent 20th May, 1812.

THIS railway was laid down by Mr. John Hodgkinson, who estimated the cost of completing the same at £12,000. The sum of £10,900 being subscribed in £100 shares, the work commenced under the sanction of the legislature in an act, entitled, '*An Act* '*for making and maintaining a Railway from the End of the* '*Llawihangel Railway in the parish of Llawihangel Crucorney,* '*in the county of Monmouth, to or near to the Twelfth Mile-stone,* '*in the Road leading from the town of Abergavenny, in the county* '*of Monmouth, to the city of Hereford.*' The clause for remunerating the proprietors enacts the following as

TONNAGE RATES.

	d.	
Dung, Compost, Limestone, Manure and Materials for Roads..	2 per Ton, per Mile.
Lime, Chalk, Marl, Ashes, Peat, Clay, Bricks and Sand	3 ditto. ditto.
Coal, Cinders, Coke, Culm, Charcoal, Tin, Copper, Lead-ore, Pig or Sheet-lead, Iron-stone or Ore, Pig and Bar-iron, Timber, Tiles, Slates, Flag-stones and other Stones	4 ditto. ditto.
All other Goods, Wares, Merchandize and Things whatsoever..	6 ditto. ditto.

A Fraction of a Ton to be considered as the Quarters contained in such Fraction; and a Fraction of a Quarter as One Quarter. A Fraction of a Mile to be considered as the Quarters contained in it, and of a Quarter as One Quarter.

TOLLS TO BE TAKEN ON THE RAILWAY.

	s. d.
For every Horse, Mare, Gelding, Colt, Mule, Ass, or other Beast carrying or drawing Goods, Wares or Merchandize liable to pay Tonnage Rates, and passing through any Stop-gate or other Gate on the Railway.............	0 3 each.
For all Cows and Horned or Neat Cattle, except Sheep or Swine, driven loose on the said Railway..............................	0 2 ditto.
For all Sheep and Swine...	1 3 per Score.
All Waggons and Carriages carrying Persons for Hire on the said Railway, for each Passenger................................	0 2 per Mile.

This tramroad, which may be considered a continuation of the Llawihangel Railway, was designed to facilitate the communication with Herefordshire, and thereby contribute to the easier transit of the various products and commodities, both of import and export, and is nearly seven miles in length, from its commencement at the Llawihangel Railway to its termination at Llangua Bridge.

The fund to be raised for the purposes of the act is £13,000, in £100 shares, with the power of raising a further sum of £7,000, either amongst themselves, or by creating new shares, or by mortgage.

When it is stated, that by this railway a difference in the level
of from 166 to 168 feet is made in the distance above specified, it
is hardly necessary to add, that were it even for nothing but the
saving of time and labour in the conveyance of goods, the work
could not fail to be of very great utility.

HAMOAZE RIVER OR ESTUARY.

This river is navigable for ships of war of the greatest size,
and, in consequence of its connection with Plymouth Sound, is of
great service as a harbour.   It extends in a direction almost due
north from Cawsand Bay to the Tamar River near St. Mellion,
a distance of about nine miles, leaving as its branches Cat Water,
Sutton Pool, and Stone-House Creek; communicating also with
the River Tavey, near Warley, and passing, in its course, by
Plympton Earle, and Saltash, both considerable towns.   Several
improvements have been contemplated and undertaken on this
river and its branches, amongst which may be mentioned the
bridge and causeway over Stone-House Creek, projected by Mr.
Smeaton in 1767; a pier from Penlee Point to protect the ships
in Cawsand Bay from the east and south-east winds; the deepening and cleansing of Cat Water and Sutton Pool, for which
£4,000 was granted in the 45th George III.; and the construction
of a floating dock in Sutton Pool, capable of holding one hundred
merchantmen afloat.

HARTLEPOOL CANAL.

This canal, three hundred yards long and 19 feet deep, the
whole of which is cut through the solid rock, was executed in the
year 1764, at the expense of Sir J. H. Duval, for the purpose of
connecting Hartlepool Harbour, on the coast of Durham, with the
sea.   As a private work, it is not necessary for us to enter into
details of its construction, or the cost of its execution.   It has been
the means of saving many valuable lives; for in stormy weather,
vessels now can enter the harbour, where they lie in security.

HAY RAILWAY.

51 George III. Cap. 122, Royal Assent 25th May, 1811.
52 George III. Cap. 106, Royal Assent 20th May, 1812.

THIS railway commences at the wharf of the Brecknock and Abergavenny Canal, not far from the town of Brecon, and pursuing a circuitous course through a mountainous district, in some parts 670 feet or more above the level of the sea, it ends at the village of Eardisley, in the county of Hereford, where a junction of the Kington Railroad has since been made with it.

This undertaking was commenced in the latter end of the year 1811, under the authority of an act of the legislature, entitled, ' *An Act for making and maintaining a Railway from or* ' *near the public Wharf of the Brecknock and Abergavenny Canal,* ' *in the parish of St. John the Evangelist, in the county of Brecon,* ' *to or near to a certain Place called Parton Cross, in the parish of* ' *Eardisley, in the county of Hereford.*' But before the proprietors had advanced far in their work, they perceived the necessity of varying the line of their original design, and, consequently, went again to parliament for the purpose of obtaining a second act, which received the royal assent in 1812, and is styled, ' *An* ' *Act for enabling the Company of Proprietors of the Hay Rail-* ' *way to amend, vary, and extend the Line of the said Railway, and* ' *for altering and enlarging the Powers of an Act passed in the* ' *Fifty-first Year of the Reign of his present Majesty, for making* ' *and maintaining the said Railway.*'

By the first act the proprietors have power to raise £50,000 in shares of £100 each, and a further sum of £15,000, if necessary, amongst themselves, or by the admission of new subscribers, or by mortgage, or by promissory notes. The work commenced with a subscription, in £100 shares, of £47,500. Under the provisions of these acts the work has been completed; and the following are fixed as

TONNAGE RATES.

	d.
For all Lime-stone, Stone for repairing Turnpike-Roads and Highways, Dung, Compost and all Sorts of Manure, except Lime, such a Sum as the Company shall direct, not exceeding	2 per Ton, per Mile.

TONNAGE RATES CONTINUED.

d.

For all Coal, Coke, Culm, Stone, Cinders, Marl, Lime, Sand, Clay, Peat, Iron-stone and other Minerals, Building-stone, Pitching and Paving-stone, Bricks, Tiles, Slates, Timber, Lead in Pigs or Sheets, Bar-iron, Waggon-tire, and all Gross and Unmanufactured Articles, a Sum not exceeding...... } 4 per Ton, per Mile.

For all other Goods, Commodities, Wares and Merchandize whatsoever, a Sum not exceeding .... } 6 ditto. ditto.

Fractions of a Ton to be considered as Quarters of a Ton, and of a Mile as Quarters of a Mile. The Rate of Charge for small Parcels not exceeding Five Hundred Weight, to be fixed by the Company.

Owners and Occupiers of Land may pass on the said Railway free of Toll, as far as the same extends through their Lands, and may drive Cattle and Sheep along the same.

Lords of manors and owners of land, through which the road passes, may erect wharfs, &c. on the line ; and if they refuse to do so, then the company are authorized. In case of lords of manors and others erecting wharfs, &c. the following rates will be allowed.

WHARFAGE AND WAREHOUSING RATES.

d.

For Wharfage of all Goods mentioned as above .... 1 per Ton.
For Warehousing of all Parcels not weighing more than Fifty-six Pounds 1 each.
For ditto of all above Fifty-six Pounds, and not more than Five Hundred Weight.. } 2 ditto.
For ditto of all Packages above Five Hundred Weight .... 6 ditto.

If they remain on a Wharf or in a Warehouse above Forty-eight Hours, then a further Charge may be made for the first Ten Days, of One Penny per Ton for Wharfage, and Three-pence per Ton for Warehousing; after the Space of Ten Days, the same Rates for *every* Day till removed.

The railroad was laid down by Mr. John Hodgkinson, who designed two lines of road, one twenty-six miles in length, without a tunnel, the estimate for which was £50,375, 12*s.*; the other twenty-four miles long, with a tunnel, and on a line which does not rise more than 7 inches in the chain, estimated at £52,743, 18*s.* This latter is the one adopted ; and, taking the level line from the wharf of the Brecknock and Abergavenny Canal, where the road commences, the rises and falls thereof, are as here stated, viz. from the wharf to the tunnel, (which latter is two furlongs five chains long,) in a distance of three miles and three quarters, a rise of 169 feet 2 inches above the level; from the outlet of the tunnel, which is 184 feet 2 inches above the level line, there is a descent in eight miles of 154 feet 2 inches below the same; for the next four miles and three quarters, the road has a further fall of 95 feet; from that fall to the termination of the railroad at Eardisley village, being a distance of nearly seven miles and a half, there is a rise of 78 feet.

The advantages of this railroad to the owners of property on its line are very considerable, independent of the facilities it affords for the transit of goods, minerals, and other produce, by means of its connection with the Brecknock and Abergavenny Canal, the Kington Railroad, and, through it, with the Leominster Canal, and the extended line of country to which it thereby transfers the produce carried along it.

HECK AND WENTBRIDGE RAILWAY.

7 George IV. Cap. 46, Royal Assent 5th May, 1826.
8 George IV. Cap. 20, Royal Assent 12th April, 1827.

THIS work commences at a place called Wentbridge, adjoining the turnpike-road from Doncaster to Ferrybridge; and, pursuing a circuitous course in a north-east direction, arrives at its termination in the basin communicating with that part of the Aire and Calder Navigation called the Knottingley and Goole Canal, in the township of Heck, after having completed a distance of seven miles and thirty-five chains.

The first proceeding in this work was under authority of an act, entitled, ' *An Act for making and maintaining a Railway or Tram-* ' *road from Heckbridge, in the parish of Snaith, to Wentbridge, in* ' *the parish of Kirksmeaton, all in the West Riding of the county* ' *of York.*'

By this act it was determined that the subscribers, who were called " The Heck and Wentbridge Railway Company," should make and maintain a railway or tramroad from Far Fleet Close, at or near Heckbridge, in the parish of Snaith, and passing through the parishes of Womersley, Campsall, Kirksmeaton and Darrington, and through or into the hamlets or townships of Pollington, Heck, Whitley, Balne, Stubbs Walden, Stapleton, and Wentbridge, terminating in the great north road, at the last-mentioned place.   They are also required to make a dock or basin at the communication of their railway with the canal from Knottingley to Goole, for loading and unloading vessels, together with a bridge for haling horses to pass over the cut joining such basin or dock with the canal.   For these and other purposes of the act,

they are empowered to raise amongst themselves in shares of
£100 each, a sum not exceeding £11,300; and they may, if
needful, raise a further sum of £2,800, by borrowing on mortgage of the rates. For paying interest of capital, and monies
borrowed, they have authority to demand the following

TONNAGE RATES.

	d.		
For all Materials for repairing Roads, and for all Dung, Com- post and Stable Manure	1	per Ton, per Mile.	
For all Stone of every Description, except for repairing Roads, Lime-stone, Lime, Coal, Coke, Culm, Charcoal, Cinders, Sand, Clay, Bricks, Tiles, Earth, Timber, Staves, Deals, Lead, Iron or other Metal	3	ditto.	ditto.
For all Manufactured Goods, and all other Goods, Wares, Mer- chandize, Matters or Things whatsoever	4	ditto.	ditto.

No Toll to be taken for Manure of any Description used on the Lands in Heck, Balne,
Womersley, Stubbs Walden, Little Smeaton, Kirksmeaton and Stapleton, if brought
from Heckbridge into these Townships.

In Addition to the above Rates, the Proprietors are authorized to charge Sixpence per
Ton on all Goods, Wares, Merchandize, and Things whatsoever, which shall pass
any Inclined Plane on the Railroad. Fractions of a Ton to be taken as Quarters
of a Ton, and of a Quarter as One Quarter; Fractions of a Mile to be taken as
Quarters, and of a Quarter as One Quarter. Small Parcels and Packages not
exceeding Five Hundred Pounds to be charged for according to Rates determined
by the Company, who also have Power to reduce the Tolls, and again to advance
them, as Circumstances may demand.

Owners and Occupiers of Land have the usual Power of passing along the Railway
without paying Tolls; they may also erect Wharfs, Warehouses, &c. on their
Lands adjacent to the Railway, for Warehousing Goods; or, in Case they refuse
so to do, the Proprietors may erect the same, paying for the Land taken for such
Purposes.

The company, or other persons erecting wharfs, warehouses,
&c. are empowered to demand the following

WHARFAGE AND WAREHOUSING RATES.

	d.	
For Coals, Culm, Lime, Lime-stone, Clay, Iron, Iron-stone, Copper-ore, or other Ores, Timber, Stone, Brick, Tiles, Slates, Gravel, or other Things..	2 per Ton.	
For every Package not exceeding Fifty-six Pounds Weight	2 each.	
For ditto exceeding Fifty-six Pounds, and not more than Three Hun- dred Pounds...	3 ditto.	
For ditto exceeding Three Hundred Pounds, and not more than Six Hundred Pounds	4 ditto.	
For ditto exceeding Six Hundred Pounds, and not more than One Ton	6 ditto.	
For all Packages exceeding One Ton	6 per Ton.	

After remaining Forty-eight Hours on the Wharfs or in Warehouses, the Owners are
to pay One Penny per Ton Wharfage, and Two-pence per Ton Warehousing for
the next Seven Days, and the said Sums respectively for every succeeding Seven
Days.

The estimate for this work was made by Mr. Enoch Taylor,
who omitted to calculate the expense of making the basin or dock,
and the cut joining it to the canal, with the bridge over the same,
and other works connected therewith; indeed the proprietors

themselves, in their first scheme, had no intention of making either basin, cut or bridge, excepting a swivel bridge for the towing-path, and therefore found their original stock too small for the purposes of their act; to remedy the first omission, they obtained, on the 12th April, 1827, another act, entitled, ' *An Act to amend* ' *and enlarge the Powers and Provisions of an Act relating to the* ' *Heckbridge and Wentbridge Railway.*' By this they were em-powered to purchase twenty acres of land, in addition to the six acres for which the former act made provision, for making the dock or basin, cut and bridge before-mentioned, as also coal-yards, warehouses, wharfs, and other buildings and conveniences; they may also raise a further sum of £7,600 amongst themselves, or by the creation of new shares, or by borrowing of the Commissioners of Exchequer Bills, for the purposes of the said act.

The original object for constructing this railway, was to bring the stone situate at Wentbridge and Smeaton into the London and other distant markets.

HEDON HAVEN.

14 George III. Cap. 106, Royal Assent 20th May, 1774.

THE harbour of Hedon having, from the accumulation of warp, &c. in the bed of the River Humber for a long series of years, become unnavigable, an act, entitled, ' *An Act for recovering,* ' *improving, and maintaining the Navigation of the Haven of* ' *Hedon, in Holdernesse, in the East Riding of the county of York,*' was obtained in the year 1774, for the purpose of remedying this inconvenience, and to render the harbour again navigable from low-water-mark to the turnpike-road near the town of Hedon, leading to Patrington; and also for making a reservoir or basin near the said road. For these purposes, the commissioners named in the act were empowered to borrow money on security of the tolls; and the following were determined on as

TONNAGE RATES.

	s.	*d.*	
Wheat, Rye, Beans, Peas or Rapeseed...........................	0 ·	6	per Quarter.
Malt, Oats, Barley, or other Grain not before named	0	4	ditto.
For every Sack of Meal or Flour containing Five Bushels	0	6	per Sack.

TONNAGE RATES CONTINUED.

	s.	d.
Coals, Culm or Cinders, of Forty-eight Bushels to the Chaldron	3	6 per Chaldron.
Brick, Stone, Tile, or Lime for Building..................	3	6 per Ton.
All other Goods, Wares, Merchandize or Commodities whatso-ever, not before enumerated .... }	4	0 ditto.

And in Proportion for lesser Weights and Quantities.

Goods remaining on the Wharfs, &c. above Twenty-four Hours, are to pay Wharfage Rates appointed by the Commissioners. Manure, Hay and Straw not for Sale, but to be used by the Owners, are exempt from the Tolls.

The commissioners appear to have proceeded in the execution of the plan for which the act was obtained; but the trade of Hedon having greatly declined, the advantages accruing are only of a limited nature.

HEREFORD RAILWAY.

7 George IV. Cap. 100, Royal Assent 26th May, 1826.

WE have, in a former page, given an account of the Grosmont Railway, to which the present may be properly considered an addition. The act for executing it was obtained in 1826, and bears for its title, ' *An Act for making and maintaining a Tramroad or* ' *Railway from the End of the Grosmont Railway, at Monmouth* ' *Cap, in the parish of Llangua, in the county of Monmouth, to* ' *Wye Bridge, in the parish of Saint Martin, within the Liberties* ' *of the city of Hereford.*' Locomotive engines are allowed by the act, and the following are appointed as

TONNAGE RATES.

	d.	
For all Dung, Compost, Lime-stone, Manure and Materials for repairing Roads .... }	2 per Ton, per Mile.	
For all Lime, Chalk, Marl, Peat, Ashes, Clay, Bricks and Sand,	3 ditto.	ditto.
For all Coals, Cinders, Coke, Culm, Charcoal, Tin, Copper, Lead-ore, Lead in Pigs or Sheets, Iron-stone or Ore, Iron in Pigs, Bar-iron, Timber, Tiles, Slates, Flag-stones and other Stone...................................... }	4 ditto.	ditto.
For all other Goods, Wares, Merchandize and Things what-soever .... }	6 ditto.	ditto.

Fractions of a Ton to be taken as the Number of Quarters in the Fractions, and of a Quarter as a Quarter. Fractions of a Mile as Quarters, and of a Quarter as a Quarter.

For passing along the road with cattle, &c. the following are the authorized tolls.

TOLLS.

	s.	d.
For every Horse, Mule, Ass or other Beast, (not carrying or drawing Goods, &c. liable to the previously stated Rates), which shall pass any Stop-gate or Toll-house................................	0	3 each.
For all Cows, Horned or Neat Cattle, except Sheep and Swine	0	2 ditto.
For all Sheep and Swine	1	3 per Score.
For all Waggons and Carriages carrying Persons for Hire on the said Railway, for each Person so carried	0	2 per Mile.

Small Parcels under Five Hundred Weight are to be paid for according to a Rate to be fixed by the Company.

The proprietors are empowered to raise £23,200 in shares of £100 each; and if need be, an additional sum of £12,000 by mortgage.

From an inspection of the communication with various parts of the kingdom, which will appear by referring to the map, it is evident that the execution of this railroad will prove of very great convenience to the owners of property on its line; the various productions of the particular district through which it is designed to be made, will thus have a ready conveyance, while, by the same means, the staple commodities of other places will be as easily conveyed to the towns in its vicinity.

HEREFORD AND GLOUCESTER CANAL.

31 George III. Cap. 89, Royal Assent 11th April, 1791.
33 George III. Cap. 119, Royal Assent 11th July, 1793.

THIS useful branch of inland navigation, which is about thirty-five miles and a half in length from its commencement at Hereford to the tideway of the Severn at Gloucester, was projected under the superintendence of Mr. Joseph Clowes, civil engineer, in the latter end of 1790; and the first act obtained for the execution of the work, was passed in the following year, under the title of '*An* '*Act for making and maintaining a navigable Cut or Canal from* '*the city of Hereford to the city of Gloucester, with a collateral Cut* '*from the same to the town of Newent, in the county of Gloucester.*'

The act being obtained, the necessary works were soon after commenced; but it having been found necessary to vary the original line, and to make other alterations, a second act was obtained in 1793, entitled, '*An Act to vary and extend the Line of the* '*Canal authorized to be made by an Act passed in the Thirty-first*

' *Year of the Reign of his present Majesty, entitled, An Act for*
' *making and maintaining a navigable Cut or Canal from the city of*
' *Hereford to the city of Gloucester, with a collateral Cut from the*
' *same to the town of Newent, in the county of Gloucester.*'

This canal pursues a northerly direction from Byster's Gate in
Hereford, near to the banks of the Wye, till it comes to the River
Lugg, near Sulton St. Michael and Sulton St. Nicholas; having
crossed this river, it takes an easterly course to Munsley; thence
crossing the River Leadon, it proceeds in a southerly direction, till
it again crosses the Leadon, two miles below Ledbury; after pursuing its course to Denimoch easterly, it crosses the same river for
a third and fourth time at four miles from the last-mentioned place;
proceeding onwards to its termination, it passes by Pountley,
Newent, Rudford and Lassington, crossing for the last time the
Leadon, and also a branch of the Severn, in which river, after
going through a cut across Alney Island, it terminates opposite to
Gloucester.

By the first act the proprietors of this canal were authorized to
demand the following

TONNAGE RATES.

		d.		
For Manure, Bricks, Rubble, Lime and Clay		1	per Ton, per Mile.	
For Coals		2	ditto.	ditto.
For Corn, Meal, Hewn-stone, Hops, Wool, and other Goods, Merchandize and Wares	}	3	ditto.	ditto.

And so on in Proportion for different Distances.

The original sum granted by the act for completing this work
was £25,000, with power to raise £30,000 more, if necessary;
shares to be £100 each.

The advantages of the amended act are, the nearer approach
to Hereford and the tunnel at Oxenhall, which saves the collateral
cut to Newent, and avoids a great deal of circuitous navigation.

We have stated above that the length of canal, when finished,
will be thirty-five miles and a half, which is on the following
levels,—from Hereford to Withington March, six miles of level
canal; from thence to Monkhide, (which is a summit level at an
elevation of 195½ feet above low water of the Severn,) there is a rise
of 30 feet in a distance of three miles: the canal continues on the
summit level for eight miles and a half to Ledbury; from that

place to Gloucester, where it terminates, there is a fall of 195½ feet
in the remaining eighteen miles. The proposed cut from Newent
to the canal has a fall into it of 10 feet in a length of three miles.
The total lockage is 226 feet nearly; and the number of tunnels on
the canal three, all of considerable size; the first, near Hereford,
being four hundred and forty yards long ; the second on the high
ground at Asperton, near Frome Cannon, the middle of the summit
level, thirteen hundred and twenty yards; and the third at Oxenhall, two thousand one hundred and ninety-two yards.

In 1796 the line from Newent to the Severn was completed;
and, after two years' interval, the Oxenhall Tunnel was opened, by
which means the navigation became practicable to Ledbury. The
expense of cutting, &c. was very great; but the advantages derived from this work are great in proportion; as an instance, we
may mention, that the opening of the Oxenhall Tunnel effected
an immediate reduction in the price of coals at Ledbury of no less
than 10s. 6d. per ton; that quantity being sold for 13s. 6d., when,
before the opening of the navigation, 24s. was the price.   Nor is
it with the coal mines alone that this canal opens a ready communication; lime-stone, iron, lead, and other productions of South
Wales, as well as those of the immediate neighbourhood of Hereford, may, by means of this canal, be conveyed to London, Bristol, Liverpool, Hull, and various other parts of the kingdom,
entirely by water carriage.

HERTFORD UNION CANAL.

5 George IV. Cap. 47, Royal Assent 17th May, 1824.

This canal, designed to make a communication from the River
Lea Navigation at White Port Bridge, in the parish of St. Mary
Stratford Bow, with the Regent's Canal at Old Ford Lock, Bethnal Green, was projected by Sir George Duckett, Bart: who, in
1824, obtained the sanction of parliament by the following act,
entitled, ' An Act for making and maintaining a navigable Canal
' from the River Lee Navigation, in the parish of St. Mary Strat-
' ford Bow, in the county of Middlesex, to join the Regent's Canal
' at or near a Place called Old Ford Lock, in the parish of St.
' Matthew Bethnal Green, in the said county of Middlesex.'

By this act Sir George Duckett, his heirs and assigns, may borrow on mortgage of the canal and rates, any sum not exceeding £50,000; and for defraying the cost of completing the work, authority is given to charge all persons using the said canal the following

TONNAGE RATES AND TOLLS.

	s.	d.
For all Goods, Wares, Merchandize, Articles, Matters and Things whatsoever, entering the Canal either from the River Lea Navigation or the Regent's Canal	1	0 per Ton.
For every Horse, Mule, or Ass, except those used for drawing or haling Boats and Barges..	0	6

Fractions of a Ton to be taken as Quarters, and of a Quarter as a Quarter; and Barges or other Vessels not carrying Twenty Tons, to pay for Twenty Tons. Tolls for Horses and other Animals to be paid only once a Day.

Lords of manors and proprietors of lands may erect wharfs and warehouses; and if not, Sir George Duckett, his heirs or assigns, may do so, and claim the following

CRANAGE AND WHARFAGE RATES.

	d.
For all Goods, Wares, Merchandize and Things whatsoever, not remaining on the Wharfs above Forty-eight Hours	3 per Ton.
For ditto remaining more than Forty-eight Hours	6 ditto.

If Goods are left more than Forty-eight Hours upon the Wharfs, without Permission of Sir George or his Agents, they may be removed into a Place of safety at the Owner's Expense, and detained till such Costs are discharged; and, in Case the Rents and Charges for Warehousing shall not be liquidated within Two Months, the Goods are to be sold to pay the same.

The summit level of this canal is to be 6 inches above the top water mark of the Regent's Canal; bridges are to be erected over the towing-paths of the same; and a stop-lock is to be made within a hundred yards of the same. Various other regulations are made for the preservation of the Lea Navigation and the Regent's Canal, which it is unnecessary to state; we may therefore briefly remark, that the work is of very great utility as well to the vicinity of the metropolis as to other parts of the country; more especially by connecting the Paddington Canal, through the Regent's Canal, with the Lea Navigation, without locking down into the Thames.

HORNCASTLE NAVIGATION.

32 George III. Cap. 107, Royal Assent 11th June, 1792.
39 & 40 George III. Cap. 109, Royal Assent 9th July, 1800.

The Horncastle Navigation commences in the Old Witham River, near Tattershall, in the county of Lincoln, and in part occupies the site of a cut formerly called the Tattershall Canal, made by Messrs. Dyson and Gibson, of whom the present company purchased it.

The first act obtained for the purposes of this undertaking was passed in 1792, and is entitled, ' *An Act for enlarging and im-* ' *proving the Canal called the Tattershall Canal, from the River* ' *Witham to the town of Tattershall, and extending the same into* ' *the River Bain, and for making the said River Bain navigable* ' *from thence to or into the town of Horncastle, all in the county of* ' *Lincoln, and also for amending and rendering complete the Navi-* ' *gation communicating between the said River Witham, and the* ' *Fosdyke Canal, through the High Bridge, in the city of Lincoln.*'

By this act the company were incorporated under the title of " The Company of Proprietors of the Horncastle Navigation," and were empowered to purchase, deepen, widen, and enlarge the cut made by Messrs. Dyson and Gibson; and to make any new cuts on the sides of the river, to straighten the same, and to avoid mills or other obstructions. The commissioners of the River Witham, in order to render the navigable communication complete at all times, are authorized to make that river navigable through the High Bridge in Lincoln, into the Fossdike Canal. For putting these plans into execution, the proprietors are empowered to raise, in shares of £50 each, the sum of £15,000; and, in case this sum should not be sufficient, they are to raise £10,000 more in the usual way; the expenses of the improvement of the Witham River are for seven years, to be borne jointly by the Witham Company and those of the Sleaford and Horncastle Navigations; and for remunerating the latter, the following are to be their tonnage rates.

TONNAGE RATES.

	s.	d.	
For Goods, Wares, Merchandize and other Things whatsoever, navigated from above the Seventh Lock at Dalderby, downwards, or from below to above the same Lock	2	0	per Ton.
For ditto ditto, or between the Seventh and Fourth Lock near Fulby Mill..	1	9	ditto.
For ditto navigated from or to below the Fourth Lock	1	3	ditto.

For Lime, Lime-stone, Manure, or Materials for Roads, Half the above Tolls.

The necessary preparations being made, and the plans, projected in the outset of the undertaking, being completed, the company entered upon the work, but after they had proceeded for some time in the execution of the powers invested in them, they found that the funds raised under the authority of this act were insufficient for the extent and magnitude of their scheme; they therefore again applied to parliament, and obtained a second act, which received the royal assent on the 9th July, 1800, entitled, ' *An Act for enabling the Horncastle Navigation Company to raise* ' *a further Sum of Money to complete the said Navigation, and for* ' *amending an Act passed in the Thirty-second Year of the Reign* ' *of his present Majesty, for making and maintaining the said Na-* ' *vigation.*'

The preamble of this second act states that they have raised, under the first act, the sum of £15,000, and great part of the further sum of £10,000 therein directed to be raised; all which monies have been expended on the works; they are therefore authorized to raise, by subscription amongst themselves, or by the admission of new subscribers, or by mortgage, or on bond, the further sum of £20,000 for the purposes of the said act, and for remunerating the subscribers for the additional contributions, the following are granted as

ADDITIONAL TONNAGE RATES.

	s.	d.	
For all Goods, Wares, Merchandize and Commodities, conveyed from any Part above the Seventh Lock at Dalderby Ford to the River Witham, or any less Distance, and *vice versa*	1	3	per Ton.
For Goods as aforesaid, from any part between the Seventh Lock and the Fourth at Fulby Mill to the Witham, or any less Distance, and *vice versa*...	0	10	ditto.
For the same from any part below the said Fourth Lock to the Witham, and *vice versa*..	0	5	ditto.

For all Lime or Lime-stone used for Manure, and for all other Kinds of Manure or Materials for repairing Highways, in the various Cases as above, Half of the said additional Rates per Ton shall only be charged.

Y 2

In the former act it was directed, that after the payment of
£8 per centum to the proprietors for money advanced, the surplus of the rates should be funded, and when this fund amounted
to £1,000, the rates should be reduced; but in the present that
clause is repealed.

There is a considerable basin at Horncastle, and the work was
opened in the year 1802. The length of the canal is eleven miles,
at no great elevation above low water mark, and the direction it
pursues is nearly north-east. The advantages it affords, by the easy
conveyance of agricultural produce, and the importation of coals,
timber, and other goods through the River Trent, are of great
consequence to a portion of the county of Lincoln, and to Horncastle and its neighbourhood in particular.

HUDDERSFIELD CANAL.

34 George III. Cap. 53, Royal Assent 4th April, 1794.
40 George III. Cap. 39, Royal Assent 30th May, 1800.
46 George III. Cap. 12, Royal Assent 31st March, 1806.

BEFORE we enter on a description of this bold, stupendous
and useful undertaking, it may be neccessary to premise that, in
the year 1774, Sir John Ramsden, Bart. obtained an act for
making and maintaining a navigable canal from the River Calder,
at a certain point between a bridge called Coopers Bridge and the
River Colne, to the King's Mill, near the town of Huddersfield,
in the West Riding of the county of York. Sir John was then a
minor; but the measure met with the approbation of his trustees,
inasmuch as it tended greatly to the convenience of the town of
Huddersfield, whereof Sir John is nearly the sole proprietor.
This canal was executed in due course; and, in the year 1792, an
act of parliament passed for making and maintaining a canal from
Manchester to or near Ashton-under-Lyne and Oldham; and, in
the year 1793, the work of this canal was in a great state of for-
wardness. It was then discovered, that if a communication could
be formed between Sir John Ramsden's Canal and the Ashton, it
would be the most direct line of conveyance between the east and
west seas, provided a short cut was made extending the Ashton
Canal at Manchester to the Duke of Bridgewater's Canal, which

defect was obviated by the formation of the Rochdale Canal. With this impression a survey was made, in the year 1793, by Mr. Nicholas Brown; and the measure obtained legislative sanction in an act, entitled, ' *An Act for making and maintaining a navigable* ' *Canal from and out of the Canal of Sir John Ramsden, Bart.* at ' *or near the town of Huddersfield, in the West Riding of the* ' *county of York, to join and communicate with the Canal Naviga-* ' *tion from Manchester to or near Ashton-under-Lyne and Oldham,* ' *at or near the town of Ashton-under-Lyne aforesaid, in the county* ' *palatine of Lancaster.*' Under the above act the proprietors, who are incorporated by the title of the " Huddersfield Canal Com- " pany," are enabled to raise in shares of £100 each, the sum of £184,000; and in case such sum should prove insufficient, they may raise £90,000 in addition, amongst themselves, or by creating new shares, or by mortgage. By the same act the following are to be collected as

TONNAGE RATES.

	s.	*d.*	
For all Dung, Manure, Clay, Sand and Gravel, not passing a Lock	0	½	per Ton, per Mile.
For ditto passing a Lock	0	1½	ditto. ditto.
For all Lime, Stone, Coal, Cannel, or other Minerals, not passing a Lock	0	1	ditto. ditto.
For ditto passing a Lock	0	2	ditto. ditto.
For all Timber, Goods, Wares, Merchandize and other Articles, not before mentioned	0	3	ditto. ditto.
For all Stone, Lime, Coal, Cannel, Timber, Minerals, Goods, Wares, Merchandize, and all other Articles passing along or through the Tunnel on the Summit Level, or any part thereof, in Addition to the above Rates the further Sum of	1	6	per Ton.

Fractions of a Mile to be taken as a Mile; of a Ton as the Quarters of a Ton contained therein; and of a Quarter as a Quarter.

Wharfage Rates to be demanded by the Company, or others having Wharfs on the Line of the Canal, shall not exceed Three-pence per Ton for the Space of Ten Days, after which Time an Additional Charge may be made for every succeeding Day of One Half-penny per Ton per Day. Vessels of less than Ten Tons are not to pass a Lock when the Water does not run over the Weir, nor of Fifteen Tons when it does, without Leave of the Company's Agent, to be given in Writing.

The company are required to make reservoirs for supplying the canal, sufficient to contain not less than twenty thousand locks of water, each lock containing one hundred and eighty cubic yards; but none of this water, except in times of flood, is to be taken from rivers on the line. In case Sir John Ramsden sustains any loss in the annual income of his canal, in consequence of this company's building of warehouses, wharfs, &c. such loss is to be made good by the Huddersfield Canal Company.

As many mills are upon the streams and brooks from which the reservoirs of the company are to be supplied, it is provided that all persons concerned shall have access to the company's works, and that damages done shall be immediately repaired; and as it is also proposed that a tunnel should be made on the summit level, under Pule Moss and Brunn Top, in the townships of Marsden and Saddleworth, whereby the waters in Brunn Clough and Red Brook Vallies may be diminished, such diminution shall be, from time to time, made up by water supplied to the streams running thereto, from the company's reservoirs on or above the summit level aforesaid. A lock not more than 8 feet wide, with a fall of not less than 6 feet, shall be made at the communication with Sir John Ramsden's Canal; and that part of his canal between his navigation warehouses and the Huddersfield Canal, shall be cleansed and kept navigable by the said company at their will and pleasure, should the said Sir John Ramsden, his heirs or assigns, fail or refuse so to do; and the said Sir John Ramsden is not to receive any tolls or rates for goods navigated from this canal to his warehouses. The provision respecting the supply of water to the streams in Brunn Clough and Pule Moss is necessary on account of the mills thereon.

If the interests of Sir John Ramsden, the Aire and Calder Proprietors, or the Calder and Hebble Navigation, should be injured by making, at any future time, a canal to the eastward, communicating with this or Sir John Ramsden's, full recompense is to be made to the injured parties by the Huddersfield Company, by authorizing them to receive all rates and tolls, in proportion to the length of such navigation and the tonnage thereon collected. In 1798 the part of this canal which lies between Huddersfield and Marsden was completed and opened; and also the part between Ashton-under-Lyne and Stayley Bridge; besides these, another part from Stayley Bridge towards the west end of the tunnel was navigable; but, owing to the very heavy expense incurred in the works of the tunnel, and the deficiency arising from many of the subscribers not being able to pay up their calls, the canal was

greatly retarded. Besides this deficiency, the company were only
able to borrow £14,182 on mortgage, which sum, with the
amount actually paid by the subscribers, had all been expended on
the works, they therefore obtained, in 1800, a second act, entitled,
' *An Act for enabling the Huddersfield Canal Company to finish*
' *and complete the Huddersfield Canal; and for amending the Act,*
' *passed in the Thirty-fourth Year of the Reign of his present*
' *Majesty, for making and maintaining the said Huddersfield Canal.*'
By this second act the committee are empowered to make calls,
from time to time, not exceeding £20 per share in the whole, and
they may raise, by new shares, or on promissory notes payable at
distant times, and bearing lawful interest, any sum or sums necessary for completing the said canal, not exceeding in the whole, the
sum of £274,000, mentioned in the first recited act.

The work being thus supplied with funds, proceeded towards
completion; but the cost and difficulties attendant on its execution
were so much beyond calculation, that the proprietors were, six
years afterwards, compelled to apply a third time to parliament,
and obtained, in 1806, another act, bearing as title, ' *An Act to*
' *enable the Huddersfield Canal Company to raise a further Sum of*
' *Money for the Discharge of their Debts, and to finish and com-*
' *plete the Huddersfield Canal, and for amending the several Acts*
' *passed for making and maintaining the said Canal.*'

This canal, which is fitted for small craft of 7 feet wide, and
such as navigate upon the Staffordshire and southern canals, and
what Dupin calls of the narrow section, is capable of passing boats
with twenty-four tons burthen; and, by a reference to the map,
it will be seen that it commences on the south of the town of Huddersfield, and pursues a south-west direction, winding its course
past Slaithwaite, nearly parallel with one of the branches of the
River Colne, for the distance of seven miles and a half, which
river it crosses in three places by appropriate aqueducts, and, by
an ascent of 436 feet, distributed among forty-two locks, it arrives,
near Marsden, at the summit level, which is higher than that of
any other canal in the kingdom, being at an elevation of 656 feet
above the level of the sea; the summit level is thence continued
for nearly half a mile, when the canal enters that extensive chain
of mountains well known to travellers going from Manchester to

Huddersfield, (through which it passes under the part designated Pule Hill and Brunn Top, generally called Standedge,) for the distance of five thousand four hundred and fifty-one yards, and emerges therefrom into the vale of Diggle in Saddleworth, continuing to near Wrigley Mill, making the whole summit level four miles; it then glides along the valley, alternately on the north and south sides of the River Tame, past Dobcross, Scout, and Stayley Bridge, to its junction with the Manchester, Ashton-under-Lyne and Oldham Canal, near Duckinfield Bridge, having passed a further distance of eight miles and a quarter, and through a descent of $334\frac{1}{2}$ feet, which is equally divided among thirty-three locks; crossing the River Tame in four different places, and making the whole length of canal nineteen miles and three quarters.

In passing from the summit level to Ashton-under-Lyne, there are two other tunnels; one at Scout, two hundred and four yards long, excavated through a strong sand rock, and the other near its extremity at Ashton, one hundred and ninety-eight yards long, cut through a complete body of fine sand.

The principal tunnel at Standedge, or, as it is generally called, the Marsden Tunnel, is 9 feet wide and 17 feet high; the depth of water through it is 8 feet, leaving 9 feet from the surface of the water to the spring of the arch; there is no towing-path in the tunnel; the boats are therefore haled through by manual labour, which is effected in about one hour and twenty minutes; those at Scout and Ashton have each a towing-path.

There are now four lines of communication between the east and west coasts; first by way of the River Trent, and the Trent and Mersey; second, by way of the Aire and Calder, and the Leeds and Liverpool; third, by the Aire and Calder, Calder and Hebble, the Rochdale, and the Duke of Bridgewater's; and fourth, by the Aire and Calder, Calder and Hebble, that of Sir John Ramsden, the Huddersfield, Ashton-under-Lyne, Rochdale, and the Duke of Bridgewater's; which last line is the shortest by nine miles and three quarters. This canal passes through a very populous and manufacturing district, full of valuable stone, but nearly void of every article for manufacturing purposes; its beneficial effects are therefore very obvious, not only as being the shortest line of communication from Manchester to Hull; but, at the same

time, affording the greatest facility to the manufacturers in procuring coal, lime, timber, cotton, wool, dye-wares, iron, &c. and
that of exporting their goods in a manufactured state.

Mr. Outram was the engineer who made the original estimate,
which amounted to £184,000 ; but it appears that upwards of
£300,000 has been expended. Mr. Clowes, Mr. Nicholas Brown,
and other engineers, have also been engaged in prosecuting the
works; and although the proprietors have not reaped the fruits of
their patriotic undertaking, there is a prospect it will eventually be
productive, as the revenue has of late years greatly increased.

HULL, PORT OF.
(SEE KINGSTON-UPON-HULL.)

HULL RIVER.
(SEE DRIFFIELD NAVIGATION.)

HUMBER AND OUZE.

23 Henry VIII. Cap. 18, Royal Assent ———— 1531–2.

THIS article is merely introduced for the purpose of shewing
that an act for keeping clear the navigation of these rivers, was
passed as above in the reign of Henry VIII. bearing for title,
‘ *An Act for pulling down and avoiding of Fish-garths, Piles,*
‘ *Stakes, Hecks, and other Engines, set in the River and Water of*
‘ *Ouze and Humber.*’

HUMBER RIVER.
(SEE LOUTH NAVIGATION.)

HYTHE RIVER.
(SEE COLNE RIVER.)

IDLE RIVER.

6 George I Cap. 30, Royal Assent 7th April, 1720.

THAT part of the Idle River which we have to notice, and for
rendering which navigable, an act was passed as above, entitled,
‘ *An Act for making the River Idle navigable from East Retford,*

' *in the county of Nottingham, to Bawtry Wharf, in the county of*
' *York*,' commences in the River Trent at West Stockwith, at a
very short distance from the junction of the Chesterfield Canal
with that river, and, pursuing a westerly direction for about ten
miles. reaches the wharf in Bawtry by a circuitous course. There
is nothing in this navigation worthy of much remark, save the
sluice and locks at Misterton, half a mile from the Trent, which
were constructed for the purpose of keeping the water of the
Trent, in time of floods, out of the low lands through which the
Idle passes. As an easy communication between the towns of
East Retford and Bawtry, it may be considered an useful undertaking.

INVERNESS AND FORT WILLIAM CANAL.

(SEE CALEDONIAN CANAL.)

ISLE OF DOGS CANAL.

47 George III. Cap. 31, Royal Assent 1st August, 1807.

THIS canal was made by government, the funds being raised
under the authority of an act, entitled, ' *An Act to authorize the*
' *Advancement of further Sums of Money out of the Consolidated*
' *Fund, to be applied in completing the Canal across the Isle of*
' *Dogs, &c. &c.*' It was then called the City Canal, and, in 1829,
was purchased by the West India Dock Company for £120,000.
It crosses the Isle of Dogs, entering from Blackwall Reach, just
below the communication of the Thames with the West India
Docks, and again unites with the Thames at the upper part of
Limehouse Reach, being three quarters of a mile long, and having
a tide-lock at each end.

The original object in making this canal was to facilitate the
passage of vessels round the Isle of Dogs; however, after it was
completed, government found that mariners would rarely pass
through it, on account of having a small sum to pay for dues.
The project therefore failed to answer the original intention.

ITCHIN NAVIGATION.

16 & 17 Char. II. C. — R. A. —— 1662.   7 Geo. III. C. 87, R. A. 15th Apr. 1767.
35 Geo. III. C. 86, R. A. 2nd June, 1795.   42 Geo. III. C. 111, R. A. 26th June, 1802.
51 Geo. III. C. 202, R. A. 26th June, 1811.   1 Geo. IV. C. 75, R. A. 15th July, 1820.

THE first attempt towards the formation of this navigation was
a clause in the general act of the 16th and 17th of King Charles
II. wherein Sir Humphrey Bennet, Knight, and others, were
authorized to make the Itchin navigable for boats and barges; the
goods conveyed by which were declared to be liable to carriage
rates not exceeding one half of the expense of conveying the same
by land, and they executed the powers entrusted to them; but in
lapse of time, by purchase, transfer and other means, the whole
property of the navigation became vested in one individual, who of
course demanded the rates he thought fit; in consequence of this,
the inhabitants of Winchester applied to parliament for an act,
whereby, in pursuance of the provisions of the first act, commissioners might be appointed to determine the rates he should in
future charge for carriage on this navigation. The Mayor,
Recorder, and Aldermen of the city of Winchester, the Dean of
the same, the Warden of Winchester College, together with the
Justices of the Peace for the county of Southampton, all for the
time being, were accordingly appointed commissioners for regulating the rates, under an act bearing for its title, ' *An Act to*
' *explain, amend, and render more effectual an Act made in the*
' *Sixteenth and Seventeenth Years of King Charles the Second,*
' *entitled, An Act for making divers Rivers navigable, or otherwise*
' *passable for Boats, Barges, and other Vessels, so far as the same*
' *relates to the River Itchin, running from Alresford through Win-*
' *chester to the Sea, near Southampton, and for better regulating the*
' *said Navigation.*' By this act the extent of the navigation is
declared to be from Black Bridge, near the city of Winchester, to
Northam, in the parish of St. Mary's, near the town of Southampton; and the commissioners apportioned the rates of carriage on
the canal so much to the satisfaction of the parties concerned, that
when, on account of making further improvements, and concluding
certain agreements with Mr. James D'Arcy and his tenant, Mr.

Edward Knapp, a third act, which is entitled, '*An Act to explain,* '*amend, and render more effectual the several Acts of the Sixteenth* '*and Seventeenth of King Charles the Second, and of the Seventh* '*of his present Majesty, relating to the Navigation of the River* '*Itchin, in the county of Southampton, and for improving the* '*Navigation thereof, and for ascertaining the Rates of Carriage,* '*Riverage, and Wharfage payable thereon,*' was obtained in 1795, these rates were adopted as approved of by the proprietor and the inhabitants of Winchester. By this act also, Mr. D'Arcy engaged to make the river navigable from Woodmill to the Roman Ditch, by widening the same, and also to render the same ditch navigable by diverting the river from its old bed into the Roman Ditch aforesaid; the navigation was also vested in Mr. D'Arcy, and he was authorized to demand the following

TONNAGE RATES.

	s	d.	
For all Coals brought from Northam to the Wharf near Winchester, or from thence to Northam, and in Proportion for intermediate Distances	3	0	per Chaldron.
For all Culm, Stone, Coal, Scotch Coal, and all other Weighable Goods and Corn, except Oats, and so on, rateably	3	9	per Ton.
For Oats brought the same Distance, and so on, rateably	0	6	per Quarter.

By this act also the navigation is declared to consist of one hundred and sixty equal shares or parts, any or all of which the said Mr. D'Arcy, his heirs or assigns, may dispose of. Persons purchasing the same are entitled to proportional shares of the rents and profits, deducting annuities and various other incumbrances on the same, which Mr. D'Arcy undertakes to liquidate. By this and the former acts, the proprietors of the river were also appointed sole carriers thereon; but, in the year 1801, when the property fell into the hands of Mr. George Hollis of Winchester, and Mr. Harry Baker of Westminster, these gentlemen consented to relinquish the power thus vested in them; and accordingly a fourth act was obtained in 1802, which is styled, '*An Act for explaining,* '*amending, and rendering more effectual several Acts of the Sixteenth* '*and Seventeenth of Charles the Second, and of the Seventh and* '*Thirty-fifth of his present Majesty, relating to the Navigation of* '*the River Itchin, in the county of Southampton.*' By this act the river is declared navigable by all persons; and the wharf at Northam is free to the public for taking in lading or to land the same,

and the commissioners therein named, are empowered to direct
new wharfs and storehouses, if necessary, to be made at Northam
by the said Messrs. Hollis and Baker, their heirs and assigns. For
the surrender of their privileges, these gentlemen are empowered
to collect the following

TONNAGE RATES.

		d.
For all Culm, Coals, Corn, Iron, Stone, Timber, and all other Goods, Wares, Merchandize, or Things whatsoever, except Chalk carried down the River, in Boats or Vessels going for Freight to be carried on the said River, and which shall be free of Tonnage..	}	½ per Ton, per Mile.

And so on in Proportion for a greater or less Quantity than a Ton, and a greater or less
Distance than a Mile.

WHARFAGE RATES.

	d.
For Coals at the Wharf near Winchester........................	2 per Chaldron.
For all other Goods, Wares and Merchandize	2 per Ton.

Additional Charges, after the Space of Ten Days, to be made, with the Consent of the
Commissioners, by the said Proprietors.

The owners of boats and vessels navigating on this river are
authorized, by this act, to take, in addition to the before-mentioned
rates payable to the proprietors, the following

RIVERAGE RATES.

	s.	d.	
For Coals carried or conveyed from Northam to Mansbridge or West End Mills .... }	1	3	per Chaldron.
For ditto ditto from Northam to Bishops Stoke...............	2	0	ditto.
For ditto ditto from Northam to Shawford	2	9	ditto.
For ditto ditto from Northam to Winchester	3	0	ditto.
For Corn or other Goods carried or conveyed from Northam to Mansbridge or West End Mills .... }	1	3	per Ton.
For ditto ditto from Northam to Bishops Stoke...............	1	9	ditto.
For ditto ditto from Northam to Winchester	2	3	ditto.
For ditto ditto from Bishops Stoke to Winchester.	1	6	ditto.
For ditto ditto from Mansbridge or West End Mills to Winchester .... }	2	0	ditto.
For ditto ditto from Winchester to Shawford	1	3	ditto.
For ditto ditto from Winchester to Bishops Stoke.............	1	6	ditto.
For ditto ditto from Winchester to Mansbridge or West End Mills	2	0	ditto.
For ditto dittó from Winchester to Northam	2	3	ditto.
For ditto ditto from Mansbridge or West End Mills to Northam	1	0	ditto.
For ditto ditto from Bishops Stoke to Northam...............	1	6	ditto.
For ditto ditto from Shawford to Northam	2	0	ditto.

Exclusive of Tonnage, Wharfage, Porterage, Cranage, Weighing, and such like Extra
Charges.

And all Packages or Light Articles shall be estimated and paid for, at and after the
Rate of Thirty Tons for each Barge Load of Thirty Tons Burthen, and so in Proportion for the Space that such Light Goods shall occupy in the Stowage Room
thereof.

The river being made navigable, and the rates settled as above, the undertaking went forward with considerable success till the year 1810, when the two proprietors, in whom the work was now vested, petitioned parliament for an additional rate on coals; an act was accordingly passed in the following year, entitled, ' *An* ' *Act for increasing the Rates on Coals conveyed on the River* ' *Itchin, in the county of Southampton, and for amending and* ' *rendering more effectual the several Acts relating thereto.*'

By this act the proprietors were empowered to take an additional toll of one halfpenny per chaldron per mile on all coal navigated on the river, over and above their former rates.

In 1820 Mr. Hollis, who had now become sole proprietor of the work, obtained a further advance by an act, entitled, ' *An Act* ' *for increasing the Rates on Goods and Commodities conveyed on* ' *the River Itchin, in the county of Southampton.*' Under which act the following, over and above all former tolls, are directed to be paid as

TONNAGE RATES.

	d.	
For all Coals navigated on the said River	½ per Chaldron, per Mile.	
For all Corn, Salt, Iron, Timber, and all other Commodities or Things whatsoever	¼ per Ton,	ditto.

And so on in Proportion for a greater or less Quantity than a Chaldron or a Ton, and for a longer or shorter Distance than a Mile.

The advantages attendant upon this navigation, which is fourteen miles long, in a northerly direction from the tideway in Southampton Water to Winchester, at a small elevation above the sea, are the facility wherewith Winchester is supplied with deals, coal, timber, &c. and the furnishing Southampton in return with flour, corn, and agricultural produce.

IVEL RIVER.

30 George II. Cap. 62, Royal Assent 17th May, 1757.

The Ivel River, which commences in the River Ouse, or Ouze, at Tempsford, in the county of Bedford, and proceeds for about eleven miles in a southerly direction, to the town of Shefford, in the same county, was made navigable under the powers of an act of the

30th George II. entitled, ' *An Act for making the River Ivel, and the*
' *Branches thereof, navigable from the River Ouze at Tempsford,*
' *in the county of Bedford, to Shottling Mill, otherwise called*
' *Burnt Mill, in the parish of Hitchen, in the county of Hertford,*
' *and to Black Horse Mill, in the parish of Bygrave, in the said*
' *county of Hertford, and to the South and North Bridges in the*
' *town of Shefford, in the said county of Bedford.*' By this act,
which is of considerable length, on account of the many clauses
respecting privileges of proprietors of estates in the course of the
river, a number of commissioners are appointed to execute the
work, to make reservoirs, collateral cuts, and other requisite addi-
tions which may be deemed necessary. They have also power to raise
money for defraying the expenses incurred, by mortgage of the tolls
on all goods navigated on this river; such tolls to be determined
by the commissioners according to the money wanted or already
disbursed. The powers of this act were put in force soon after it
received the royal assent, and the navigation was completed as far
as Biggleswade; the money raised being then expended, no further
progress was made for some time. In the year 1805, Mr. B.
Bevan surveyed the part unexecuted, between Biggleswade and
Shefford, and estimated the cost for that part, with five locks, at
£5,900. The distance of these two towns from each other is five
miles and a quarter, in which there is a rise of 26 feet; and on this
part of the line the commissioners charge for all goods a tonnage
rate of 1*s.* 6*d.* per ton. The surplus of tolls remaining after all
costs of repairs, &c. are discharged, is reserved as a sinking fund
for the reduction of the debt; and the Biggleswade Branch alone
netted, for many years, £400 per annum towards this reduction.
The sluices at the lower part of this navigation are furnished with
separate upright planks, instead of lock gates usually employed for
such purposes.

The purposes for which this river was made navigable, viz. for
supplying coals, timber, &c. to the towns of Biggleswade and
Shefford, and the various hamlets on the line, and for the exporting
of produce, have been fully answered; and, as far as this, the work
is of considerable utility.

IVELCHESTER AND LANGPORT CANAL.

35 George III. Cap. 105, Royal Assent 22nd June, 1795.

THE act for commencing this canal is entitled, ' *An Act for*
' *improving and supporting the Navigation of the River Ivel, other-*
' *wise Yeo, from the town of Ivelchester to Bicknell Bridge, in the*
' *parish of Huish Episcopi, in the county of Somerset ; and for*
' *making a navigable Cut from thence into a certain Drain called*
' *Portlake Rhine, in the parish of Langport, in the same county ;*
' *and for making the said Drain navigable from thence to the River*
' *Parrett, below Great Bow Bridge, in the town of Langport.*'

The length of this navigation is nearly seven miles from its
commencement in the River Parrett, below the town of Langport, to Ivelchester or Ilchester, both in Somersetshire; its direction is nearly due east for the whole distance, with very little
elevation throughout. By the act the proprietors are authorized
to raise £6,000 in shares of £50 each; and, in case this should
not prove sufficient, a further sum of £2,000.

TONNAGE AND WHARFAGE RATES.

		d.	
For all Coal, Culm, Coke, Cinders, Charcoal, Timber, Iron, and Iron-stone	}	2 per Ton, per Mile.	
For all Lime, Dung, Manure, Stone, and Lime-stone when used for Manure	}	1 ditto.	ditto.
For all other Goods, Wares, Merchandize and Things		3 ditto.	ditto.
For all Goods, Wares or Merchandize, deposited on the Pro- prietors' Wharfs, for the first Twenty-four Hours	}	2 per Ton.	
For every Week beyond that Time		6 ditto.	

And so on in Proportion for a greater or less Distance than a Mile, and for a greater
or less Quantity than a Ton.

Fifty Cubic Feet of Round, and Forty Cubic Feet of Square Oak, Ash, Elm, or Beech
Timber, and Fifty Cubic Feet of Fir, Deal, Balk, Poplar, or Birch not cut into
Scantlings, and Sixty Cubic Feet of Light Goods, to be deemed and rated as One
Ton Weight.

The principal object for which this canal was undertaken, was
the introducing into the different places on its line, coal and other
articles of home consumption, and the return of corn and other
agricultural produce.

KENNET AND AVON CANAL.

34 Geo. III. C. 90, R. A. 17th Apr. 1794.   36 Geo. III. C. 44, R. A. 24th Mar. 1796.
38 Geo. III. C. 18, R. A. 7th May, 1798.   41 Geo. III. C. 23, R. A. 21st May, 1801.
45 Geo. III. C. 70, R. A. 27th June, 1805.   49 Geo. III. C. 64, R. A. 3rd, June, 1809.
53 Geo. III. C. 119. R. A. 3rd June, 1813.

THE truly useful and highly important work which we have now to describe, had its first commencement in an act which received the royal assent on the 17th April, 1794, and is entitled, ' *An* ' *Act for making a navigable Canal from the River Kennet, at or* ' *near the town of Newbury, in the county of Berkshire, to the River* ' *Avon, at or near the city of Bath; and also certain navigable Cuts* ' *therein described.*' By this act the proprietors are incorporated under the title of " The Company of Proprietors of the Kennet " and Avon Canal Navigation," and have the usual powers granted on such occasions. In consequence of an agreement with the proprietors of the Wilts and Berks Canal, conformably to a clause in this act, the line first laid down was proposed to be altered, and the sanction of parliament to this alteration was obtained in the year 1796, in an act under the title of ' *An Act to vary and alter* ' *the Line of the Canal authorized to be made by an Act passed in* ' *the Thirty-fourth of his present Majesty, entitled, An Act for* ' *making a navigable Canal from the River Kennet, at or near the* ' *town of Newbury, in the county of Berkshire, to the River Avon,* ' *at or near the city of Bath, and also certain navigable Cuts* ' *therein described, and to amend the said Act, and also to make a* ' *certain navigable Cut therein described.*'

By the first act the company were authorized to raise £420,000, in three thousand five hundred shares of £120 each, part of which might be divided into half shares of £60 each, two of these to have one vote; and should the above sum prove insufficient, they were empowered to raise £150,000 in addition. By the second act no further sums of money were required to be raised. In the year 1798 the company found it necessary to make further alterations in the line of canal; and they, in consequence, obtained the requisite authority by a third act, entitled, ' *An Act to vary the Line of the* ' *Kennet and Avon Canal, authorized to be made by Two Acts* ' *passed in the Thirty-fourth and Thirty-sixth of his present Ma-* ' *jesty, and also to extend the Powers of, and to amend the said Act.*'

z

Various circumstances, which it is not necessary here to enumerate, having rendered an additional sum of money requisite for the completion of the work, by an act called ' *An Act for enabling* ' *the Company of Proprietors of the Kennet and Avon Canal* ' *Navigation to complete the same; and for amending the several* ' *Acts passed for making the said Canal,*' the company were empowered to raise £240,000 by creating new shares and half shares, making in the whole four thousand new shares; three thousand to be taken by the original subscribers or their friends, and the remaining thousand to be sold by auction; but no interest was to be paid on the new shares, the tolls being directed to be applied towards completing the canal.

In 1805, a further sum being still wanting to complete the works, an act was obtained for that purpose, under the title of ' *An* ' *Act for enabling the Company of Proprietors of the Kennet and* ' *Avon Canal Navigation to complete the same, and for altering* ' *and enlarging the Powers of the several Acts passed for making* ' *the said Canal.*' By this act £200,000 more was directed to be raised for completing the canal, and for paying off the debts already incurred. A deficiency, however, still existed; and application was again made to parliament; and by an act, entitled, ' *An Act for enabling the Kennet and Avon Canal Company to* ' *raise a sufficient Sum of Money to complete the said Canal, and* ' *for amending the several Acts for making the same,*' an additional sum of £80,000 was directed to be raised, and to authorize the borrowing of £50,000 as granted by the act previously obtained in 1805. But, to render the undertaking complete, the various sums already recited did not prove adequate; the company also determined that it would be advisable to purchase the River Kennet Navigation; they, therefore, again obtained the sanction of parliament to their proceedings in 1813, in an act entitled, ' *An Act* ' *for enabling the Kennet and Avon Canal Company to raise a fur-* ' *ther Sum of Money to purchase the Shares of the River Kennet* ' *Navigation, and to amend the several Acts passed for making the* ' *said Canal.*' By this last enactment, £132,000 were to be raised by creating five thousand five hundred new shares of £24 each. Power was also given to create a sinking fund; and those proprietors of shares, resident within the bills of mortality, were directed to be called "The Proprietors of the London District," and to elect from amongst themselves three members of the committee of management. The following are the

TONNAGE RATES.

		s.	d.	
For all Hay, Straw, Dung, Peat, and Peat-ashes, and all other Ashes used for Manure, Chalk, Marl, Clay, and Sand, and all other Articles used for Manure and for the repair of Roads		0	1	per Ton, per Mile.
For all Coals, Culm, Coke, Cinders, Charcoal, Iron-stone, Pig-iron, Iron-ore, Copper-ore, Lead-ore, Lime, (except used for Manure,) Lime-stone, and other Stone, Bricks and Tiles		0	1½ ditto.	ditto.
For all Corn and other Grain, Flour, Malt, Meal, Timber, Bar-iron, and Lead, (except such Corn, and other Grain, Flour, Malt, and Meal, as shall be carried Westwards, on such part of the Canal as shall be situate between the Town of Devizes and the City of Bath)		0	2 ditto.	ditto.
For all Corn, and other Grain. Flour, Malt, and Meal, which shall be carried from the Town of Devizes to the City of Bath		3	0 per Ton.	
For all Corn and other Grain, Flour, Malt, and Meal, which shall be carried Westwards on any part of the said Canal between the Town of Devizes and the City of Bath, and shall not pass the whole way between Devizes and Bath		0	1½ ditto, per Mile.	
For all other Goods, Wares, Merchandize, and Commodities whatsoever, in respect of which no Toll, Rate, or Duty is hereinbefore made payable		0	2½ ditto.	ditto.

And so on in Proportion for any Quantity greater or less than a Ton, and for any Distance more or less than a Mile.

Having thus presented our readers with the leading features of the various acts, obtained for completing this stupendous work, it may be useful to add the following scale of particulars respecting the money subscribed, before we proceed to describe the work itself. By the different acts obtained for this canal, the following sums have been raised, viz.

By 34 Geo. III. c. 90.

			£.	s.	d.
Shares designed to be in Number.......................		3500			
Of this Number there were lost by Failures, &c.	514				
And by Consolidation with other Classes, 32 Half Shares...............................	16				
		530			
Remaining Shares...............		2970			

These were first created at..£120 0s. 0d. per Share, And subjected to a further Call of................. } 17 4s. 7½d. at £137, 4s. 7½d. per Share. } 407,576 16 3

Carried over....................£407,576 16 3

	£.	s.	d.
Brought over...................	407,576	16	3

By 41 Geo. III. c. 43.

Shares created; intended to be......................... 3000
Lost of these.................................... 42
And by Consolidation with other Classes, 4 Half } 2
Shares .... } 2
         ——   44

Remaining Shares .... 2956 } 177,360   0   0
           at £60 per Share, }

By 45 Geo. III. c. 70.

Shares were created................................... 8458 } 169,160   0   0
           at £20 per Share, }
And Optional Notes...................................... 99 } 3,300   0   0
           at £33, 6s. 8d. }
Shares.. 1377 } 27,540   0   0
           at £20 per Share, }

By 49 Geo. III. c. 138.

Shares were created 4000
Gained by Consolidation from the Two first Acts, 36 Half } 18
Shares... }
         ——   } 96,432   0   0
Shares............................ 4018 }
           at £24 per Share, }

               CAPITAL.......... ... £881,368 16 3

The Kennet and Avon completes a circuit of navigable canals, which traversing the northern, midland, and south-western counties of England, connect together its four largest rivers, viz. the Trent, the Mersey, the Severn, and the Thames. Viewed in this light, it forms an important link in that great chain of inland navigation, which has been rapidly increasing in this kingdom for the last fifty years, and which seems to know no other boundary than what the rugged and mountainous parts of the country naturally present. This canal, by uniting the Rivers Kennet and Avon, the former of which runs into the River Thames at Reading, and the latter into the Severn a few miles below Bristol, becomes, in conjunction with the Bristol Channel and the estuary of the Thames, the central line of communication between the Irish Sea and German Ocean. The line of navigation, which thus joins these two seas, passes through a very fertile and populous district. Upon the banks of it lie not only the metropolis, but a great many large towns and cities, the ordinary intercourse between which must necessarily produce a very extensive traffic; and if we take into consideration the numerous collateral branches from this grand line, the whole together forms a comprehensive system of water communication, which pervades the southern division of England, and connects the remotest parts of South Wales and Cornwall, with the counties of Essex and Kent. Thus favourably circumstanced, the Kennet and Avon Canal is highly beneficial to the commerce, manufactures, and agriculture of the south-western counties of this kingdom; in the same manner as the Trent and Mersey and Grand Junction Canals have contributed to the improvement and prosperity of the northern and midland counties.

The Kennet and Avon Canal commences at the head of the Kennet Navigation, at Newbury in Berkshire, and passes up the vale of the River Kennet, by Hungerford and Great Bedwin, to Crofton. The distance between Newbury and Crofton is sixteen miles and a half; and the difference of level between these two places is 210 feet, which is effected by means of thirty-one locks. The summit level begins near Crofton, and extends for two miles and a half to the village of Brimslade, passing, in its way, through a tunnel five hundred and ten yards in length, which is cut through the highest part of the intervening hill.

From the western extremity of the summit level, the canal begins to descend to Wootten Rivers, a distance of only one mile, in which there is a fall of 33 feet, which is divided into four locks. From Wootten Rivers it is carried along the vale of Pewsey to Devizes, a distance of fifteen miles, upon one level. From Devizes to a place called Foxhanger, there is a fall of 239 feet, within the short distance of two miles and a half; along this abrupt descent it is carried by a flight of locks, twenty-nine in number. From Foxhanger the canal proceeds to the village of Semington, where it is joined by the Wilts and Berks Canal; the distance is four miles and a half; the fall 56 feet, comprehended in seven locks. From Semington it runs along a rich vale for five miles, upon one level, to Bradford; and at the latter place it descends into the vale of Avon by a lock of 10 feet. After this, it proceeds upon one level for nine miles, along the vale, to Sidney Gardens, Bath. About a mile beyond these gardens, it descends into the Avon, near the Old Bridge, sustaining, in this short distance, a fall of 66½ feet, by means of seven locks. From this

point that river is navigable to Bristol, as already described under
the River Avon. Its whole length is fifty-seven miles; its total
rise 210 feet, effected by thirty-one locks; and its whole fall $404\frac{1}{2}$
feet, effected by forty-eight locks. Its breadth at bottom is 24
feet; at the surface, 44 feet; and the least depth of water is 5
feet, but through a considerable length, 6 feet. The locks are 80
feet long, and 14 feet wide; and the barges which navigate it
carry from fifty to seventy tons.

Few canals afford more specimens of deep cutting, aqueducts
and tunnels, than the Kennet and Avon, and we shall proceed to
enumerate them, according to the order in which they arise from
Newbury to Bath. Much labour has been expended upon this
part of the canal, to prevent its interference with the channels,
which have been made for the purpose of conveying water to the
meadows, (usually called Water Meadows,) between Newbury
and Hungerford; and the River Kennet has within the same
distance been three times crossed by means of weirs; once to
avoid Hampstead Park, and twice to prevent its passing through
the village of Kentbury. At a little distance above Hungerford
the level of the canal has acquired a sufficient elevation to be carried over the Kennet by means of an aqueduct, consisting of three
arches. Ascending from this aqueduct to the eastern extremity
of the summit level, it is carried in its passage from thence to the
western extremity through the hill at Burbage, by a great deal of
deep cutting, and a tunnel of five hundred yards long and $16\frac{1}{2}$
feet wide. From the extremity of this tunnel to the town of
Devizes, no work of consequence occurs. From Devizes to Bath
the country assumes a more hilly and rugged character. At the
former place there has been an extensive piece of deep cutting.
Between the locks near Foxhanger, it has been found necessary to
make very large side ponds, in which the water is permitted to
expand itself, after it is let out of the locks, and is thus prevented
from running to waste. From Foxhanger, the line of the canal is
continued through the long vale of Somerham Brook, by an
expensive embankment. On leaving this vale, it proceeds along
the valley of the Semington River, and at Semington is conveyed
across the river by a stone aqueduct, having an arch of 30 feet span,
with a long embankment at each end of it. From hence there is

a considerable piece of cutting, as far as the River Biss, below Trowbridge; it then crosses that river over an aqueduct of the same dimensions as that at Semington, with a large embankment, 30 feet high, on each side of it.

From the aqueduct over the River Biss, the canal passes by Bradford, through a tract of country abounding with hills and rocks, to Sidney Gardens, Bath: and in its course is twice conveyed across the River Avon by handsome stone aqueducts, the centre arches of which are about 60 feet span each. It enters and departs from Sidney Gardens through tunnels, which pass under the houses and rides. The walks of the gardens are carried over it by two iron bridges. The seven locks upon the remainder of the canal, between these gardens and its entrance into the Avon, have been made at considerable expense; several of them being so near to each other, that large side ponds have been required.

This canal, at its highest elevation at the Crofton Tunnel, is 474 feet above the level of the sea. In its course it passes within a short distance of Hungerford House, Tottenham Park, Wilcot Park, East Stowel, Hewish, New Park, Mount Pleasant, and a number of other seats of the nobility and gentry. The direction it takes, from its junction with the River Kennet Navigation, is nearly west. It has communication with the Wilts and Berks Canal at Semington; with the Frome Canal at Widbrook; and with the Somerset Coal Canal near Bradford, all upon its line. From these and many other advantages, the traffic on it in coal, corn, stone, copper and iron, is of very considerable extent, and, from the almost daily addition to its communication with different parts of the kingdom, by connecting canals and railroads, must continue to increase as long as Great Britain maintains its character as a commercial nation.

Mr. Rennie was engineer for the canal, by whose abilities the most formidable obstacles were overcome. The aqueduct over the River Avon, about a mile from Limpley Stoke, and six miles from Bath, is greatly admired for its architectural beauty; and, indeed, wherever there is an aqueduct or a bridge upon the line, they are invariably distinguished by the excellent workmanship employed in their construction. The execution of the locks and tunnels is deserving of similar commendation.

Of the good effects arising from a well-regulated system of inland navigation there can be no doubt; but at the same time it should be recollected, that in most instances these effects must be produced by slow and gradual means. There is probably no canal in Great Britain to which this observation may be applied with greater propriety than the Kennet and Avon. The difficulties to be encountered have sometimes been so great, as to present a very unpromising appearance as to its ultimate execution; but they have all been surmounted by the skill, perseverance and good management of the persons to whom its affairs have been entrusted. It was opened on the 28th of December, 1810, for public accommodation ; and, when considered in connection with the other works which are now carrying on in the western counties, it promises to continue one of the most profitable concerns of the kind in this part of the united kingdom.

KENNET RIVER.

2 George I. Cap. 24, Royal Assent 21st September, 1715.
7 George I. Cap. 8, Royal Assent 23rd March, 1720.
3 George II. Cap. 13, Royal Assent 15th May, 1730.

As the interests of this navigation are merged in those of the Kennet and Avon Canal, in consequence of the provisions of an act obtained by that company, it will not be necessary to do more than recite the three acts obtained as above; the first is entitled, ' *An Act to make the River Kennet navigable from Reading to* ' *Newbury, in the county of Berks.*' The second, ' *An Act for* ' *enlarging the Time for making the River Kennet navigable from* ' *Reading to Newbury, in the county of Berks.*' A third act was obtained in the 3rd of George II. entitled, ' *An Act for making* ' *the Acts of the Second and Seventh of his late Majesty's Reign,* ' *for making the River Kennet navigable from Reading to New-* ' *bury, in the county of Berks, more effectual.*' By these acts, the proprietors of the Kennet River were empowered to demand a rate of 4s. per ton on goods of every description conveyed thereon, but the Kennet and Avon Canal Proprietors, since they purchased this work, have only charged a rate of $1\frac{1}{2}d.$ per ton per mile.

The Kennet River Navigation, commencing from its junction with the Kennet and Avon Canal at Newbury, to its fall into the Thames a mile and a half below Reading, is twenty miles in length. Its elevation at the highest point is 264½ feet above the level of the sea. From Newbury to the High Bridge at Reading, in a distance of eighteen miles and a half, there are twenty locks, with a fall of 126 feet; this constitutes the River Kennet Navigation. These eighteen miles and a half may now be reckoned as a continuation of the Kennet and Avon Canal.

From Reading to the Thames, about a mile and a half, the river is under the control of the Thames Commissioners, who have made a cut and lock on this part. The breadth of the water in the river is between 60 and 70 feet; on the cuts, 54 feet; the average depth about 5 feet. The locks are 120 feet long, by 19 feet broad, thus allowing the passage of vessels 109 feet long and 17 wide, drawing 4 feet water. In its course it passes Sandleford Priory, Padworth House and White Knights.

Its utility for the transit of corn and other agricultural produce, coals and various articles of home consumption is very great, particularly when considered in conjunction with the various canals of which it forms a part. The turf and peat pits between Reading and Newbury afford the opportunity of producing an abundance of peat ashes, which, by means of this navigation, is distributed over a large district of country, and found highly beneficial for manure.

KENSINGTON CANAL.

5 George IV. Cap. 65, Royal Assent 28th May, 1824.
7 George IV. Cap. 96, Royal Assent 26th May, 1826.

THE first act granted for the purposes of this work was obtained in 1824, and bears for title, ' *An Act for widening, deepening,* ' *enlarging and making navigable a certain Creek called Counter's* ' *Creek, from or near Counter's Bridge, on the Road from London* ' *to Hammersmith, to the River Thames in the county of Middlesex,* ' *and for maintaining the same.*' By the preamble of this act it is stated, that the town and parish of St. Mary Abbot's Kensington, would be greatly benefited by the forming of Counter's Creek into a canal, for the conveyance of goods through the same to the Thames. Commissioners were, therefore, appointed to take measures for executing the same, with powers to make tunnels, erect steam engines, take down bridges and divert roads for this purpose; and in order to meet the cost of the undertaking, the proprietors were to raise amongst themselves the sum of £10,000, in one hundred shares of £100 each. In case this should not prove sufficient, they may raise a further sum of £5,000, either of which sums may be borrowed on mortgage of the tolls, and the £5,000, last directed to be raised, may be obtained on promissory notes, or by such other means as shall appear most eligible.

For paying interest and other expenses, the proprietors, who are by the act called " The Kensington Canal Navigation Com- " pany," are to collect the following

TONNAGE RATES.

		d.
For all Dung or Manure conveyed between the Thames and Fifty Yards Northward of Stamford Bridge	}	½ per Ton.
For ditto between the Northern Extremity of the said Fifty Yards and the Hammersmith Road	}	3 ditto.
For all Coals, Cinders, Culm, Lime, Slate, Stone, Alabaster, Potatoes, Pig-iron, Bricks, Peat, Gravel, Sand, Clay, Marl, Timber. Deals, Malleable and Wrought or Manufactured Iron, Lead and other Un-wrought Metals, Corn, Grain, Malt, Peas and Beans, Wool, Cotton Wool and Yarn, Cotton Linen, and Woollen Manufactured Goods, Hemp, Flax, Groceries, and all other Goods, Wares and Merchan-dize whatsoever, carried between the Thames and Fifty Yards Northward of Stamford Bridge	}	1 ditto.
For all the above-named Description of Goods carried between the Northern Extremity of the said Fifty Yards and the Hammersmith Road	}	6 ditto.

Fractions of a Ton to be taken as the Quarters therein, and of a Quarter as a Quarter.

The company may erect wharfs and cranes, and charge as

WHARFAGE RATES.

		d.
For all Goods, Wares and Merchandize remaining on the Wharfs Seventy-two Hours	}	9 per Ton.
For ditto after the Seventy-two First Hours		6 ditto, per Day.

The canal was to be completed in three years after the passing of this act, or the powers thereof were to cease, and the company was directed to pay a fine of £5, with an annual rent of the same sum to the Mayor and Commonalty of London, for the liberty of opening and enlarging the communication with the Thames.

The work was commenced immediately on obtaining the act; but it having been found expedient to make the canal of a greater width than at first proposed, and this alteration costing more than was originally estimated, a second act was obtained in 1826, bearing the title of ' *An Act to amend an Act for making a Canal 'from Counter's Bridge, on the Road from London to Hammer- ' smith, to the River Thames, in the county of Middlesex, and to ' enable the Kensington Canal Company to raise a further Sum for ' the completing of the said Canal.'* By this act the company were authorized to raise a further sum of £30,000 by the usual means, and the term of completing the canal was prolonged for three years.

Mr. Thomas Hollinsworth was the engineer employed, and his estimate for the canal, to be 9,000 feet long, was, for completing the same, with

Lock and Coffer Dam......................	£8,000
Draw Bridge and Lock....................	13,000
	£21,000

This canal, though of limited extent, is of great service for the purposes which gave rise to its projection.

KENYON AND LEIGH RAILWAY.

10 George IV. Cap. 36, Royal Assent 14th May, 1829.

The Kenyon and Leigh Railway was projected with a view to connect the Bolton and Leigh Railway with that of the Liverpool and Manchester, and the act for completing the same obtained the sanction of the legislature as above, under the title of ' *An Act 'for making a Railway from the Bolton and Leigh Railway in ' the township of West Leigh, to the Liverpool and Manchester ' Railway, in the township of Kenyon, with a Branch therefrom, ' in the county of Lancaster.'* By this act the company, under the title of " The Kenyon and Leigh Junction Railway Com- " pany," are empowered to make a railway from the Bolton and Leigh Railway, within the township of West Leigh, and extending to or passing through Leigh, Winwich, Pennington and Kenyon, or some of them, and terminating at the Liverpool and Manchester

Railway, five hundred yards to the west of Broseley Lane, in the
said township of Kenyon, together with a branch from a certain
field in the said township of Kenyon, belonging to the Earl of
Wilton, and extending from thence in a curved line eastwardly,
terminating at or near the said Liverpool and Manchester Railway, four hundred yards to the eastward of the said Broseley
Lane; and also, to make inclined planes, if necessary, on any
part of the line. The distance between the inside edges of the
rails of this railway to be not less than 4 feet 8 inches, and that
between the outside edges not more than 5 feet 1 inch; and at
the crossings of turnpike-roads or highways, the guiding flanch
or ledge shall not rise above or sink below the level of such road
more than 1 inch. Bridges for carrying the same over highways,
shall leave a clear width of 15 feet under the arch, and a height
of 16 feet above the surface of the road; but the bridge over the
Leeds and Liverpool Canal shall not be less than 25 feet in span;
width of towing-path 6 feet, and breast wall of the same 12 feet
in height above the level of the top water in the canal. The proprietors are empowered to raise £25,000, in shares of £100 each,
for the purposes of this act; £22,946, being the estimate of the
work, is to be raised before the act is put in force. But should
the sum of £25,000 prove insufficient, the proprietors may raise
£6,000 more in the usual way. The following are directed to be
collected as

TOLLS AND TONNAGE RATES.

	s.	d.
For every Person passing on the Road in any Coach, Cart, Waggon, or other Carriage	0	6 each.
For every Horse, Mule, Ass or other Beast of Draught or Burthen, and for every Ox, Cow, Bull or Neat Cattle, ditto, ditto	0	6 ditto.
For every Calf, Sheep, Lamb, or Pig ditto, ditto	0	1 ditto.
For all Lime-stone and Lime, Coal, Coke, Culm, Charcoal, Cinders, Stone, Sand, Clay, Building, Pitching and Paving-stones, Flags, Bricks, Tiles, Slates, Dung, Compost, and all Sorts of Manure and Materials for repairs of Roads	0	6 per Ton.
For all Sugar, Corn, Grain, Flour, Dye Wood, Timber, Staves, Deals, Lead, Iron and other Metals, Cotton and other Wool, Hides, Drugs, Manufactured Goods, and all other Wares, Merchandize, Matters or Things	1	0 ditto.

Fractions of a Ton to be taken as the Quarters therein, and of a Quarter as a
Quarter.
The Company to fix the Rates for Parcels not exceeding Five Hundred Weight.
This Railway is not to be used as a Foot Path, under Penalty of Forty Shillings, to
be paid by the Offender, but Owners or Occupiers of Lands adjoining may pass
thereon without paying Toll. No carriage to carry more than Four Tons, including its own Weight, except any one Piece of Timber, Block of Stone, Boiler,
Cylinder, Bob or Single Piece of Machinery, which may, with the Carriage,
weigh Eight Tons, and pay Four-pence per Ton per Mile.

The railway must be completed in seven years, or the powers of the act cease. The length thereof is about four miles, in a southerly direction from Leigh; in its course it passes not far from Pennington Hall and Haydock Lodge; and, connecting the Bolton and Leigh Railroad with that of the Manchester and Liverpool, it adds considerably to the facilities for conveying coal, iron and lead from various mines within reach of Bolton, Leigh, and other places, with which a communication is thereby opened. The engineering department is under the direction of Mr. Vignolles.

KETLEY CANAL.
(SEE SHROPSHIRE CANAL.)

KIDWELLY CANAL.

6 George III. Cap. 55, Royal Assent 19th February, 1766.
52 George III. Cap. 173, Royal Assent 20th June, 1812.
58 George III. Cap. 75, Royal Assent 28th May, 1818.

THE first commencement of this undertaking was an act obtained in 1766, by Thomas Kymer, Esq. to make a canal from the tideway in Kidwelly Harbour to his coal and lime works, about three miles and a half from that place. This act is entitled, ' *An* ' *Act to enable Thomas Kymer, Esq. to make a navigable Cut or* ' *Canal, from Little Gwendraeth River, near the town of Kidwelly,* ' *to the Great Forest and Pwll Llygod, in the county of Carmar-* ' *then.*' It may be strictly considered a private act, as it was for the sole purpose of affording conveyance for the produce of Mr. Kymer's estate; and the canal which was entirely cut through his own land was called Kymer's Canal. The utility of the work, however, was proved to be so great, that it was thought desirable to extend its benefits to the neighbourhood, and, in consequence, another act was obtained in 1812, entitled, ' *An Act for the im-* ' *proving of the Harbour of Kidwelly, and for making and main-* ' *taining a navigable Canal, or Tramroads, in Kidwelly, and* ' *Llanelly and other parishes therein mentioned, in the county of* ' *Carmarthen.*' By this act powers were given for a company to improve the harbour at Kidwelly, and to make a canal and tramroads in Kidwelly, Llanelly, and other parishes of the vicinity. The company was by this act incorporated under the name of " The Kidwelly and Llanelly Canal and Tramroad Company," with the usual powers. They were also authorized to restore or make a cut or channel from Salmon Scarr, on the south side of the River Towey, to the united rivers of Great and Little Gwendraeth, near Bertwyn House. For all the purposes of this act the company may raise £60,000, in shares of £100 each; and should that prove insufficient, they may raise a further sum not exceeding £20,000 in like manner, or on mortgage. For enabling them to keep up the works, and to pay the interest of money advanced, the proprietors are authorized to demand as under for

TONNAGE RATES.

			_d._
For all Goods, Wares, Merchandize and other Things, navigated, carried or conveyed on the said Canal, Collateral Cuts, Railways or Tramroads, except the Articles mentioned below......		4 per Ton, per Mile.	
For all Iron Castings, navigated and carried on ditto	3	ditto.	ditto.
For all Pig-iron, ditto................	2½	ditto.	ditto.
For all Calcined Iron-ore, Rotten-stone, Coals, Culm, Stone-coal, Cokes, Cinders, Charcoal, Timber, Deals, Stones, Tiles, Slates and Bricks, ditto...............	1¾	ditto.	ditto.
For all Iron-stone, Iron-ore, Lime-stone, Lime, Sand, Clay, and all Kinds of Manure, ditto	1	ditto.	ditto.

And so on in Proportion for a greater or less Weight than a Ton, and for a longer or shorter Distance than a Mile. Parcels of less than Five Hundred Weight to be paid for according to Rates which shall be fixed by the Proprietors.

Ships, Barges, and other Vessels entering and using the Harbour of Kidwelly, to pay, as Harbour Dues, One Penny per Ton on their registered Burthens, which Dues shall be appropriated solely to maintaining and improving the said Harbour. His Majesty's Vessels of War, Post-Office Packets, Transports employed on his Majesty's Service, Vessels carrying Salt for the Fisheries, Ships carrying Stones or other Materials for the Works, and Custom-House Vessels are all exempt from paying these Dues. Vessels resorting to any Shipping Places to be hereafter erected by the Company, shall pay One Penny per Ton on all exported Goods, and One Half-penny per Ton on all imported Goods. The Company may also demand the following

TOLLS.

		_d._
For every Horse, Mare, Gelding, Mule or Ass, Cow or other Neat Cattle, travelling on the Railways or Tramroads, and not drawing any Waggon, nor passing from one Farm to another on the Line	1 each.	
For all Sheep, Swine or Calves, except when passing from one Farm to another......	8 per Score.	

Fishing Boats, Boats or Vessels carrying Coals to other Vessels in the Harbour, or bringing Supplies of Flesh or Vegetables to the Town of Kidwelly, are exempt from Duties. Goods or Merchandize are not to remain on any Quays or Wharfs of the Company for a longer Time than Twenty-four Hours; if they do, they are to be charged a Wharfage Rate of One Half-penny per Ton per Day.

In 1818 a third act was obtained to alter and enlarge the powers of those previously granted, and is entitled, ' *An Act to* ' *explain and amend an Act of the Fifty-second of his present* ' *Majesty, entitled, An Act for the improving of the Harbour of* ' *Kidwelly, and for making and maintaining a navigable Canal,* ' *or Tramroads, in Kidwelly and Llanelly, and other parishes therein* ' *mentioned, in the county of Carmarthen, and to alter and enlarge* ' *the Powers thereof.*' By this act the company are enabled to raise the harbour dues of Kidwelly, from one half-penny to one penny per ton, on the registered burthen of all vessels entering and using this harbour.

If the works are not completed in six years from the date of the act, then its powers are to cease; and if any persons, desirous of making any collateral cut, branch or railway, authorized by this or the former acts, shall advance to the company a sufficient sum of money for making the same, then they may call upon the company to complete the same, and in case of refusal, the parties themselves are authorized to make it, and shall be accounted proprietors of one £100 share, for every hundred pounds *bona fide* expended on the making of the said branch, cut or tramroad. There are two small detached tramroads, one at Machynis Pool, the other at the Loughor Mines.

KILMARNOCK RAILWAY.

48 George III. Cap. 46, Royal Assent 27th May, 1808.

THIS railway, commencing near the town of Kilmarnock, in the county of Ayr in Scotland, pursues a westerly course for about half its length; it then turns at almost right angles to the south, and terminates at the Troon, having traversed between its two points, Kilmarnock and the Troon, a distance of nine miles and six furlongs, and passing, in its way, by the estates of Fairlie and Robertland, both belonging to the family of Sir William Cunningham.

The design, for which it was projected, was to open a cheaper and easier conveyance than heretofore, for coal, lime and minerals, as well as for the goods, wares and merchandize used and manufactured by and in the large works of the county of Ayr. The act for executing it was passed in 1808, and has for title, ' *An Act* ' *for making a Railway from or near to the town of Kilmarnock,* ' *in the county of Ayr, to a Place called the Troon, in the said* ' *county.*' By this act the proprietors are incorporated under the style of " The Company of Proprietors of the Kilmarnock and " Troon Railway," and are empowered to raise in shares of £500 each, the sum of £40,000, for the purposes of the act; and should need be, they may raise a further sum of £15,000 amongst themselves, or by borrowing on security of the undertaking. The following are also directed to be paid as

TONNAGE RATES.

d.

For all Goods, Wares, Merchandize and other Things whatsoever 3 per Ton, per Mile.

Fifty Cubic Feet of Round, and Forty Cubic Feet of Square Oak, Ash, Elm or Beech Timber, and Fifty Cubic Feet of Fir or Deal, Balk, Poplar, Birch or other Timber or Wood not cut into Scantlings, to be considered as One Ton Weight. One Hundred and Twelve Pounds Avoirdupois of Coal, Coke, Lime and all other Goods, Commodities, Matters or Things to be rated as One Hundred Weight; and Two Thousand Two Hundred and Forty Pounds Weight as one Ton.

Fractions of a Ton to be reckoned as the Numbers of Quarters in it, and of a Quarter as a Quarter.

Fractions of a Mile as the Quarters in it, and of a Quarter as a Quarter.

If the yearly dividends exceed £20 per cent. on the sums expended, for three years, the rates may be reduced by order of two justices of the peace; and if, after such reduction, the dividends for any two years shall not amount to £20 per cent. per annum on the sums expended, the rates may be raised to their former amount, by order of two justices as aforesaid.

Owners of land on the line may erect wharfs and warehouses, but if they refuse after twelve months' notice, the company may erect such wharfs, &c. and demand a rate for all goods left on their wharfs or in their warehouses above twenty-four hours; such rate to be regulated at a quarter sessions of the county.

The line of this useful undertaking was laid down by Mr. William Jessop, who estimated the expense of making the same at £38,167, 10s. The whole length is, as we have before stated, nine miles and six furlongs. At a distance of seven miles, two furlongs and five chains, there is a branch to Sir William Cunningham's Coal Works at Peatland, which is four furlongs and five chains in length. There were originally only four subscribers to the work, who took shares as follow, viz.

The Marquis of Tichfield, seventy-four shares .. £37,000
Lord Montgomerie, one ditto................   500
Lord Montgomerie Eglington, one ditto.......   500
John Boyle, Esq. one ditto   500
                                             ————
                                             £38,500

KINGSTON-UPON-HULL.

14 Geo. III. C. 56, R. A. 20th May, 1774.   23 Geo. III. C. 55, R. A. ——— 1783.
42 Geo. III. C. 91, R. A. 22nd June, 1802.   45 Geo. III. C. 42, R. A. 5th July, 1805.
                6 Geo. IV. C. 107, R. A. 5th July, 1825.

THIS article is merely inserted as serving to inform our readers,
that the powers of demanding various dues and customs relating
to the Hull River and the port of Kingston-upon-Hull, together
with the building of quays, wharfs, &c. for the securing the
revenues of his Majesty's customs there, were legalized by an act
of 14th George III. entitled, ' *An Act for making and establishing*
' *public Quays or Wharfs at Kingston-upon-Hull, for the better*
' *securing his Majesty's Revenues of Customs, and for the Benefit*
' *of Commerce in the Port of Kingston-upon-Hull; for making a*
' *Basin or Dock, with Reservoirs, Sluices, Roads and other Works*
' *for the Accommodation of Vessels using the said Port; and for*
' *appropriating certain Lands belonging to his Majesty, and for*
' *applying certain Sums of Money out of his Majesty's Customs at*
' *the said Port for those Purposes, and for establishing other neces-*
' *sary Regulations within the Town and Port of Kingston-upon-*
' *Hull.*' The other acts above-noticed relate principally to making
a new dock and other regulations.

For the extent of the port we refer to the map, and for the
various dues to the acts, those particulars not coming within the
design of a work on inland navigation.

KINGTON CANAL.
(SEE LEOMINSTER CANAL.)

2 A

KINGTON RAILWAY.

58 George III. Cap. 63, Royal Assent 23rd May, 1818.

THIS railway was projected for the purpose of opening a communication between the Hay Railway near Eardisley in Herefordshire, to Kington in the said county, and from thence to the Burlinjob Lime Works, in the county of Radnor, and thereby facilitating and cheapening the conveyance of coal, iron and other commodities from the county of Brecon, to the said town and lime works ; and, in return, to facilitate the export from thence of lime, corn and other products, all which objects were not feasible by the turnpike and other roads, in consequence of their ruinous state.

The necessary powers were obtained in an act, entitled, ' *An* ' *Act for making a Railway from the Hay Railway, near Eardis-* ' *ley, in the county of Hereford, to the Lime Works near Burlinjob,* ' *in the county of Radnor ;*' by which the subscribers were incorporated under the name of " The Kington Railway Company," and empowered to make the said railway from the Hay Railway near Eardisley, through the townships of Almeley, Lyonshall, Kington and Old Radnor, in the counties of Hereford and Radnor. For accomplishing this work, the proprietors are empowered to raise £18,000, in shares of £100 each; and in case that sum should not be sufficient, they may raise £5,000 more. Any part of the said £18,000 which was not subscribed before the passing of the act, or of the additional £5,000, may be raised on promissory notes under the common seal, or by mortgage. For paying interest and maintaining the railway, they are authorized to demand the following

TONNAGE RATES.

	d.
For all Lime, Stone, Materials for the repairing of Turnpike Roads or Highways, all Dung, Compost and Manure, except Lime..........	3 per Ton, per Mile.
For all Coal, Coke, Culm, Stone, Cinders, Marl, Sand, Lime, Clay, Pier, Iron-stone and other Minerals, Building-stone, Pitching and Paving-stone, Bricks, Tiles, Slates, Timber, Lead in Pigs or Sheets, Bar-iron, Waggon-tire, and all Gross and Unmanufactured Articles and Building Materials....	5 ditto. ditto.
For all other Goods, Commodities, Wares, and Merchandize whatsoever	6 ditto. ditto.

Fractions of a Ton and a Mile as the Quarters in each respectively, and of a Quarter as a Quarter.

The Company are to fix the Rate for Parcels not exceeding Five Hundred Weight. The Railway is not to be used as a Passage for Horses or Cattle, except those crossing it to the Farms on its Line.

Wharfs and warehouses may be erected by owners of land or lords of manors, on their own lands; but if such erections are not made within three calendar months after notice given, then the said company may themselves erect them, and at such wharfs may be taken the following

WHARFAGE AND WAREHOUSING RATES.

d.

For all Coals, Culm, Lime, Lime-stone, Clay, Iron, Iron-stone, Lead or other Ores, Timber, Stone, Brick, Tiles, Slates, Gravel or other Things . . . . } 1 per Ton.

For every Package not exceeding Fifty-six Pounds in Weight. . . . . 1 each.

For ditto above Fifty-six Pounds and not exceeding Five Hundred Weight 2 ditto.

All Articles remaining above Forty-eight Hours, shall pay in addition for the next Ten Days, for Wharfage, One Penny per Ton; for Warehousing, Three-pence per Ton; and the like Sums of One Penny and Three-pence for every Day after the Expiration of the said Ten Days.

A loan of Exchequer Bills is to be deemed equivalent to a subscription, as being provided for under the clauses of an act of the 57th George III. entitled, ' *An Act to authorize the Issue of* ' *Exchequer Bills, and the Advance of Money out of the Consoli-* ' *dated Fund to a limited Amount, for the carrying on of Public* ' *Works and Fisheries in the United Kingdom, and Employment of* ' *the Poor in Great Britain.*'

This railway is about fourteen miles long, in a direction from Burlinjob to Castle Weir, west, and from thence to the Hay Railway, south. It is 505½ feet above the level of the sea, and well calculated for the purposes for which it was projected.

KIRKINTILLOCH, OR MONKLAND AND KIRKINTILLOCH RAILWAY.

5 George IV. Cap. 49, Royal Assent 17th May, 1824.

THIS useful work was undertaken in the year 1824, under the authority of ' *An Act for making a Railway from Palace* ' *Craig, in the parish of Old Monkland, in the county of Lanark,* ' *to the Forth and Clyde Canal, near Kirkintilloch, in the county of* ' *Dumbarton.*' The design of the projectors was to open a communication between the iron works at Palace Craig, near Old

Monkland, and the Forth and Clyde Canal, for the purpose of exporting the minerals and manufactures of that place and vicinity, and it has fully answered the end proposed. It traverses a distance of more than ten miles, in a northerly direction from Monkland to Kirkintilloch. Taking the surface water of the Forth and Clyde Canal as a level, there is a rise, from the basin where the railway communicates with that work, to its termination at Palace Craig, of 133 feet 11 inches. In its way it passes by Howes, at which place there is a branch of three quarters of a mile in length, with a rise, from the aforesaid level, of 161 feet 3 inches to Kipps' Colliery. It connects with the Garnkirk and Glasgow Railway, and with the Ballochney Railway, and also with the Wishaw and Coltness Railway; besides connecting the Monkland Canal with the above railroads and the Forth and Clyde Canal, thus giving facility to the export of immense quantities of coal, ironstone and limestone, with which this district abounds.

Mr. Thomas Grainger was the engineer employed, whose estimate for the whole, including the basin at the Forth and Clyde Canal of one hundred yards square, was £24,953, 1s. 5d.; the necessary funds for which were raised by shares of £50 each.

LANCASTER CANAL.

32 Geo. III. C. 101, R. A. 11th June, 1792.   33 Geo. III. C. 107, R. A. 10th May, 1793.
36 Geo. III. C. 97, R. A. 14th May, 1796.   40 Geo. III. C. 57, R. A. 20th June, 1800.
47 Geo. III. C. 113, R. A. 13th Aug 1807.   59 Geo. III. C. 64, R. A. 14th June, 1819.

THIS stupendous undertaking commences, at 144 feet 9 inches above the level of the sea, near Kirkby Kendal, to the north of which place it has a feeder from the Mint Beck; it proceeds in a southerly direction to the tunnel at Hincaster Green; from this tunnel it turns directly eastward till it crosses Stainton Beck, where it again bends to the south and continues a sinuous course in that direction past Beetholme, Milthorp and Burton-in-Kendal, near the division of the counties of Westmoreland and Lancaster; it then locks down 75 feet by nine locks, in a place named Tewit Field; here a branch was intended to run off westward to the lime rocks of Warton Cragg, the main line proceeding in a south-easterly direction to Barwick, not far from which place it crosses the River

Keer; from Barwick, passing near Over Kellet, it runs south-west to Bolton-by-the-Sands and Hest; bending to the east from this place and winding round Lancaster, where it crosses the Lune or Loyne by a magnificent aqueduct, it proceeds to Galgate, leaving Quern Moor Park on the east. From Galgate a branch 79 feet 4 inches above low water goes off westerly by Thornham to Glasson New Dock, locking down 51 feet to the sea lock at Glasson, the sill of which is 3 feet 10 inches above low-water-mark. Leaving the Galgate Branch the main line comes to Garstang, where it crosses the River Wyre, a branch of which it again passes near Kirkland Hall. From Garstang it runs easterly by Greenhalgh Castle past Myerscough Hall; thence making a detour westward it winds round the estate of Salwick Hall, whence it runs eastwardly to Preston, traversing from Tewit Field to that town a distance of forty miles on one level, generally called the Lancaster Level. Here the canal is interrupted for about four miles and a half: but a railroad crossing the Ribble, and ascending the high ground, connects this part of the line with the continuation thereof at the summit level at Thorpe Green. This railroad rises 222 feet; at its termination, where the head level of the canal commences, there is a commodious basin, and immediately adjoining commences a tunnel three hundred yards in length. From this junction of the railroad and canal, the latter proceeds almost due south to Bark Hill near Wigan, a distance of thirteen miles and a half. The remainder of the projected line to West Houghton was never executed, being rendered unnecessary by the junction of the Leeds and Liverpool with the Lancaster Canal, at Johnson's Hillock, near Shaw Hall, two miles and a half from the tunnel. At this place the Lancaster Company made a short branch or junction on which there are seven locks, with a rise of 67 feet 3 inches, from their summit level into the Leeds and Liverpool Canal. A communication is thus made between Kendal and Manchester, and all the navigations connected with that town, through the Leeds and Liverpool Branch to Leigh, by way of Bark Hill and Wigan. The canal in its progress passes through a noted agricultural district, generally called the Fylde Country.

Having thus given the route of the canal, we proceed to notice the acts of parliament connected with it, in their order. The first

obtained for this purpose, bearing date in 1792, is entitled, ' *An*
' *Act for making and maintaining a navigable Canal, from Kirkby*
' *Kendal in the county of Westmoreland, to West Houghton in the*
' *county palatine of Lancaster, and also a navigable Branch from*
' *the said intended Canal at or near Barwick, to or near Warton*
' *Cragg, and also another navigable Branch, from, at or near,*
' *Galemoss, by Chorley, to or near Duxbury in the said county*
' *palatine of Lancaster.*' It incorporates the proprietors under
the style of " The Company of Proprietors of the Lancaster Canal
" Navigation," and gives them power to cut the line as we have
described to West Houghton, with branches from Barwick Hall to
Warton Cragg, and from Galemoss in the parish of Crofton, to
or near Duxbury in the parish of Standish. The part to West
Houghton was rendered unnecessary as we before stated, and the
Duxbury Branch has also been left unexecuted.

By this act the proprietors were empowered to raise £414,100,
in £100 shares, £60,000 thereof to be applied solely to complete
the Westmoreland part of the canal, with a power of raising by
further subscription amongst themselves, or by mortgage, the additional sum of £200,000, if required. This act also established
the following rates.

TONNAGE AND WHARFAGE RATES.

	s.	d.	
For Coals navigated on the Canal	0	1½	per Ton, per Mile.
For Lime-stone, Slate, Salt-ores, Salt-rock, Bricks, Stone, Flags, Iron-stone, Coal-sleck, Black-bass, Iron-Cinders, Gravel, Sand, Clay, Marl and Manure..........	0	½	ditto. ditto.
For Lime, Pig-iron, Cast-iron, and Bar-Iron	0	1	ditto. ditto.
For Timber, Dying-woods, and all other Goods, Wares, Merchandize and Commodities not before-enumerated..	0	2	ditto. ditto.
For Coals passing the Locks on the South Side of the River Ribble, if they do not pass more than Eighteen Miles North of Chorley on this Canal	2	3	per Ton.
For the Wharfage of Coal, Lime, Lime-stone, Clay, Iron, Iron-stone, Timber, Stone, Brick, Tiles, Slate or Gravel....................	0	1	ditto.
For all other Goods or Things whatever..................	0	3	ditto.

Coal, Iron and Lime-stone may remain on the Wharfs Twenty-one Days ; Timber,
Clay, Lime, Iron-stone, Stone, Bricks, Tiles, Slate and Gravel, Thirty Days; all
other Goods Six Days; an additional Charge of one Penny per Ton for every Ten
Days after this Period.

And so on in Proportion for more or less than a Ton or a Mile.

Forty Feet of Round, or Fifty Feet of Square Oak, Ash or Elm Timber, and Fifty
Feet of Fir or Deal, Balk, Poplar, Beech or Birch cut into Scantlings, and Forty
Feet of Light Goods to be deemed One Ton.

In the following year a second act, the title of which sufficiently explains its purport, was granted, as ' *An Act to alter and*
' *amend an Act passed in the last Session of Parliament, entitled,*
' *An Act for making and maintaining a navigable Canal, from*
' *Kirkby Kendal in the county of Westmoreland, to West Houghton*
' *in the county palatine of Lancaster, and also a navigable Branch*
' *from the said intended Canal at or near Barwick, to or near*
' *Warton Cragg, and also another navigable Branch, from, at or*
' *near, Galemoss, by Chorley, to or near Duxbury in the said*
' *county palatine of Lancaster; and also for making a navigable*
' *Branch from the said Canal at or near Galgate, to Glasson Dock,*
' *in the said county palatine of Lancaster.*' The next act, obtained in 1796, and entitled, ' *An Act to enable his Majesty, in*
' *Right of his Duchy of Lancaster, to make a Grant of certain*
' *Lands, for the Purpose of carrying into Execution an Act passed*
' *in the Thirty-second of his present Majesty, entitled, An Act for*
' *making and maintaining a navigable Canal, from Kirkby Kendal*
' *in the county of Westmoreland, to West Houghton in the county*
' *palatine of Lancaster, and also a navigable Branch from the said*
' *intended Canal at or near Barwick, to or near Warton Cragg,*
' *and also another navigable Branch, from, at or near, Galemoss,*
' *by Chorley, to or near Duxbury in the said county palatine of*
' *Lancaster,*' was merely to enable his Majesty, as Duke of Lancaster, to grant the company certain lands in that duchy. The
fourth act, entitled, ' *An Act for enabling the Company of Proprie-*
' *tors of the Lancaster Canal Navigation to complete the same,*'
was obtained in 1800, for the purpose of enabling the proprietors
to raise the additional £200,000, mentioned in the first act, by
creating new shares.

An act, entitled, ' *An Act to enable the Company of Proprie-*
' *tors of the Lancaster Canal Navigation, to vary the Course of the*
' *said Canal, and to make Railways or Roads, and to amend and*
' *render more effectual Two Acts relating to the said Navigation,*'
was obtained in 1807, whereby the proprietors were empowered
to vary the line between Tewit Field in the parish of Warton
and a place called the World's End, in the parish of Hincaster;
also to make a railway from Farlton Knott in the parish of
Beetham, to communicate with the said variation in Kelnhall

Close in the township of Farlton, and another from the limestone
rock at Kellet Seeds in the parish of Bolton-by-the-Sands to Over
Kellet and Carnforth. By this act the power of taking water
from the River Mint, is repealed.

The last act received the royal assent in 1819, under the title
of ' *An Act to alter and amend the several Acts passed for making*
' *and maintaining the Lancaster Canal Navigation.*' It grants to
the company the power of making reservoirs and feeders in the
townships of Killington, New Hutton, Kirkby Lonsdale, and
Kirkby-in-Kendal, and to convey the water from Crookland's
Beck into the said canal; and to make a navigable branch from
the said canal in the township of Whittle-le-Woods, at a place
called Johnson's Hillock, to join and communicate with the present
southern termination of the Leeds and Liverpool Canal, which said
branch shall be accounted part of the said Lancaster Canal Navigation. By this act is repealed a clause of the 32nd George III.
authorizing the proprietors to take 2s. 3d. per ton for all coals
passing the locks on the said canal on the south side of the Ribble.
The proprietors are also empowered to raise £270,000, on mortgage of the rates and dues of the said canal, for the purpose of
completing the said navigation and works. The proprietors of
the Lancaster and the Leeds and Liverpool Canals are not to take
water either from other of these works, when the depth shall be
reduced to 5 feet upon the sill of the upper gates of the locks on
the said Leeds and Liverpool Canal, adjoining the said Lancaster
Canal, which sill is not to be lower than the bottom level of the
said Lancaster Canal. We have before mentioned, that by uniting
the two canals at Johnson's Hillock, a length of eleven miles was
common to both canals; this length is actually part of the Lancaster Canal, but that company is confined by a specific agreement, not to charge more for goods passing out of the Leeds and
Liverpool on it, than they would be liable to for the same distance,
taking it as part of the Leeds and Liverpool Canal. On the line
of this canal there are two tunnels, one at Hincaster eight hundred
yards long; the second at the Whittle Hills, not far from the
junction with the Leeds and Liverpool Canal, three hundred yards
long; there is also a remarkable piece of deep cutting at Ashton,
near Lancaster.

The Leeds and Liverpool Canal was to have crossed this canal by an aqueduct 60 feet high at Bark Mill near Wigan; and the Lancaster Canal itself was to have been conducted by an aqueduct over the Ribble at Preston; there is one over the Wyre at Garstang, the Beeloo near Bethorn, and the Lune near Lancaster, the last of which is a most wonderful piece of workmanship, being 51 feet high above the river, having five arches of 70 feet span each, and is supposed to be the largest aqueduct of the kind in England.

Mr. Brindley surveyed part of the line of the Lancaster Canal in 1772, and Mr. Whitworth soon after completed the survey. But it was not till 1791, that the promoters of the scheme resumed the subject; when they appointed Mr. Rennie engineer to the undertaking, and this was the first great work of the kind in which he had taken the direction; the magnificent aqueduct over the Lune at Lancaster, and other immense works upon this canal, established his reputation as a civil engineer.

It would be almost impossible to enumerate all the advantages accruing to the public from the execution of this undertaking. The interchange of the coals and cannel of Wigan and the southern extremity of the line, with the stone, lime and slate of its northern parts, is not amongst the least beneficial effects of its completion; whilst liquors and various other articles of foreign merchandize introduced at the port of Lancaster, are by its means conveyed with expedition and at a trifling expense to the various populous manufacturing places on its line.

LAPWORTH AND RINGWOOD CANAL.
(SEE STRATFORD-UPON-AVON CANAL.)

LARKE RIVER.

11 & 12 William III. Cap. 22, Royal Assent 11th April, 1700.
57 George III. Cap. 71, Royal Assent 10th July, 1817.

THE navigation of the River Larke or Burn extends for the distance of about fourteen miles from a place called Long Common, a little below Milden Hall Mill, to Eastgate Bridge in

Eastgate Street Bury St. Edmunds, in the county of Suffolk; its level from its situation in the flat part of the county is in no part greatly above the tideway.

The first step towards the rendering this river navigable, was an act of parliament in the year 1700, bearing as title, ' *An Act* ' *for making the River Larke, alias Burn, navigable.*' By this act power was granted to Henry Ashley, Esq. of Eaton Socon, in Bedfordshire, his heirs and assigns, to cleanse, enlarge or straighten the said river, and to construct all necessary works on the same. He was empowered to demand certain rates, and a number of commissioners were appointed to settle disputes, which commissioners were from time to time to elect others on vacancies. After the lapse of several years, the property became vested in Mrs. Susanna Palmer, and great inconvenience arose from the neglect of the commissioners in not filling up vacancies. A second act was therefore obtained in 1817, entitled, ' *An Act for amending and* ' *rendering more effectual an Act of his late Majesty, King William* ' *the Third, for making the River Larke, alias Burn, navigable ;*' by which new commissioners were appointed with the necessary powers, and the following determined upon to be paid to Mrs. Palmer, in lieu of former tolls as

TONNAGE RATES.

	s.	d.	
For Coals, by Lynn Measure	4	2	per Chaldron.
For Deals	2	7¼	per Half Hundred.
For Timber (accounting Forty Feet to the Load)	2	7½	per Load.
For Wool, (accounting Ten Tod to the Pack)	3	3¾	per Eight Packs.
For Salt	3	3½	per Weigh.
For Wheat or Barley, (reckoning Ten Coombs to the Load)	2	7½	per Load.
For Oats	3	3½	per Last.
For Beans or Peas, (reckoning Ten Coombs to the Load)	3	3½	per Load.
For Grocery Wares or Commodities	3	3¾	per Ton.
For Oil or Wine	5	0½	ditto.
For Turf	4	2	per Thousand.
For Reed, Sedge, or Hay, (reckoning Twenty Hundred Weight to a Load)	4	2	per Load.
For Hemp, (reckoning Twenty Hundred Weight to a Load)	4	2	per ditto.
For Malt	3	3½	per Last.
For Bricks, (reckoning Five Hundred to the Load)	2	7½	per Load.
For Tiles	2	11	per Thousand.
For all other Goods, Wares, Merchandize or Commodities whatsoever	2	7½	per Ton.

All these Rates to be considered as payable for Goods passing between the Sluice next above Milden Hall Bridge and Bury St. Edmunds, and in Proportion for a greater or less Weight and for a less Distance; and the Proprietor may lower or raise all or any Part of the said Tolls from time to time. And the Commissioners are empowered to raise the Tolls for the Payment of Expenses incurred by making new Works, application being made to them by the Proprietor for that Purpose.

This is a very useful navigation, and beneficial to the agriculturists of the district about Bury, as besides the advantageous mode it affords of conveying their produce down to Lynn, by its junction with the Ouse near Littleport, it conveys to them in return, and at a much lower rate than by land carriage, fuel and other articles of home consumption which their own neighbourhood cannot supply.

LEA RIVER.

3 Hen. VI. C. 5, R. A. —— 1425.	9 Hen. VI. C. 9, R. A. —— 1430.
13 Eliz. C. — R. A. —— 1561.	13 Geo. II. C. 32, R. A. 14th June, 1739.
7 Geo. III. C. 51, R. A. 29th June, 1767.	19 Geo. III. C. 58, R. A. 31st May, 1779.
45 Geo. III. C. 69, R. A. 27th June, 1805.	5 Geo. IV. C. 47, R. A. 17th May, 1824.

THE Lea or Lee Navigation commences at the county town of Hertford, at 111 feet 3 inches above the level of the sea; passing thence in an easterly direction by a bending course and leaving Ware Park on its northern bank, it arrives at Ware; from this town it proceeds in a south-easterly direction to its junction with the Stort River Navigation at no great distance from Hoddesden. From the junction, verging a little to the west, it directs its way southerly to Waltham Abbey; the line is now nearly straight in the same direction to Oil Mill; here again diverging to the east, it comes to Temple Mills, passing on its way Wanstead and Aldersbrook; a little above Temple Mills there is a cut, making a communication between this navigation and the Regent's Canal; from Temple Mills it proceeds to its fall into the Thames at Bow Creek, not far from the East India Docks; at Bromley there is a cut from this navigation into the Thames at Limehouse, which is about a mile and a half in length, with a fall of $17\frac{1}{2}$ feet. This cut, by avoiding the circuit of the Isle of Dogs, makes a ready communication with the port of London. It was cut at the expense of the city of London, and is known by the name of the Lea Cut or Limehouse Canal.

The first parliamentary enactment having reference to the Lea or Lee, bears date in 1425, under the title of '*An Act for the* '*Preservation of the River Lea;*' another act was passed in 1430, entitled, ' *To scour and amend the River Lea.*' This, according to the custom at that time, is written in the Old Norman French, and therefore need not be recited here.

In the 13th of Elizabeth, 1561, another act was sanctioned by the legislature, entitled , ' *An Act for the bringing of the River Lea* ' *to the North Side of the city of London,*' whereby the whole jurisdiction, rule and government of the said river or new cut, mentioned to have been made by the Mayor, Commonalty and Citizens of London, are vested in the said persons. The next parliamentary enactment which received the royal assent was obtained in 1739, and is designated, ' *An Act for ascertaining, preserving* ' *and improving the Navigation of the River Lea, from the town* ' *of Hertford, to the town of Ware, in the county of Hertford;* ' *and for preserving and improving the said River, from the said* ' *town of Ware to the New Cut, or River, made by the Mayor, Com-* ' *monalty and Citizens of London, and for enabling the Governor* ' *and Company of the New River, the better to supply the cities of* ' *London and Westminster, and the liberties of the suburbs thereof* ' *with good and wholesome Water.*'

As the New River, which supplies the city of London with water, is mentioned in the last-recited act, it may be proper here to state that that useful work was projected and begun by Sir Hugh Middleton, in 1608; and that in 1773 Mr. James Sharp suggested the practicability of rendering that river navigable. The New River has its rise in the Chalk Hills between Hertford and Ware, and has also a feeder near that point from the River Lea.

By the act just recited, the governor and company of the New River were directed to pay the company of the Lea River £350 per annum, in consideration of the water supplied by that company, such yearly rent or fine to be applied to the improvement and preservation of the said River Lea or Lee. But it having appeared that the powers of this act were imperfect, and that the authority vested in the Mayor and Commonalty of London by the act of Elizabeth, interfered with the powers granted to this company, to the injury of both, a further act was obtained in 1767, which is designated, ' *An Act for improving the Navigation of the River Lea,* ' *from the town of Hertford to the River Thames, and for extending* ' *the said Navigation to the Flood-Gates belonging to the Town*

' *Mill, in the said town of Hertford.*' As there are many clauses
in this act for directing new cuts or canals to be made on various parts of the line, we shall here consolidate them.   The River
Lea or Lee is to be made navigable to the Flood-gates of the
Town Mill at Hertford; and the proprietors are authorized to
make at any time the following new cuts or canals, viz. one from
the said river at a place called The Folly, into and down part
of Dicker Mill Stream, to return into the said river at any
point they may think best above Dicker Mill and between Con-
stant's Weir and Manifold Ditch; one from the lock above Ware
Mill into the said river on the south, near Priory Orchard; one
from above Ware Weir into the same on the south-west near
Stansted Bridge; one from below Stansted Bridge into the said
river above Stansted Mill; one from above Field's or Rye Bridge
Weir to any part between Archer's Weir and Field's Weir on
the north-west; one from Dobb's Weir or the New Turnpike to
the head of Broxbourn Mill; one from above Carthagena Turnpike to a little below the same; one from above King's Weir over
Cheshunt Mill Stream, into the river near the west tail stream of
Waltham Abbey Powder Mills; one from above Sotheby's Upper
Weir, or Newman's Weir, to Enfield Mill Stream one hundred
yards southwards below Enfield Lock, and thence to run through
Enfield Mill Stream, to within three hundred and forty yards
northward of and above Enfield Corn Mill; thence another cut to
the eastward of the said mill stream, again communicating with
the river two hundred and four yards below Enfield Mill, from
thence to run through as much of the said mill tail stream as shall
be necessary; one through part of Enfield and Edmonton Marshes,
across the ditch parting Edmonton and Tottenham Marshes, and
through part of Tottenham Marsh into and through the tail stream
of Tottenham Mill into the said river again; one from below
Flander's Wharf to above the tail stream of Walthamstow Mill;
one from between Lea Bridge and the buildings of the Hackney
Water Works, through part of Hackney Marsh, into the said
river between Padding Mill Stream and Hackney Brook, on the
east of Jones's Calico Grounds at Old Ford; and one from between
Bromley Lock and Bromley Hall, through the parishes and hamlets of Bromley St. Leonard's, Blackwall, Poplar, St. Dunstan

Stepney and St. Ann Limehouse, to the north of Limehouse Church, into the Thames near Limehouse Bridge Dock. The following are to be paid as

TONNAGE RATES.

	s.	d.	
For all Coals, Culm or Cinders, carried or conveyed through King's Weir or the Lock nearest thereto	0	8	per Chaldron.
For ditto conveyed through Newman's Weir or the Lock nearest thereto	0	8	ditto.
For ditto conveyed through Lea Bridge or the Lock on the New Cut below the said Bridge	0	4	ditto.
For ditto on the Cut from Bromley Lock into the Thames	0	3	ditto.
For all other Goods, Wares, Merchandize or Commodities conveyed through King's Weir, or the Lock nearest thereto	0	6	per Ton.
For ditto through Newman's Weir or the Lock nearest thereto	0	6	ditto.
For ditto through Lea Bridge, or the Lock on the New Cut below the said Bridge	0	3	ditto.
For ditto on the Cut from Bromley Lock into the Thames	0	2	ditto.
For every Pleasure Boat passing any of the above Locks or Places	1	0	each.

And in Proportion for a greater or lesser Quantity than a Chaldron or Ton.

Five Quarters of Wheat, Rye, Beans, Peas and Tares to be allowed to a Ton; Six Quarters of Barley to a Ton; Eight Quarters of Malt and Oats to ditto; Eight Sacks of Meal or Flour, each containing Five Bushels to ditto; and Ten Quarters of Bran or Pollard to a Ton. No Tonnage Rates to be demanded for any Boat, Barge, Lighter, or other Vessel carrying only Oil Cake, Malt Dust, Pigeon Dung or Manure of any Kind whatsoever.

Money for executing the work may be raised by borrowing on security of the rates, or by annuities secured thereon.

By this act also were allowed to various persons the following sums, viz. to the New River Company, in lieu of a toll taken by them for boats passing their lock at Ware Mill, at four quarterly payments for ever, one shilling for every boat, &c. passing the said lock, and also a clear annual rent of £40; to the owners of Sewardston Mills £45; to the owners of Newman's Weir £19, 5s.; to the owners of Parkinson's Weir £16, 15s. 6d.; to the owners of Enfield Mill Stream £40; to the Dean and Chapter of St. Pauls, or their lessee, £25; to Abraham Hume, Esq. £28; to John Archer, Esq. £28; to Sir William Maynard £48, and a wharf to be built for him; all the above sums are annual rents. To Sir William Wake and Peter Floyer, Esq. one penny per ton on all goods, wares and merchandize whatever, conveyed on the said river from above King's Weir to the west tail stream of the Waltham Abbey Powder Mills, in lieu of five shillings toll now taken by them for every vessel passing the lock called Waltham Turnpike.

The next act obtained was passed in 1779, under the title of
' *An Act for preserving the Navigation of the River Lea, in the*
' *counties of Hertford, Essex and Middlesex.*' This act states that
the trustees under the powers of the former enactments, from the
amount of the principal money already advanced for the prosecution of the work, and from the sums to be paid yearly as annuities,
compensations and other purposes authorized by the acts before
granted, cannot liquidate the charges upon them without an advance of the rates to meet the same, they are therefore empowered
to demand in future, the following

ADDITIONAL RATES.

	s.	d.	
For all Coals, Culm or Cinders passing King's Weir or the Lock nearest thereto	0	6	per Chaldron.
For all Malt, ditto, ditto	1	3	per Ton.
For all Flour, ditto, ditto	0	4½	ditto.
For other Goods, Wares or Merchandize whatsoever, ditto	0	6	ditto.
For all Coals, Culm or Cinders passing Newman's Weir or the Lock nearest thereto, not having paid at King's Weir	0	6	per Chaldron.
For all Malt, ditto, ditto	0	11	per Ton.
For all Flour, ditto, ditto	0	4½	ditto.
For all other Goods, ditto, ditto	0	6	ditto.
For all Coals, Culm or Cinders passing through Lea Bridge or the Lock in the said Cut below the same	0	7	per Chaldron.
For all Malt, ditto, ditto	0	5	per Ton.
For all Flour, ditto, ditto	0	3	ditto.
For all other Goods, ditto, ditto	0	3	ditto.
For all Malt passing between Bromley Lock and the Thames	0	2	ditto.
For all other Goods, ditto, ditto	0	2	ditto.
For every Pleasure Boat passing any of the above	1	0	each.
For every empty Lighter, &c. not having conveyed any Goods that have paid Dues, or not having delivered any Lading liable to the same	5	0	ditto.

Every Load of Wood to be reckoned as Five Tons.

The tolls to be reduced as the annuities fall in, and when the
tonnage payable to Sir William Wake and Mr. Floyer shall not
amount in any year to £160, the deficiency shall be made up by
the trustees; other regulations as to the height of water in various
parts are made by the said act, but as they are not of general importance, it is unnecessary to quote them.

Another act was obtained in 1805, entitled, ' *An Act for the*
' *better Preservation and further Improvement of the Navigation of*
' *the River Lea, in the counties of Hertford, Essex and Middlesex.*'
This act applies chiefly to the regulations of the depth of water,
the prevention of its waste and other particulars of a similar nature.
It also enacts that in future no vessel using this navigation, shall
carry at any one time more than forty tons of goods, &c.

Here the Lea River Navigation may be properly said to end, as the branch to join it with the Regent's Canal is known as the Lea Union or Hertford Union Canal, and was constructed by Sir George Duckett; it is, however, so connected with the Lea, that we have thought it needless to give the particulars under a separate head.

The act for forming this union was passed in May, 1824, under the title of ' *An Act for making and maintaining a navigable Canal* ' *from the River Lea Navigation, in the parish of St. Mary Strat-* ' *ford Bow, in the county of Middlesex, to join the Regent's Canal,* ' *at or near a place called Old Ford Lock, in the parish of St.* ' *Matthew Bethnal Green, in the said county of Middlesex;*' whereby Sir George Duckett, Bart. his heirs and assigns, are empowered to make the communication and all other works connected with it. They have also power to borrow money on the rates, or by mortgaging the canal and works, to the extent of £50,000. They are also authorized to demand the following

TONNAGE RATES AND TOLLS.

	s.	d.
For all Goods, Wares and Merchandize whatever, on Vessels entering the Canal from the Lea River or the Regent's Canal........	1	0 per Ton
For all Horses, Mules or Asses, passing on the Towing-paths, unless drawing or haling Barges and other Vessels.....................	0	6 each.

Parcels not exceeding Five Hundred Weight, to be charged according to Rates fixed by Order of Justices at the Quarter Sessions.

Wharfs may be erected, and the following demanded as

WHARFAGE RATES.

	d.
For all Goods, Wares and Merchandize remaining on the Wharf Forty-eight Hours	3 per Ton.
For every Day after that Time..	6 ditto.

The water in the summit level of this canal must be 6 inches above the top water mark of the Regent's Canal, and a stop-lock is to be formed within one hundred yards of that canal. The River Lea Company may, if they think fit, place a dam at the mouth of the canal, to prevent any but flood-water being taken from their navigation. The rights of the Commissioners of Sewers and of the East London Water Works Company, are also secured by separate clauses in the act.

The length of the river navigation, from its commencement to its fall into the Thames, is about twenty-six miles; and the Hertford and Lea Union Canal, from Hertford to the junction with the Stort Navigation, is about five miles; of the Lea Cut or Branch to avoid the circuit of the Isle of Dogs, one mile and a half; and of the cut made by Sir George Duckett, communicating with the Regent's Canal, one mile. The course of this navigation runs southerly from near Hoddesden to the Thames, and divides Essex from the counties of Hertford and Middlesex; the country is very flat, particularly as it approaches the Thames.

To observe that legislative enactments took place for this navigation above four hundred years ago, fully stamps the importance of this water communication, which has afforded a cheap and ready transit for corn, malt, wool and other agricultural produce to the metropolis; and in return, of coal, timber, deals, bricks, paving-stones, groceries, cloth, and various other articles of daily consumption; and by extending the navigation of the River Stort, these benefits are more widely dispersed through the country.

LEEDS AND LIVERPOOL CANAL.

6 Geo. I. C. 28, R. A. 7th April, 1720.   10 Geo. III. C. 114, R. A. 19th May, 1770.
23 Geo. III. C. 47, R. A. 24th June, 1783.   30 Geo. III. C. 65, R. A. 9th June, 1790.
34 Geo. III. C. 94, R. A. 9th May, 1794.   59 Geo. III. C. 105, R. A. 21st June, 1819.

A navigation between the east and west seas, by the Rivers Aire and Ribble, had been deemed practicable by several public spirited gentlemen, residents in the counties of York and Lancaster, who at various times had endeavoured to draw the public attention to the scheme. But while this was in contemplation, the Duke of Bridgewater formed a plan of making a navigable canal from Worsley Mill to Manchester, which was soon afterwards executed with great ability and amazing rapidity.

The Duke's success drew forth the attention of Mr. Longbotham, a native of Halifax, who, after inspecting and examining the works on the Duke's Canal, projected the scheme of making a similar canal from Leeds to Liverpool, and for this purpose he took an actual survey of the country between those two places, laid down a plan and prepared an estimate of the expense, which

2 B

he produced at sundry meetings of gentlemen and land-owners interested in promoting the scheme. It was unanimously resolved, in order to put it beyond a doubt, whether it was practicable or not, to call Mr. Brindley, to re-survey the line laid down by Mr. Longbotham; and after surveying by himself, and Mr. Whitworth, (who was engaged with him) he reported to two numerous meetings, one held at Bradford on the 5th and the other at Liverpool on the 9th of December, 1768, that it was very practicable, and might be executed for the total sum of £259,777, which he stated in detail. The canal, according to the plan and estimate, was one hundred and eight miles and three quarters in length, 42 feet wide at the top, 27 feet at the bottom, and 5 feet deep.

This canal, as its name implies, proceeds from Leeds to Liverpool, and is the most extensive of any in the kingdom. At that era of canal navigation, when first commenced, it was one of the boldest and most magnificent projects hitherto attempted in Great Britain.

The act of the 10th George III. is entitled, ' *An Act for* ' *making and maintaining a navigable Cut or Canal from Leeds* ' *Bridge, in the county of York, to the North Lady's Walk in* ' *Liverpool, in the county palatine of Lancaster, and from thence to* ' *the River Mersey.*'

In describing the line of this canal, we shall confine ourselves to the course of country through which it has been actually executed; and afterwards mention a few of the places through which it was projected by the original line. Commencing at Leeds Bridge, where the jurisdiction of the Aire and Calder Navigation terminates, and where the two navigations unite, it proceeds twenty-seven chains in the River Aire, to the first lock on the Leeds and Liverpool Canal, where the extensive warehouses, wharfs, basins and docks belonging to this concern are situate; from which circumstance, the lock here may be admitted as the commencement of the canal. From this place its course is north-westerly, passing alongside the River Aire by Armley, Kirkstall Bridge, Kirkstall Abbey and Forge, to near New Leeds, whence it makes a detour southerly to Ross Mill; from hence it again takes a north-westerly course, leaving Horsforth on the north and

Calverley on the south, to Woodhouse, when bending westerly to Apperley Bridge, it then changes its course to the north, leaving Idle to the south and Esholt Hall to the north; thence proceeding westward by Buck Mill to Shipley, where the Bradford Canal branches off; having obtained a rise, from the surface water in the River Aire, at the tail of the Leeds and Liverpool Canal Lock above Leeds Bridge, of 155 feet 7 inches. From the junction with the Bradford Canal, it proceeds westward to New Mill, at which place it crosses the River Aire by an extensive aqueduct, and runs north-westerly to Bingley, where locking up 88 feet 8 inches, it attains a level that continues above eighteen miles, without another lock.

The Great Lock, as it is commonly called, at Bingley, consisting of five rises in one range of gates and masonry, and which unfortunate arrangement requires five locks full of water to pass one vessel from the lower to the higher level, must always cause a great waste of water, till remedied by dividing the fall or side ponds.

From Bingley Great Lock the canal proceeds in a north-westerly direction, passing Rushforth Hall, Riddlesden, within a mile of Keighley, about the same distance from Steeton, close to Silsden; thence to Kildwick, Snaygill and to Skipton. At this place, which is at an elevation of 272½ feet above the River Aire at Leeds Bridge, a short branch proceeds from the canal to a limestone wharf on the north side of Skipton Castle, which ,branch belongs to the Earl of Thanet. From Skipton the canal runs north-west by Thorleby and Gargrave, and just above the latter place it again crosses the River Aire by another large aqueduct; it then bends south-westerly, passing Bank Newton, Marton, Gillchurch, Greenberfield and Rainhall Pasture, at which point, another branch of a quarter of a mile runs off southward to a limestone quarry called Rainhall Rock; this branch is upon the summit level of the canal, and at an elevation of 411 feet 4 inches above the River Aire at Leeds, which elevation is attained in a distance (from Leeds Bridge to the summit lock at Greenberfield) of forty-one miles. The canal then proceeds by Barnoldswick and Salterford to Foulridge, where the great tunnel commences, whose height is 18 feet, width 17 feet, and the length one thousand six hundred and forty yards. The surface of the ground on the

highest part over the tunnel, is at an elevation of 60 feet above
the water in the tunnel. Within a little distance of the tunnel, are
two reservoirs, for the supply of the canal, which cover one hundred and four acres of land, and will contain twelve hundred thousand cubic yards of water. From Foulridge the canal proceeds
to near Barrowford, where it locks down from the summit 70 feet
towards Liverpool; crosses Colne Water by an aqueduct; passes
near Carr Hall (a seat of Colonel Clayton's) and Dancer House to
the town of Burnley, which it circumscribes on three sides, and at
which place an embankment has been carried for one thousand
two hundred and fifty-six yards in length, at above 60 feet high,
and aqueducts made over the Rivers Brown and Calder, and a
road aqueduct under the canal; thence the canal proceeds to near
Gannah, where there is another tunnel five hundred and fifty-nine
yards in length; thence by Hapton, Altham, Clayton Hall, Henfield, to Church Valley, whence Messrs. Peels' short branch runs
to their print works at Church; now crossing the River Henburn
by an aqueduct, the main line proceeds past Rushton and White
Birch to the town of Blackburn, sweeping on the south side of
this town to a place called Grimshaw Park, where by six locks
there is a fall of 54 feet 3 inches; thence passing over Derwent
Water by an aqueduct, it runs by Livesey Hall, and passing Rod-
dlesworth Water by another aqueduct, proceeds to near Chorley;
thence to Cophurst Valley, and here locking down 64 feet 6
inches by seven locks into the head level of the Lancaster Canal,
at Johnson's Hillock. At this part of the line there is an interval
of eleven miles of the Lancaster Canal upon one level, when the
Leeds and Liverpool Canal again commences near Kirklees, at
the head of a range of twenty-three locks, which brings the canal
down 214 feet 6 inches from the level of the Lancaster Canal to
the basin at Wigan. Here it may be observed, that the basin at
Wigan is situate upon that part of the canal made under the
powers of the River Douglas Navigation Act. From this basin
to Newburgh constitutes the Upper Douglas Navigation, a distance
of seven miles, in which there is a fall to Newburgh of 30 feet.

In this last-mentioned distance the principal part of the coal
carried by the Leeds and Liverpool Canal to Liverpool, is put on
board the vessels; as also the coal sent down to the Ribble. Com-

mencing at Newburgh and tracing the canal to Liverpool, it has been executed according to the original plan and act. There it has a stretch of twenty-eight miles and a half upon the same level, passing Brier's Mill, Burscough, Scaresbrick, Halsall, Down-holland, Lidiate, Mayhull, over the Alt River, Litherland, Bootle, Bankhall, Vauxhall, the Gaol, and to the basin of this canal at the North Lady's Walk in Liverpool, being a distance from Leeds Bridge of one hundred and twenty-seven miles and thirteen chains, and containing a lockage of 844 feet $7\frac{1}{2}$ inches; that is from Leeds to the summit, a rise of 411 feet $4\frac{1}{2}$ inches; and from the summit to the basin at Liverpool a fall of 433 feet 3 inches.

Hence it appears that the basin at Liverpool is 21 feet $10\frac{1}{2}$ inches below the level of the River Aire at Leeds; and the canal basin at Liverpool is 56 feet above low-water-mark in the River Mersey.

At three miles from Newburgh, is the junction of the line of the Lower Douglas Navigation with the Leeds and Liverpool Canal; the Douglas Navigation locks into the tideway at the tail of Tarleton Cut, from whence to the Ribble is two miles and a half, and from the union with the Ribble is six miles and a half to the custom house at Preston.

As the act for making the Douglas Navigation stands in priority of date to that for making the canal from Leeds to Liverpool, we shall here recite it. It was obtained in the 6th George I. and is entitled, ' *An Act for making the River Douglas, alias* ' *Asland, navigable, from the River Ribble to Wigan, in the county* ' *palatine of Lancaster;*' wherein it is stated, that the making of this river navigable from the River Ribble to a place called Mirey Lane End, in the township of Wigan, will be very beneficial to trade, advantageous to the poor, and convenient for the carriage of coals, cannel, stone, slate, and other goods and merchandize.

The only proprietors were William Squire, Esq. and Thomas Steeres, Gentleman, both of Liverpool, who were by the act nominated and appointed undertakers to make the said River Douglas, alias Asland, navigable; and they and their heirs and assigns have power to charge for goods conveyed thereon, the following tonnage rates.

TONNAGE RATES.

	s.	d.
For Coal, Cannel, Slate, Stone, or other Goods, Wares, Merchandize or Commodities, from the River Ribble to the Town of Wigan, or *vice versa*, or any intermediate Distance	2	6 per Ton.

And so in Proportion for a greater or lesser Weight.

But no Rates shall be charged to the Land-owners within Five Miles of the said River, upon Manure for Land only.

The next act respecting the Douglas Navigation is that of the 23rd George III. and is entitled, '*An Act for altering and varying* '*the Powers of an Act, passed in the Sixth Year of the Reign of* '*King George the First, for making the River Douglas, alias* '*Asland, navigable, from the River Ribble, to Wigan, in the* '*county palatine of Lancaster; and for enabling the Company of* '*Proprietors of the Leeds and Liverpool Canal, incorporated by an* '*Act passed in the Tenth Year of his present Majesty's Reign, to* '*purchase the said River Navigation; for amending the said last-* '*mentioned Act; for incorporating and consolidating the said two* '*Navigations; and for other Purposes.*' By this act, as its title imports, the Douglas Navigation became incorporated with the Leeds and Liverpool Canal; which company, in January, 1772, purchased twenty-eight shares out of the whole thirty-six shares of the Douglas Navigation, and they now have the power to purchase the remaining eight shares. They had already made the connecting branch with the Leeds and Liverpool Canal, a length of three miles and a half, with 12 feet lockage; but, upon becoming possessed of the remainder of this property, which took place in 1780, they extended the canal, and altogether abandoned the river from Wigan to the low end of Tarleton Cut, which, out of a distance of sixteen miles and three quarters, leaves only two miles and a half of river navigation, and that in the tideway. The Leeds and Liverpool Canal Company had a power to make a call of £14 per share upon their proprietors, for the purpose of purchasing the Douglas Navigation and improving the same. And by the time they had finished all the improvements, it had cost altogether about £74,000.

The length from Wigan to Newburgh (now made the line of the Leeds and Liverpool Canal, as stated before) is seven miles, and has a fall of 30 feet; this part is usually called the Upper Douglas. From Burscough to the Ribble is nine miles and a half, and has a fall of 42 feet; this is called the Lower Douglas Navigation.

Now recurring back to the Leeds and Liverpool Canal, the first act relating thereto passed in the 10th George III. as stated above, and the number of subscribers when the act was obtained, amounted to five hundred and twenty-nine, (amongst whom appears only one nobleman, the Earl of Thanet) who are incorporated by the name of " The Company of Proprietors of the " Canal Navigation from Leeds to Liverpool." Under this act the company were empowered to raise the sum of £260,000, to be divided into two thousand six hundred shares of £100 each, and the said shares to be deemed personal estate; and in case the above sum be found insufficient, the company may raise the additional sum of £60,000 in the same manner. The act authorizes the proprietors to receive five per cent. interest upon the sums advanced during the execution of the canal. Proprietors to have a vote for every share; but not to vote by proxy for more than fifty shares.

The estimate for this canal, as before stated, was made by the celebrated Mr. Brindley, and amounted to only £259,777 ; but as he could not attend to the execution thereof, it was put under the direction of Mr. Longbotham, who completed in less than seven years, (commencing July, 1770,) that part from Leeds to a place called Holmbridge, near Gargrave, on the Yorkshire side, a distance of thirty-three miles and a half, at a cost of £175,000; and from Liverpool to Newburgh, on the Lancashire side, twenty-eight miles, at an expense of £125,000. The canal was opened for trade from Liverpool to Newburgh in 1775, and from Leeds to Holmbridge on the 4th June, 1777. At that time it appears this company had expended in the works and in purchasing the Douglas Navigation, the whole of the money they had a power to raise ; and therefore applied for another act in the 30th year of George III. for authority to raise more money and to vary the line; which act is entitled, ' *An Act to enable the Company of* ' *Proprietors of the Canal Navigation from Leeds to Liverpool, to* ' *vary the Line of the said Canal Navigation; and to raise a further* ' *Sum of Money for the Purpose of completing the said Canal* ' *Navigation; and for other Purposes.*' This act enables the company to vary the original line of canal commencing at a place called Lomishay in the township of Marsden, through the several parishes and places called Marsden, Pendle Forest, Ighten Hill Park, Gawthrop, Padiham, Hapton, Altham, Clayton and Harwood, in the county of Lancaster, to a place called Nut or Banks Wood, there to communicate again, with the original line. Under this act the company were authorized to borrow the further sum of £200,000 on the credit of the said canal and of that of the River Douglas Navigation, by assigning over the tolls, rates or duties; the interest on which to be paid in preference to any dividend.

There yet remained the most difficult and most expensive part of this canal to execute : and after an interval of near thirteen years, the company, on resuming the prosecution of the work, appointed Mr. R. Whitworth their engineer, under whose direction it recommenced at Holmbridge in the year 1790. He re-surveyed the whole line and made an estimate for completing the same amounting to £169,817, 15s. 5d.; he also recommended various improvements, the most important of which was to make a tunnel at the summit level near Foulridge, in lieu of following the original plan, by which a head level of above six miles in length was obtained instead of one mile; he also made this part of the canal 2 feet extra depth, which answers the purpose of a reservoir in dry seasons. The work from Holmbridge to Wanlass Banks, near Barrowford, a distance of fourteen miles, in which are 208 feet of lockage, cost £210,000, including £40,000 the expense of the tunnel at Foulridge.

At this period the trade of Lancashire had become so important as to induce the proprietors of this canal to turn their attention to the accommodation of the established manufactories; for which purpose they abandoned the idea of pursuing their original scheme of connecting the east and west sides of the island by the shortest route, and directed their engineer to take a survey through a new line of country which would embrace both the coal and manufacturing districts.

Hence the company, in 1794, again applied to parliament for power to make the proposed deviation in the line of their canal, and obtained an act, entitled, ' *An Act to enable the Company of* ' *Proprietors of the Canal Navigation from Leeds to Liverpool, to* ' *complete the said Navigation, and to vary the Line thereof, and to* ' *raise a further Sum of Money for those Purposes; and to make*

' *a navigable Branch, therein described, from the intended new*
' *Line of the said Canal.*' The branch above-mentioned was intended to have been cut into Ighten Hill Park, near Burnley, for
the purpose of opening a valuable bed of coal; but this has not
been done. By this act several land-owners have a power to cut
side branches in their own estates, subject to certain restrictions.
They have also the power to make railways within one thousand
yards of the canal.

The company is authorized to borrow, or raise amongst themselves, or by the admission of new subscribers, the further sum of
£280,000, which is to be applied in paying off £101,394, being
part of the £200,000 borrowed under the powers of the 39th
George III. and in completing and finishing the said canal. They
are also restricted by this act from taking more than twenty-six yards
in breadth for the canal and towing-path, except in certain cases.

The works were now prosecuted with great vigour, and in
May, 1796, the canal was opened for trade from the east end of
the Foulridge Tunnel to Burnley, a distance of eight miles, in
which space there is a lockage westwards of 70 feet. Again in
April, 1801, the canal was opened for trade from Burnley to
Henfield Warehouse, a distance of nine miles and thirty-seven
chains, and level. In this seventeen miles and a half, from Foulridge to Henfield, is embraced the most expensive, as well as the
most difficult work on the whole navigation, having cost no less
than £120,000; but this sum includes for extraordinaries £40,000
for the tunnel at Foulridge; £9,000 for reservoirs there; £22,000
for an embankment at Burnley; and £10,000 for another tunnel
of five hundred and fifty-nine yards in length, at a place called
Ridge near the last-mentioned town.

During the succeeding nine years the execution of the canal
proceeded slowly, but in June, 1810, another stretch of eight
miles upon the same level, that is, from Henfield to Blackburn,
was opened for trade. This last work and the remainder of the
canal from Blackburn to Wigan was executed under the direction of Mr. J. Fletcher. And lastly, having completed the remainder of the canal, it was opened for trade in October, 1816,
between Blackburn and Wigan, when vessels could then proceed
direct from Leeds to Liverpool.

Here it may be observed, that this company abandoned their own line of canal for the space of eleven miles, and locked down 64 feet 6 inches at Cophurst, into the head level of the Lancaster Canal; consequently, every vessel going through the Leeds and Liverpool Canal, must pass eleven miles along the Lancaster Canal, that is, from Cophurst or Johnson's Hillock to Kirklees. To establish this junction, an agreement between the two companies was entered into,' stipulating that such junction should be made, and the same was confirmed by an act obtained by the Lancaster Canal Company in the 59th George III.

This gigantic concern, which was no less than forty-six years in executing, and which has cost £1,200,000, has proved highly beneficial to the country through which it passes, giving facility to the transport of coal, limestone, lime for manure, and all agricultural produce, connecting the trade of Leeds with Liverpool and with Manchester, Wigan, Blackburn, Burnley, Colne, Skipton, Keighley, Bingley and Bradford; and by opening a communication between the eastern and western sides of the island, which in a great measure was the original object of the first promoters, now bids fair to remunerate the proprietors for their risk and patient endurance through a long and difficult struggle, having had to borrow above £400,000, at a time when the public funds were very low.

Although they only applied for tolls to remunerate them upon the original estimate made by Mr. Brindley, those rates have never been increased, and now stand the same as by the first act of 10th George III. which empowered them to take the following

TONNAGE RATES.

		d.	
For Clay, Brick or Stones		½	per Ton, per Mile.
For Coal or Lime		1	ditto. ditto.
For Timber, Goods, Wares, Merchandize or other Commodities		1½	ditto. ditto.
For Soap Ashes, Salt, Salt Scrow, Foul Salt and Grey Salt, Pigeon Dung, Rape or Cole Seed; Dust, Rags or Tanners' Bark to be used for manuring Lands of any Person whose Lands shall be cut through, lying in the Township through which the Canal passes		¼	ditto. ditto.

All small Rubbish, Waste Stones from Quarries, Gravel and Sand employed for repairing Roads, not being Turnpike, if not carried more than Five Miles; also all Dung, Soil, Marl, Ashes of Coal and Turf for the Improvement of Lands belonging to Persons through whose Lands the Canal passes, but not to pass any Lock unless the Water flows over the Gauge, Paddle, or Niche of such Lock, are exempt from Toll.

Fifty Feet of Round, or Forty Feet of Square Oak, Ash or Elm Timber, or Fifty Feet of Fir or Deal, Balk, Poplar and other Timber Wood, to be deemed One Ton Weight; and the Ton of Coals and Lime-stone to be Twenty-two Hundreds of One Hundred and Twelve Pounds each.

Lords of manors or land-owners have a power to erect wharfs, warehouses, &c. upon their lands; and if such lords of manors or owners of land shall not do so within twelve months after notice given them by the company, then the company may erect the same.

WHARFAGE RATES.

	d.	
For Coals, Stone or Brick, not longer than Six Days	1½	per Ton.
For Goods or Merchandize, ditto	3	ditto.

No Charge whatever if the Articles do not lie longer than Six Hours.

Fractions of a Mile to be reckoned as a Mile. Fractions of a Ton as the Quarters of a Ton, and of a Quarter as a Quarter.

Every Vessel passing the Leeds Lock, to pay the Tonnage of Eight Miles.

When the Canal shall communicate with the Douglas Navigation at or near the Warehouses in Wigan, the Coals, Stones, Timber, Goods, Wares and Merchandize passing upon any Part of it, shall be charged no more than if the same had been carried the like Distance on the Leeds and Liverpool Canal.

The Leeds and Liverpool Canal Company having finished their main line of navigation in the year 1816, they now turned their attention to forming a communication with the town of Manchester, a subject which had engaged their consideration prior to the death of the late Duke of Bridgewater; and for this purpose they again applied to parliament and obtained an act, entitled, ‘ *An Act to enable the Company of Proprietors of the Canal Navi-* ‘ *gation from Leeds to Liverpool, to make a navigable Cut, and also* ‘ *a collateral Branch or Railway, from their said Canal at Hennis* ‘ *Bridge near Wigan, to join the Duke of Bridgewater's Canal at* ‘ *Leigh, all in the county palatine of Lancaster, and to amend the* ‘ *several Acts relating to the said Leeds and Liverpool Canal, so far* ‘ *as relates to certain Powers, therein given to the late Duke of* ‘ *Bridgewater.*’ This branch proceeds from the main line of the Leeds and Liverpool Canal, at a point half a mile from the basin at Wigan, southward to Brin Moss, then easterly, passing between Platt Bridge and Bamferlong Hall, intersecting Hindley Brook, and passing Strangwood, West Leigh House, and terminates in that part of the Duke of Bridgewater's Canal which extends from

Manchester to Leigh, at the south end of the town of Leigh, being
a distance of six miles, seven furlongs and twenty-one poles, and
with a lockage down to the Duke's Canal of 15 feet 2 inches, by
two locks. At the road leading from Ashton to Platt Bridge, the
side cut or railway branches off nearly north for about a mile in
length. By this branch another communication by water is made
between Liverpool and Manchester; it also affords the first communication which had ever been made to connect Kendal, Lancaster
and Preston, with Manchester, Rochdale and other trading towns
in that part of the country. In the execution of this branch, which
was completed by the end of the year 1821, above £50,000 was
expended. The tonnage rates are the same as upon the main line
of the Leeds and Liverpool Canal, excepting the side cut or
railway, which shall not exceed 4d. per ton for any article whatever; and the fractions of tons and miles to be reckoned as on the
Leeds and Liverpool Main Line; but the devisees of the late Duke
of Bridgewater have authority by this act to charge and receive
for articles passing into or out of the said Leigh Branch, as under.

TONNAGE RATES.

	s.	d.
For every Article, except Flags	1	2 per Ton.
For Flags..	0	2 ditto.

Fractions of a Quarter of a Ton to be paid for as a Quarter of a Ton.
These Rates shall exempt the above-named Articles from any Charge at the Castlefield
Lock, situate upon the Rochdale Canal in the Town of Manchester.

The reservation clause in the Leeds and Liverpool Canal Acts,
and in those for making the River Douglas navigable, which
restrained any boat or vessel from passing locks, without tonnage
was paid for a burthen of twenty tons, is by this act repealed;
and in lieu thereof, it is enacted, that empty boats or vessels shall
each pay at the first lock they shall arrive at, the sum of five
shillings only; provided also, that every empty boat or vessel
passing through or returning out of the summit level upon the line
of the Leeds and Liverpool Canal, either through the Greenberfield
Lock on the Yorkshire side, or through the Barrowford Lock on
the Lancashire side of the said summit level, shall pay a further
sum of five shillings.

By this act for making the Leigh Branch the company obtained
power to raise £50,000, either by admission of new subscribers, or

by contributing amongst themselves in such manner as they may direct, or by mortgage of the navigations, cuts and works, conformably to any order of a general assembly of the said proprietors, where there shall be present, as principals or proxies, the holders of not less than twelve hundred shares in the said navigation. It may be observed, that when the first parts of the canal opened for business, the interest ceased on the money advanced for calls, which was made stock, thereby causing an original share to amount, on the 1st of January, 1779, to £139, 8s. 9d.

Upon inspection of the map, it will appear that this canal connects the Irish Sea with the German Ocean, and the great ports of Liverpool and Hull, by which a cheap and ready transit is afforded to the Foreign Trade to and from the Baltic, Holland, Hanseatic Towns, the Netherlands, France and Germany; also with Ireland, the West Indies and America. Besides, the public are greatly benefited by the ease with which the interior trade is carried from Leeds and the West Riding into the manufacturing districts of Lancashire and to Liverpool, and *vice versa.* Moreover, upon the banks of this canal are found immense quantities of stone for paving and building, limestone for repairs of roads and for burning into lime for manure; inexhaustible beds of coal, which not only supply the neighbouring districts, but furnish an abundance for exportation at Liverpool; in short no part of the kingdom is more benefited by a public work of this kind than the country, through which the Leeds and Liverpool Canal passes.

LEEDS AND SELBY RAILWAY.

11 George IV. Cap. 59, Royal Assent 29th May, 1830.

THIS railway commences from the east side of Marsh Lane, in Leeds, and immediately enters a tunnel, eight hundred yards in length, to be made through a hill the apex of which is 72 feet ᶠabove the base of the railway. Its course is eastwardly, approaching the Waterloo Colliery, and passing the Osmanthorp Colliery to Halton Dial; thence by Cross Gates, the villages of Moor Garforth and Church Garforth, Newthorp and South Milford; and thence in nearly a straight line to the town of Selby, where it terminates at the banks of the Ouse, about two hundred and forty yards south of the bridge, and about three hundred and thirty north of the place where the Selby Canal locks down into that river.

Its total length is nineteen miles and seven furlongs. Its commencement is at a point 38 feet 8 inches above the level of the surface water of the River Aire at Far Bank Ferry, from whence there is a gradual rise of 63 feet 4 inches in the first length of two miles, two furlongs and six chains; and in the next two miles, one furlong and nine chains there is a further rise of 76 feet; thence to its greatest elevation at the seven mile point, it is nearly level, there being in this length a rise of only 7 feet 6 inches.

From thence the railway descends, in one regular plane, 232 feet in a distance of six miles, four furlongs and six chains; and in the remainder of the railway there is a further descent of 10 feet only, although it is six miles, two furlongs and four chains to its termination.

When this railway was first projected, Mr. Stephenson was employed to lay out the line; but previous to an application to parliament, James Walker, Esq. F.R.S. L.&E. was consulted, who designed the present course, and estimated its cost at £200,000, and of this sum £177,000 was subscribed at the time the bill was brought into parliament, though it is required that the whole sum shall be subscribed before any of the provisions of the act are put in execution.

The act received the royal sanction on the 29th May, 1830, and is entitled, ' *An Act for making a Railway from the town* ' *of Leeds to the River Ouse, within the parish of Selby, in the* ' *West Riding of the county of York.*' The act was obtained by a company consisting of one hundred and five persons, amongst whom we find the Earl of Mexborough, Lord Reay and the Honorable E. R. Petre, who were incorporated by the name of " The Leeds and Selby Railway Company," with power to raise amongst themselves the sum of £210,000, in two thousand one hundred shares of £100 each; and should not this prove sufficient, they may borrow, on mortgage of the undertaking, the further sum of £90,000.

TONNAGE RATES.

d.

For Lime to be used as Manure, Dung, Compost or other Manure, and for Materials for the repair of Roads............ } 1 per Ton, per Mile.

For Coal, Lime, Lime-stone to be used otherwise than as Manure, Coke, Culm, Charcoal, Cinders, Stone, Sand, Clay, Fuller's-earth, Building, Pitching and Paving-stones, Flags, Bricks, Tiles and Slates, Pig-lead, and Pig and Old Iron... } 1½ ditto. ditto.

For Sugar, Corn, Grain, Flour, Dye Woods, Timber, Staves, Deals, Lead, Bar-iron, and other Metals................. } 2½ ditto. ditto.

For Cotton and other Wool, Hides, Drugs, Manufactured Goods and for all other Wares, Merchandize, Articles, Matters and Things...................................... } 3 ditto. ditto.

Where the Rates do not amount to Sixpence per Ton, by reason of passing a short Distance only, the Proprietors have authority to demand it.

TOLLS.

s. d.

For every Person passing in or upon any Carriage for any Distance not exceeding Five Miles... } 0 6

For ditto not exceeding Ten Miles.. 1 0

For ditto exceeding Ten Miles.. 1 6

For every Horse, Mule, Ass or other Beast of Draught or Burthen, and for every Ox, Cow, Bull or Neat Cattle, carried in or upon such Carriage for any Distance not exceeding Five Miles................................. } 0 9

For ditto not exceeding Ten Miles.. 1 6

For ditto exceeding Ten Miles.. 2 6

For every Calf, Sheep, Lamb or Pig carried on the same any Distance........ 0 6

Fractions to be taken as for a Quarter of a Mile and Quarter of a Ton.

COMPANY'S CHARGE FOR CARRYING UPON THE RAILWAY, INCLUDING TONNAGE AND TOLLS.

s. d.

For Lime, Lime-stone, Dung, Compost and other Manure, and for Materials for the repair of Roads, Stone, Sand, Clay, Building, Pitching and Paving-stones, Tiles, Slates, Timber, Staves and Deals... } 6 0 per Ton.

For Sugar, Corn, Grain, Flour, Dye Woods, Lead, Iron and other Metals... } 7 0 ditto.

For Cotton and other Wool, Hides, Drugs, Groceries, and Manufactured Goods.................................... } 8 6 ditto.

For Hops, Tea, Wines, Spirits, Vitriol, Glass and other hazardous Goods... } 10 6 ditto.

And for any Distance short of the whole Length of the Railway, a rateable Proportion of such several Sums, according to the Distance.

d.

For Coal, Coke, Culm, Charcoal and Cinders.................... 2½ per Ton, per Mile.

For Persons, Cattle and other Animals, such reasonable Charge as shall from Time to Time be determined by the Company.

Company not compelled to receive less for short Distances than.. 9 per Ton.

For the Carriage of small Parcels not exceeding Five Hundred Pounds Weight, the Company have power to fix the Charge at any general Meeting.

For ascertaining the Weight of Tonnage, One Hundred and Twelve Pounds is deemed a Hundred Weight, and Twenty Hundred Weight a Ton; Fourteen Cubic Feet of Stone, Forty Cubic Feet of Oak, Mahogany, Beech and Ash, and Fifty Cubic Feet of all other Timber, shall be deemed a Ton Weight.

The act allows five years for the completion of the railway, and if not then made, the powers of the act are to cease, except as to such part as may have been executed.

The proposed object of this railway is to facilitate the transit of merchandize in general, by opening a more expeditious line of conveyance between Leeds and the port of Hull, and *vice versa.*

LEICESTER NAVIGATION.

31 George III. Cap. 65, Royal Assent 13th May, 1791.
37 George III. Cap. 51, Royal Assent 3rd May, 1797.

THE first parliamentary sanction of this useful work was obtained in 1791, under the title of ' *An Act for making and main-* ' *taining a navigable Communication between the Loughborough* ' *Canal and the town of Leicester, and for making and maintaining* ' *a Communication by Railways or Stone Roads, and Water Levels,* ' *from several Places and Mines to the said Loughborough Canal,* ' *and for continuing the same, by passing along the said Canal, to* ' *the said Navigation, commencing all in the county of Leicester.*' By this act the proprietors, who are incorporated as " The Com- " pany of Proprietors of the Leicester Navigation," have authority to make a navigable canal, from the basin of the Loughborough Canal on the north of the town of that name to the River Soar at Quorndon Village; from this point they are empowered to make the Rivers Soar and Wreak navigable, and to cut such branches and deviations therefrom as may render the water communication, between Loughborough and Leicester, most convenient. The canal and improvements have consequently been made, and the navigation is complete, uniting, as before-mentioned, with the Loughborough Canal at that town, and joining the Soar at the West Bridge in Leicester. There are other branches, railroads and water levels connected with the work, which will be mentioned below. For executing the powers invested in them, the proprietors were authorized to raise the sum of £46,000 in shares, and an additional sum of £20,000 should the former prove insufficient. For paying interest and other current expenses they were also empowered to collect the following rates.

TONNAGE RATES.

	s.	d.	
For all Coal conveyed from Loughborough to Leicester......	1	2	per Ton.
For ditto any shorter Distance............................	0	1	ditto, per Mile.
For ditto passing to the River Wreak for Melton Mowbray...	0	7	per Ton.
For all Timber, Iron, &c. from Loughborough to Leicester...	2	6	ditto.
For ditto any shorter Distance............	0	2	ditto, per Mile.
For ditto passing to the River Wreak and Melton Mowbray...	1	3	per Ton.
For all Coal conveyed on the Railroads and Water Levels from the several Places to Loughborough................	0	1	ditto, per Mile.
For Lime and Lime-stone on the Railroads..................	0	1½	ditto. ditto.
For ditto on the Water Levels...........................	0	0¾	ditto. ditto.

For all Lime, Lime-stone, Stones for Building and Materials for making or repairing Roads, Half the above Tolls.

The tolls may be lowered, if circumstances permit, and in that case such goods as pass along this line to the Melton Mowbray Navigation or Branch, which will be noticed in its place, are not to pay more than half the regulated tolls.

The proprietors having not only expended the sums directed to be raised under this act, but also contracted a debt of £14,000 without completing the work; they made another application to parliament and obtained a second act in 1797, entitled, ' *An Act* ' *for enabling the Company of Proprietors of the Leicester Navi-* ' *gation to finish and complete their several Works, and to discharge* ' *the Debts contracted in the making thereof, and for amending an* ' *Act passed in the Thirty-first of his present Majesty, for making the* ' *said Navigation, and several other Works, in such Act mentioned.*' By this second act they are enabled to raise a further sum of £18,000, by an additional call on the shareholders, or by mortgage or annuities as may seem best; and as it appears that some of the proprietors had voluntarily advanced £5 per share for the purpose of making a reservoir on Charnwood Forest, it is provided by this act that such advance shall be accounted as part of their calls for raising the additional sum of £18,000; and if it should be deemed expedient not to call for an advance on the original shares, but to borrow the £18,000, then the £5 per share advanced by the proprietors as above shall be repaid them. The company are also to collect the following

ADDITIONAL TONNAGE RATES.

		d.	
For all Coals carried from the Loughborough Canal to Lady Bridge or West Bridge, Leicester.........................		6	per Ton.
For ditto a less Distance between the same....................		½	ditto, per Mile.
For ditto when navigated from the Loughborough Canal to the Junction of the Wreak and Soar and along the Wreak and on the Navigation to Melton Mowbray		3	per Ton.

When this Company shall receive what will produce a Nett Income of £5 per Cent.
per Annum, then the additional Rates are to be taken off Coals which pass on the
Leicestershire and Northamptonshire Union Canal beyond Aylpston Mill. Coals
passing through the Oakham Canal are also exempt from the additional Tolls.
The Proprietors of this Navigation are directed to guarantee £2,000 per Annum to the
Loughborough Canal Company, on Condition of their taking any Sum not more
than One Shilling and Sixpence, nor less than Ten-pence per Ton on Coals passing
from Loughborough to the Trent.

The Leicester Canal or Navigation commences, as we have
before stated, at the basin of the Loughborough Canal on the north
side of that town, at an elevation of 125 feet above the sea;
passing the town it proceeds in a south-west direction to near
Barlow-upon-Soar, leaving Beaumanor Park on the west, and
falling into the Soar at Quorndon. Here the River Soar becomes
navigable and continues so to its junction with the Wreak River
near Wanley Hall; the united rivers being navigable to Turnwater
Meadow. In this meadow the navigation is joined by the Leicester
and Melton Mowbray Navigation, of which we shall have to speak
below; here also a cut is made across the meadows to avoid the
shallows, and passing through the parishes of Syston, Barkley and
Thurmanston, and leaving Wanlip Hall and Birstal Hall on the
east and Beaumont Lees on the west, it terminates at Leicester in
the Soar, thus communicating with the Leicestershire and Northamptonshire Union Canal.

From the basin at the Loughborough end of the line there is a
railway two miles and a half long, with 185 feet rise to a basin at
Forest Lane, at the east end of the Charnwood Forest Water
Level. This level extends to Barrow Hill, a distance of nearly nine
miles, having a side cut of a quarter of a mile long to Thringstone
Bridge. At the west end of the Great Level there is a railway to
the Clouds Hill Lime Works, effecting by these means a communication with the Ashby-de-la-Zouch Canal; here also is a railroad
to the Barrow Hill Lime Works; the Thringstone Branch also
extends a mile and a half to Coal Orton, and by a diversion of half
a mile to Swannington Common Coal Works.

From Loughborough to its junction with the Leicester and
Melton Mowbray Navigation, this navigation is level for three
miles, and from that point, to its termination in the Leicestershire
and Northamptonshire Union Canal, the distance is eleven miles,
with a rise of 45 feet.

At Leicester there is a basin, and on Charnwood Forest a reservoir for supplying the water-level with a feeder for the same, to
which water-level the company are empowered to make railways
from coal works two thousand yards distant therefrom; and since
the commencement of the Ashby Canal, this company has had
power to charge a toll of 2s. 6d. per ton on all coals dug in Swannington, Coal Orton or Thringstone, if carried through Blackfordby
or the last named canal.

This navigation was laid down by Mr. William Jessop, and in
December, 1793, the line from Loughborough to near Mount
Sorrel was opened, the remainder not being completed till Feb-
ruary of the succeeding year.

The work is of considerable utility, affording an easy transit
for the coal, limestone and granite of its neighbourhood, and supplying Leicester and other places on its line with timber, deals and
various articles of home consumption.

LEICESTER AND MELTON MOWBRAY NAVIGATION.

(SEE WREAK AND EYE NAVIGATION.)

LEICESTERSHIRE AND NORTHAMPTONSHIRE UNION CANAL.

33 George III. Cap. 98, Royal Assent 30th April, 1793.
45 George III. Cap. 71, Royal Assent 27th June, 1805.

WE have mentioned in the preceding article, that the Leicester
Navigation communicates with the present work at or near the
West Bridge in the town of Leicester, and we have now to describe
the extent of this undertaking, and the acts under which it was
commenced.

The first enactment, for the formation of the Leicestershire and
Northamptonshire Union Canal, obtained the royal assent in April,
1793, under title of ' *An Act for making and maintaining a Naviga-*
' *tion from the town of Leicester to communicate with the River Nen,*
' *in or near the town of Northampton, and also a certain collateral*
' *Cut from the said Navigation.*' By this act the proprietors were

incorporated under the style of " The Company of Proprietors of " the Leicestershire and Northamptonshire Union Canal," with powers to make navigable the River Soar, from the West Bridge in the parish of St. Mary, Leicester, to Ayleston Bridge in the county of Leicester, and from thence to make a navigable canal to the parish of Hardingstone in the county of Northampton, to communicate with the River Nen or Northern River, and to proceed along the said river to the town of Northampton, and from that town to make a navigable canal to and into another part of the River Nen, and after crossing the said river to communicate with an intended branch from the Oxford Canal at Braunston, to join the Thames at New Brentford; also to make a collateral cut from the before-named canal in the parish of Lubenham, in Leicestershire, to Market Harborough. For executing these plans the sum of £200,000 was directed to be raised in shares of £100 each; and should this prove insufficient, a further sum of £100,000. With these powers the proprietors commenced the work; but after having rendered the River Soar navigable as far as Ayleston Bridge, and after completing part of the canal from that place, they found that great advantages would be gained by varying the original line of the projected cut to Market Harborough, they therefore applied to parliament for a second act, which was obtained in 1805, under the title of ' *An Act to enable the Company* ' *of Proprietors of the Leicestershire and Northamptonshire Union* ' *Canal, to vary the Line of the said Canal, and to alter and amend* ' *the Powers of the Act passed for making the said Canal.*'

The second act being obtained, the proprietors continued the execution of their plan as far as Foxton, and the collateral cut to Market Harborough was completed. The remainder of the work was rendered unnecessary by the junction with the Grand Union at Foxton as above-mentioned. By the first act the company had authority to collect the following

TONNAGE RATES.

	d.	
For all Coal and Coke...................................	2½	per Ton, per Mile.
For all Lime, Lime-stone, Dung and Manure	1½	ditto. ditto.
For all Live Cattle, Stones, Bricks, Tiles, Sand, Iron-stone, Pig-iron and Pig-lead....................................	2	ditto. ditto.
For all other Goods, Wares and Merchandize whatever......	3	ditto. ditto.

Materials for Roads, Manure for the use of Proprietors of Land on the Line, Troops, and Government Stores are exempt from all these Rates.

This navigation, commencing at the junction with the Leicester Navigation at 175 feet above the level of the sea, proceeds to Ayleston Bridge in the bed of the Soar River, in a south-westerly direction; at Ayleston Bridge the cut commences, and pursues the same course as the river to a short distance beyond Enderby Hall, where the Soar divides into two branches; from this point it runs parallel to the eastern branch as far as Wistow Hall, having that mansion on its western bank and an aqueduct opposite to it on the eastern. From Wistow Hall it runs in a circuitous easterly course of twelve miles and three quarters, with 160 feet rise to the tunnel at Saddington, where it is 295 feet above the level of the sea. Leaving Saddington Tunnel, it proceeds in a sinuous line on the same level to Foxton and Gumley Hall, where it falls into the Grand Union Canal, having completed a line of seventeen miles. At this point also the branch to Market Harborough commences, running at first in an easterly course for about half its length and afterwards to the south, the whole distance being nearly four miles on one level.

There are warehouses and a basin at Gumley, and the tunnel at Saddington is eight hundred and eighty yards in length; this tunnel was completed in 1800, and the line from Leicester to Gumley opened soon after.

The work, which was executed under the management of Mr. John Varley, Sen. and Mr. C. Staveley, Jun. is of great utility in the supply of timber, deals, &c. and the export of the agricultural produce of the district through which it passes.

LEICESTER AND SWANNINGTON RAILWAY.

11 George IV. Cap. 58, Royal Assent 29th May, 1830.

THIS railway commences from that part of the River Soar near West Bridge, in the town of Leicester, called the Leicestershire and Northamptonshire Union Canal, whence it takes a northwardly course by Freaks Grounds, where it enters a tunnel one mile and three quarters in length; thence in a westwardly course, running parallel with and on the south side of the turnpike-road leading from Leicester to Ashby-de-la-Zouch; thence across a small rivulet north of the village of Glenfield, along the western bank of which it pursues its course by the villages of Ratby and Newton-Unthank to Desford, where it again takes a northwardly course by Merry Lees, Thornton and Bagworth; thence by the Birch Tree Inn, on the above-mentioned road, and westward by the Red House to the turnpike-road leading between Hinchley and Melbourne, at the north end of the village of Swannington, where it terminates. It is fifteen miles and three quarters in length, and the various inclinations which are rendered necessary by reason of the irregularities of the ground, over which it is intended to be made, are as follows; from the Leicester end of the railway it ascends 2 feet 10 inches in the distance of five furlongs; in the next six furlongs and one chain it rises 38 feet 9 inches; there is a rise of 5 feet 3 inches only, in one mile, three furlongs and two chains; then a long stretch of four miles, five furlongs and seven chains gradually rising 79 feet, and a further ascent of 57 feet 2 inches in the next distance of one mile, two furlongs and nine chains. From this point the railway gradually ascends 65 feet 7 inches in three quarters of a mile, and 22 feet further in the next one furlong and five chains; then a rapid ascent of 72 feet 3 inches in the short distance of three furlongs and seven chains. It is then level for the space of one furlong and three chains; but in the next seven furlongs and two chains there is a rise of 49 feet; from which point it descends 43 feet in one mile, six furlongs and four chains, and at the foot of this plane is a level course of five furlongs; then a further fall of 28 feet in the next one mile and two furlongs; and at the end of that another level course of two furlongs and one chain. From this point the line descends 133 feet in the short space of two furlongs and seven chains; whence, the remaining portion of the line, viz. one furlong and two chains, is level.

There are four branches from the main line above described, viz. one, in a distance of two furlongs and seven chains, extending eastward from the Freaks Grounds to the River Soar, near the North Bridge, Leicester; another of the same length to the collieries belonging to Lord Viscount Maynard, at Bagworth; and a short distance beyond which there is a third branch of one mile, four furlongs and eight chains in length, extending to Ibstock

Collieries; and within three quarters of a mile of Swannington there is a fourth branch, three furlongs and two chains in length, extending westward to Long Lane Colliery.

These proposed works were designed by Mr. Robert Stephenson, who estimated the cost at £75,453, of which sum it appears that £61,950 was subscribed before the application to parliament.

The act authorizing the execution of this railway received the royal assent on the 29th May, 1830, and is entitled, ' *An Act for* ' *making and maintaining a Railway or Tramroad from the River* ' *Soar near the West Bridge, in or near the borough of Leicester, to* ' *Swannington, in the county of Leicester, and four Branches there-* ' *from.*' The subscribers were by this act incorporated as " The " Leicester and Swannington Railway Company," with power to raise amongst themselves the sum of £90,000, in eighteen hundred shares of £50 each; and if this is not sufficient, they may borrow on mortgage the further sum of £20,000 ; but previous to commencing the works, the amount of the original estimate is to be subscribed.

The distance between the inside edges of the rails to be not less than 4 feet 8 inches; and between the outside edges not more than 5 feet 1 inch.

TONNAGE RATES.

	d.		
For all Dung, Earth, Compost, Manure and Materials for Roads, which shall be drawn or propelled and carried by and at the expense of the Company	2	per Ton, per Mile.	
If only drawn or propelled at the expense of the Company..	1¾	ditto.	ditto.
If drawn or propelled by Engines or other power, and not carried in the Waggons of the Company	1½	ditto.	ditto.
For all Coal, Coke, Culm, Charcoal, Cinders, Lime, Stone, Slate, Marl, Sand, Clay, Building, Pitching and Paving-stones, Flags, Bricks, Tiles, Deals, Lead and Iron in Pigs, or other Metals, which shall be drawn or propelled and carried by and at the expense of the Company	3	ditto.	ditto.
If only drawn or propelled at the expense of the Company...	2¼	ditto.	ditto.
If drawn or propelled by Engines or other power, and not carried in the Waggons of the Company................	2	ditto.	ditto.
For all Timber, Wool, Corn, Grain, Flour, Manufactured Goods, Lead in Sheets or Iron in Bars, and all other Wares or Merchandize which shall be drawn or propelled and carried by and at the expense of the Company......	4	ditto.	ditto.
If only drawn or propelled at the expense of the Company..	3½	ditto.	ditto.
If drawn or propelled by Engines or other power, and not carried in Waggons belonging to the Company..........	3	ditto.	ditto.
For all Goods and Merchandize whatever, (except Lime) and also except all such Goods in respect of which the Mile Tonnage shall be paid for passing Twelve Miles at least on the Railway, over and above the respective Rates and Tolls..........	6	ditto.	

TONNAGE RATES CONTINUED.

d.

For all Goods, Wares and Commodities whatsoever, and for all Carriages which shall pass any of the Inclined Planes, (by Steam Power) over and above the preceding Rates, upon each of the Inclined Planes............... } 4 per Ton.

This last-mentioned Toll upon the Inclined Planes is not to be levied, if the other Rates produce £10,000 per Annum.

TOLL FOR COACHES OR OTHER CARRIAGES,

d.

For every Person passing in any Carriage not drawn or propelled, and provided by and at the expense of the Company.................. } 2½ per Mile.

For every Person passing in any Carriage drawn or propelled and provided by the Company .... } 3 ditto.

For every Horse, Mule, Ass or other Beast of Draught or Burden, and for every Ox, Cow, Bull or other Cattle carried in or upon such Carriage, not drawn or propelled or provided by the Company.... } 2 ditto.

But if provided by the Company .... 3 ditto.

For every Calf, Sheep, Lamb or Pig passing in any Carriage, not drawn or propelled or belonging to the Company .... } ½ ditto.

But if provided by the Company.................................... 1 ditto.

Fractions to be taken as for a Quarter of a Mile and Quarter of a Ton.

The Company are not compelled to receive less than Sixpence per Ton for short Distances, and have power to regulate and fix the Prices of small Parcels of less than Five Hundred Pounds Weight.

WHARFAGE RATES.

d.

For every Description of Goods loaded, landed or placed upon any of the Wharfs of the Company, which shall not remain more than Seventy-two Hours... } 1 per Ton.

But if more than Seventy-two Hours, the further Sum of .... 1 ditto.

And for the Warehousing for the next so succeeding Week.............. 6 ditto.

And the like Sum of One Penny and Sixpence per Ton respectively, for every further and subsequent Week such Articles shall remain upon the said Wharfs or Warehouses.

CRANAGE TOLL.

s. d.

At one single Lift of the Crane, being less than Two Tons .... 0 6 per Ton.
Ditto of Two Tons and less than Three .... 1 0 ditto.
Ditto of Three Tons and less than Four .... 1 6 ditto.

And so progressively advancing Sixpence per Ton.

Lords of manors and others may erect wharfs, and charge the same rates as the company of proprietors. The railway to be completed in five years or the powers to cease.

The object sought by the execution of this railway and branches, is a cheap and expeditious conveyance of the coal, lime and other minerals which abound at the upper portion of the railway, to the town of Leicester, and thence by the canals and navigable rivers with which it will immediately communicate to other districts.

LEOMINSTER, OR KINGTON AND LEOMINSTER CANAL.

31 Geo. III. C. 69, R. A. 13th May. 1791.   36 Geo. III. Cap. 70, R. A. 26th April, 1796.
43 Geo. III. C. 141, R. A. 11th Aug. 1803.   7 Geo. IV. Cap. 94, R. A. 26th May, 1826.

THE Leominster, or as it has sometimes been called the Kington and Leominster Canal, commences at the town of Kington,
505½ feet above the sea, where it meets the Kington Railway;
from that place, pursuing an easterly direction, it passes by the
seats of Eywood, Titley, Staunton Park and Shobdon Court to the
aqueduct over the River Lugg at Kingsland, from which point it
bends towards the south to near the town of Leominster; from
Leominster it runs almost due north for a considerable distance
past Berrington House, then making a detour to the east, it continues its course in that direction, with many windings, past Tenbury to the aqueduct over the Rea River, and the adjoining tunnel
at Sousant; from the tunnel, which is 264½ feet above the level of
the sea, it pursues an easterly direction to Stourport, where it
unites with the Severn and the Stafford and Worcester Canal,
having traversed a distance of forty-six miles. From Kington
to Staunton Park it is level for four miles; from Staunton Park to
Milton two miles and a half with a fall of 152 feet; from that
place to Kingsland Aqueduct three miles and a half with 37 feet
fall; from the aqueduct to Leominster four miles and a half with
64 feet fall; in one mile and a half from Leominster there is a
rise of 18 feet; the next five miles and a half to Wiston is level;
from Wiston to Letwich Brook four miles and a half with a fall of
36 feet; from Letwich Brook to the Rea there is a level of seven
miles; from this point to the Sousant Tunnel there is a rise of 35
feet in the length of a mile; from this tunnel to the east end of
the Great Pensax Tunnel nine miles and level; from the east end
of this tunnel to the junction of the Severn and the Stafford and
Worcester Canal, being above three miles, there is a fall of 207
feet. The total length therefore, as above stated, is forty-six
miles, and the lockage 544 feet, being 496 feet of fall and 48 of
rise. In the line there are two considerable tunnels; the one

near Sousant is twelve hundred and fifty yards long; the other at Pensax three thousand eight hundred and fifty yards. There are also two collateral cuts near Tenbury for the use of the mills there.

The first act obtained for the formation of this canal, was passed in the year 1791, under the title of ' *An Act for making* ' *and maintaining a navigable Canal from Kington in the county* ' *of Hereford, by or through Leominster, to join the River Severn* ' *near Stourport Bridge, in the county of Worcester.*' By this act the proprietors are incorporated as " The Company of Proprie- " tors of the Leominster Canal Navigation," and are empowered to raise the sum of £150,000, in shares of £100 each, with the option of obtaining £40,000 more if needful. They are also authorized to demand the following

TONNAGE RATES.

	s.	d.		
For all Timber, Stone, Marble, Lime, Lime-stone for Ma- nure, Iron-stone, Raw Materials, Bricks, Brick-tiles, Slate, Gravel, Sand, Clay, Manure and Rubbish, navi- gated between the Severn and Milton Cross..........	0	1½	per Ton, per Mile.	
For ditto from Milton Cross to Kington..................	0	3	ditto.	ditto.
For Coke and Charcoal.................................	0	4	ditto.	ditto.
For all Coal carried on any part between the River Rea and Leominster, or between the Teme and Leominster	3	4	ditto.	
For ditto on any part between the Severn and Rea to Leominster or between the Teme and Leominster, in addition to the above	0	11	ditto.	
For ditto conveyed out of the Severn and navigated to Leominster or between that place and the Teme in addition..	1	2	ditto.	
For ditto navigated between Leominster and Milton Cross	0	2½	ditto, per Mile.	
For ditto between Milton Cross and Kington............	0	6	ditto.	ditto.
For ditto between the Rea and Teme....................	0	2½	ditto.	ditto.
For ditto eastward between the Rea and Severn..........	1	9	ditto.	ditto.
For ditto westward between the Severn and Rea........	0	2½	ditto.	ditto.
For Merchandize in general navigated between the Se- vern and Milton Cross...............................	0	2½	ditto.	ditto.
For ditto from Milton Cross to Kington..................	0	6	ditto.	ditto.

Slack Coal for the Purpose of burning Lime for Manure is to be charged only Half the usual Rates, and the Proprietors have authority to lower the Rates, when able so to do.

By this act power was given for taking supplies of water from springs, &c. within two thousand yards of the line; there was also a power of constructing inclined planes instead of locks upon some parts.

In less than five years after the passing of the first act, this company obtained another, entitled, ' *An Act to enable the Com-* ' *pany of Proprietors of the Leominster Canal Navigation to finish* ' *and complete the same.*' By this act the proprietors are authorized to raise a further sum of £180,000 by new shares of the same value as those created under the former act; or if the proprietors think it more advisable, they may borrow the said sum on mortgage of the canal and rates.

The means of increasing their funds, thus afforded, did not prove effectual, and accordingly in 1803, a third act was obtained under the title of ' *An Act for enabling the Company of Proprie-* ' *tors of the Leominster Canal to raise Money to discharge their* ' *Debts, and to complete the Canal, and for explaining and amend-* ' *ing the Acts for making and maintaining the said Canal, and* ' *for granting to the said Company further and other Powers.*'

From this act it appears that only £68,582 had been raised under the last, and that sundry new debts had been incurred in the prosecution of the work, amounting to £25,000 and upwards, and that the canal was still unfinished; the proprietors of the new shares already subscribed and paid for, are therefore protected from any disadvantage which might happen from their being liable to additional calls, by reducing the number of shares to the same number as the holders of the present shares, viz. six hundred and eighty-six, and the said six hundred and eighty-six share-holders are hereby declared to be the company. The company are empowered, over and above the tolls granted by the first act, to demand the following

TONNAGE RATE.

	d.
For all Coal, Goods, Wares, Merchandize and Things whatsoever, passing through the Locks intended to be made between the River Severn and the Canal Basin	1 per Ton.

They have also authority to make a railway from the canal at or near Stockton in the county of Worcester, to the basin at or near Stourport Bridge in the same county; and also one from Milton Cross to the town of Kington. And certain commissioners are appointed to superintend the works from Sousant Tunnel to the Severn. By this act also the proprietors have authority to raise by additional calls £50,000, and by mortgage, if necessary, £30,000; and the select committee may, if requisite, raise a still further sum of £10,000 by mortgage as aforesaid. All debts now due are to be secured by bonds payable with interest in five years.

Notwithstanding all these additional means of raising money, the funds still proved inadequate to the completion of the work, and the aid of parliament was again applied for in 1826, this application was answered by an act, entitled, ' *An Act to enable the* ' *Company of Proprietors of the Leominster Canal to raise further* ' *Sums of Money to discharge their Debts, and to complete the* ' *Canal, and for amending the Acts for making and maintaining* ' *the said Canal, and for granting to the said Company further and* ' *other Powers.*' By this act the proprietors may raise £60,000 by creating six hundred new shares of £100 each, such sum to be applied to the liquidation of debts already incurred. This and one or two clauses relating to the election of committees, and the compensation to be made for lands, &c. taken for the use of the company, comprize the substance of the act last obtained.

Mr. Thomas Dadford, Jun. was the engineer, under whose able superintendence the work has been put into execution. The tunnel at Sousant was finished in 1796, and in November of the same year twenty miles of the canal, from Leominster to Mamble Coal Works, were opened; the consequence of which was an immediate reduction of the price of coal from 1*s*. 6*d*. to 9*d*. per cwt. In 1797 the entrance into the canal from the Severn was opened and the work has gone on progressively since that time.

The design for which it was projected was the transit of stone, lime and iron-ore, and the agricultural produce of the country on its line to London, Liverpool, Hull and Bristol, and also the supply of Leominster and its vicinity with coal and coke. These purposes, it is hardly necessary to state, have been fully answered.

LEVEN CANAL.

41 George III. Cap. 32, Royal Assent 21st May, 1801.
45 George III. Cap. 43, Royal Assent 5th June, 1805.

THIS canal which is little more than three miles in length, was undertaken, at the sole charge of Mrs. Charlotte Bethell, of Rise, for the purpose of opening a communication between Leven and the port of Kingston-upon-Hull, and of thus affording an easier conveyance for goods and agricultural produce. Its direction is due west from the village of Leven to the Hull River Navigation near Ayke Beck Mouth, and the expense of making it, as estimated by Mr. William Jessop, was £4,041. Mrs. Bethell also consulted Mr. Rennie and Mr. Creassy as to the practicability of the undertaking.

An act for its execution was obtained in 1801, entitled, ' *An* ' *Act for enabling Charlotte Bethell, Widow, to make and maintain* ' *a navigable Canal from the River Hull, at a point in the parish* ' *of Leven, near the Boundary between Eske and Leven Carrs, in* ' *the East Riding of the county of York, to Leven Bridge in the* ' *said Riding.*'

By this act Mrs. Bethell was authorized to demand the following

TONNAGE RATES.

	s.	d.	
For all Lime and Lime-stone, Dung, Soot, Rape-Dust and other Manure	0	6	per Ton.
For all Coal and Coke	0	9	ditto.
For all Wheat, Rye, Beans, Peas, Malt, Oats, Barley, Rapeseed, Mustard-seed, Linseed and other Grain and Seeds of all Sorts, Bricks, Stones, Tiles, Slate and Sand, and all other Goods, Wares, Merchandize and Things whatsoever	1	0	ditto.

Fractions of a Ton to be taken as the Quarters therein, and of a Quarter as a Quarter.

The proprietor is also empowered to erect wharfs and quays, and to charge a wharfage rate for all goods left thereon above twenty-four hours; such rate to be determined between the parties.

The cost of this canal appears to have exceeded the estimate, for in 1805 Mrs. Bethell obtained a second act, entitled, ' *An Act* ' *for altering and amending an Act passed in the Forty-first of his* ' *present Majesty for enabling Charlotte Bethell, Widow, to make* ' *and maintain a navigable Canal from the River Hull to Leven* ' *Bridge, in the East Riding of the county of York;*' whereby, in consideration of the great expense she had incurred in completing the same, she is empowered to receive the following additional tolls as

WHARFAGE RATES.

	s.
For every Barge or Boat, using the Canal and laden with Lime, Lime-stone, Dung, Soot, Rape-Dust and other Manure, Coke, Coal, Wheat, Rye, Beans, Peas, Malt, Oats, Barley, Rapeseed, Mustard-seed, Linseeed and other Grain and Seeds of all Sorts, Stones, Bricks, Tiles, Slate and Sand	7 each.

The work as far as it extends is useful, and answers the design for which it was projected, by supplying lime and manure, and conveying of corn and other produce of the land to Hull, Beverley, and other places.

LEWES NAVIGATION.
(SEE OUZE RIVER, SUSSEX.)

LIDBROOK AND LYDNEY RAILWAY.
(SEE SEVERN AND WYE RAILWAY.)

LISKEARD AND LOOE CANAL.

6 George IV. Cap. 163, Royal Assent 22nd June, 1825.

THE Liskeard and Looe Canal commences at Tarras Pill, and proceeds from thence in a northerly direction to the parish of Liskeard, terminating at Moorswater, 156 feet above the level of the sea. The distance which it passes over is five miles and seven furlongs, and in its course there are twenty-five locks. The estimated cost of completing the works, as made by Mr. John Edgécumbe, was £12,577, 6s. There is a short branch of about a mile in length to Sand Place.

An act for executing this canal was obtained in 1825, under the title of ' *An Act for making and maintaining a navigable* ' *Canal from Tarras Pill, in the parish of Duloe, in the county of* ' *Cornwall, to or near Moorswater, in the parish of Liskeard, in* ' *the said county, and for making several Roads to communicate* ' *therewith.*' By this act the proprietors are incorporated as " The " Liskeard and Looe Union Canal Company," and have power to cut the canal, roads and other works connected therewith, to take water from the River Looe and Crylla Rivulet, and to use part of the latter as a feeder, under certain restrictions; and that no injury may be done to the navigation of the Fowey, of which river the Crylla is a tributary stream, two engineers are to be appointed, one by the company, the other by the Mayor and Corporation of Lostwithiel, to inspect the same. The company are also empowered to make rollers and inclined planes, and to dig the canal 4 feet deep, with a width of 14 feet at the bottom and 26 feet at the surface. For accomplishing these purposes, the act directs a sum of £13,000 to be raised in shares of £25 each; and in case that sum should prove insufficient, the company may raise £10,000 in addition, by mortgage. For paying interest and contingent expenses the following are to be received as

TONNAGE AND WHARFAGE RATES.

	s.	d.		
For all Lime-stone, Culm or Coal for burning Lime, Sand, Oreweed, Dung or any other Manure, except Salt and Burnt Lime, Building-stone, Free-stone, Granite, Clay and Stone for making Roads......................	0	3½	per Ton, per Mile.	
For Lime...	0	7	ditto.	ditto.
For all Wheat, Barley, Oats, Bran, Flour, Meal and Potatoes	0	10	ditto.	ditto.
For all Tin-ore, Copper-ore, Lead-ore, Iron-stone, Antimony, Manganese, and all other Metals, Semi-Metals and Minerals not smelted, Coals and Culm not used for burning Lime...................................	0	7	ditto.	ditto.
For all Tin, Copper, Lead, Iron, and all other Metals having been smelted, Bricks, Tiles, Timber, Charcoal, Deals, Wood, Faggots, Bark, Seeds, Vetches, Peas, Paper, Old Junk or Rags, Salt and all other Goods, Wares, Merchandize and Things whatever, Hay, Straw, Cattle, Calves, Sheep, Swine and other Beasts..............	1	1½	ditto.	ditto.
For all Goods, Wares, Merchandize and Things landed on any Wharf, but not remaining more than Seventy-two Hours......................................	0	9	per Ton.	
For ditto after the first Seventy-two Hours...............	0	6	ditto, per Day.	

Fractions of a Ton to be taken as the Quarters therein, and of a Quarter as a Quarter.
Fractions of a Mile as the Quarters, and of a Quarter as a Quarter.

Lords of manors and others may erect wharfs and warehouses on the line, having first obtained the company's consent. And should the work not be completed in five years from the date of the act, the powers thereof are to cease.

This canal was projected for the purpose of facilitating the transport of coals, timber, stone, minerals and other products of the mines and lands on its line and in the vicinity, and of various composts and manure for the use of the farmer, and it fully answers the intention of the projectors.

LIVERPOOL AND MANCHESTER RAILWAY.

7 Geo. IV. C 49, R. A. 5th May, 1826.   7 & 8 Geo. IV. C. 21, R. A. 12th April, 1827.
9 Geo. IV. C. 7, R. A. 26th Mar. 1828.   10 Geo. IV. C. 35, R. A. 14th May, 1829.

AFTER various disappointments, and at above £30,000 expenditure, this company succeeded in their application to parliament, and obtained an act in the year 1826, under the title of ' *An Act* ' *for making and maintaining a Railway or Tramroad from the* ' *town of Liverpool to the town of Manchester, with certain* ' *Branches therefrom, all in the county of Lancaster.*' By this act, obtained for constructing this magnificent work, certain subscribers were incorporated as " The Liverpool and Man- " chester Railway Company," with powers to make and maintain a railway or tramroad with collateral branches, commencing on the east side of Wapping in the town of Liverpool, and passing through the several parishes of Liverpool, Walton, Childwall, Huyton, Prescot, Winwick, Warrington, Leigh, Eccles and Manchester, in the county palatine of Lancaster; and extending to or passing through the townships of Liverpool, West Derby, Wavertree, Much Woolton, Thingwall, Roby, &c. &c. to Salford and Manchester, terminating near the south-west side of the New Bailey Prison in Salford, in the parish of Manchester, near the New Bailey Bridge over the Irwell. The branches mentioned in the act are one from certain closes called the Ridings, in the parish of Prescot, running northwardly to Whiston Potteries; the other running southwardly from the same place and terminating in the Lower Houghton Hays in Whiston aforesaid. The proprietors have power also to make inclined planes on any part of the work; they are likewise directed to make that part of the line, which shall be in the town of Liverpool by means of a tunnel under the same, in a direction laid down on the original plan, subject to the inspection and approval of the corporation surveyor, and to purchase houses undermined, if the owners require it. Locomotive engines are not to be used in the town, nor are steam engines to be set on certain lands therein specified. Not more than twenty-two yards in breadth to be taken, except in certain cases.

For completing the work the company are authorized to raise £510,000, in shares of £100 each, of which the Marquis of Stafford shall hold one thousand, and which shall be subscribed for before the work commences; and should that sum prove insufficient, they may raise £127,500 additional, on mortgage of the works.

Before any dividends out of the profits are declared, the proprietors are to invest one-tenth part of such profits in government securities as a fund to be used in future, instead of making additional calls; and when such fund shall amount to £100,000, then the whole of the profits shall be divided, and until the fund shall amount to the said sum of £100,000, the dividends on the reserved fund shall be added thereto ; but when by these means the £100,000 is made up, then the nett profits of the work and the dividends on the fund shall both be divided amongst the subscribers. When the annual dividends on shares amount to £10 per share, the company are bound to lower their tonnage rates £5 per cent. and when the profits do not amount to £10 per share per annum, then the deficiency shall be made up from the reserved fund. The following are to be taken as

TONNAGE RATES.

		d.	
For all Lime-stone		1	per Ton, per Mile.
For all Coal, Lime, Dung, Compost, Manure, and Materials for Roads	}	1½ ditto.	ditto.
For all Coke, Culm, Charcoal, Cinders, Stone, Sand, Clay, Building, Paving and Pitching-stones, Flags, Bricks, Tiles and Slates	}	2 ditto.	ditto.
For all Sugar, Corn, Grain, Flour, Dye Woods, Timber, Staves, Deals, Lead, Iron and other Metals	}	2½ ditto.	ditto.
For all Cotton and other Wool, Hides, Drugs, Manufactured Goods, and all other Wares, Merchandize, Matters or Things	}	3 ditto.	ditto.

Where the Amount of Tolls from shortness of Distance do not amount to One Shilling per Ton, the Proprietors are empowered to demand that Sum.

Chaises, Gigs, Coaches and Passengers and Cattle, may pass on the Railroads on paying

	s.	*d.*
For every Person travelling thereon, not more than Ten Miles, in any Vehicle	1	6
For ditto exceeding Ten Miles but not above Twenty Miles	2	6
For ditto above Twenty Miles	4	0
For every Horse, Mule, Ass or other Beast of Draught or Burthen, and for every Ox, Cow, Bull or Neat Cattle, carried in or on such Carriage, not exceeding Fifteen Miles	2	6
For ditto exceeding Fifteen Miles	4	0
For every Calf, Sheep, Lamb or Pig, any Distance	0	9

Fractions of a Ton and of a Mile to be reckoned as the Quarters in that Fraction, and of a Quarter as a Quarter.

The proprietors may carry goods, &c. of all descriptions upon the said railroad, and charge for the same, including the before-mentioned rates, the following

CARRIAGE RATES.

	s.	*d.*	
For all Lime, Lime-stone, Dung, Compost, Manure and Materials for Roads, Stone, Sand, Clay, Building, Pitching and Paving-stones, Tiles, Slates, Timber, Staves and Deals	8	0	per Ton.

2 D

CARRIAGE RATES CONTINUED.

	s.	d.
For all Sugar, Corn, Grain, Flour, Dye Woods, Lead, Iron and other Metals	9	0 per Ton.
For all Cotton and other Wools, Hides, Drugs, Groceries and Manufactured Goods	11	0 ditto.
For all Wines, Spirits, Vitriol, Glass and other hazardous Goods	14	0 ditto.
For all Coal, Coke, Culm, Charcoal and Cinders	0	2½ ditto, per Mile.

All shorter Distances in Proportion.

For all Persons, Cattle and other Animals, such Rates as the Company may decide upon.

The Company are not, however, compelled to receive less than Two Shillings per Ton, for short Distances; they may also fix the Rates for Parcels not exceeding Five Hundred Weight, and may from time to time vary and repeal the said Rates.

This act, which is very long, comprising not less than two hundred clauses, contains nothing more of interest to general readers, the parts not mentioned being for the protection of private individuals.

In 1827 another act was obtained under the designation of ' *An Act for amending and enlarging the Powers and Provisions of* ' *an Act, relating to the Liverpool and Manchester Railway ;*' by which the former act was amended and enlarged, and leave was given to the company to borrow £100,000 of the Exchequer Bill Commissioners, or of other persons; and it is provided that subscribers who do not pay their calls at the appointed time, shall pay interest on the sums due; it is also provided that the subscribers shall receive interest at five per cent. upon the amount of their subscriptions, besides the £10 per share dividend, without making any deduction from their maximum tonnage rates.

Another act was obtained in 1828, having for title, ' *An Act to* ' *enable the Company of Proprietors of the Liverpool and Manchester* ' *Railway to alter the Line of the said Railway, and for amending* ' *and enlarging the Powers and Provisions of the several Acts* ' *relating thereto.*' By this act alterations were made in the line of the railway originally laid down; one of the deviations is in the township of Sutton; another alteration from a field in that township to a field in Burtonwood; another in the townships of Newton and Culcheth; and the same was now directed to be made according to an amended plan, the details of which it is unnecessary to enter into.

However, the company still found that their line might be improved, for in the following year a fourth act was passed, as ' *An Act for enabling the Liverpool and Manchester Railway*

' *Company to make an Alteration in the Line of the said Railway,*
' *and for amending and enlarging the Powers and Provisions of*
' *the several Acts relating thereto.*'

By this act the line was varied again, so as to pass from Oldfield Road across Ordsall Lane and the River Irwell to Water Street, instead of passing over the Bolton, Bury and Manchester Canal to Irwell Street, near the New Bailey Prison; and the proprietors were authorized to build bridges over the Irwell and Water Street in Manchester.   The estimate for this part of the line, abandoned for the one substituted by this act, was £11,802, of which £10,216, 16*s.* was for land purchased.   Mr. George Stevenson calculated the expenses of the present line to be £10,229, 10*s.* in which sum £500 is considered as two years' rent of the land on the line, which, being already contracted for at an annual chief rent, would not be paid for in a gross sum; and the cost of building the bridges at £9,000, leaving together a balance of £729, 10*s.* for contingent costs.   In the former part of this description of the Liverpool and Manchester Railway, we have quoted the carriage rates which the company are empowered to take.

In making the estimates of the cost of this work, no contemplation was had of the expense of forming an establishment for the carriage of goods; by this act, therefore, it is provided that a fund of £127,500 shall be raised for that purpose, in shares of £25 each, either amongst themselves or by the admission of new members. The accounts of this department are to be kept separate, and separate dividends are to be made in respect thereof.   The raising of this fund is not to prejudice the power of borrowing money for completing the railroad, granted by the first act.   The length of the deviated line, as stated by Mr. G. Stevenson, and Mr. Joseph Lock his assistant, according to the plan adopted by the act of 1828, is eleven miles and nine hundred and seventy yards, and the estimate of the deviation £167,009, 4*s.* 4*d.*

The whole length of the railway, including the tunnel under Liverpool, is thirty miles and three quarters, in which distance there are three inclined planes, viz. at Sutton, Rainhill and the tunnel at Liverpool.   The rise at the tunnel is 110 feet in one thousand nine hundred and seventy yards; the next one thousand yards is level; then in five miles and one furlong, there is a fall of

24 feet 7 inches; then in one mile and a half up the Rainhill Inclined Plane, there is a rise of 82½ feet; and from Rainhill to Sutton, a distance of one mile and seven furlongs, is level; then a fall of 82½ feet in one mile and a half; in the next two miles and a half there is a fall of 5 feet; and in the following six miles and a half there is a fall of 37 feet; this is the lowest point on the railway; from whence, in the next five miles and a half, is a rise of 21 feet 1½ inches; the last four miles and a half to Manchester, are level. Adjoining the great tunnel at Liverpool there is also constructed another short one, for the accommodation of carriages taking passengers. Mr. George Stevenson has been the engineer to this undertaking, under whose superintendence the work has been ably conducted; Messrs. G. and J. Rennie were also called in upon particular occasions by the promoters of the undertaking.

The utility of the work cannot yet be fairly estimated; but if it should answer the high expectations now entertained, it will be one of the most lucrative concerns in the kingdom, and of the utmost importance to the great trading towns of Liverpool and Manchester, as well as to the district of country through which it passes.

LIVERPOOL DOCKS AND HARBOUR.

8 Anne, C. 12, R. A. ——— 1710.	3 Geo. I. C. 1, R. A. ——— 1716.
11 Geo. II. C. 32, R. A. ——— 1737.	2 Geo. III. C. 86, R. A. ——— 1762.
25 Geo. III. C. 15, R. A. ——— 1785.	39 Geo. III. C. 59, R. A. 21st June, 1799.
51 Geo. III. C. 143, R. A. 10th June, 1811.	59 Geo. III. C. 30, R. A. 19th May, 1819.
6 Geo. IV. C. 187, R. A. 27th June, 1825.	9 Geo. IV. C. 114, R. A. 27th June, 1828.

The acts for improving the port of Liverpool and for completing and maintaining the docks, quays, basins, works and buildings erected and made there, are of too general a nature to be stated at large in these pages, particularly as they do not form an essential part of a work exclusively on inland navigation. It may therefore suffice to remark, that trustees for the management of these works are incorporated under the title of " The Trustees " of the Liverpool Docks," and have powers to purchase land, enlarge such docks as are necessary, to make others with their accompanying buildings, and to raise monies for the execution of the trusts confided to them. To enter more particularly into the precise terms of these acts and the sums of money each directs to be raised, would not be of general interest; the works are executed with due regard to the trade and interests of that flourishing town, and the whole are of the most magnificent description. The harbour here, as may be seen from the map, is entirely artificial, being formed within the town and communicating with the river. Few ports in Europe can vie with these works, or with the conveniences for loading and unloading of vessels. There are both wet and dry docks, with graving docks and other requisites for repairing vessels. The warehouses are of uncommon size, comprising several stories, with cranes, &c. to each. Government has here a large warehouse for tobacco, and each part of the docks and buildings is eminently adapted to the purpose for which it is designed.

LLANELLY RAILWAY AND DOCK.

9 George IV. Cap. 91, Royal Assent 19th June, 1828.

THIS work was projected for the purpose of conveying the minerals and other productions of the country near its line to the sea, and the dock was for the readier shipment and landing of the exports and imports to be conveyed thereon.

The scheme met with the approbation of parliament in an act, entitled, ' *An Act for making and maintaining a Railway or Tram-* ' *road from Gelly Gillie Farm, in the parish of Llanelly, in the* ' *county of Carmarthen, to Machynis Pool in the same parish and* ' *county; and for making and maintaining a Wet Dock at the* ' *Termination of the said Railway or Tramroad at Machynis Pool* ' *aforesaid.*' By this act the proprietors are incorporated under the style of " The Llanelly Railroad and Dock Company," and have authority to complete the projected railway and dock, the cost of which is estimated at the sum of £14,000, to be raised in shares of £100 each; and in case the said £14,000 should prove to be insufficient for the completion of the works, they are empowered to raise, on mortgage or by annuity, a further sum of £6,000. The dock to be so constructed as to be large enough for ships of three hundred tons burthen, with slips, poles, beacons, warping and

mooring buoys, chains and capsterns, and the company are to build
wharfs, warehouses and other works necessary for the purposes of
the act.   The following are to be taken as

DOCK, WHARFAGE, WAREHOUSING AND TONNAGE RATES.

	s.	*d.*	
For all Ships or Vessels entering the Dock or Basin, and not continuing therein above Twenty-one Days............	0	2	per Ton.
Above that Time, per Week additional.....................	0	1	ditto.
For all Goods, Wares, Merchandize and other Things, navigated into or out of the Dock or Basin................	0	1	ditto.
For all Sand, Lime-stone and Lime for Manure, Dung, Compost and other Manures and Materials for Roads, conveyed on the Railway................................	0	1	ditto, per Mile.
For all Copper, Tin, Lead and other Ores, and all Matters containing Ore, Copper, Lead, Iron and other Metals; Timber, Coal, Coke, Culm, Cinders, Stone, Bricks, Earth, Clay, Chalk, Marl, Lime and Sand, not used for Manure..	0	0½	ditto. ditto.
For Parcels or Packages lying Seven Days in the Company's Warehouses, if not exceeding One Hundred Weight....	0	4	each.
Above that Weight......................,.................	0	4	per Cwt.
Coarse Goods not in Packages............................	3	6	per Ton.
For every Horse, Mule and Ass, not drawing Goods nor going from Farm to Farm or to the Commons.........	0	2	each.

The Rates of small Parcels, not weighing more than Five Hundred Weight, are to be
regulated by the Company.

Fractions of a Ton and a Mile to be taken as the Quarters therein, and of a Quarter as
a Quarter.

All Vessels belonging to his Majesty, or conveying Soldiers, Arms and Baggage, or
belonging the Ordnance, Customs, Excise or Post-Office, are exempted from
these Rates; as are also Owners of Lands on the Line and their Servants and
Cattle.

The length of the railway is two miles and three hundred
yards, in which distance there is a rise of 68 feet above high-
water-mark; the dock is two hundred yards by fifty-five at the
bottom, calculated to hold twenty-one vessels of three hundred tons
as mentioned above; the depth is 16 feet below high-water-mark
of the highest spring tides, and the flood-gates at the entrance are
36 feet wide.   Mr. F. Foster estimated the whole at £11,736, 3s.
4d. including £8,074, 10s. the cost of the dock and other conveniences.   The engineer's estimate was subscribed for in equal
portions by Messrs. D. T. Shears, J. H. Shears, T. Margrave and
W. Ellwood, Jun.

The work is completed and is found useful for the intended
objects of its projection.

LLANLLYFIN AND CARNARVON RAILWAY.
(SEE NANTLLE RAILWAY.)

LLANFIHANGEL RAILWAY.

51 George III. Cap. 123, Royal Assent 25th May, 1811.

THIS railway commences at a level of 447 feet above the sea, on the banks of the Brecknock and Abergavenny Canal, with which it communicates, and proceeds from thence in a circuitous course nearly north-east to its junction with the Grosmont or Llanfihangel Crucorney Railroad at Llanfihangel Crucorney Court, in the county of Monmouth.

The act for this work was passed in 1811, under the title of ' *An Act for making a Railway from the Brecknock and Aberga-* ' *venny Canal, in the parish of Llanwenarth, to or near to Llanfi-* ' *hangel Crucorney in the county of Monmouth,*' whereby the proprietors are incorporated as " The Llanfihangel Railway " Company," and empowered to make a railway from the coal wharf of the Brecknock and Abergavenny Canal, in the parish of Llanwenarth, to the village of Llanfihangel Crucorney, in the county of Monmouth, by or near the Cadvor, Penyr Worlod, Lanforst, and Maerdy, across the Usk, by or through the town of Abergavenny and other places, and to make inclined planes on the line. For the purposes of this act it is directed that £20,000 shall be raised in shares of £200 each, and if that sum should prove insufficient, they may obtain an addition of £15,000 by borrowing on mortgage of the work.

TONNAGE AND OTHER RATES.

		d.	
For all Dung, Compost, Lime-stone, Manure and Materials for Roads		2 per Ton,	per Mile.
For all Lime, Chalk, Marl, Ashes, Peat, Clay, Bricks and Sand		3 ditto.	ditto.
For all Coals, Cinders, Coke, Culm, Charcoal, Tin, Copper, Lead-ore, Lead in Pigs or Sheets, Iron-stone or Ore, Iron in Pigs and Bars, Tiles, Slates, Flag-stones and other Stones		4 ditto.	ditto.
For all other Goods, Wares, Merchandize and Things whatsoever		6 ditto.	ditto.
For Horses, Colts, Mules or Asses, not drawing any Goods liable to Toll, and for Cows, and Horned and Neat Cattle, except Swine or Sheep		1 each.	
For all Swine and Sheep		6 per Score.	
For Persons travelling in all privileged Waggons, carrying Passengers for Hire		1 per Mile, each.	

Parcels under Five Hundred Weight to be paid for according to a Rate fixed by the Proprietors.

Tickets to be delivered by the Collector of Tolls, and no Toll to be paid for the same Horse or other Animal more than once in the Day.

Lords of manors or the company may erect wharfs and warehouses on the line, for using which they shall charge the following

WHARFAGE AND WAREHOUSING RATES.

		d.
For Coal, Culm, Lime, Lime-stone, Clay, Iron, Iron-stone, Lead or other Ores, Timber, Stone, Bricks, Tiles, Slates, Gravel or other Things.. }	1	per Ton.
For Packages of not more than Fifty-six Pounds......................	1	each.
For ditto above Fifty-six Pounds and not exceeding Five Hundred Weight	2	ditto.
For ditto exceeding Five Hundred Weight.............	6	per Ton.

But if the same shall remain on any Wharf or in any Warehouse for a longer Time than Forty-eight Hours, then the Proprietors may charge, in addition, One Penny per Ton for Wharfage and Three-pence per Ton for Warehousing, for the next Ten Days, and the same Sums respectively for every Day the said Goods shall remain on the Wharfs or in the Warehouses.

There are other clauses, but of no general interest. Mr. William Crossley made the estimate of this railroad in 1810, and stated that a single railroad would cost £13,390, 12s. and a double one £17,862. The length of the road is eleven thousand six hundred and six yards, and the money originally subscribed £15,400.

LONDON AND CAMBRIDGE JUNCTION CANAL.

52 George III. Cap. 141, Royal Assent 9th June, 1812.
54 George III. Cap. 168, Royal Assent 20th June, 1814.

As far back as the year 1778 Mr. Whitworth pointed out to the Common Council of the City of London, the public advantage which would accrue by making a canal from Bishop's Stortford to Cambridge; and that body gave him orders, as their engineer, to make a survey of the country between those places, which he did in the years 1779 and 1780. He reported this line to be very practicable; the length whereof by his survey was twenty-eight miles and a quarter, with a rise from Bishop's Stortford to the head level at Elsenham of 84 feet, and a fall from thence to the River Cam at the low end of Cambridge of 141 feet 2 inches. This scheme has lain dormant till the present proprietors saw the great advantage the public would derive by accomplishing an easy communication between the metropolis and the various towns and districts in the line of this projected canal down to Lynn and the Isle of Ely; and for the purpose of putting into execution so important a work, they applied and obtained an act in 1812, under the title of ' *An Act for making and maintaining a navigable*

' Canal, with Aqueducts, Feeders and Reservoirs, from the Stort
' Navigation at or near Bishop's Stortford, in the county of Hert-
' ford, to join the River Cam, near Clayhithe Sluice, in the county of
' Cambridge, with a navigable Branch or Cut from the said Canal
' at Sawston to Whaddon, in the county of Cambridge;' by which
certain subscribers were incorporated as " The Company of Pro-
" prietors of the London and Cambridge Junction Canal," and
empowered to complete a navigable canal from Sir George
Duckett's Canal, called the Stort Navigation, at or near Bishop's
Stortford, through the-parishes and hamlets of Bishop's Stortford,
Hockerill, Birchanger, Stansted, Mount Fitchet, Ugley, Newport,
Saffron Walden, Littlebury, Little Chesterford and Great Chesterford, Hinxton, Ickleton, Duxford, Whittlesford, Great Shelford,
Trumpington, Cherry Hinton, Fen Ditton and Horningsea, to
join the Cam below Clayhithe Sluice, in the parish of Horningsea
aforesaid; and to make a branch or cut with proper aqueducts
and other works, from the said canal at Great Shelford to Whaddon; and to make necessary works for supplying the said canal
and branch with water. The company may also construct railways and inclined planes, should the same appear more advantageous, in any part of the line; but the proprietors are not to make
any works within the park of Lord Braybrook, at Audley End,
nor to take water from streams flowing into the same; nor to
erect buildings between the park walls and the banks of the canal.
There are also similar clauses respecting the estates of Shortgrove,
Elsenham Hall, Elsenham Leys, and many others, the property
of gentlemen living near the intended line. The streams, which
feed that valuable conduit in the market place of Cambridge,
called Hobson's Conduit, from which great part of the town and
university obtain water, are by this act to be kept from injury or
diminution. For completing the undertaking, the proprietors are
empowered to raise £570,000 in shares of £100 each; and should
this prove insufficient they may raise an additional sum of £300,000,
either amongst themselves, or by the creation of new shares, or
by mortgage, or by promissory notes; but no proceeding is to
take place before £425,250 shall have been actually subscribed.
For defraying the necessary expenses and paying interest the
company may demand the following rates.

TONNAGE RATES.

		d.
For all Goods, Wares, Merchandize, and all other Matters or Things whatsoever......	}	3 per Ton, per Mile.

Fractions of a Mile to be taken as a whole Mile, and Vessels having on Board a less lading than Twenty Tons, shall pay for Twenty Tons.

The proprietors of the canal, lords of manors or others may erect wharfs and warehouses on the line; and for the accommodation thus afforded, rates shall be paid according to agreement between the company and the owners of goods. Owners and occupiers of land may convey corn and grain and manure, the actual produce of their lands, on the levels of the canal, free from tolls, provided they pass no lock; and they may carry back manure for their lands tonnage free.

In the year 1814 a second act was obtained, under the title of ' *An Act to alter and amend an Act made in the Fifty-second of his* ' *present Majesty, for making a Canal from the Stort Navigation,* ' *at or near Bishop's Stortford, to the River Cam.*' By this act it appears that the sum of £425,250 had not been subscribed, therefore the works were not commenced; but as an amount had been raised, nearly sufficient for making the part between Clayhithe Sluice and Saffron Walden, it is provided by this second act, that the clause, insisting on the amount above stated, should be repealed, and this part of the work, with the cut from the canal from Sawston to Great Shelford, should be commenced; but that part between Saffron Walden and the Stort Navigation shall not be commenced before three-fourths of the estimate for the whole work is subscribed. By this act also fifteen additional subscribers are to be elected into the committee, as directors, at the next general assembly of the company.

Commencing at the level of the Bishop's Stortford Canal, there is a rise of 72 feet to the summit of this canal, by twelve locks of 6 feet each, bringing the work to the west end of the summit level, near to the large tunnel, which is a mile and three hundred and forty yards in length. The distance from the commencement to the summit level has four of these locks in the first mile and a half; there is then a level of six furlongs and eight chains; in the remaining space of one mile and two furlongs there are the remaining eight locks; the summit level is four miles, six furlongs and two chains long, and from it there are ten locks descending to the east a distance of three miles, six furlongs and three chains to a second tunnel four hundred and eighteen yards in length. At thirteen miles, three furlongs and one chain from the Bishop's Stortford Canal is a third tunnel seven hundred and four yards long, and the canal locks down by twenty-two locks in twelve miles, four furlongs and six chains from the west end of this third tunnel; at the distance of eight miles, six furlongs and seven chains from which the branch to Whaddon commences; this is near to Shelford Magna, whence to the entrance into the Cam at Clayhithe Sluice there are eight locks in a distance of ten miles, one furlong and nine chains, making a total fall of 165 feet 9 inches. The Whaddon Branch has thirteen locks.

The dimensions of the canal and branch are 5 feet in depth, 24 feet breadth at the bottom and 44 feet at the top; the summit level is the same breadth at the bottom, but 6 feet deep and 48 feet at the surface. The estimate for the main line was £523,838, including reservoirs, feeders and steam engines; of this sum £121,300 was subscribed at first in shares of £100 each. The estimate for the Whaddon Branch, including an aqueduct over the Grant or Granta River, was £44,848. The line was surveyed and laid down in 1811 by Messrs. Netlam and Francis Giles, under the direction of Mr. Rennie.

The completion of this canal will be found highly advantageous to the agricultural counties of Cambridge, Norfolk, Suffolk, Essex and Hertford, and very beneficial to the metropolis.

LOUTH CANAL.

3 George III. Cap. 39, Royal Assent 24th March, 1763.
9 George IV. Cap. 30, Royal Assent 9th May, 1828.

THE first act for making the Louth Canal was obtained in 1763, under the title of ' *An Act for making a Navigation from the* ' *River Humber, by a Canal or Cut at or near Tetney Haven, to the* ' *River Ludd in the parish of Alvingham, in the county of Lincoln,* ' *and for continuing the said Navigation in or near the said River,* ' *from thence to or near the town of Louth, in the said county,*' which sufficiently declares the proposed line of the same. The length thereof is about fourteen miles, in a south-west direction, at a very trifling elevation above the sea; for the first nine miles and three quarters, commencing at the sea-lock gates in Tetney Haven, the line is on a level; in the next two miles and three quarters there is a rise of 24 feet, and in the remaining mile and a half a rise of 32½ feet. The line was surveyed by Mr. John Grundy and afterwards revised by Mr. Smeaton; the estimate for which amounted to £16,500. For putting this work into execution, certain commissioners were empowered to raise money on mortgage of the tolls, which are directed to be paid as below.

TONNAGE RATES.

	s.
For all Goods, Wares, Merchandize or Commodities, except Groceries..	4 per Ton.
For all Groceries..	8 ditto.

A Chaldron of Coals containing Forty-eight Winchester Bushels to be estimated as One Ton.
Less Weights than a Ton to pay in Proportion.

The sum borrowed under this act was altogether £28,000; but though this amount had been expended, the canal was found to be so defectively constructed, that a further outlay was required, in consequence whereof meetings of the commissioners were held in the year 1777, for devising means to procure the necessary funds, and Mr. Chaplin having proposed to advance the sums required, on condition that he should have the tolls on lease for ninety-years, the act for sanctioning which agreement should be obtained at his cost, when required, that proposal was, with the exception of two subscribers, agreed to, and the lease granted to Mr. Chaplin, he covenanting on his part to make all repairs, to pay all wages and legal interest for all sums previously subscribed.

Mr. Chaplin accordingly took the works into his own hands, but doubts as to the validity of this agreement were entertained, and it having become expedient on other accounts to repeal the first act, a second was obtained in 1828, entitled, ' *An Act for* ' *improving and maintaining the Navigation from the River* ' *Humber to Alvingham in the county of Lincoln, and from thence* ' *to Louth in the same county.*' By this act the remainder of the term of Mr. Chaplin's lease, subject to a reduction of the tolls, is continued to him and his heirs or assigns. Instead of the former rates, there shall be demanded according to the following list, for goods, &c. conveyed on the canal from the Humber to and above the lock, called the Basin Lock, as in the first column of the list, and for all goods, &c. conveyed a less distance, as in the second column of the said list.

LIST OF TONNAGE RATES BEFORE REFERRED TO.

	s. d.	d.
For all Sugar, Molasses, Plums, Currants, Raisins and Figs..................................	4 0	4 per Ton, per Mile.
For all Slate, Timber, Deals and Free-stone........	2 8	3 ditto. ditto.
For every Chaldron of Coals of Forty-eight Bushels Imperial Measure..............................	2 8	3 per Mile.
For every Forty Bushels of Cinders, Coke or Culm	1 4	1½ ditto.
For every Eighty Tods of Wool, Twenty-eight Pounds each Tod..............................	2 8	3 ditto.
For every Thousand of Stock Bricks, Paving Bricks, Floor Bricks or Pantiles........................	2 8	3 ditto.
For every Thousand Common Bricks...............	1 4	1½ ditto.
For every Quarter of Rye Grass Seed and Hay Seed..	0 2	
For every Four Quarters of ditto...................		1 ditto.
For every Twelve Bunches of Plaster Laths........	0 4	
For every Fifteen ditto............................		½ ditto.
For every Quarter of Wheat, Beans, Peas, Rye, Lentils, Barley, Malt, Oats, Rapeseed or Linseed....	0 6	½ ditto.
For all other Goods, Wares, &c. whatsoever........	2 8	3 per Ton, per Mile.

And so in Proportion for a greater or less Quantity than above.

If Goods remain on the Wharfs or in the Warehouses for more than Twenty-four Hours and not exceeding Six Days, the Company may charge the Owners Threepence per Ton, over and above the Tonnage Rates for the same.

Provision is also made for keeping the water of the River Ludd at a certain level, and for protecting the low lands between Tetney Haven and Alvington Out Fen. After the debt charged upon the work shall have been paid off, the commissioners and their successors, named and appointed in the act, may invest any part of the surplus monies, not exceeding £3,000 in each year, in the Public Funds or Exchequer Bills, as a fund for repairs.

There are other clauses for the protection of private property, which being such as are usually inserted, it is needless here to enumerate.

This, as far as it extends, is an useful work, and highly beneficial to the town of Louth, and the adjoining district.

LOYNE OR LUNE RIVER.

23 Geo. II. C. 12, R. A. 14th March, 1749.   12 Geo. III. C. 81, R. A. 1st April, 1772.
29 Geo. III. C. 39, R. A. 24th June, 1789.   47 Geo. III. C. 37, R. A. 1st Aug. 1807.

THE first enactment for improving the Loyne or Lune took place as far back as the year 1749, under the title of ' *An Act for* ' *improving the Navigation of the River Loyne, otherwise called* ' *Lune, and for building a Quay or Wharf, &c. ;*' wherein it is stated that the Loyne or Lune has become dangerous for navigators, and very inconvenient for the town and port of Lancaster, now becoming a place of considerable trade to the West Indies and other foreign parts; it is therefore necessary that a quay or wharf, with other conveniences, should be built on the west side of the river, and that buoys should be placed at the entrance into the said river and other places thereof, and land-marks erected for guiding ships and vessels to and from the said town; this act therefore appoints certain trustees to build a quay or wharf with other works and conveniences, and to erect piers or moles at the mouth of the said river, and for raising the necessary funds. The following rates are to be collected during twenty-one years for all ships and vessels coming into or going out of the port.

TONNAGE RATES.

	s.	d.	
For every Vessel trading to or from any Port or Place in Europe within the Streights or Mediterranean Sea, into or from any Port or Place in Africa, America or Greenland	1	0	per Ton.
For ditto trading to any Foreign Port in Europe, except Ireland, the Isle of Man or the Streights....................................	0	8	ditto.
For ditto to any Port or Place in Great Britain, South of Holly Head or North of the Mull of Galloway	0	6	ditto.
For ditto in Ireland or the Isle of Man.............................	0	4	ditto.
For ditto in Great Britain, North of Holly Head or South of the Mull of Galloway...	0	2	ditto.

For ditto coming into the River in Ballast and not lading or unlading in the Port,
One-fourth of the said Rates.
Vessels of War and Ships driven in by Stress of Weather, are exempt.

At the end of twenty-one years half the above rates are to cease. Trustees are empowered to borrow £2,000 on security of the duties, and to pay interest thereon at £5 per cent.

A second act was obtained in 1772, under the title of ' *An Act* ' *to explain and amend an Act made in the Twenty-third Year of the* ' *Reign of his late Majesty George the Second, for improving the*

'*Navigation of the River Loyne, otherwise called Lune, &c. &c. in*
'*the county palatine of Lancaster.*' By this act the rates of the
former act were confirmed, with power to the commissioners or
trustees, of lowering them when expedient to half the original
sums; the other clauses, merely confirming the former act, need
not be quoted.

The next application to parliament was made in 1789, when a
third act was obtained under title of '*An Act to explain, amend,*
'*and render more effectual several Acts, made in the Twenty-third*
'*of George the Second, and Twelfth of his present Majesty, for*
'*improving the Navigation of the River Loyne, otherwise called*
'*Lune, &c. &c. and for other Purposes therein mentioned.*' By this
act it is stated that the commissioners have borrowed £6,000 under
authority of the former acts, and have expended the same on the
works, as directed, and particularly on the making of a wet dock
at Glasson, and other improvements of the said river, in doing
which a debt of £1,560 has been contracted; and since it will be
advantageous to build a stone land-mark in place of the present
wood one at Rossall Point, as well as one or more light-houses
near Lancaster Bay, it is by this act provided that the rates levied
under the former acts shall be collected, together with the following

ADDITIONAL RATES.

	d.
For every Vessel trading to or from any Port or Place in Europe within the Streights or Mediterranean Sea, into or from any Port or Place in Africa, America or Greenland...	6 per Ton.
For ditto trading to any Foreign Port in Europe, except Ireland, the Isle of Man or the Streights...	4 ditto.
For ditto to any Port or Place in Great Britain, South of Holly Head or North of the Mull of Galloway...	3 ditto.
For ditto in Ireland or the Isle of Man...	2 ditto.
For ditto in Great Britain, North of Holly Head or South of the Mull of Galloway...	1 ditto.

These additional rates to cease when the sum of £2,500,
which this act directs to be borrowed, shall have been paid off,
and the old debt reduced to £4,000. One penny per ton is to be
paid by every vessel as a light-house duty, which sum shall be
applied to the maintenance of the said light-house; the overplus,
if any, to be employed in reducing the debt. By this act it is

also provided that the port of Lancaster shall from time to time be cleansed and scoured, and the entrance from the sea kept clear and open.

A fourth act was obtained in 1807, entitled, ' *An Act to ex-* ' *plain, amend, and render more effectual several Acts, for im-* ' *proving the Navigation of the River Loyne, otherwise Lune, and* ' *for building a Quay or Wharf near Lancaster, in the county pala-* ' *tine of Lancaster.*' By this act it appears that the commissioners cannot, out of the present rates, pay the interest, &c. due from their trust, or carry on and uphold the necessary works, they are therefore empowered to take, in lieu of all former rates, except the light-house dues, which are to continue the same, the following

TONNAGE RATES.

	s.	d.	
For every Vessel trading to or from any Port or Place in Europe within the Streights or Mediterranean Sea, into or from any Port or Place in Africa, America or Greenland....................	3	0	per Ton.
For ditto trading to any Foreign Port in Europe, except Ireland, the Isle of Man or the Streights......................................	2	0	ditto.
For ditto to any Port or Place in Great Britain, South of Holly Head or North of the Mull of Galloway.............................	1	6	ditto.
For ditto in Ireland or the Isle of Man.............................	1	0	ditto.
For ditto in great Britain, North of Holly Head or South of the Mull of Galloway..	0	6	ditto.

The same Exemptions as before are made by this Act, and Vessels conveying Coal or Fuel are also declared free from the Dues or Rates.

By this act the commissioners are empowered to appoint or license a sufficient number of pilots to conduct vessels in and out of the port, and to enforce the pilotage dues from all masters of vessels refusing to take on board a pilot, licensed according to the powers of this act.

MACCLESFIELD CANAL.

7 George IV. Cap. 30, Royal Assent 11th April, 1826.

During the progress of the Peak Forest Canal, it appeared desirable that another should be made between the summit levels of that work and of the Trent and Mersey Canal, thereby forming a more direct communication between the southern canals and the town of Manchester; no resolution, however, was come to on this subject before the year 1825, when a line was determined upon, under the direction of Mr. Telford, and in the following year parliamentary sanction was obtained under the title of ' *An Act for* ' *making and maintaining a navigable Canal from the Peak Forest* ' *Canal in the township of Marple, in the county palatine of* ' *Chester, to join the Canal Navigation from the Trent to the* ' *Mersey, at or near Hardings Wood Lock, in the township of Talk,* ' *or Talk-on-the-Hill, in the county of Stafford.*' By this act the company were incorporated by the name of " The Company of " Proprietors of the Macclesfield Canal."

The work, designed for the passage of narrow vessels of 7 feet wide, commences near the northern extremity of the summit level of the Peak Forest Canal, in the township of Marple, and passes upon that level through a very undulating part of the county of Chester, crossing at a considerable elevation several vallies whose streams afford it supplies of water; leaving Lime Hall on the east and Macclesfield on the west, it proceeds to the turnpike-road from Buxton to Congleton, having completed a distance of seventeen miles and a half; it then descends by locks to its lowest level, crossing the River Dane on the east of Congleton, and after pursuing a south-west direction to the Trent and Mersey Navigation, enters the summit level of that canal, making the total fall 113 feet 9 inches, and its total length twenty-nine miles, four furlongs and eleven poles.

The original estimate was £295,000, and the proprietors are empowered to raise by shares £300,000; should this be inadequate, they may raise a further sum of £100,000, on mortgage of the tolls.

By the act they are restricted from taking any water out of the summit levels of the Peak Forest Canal and of the Trent and Mersey, except under certain limitations. The canal is to be supplied with water from certain rivers, brooks, rivulets and water-courses, &c. but without injury to any mills thereon; and for the purpose of defining when the water shall be taken out, Mr. Nicholas Brown, of Wakefield, and Mr. Thomas Brown, of Manchester, civil engineers, are to determine under what state of the rivers, brooks, &c. the surplus water may be taken without injury to the mill-property thereon. Five reservoirs are to be constructed for the supply of the canal, and the following are fixed as tonnage rates.

2 E

TONNAGE RATES.

	d.	
For all Sand, Gravel, Paving-stones, Brick, Clay, Coal for burning Lime-stone, and Rubble-stone for Roads	1	per Ton, per Mile.
For all Ashler-stone, Slate, Flags, Spar, Coal, except for burning Lime, and other Materials.	1½	ditto. ditto.
For all Timber, Lime, Goods, Wares and all other Merchandizes, Articles, Matters and Things not mentioned above	2	ditto. ditto.

Fractions of a Ton and of a Mile to be taken as the Quarters therein, and of a Quarter as a Quarter.

Dung, Soil, Marl and Ashes of Coal or Turf for Land upon the Line, are exempt from Toll, provided no Lock be passed, or if passed, when the Water flows over the Waste Weir.

The advantages of this canal, when completed, will be seen from an inspection of the map, as it will be found to form the shortest line of communication between the Peak Forest and Trent and Mersey, and to lessen the distance thirteen miles between London and Manchester.

MAMHILAD RAILWAY.

54 George III. Cap. 101, Royal Assent 17th June, 1814.

THIS railroad, commencing in the Brecon and Abergavenny Canal, at an elevation of 447 feet above the level of the sea, runs in an easterly direction for a short distance, and then taking a detour, proceeds southerly to its termination near Usk Bridge, over the river at that place. The country abounds in limestone, and by means of this railroad an easy conveyance is found for this material and ironstone, which is also a produce of the neighbourhood.

As it is connected so intimately with the Abergavenny Canal, it will only be necessary here to quote the title of the act obtained for its completion, which is ' *An Act for making and* ' *maintaining a Tramroad or Railway from the parish of Mamhi-* ' *lad, in the county of Monmouth, to or near Usk Bridge, in the* ' *said county.*'

The railroad is five miles and three chains in length, and there is a descent, from its junction with the Brecon and Abergavenny Canal to Usk Bridge, of 308 feet 6 inches. The work was estimated by Mr. John Hodgkinson at £6,000, of which £4,150 were subscribed in shares of £50 each.

MANCHESTER, ASHTON AND OLDHAM CANAL.
(SEE ASHTON-UNDER-LYNE CANAL.)

MANCHESTER, BOLTON AND BURY CANAL.

31 George III. Cap. 68, Royal Assent 13th May, 1791.
45 George III. Cap. 4, Royal Assent 12th March, 1805.

THIS canal was projected for the purpose of making a communication, by narrow boats of 7 feet wide, between the towns whose names it bears; but by an agreement entered into in 1794, with the Leeds and Liverpool Canal Company, for making a junction at Redmoss, the proprietors of the Manchester, Bolton and Bury Canal were induced to make their canal capable of navigating vessels 14 feet wide, the same as those on the Leeds and Liverpool Canal.

By the first act obtained in 1791, and entitled, ' *An Act for* ' *making and maintaining a navigable Canal from Manchester to* ' *or near Presto-lee-Bridge, in the township of Little Lever, and* ' *from thence by one Branch to or near the town of Bolton, and by* ' *another Branch to or near the town of Bury, and to Weddell Brook* ' *in the parish of Bury, all in the county palatine of Lancaster,*' the proprietors were incorporated as " The Company of Proprie- " tors of the Canal Navigation from Manchester to Bolton and " to Bury." They were also empowered to make a canal from the River Irwell, near the Sugar House or Old Quay in Manchester, to a certain meadow near Presto-lee-Bridge, in the parish of Bolton, and from thence by one branch to Church Bridge in Bolton and to Bury Bridge in the parish of Bury, and from thence to Weddell Brook, in the same parish, and to make reservoirs, steam engines and other machines for supplying the same with water.

For completing the various works, the proprietors have power to raise £47,000, in shares of £100 each; and should this not prove sufficient they may raise a further sum of £20,000 either by themselves, or by the admission of new subscribers, or by mortgage. They are also empowered to demand the following tonnage rates.

TONNAGE RATES.

	d.	
For all Lime, Lime-stone, Clay, Bricks, Stone, Coal or other Minerals..................... }	2	per Ton, per Mile.
For all Timber, Goods, Wares, Merchandize and other Commodities..................... }	3	ditto. ditto.
For all Lime and Lime-stone, if passing the Locks when the Water flows over the Lock Weir, instead of the Rate above quoted .... }	$\frac{1}{2}$	ditto. ditto.
For all Coal, Clay, Bricks or Stones, except Lime-stone, not passing any Lock, in lieu of the above quoted Rate ..... }	$1\frac{1}{2}$	ditto. ditto.

Wharfage Rates to be determined by the Company.

A junction having been proposed between the Mersey and Irwell Navigation and this canal, it is provided, that the proprietors of the Mersey and Irwell Navigation are exempted from all rates for conveying stone on this canal, when the water flows over the lock weirs, such stone being for the repair of the banks, &c. of the said Mersey and Irwell Navigation; and the proprietors of this canal may lock down into the Mersey and Irwell without paying any rates or dues, for any distance between Hunt's Bank and Throstle Nest. When this company's vessels pass below the first lock on the Irwell, they are to pay the following

TONNAGE RATES.

	d.	
For all Coals, Stone, Lime, Lime-stone, Bricks, Slate, Iron and other Minerals..................... }	$\frac{1}{2}$	per Ton, per Mile.
For Timber and all other Goods.....................	1	ditto. ditto.

Additional Rates to the same Amount as above may be demanded by the Mersey and Irwell Company, when the Rate of Carriage between Liverpool and Manchester shall be Six Shillings per Ton.

Proprietors of mines may make cuts to communicate with the canal. Lords of manors, and proprietors of land on the line may build wharfs, cranes, weigh-beams and warehouses, and if not, then the company may build the same. Proprietors of wharfs may demand the following

WHARFAGE RATES.

	d.	
For all Coal, Lime, Lime-stone, Clay, Iron, Iron-stone, Timber, Stone, Brick, Tile, Slate, Flags, Sand or Gravel..................... }	1	per Ton.
For all other Goods.....................	3	ditto.

Coal, Iron and Lime-stone may remain for Three Weeks on the Wharf; the other Goods may remain not longer than Six Days, without paying an additional Sum of One Penny per Ton for the next Thirty Days.

The company having received the powers above recited, commenced their operations; but after having carried on the work for some time, it was found that not only the sums, directed

by the act to be raised, had been expended, but that a debt of
£31,345 was also incurred; they therefore applied a second time
to parliament and obtained an act, entitled, ' *An Act to enable the*
' *Company of Proprietors of the Canal Navigation from Manchester*
' *to Bolton and to Bury, to raise Money to complete the same.*' By
this act they were empowered to raise an additional sum of
£80,000 amongst themselves, for paying off the debt and for
completing the work; and for the readier obtaining of this sum,
they had authority to borrow any part thereof on mortgage. This
act having only the usual clauses, it is unnecessary to quote any
other part of it.

The direction of the canal is north-west; from its commencement in the Mersey and Irwell Navigation there is a rise to the
basin in Salford, of 68 feet 4 inches by six locks; thence it runs
nearly parallel with the Irwell on a level for about four miles; in
the next three miles there are twelve locks; the remaining part of
the line and the branch to Bury is level. The whole rise is 189
feet 6 inches. It crosses the Irwell by an aqueduct near to Clifton
Hall, and there are two other aqueducts, one over the River Roach,
not far from Darley Hall, and another over the Irwell near Bolton.
The length of the line is above fifteen miles. At first the canal
was designed, as stated above, for narrow boats, and some locks
were built accordingly; but these were afterwards pulled up and
rebuilt, and the canal widened. There is a feeder from the Irwell,
with a reservoir at Bury, and another at Radcliffe.

The work is of great utility, not only to the towns it connects, but
also to the adjacent country, abounding in coals and minerals, for
which it affords a ready conveyance; and also to the cotton trade
which is carried on very extensively in this part of Lancashire.

MANCHESTER AND OLDHAM RAILWAY.

7 George IV. Cap. 99, Royal Assent 26th May, 1826.

THE act for making this railway was obtained in the year 1826,
under title of ' *An Act for making and maintaining a Railway or*
' *Tramroad from Manchester to Oldham, with a Branch from*
' *Failsworth Pole, to or near to Dry Clough, in the township of*

' *Royton, all in the county palatine of Lancaster ;*' whereby the proprietors are incorporated as " The Manchester and Oldham " Railway Company," with powers to make and maintain a railway or tramroad, for carriages to be moved by stationary or locomotive steam engines or other power, commencing in St. George's Road, Manchester, and passing through Manchester, Newton, Failsworth, Prestwich-cum-Oldham, Woodpark and Knott Lanes in the parish of Ashton-under-Lyne, and terminating at the Manchester and Austerlands Turnpike Road, at Mumps Brook, in the parish of Oldham. Also a branch from Failsworth Pole to Dry Clough in the township of Royton, and all inclined planes, steam engines, wharfs, warehouses and all other buildings, &c. necessary for the same. For executing these powers, the company may raise a capital of £75,000, in shares of £100 each, together with a further sum of £20,000 on mortgage, should the former amount prove insufficient to complete the work. The following are to be collected as

TONNAGE RATES.

	d.		
For all Lime, Dung, Earth, Compost, Manure, Materials for Roads drawn and carried by the Company..............	2	per Ton, per Mile.	
For ditto only drawn or propelled by their Engines..........	1¼	ditto.	ditto.
For ditto drawn or propelled by the Company's Engines, but in the Waggons of other Persons.......................	1	ditto.	ditto.
For all Coal, Culm, Coke, Charcoal, Cinders, Stone, Clay, Lime, Marl, Sand, Building, Pitching and Paving-stones, Flags, Bricks, Tiles, Slates, Earth, Staves, Deal, Lead, Iron in Pigs and other Metals drawn or propelled and carried by the Company...................................	3	ditto.	ditto.
For ditto only drawn or propelled by their Engines.........	2½	ditto.	ditto.
For ditto drawn by their Engines in Waggons of other Persons	2	ditto.	ditto.
For all Timber, Cotton, Wool, Hides, Drugs, Dye Woods, Sugar, Corn, Grain, Flour, Manufactured Goods, Lead in Sheets, Iron in Bars, and all other Wares, Merchandizes, Matters or Things drawn or propelled and carried by the Company......................................	3½	ditto.	ditto.
For ditto only drawn or propelled by their Engines.........	3	ditto.	ditto.
For ditto drawn by their Engines in Waggons of other Persons	2½	ditto.	ditto.
For all Goods, Wares and Merchandize, and all other Commodities, Matters and Things, and for all Carriages conveying Passengers or Cattle, carried upon any Inclined Plane where the same shall be conveyed by Steam Power	6 ditto, at each Plane.		
For ditto when not conveyed by Steam Power..............	3	ditto.	ditto.
For every Person passing in or on any Carriage on the Railway, Branches or Parts thereof	2½	per Mile each.	
For every Horse, Mule, Ass or other Beast of Burden, and for every Ox, Bull, Cow or Cattle carried in such Carriage	1½	ditto.	
For every Calf, Sheep, Lamb or Pig ditto....................	¼	ditto.	

Fractions of a Ton and of a Mile as the Quarters in them, and of a Quarter as a Quarter.

Parcels not exceeding Five Hundred Weight, to pay Rates to be fixed by the Company.

The company are to build, at their own cost, a sufficient bridge over the Rochdale Canal in Failsworth, and another over the Ashton-under-Lyne Canal from Manchester to Hollinwood. Lords of manors may erect wharfs and warehouses, and if they refuse, the company may do so, and charge the following

WHARFAGE AND WAREHOUSING RATES.

	s.	d.	
For all Coals, Culm, Lime, Lime-stone, and other Minerals, Timber, Stone, Clay, Tiles, Bricks, Slate, Goods, Merchandize or other Things, not remaining more than Seventy-two Hours on the Wharfs	0	1	per Ton.
For ditto beyond Seventy-two Hours on the Wharf	0	1	ditto, per Week.
For ditto Warehousing	0	6	ditto. ditto.
For the use of Cranes, at One Lift under Two Tons	0	6	ditto.
For ditto under Three Tons................................	1	0	ditto.
For ditto under Four Tons	1	6	ditto.

And so on, advancing Sixpence per Ton additional.

This railway which was expected to be of great utility in conveying coals from Greenacre Moor to Manchester, and merchandize throughout the populous district on its line, turns out not to answer the expectations of the proprietors; and it is reported that all or a considerable part of it will be abandoned. It is to commence, as before stated, in St. George's Road, Manchester; thence pursuing a north-easterly course and running nearly parallel with the turnpike-road, is to terminate at Mumps Brook, about half a mile on the east side of Oldham.

MANSFIELD AND PINXTON RAILWAY.

57 George III. Cap. 37, Royal Assent 16th June, 1817.

THE Mansfield and Pinxton Railway, commencing in the town of Mansfield, proceeds from thence in a westerly direction, leaving Skegby Hall, Unwins Hall and Brook House on the north, to Pinxton Basin near to Pinxton Mills, and not far from Alfreton in the county of Derby, where it communicates with a branch of the Cromford Canal; about a mile and a half from this point a branch passes easterly towards Codnor Park Works, which it passes, and communicates again with the Cromford Canal at a short distance from those works, at $278\frac{1}{2}$ feet above the level of the sea.

The act for this undertaking was passed in 1817, as ' *An Act*
' *for making and maintaining a Railway or Tramroad from Bull's*
' *Head Lane, in the parish of Mansfield, in the county of Not-*
' *tingham, to communicate with the Cromford Canal, at Pinxton*
' *Basin, in the parish of Pinxton, in the county of Derby.*' By it
the proprietors, who are styled " The Mansfield and Pinxton
" Railway Company," are empowered to make the road and to
alter, repair, and manufacture materials for the same; for doing
which they are to raise the sum of £22,800, in shares of £100
each; and in case that should not prove sufficient for completing
the same, they may raise an additional fund of £10,000 amongst
themselves, or by creating new shares, or by mortgage of the
work and tolls. The following are to be demanded as

TONNAGE RATES.

	s.	d.		
For all Stone for repairing Roads and for all Manure.......	0	2	per Ton, per Mile.	
For all Stone, Cinders, Chalk, Marl, Sand, Lime, Clay, Ashes, Peat, Lime-stone, Iron-stone and other Materials, Building-stone, Pitching and Paving-stone, Bricks, Tiles, Slates, Timber, Lead in Pigs or Sheets, Bar-iron, Waggon-tire, all Gross and Unmanufactured Articles and Building Materials....................................	0	3	ditto.	ditto.
For all Coal, Coke and Slack carried into the parish of Mansfield along any Part of the Railroad..............	2	0	ditto.	
For ditto in that Direction but not into that Parish........	0	3	ditto.	ditto.
For ditto towards or to the Cromford Canal at Pinxton Basin	0	3	ditto.	ditto.
For all other Goods, Wares and Merchandize..............	0	6	ditto.	ditto.

Fractions of a Ton and of a Mile to pay as the Quarters therein, and of a Quarter as a Quarter.

Carriage of Parcels, not exceeding Five Hundred Weight, to be fixed by the Proprietors.

Owners of land on the line, and lords of manors are to erect
wharfs, on their own lands, if required by the company; and in
case of refusal the company may do so. The company is also
directed by the act to build sufficient wharfs, warehouses and
landing places at Pinxton, for the reception of goods; and for the
expenses so incurred they are to demand as

WHARFAGE RATES.

	d.	
For all Packages not exceeding Fifty-six Pounds in Weight............	1	each.
For ditto Five Hundred Weight......................................	2	ditto.
For all above the last quoted Weight.....................................	6	per Ton.

Private individuals building wharfs and warehouses are authorized to claim the following as wharfage rates.

d.

For all Coals, Culm, Lime-stone, Clay, Iron, Iron-stone, Lead-ore or } 1 per Ton.
   other Ores, Timber, Stone, Bricks, Tiles, Slates and Gravel.........}

For all other Goods and Merchandizes .... 2 ditto.

If the said Goods shall remain above Twenty-one Days, then One Penny per Ton additional is to be paid for the succeeding Ten Days, and a further Sum of One Penny per Ton per Day for every Day afterwards.

The railway is double; the length, eight miles, two furlongs and four chains. At the commencement in Mansfield it is 101 feet 8 inches above the level of the Cromford Canal at Pinxton Basin; from Mansfield to the summit level there is a rise of 88 feet 10 inches; from the summit to the Pinxton Basin, a distance of four miles and nine hundred and twenty yards, there is a fall of 80 feet 10 inches; the railway at its termination there, being 8 feet above the level of the canal.

This work cannot fail of being useful, passing as it does through a country abounding with minerals, and where no other line of conveyance exists.

MARKET WEIGHTON CANAL.

12 George III. Cap. 37, Royal Assent 21st May, 1772.

THE Market Weighton Canal is of a two-fold benefit to the country through which it passes, affording an easy mode of conveying agricultural and other produce, more especially that beautiful fine white durable brick, usually called Walling Fen Brick; and at the same time draining the low lands and fens which abound in its vicinity. Its length is rather more than eleven miles, commencing at a point called New River Head, near Market Weighton, and pursuing an almost straight line from north to south, and passing through the parishes of Blacktoft, Everingham, Seaton, Ross, Holme-upon-Spalding Moor, Frog-gathorp, Hootham, and other places of minor importance, to the extensive fen, which is called Walling Fen, and contains twenty thousand acres of land; it then terminates by locking down into the Humber, at Fossdike Clough, opposite the mouth of the Trent. The whole line, as may be concluded from the nature of the country it passes through, is low and flat; there is, however, a little elevation near Market Weighton, and a lock on the Warren at Wolsea, besides the sea lock at its opening into the Humber.

The act for executing this useful work is entitled, ' *An Act for* ' *draining and preserving certain Commons, Low Grounds, and* ' *Carrs, in the parish of Market Weighton, and other adjacent* ' *parishes in the East Riding of the County of York; and for* ' *making a navigable Cut or Canal, from Market Weighton to the* ' *River Humber.*' By this act certain persons are appointed as trustees or commissioners for executing the work and other purposes connected therewith, to have the direction and management of the drainage and navigation, and from time to time to tax or assess the owners and occupiers of the low lands, according to the number of acres they occupy, for the benefit they receive from the said drainage, such acre-tax not to exceed forty shillings per acre; the proceeds to be employed in maintaining and completing the same. They are also empowered to inclose part of the commons or waste lands, for defraying the tax. They also have power to take away, if necessary, certain drains or sewers, and, if requisite, others may be substituted and maintained out of their funds. The locks, to be erected, are not at any time to pen up the water higher than within 3 feet of the surface of the land. The commissioners are empowered to demand for the navigation of the main drain or canal, the following

TONNAGE RATES.

	s.	d.	
For all Groceries, Goods, Wares, Merchandize and Commodities	4	0	per Ton.
For Stone	1	0	ditto.
For Manure	0	6	ditto.
For Coals, each Chaldron containing Thirty-two Bushels	2	0	per Chaldron.
For Lime ditto	1	6	ditto.
For Tiles	2	0	per Thousand.
For Bricks	1	0	ditto.
For Wool, each Pack containing Sixteen Stones	0	8	per Pack.
For Wheat, Rye, Beans, Peas, Lentils, Barley, Oats, Malt, or any Seeds or Grain whatsoever }	0	8	per Quarter.
For Flour, each Sack containing Five Bushels	0	6	per Sack.

And so on in Proportion for a less Distance than the whole Line, as may be agreed on by the Commissioners.

Certain persons having agreed to advance money for the immediate execution of the work, it is provided, that they shall receive a share of the rates, equal to the proportion of money by them so contributed, together with interest on the sums advanced.

The commissioners may also tax the lands to the extent of five shillings per acre, for maintaining the canal and drainage, and for the payment of salaries and other expenses. The accounts of the drainage and of the navigation are to be kept separate.

Mr. Whitworth was the engineer. The work is well suited for the purposes intended, and highly beneficial to the town of Market Weighton and the neighbouring district.

MEDWAY RIVER.

17 Char. II. C. 6, R. A. 2nd Mar. 1664.   14 Geo. II. Cap. 26, R. A. 29th Apr. 1740.
32 Geo. III. C. 105, R. A. 15th June, 1792.   42 Geo. III. Cap. 94, R. A. 22nd June, 1802.
5 Geo. IV. C. 148, R. A. 21st June, 1824.

It will not be necessary in the present instance to take particular notice of the first and second acts relating to this river, which were passed in the 17th of Charles II. and the 14th George II. more than to state that by these acts a company was incorporated under title of " The Company of Proprietors of the Naviga- " tion of the River Medway;" we shall therefore commence our remarks by quoting the act passed in 1792, entitled, ' *An Act for* ' *improving the Navigation of the River Medway, from the town of* ' *Maidstone, through the several parishes of Maidstone, Boxley,* ' *Allington and Aylesford, in the county of Kent.*'

By this act certain persons were named as a committee for improving the navigation of the Medway, from the lock in Maidstone to the lower part of an orchard belonging to Mr. G. Hunt, Jun. on the west side of the river below Aylesford Bridge, in Kent. They have the requisite powers for enlarging, widening and rendering straight the channel of the said river, and to make all necessary bridges, tunnels, and dams; they may also, with consent of the quarter sessions, alter or rebuild Aylesford Bridge, and make a collateral cut from a shoal in the river, called Preston Shelf, below the town of Maidstone, on the east side of the river, to any part of the same above and near the said bridge; they may likewise build a bridge or establish a ferry at Castle Shelf, purchasing the site thereof of Lord Romney; and for defraying all necessary expenses they are empowered to demand the following tonnage rates.

TONNAGE RATES.

	d.	
For Stone, Chalk and Manure...................................	1	per Ton.
For Lime...	2	ditto.
For all other Goods, Wares and Merchandize......................	3	ditto.
For Coal	2	per Chaldron.

Timber, Knee Timber, Planks and Pannels are free from Dues; and Goods, Wares, &c. belonging the Inhabitants of Aylesford, and landed at the German Forestall, are exempted from Rates; and all Goods landed or shipped at Castle Shelf, shall only pay Half the above Rates.

The committee may also borrow £8,000, for the purposes of this act, on the credit of the tolls and rates.

This act was repealed and a new one granted in 1802, under the title of ' *An Act for repealing an Act passed in the Thirty-* ' *second of his present Majesty, for improving the Navigation of the* ' *River Medway, from the town of Maidstone, through the several* ' *parishes of Maidstone, Boxley, Allington, and Aylesford, in the* ' *county of Kent, and for the better and more effectual improving the* ' *Navigation of the said River;'* whereby the proprietors are incorporated afresh as " The Company of Proprietors of the Lower " Navigation of the River Medway," and are empowered to improve and maintain the navigation and towing-paths, and execute other works entrusted to the committee under the former acts; they may also provide money for expenses by shares of £100 each; £5,000 to be thus raised in addition to the former sum of £8,000; or any part of the said £5,000, or the whole thereof, may be raised on mortgage; the following are directed to be levied as

TONNAGE RATES.

	d.	
For Stone, Chalk and Manure, except Lime	1½	per Ton.
For Lime, Timber, Deals, Bricks and Iron	4	ditto.
For all other Goods, Wares and Merchandize....................	6	ditto.
For Coals	4	per Chaldron.

The rights of the persons incorporated under the act of Charles II. are to be reserved, as far as they are authorized to scour, cleanse and deepen the Medway from below Shepherd's Wharf in Maidstone; and the said persons, who in that act were styled " The Company of Proprietors of the Navigation of the River " Medway," may convey all goods, &c. on paying the rates first quoted in this article. The proprietors are restricted by this act from dividing more than £10 per cent. on their shares; when the profits amount to more, then the rates are to be forthwith reduced.

Another act was obtained in 1824, entitled, ' *An Act for the* ' *more effectually improving the Navigation of the River Medway,* ' *from Maidstone to Halling in the county of Kent, and to alter* ' *and enlarge the Powers of an Act of the Forty-second of his late* ' *Majesty, for improving the Navigation of the said River.*'

Having recited the title of the former act, the present one goes on to state that the company have raised a capital stock of £16,000, and have expended the whole thereof, besides contracting sundry debts in the execution of the works directed by the said act, and that the company cannot, in consequence, effect that improvement of the navigation which is required by the interests of the parties concerned therein; they are therefore authorized by this act to borrow £12,000 on mortgage of the rates, and to make and maintain a cut or canal from Ozier Bed Reach to East Malling, and another from Haystack Hole to Occupells; to remove Preston Shoal; to alter Aylesford Bridge, and to make a towing-path from Occupells to Lower Town Wharf in St. Faith's Street, Maidstone.

They are also empowered to cleanse, scour, deepen and improve the channel of the river from Maidstone to Halling, through the parishes of Maidstone, Boxley, Allington, Aylesford, Ditton, East Malling, Burham, Birling Snodland, Wouldham and Halling.

The shoals and obstructions in the river are to be removed so as to leave it 90 feet wide and 3 feet deep in the middle; then Aylesford Bridge is to be altered; afterwards the navigable cut from Ozier Bed Reach to Newhythe and the towing-path from Haystack Hole to Maidstone are to be completed. All this is to be done within five years; and in case sufficient should remain, out of the sum of £12,000 and any interest thereon, it is to be employed in making the navigable cut from Haystack Hole to Occupells, within five years afterwards; if a sufficient sum does not remain, the residue is to accumulate for that purpose. In lieu of the former rates, which are repealed, the following are to be taken as tonnage rates.

TONNAGE RATES.

		d.	
For Stones, Chalk, Sand and Manure	....	2½	per Ton.
For Lime, Timber, Deals, Bricks and Iron	....	6	ditto.
For all other Goods, Wares and Things whatsoever	....	10	ditto.
For Coals	....	6	per Chaldron.

Pleasure Boats and Boats used for Husbandry are to pass without paying Tolls.

The company are not to divide above £7, 10s. per cent. on their shares in any one year; but the excess, if any, is to be applied to the completion of the works, and after that to the paying off the debts due by the company. And when the mortgage debts are paid off, the tolls are to be reduced as below.

REDUCED RATES.

		d.	
For Stones, Chalk, Sand and Manure	....	1¾	per Ton.
For Lime, Timber, Deals, Bricks and Iron	....	4¼	ditto.
For all other Goods	....	7	ditto.
For Coals	....	4½	per Chaldron.

The exemptions mentioned in the former act are continued in this, as are also the rights of the Medway Navigation Company, who are to pay for navigating the whole or any part of the Lower Navigation, the following

TONNAGE RATES.

		d.	d.	
For Stone	....	2	1¼	per Ton.
For Chalk and Manure	....	1	1	ditto.
For Lime	....	3	2¼	ditto.
For all other Goods, &c.	....	5	3½	ditto.
For Coal	....	4	2½	per Chaldron.

And when the mortgage debt is paid off, then these rates also are to be reduced to the amount above-stated in the second column.

This is a work of considerable utility, and one which has added greatly to the facilities of water carriage; and when the intended Weald Canal is made, will be a means of bringing the produce of the southern part of Kent to the great victualling place of Chatham.

In consequence of the recent discovery of a very valuable quarry of building stone on the south side of this river near Penshurst, a company, unconnected with the proprietors of the Medway Navigation, have at very considerable expense rendered this river navigable from Tunbridge up to Penshurst Bridge, by widening, deepening and straightening, and by making a cut of about a mile in length through the estate of Sir John Sidney, Bart.

By this means the navigation of this fine river is extended about six miles further into the interior; and as good building stone is a rare commodity within this distance of the metropolis, it will doubtless amply repay the spirited individuals who have, without any parliamentary enactment, produced the means by which it may be introduced to market.

MERSEY RIVER.

45 George III. Cap. 62, Royal Assent 27th June, 1805.

This may properly be considered a private bill, being only passed to enable Joseph White, Esq. lord of the manor of Higher Bebington, owner of property on the Cheshire and Lancashire sides of the River Mersey, and proprietor of the Rock Ferry House at Liverpool, to demand rates for the passage of the river there, and to erect slips, wharfs and piers on both sides for the convenience of passengers and goods conveyed over the said river. The following are the

FERRY RATES.

	d.	
For all Persons passing over..	1	each.
For all Calves, Pigs and Sheep..	1	ditto.
For all Bulls, Cows, Steers or Heifers................................	2	ditto.
For all Horses, Mares, Geldings, Colts, Fillies, Mules or other Beasts..	3	ditto.
For all Wheels of Carts, Coaches, Chaises or other Carriages..........	6	ditto.
For all Marl, Manure, Stone, Lime and other Articles................	1	per Ton.
For all other Goods, Wares and Merchandize, Corn and other Articles of Provision excepted	1	per Cwt.
For Corn	1	per Sack.
For every Hamper or Basket of Fowls, Potatoes and other Vegetables, not carried on the Knee of a Passenger.............................	1½	each.
If so carried...		No charge.

If the piers, &c. are not kept up, the tolls are to cease. The daily use of the ferry stamps its utility; but as it does not come within the scope of this publication, any further observations are unnecessary.

MERSEY AND IRWELL NAVIGATION.

7 George I. Cap. 15, Royal Assent 17th June, 1720.
34 George III. Cap. 37, Royal Assent 28th March, 1794.

THE first attempt towards making navigable the Rivers Mersey and Irwell from Liverpool to Manchester, was the obtaining an act in the year 1720, under the title of ' *An Act for making* ' *the Rivers Mersey and Irwell navigable, from Manchester to* ' *Liverpool, in the county palatine of Lancaster.*' By this act certain persons were appointed undertakers, with power to scour and cleanse the rivers, and to make the necessary cuts and branches, build bridges, sluices, locks and weirs; all these necessary works were done, and a navigable communication made between Liverpool and Manchester, to the incalculable benefit of those towns; and for defraying the cost of such works, the undertakers are empowered to demand the following

TONNAGE RATES.

	s.	*d.*
For all Coal, Cannel, Stone, Slate, Timber or other Goods, Wares and Merchandizes, conveyed between Bank Quay and Hunt's Bank in Manchester	3	4 per Ton.

Dung, Marl and Manure carried on the Navigation for the use of the Owners or Occupiers of Lands within the Distance of Five Miles from the said Rivers, are free from the Rates; and since the River Mersey has been before navigable from Liverpool to Bank Quay, all Goods, Wares and Merchandize passing between those two Places, are not to be liable to the Rates.

This act was amended in 1794, by another act, entitled, ' *An* ' *Act for altering an Act passed in the Seventh of George the First,* ' *entitled, An Act for making the Rivers Mersey and Irwell navi-* ' *gable, from Liverpool to Manchester, in the county palatine of* ' *Lancaster ; by incorporating the Proprietors of the said Naviga-* ' *tion, and to declare their respective Shares therein to be personal* ' *Property.*' By this second act, the undertakers and other persons therein named are incorporated as " The Company of Proprietors " of the Mersey and Irwell Navigation," and are invested with the powers of the former act; the navigation, its tonnage rates and duties, buildings, wharfs, warehouses, quays and all other appurtenances thereto belonging are granted to the said company, as are also all boats, barges, vessels and other effects, matters and things pertaining to the same.

Commencing on the west side of the town of Manchester, at 93¼ feet above the level of the sea, the Irwell takes a very sinuous course to the west, passing Chat Moss and uniting with the Mersey after having left Flixton House to the east; from their junction the united rivers continue their progress towards Liverpool, making many turnings in their course to Warrington, at a short distance from which town a navigable cut called the Mersey and Irwell Canal opening from the rivers takes a course nearly south for a short distance, then turning to the south and again to the south-east and passing Norton Priory, it enters the estuary of the Mersey at Runcorn Gap. From Warrington the united rivers make a great detour to the south and back again northward, after which they open into the estuary before-mentioned near Sankey Bridge. Owing to the very winding course of the rivers, the length of this navigation may be reckoned fifty miles, but the distance is in many places shortened by side-cuts across the loops or bends. The elevation is not great, the whole rise being only 70 feet. The various canals and navigations connected with the Mersey and Irwell, or so near as to make a communication extremely easy, render this an undertaking of vast importance and utility.

The navigation, for which the acts quoted were obtained, has been one of very great cost to the proprietors; in many instances, as will be seen on the map, cuts of considerable dimensions have been made to shorten the winding course of the river; the want of water, also, which was severely felt in dry seasons, has been another source of expense to the undertakers; they have however conducted the work with great spirit and perseverance; and when their expensive works near Runcorn Gap are completed, this navigation will be one of the first importance.

MONKLAND CANAL.

10 George III. Cap. 105, Royal Assent 12th April, 1770.

THE act for executing this work was obtained so long back as the year 1770, under the title of ' *An Act for making and main-* ' *taining a navigable Cut or Canal and Waggon Way, from the*

2 F

' *Collieries in the parish of Old and New Monkland, to the city of*
' *Glasgow.*' By this act the proprietors are incorporated as " The
" Company of Proprietors of the Monkland Navigation," and are
empowered to raise £10,000, in shares of £100 each; and in case
this should prove inadequate to the completion of the work, then
the further sum of £5,000 may be subscribed. The following are
the authorized

TONNAGE AND WHARFAGE RATES.

	d.	
For all Coals, Stones, Timber, Dung, Fuel, and all other Goods, Wares and Merchandize whatever, conveyed on the Canal	1	per Ton, per Mile.
For ditto on the Waggon Way	1	ditto. ditto.
Limestone	½	ditto. ditto.
Ironstone	¼	ditto. ditto.

Gravel, Paving-stones and other Materials, except Limestone for repairs of Roads, and Dung, Soil, Marl and all Sorts of Manure for improving Lands and Grounds, are exempted from the Rates.

The Monkland Canal begins at Old Monkland Coal Works, about 290 feet above the level of the sea, and proceeds in a course nearly direct from east to west, to Glasgow, where it communicates with a branch of the Forth and Clyde Canal, 156½ feet above the sea level. In its course it receives the Monkland and Kirkintilloch, Garnkirk and Glasgow, and Airdrie Railroads, thus opening an easy way for the transit of coals and the import of other goods into the interior.

The intent of this work, as the preamble of the act declares, is to facilitate the conveyance of coal, &c. from the interior parts of the country, and to make a better communication between the collieries in the parishes of Old and New Monkland to the city of Glasgow, and it has answered the original intention and fully proved the utility of the work.

MONKLAND AND KIRKINTILLOCH RAILWAY.

(SEE KIRKINTILLOCH, OR MONKLAND AND KIRKINTILLOCH RAILWAY.)

MONMOUTH RAILWAY.

50 George III. Cap. 123, Royal Assent 24th May, 1810.

THE act for this work, obtained in 1810, and entitled, ' *An* ' *Act for making and maintaining a Railway from Howler Slade* ' *in the Forest of Dean, in the county of Gloucester, to the town of* ' *Monmouth; and for making other Railways therein mentioned, in* ' *the county of Gloucester and Monmouth;*' provides for the making of a railway or tramroad from Howler Slade in the Forest of Dean, by the villages of Newland and Redbrook and the town of Coleford to May Hill, near Monmouth, or to a place in the said town of Monmouth, extending north-eastward from Wyebridge to the Nag's Head near Dixon Gate, by passing the bridge over the Wye or by passing the river itself by a boat; and also to make branches out of the said main railway, viz. one from Winnall's Hill southwards to Winnall Colliery, with a collateral line to the mine in Clear-Well-Mead; another line from the same place northward to Wymberry Slade; one from the said line at Swan Pool to the village of Staunton; one other from the same in Lord's Grove to Redbrook Tin Mines, there branching into two railways, one extending to Lower Redbrook Tin Mines, the other to the Wye at Cinder Bank in Newland, there crossing the river to Pool Dee in the parish of Penallt, in the county of Monmouth, and also the necessary wharfs; thus rendering easy the communication between those several places, and facilitating the conveyance of coal, stone and other products of the said forest.

The proprietors are incorporated as " The Monmouth Railway " Company," with the usual powers, and have authority to raise £22,000, in shares of £50 each; and should this prove insufficient, they may borrow £6,000 additional, by promissory notes or mortgage; and when the Lydney and Lidbrook (now the Severn and Wye) Railway Company shall have completed certain branches mentioned in their act, then the present company may unite their works therewith, on the payment of a yearly rent of £50 to the aforesaid company. They are also empowered to collect the following tonnage rates.

2 F 2

TONNAGE RATES.

		d.
For all Stone for the repairs of any Turnpike-Roads, Streets or Highways; Lime for Manure and all other Manure	}	8 per Ton.
For all Coal, Coke, Culm, and for all other Stone, Coal, Cinders, Chalk, Marl, Sand, Lime, Clay, Ashes, Peat, Limestone, Pitching and Paving-stone, (not being for Manure, or for the repair of any Turnpike-Roads, Streets or Highways) Iron-stone, Iron or other Ore and other Minerals, and Brick, the Produce of the said Forest, which shall be carried or borne on the said Railways, from any Place within the said Forest, and not passing beyond Staunton Lane End, in Coleford, or to any other Place of less Distance than aforesaid, at which such Goods shall be deposited for Sale, or to be from thence conveyed by any other Means than on the said Railway or Railways	}	6 ditto
For all Coal, Coke, Culm, and for all Stone, Coal, Cinders, Chalk, Marl, Sand, Lime, Clay, Ashes, Peat, Lime-stone, Pitching and Paving-stone, (not being for Manure, or for the repair of any Turnpike-Roads, Streets or Highways) Iron-stone, or other Ore and other Minerals, and Bricks, the Produce of the said Forest, which shall be borne or carried from the said Place called Staunton Lane End, along the said Railways or either of them	}	6 per Ton, per Mile.
For all Goods, Commodities, Wares or Merchandizes whatsoever carried from Redbrook aforesaid, to or near Pool Dee aforesaid, or back again from thence to the River Wye....	}	6 ditto.
For every Carriage conveying Passengers, or light Goods or Parcels, not exceeding Five Hundred Weight	}	6 per Mile.
For all other Goods, Commodities, Wares and Merchandizes whatsoever carried on the said Railways or either of them, whether the Produce of the said Forest or not	}	6 per Ton, per Mile.

Fractions of a Ton and a Mile to be reckoned as the Quarters therein, and of a Quarter as a Quarter.

Coal brought up the Lines of the Lydney and Lidbrook Company to pay only Three-fourths of the above Rates, except those carried from Redbrook to Pool Dee.

Several clauses are inserted for preservation of the timber in the forest, and for securing his Majesty's rights to shares of the mines. Inspectors are to be appointed by the King's Surveyor General for searching suspicious persons and their carriages, for the maintenance of which inspectors and for the enjoyment of certain privileges, the proprietors are to pay certain annual and weekly rentals or allowances. Wharfs, &c. may be erected by the company, who are to receive according to the annexed scale of wharfage rates.

WHARFAGE RATES.

		d.
For Coals, Culm, Lime, Lime-stone, Clay, Iron, Tin-plates, Iron-stone, Lead and other Ores, Timber, Stone, Bricks, Tiles, Slates, Gravel, Hay, Straw, Corn, Corn in the Straw or Manure....................	}	1 per Ton.
For all other Goods, Wares, Merchandizes or Things whatsoever.......		3 ditto.

None but the first enumerated Articles may remain on the Wharfs above Six Days, but these may lie thereon for One Month on the Payment of Sixpence per Ton. After the other Articles have remained Ten Days more than the Six before-mentioned, they shall pay One Penny per Ton, and One Penny per Ton for every further Day

An inspection of the map will shew that the plan is well designed to answer the purposes of the subscribers thereto.

MONMOUTHSHIRE CANAL.

32 George III. Cap. 102, Royal Assent 3rd June, 1792.
37 George III. Cap. 100, Royal Assent 4th July, 1797.
42 George III. Cap. 115, Royal Assent 26th June, 1802.

THIS extensive undertaking of canal and railroads, for the company have powers to construct both, was first authorized by the legislature in 1792, by ' *An Act for making and maintaining a* ' *navigable Cut or Canal from or from some Place near, Pont-* ' *newynydd into the River Usk, at or near the town of Newport, and* ' *a collateral Cut or Canal from the same, at or near a Place called* ' *Cryndaw Farm, to or near to Crumlin Bridge, all in the county of* ' *Monmouth; and for making and maintaining Railways or Stone* ' *Roads from such Cuts or Canals to several Iron Works and Mines,* ' *in the county of Monmouth and Brecknock.*' By this act the proprietors are empowered to raise £120,000, in shares of £100 each, and a further sum of £60,000, if required. The company is designated " The Company of Proprietors of the Monmouth-" shire Canal Navigation," and has power to make new railways to iron-works, limestone quarries, or coal mines within eight miles of the line of their canal. The proprietors commenced their undertaking under the superintendence of Mr. J. Dadford, Jun. the engineer who made the estimate; and the work proceeded, but it afterwards being found advantageous to extend the original design, a second act was obtained in 1797, under the title of ' *An Act for* ' *extending the Monmouthshire Canal Navigation, and for explain-* ' *ing and amending an Act passed in the Thirty-second of his* ' *present Majesty, for making the said Canal.*' The powers of this last act, however, were soon found insufficient for the purposes designed, a third was therefore obtained in 1802, entitled, ' *An Act* ' *for making and maintaining certain Railways to communicate with* ' *the Monmouthshire Canal Navigation, and for enabling the* ' *Company of Proprietors of that Navigation to raise a further* ' *Sum of Money to complete their Undertaking, and for explaining* ' *and amending the Acts passed in the Thirty-second and Thirty-*

' *Seventh of his present Majesty, relating thereto.*' By this act the proprietors were enabled to borrow a further sum of money, and to make additional railways communicating with their canal. Five per cent. of the clear profits of the undertaking are to be invested in government securities, till a fund of £1,000 shall have accumulated for repairs of the works. The rates on various articles are to be reduced, when the proprietors are able to divide £10 per cent. on their shares, and coal is the first article so to be reduced; but when the dividend shall fall below £10 per cent. then the rates are to be advanced again. The following are the

TONNAGE RATES.

	d.	
Iron-stone, Iron-ore, Lead-ore, Coal, Coke, Culm, Stone-coal, Cinders, Charcoal, Lime, if not intended for Manure; Tiles, Bricks, Lime-stone, Flags and other Stone, conveyed on the Canal or Railways	2½	per Ton, per Mile.
Hay, Straw, Corn in the Straw, Materials for Roads, Lime and other Manures	1½	ditto. ditto.
Iron, Lead, Timber and all other Goods, Wares and Merchandize	5	ditto. ditto.
Horses, Mules or Asses passing the Toll-Gates on the Railroads	1	each.
Cows, Horned or Neat Cattle ditto	½	ditto.

Vessels not to pass the Locks, unless the Water flows over the Waste Weir above, without special Permission.

The whole sum raised under the different acts amount to £275,330, in £100 shares. The company made nine miles of the Sirhowey Railroad, of which distance they receive the rates; they have also an annual rent of £110 from the Sirhowey Company, for allowing them to connect their railroad with these works; and they allowed £3,000 to the Brecknock and Abergavenny Company for permission to unite with that work.

This canal and its branches and railroads commence in the Usk River, not a great distance below the town of Newport, close to the termination of the Rumney and Sirhowey Railroads; passing on in a direction nearly full north and leaving Newport to the east, the canal extends by Pontypool to Pontnewynydd, a distance of more than seventeen miles and three quarters. Near this place it connects with the Abergavenny and Brecknock Canal. In its course it passes Malpas, opposite which at Crynda-Farm, is a branch canal to Crumlin Bridge. At Count-y-Billa Farm, at Risca and at Pill-Gwenlly it joins the Sirhowey Tramroad; from the Crumlin Bridge Branch there is a railroad to Beaufort Iron Works; a branch to Sorwy Furnace, another to Nant-y-glo Works, and a third to the Sirhowey Railroad to Risca. Near Pontypool is a railway branch to Tronsnant Furnace and another to Blaen-Din Works. From the Usk to Pontnewynydd in a distance of twelve miles and a half, there is a rise of 447 feet by the canal; in its railway continuation to Blaen-Ason, there is a rise of 610 feet in a distance of five miles and a quarter. From Crynda-Farm to Crumlin Bridge the canal rises 358 feet in eleven miles; the railway from Crumlin Bridge to Beaufort rises 619 feet in ten miles; the Nant-y-glo Branch has a rise of 518 feet.

This is an extensive and useful undertaking, being in the very centre of a country abounding in limestone, stone, coal, iron, tin and lead, which before this work was executed were permitted to remain undisturbed, for want of a conveyance for the produce of the mines. The cost of the work has been great, but it is a speculation which will not fail, eventually, of proving highly beneficial to the parties who have embarked their property in it; for by a most singular clause in the act, the coal from Newport can be carried to supply the Bristol Market without paying the sea duty, notwithstanding all other coal brought *down* the Severn, which does not approach within many miles so near the sea, as the Newport Coal, cannot be carried to Bristol, without payment of the duty on sea-borne coal.

MONTGOMERYSHIRE CANAL.

34 George III. Cap. 39, Royal Assent 28th March, 1794.
55 George III. Cap. 83, Royal Assent 22nd June, 1815.
2 George IV. Cap. 119, Royal Assent 23rd June, 1821.

THE Montgomeryshire Canal was commenced under an act of parliament obtained in the year 1794, with the title of ' *An Act* '*for making a navigable Canal from or near Porthywain Lime* ' *Rocks in the parish of Llanyblodwell, in the county of Salop, to* ' *or near Newtown, in the county of Montgomery, and also certain* ' *collateral Cuts from the said Canal.*' By this act the proprietors were incorporated as " The Company of Proprietors of the Mont- " gomeryshire Canal," and authorized to raise £72,000, in shares of £100 each, and a further sum of £20,000, if required, to complete the same. The company thus empowered began their projected work, but after having expended £71,100, in the main line of the canal and a collateral cut to Guilsfield, they found their funds insufficient for the completion of the undertaking, and therefore applied for a second act, which was granted in 1815, as '*An Act to authorize the raising of a further Sum of Money to complete the Montgomeryshire Canal, and to extend the Power of deviating from, and making certain Alterations in, part of the original Plans, and for explaining and rendering more effectual, an Act of the Thirty-fourth of his present Majesty, for making the said Canal.*'

By the second act the company are authorized to vary the line and to continue it; their title was also changed into that of " The " Company of Proprietors of the Western Branch of the Mont- " gomeryshire Canal," with the powers of the former company secured to them. The former part of this canal is by the present act distinguished as "The Eastern Branch of the Montgomeryshire " Canal," and is to be supplied by the present company, with water from the Severn Feeder, the property of the former company, but now transferred to the present. This act directs the raising of £40,000 in new shares, to form one capital stock with the former capital. The same officers are to be appointed for both, and in fact it is now to be considered one concern, with this exception, that the expenses of the Eastern Branch are to be paid out of the stock and profits of that branch exclusively, and the cost of the Western out of the funds raised under this act. The old shareholders are to divide five per cent. annually on their stock, and the surplus profits are to form a fund for completing the Western Branch.

The new shareholders of the Western Branch are to divide their own profits, till they receive an annual dividend of £5 per cent. when the two shall be consolidated and pass as one.

TONNAGE RATES.

	d.	d.		
For all Lime-stone	1½	2¼	per Ton, per Mile.	
For all Coal, Culm and Lime	2¼	3	ditto.	ditto.
For all other Stone, Pig-iron, Brick, Timber, Tiles, Slates, Gravel, Sand, Lead and Iron-ore, and all other Minerals	3	5	ditto.	ditto.
For all Bark, Cordwood, Coke, Charcoal, Lead, Wrought-iron, Balk and Deals	3½	5½	ditto.	ditto.
For all other Goods, Wares and Merchandize	4	6	ditto.	ditto.

These rates in the first column only apply to the portion of canal and cuts already made; for the extension from the present termination at Garth Mill and Newtown, the rates in the second column are allowed.

A third act was obtained in 1821, entitled, ' *An Act to enable* ' *the Company of Proprietors of the Eastern Branch of the Mont-* ' *gomeryshire Canal, to alter the Line of the Tannat Feeder; to* ' *make a navigable Cut from the Guilsfield Branch, to improve the* ' *same; and to amend Two several Acts respecting the said Canal.*' The design of this act is to enable the proprietors of the Eastern Branch to alter the line of the Tannat Feeder, and to make a cut from the Guilsfield Branch, in order to improve the same. By this act also, the clauses whereby the two branches were to be consolidated, is repealed, and the consolidation is not to take place unless by consent of the proprietors of each. The point of commencement of the Eastern Branch, which before was doubt-ful, is now to be taken at the distance of thirty-five yards from the sill of the upper gate of the higher of the two Carreghofa Locks.

The length of this canal is twenty-seven miles, and was exe-cuted under the direction of Mr. J. Dadford, Jun. It has a lock-age of 225 feet, in the main line from Llanymynach to Newtown. Commencing at Portywain Lime Works in Llanyblodwell Parish, in which place it unites with a branch of the Ellesmere Canal, it passes near the village of Llanymynach and crosses the Verniew River, joining at this place another branch of the Ellesmere Canal; thence running to Gwern-felu, where the branch to Guils-field turns off, it proceeds to Welch Pool; after this it runs parallel to the Severn, past Beniew, through Garth Mill to its union with the Severn on the east side of Newtown. Its direction, by in-specting the map, will be found nearly south-west.

The estimate for the branch from Garth Mill to Newtown, was made by Mr. Josias Jessop, and amounted to £28,268, in-cluding six locks of 8 feet each, and an aqueduct at Llyvior Brook; the cut to be 15 feet wide at the bottom, and 4 feet 6 inches deep.

The estimate for the cut from the upper end of the Guils-field Branch to Pool Quay and widening the Guilsfield Branch, was made by Mr. G. W. Buck, at £9,140, 11s. 11d. including

£5,592, 1s. for the cut; £1,134, 14s. 6d. for deepening and widening the Guilsfield Branch; and £2,413, 16s. 5d. for making the Eastern Branch, or Tannat Feeder, navigable.

The northern parts of the line in particular, and the whole line generally, is situated in the midst of quarries of limestone, slate and freestone, and near mines of coal, lead-ore and other minerals; the advantages of the work, therefore, are of much importance, as well to the proprietors of land on its banks as to the public in general; particularly when we take into consideration its connection with the Ellesmere Canal, and the extent of country traversed by this useful line of navigation.

NANTLLE RAILWAY.

6 George IV. Cap. 63, Royal Assent 20th May, 1825.
7 & 8 George IV. Cap. 3, Royal Assent 21st March, 1827.
9 George IV. Cap. 62, Royal Assent 23rd May, 1828.

THIS railway commences at the Gloddfarlon Slate Quarries, near Nantlle Pool, and proceeding in a westerly direction for some distance, it turns at right angles to the north, in which direction it proceeds to its termination at the shipping quay at Carnarvon.

The first act for this work is entitled, ' *An Act for making and* ' *maintaining a Railway or Tramroad, from or near a certain* ' *Slate Quarry called Gloddfarlon, in the parish of Llandwrog, in* ' *the county of Carnarvon, to the town and port of Carnarvon, in* ' *the same county.*' By this act the proprietors are incorporated as " The Nantlle Railway Company," with power to make the necessary works; they are also directed to raise £20,000 in shares of £100 each, for paying the interest of which, and other current expenses, they are entitled to the following

TONNAGE RATES.

For all Copper, Tin, Lead, Iron and other Ores, and all Matters containing Ores of Copper, Tin, Lead, Iron and other Metals; and all Slates, Slate-stones, Blocks of Slate, Tiles and Tile-stone } 6d. per Ton, per Mile.

For all Lime, Lime-stone, Dung, Compost and all Sorts of Manure, Materials for the repair of Public Roads and Highways; Timber, Coals, Coke, Culm, Cinders, Stones, Bricks, Earth, Clay, Chalk, Marl, Lime, Sand, Corn, Grain, Flour, and all other Goods, Wares and Commodities whatever.... } 3 ditto. ditto.

Fractions of a Ton and of a Mile to be taken as the Quarters therein, and of a Quarter as a Quarter.

Occupiers and Owners of Land on the Line, are not to pay Tolls for their Carriages or Cattle.

When the sum annually raised for the necessary expenses shall exceed what is required for carrying on the work, and for paying a dividend on the shares at the rate of £5 per cent. then the remainder shall be appropriated to paying off the sums originally subscribed; and when these are all paid off, the rates are to be reduced, as far as regards the first articles described in the foregoing scale of rates, to $3\frac{1}{2}d.$ per ton per mile; the other articles to be paid for as before.

The sum, estimated under the first act, does not appear to have been sufficient for completing the road, as in 1827 a second was obtained under the title of ' *An Act for enabling the Com-* ' *pany of Proprietors of the Nantlle Railway to raise a further* ' *Sum of Money for completing the said Railway and other Works.*' By this act the further sum of £20,000 was directed to be raised by mortgage of the works, and the rates were ordered not to be reduced till all the debt both of shareholders and mortgagees should be paid.

A third act was obtained in 1828, entitled, ' *An Act for ex-* ' *tending the Time of completing the Nantlle Railway and other* ' *Works connected therewith, in the county of Carnarvon.*' This act, like the second, is very short, merely giving the further space of five years for completing the work.

NARR RIVER.

24 George II. Cap. 19, Royal Assent 22nd May, 1751.
10 George III Cap. 27, Royal Assent 12th April, 1770.

THE River Narr Navigation, commencing at King's Lynn, runs for some distance from that town towards the south, in a direction nearly parallel with the Eau Brink Cut on the Ouse; it then makes a detour to the south-east, after which it proceeds in a sinuous course to the east, leaving on the north Bilney Lodge and West Acre Abbey; on the south Narborough and Narford Halls; and terminating at Castle Acre, all in the county of Norfolk.

The first act for this undertaking passed in the year 1751, as ' *An Act for making the River Narr navigable from the town and* ' *port of King's Lynn to Westacre, in the county of Norfolk,*' whereby certain commissioners were appointed for making navigable the River Narr from King's Lynn to West Acre, and for borrowing £3,500 on security of certain tolls to be levied on vessels using the navigation. The work was commenced, and the various sums of money so borrowed became, in process of time, the property of the Rev. Henry Spelman, to whom also, in December, 1769, an arrear of interest amounting to £1,154, 19s. 7d. was due, without the works being completed. The commissioners applied to parliament for another act, authorizing the said interest to be reckoned in future as a capital sum due to the said Mr. Spelman, who also engaged to furnish a further sum of £1,345, 0s. 5d. in order to pay the cost of the said second act and to complete the works. The act was in consequence obtained under the title of ' *An Act to enlarge the Powers of an Act of the Twenty-fourth of* ' *his late Majesty, for making the River Narr navigable from the* ' *town and port of King's Lynn to Westacre, in the county of Nor-* ' *folk, and for making the said Act more effectual.*' By this act £800 are to be forthwith expended in repairs; £600 thereof in the river above Narborough, and £200 below. The debt owing to Mr. Spelman, his heirs or assigns, may be reduced by a notice of six months, signed by nine or more of the commissioners.

At the time this work was finished, it was an important benefit to the port of Lynn, and has apparently answered the purpose for which it was undertaken.

NEATH CANAL NAVIGATION.

31 George III. Cap. 85, Royal Assent 6th June, 1791.
38 George III. Cap. 30, Royal Assent 26th May, 1798.

By the first act passed in 1791, and entitled, ' *An Act for* ' *making and maintaining a Canal or navigable Communication* ' *from or near a certain Place called Abernant, in the county of* ' *Glamorgan, to or through a certain Place called the Brickfield,* ' *near Melincrytham Pill, into the street of Neath, near the town* ' *of Neath, in the said county,*' power was given to certain persons, incorporated as " The Company of Proprietors of the Neath " Canal Navigation," to purchase lands and to undertake the necessary works for making and completing a navigable canal from Abernant, in Glamorganshire, to communicate with the River Neath in the town of that name, which canal will facilitate the conveyance of coals, ores, stone and timber, from the mines, quarries, woods and collieries on its line. They are also empowered to make use of the bed of the River Neath, wherever that may be useful or necessary for the completion of their plan, and they may make inclined planes, railways or rollers in any part, if deemed requisite. For these purposes they may raise £25,000, in shares of £100 each; and in case such sum should not prove sufficient, they may raise £10,000 additional, either amongst themselves, or on assignment of the rates. The shareholders are to receive £5 per cent. per annum, every year until the work is finished.

TONNAGE RATES.

	d.	
For all Iron, Goods, Wares, Merchandize and other Things, except as specified below	4 per Ton, per Mile.	
For all Iron Castings	3 ditto.	ditto.
For all Pig-iron	2½ ditto.	ditto.
For all Iron-stone, Iron-ore, Coals, Culm, Stone-coal, Coke, Cinders, Charcoal, Timber, Stone, Tiles, Clay, Bricks, Lime-stone, Lime and Manure of all Sorts	1½ ditto.	ditto.

Fractions of a Mile and of a Ton to be taken as the Quarters therein, and of a Quarter as a Quarter.

No Tolls are to be paid by the Owners or Occupiers of the Melyn-y-Court Furnace, Ynis-y-Gerwn Tin Mills and Aberdulais Forges, for any Goods conveyed between the last-named Place and the Ynis-y-Gerwn Tin Mills, or between the Weir at the last-named Place and the Upper End of Llyntwrch.

Wharfs may be made and the charge for using them is to be determined by the company. Five pounds per cent. is to be reserved out of the clear annual profits, as a fund for repairs, till the same shall amount to £1,000, when it shall cease to be funded till the £1,000 is reduced to £500, and then it shall commence again. The company may also make railways and collateral cuts, with inclined planes on the same. Private individuals may build wharfs, &c. and charge the following

WHARFAGE RATES.

	d.
For Coals, Culm, Lime-stone, Clay, Iron, Iron-stone, Lead or other Ores, Timber, Stone, Bricks, Tiles, Slates or Gravel	1 per Ton.
For all other Goods, Wares or Things	3 ditto.

None of these to remain on the Wharfs, &c. more than Six Days, except those first enumerated, which may remain One Month on paying Three-pence per Ton. After the first Six Days the Owners are to pay for the next Ten Days, One Penny per Ton additional; after that Time, One Penny per Ton for every succeeding Day. Pleasure Boats and Boats used for the Purposes of Husbandry, are to pass on the Canal and Cuts free of Toll.

The company having nearly completed their first plan, applied in 1798 for ' *An Act for extending the Neath Canal Navigation,* ' *and for amending an Act, passed in the Thirty-first of his pre-* ' *sent Majesty, for making the said Canal,*' by which they had authority to continue the canal from the town of Neath to Giant's Grave Pill, in the parish of Briton Ferry, and to make and build all necessary inclined planes, collateral cuts, warehouses and wharfs, with certain restrictions, on behalf of certain proprietors of estates on the line. There is a remarkable clause in the act which is this, that the warehousing rates shall be the same as those charged by the Staffordshire and Worcestershire Canal Company at Stourport.

This canal commencing near Abernant, is about fourteen miles long; at its head there are two short railways, branching off to the mines on the east and west of Abernant House, which is situated in the fork made by them. The canal proceeds parallel to the River Neath in a south-west direction, leaving Maesgwn and Rheola on the west, and Melincourt Furnaces on the east; at the commencement it is considerably elevated, but falls considerably in its progress to Neath River Harbour. A few miles above Neath the canal has a branch to the west, with which the Aberdulais Railway communicates, as do also two other railroads from copper works on the same side of the canal. The main branch continues its course to Neath, where the two branches communicate and are crossed by the turnpike-road; they then run parallel on opposite sides of the river to their termination—the main canal in the Neath River, the branch to its union with the short canal called the Briton Canal, at Briton Ferry House, near Giant's Grave Pill. This canal was within two miles of its completion in 1798. Its object is the export of coals, iron, copper, limestone and other produce of the mines which abound in its vicinity.

The act for the Neath River and Harbour not coming within the design of an account of inland navigation, need not be noticed here, further than stating it to be the termination of the main line of the Neath Canal; the other branch ending at the Briton Canal, which communicates with Swansea Harbour.

NYNE OR NEN RIVER.

12 Anne, C. 7, R. A. 28th May, 1714.   11 Geo. I. C. 19, R. A. 20th Apr. 1725.
29 Geo. II. C. 69, R. A. 15th Apr. 1756.   34 Geo. III. C. 85, R. A. 17th Apr. 1794.

THE nature of the country through which this work is carried, and the multiplicity of small navigable cuts branching off in every direction, will render an inspection of the map more necessary than a detail of its course in these pages; we shall therefore content ourselves with giving a few of the leading points in the history of the navigation, and for a minute description of its course, refer our readers to the line laid down on our map.

The first attempt towards the object of the present account, was an act obtained in the reign of Queen Anne, entitled, ' *An Act for* ' *making the River Nyne, or Nen, running from Northampton to* ' *Peterborough, navigable;*' wherein certain commissioners were appointed to conduct the work, and to fix such rates and tolls for the navigation of the same, as they should from time to time judge necessary.

In the 11th of George I. a second act was obtained, in which it is recited that two clauses, in the former act, the one restraining the commissioners from making *any* part of the river navigable until they had agreed with some person or persons to complete the whole; the other compelling the said commissioners or contractors to make good any damage that might occur in endeavouring to render the whole navigable, but failing so to do, had been found so prejudicial, that no one would undertake the work, and in consequence nothing had been done. These clauses are therefore repealed, and leave is given to make any part navigable, and particularly that from Peterborough to Northampton. This act is entitled, ' *An Act for making more effectual an Act passed in* ' *Parliament holden in the Twelfth Year of the Reign of her late* ' *Majesty Queen Anne, entitled, An Act for making the River* ' *Nyne, or Nen, running from Northampton to Peterborough,* ' *navigable.*'

In 1756 an act to amend and explain the two former was obtained under the title of ' *An Act for explaining and amending* ' *and rendering more effectual, Two several Acts of Parliament,*

' one of them passed in the Twelfth Year of her late Majesty Queen
' Anne, for making the River Nyne, or Nen, running from North-
' ampton to Peterborough, navigable; and the other made in the
' Eleventh Year of his late Majesty King George the First, for
' making more effectual the said former Act.' In this act it is recited
that that part of the river between Peterborough and Thrapston
Bridge has been made navigable, and distinguished by the name
of " The Eastern Division of the Nyne or Nen Navigation;" in
our map it is called " The Lower District;" and the other part of
the navigation, that is, from Thrapston Bridge to Northampton, is
distinguished in the act as " The Western Division;" in our map
as " The Upper District;" and it appearing that the completion
of this Upper District would be highly beneficial to the towns of
Peterborough and Northampton, and to other places, commissioners
are appointed for carrying the same into effect, and the clauses of
the former acts are for this purpose extended and enlarged.   It is
required that the navigation be commenced in the first instance at
Thrapston Bridge, and not in any other part of the river, and shall
proceed upwards from that place towards Northampton.   Locks
are to be built, where required, and rates for passing them to be
settled by a majority of the commissioners, who are to proportion
the same according to the distance from Thrapston Bridge and
to the expense of building the locks; and they are authorized to
borrow money on security of such rates, in order to the more
speedy completion of the work; the lenders of such money to be
nominated proprietors of the navigation.   Interest of the money
borrowed is not to exceed four per cent. and when the tolls, after
the interest is paid on all monies borrowed, shall exceed the expenditure, then the residue is to be applied towards paying off the
principal.

Some difficulties still occurring, another act was obtained in
1794, as ' An Act to remove certain Difficulties in the Execution of
' the Powers vested in the Commissioners appointed by Two Acts,
' passed in the Twelfth of Anne and Eleventh of George the First,
' for making the River Nyne, or Nen, running from Northampton
' to Peterborough, navigable, so far as the same relates to the Na-
' vigation between Peterborough and Thrapston Bridge.'   At this
time it appears that the work from Peterborough to Oundle

North Bridge was undertaken by certain persons contracting for the execution thereof, and the other part from the North Bridge in Oundle to Thrapston by another person, it is therefore in this act provided, that the commissioners shall appoint a clerk and overseers, whose salaries shall be paid, one moiety out of the tolls arising from the navigation between Peterborough and Oundle, the other from that between Oundle and Thrapston.

Commencing on the south side of Peterborough, the Lower District of the Nen runs for some distance in a crooked course towards the west, leaving Earl Fitzwilliam's noble seat at Milton on the north bank, and Overton Longville on the east; its direction then varies a little to the north, and after intersecting the turnpike-road between Stamford and Huntingdon, it takes an easterly course to its termination at Thrapston Bridge, passing Water Newton Lodge, Elton Hall, the town of Oundle, Lilford Hall, Barnwell Castle, Sadborough and Clapton in its course. The river is throughout very winding, and between Peterborough and Thrapston there are eight cuts to avoid bends and reaches in the river. At Thrapston the connection with the Upper District commences. This part of the line is not greatly elevated above the level of the sea; its direction is south-west, leaving Higham Ferrers on the east and Wellingborough on the west; running by Ecton Hall and various other seats of the nobility and gentry to Northampton, where it connects with the railway branch of the Grand Junction Canal.

This line of navigation is on many accounts highly beneficial; it supplies at an easy expense the towns and villages on the line with coals, wood and other articles of domestic consumption; whilst it affords equal facilities for the export of agricultural produce, making a link in the chain of communication between Lynn, Liverpool, Manchester, London, and a great number of other commercial places.

NYNE OR NEN RIVER, BEDFORD LEVEL.

27 George II. Cap. 12. Royal Assent 6th April, 1754.

THE original navigation from King's Lynn to Standground Sluice, near Peterborough, was carried from Salter's Load Sluice, through Well Creek and the River Nen to Flood's Ferry, and from thence through Ramsey, Ugg and Whittlesea Meres, a passage at all times tedious and frequently difficult as well as dangerous. An act was therefore obtained in the 27th of George II. entitled, ' *An Act for improving and preserving the Navigation* ' *from Salter's Load Sluice, in the county of Norfolk, to Stand-* ' *ground Sluice, in the county of Huntingdon; and from Flood's* ' *Ferry, in the Isle of Ely, in the county of Cambridge, to Ramsey* ' *High Load, in the said county of Huntingdon; and also the* ' *Navigation from Old Bedford Sluice, in the said county of Nor-* ' *folk, to the River Nene, in the parish of Ramsey, in the said* ' *county of Huntingdon.*' By this act certain persons are appointed commissioners for managing a new line from Salter's Load, through Well Creek to the town of Outwell; from thence, through the Nen by the towns of Upwell and March to Flood's Ferry aforesaid; and from thence to Ramsey High Load; and for preserving the navigation from Flood's Ferry, through Whittlesea Dyke to Standground Sluice, and also the navigation from Old Bedford Sluice through the Old Bedford River and the Forty Foot Drain, to the River Nen, in the parish of Ramsey. The inhabitants of Peterborough and other towns named in the act, are required to meet annually in their respective vestries on Easter Monday, to chuse commissioners for this act. The commissioners are empowered to demand rates at Salter's Load Sluice, Standground Sluice and Old Bedford Sluice, for the purpose of defraying the necessary charges.

TONNAGE RATES.

d.

For every Chaldron of Coals, Lynn Measure ; Hundred of Battens ; Half Hundred of other Deals ; Load of Timber, at Forty Feet to the Load ; Eight Packs of Wool, of Ten Tod to the Pack ; Weigh of Salt ; Load of Wheat, Rape, Lineseed, Coleseed, Barley, Rye, Peas or Beans, of Five Quarters to the Load ; Last of Oats, or Barley Bigs ; Two Thousand of Turf ; Load of Reed, Sedge, Hay, Flax or Hemp, of Twenty Hundred Weight to the Load ; Last of Malt ; Thousand of Tiles ; Five Hundred of Bricks ; Twenty Feet of Stone ; and Chaldron of Lime.. 3

For every Ton of all other Goods, Wares, Merchandize or Commodities whatsoever   3

TONNAGE RATES CONTINUED.

Greater or less Quantities in Proportion. Pleasure Boats are exempted from this Rate,
as also are all Manures and Compost, Malt Dust, Pigeons' Dung and Oil Cake,
excepting that made of Lineseed.

The commissioners may borrow £3,000 on credit of the rates,
and mortgage them as security for the same. The tolls of the
different sluices to be kept separate, and the proceeds employed
on the distance between them. There are several other clauses in
the act, besides those which we have quoted, but they are not of
general interest. This navigation is very convenient for the export of corn, and for obtaining coal, timber and groceries in return.

NENE AND WISBECH RIVERS.

8 George IV. Cap. 85, Royal Assent 14th June, 1827.
10 George IV. Cap. 104, Royal Assent 1st June, 1829.

THE improvements which the acts, obtained as above, were
intended to produce, are of a very important nature, as will appear
from our map.

The cut which is to obviate the necessity of following the
channel of the river from Kinderley's Cut to the Eye, begins at
Gunthorpe Sluice, near the termination of Kinderley's Cut; intersecting in its course the Sutton Sluice, it passes by Sutton Wash to
Crab Hole, in nearly a straight line. The depth from the low-
water-level in the Eye to the surface of the water at Kinderley's
Cut is 13 feet 8 inches; the bottom of the channel at Sutton Wash
is 8 feet 6 inches. Mr. Rennie and Mr. Telford were both employed in forming the plan, and the estimate was £127,890. At
Kinderley's Cut the high water is calculated to be 11 feet above
low water. On one occasion, in 1810, the high water at Crab
Hole was 25 feet.

The first act obtained for this improvement is entitled, ' *An*
' *Act for improving the Outfall of the River Nene, and the Drain-*
' *age of the Lands discharging their Waters into the Wisbech River,*
' *and the Navigation of the said Wisbech River, from the Upper*
' *End of Kinderley's Cut to the Sea, &c. &c.*'

It recites various acts for the general improvement of this
district, and then goes on to state the powers given to the parties

interested in the present work. These are the making of a new
cut from the north end of Kinderley's Cut, to be continued from
thence to low water near Crab Hole, with proper banks and other
works. They are to raise £130,000; and of this sum certain
proportions named in the act, but not necessary here to be recapi-
tulated, are to be contributed by certain districts, which will be
benefited by the work. Commissioners are appointed for the
execution of the undertaking, and the different places which contribute have their own commissioners.

They are to complete the works with as little delay as possible, and build the Cross Keys Bridge according to the plan of
Messrs. Rennie and Telford. The building of this bridge and the
other works are to proceed together.

The Cross Keys Bridge Company are to pay these commissioners £3,000, the amount of estimate under their own act,
for building the bridge, or in default, the bridge-tolls are to be
received by the commissioners. The burgesses of Wisbech are
also to pay £30,000, by three instalments to the said commissioners
for the said work, and are to receive an additional tonnage of 6d.
per chaldron on all coals arriving in their port, exclusive of what
they were before entitled to, under their own private act. The
burgesses may borrow this sum of £30,000, or any part of it, on
credit of the tolls directed to be received by their act, or the commissioners may do so, in default of the burgesses so doing, by
mortgage of all duties mentioned in this act. After the £30,000
have been paid, the burgesses are to appropriate the surplus of
their rates to the liquidation of the sums they have borrowed.
The lands in the Hundred of Wisbech are to contribute £15,000;
South Holland Hundred £7,000; Sutton St. Edmond's Hamlet
£1,700; Sutton St. James' Hamlet £550, and in case they contract for the perpetual right of drainage, £600 additional. The
commissioners may borrow money on mortgage or annuities, and
the rates are to be reduced when mortgages are paid off and
annuities redeemed. As the sands and marshes are embanked and
made productive, it is ordered that when the commissioners shall
receive any sums for sale, rent or profit of the same, after necessary repairs and current expenses have been paid, then the residue
shall be applied to paying off borrowed monies; to forming a

fund of £30,000, to be invested for maintaining the works; and to paying off, proportionably, the sums levied on the different places and hundreds before named.

Before the fund is raised, all costs and charges incident to the works and repairs shall be defrayed by an acre-rate upon the lands entitled to drain through the work to the sea, to be determined by a meeting of not less than forty of the commissioners; and in case of non-payment, the said commissioners have the power of levying a penalty on defaulters.

A second act was passed in 1829, entitled, ' *An Act for altering,*
' *amending and enlarging the Powers granted by an Act passed in*
' *the Seventh and Eighth Years of the Reign of his present Majesty,*
' *for improving the Outfall of the River Nene, and the Drainage*
' *of the Lands discharging their Waters into the Wisbech River and*
' *the Navigation of the said Wisbech River, from the Upper End*
' *of Kinderley's Cut to the Sea, and for embanking the Salt Marshes*
' *and Bare Sands lying between the said Cut and the Sea.*'

This act recites the progress of the work under the powers of the former act, and states the great improvement which would accrue to the lands and country generally from the adoption of a new line, which it is unnecessary here to describe, being laid down on the map; it also authorizes the commissioners to take the improved line, and to erect light-houses or beacons without the sanction of the Trinity House. It gives them power to remove Gunthorpe Sluice and erect a new one, to be vested in the North Level Commissioners, who are to repay them all expenses attendant thereon, except £2,000 which the Nene Outfall Commissioners themselves agree to disburse. For carrying on the work, his Majesty is to have power to convey or sell to the said commissioners the sixth part of the sands, vested in the crown. They have power to make warping works, and to allow contiguous lands to be warped. They may borrow not more than £10,000 at any one time, as a temporary loan, on bond payable in two years; and they may also borrow on mortgage of certain lands vested in them. The rights of the Cross Keys Bridge Company, and of a great number of other public bodies and individuals, are saved by clauses in both acts, which on this account are of very great length.

The work is one of infinite importance, whether considered as a drainage or as a ready means of communication between the country through which it passes, and other parts of the kingdom.

NEWCASTLE-UNDER-LYNE CANAL.

35 George III. Cap. 87, Royal Assent 2nd June, 1795.

THIS canal was projected for the purpose of supplying the potteries with coal from the mines near Newcastle, and for opening an easier transit for the limestone from Caldon Lowe, through the Trent and Mersey Canal. The act for this work is entitled, ' *An* ' *Act for making and maintaining a navigable Canal, from and* ' *out of the Navigation from the Trent to the Mersey, at or near* ' *Stoke-upon-Trent, in the county of Stafford, to the town of New-* ' *castle-under-Lyne, in the said county,*' and by it the proprietors, incorporated as " The Newcastle-under-Lyne Canal Company," are empowered to raise the sum of £7,000, in shares of £50 each, with an additional £3,000 on mortgage of the rates, if necessary, for completing the same. They have also power to collect the following

TONNAGE RATES.

		d.	
For all Coal, Lime-stone and Iron-stone......................	1½	per Ton, per Mile.	
For all other Goods...	2	ditto.	ditto.
If less than a Ton in a Boat.................................	6	per Mile.	

The canal is about three miles long, in a direction nearly west, commencing at Stoke-upon-Trent, in the Trent and Mersey Canal, and ending at the town of Newcastle, in the Newcastle-under-Lyne Junction Canal.

NEWCASTLE-UNDER-LYNE JUNCTION CANAL.

38 George III. Cap. 29, Royal Assent 26th May, 1798.

THE act for making this canal, was obtained in 1798 under the title of ' *An Act for making and maintaining a navigable Canal,* ' *and Inclined Plane or Railway, from and out of the Newcastle-* ' *under-Lyne Canal to the Canal of Sir Nigel Bowyer Gresley, Bart.* ' *near the town of Newcastle-under-Lyne, and also another Branch* ' *of Canal, or Inclined Plane or Railway, from and out of the said*

' *last-mentioned Canal, at or near Apedale, to certain Coal and*
' *other Works, all in the county of Stafford;*' in which is pointed
out the utility of a canal, with inclined planes or railways, from
the Newcastle-under-Lyne Canal to that of Sir Nigel Bowyer
Gresley; as also of another, from the last-mentioned canal at
Apedale to the works of Sir John Edensor Heathcote, Thomas
Kinnersley and John Wedgwood, Esquires. A company is therefore incorporated, as " The Newcastle-under-Lyne Junction Canal
" Company," with power to execute the same, and to raise for that
purpose £8,000, in shares of £50 each; and if needful, they may
raise £4,000 additional, either by new shares, or by mortgage of
the rates. For paying interest and other charges they are empowered to demand the following

TONNAGE RATES.

		d.	
For all Coal, Lime-stone, Iron-stone, Iron, Bricks, Sand, Clay and Furnace Cinders....	}	2	per Ton, for the First Mile.
For ditto the whole Distance		4	ditto.
For all other Goods, Wares and Merchandize........		3	ditto, per Mile.
For a less Quantity than a Ton		6	

Fractions of a Mile to be considered as a Mile.

The company may convey water through Sir Nigel Bowyer
Gresley's Canal to supply their own, but are not to draw it down
below the highest present level. The direction of the canal is
north-west, commencing in the Newcastle-under-Lyne Canal at
the south-east part of that town, and terminating in the south-west
in Gresley's Canal; in which canal at Apedale its western part commences and extends to Partridge Nest and Bignel-End Collieries.

NEWCASTLE-UPON-TYNE AND CARLISLE
RAILWAY.

10 George IV. Cap. 72, Royal Assent 22nd May, 1829.

THE projectors of the Newcastle-upon-Tyne Railway, fore-
seeing the advantages likely to arise from a communication between
that place and Carlisle, applied to parliament for a legislative authority for the same, which was obtained under title of ' *An Act*
' *for making and maintaining a Railway or Tramroad, from the*
' *town of Newcastle-upon-Tyne, in the county of the town of New-*

' castle-upon-Tyne, to the city of Carlisle, in the county of Cumber-
' land, with a Branch thereout.' Commencing in a street called
the Close, in the parish of St. Nicholas, Newcastle, this railroad
proceeds in a winding course, occasionally bending to the north
and south, but mainly westward by the side of the turnpike-road
from Newcastle to Hexham, and nearly parallel to the River Tyne,
passing on its way many collieries and mines with which the district
abounds.   At Hexham it makes a curve to the north to a little
beyond Acomb Hermitage, still continuing near and parallel to the
Tyne, which river it follows in its westerly direction to Thropwood
House; here it crosses the turnpike-road and runs close to the
southern side thereof as far as Haltwhistle; it then diverges to the
south-west for a short distance, when turning again towards Green
Head on the north of the turnpike-road, which it again crosses, it
leaves the Tyne.   From Green Head the direction is south-west,
again crossing the turnpike-road at Naworth Castle; this direction
it keeps to the town of Carlisle, where it terminates in the Carlisle
Canal, 75 feet above the level of the sea.   The branch is from
Elswick Dean in the township of the same name, in the parochial
chapelry of St. John and that part of the parish of St. Nicholas
terminating at the west side of Thornton Street, in Westgate, in
the county of Northumberland.

The extent of the undertaking may be estimated from the
circumstance of having authority to raise £300,000, in shares of
£100 each; and in case this should not prove sufficient to meet the
expenses, £100,000 may be raised in addition by way of mortgage
on the works. The main line of this intended railway is sixty-two
miles, one furlong; the Thornton Street Branch is near a mile in
length, with a rise of 114 feet 6 inches.   From Newcastle the
main line proceeds in nearly one regular inclination for forty-two
miles and three quarters, rising 437 feet 6 inches.   From the
summit level there is a fall of only 2 feet 6 inches, in six miles
and a quarter; the remaining distance of thirteen miles and one
furlong is divided into several planes of various inclinations, and
altogether descending to the London Road at Carlisle, which is 45
feet higher than the commencement at Newcastle, 392 feet 6
inches.   At thirteen miles from Carlisle the line crosses a private
colliery railway belonging to the Earl of Carlisle.   The survey

for this undertaking was made by Mr. J. O. Blackett and Mr. J. Stedholme, under the direction of Benjamin Thompson, Esq. who estimated the cost at £272,633, 0s. 10d.; of which the item for bridges alone amounts to £49,950, 3s. 9d.

The subscribers are to be allowed £4 per cent. as interest on the sums advanced, till the annual dividends shall amount to that sum per cent. The usual clauses are inserted in this act, and the tonnage rates are declared as below.

TONNAGE AND CARRIAGE RATES.

	s.	d.		
For Dung, Compost, Lime and all other Manure	0	1	per Ton, per Mile.	
For Coal, Lime-stone not used as Manure, Iron-stone, Iron and other Ores, Timber, Deals, Building, Pitching and Paving-stones, and Clay.............................	0	1½	ditto.	ditto.
For Coke, Culm, Charcoal, Flags, Bricks, Tiles, Slates, Lead, Iron and other Metals	0	2	ditto.	ditto.
For Corn, Grain, Flour, Hay and all other Agricultural Produce	0	2½	ditto.	ditto.
For Sugar, Dye-woods, Groceries, Cotton and other Wool, Hides, Drugs, Manufactured Goods, and all other Wares, Merchandize, Matters or Things..............	0	3	ditto.	ditto.
For all Persons Travelling on the Railroad in any Coach, Waggon or other Carriage, not more than Five Miles	0	6	each.	
For ditto above Five Miles and not exceeding Ten........	1	0	ditto.	
For ditto above Ten Miles and not exceeding Fifteen	1	6	ditto.	
For ditto above Fifteen Miles and not exceeding Twenty..	2	0	ditto.	
For ditto above Twenty Miles and not exceeding Twenty-five..	2	6	ditto.	
For ditto above Twenty-five Miles and not exceeding Thirty	3	0	ditto.	
For ditto above Thirty Miles and not exceeding Forty....	3	6	ditto.	
For ditto above Forty Miles and not exceeding Fifty	4	0	ditto.	
For ditto any Distance exceeding Fifty Miles	5	0	ditto.	
For all Horses, Mules, Asses, Beasts of Draught or Burthen, and for all Oxen, Cows or Neat Cattle carried in such Carriage, not exceeding Fifteen Miles...........	2	6	ditto.	
For ditto not exceeding Forty Miles.....................	4	0	ditto.	
For ditto above Forty Miles..............................	6	0	ditto.	
For every Calf, Sheep, Lamb or Pig, any Distance	0	9	ditto.	
For all Lime-stone, Lime, Iron-stone, Iron and other Ores; all Sorts of Dung, Compost and Manure; all Materials for repairing Roads; all Stone, Sand, Clay, Building, Pitching and Paving-stones, Tiles and Slates; all Timber, Staves and Deals carried on the Road by the Company	12	0	per Ton.	
For all Sugar, Corn, Grain, Flour, Dye-woods, Lead, Iron and other Metals ditto	14	0	ditto.	
For all Cotton and other Wool, Hides, Drugs, Groceries and Manufactured Goods ditto	16	0	ditto.	
For all Wines, Spirits, Vitriol, Glass and other Hazardous Goods ditto	20	0	ditto.	
For all Coal, Coke, Culm, Charcoal and Cinders..........	0	3	ditto, per Mile.	

For all Persons, Cattle and other Animals, according to such Rates as the Company shall determine.

The company, if they should build bridges at Corby and Scotswood, which under certain restrictions they may do, are entitled to receive, in addition to the above tonnage rates, a pontage on goods, &c. conveyed on the railway and over the bridges connected therewith; they are also to charge, for the passage of carriages over the general road-way to be made over Scotswood Bridge, the following

PONTAGE RATES.

	s.	d.	
For Six or more Horses or other Beasts, drawing any Coach, Chaise, Chariot, Berlin, Landau, Calash or Hearse	2	0	
For Three or Four ditto	1	6	
For Two ditto	1	0	
For One ditto	0	6	
For Four or more Horses or Beasts drawing any Wain, Dray, Cart or Carriage	0	8	
For Three ditto	0	6	
For Two ditto	0	4	
For One ditto	0	2	
For every Horse, Mule or Ass laden or unladen, not drawing	0	1	
For every Drove of Oxen, Cows or Neat Cattle	0	10	per Score.
For every Drove of Calves, Swine, Sheep or Lambs	0	5	ditto.
For every Foot Passenger	0	1	

The Prices of Carriage for small Parcels to be determined by the Company.

This is an important project, and one which, though very expensive in the commencement, is considered likely to repay the spirited persons who have ventured to undertake it.

NEWPORT PAGNELL CANAL.

54 George III. Cap. 98, Royal Assent 17th June, 1814.

THIS canal was designed, as the preamble of the act declares, for the purpose of forming a communication with the Grand Junction Canal. The act was obtained in 1814, under title of ' *An Act for making and maintaining a navigable Canal from* ' *Newport Pagnell to the Grand Junction Canal, at Great Linford,* ' *in the county of Buckingham.*' The proprietors are incorporated as " The Company of the Proprietors of the Newport Pagnell " Canal," and have the usual powers granted to such companies. Water for the supply of this canal may be taken from the Grand Junction Canal, under certain restrictions, the Newport Company making a lock at the union of the canals, with its upper gates 1 foot above the top water level of the Grand Junction, such lock to be maintained at the cost of the Newport Company.

For executing the work, £13,000 is to be raised in shares of £100 each; and should this prove insufficient, a further sum of £7,000 may be provided, by the creation of new shares or by mortgage of the rates.   The following are allowed as

TONNAGE RATES.

	s.	*d.*	
For all Goods, Wares, Merchandize and Things	2	0	per Ton.
For all Coals or Coke	1	6	ditto.
For all Manure	0	6	ditto.

Fractions of a Ton to be reckoned as the Quarters therein.   Land-owners to carry Manure free of Toll.

Lords of manors and others may build wharfs for public use, and charge the following

WHARFAGE RATES.

	d.	
For all Minerals, Timber or other Goods, remaining not longer than Twenty-four Hours	3	per Ton.
For ditto remaining above Twenty-four Hours and not above Thirty Days	6	ditto.
After that Time	¼	ditto, per Day.

Coal, Iron and Lime-stone may remain on the Wharfs for Three Months, on payment of Sixpence per Ton.

This canal begins at the town of Newport Pagnell, 180½ feet above the level of the sea, and proceeding in a north-easterly direction it unites with the Grand Junction Canal at Linford, at a level of 232¼ feet above the sea.   The estimate for this work was made in 1813 by Mr. B. Bevan.   He calculated the cost to be £12,650, of which, £9,700 was subscribed; the shares were made of the value of £100 each, but half and quarters were allowed. The canal from Newport to its opening into the Grand Junction Canal is only a mile and a quarter long, with a rise of 50 feet 9 inches, from Newport to the level of the Grand Junction near the Swing Bridge, which is effected by seven locks of 7 feet 3 inches each.

The conveniences afforded by this communication with the Grand Junction Canal in the transit of coal, agricultural produce, timber, deals, stone and groceries, are important to the town and neighbourhood of Newport Pagnell.

NITH OR NIDD RIVER NAVIGATION.

51 George III. Cap. 147, Royal Assent 10th June, 1811.

THE River Nith or Nidd Navigation commences in the Solway
Frith, and continues a course of about nine miles, in a direction
nearly north, between the counties of Dumfries and Kirkcudbright,
to its termination at Dumfries Bridge, through the whole of which
distance the tide flows. The act which refers to this work is entitled, '*An Act for improving the Harbour of Dumfries, and the
' Navigation of the River Nith ;*' by which it appears that, though
two several acts of George II. and III. had awarded a proportion
of the taxes on beer and ale levied on the authority of those acts,
for the purpose of improving Dumfries Harbour, the said harbour
stands in need of repairs; the preceding acts are hereby repealed
and the present substituted for them. By this act certain commissioners therein named have the requisite powers to cleanse,
deepen and improve the said harbour and the River Nith, including
both sides thereof from Southerness to the caul of Dumfries. The
following are to be levied as

HARBOUR RATES.

	s.	d.	
For all Goods, Wares and Merchandize, including Slate and Foreign Timber, imported into or exported out of the said River, except Coals, Lime or Lime-stone	1	2	per Ton.
For Coals, Lime and Lime-stone	0	6	ditto.
For all Vessels coming into the River from Foreign Parts	0	6	ditto.
For ditto from any Part of Great Britain, Ireland and the Isle of Man	0	2	ditto.
For ditto coming to an Anchor at or near Carse-thorne, except chartered to Dumfries...	0	1	ditto.

All Custom-House, Excise or Post-Office Ships and Ships in his Majesty's Service, are
exempted from the Rates.

Commissioners have power to license pilots, meters of timber
and weighers on the river; they may also erect light-houses,
quays and harbours, and make the improvements laid down by
Mr. James Holinsworth, viz. throwing the course of the channel as
close as possible to Glencaple Quay; lengthening the pier at Kirk-
connel Banks, and making a new channel of the river from
Glencaple Quay by Conheath to Kelton, from thence in nearly a
straight line to the mouth of Cargenfrew; and from thence in a

straight line from Netherton Merse to New Quay; thence through
the west corner of Kingholme and through the east corner of the
lands of Moat, into the dock.

Commissioners may borrow £16,000 for the purpose of executing the work, on security of the rates, paying £5 per cent.
per annum interest for the same.

NORTH WALSHAM AND DILHAM CANAL.

52 George III. Cap. 69, Royal Assent 5th May, 1812.

THE North Walsham and Dilham commences at Wayford
Bridge in the parish of Dilham in Norfolk, where it communicates
with the River Ant; from this place it runs in a north-west direction, parallel to a branch of the Ant River, by a very sinuous
course, passing Worsted, Westwick, Honing and Corstwick Halls,
leaving North Walsham and Suffield Hall on the west, and proceeding by Witton Park to its termination at Antingham, being a
distance of seven miles. The act for forming it was obtained in
1812, under the title of '*An Act for making a navigable Canal
'from the Rivers Ant and Bure, at or near Wayford Bridge, near
'Dilham, to the towns of North Walsham and Antingham, in the
'county of Norfolk.*' The proprietors are incorporated as "The
"Company of Proprietors of the North Walsham and Dilham
"Canal Navigation," and have power to raise £30,000, in shares
of £50 each; and in case this should be insufficient, they may
obtain £10,000 in addition, by contributing amongst themselves,
or by mortgaging the rates and dues. They may also demand the
following

TONNAGE RATES.

		d.		
For all Lime-stone, Dung, Peat or Soap Ashes, Chalk, Marl, Clay, Sand and all Lime or other Articles used as Manure or for repairing Roads...........................	}	$2\frac{1}{2}$	per Ton, per Mile.	
For all Coals, Culm, Pig-iron, Iron-stone, Iron, Copper and Lead-ores, Lime not for Manure, Kelp, Ashes, Barilla, Tallow, Building-stone, Bricks, Tiles, Paving-stone and Pipe-clay	}	3	ditto.	ditto.
For all Coke, Cinders, Charcoal, Corn and other Grain, Flour, Malt, Meal, Cider, Hay, Straw, Raw Hemp and Tanners' Bark, Porter and Beer, Timber, Ochre, Calamine, Bar-iron, Lead, Kelp, Sand except for Manure, Pitch, Tar, Turpentine and Rosin	}	4	ditto.	ditto.
For all Wines and Spirituous Liquors		5	ditto	ditto.

TONNAGE RATES CONTINUED.

	d.	
For all Passengers in Boats or Barges	1	per Mile each.
For all Cattle, Horses and Asses	½	ditto. ditto.
For all Sheep, Swine and other Beasts	6	ditto, per Score.
For all other Goods, Wares, Merchandize and Commodities..	6	per Ton, per Mile.

No less Fraction than Half a Mile or a Quarter of a Ton to be paid, and Wharfage to be charged if Goods remain longer than Forty-eight Hours.

Lords of manors and occupiers of land may erect wharfs and quays, but if they refuse, the company have power to do so, charging rates according to their own discretion.

This work is highly beneficial to the district through which it passes, by affording a communication with Great Yarmouth and London, and thus connecting with most parts of the kingdom.

NORTH WILTS CANAL.

53 George III. Cap. 182, Royal Assent 2nd July, 1813.

THIS canal is marked in our map a branch of the Wilts and Berks Canal; having been made under the authority of a distinct act of parliament, we shall here only describe its course, and state the sum to be raised for the execution of the work.

It commences in the Wilts and Berks Canal, near Swindon, 345⅓ feet above the level of the sea, and proceeding in a pretty direct line towards the north-west, terminates in the Thames and Severn Canal at Weymoor Bridge, having passed the town of Cricklade in its way. The length is eight miles and three furlongs, and falls, from the Wilts and Berks Canal to the Thames and Severn, 58 feet 8 inches. The act obtained for making it is entitled, ' *An Act for making and maintaining a navigable Canal* ' *from the Wilts and Berks Canal, in the parish of Swindon, in the* ' *county of Wilts, to communicate with the Thames and Severn* ' *Canal in the parish of Latton, in the same county;*' whereby the proprietors, who are styled " The Company of Proprietors of the " North Wilts Canal Navigation," are empowered to make and complete the same. They are to raise £60,000, in shares of £25 each; but the sum of £44,000, being five-sixths of the estimate, is to be subscribed before the work commences. If the said £60,000 should not be sufficient, they may raise a further sum of

£30,000, either amongst themselves, or on mortgage of the rates, or by promissory notes bearing interest. The estimate for this work was made by Mr. Whitworth, under whose superintendence it was executed for less than the estimate, (an unusual thing.) Near Cricklade this canal is carried over the River Thames by an aqueduct peculiarly constructed, so as to meet the difficulty of passing that river at little more than 2 feet above its surface. But as this act is repealed by an act of the 1st and 2nd George IV. which consolidates this work with the Wilts and Berks Canal, we therefore refer to that article.

NORWICH AND LOWESTOFT NAVIGATION.

8 George IV. Cap. 42, Royal Assent 28th May, 1827.

THE object of this undertaking is to open a much superior communication for sea-borne vessels between Norwich and the sea, than the present navigation of the River Yare from that town to Yarmouth affords. The present state of the River Yare, which for thirty miles affords sufficient depth of water for a larger class of vessels than the wherries now navigated upon it, but which, from the insurmountable difficulty of passing over that shallow part called Breydon Lake, although carrying not more than from twenty-six to thirty-six tons, are frequently retarded, thereby causing an interruption to the regular despatch of business. To avoid this and other impediments, and to save the time and the trouble of re-shipment of all sea-borne articles, this company obtained powers to make a Ship Canal from Norwich to Lowestoft, calculated for vessels drawing 10 feet water; a principal part of which will be the river navigation deepened, widened, and improved by short cuts of about four miles in length; commencing in the Wensum or Yare River, at Norwich, it follows the course of that river to a bend where the road from Norwich to Yarmouth, in the township of Thorpe, leaves it, at which place is a canal of about thirty chains in length, cutting off two bends of the river; it then proceeds along the winding course of the river, passing Wood's End to Surlingham Ferry, at which is another short cut of sixteen chains; passing on

to Bradestone, there is another cut thirty-four chains in length
to Coldham Hall; and from thence it pursues the windings of
the river, passing Buckenham, Horseshoes, Devil's Round and
Hardley Cross, to Raveningham Mill, where the River Yare
continues its course easterly, and a canal is cut of two miles and a
half in length, to the River Waveney, at about a quarter of a
mile from St. Olaves; thence following the course of the Waveney
to Oulton Dyke, at which is a new cut of three quarters of a mile
in length to Oulton Broad, which connects it with Lake Lothing,
at the eastern end of which is a cut of half a mile in length and
120 feet wide, to the sea, where there is a tide-lock which will
admit vessels 84 feet long and 21 feet beam.

The level of this navigation is 4 feet above low water, and
4 feet below high water of spring tides, with 10 feet water on the
bottom-sill at low water; indeed this country is so flat that not
one lock is required on the old navigation between Yarmouth and
Norwich.

The act for this work was obtained in 1827, as ' *An Act for
' making and maintaining a navigable Communication for Ships
' and other Vessels, between the city of Norwich and the Sea, at or
' near Lowestoft, in the county of Suffolk.*' By this act the subscribers, incorporated as " The Company of Proprietors of the
" Norwich and Lowestoft Navigation " are empowered to make
the necessary works, when £100,000 shall be raised in £100
shares; and in case the said £100,000 shall not be sufficient to
complete the works, they may raise £50,000 more by mortgage
of the rates, or by granting annuities, or by borrowing of the
Exchequer Commissioners for carrying on public works. The
following are directed to be taken as

TONNAGE, WHARFAGE AND WAREHOUSING RATES.

The Column marked thus * are the Harbour and River Rates.

The Column marked thus † are the Rates of Wharfage at the Harbour, and all other
Places throughout the Line of Navigation respectively, for any Time not exceeding
the first Twenty-four Hours; an additional Rate or Duty to the same Amount, for
every Forty-eight Hours beyond the first Twenty-four Hours, or for any shorter period
of Time after the first Twenty-four Hours, or after any one complete Term of Forty-
eight Hours.

The Column marked thus ‡ are the Rates on Goods warehoused in the Warehouses, at the Harbour, or on the Line of Navigation, for any Time not exceeding the
first Twenty-four Hours, and at per Week exceeding the first Twenty-four Hours.

RATES CONTINUED.

DESCRIPTION OF GOODS.	(*)		(†)		(‡)	
	s.	d.	s.	d.	s.	d.
For every Quarter (containing Eight Bushels) of Wheat, Barley, Malt, Beans, Peas, Tares, Canary, Mustard and other Seeds	0	3	0	0½	0	1
For every Quarter of Oats	0	3	0	0½	0	1
For every Sack containing Five Bushels of Flour	0	2	0	0½	0	1
For every Quarter of Meal, Middlings and Sharps	0	2	0	0½	0	1
For every Quarter of Pollard and Bran	0	2	0	0½	0	1
For every Sack of Clover, Trefoil and other heavy Seeds	0	3	0	0½	0	1
For every Sack of Potatoes, Onions, &c.	0	1	0	0½	0	1
For every Bushel of Apples, Pears, &c.	0	1	0	0½	0	1
For every Bag of Hops	0	6	0	1	0	2
For every Pocket of Hops	0	3	0	0½	0	1
For every Thousand of English Oil Cakes	2	0	0	6	1	0
For every Thousand of Foreign ditto	2	0	0	6	1	0
For every Pack of Wool, Cotton, &c. containing Two Hundred and Forty Pounds	0	4	0	1	0	2
For every Hundred Weight of Tanned Hides and Calf Skins	0	2	0	0½	0	1
For every Raw Hide	0	1	0	0½	0	1
For every Hundred of Pelts	0	9	0	2	0	4
For every Ton of Tan or Bark	2	0	0	4	0	8
For every Ton of Sugar, Fruits, Bacon, Cheese, Butter, Pork, Hams, Tongues, Salt, Salted Fish, Tallow, Soap, Candles, and all heavy Grocery Goods not herein specified	2	0	0	4	0	8
For every Hundred Weight of Tea, Coffee and Spices	0	3	0	0½	0	1
For every Chest of Oranges, Lemons, &c.	0	2	0	1	0	2
For every Puncheon of Molasses	1	0	0	3	0	6
For every Butt of Ale, Porter, Cider, Perry, Vinegar and Oil	1	0	0	3	0	6
For every Puncheon of ditto	0	9	0	2	0	4
For every Hogshead of ditto	0	6	0	1½	0	3
For every Barrel of ditto	0	4	0	1	0	2
For every Kilderkin or Runlet of ditto	0	2	0	0½	0	1
For every Dozen of ditto in Hampers	0	2	0	0½	0	1
Madder, per Cask, per Cwt.	0	2	0	0½	0	1
Pipe Clay, per Ton	2	0	0	4	0	8
For every Pipe or Butt of Spirits and Wines	1	0	0	6	1	0
For every Hogshead of ditto	0	6	0	4	0	10
For every Half of ditto	0	3	0	3	0	6
For every Quarter of ditto	0	2	0	2	0	4
Under Twenty Gallons, per Gallon	0	1	0	0½	0	1
Per Dozen, in Hampers	0	2	0	0½	0	3
For every Four-wheeled Carriage	7	0				
For every Two-wheeled ditto	3	6				
For every Horse, Mare or Gelding	7	0				
For every other Beast	3	0				
For every Chaldron (containing Thirty-six Bushels) of Coal, Coke, Culm, Cinders or Breeze	2	0	0	3		
For every Ton of Hay, Cinquefoil, Clover or Straw	2	0	0	6	0	4
For every Load of Oak, Elm, Pine, Beech and Fir Timber	2	0	0	6	0	4
For every Load of Deals, Battens and Lath-wood	2	0	0	6	1	0
For every Cubic Foot of Mahogany, Teak-wood, or other valuable Woods	0	1	0	0½	0	4
For every Ton of Hemp, Cordage and Yarn	2	0	0	6	0	4
For every Barrel of Pitch, Tar, Grease, Rosin, &c.	0	3	0	2	0	3
For every Ton of Stone, Slate, Plaster of Paris, Alum, unwrought Iron, Bar-iron, Lead, &c.	2	0	0	6	0	6
For every Cubic Foot of Marble	0	3	0	1	0	1
For every One Thousand of Gutter, Pan, Mathematical and Plain Tiles	3	0	0	9	0	6

RATES CONTINUED.

DESCRIPTION OF GOODS.	(*)		(†)		(‡)	
	s.	*d.*	*s.*	*d.*	*s.*	*d.*
For every One Thousand of Bricks and Paving Tiles......	4	0	1	0	1	0
For every Crate of Glass or Earthenware..................	0	9	0	3	0	6
For every Carboy of Vitriol or Oil	0	3	0	1	0	2
For every Corpse	21	0	5	0	10	0
For every Organ	20	0	5	0	5	0
For every Piano-forte, Harpsichord, Harp or Bass Viol	5	0	1	0	2	0
For every One Hundred Pipe Staves	2	0	0	6		
For every Ton of Copper, Pewter, Brass or Metals	2	0	0	6	1	0
For every Ton of Ballast	1	0				
For Bale Goods, and all other Articles, Wares or Merchandize, not specified in this Schedule, according to the Amount of Freight, at per Cwt.	0	2	0	6	0	6

This navigation, which is thirty miles in length, connects Norwich with the sea at Lowestoft, and will be highly advantageous to the city of Norwich, by the importation of coal, timber, and general merchandize, and the exportation of the manufactures of Norwich, with the agricultural produce of the surrounding district; and a national benefit by the shelter it will afford to shipping in tempestuous weather. It is ascertained, that, at present, more than 300,000 quarters of corn and 50,000 sacks of flour are carried, in wherries, annually down the river to Yarmouth, and 60,000 chaldrons of coal and 20,000 tons of goods up the river to Norwich.

NOTTINGHAM CANAL.

32 George III. Cap. 100, Royal Assent 8th May, 1792.

THE original plan of this work was to make a canal from the Cromford Canal to the navigable River Trent, with collateral cuts from the same to the Earl of Stamford's estate in the parish of Greasley; another from the same to the estate of Edward Willoughby, Esq. in the parish of Cossall; and a third from Leen Bridge, in the town of Nottingham, to the west end of Sneinton Hermitage.

The necessary powers for executing the canal and cuts, were given to the proprietors as "The Nottingham Canal Company," by ' *An Act for making and maintaining a navigable Canal, from* ' *the Cromford Canal in the county of Nottingham, to or near to*

' *the town of Nottingham, and to the River Trent, near Nottingham*
' *Trent Bridge, and also certain collateral Cuts therein described,*
' *from the said intended Canal.*' Under this act the company are
directed to make a lock near the junction with the Cromford
Canal and reservoirs for re-supplying water taken from the said
Cromford Canal, but no reservoirs are to be made where the
Erewash Company have a previous right, nor is any reservoir to
be made in the Earl of Stamford's land. Proprietors of land have
power to make railways to the canal, or the company may make
the same, provided that none shall be made by them, without
their forming another at the same time, for the use of the Duke of
Newcastle's Collieries at Brinsley; collateral cuts may also be
made, and lords of manors or owners of lands may build warehouses on the line; if they refuse, the company may do so. The
following are ordered to be taken as

WHARFAGE RATES.

<table>
<tr><td></td><td align="right">d.</td></tr>
<tr><td>For Coal, Lime, Lime-stone, Clay, Iron, Iron-stone, Timber, Stone, Brick, Tile, Slate or Gravel for Six Days ....</td><td>1 per Ton.</td></tr>
<tr><td>All other Goods, Wares and Merchandize ditto ....</td><td>3   ditto.</td></tr>
</table>

Coal, Iron and Lime-stone may remain on the Wharf Six Months; and Timber, Clay,
Lime, Iron-stone, Stone, Brick, Tile, Slate or Gravel, may remain Thirty Days with-
out further Charge; but all other Goods are to pay One Penny per Ton for the
Space of Ten Days after the first Six, and One Penny per Ton for every additional
Day they remain.

The company is empowered to raise £50,000 in shares of
£100 each; and in case that should be insufficient, a further sum
of £25,000 may be procured on mortgage, or assignment of the
navigation; and for the payment of necessary expenses and the
interest of monies employed, the following are to be demanded as

TONNAGE RATES.

<table>
<tr><td></td><td align="right">d.</td><td></td><td></td></tr>
<tr><td>For Coal and Coke navigated on the Canal or Collateral Cuts</td><td>4½ per Ton.</td><td></td><td></td></tr>
</table>

In Addition to which they are to pay a Rate of One Half-penny per Ton, per Mile,
provided that the whole does not exceed One Shilling per Ton.

<table>
<tr><td>For all Lime and Lime-stone for burning, provided that Sum does not exceed the Tonnage for Twelve Miles ....</td><td>½</td><td>ditto,</td><td>per Mile.</td></tr>
<tr><td>For all Bricks ....</td><td>6</td><td>ditto.</td><td></td></tr>
<tr><td>For all Stone, so that the Rate does not amount to more than the Carriage would be for Ten Miles ....</td><td>1</td><td>ditto.</td><td>ditto.</td></tr>
<tr><td>For all Iron, Iron-stone, Lead and other Minerals, Timber, Corn and other Goods, and Merchandize, so that the Amount is not more than the Charge for Twelve Miles ..</td><td>1</td><td>ditto.</td><td>ditto.</td></tr>
<tr><td>For all Goods and other Things, except Slate, Lime and Lime-stone to be burnt, and Plaster, passed from the Trent into this Canal, and vice versa..............................</td><td>2</td><td>ditto.</td><td></td></tr>
</table>

Fractions of a Mile to be taken as a Mile; of a Ton as the Quarters therein, and of a
Quarter as a Quarter.

Tillage, Dung, Soil, Marl, Coal Ashes, Turf, and all other Manure, except Lime, to be used on Lands near the Line, are free from Tolls.

Goods passing into or out of this Canal, or out of or into the Cromford, are to pay the same Rates as are paid for Goods passing to or from the Erewash from or into the said Cromford Canal.

The company may divide £8 per cent. per annum on the sums subscribed, and the surplus is to be funded to answer the deficiencies of any succeeding year; and when there is no deficiency for three successive years, then the rates are to be reduced. The Trent Undertakers may make a cut or communication into the canal at Sneinton Meadow, and boats may pass thereon, paying the rates as above.

This canal is about fifteen miles in length, its direction being nearly north-west, at no great elevation in any part. It was completed in 1802, and has a large reservoir at Amsworth, with a self-regulating sluice, whereby 3,000 cubic feet of water are let out per hour, for the purpose of supplying the Erewash Canal and certain mills on the line.

As affording a ready way for the export of farming produce and coal, and for importing timber, deals and other articles of home consumption, this is an useful work.

NUTBROOK OR SHIPLEY CANAL.

33 George III. Cap. 115, Royal Assent, 3rd June, 1793.

THIS canal commences at the collieries belonging to Sir Henry Hunloke, Bart. and E. M. Mundy, Esq. which collieries are situate in the township of Shipley, whence proceeding in a southerly direction, leaving Ilkestone on the east and Kirk Hallam on the west, it falls into the Erewash Canal in the parish of Stanton-by-Dale, not far from Trowen, traversing a distance of about four miles and a half.

The act for this work was made in the year 1793, under the title of ' *An Act for making and maintaining a navigable Canal* ' *from the Collieries at Shipley and West Hallam, in the county of* ' *Derby, to the Erewash Canal in the parish of Stanton-by-Dale,* ' *in the said county.*' By this act the following are directed to be received as tonnage rates.

TONNAGE RATES.

	d.	
For all Coal and Coke, not navigated on the Erewash	4	per Ton.
For ditto, if got within the Liberties of Shipley and West Hallam, navigated on this Canal and the Erewash	8	ditto.
For ditto within the Liberties of Mapperley, Kirk Hallam, Ilkestone and Little Hallam, navigated on this Canal and the Erewash	1	ditto.
For all other Goods, Wares, &c.	8	ditto.

The Earl Stanhope and his Tenants in the parishes of Stanton-by-Dale and Dale Abbey may carry, free of Rates, any Iron-stone got within the Lordships of Shipley, Mapperley, West Hallam, Kirk Hallam, Ilkestone and Little Hallam, and used within Stanton-by-Dale and Dale Abbey, and also navigate on as much of the Canal as is in those Two Parishes, free of Rates, all Iron, Coal, Coke and Iron-stone, the Produce of the said Parish, or brought from the Erewash, and all other Goods, Wares and Articles whatever.

For completing the canal, the proprietors may raise £13,000, in shares of £100 each, and £6,500 if the first sum be not sufficient.

Railroads are laid from various parts of this canal to the coal mines near; but as the situation and number of these are changed as circumstances require, it would be impossible to describe them fully or correctly. The intention of the projectors was to afford a cheap and ready conveyance of coals and minerals from their works to the Erewash Canal, for the purpose of exporting; and though, as will be seen from what we have stated above, that this is exclusively a private speculation, it is not on that account an undertaking devoid of benefit to the public. The facilities which it affords the proprietors of conveying the produce of their mines, at the same time guarding the consumers from any additional cost of carriage, which land conveyance would add to the other charges incurred, will appear more evident on reference to our map.

OAKHAM CANAL.

33 George III. Cap. 103, Royal Assent 7th May, 1793.
40 George III. Cap. 56, Royal Assent 20th June, 1800.

THE first act for executing this advantageous undertaking was obtained in 1793, under the title of '*An Act for making and main-* *' taining a navigable Cut or Canal from the Melton Mowbray* *' Navigation, in the county of Leicester, to Oakham, in the county* *' of Rutland;'* by which certain proprietors, incorporated as "The "Company of Proprietors of the Oakham Canal," are authorized to raise £56,000, in shares of £100 each, for executing the same; and in case that should not be sufficient, they may obtain a further sum of £20,000, either by the admission of new subscribers, or by mortgage of the rates of the same. For the payment of interest and other necessary contingencies, the company have authority to demand as

TONNAGE RATES.

		d.
For all Coals, so that the gross Rate does not exceed Three Shillings.	}	3½ per Ton, per Mile.
For all Iron, Timber, Coke and other Goods, so that the gross Rate does not exceed Four Shillings	}	4 ditto. ditto.

For all Lime, Lime-stone and Stones used for Building, and Materials for Roads, Half the Rates for Coal are to be paid.

The Owners of Land through which the Canal passes are exempted from the Payment of Tolls for Dung, Soil, Marl, Ashes of Coal and Turf and all other Manures, except Lime, used on their Lands; and all Materials for Roads are to pass Toll Free, provided they pass no Lock, except when the Water flows over the Waste Weir.

Proprietors of lands and others may erect quays, wharfs and warehouses, the rates for using which are to be determined by certain commissioners appointed by the act.

Lord Winchelsea having a right of dues on all coals sold in the manor of Oakham, this act provides that the company shall pay him the sum of £15 per annum in lieu of the said dues.

Having obtained the act, the company proceeded immediately to put the work into execution, but when about ten miles of the line had been finished, they were obliged, by want of funds, to apply a second time to parliament for a fresh act, which was obtained in June, 1800, under the title of ' *An Act to enable the Company of* ' *Proprietors of the Oakham Canal to raise Money for completing* ' *the said Canal, and also for altering and amending an Act passed* ' *in the Thirty-third of his present Majesty, for making the said* ' *Canal.*' By this last act they are enabled to raise a further sum of £30,000, either by the admission of new subscribers, or by bond, or by promissory notes, or they may, if more eligible, admit persons, to whom they already owe money, amongst the number of shareholders, by way of payment of their debt, assigning the interest of one share for every £100 they are so indebted to the said persons; or they may make a call on the present subscribers to the amount of £15,000, being half of the £30,000 ordered by this act to be raised. They are also entitled to the following additional tonnage rates.

TONNAGE RATES.

d.

For all Coals, so that the gross Amount does not exceed One } 1½ per Ton, per Mile.
  Shilling and Sixpence per Ton ....

For all Iron, Timber, Coke and other Goods, the gross Amount } 2 ditto.   ditto.
  not exceeding Two Shillings per Ton....................

For all Lime, Lime-stone, Stone and Bricks for Building, Half the Rates for Coal.

It is also provided, that whenever the Leicester and Melton Mowbray Canal Company shall reduce their additional rates, the additional rates on this canal shall have a corresponding reduction.

This canal is fifteen miles in length; commencing in the town of Oakham, in the county of Rutland, it pursues a course nearly due north, by Burley Hall to Greetham, a little beyond which it makes a turn to the west and enters the county of Leicester, near Edmonthorpe Hall, having, from Oakham to this place, traversed a distance of six miles and a half, on a level; from Edmonthorpe it verges to the north-west, leaving Stapleford Park on the east; it then turns toward the west, which direction it pursues to its junction with the Melton Mowbray Navigation in Mill Close on the west of that town, having, from Edmonthorpe to its termination, passed a distance of eight miles and a half, parallel to the River Wreak, and with a fall of 126 feet from the level at Edmonthorpe.

This work, by its connection with Melton Mowbray, opens an easy and cheap passage for the produce of the country situate both north and south of Oakham and of the adjacent country, and consequently is attended with much advantage to the district through which it is carried.

OUSE RIVER, SUSSEX.

30 Geo. III. C. 52, *R. A.* 28th April, 1790. 31 Geo. III. Cap. 76, R. A. 6th June, 1791.
40 Geo. III. C. 54, R. A. 20th June, 1800. 46 Geo. III. Cap. 122, R. A. 12th July, 1806.
    54 Geo. III. C. 176, R. A. 28th June, 1814.

THIS river has its source in Slaugham, in Sussex, and running easterly, passes through the parish of Cuckfield-by-Paxhill; thence it runs nearly south by Buckham Hall, Newick Place, Isfield Place, Coombe Park, and Landport, to Lewes; and thence continues in a southerly course to the sea at Newhaven Harbour.

The first act of parliament for improving this navigation was passed in 1790, and is entitled, ' *An Act for improving, continuing*

‘ and extending the Navigation of the River Ouse, from Lewes
‘ Bridge, in the town of Lewes, to Hammer Bridge, in the parish of
‘ Cuckfield, and to the Extent of the said parish of Cuckfield, and
‘ also of a Branch of the said River, to Shortbridge, in the parish
‘ of Fletching, in the county of Sussex.’ It incorporates a number
of persons, amongst whom are Lord Sheffield, Sir Godfrey Webster,
Sir Peter Burrell, and Sir William Burrell, by the name of “ The
“ Company of Proprietors of the River Ouse Navigation,” and
empowers them to raise, amongst themselves, for carrying into
effect this act, the sum of £25,000, in shares of £100 each, of
which sum, £10,000 is to be subscribed before the work is commenced, and to collect the following

TONNAGE RATES.

	d.	
For all Chalk, Lime, Dung, Mould, Soil, Compost or other Manure, Timber, Planks, Fire Wood, Corn or Grain, ground or unground, or any other Article manufactured at Barcombe Mill; Beech, Gravel and Materials for Roads, conveyed between Lewes Bridge and Barcombe Mill	½	per Ton, per Mile.
For the same Goods above Barcombe Mill	1	ditto. ditto.
For all other Goods, Wares and Merchandize between Lewes Bridge and Barcombe Mill	1	ditto. ditto.
For the same Goods above Barcombe Mill	1½	ditto. ditto.

And in the same Proportion for any greater or less Distance or Quantity.

No tolls to be taken between Barcombe Mill and Lewes, until
£500 have been expended on the improvement of the river.

WHARFAGE RATES.

	s. d.	
For all Goods, Wares and Merchandize for a Period of Two Months ..	0 6	per Ton.
For a longer period than Two Months	1 0	ditto.

If left for a longer Period than Twelve Months, the same Rates to be paid as the
Tonnage Rate for such Goods.

No Vessel of less than Ten Tons to pass through the Locks, without leave of the
Proprietors.

The next act of parliament respecting this river was passed in
1791, and is entitled, ‘ An Act for improving the Navigation of the
‘ River Ouse, between Newhaven Bridge and Lewes Bridge, in the
‘ county of Sussex; and for the better Draining of the Low Lands,
‘ lying in Lewes and Laughton Levels, in the said county,’ and
appoints certain persons therein named, together with the commissioners of the Lewes and Laughton Levels, trustees for carrying it
into effect, who are authorized to collect the following tonnage
rates.

TONNAGE RATES.

		d.	
For all Beech, Gravel and other Materials to be used for repairing Roads..	3	per Ton.
For all Chalk, Lime, Dung, Mould, Soil, Compost, and other Manure ..	2	ditto.
For all other Goods, Wares and Merchandize	4	ditto.

And so in Proportion for a greater or less Quantity than a Ton.

Vessels passing between Lewes Bridge and Southerham Corner, and Newhaven Bridge and Lock Hole, to be exempted from Tolls.

The land in the neighbourhood of this navigation is divided into five districts, which may be taxed to pay the expense of the drainage, in the following proportions, viz.—

	s.	d.	
First District	1	0	per Acre
Second ditto..	1	6	ditto.
Third ditto	1	0	ditto.
Fourth ditto...	0	4	ditto.
Fifth ditto...	0	4	ditto.

And in the same Proportion for each District.

The trustees are not to reduce the tolls or tonnage rates, without reducing in the same proportion the rates and assessments on the land, except the tonnage rates are more than double the amount of the drainage rates, and the tonnage must be reduced in the same proportion as the drainage rates, except when the latter exceeds half the amount of the former, nor shall the tonnage rates be reduced until the money borrowed does not exceed £6,000. The tolls of this navigation to be exempted from all taxes whatever; and the trustees may borrow money on the security of the tolls, rates and duties, and may also sell the old parts of the river, in lieu of which they have substituted new cuts.

By the 40th George III. which is entitled, ' *An Act to alter,* ' *amend, and enlarge the Powers of an Act, passed in the Thirty-* ' *first Year of the Reign of his present Majesty King George the* ' *Third, for improving the Navigation of the River Ouse, between* ' *Newhaven Bridge and Lewes Bridge, in the county of Sussex, and* ' *for the better Draining of the Low Lands lying in Lewes and* ' *Laughton Levels, in the said county,*' it is stated, that in consequence of the pressure of the drainage rates on the owners of the land in the level for the purposes of this act, it is expedient to increase the tonnage rates on the river; the former tolls are therefore repealed, and in lieu thereof may be taken the following tonnage rates.

TONNAGE RATES.

	d.
For all Beech, Gravel and all other Materials for repairing Roads, Chalk, Lime, Dung, Mould, Soil, Compost or any other Manure.... }	4 per Ton.
For all other Goods, Wares, and Merchandize	8 ditto.

And so in Proportion for a greater or less Quantity than a Ton.

When the tonnage rates exceed the amount of the drainage
rates by £20, the trustees may lower them, and if lower may raise
them, so as to keep the amount levied from each as nearly equal as
possible, provided that the tonnage rates in no instance exceed the
sums above stated.

The act passed in 1806 is entitled, ' *An Act for altering, amend-*
' *ing, and rendering more effectual an Act passed in the Thirtieth*
' *Year of his present Majesty, for improving the Navigation of the*
' *River Ouse, in the county of Sussex ;*' and repeals that part of the
former act which authorizes the company to continue the navigation
of the river from Hammer Bridge, in the parish of Cuckfield, to
the extent of the said parish. It empowers the company to raise
a further sum of £30,000, and to mortgage the tolls and rates as
a security for it, or by annuity ; and it allows the proprietors of
lands on the western side of Isfield Lock, and the occupiers or
owners of Barcombe Mill, near Primmer Wood Lock, to take and
use the surplus or waste waters at those locks.

The last act relating to this navigation was passed in 1814, and
is entitled, ' *An Act for altering and enlarging the Powers of Two*
' *Acts of his present Majesty, for improving the Navigation of the*
' *River Ouse, in the county of Sussex ;*' and after stating that the
tolls and rates authorized to be taken by former acts were insufficient for supporting the navigation, it repeals such tolls and rates,
and authorizes the company to take the following

TONNAGE RATES.

	d.		
For all Chalk, Dung, Mould, Soil, Compost, Lime-stone, Ashes or other Manure (Lime excepted) carried between Lewes Bridge and Sharps Lock .... }	2	per Ton, per Mile.	
From Sharps Lock to Goldbridge	1½	ditto.	ditto.
From Goldbridge to the extremity of the Navigation........	1	ditto.	ditto.
For all Beech, Gravel, Flints, Stone and other Materials for repairing Roads .... }	1	ditto.	ditto.
For Hay, Straw, Timber, Planks, Coal, Culm or Fuller's-earth	1½	ditto.	ditto.
For Lime	2	ditto.	ditto.
For Corn or Grain ground or unground, Flour, Wheat or Seeds	3	ditto.	ditto.
For every Hundred of Faggots and Hop Poles, and for every Cord of Fire or other Wood .... }	2	per Mile.	
For all other Goods, Wares and Merchandize	¼	ditto, per Cwt.	

And so in Proportion for greater or less Distances, or greater or less Quantities.

TONNAGE RATES CONTINUED.

	d.
For every Package or Parcel under Fifty Pounds Weight.............	¼ per Mile.
For every Person in a Boat or Barge, except the Person having the Management thereof..	1 ditto.

For every Boat, Barge or other Vessel of less Burthen than Ten Tons passing through any Lock, the Sum of Sixpence for each Lock it passes through ; but if laden with any of the Articles above enumerated, instead of this Sixpence, the Rates on such Articles to be paid.

Only Half of these Tolls to be taken on Goods passing between Lewes Bridge and Barcombe Mill.

In the year 1767, Mr. Smeaton states that the high-water-mark at the pier head at Newhaven was 15 feet 6 inches, on the moon's quarter day; and at the same time at Lewes Bridge, 13 feet 4 inches. The length from Newhaven to the top of the navigation near Cuckfield, is near thirty miles.

OUSE RIVER, YORK.

2 Edward IV. Charter —— 1462.   The Lord Protector, Charter, 26th June, 1657.
13 George I. C. 33, R. A. 15th May, 1727.   5 George II. C. 15, R. A. 1st June, 1732.
7 George III. C. 96, R. A. 15th April, 1767.

THE River Ouse rises on the borders of Yorkshire and Westmoreland. Its most northern branch called the Swale commences near Lady's Pillar; another branch rises at Shunner Fall, 2,329 feet above the level of the sea. The river runs by Reeth, Richmond and Catterick to Morton Bridge, a little below which the Bedale River unites with it. Passing on by Newby Park to Topcliffe Bridge, it is joined by the Codbeck, and proceeds to near Myton Hall, where it receives the Ure, and being augmented by many other streams in its route, it arrives at Linton, where it first takes the name of Ouse. Thence continuing in a southerly direction to Benningbrough Hall, it is joined by the River Nidd and proceeds south-easterly to the city of York, where the River Foss runs into it. Passing through the city, it runs by Bishopthorpe Palace, Naburn, and Moreby Hall; not far from Nun-Appleton Hall it is joined by the River Wharfe, and passing Cawood takes a winding and very circuitous direction to Selby; thence it proceeds in a south-easterly course until it meets the River Derwent near Barnby-on-the-Marsh; passing on, at the village of Armyn it receives the River Aire, thence proceeding easterly it runs near the town of Howden, at which place it takes a southerly direction to the port of Goole, where it is joined by the River Dunn or New Dutch River; winding by Swinefleet and Saltmarshe Hall to a place called Flaxfleet, it there receives the Trent, and from this point loses its name in the River Humber.

By charter of Edward IV. granted in 1462, the Lord Mayor and Aldermen of York were appointed to oversee and be the conservators of this river, as well as of the Aire, Wharfe, Derwent, Dunn and Humber, which are connected with it.

The first act of parliament relating to this river was passed in 1657, when Cromwell was Protector, and is entitled, '*An Act for* ' *amending the River of Ouse, at or near the city of York.*' The next act was obtained in 1726—7, and entitled, '*An Act for improving* ' *the Navigation of the River Ouse, in the county of York.*' This was followed by another in 1732, entitled, '*An Act for rendering* ' *more effectual an Act passed in the Thirteenth Year of the Reign* ' *of his late Majesty King George the First, entitled, An Act for* ' *improving the Navigation of the River Ouse, in the county of* ' *York ;*' which authorized the following to be taken above Wharfe's Mouth, as

TONNAGE RATES.

	s.	d.	
For all Salt, Lead, Wool, Corn, Flour, &c. &c.	0	6	per Ton.
For all Steel and Iron	1	0	ditto.
For all Wine, Groceries and other Things	2	6	ditto.

Another act was passed in 1767, entitled, '*An Act for making* ' *navigable the River Ouse from below Widdington Ings, at or near* ' *Linton, to the Junction of the Rivers Swale and Ure ; and for* ' *making navigable the said River Swale from the said Junction to* ' *Morton Bridge; and also the Brook running from Bedale into the* ' *River Swale, in the county of York ;*' wherein it is stated that the navigation of the said river has been improved above the city of York to Linton-upon-Ouse, in the said county ; and that the continuing the said navigation from below Widdington Ings, near Linton, to the junction of the Rivers Swale and Ure, and from thence up the River Swale, to Topcliffe and Morton Bridge, and also making navigable the brook below the said bridge to the town of Bedale, will be of great utility to the public ; and a great number of persons are appointed commissioners for carrying the provisions of the act into effect, who are to erect a lock at Linton which will admit a vessel of not less than 60 feet long, 15 feet 4 inches in breadth, and which draws four feet water, upon passing which the following must be paid as

TONNAGE RATES.

	d.
For all Coal, Cinders, Lime and Lime-stone, Stone, Gravel, and Manure, carried on the said River, Cuts or Canals, from below Widdington Ings to the Junction of the Ure and Swale	4 per Ton.
For all Butter and other Goods, Wares and Merchandize................	9 ditto.

TOLLS ON THE SWALE AND BEDALE BROOK.

	s.	d.
For all Coal, Cinders, Lime and Lime-stone or other Stone, Slate, Gravel or Manure, carried upon the River Swale, Brook, Cuts or Canals, from the Junction of the Swale and Ure to Bedale, or from Bedale back to the said Junction	1	$10\frac{1}{2}$ per Ton.
For all Butter and other Goods, Wares and Merchandize...........	3	9 ditto.

And so in Proportion for a less Distance, and for a greater or less Quantity than a Ton.

The commissioners have power to borrow money, for executing the work, upon security of the tolls, or by annuities.

Another act was passed in the same year as the preceding act, entitled, ' *An Act for making navigable a Brook called Codbeck,* ' *from the River Swale to the borough of Thirsk, in the county of* ' *York.*' The same commissioners as named in the act last mentioned are appointed to carry the act into execution, and are empowered to take the following

TONNAGE RATES.

	s.	d.
For all Coal, Cinders, Lime and Lime-stone or other Stone, Slate, Gravel and Manure, from the Junction of the said Brook and the River Swale to the Borough of Thirsk, or from Thirsk to such Junction..	1	6 per Ton.
For all Butter, and all other Goods, Wares and Merchandize........	2	6 ditto.

And so in Proportion for a less Distance, or a greater or less Quantity than a Ton.

They may borrow money for the purposes of the undertaking on security of the tolls.

The last act of parliament relating to the navigation connected with this river, was passed in 1770, and is entitled, ' *An Act for* ' *completing the Navigation of the River Swale, from its Junction* ' *with the River Ure to Morton Bridge, and of Bedale Brook, in* ' *the county of York ; and for repealing part of an Act made in* ' *the Seventh Year of his present Majesty's Reign, relating thereto.*'

It incorporates certain persons therein named, as " The Company
" of Proprietors of the River Swale and Bedale Brook Naviga-
" tion." This company are empowered to raise, amongst themselves, or by the creation of new shares, or by mortgage of a
moiety of the tolls and rates, the sum of £30,000; and they are
authorized to take the following

TONNAGE RATES.

	s.	d.	
For all Coal, Cinders, Lime and Lime-stone or other Stone, Slate, Gravel or Manure, from the Junction of the Swale and Ure to Bedale, or from Bedale to such Junction	1	10½	per Ton.
For all Butter and all other Goods, Wares and Merchandize........	3	9	ditto.

And so in Proportion for a less Distance, or a greater or less Quantity.

The act limits the amount of dividend to be paid on the shares
to £10 per cent. per annum, and when the receipts from the tolls
exceed that sum, the highest rate of tolls to be reduced one-eighth.

Lords of manors and owners of land may erect wharfs and
warehouses, and on their failing to do so, when required, the company have the power of erecting them, and they, as well as such
owners, may take for every ton of goods, remaining not longer
than ten days, sixpence; and for every subsequent day one half-
penny per ton.

Half a century back a lock 21 feet wide and 70 feet long was
erected on this river at Naburn, four miles below York, at which a
small toll of 1s. 2d. is taken on every vessel. Before the erection
of this lock the tide flowed 4 feet at Ouse Bridge in York, being
a distance of eighty miles from the sea.

The River Ouse, notwithstanding the limited trade of that portion above the city of York, has such an immense traffic in the
lower part, by reason of the numerous rivers and canals immediately communicating with the manufacturing districts of Yorkshire
and Lancashire, in addition to the coal mines, stone quarries, and
various iron works situate in the West Riding, as will undoubtedly
rank it the second river of the kingdom in importance and utility;
whilst by its union with the estuary of the Humber, merchandize
is exported to and imported from all parts of the world.

OUSE RIVER, BEDFORD LEVEL.

22 Char. II. C. 16, R. A. 11th April, 1670.   24 Geo. II. C. 12, R. A. 22nd May, 1751.
35 Geo. III. C. 77, R. A. 19th May, 1795.   36 Geo. III. C. 73, R. A. 7th Mar. 1796.
45 Geo. III. C. 72, R. A. 27th June, 1805.   50 Geo. III. C. 166, R. A. 9th June, 1810.
56 Geo. III. C. 38, R. A. —— 1816.   58 Geo. III. C. 48, R. A. —— 1818.
59 Geo. III. C. 79, R. A. 14th June, 1819.   2 Geo. IV. C. 64, R. A. 28th May, 1821.
7 & 8 Geo. IV. C. 47, R. A. 28th May, 1827.   11 Geo. IV. C. 53, R. A. 29th May, 1830.

LITTLE OUSE OR BRANDON AND WAVENEY RIVER.

COMMENCING with the head of this navigation at Thetford, it runs from thence in a northerly direction about three miles and a half; thence westerly, passing Santon, Downham and Brandon, a distance of thirteen miles, and thence by a north-westerly course for six miles, to its junction with the River Ouse at Brandon Creek Bridge, making the whole about twenty-two miles and a half, in the greater part of which distance it divides the counties of Norfolk and Suffolk. Its elevation above the level of the sea is very slight, the country through which it passes being generally flat.

The first act relating to this river was passed in 1670, and entitled, ' *An Act for making navigable the Rivers commonly* ' *called Brandon and Waveney.*' This was followed in 1751, by an act, entitled, ' *An Act for appointing Commissioners to put in* ' *Execution an Act made in the Twenty-second Year of the Reign* ' *of King Charles the Second, for making navigable the Rivers* ' *commonly called Brandon and Waveney; so far as the same relates* ' *to the Navigation of the River commonly called the Lesser Ouse,* ' *from Thetford to Brandon, and from Brandon to a Place called* ' *the White House, near Brandon Ferry, in the counties of Norfolk* ' *and Suffolk ;*' which states that disputes have arisen amongst the land-owners on this river respecting the navigation, and the commissioners appointed under the act of Charles II. being dead, it is necessary to appoint fresh commissioners, and it then goes on to name a number of persons, amongst whom are the Duke of Grafton, Lord Cornwallis, the Marquis of Granby, Lord Euston, and Lord Henry Beauclerk, to be the commissioners for putting the act in execution.

The last act of parliament relating to this navigation was passed in 1810, and is entitled, '*An Act for amending an Act of* '*the Twenty-second Year of his late Majesty King Charles the* '*Second, so far as the same relates to the River Brandon, otherwise* '*the Lesser Ouse, from the White House, near Brandon Ferry,* '*to Thetford, in the counties of Norfolk and Suffolk, and for* '*improving the Navigation of the said River.*' It states that the act passed in the reign of Charles II. authorized the mayor, burgesses and commonalty of Thetford to make navigable this river, and for so doing to receive and take such tolls and rates thereon as should be fixed by commissioners named in the act, and that if the mayor, &c. declined the undertaking, the commissioners should appoint some other person who would accept the same; that the mayor, &c. not being in a situation to make this navigation, the commissioners appointed the Earl of Arlington to carry the purposes of the act into effect, and authorized him, for so doing, to take the following

TOLLS.

d.

For every Last of Corn or Grain; every Chaldron of Coal, (Forty Bushels;) every Load of broad Plank and Timber, and every Ton of all other Goods, Wares and Commodities .... } 6

And the commissioners named under the act, and the mayor, burgesses and commonalty of Thetford, granted and assigned the above tolls to the Earl of Arlington, by a deed dated 20th January, 1677, which tolls were, by an indorsement on this deed dated 10th March, 1796, demised and released by the Duchess Dowager of Grafton (sole executrix of the will of the late Duke of Grafton, who was sole executor of the Earl of Arlington) to the mayor, &c. of Thetford; and they have made considerable improvements in the navigation.

The act then appoints certain commissioners, in addition to those appointed by the last act, repeals the tonnage rates before fixed, and empowers them to collect the following

TONNAGE RATES.

The Column marked thus (*) are the Rates to be paid between Whitehouse and the Sluice called the Cross Gravel Haunch.

The Column marked thus (+) between the Cross Gravel Haunch and Brandon Ferry.

The Column marked thus (‡) between Brandon Ferry and Thetford.

RATES CONTINUED.

DESCRIPTION OF GOODS.	(*)		(+)		(‡)	
	s.	*d.*	*s.*	*d.*	*s.*	*d.*
For every Last of every Sort of Corn or Grain	0	2	0	4	1	0
For every Chaldron of Coal, Thirty-six Bushels	0	2	0	4	1	0
For every Hundred of single Deals and Battens............	0	3	0	6	1	6
For every Hundred of double Deals	0	6	1	0	3	0
For every Thousand of Reed.............................	0	4	0	8	2	0
For every Thousand of Pantiles.........................	0	4	0	8	2	0
For every Hundred of Spars or Poles, of less than Sixteen Feet in Length	0	3	0	6	1	6
For ditto, exceeding Sixteen Feet in Length...............	0	6	1	0	3	0
For every Ton or Load of other Goods, Wares and Commodities.......................................	0	2	0	4	1	0

The act also authorizes the commissioners to borrow £10,000 on security of the tolls and rates, for the purposes of improving this navigation.

OUSE AND LARKE.

It is unnecessary to recite the early enactments for this work, as they are consolidated in the act of 1827, entitled, ' *An Act for* ' *improving the Drainage of Part of the South Level of the Fens* ' *within the Great Level commonly called Bedford Level, and the* ' *Navigation of the Rivers passing through the same, in the coun-* ' *ties of Cambridge, Suffolk, and Norfolk, and in the Isle of Ely.*' Certain persons are appointed navigation commissioners, with power to make a cut from a little below Ely to Sand Hill End, in the parish of Littleport, such cut to be 50 feet wide at the bottom, 74 at the top, and 6 feet deep at least; the base of the bank to be 36 feet broad and the top 12 feet, such bank to be 12 feet high from the bottom of the cut. They are also empowered to scour, cleanse and deepen such parts of the Cam and Ouse between Clayhithe and Hermitage Sluices and Littleport Bridge, and as well the present course of the Larke between Swale's Reach and Littleport Bridge, as the intended course of the river from Prick Willow to Sandy's or Sandall's Cut, and also such parts of the several navigable lodes, communicating with the said Rivers Cam and Ouse above Littleport Bridge, as may be necessary. An acreage tax of five shillings per acre in certain parts and sixpence

per acre in others is ordered to be collected. Towing-paths are
to be made and maintained by the said commissioners. They are
also to charge as

BANKAGE RATES.

	s.	*d.*	
For every Horse, Mule, Ass or other Beast	0	3	each.
For every Drove of Neat Cattle	1	0	per Score.
For every Drove of Calves, Sheep or Lambs, Hogs or Pigs	0	8	ditto.

The following are directed to be paid by all vessels and rafts
navigated on the Ouse between Littleport Bridge and Upware
Sluice, or on the Larke between Littleport Bridge and Prick
Willow, as

TONNAGE RATES.

	s.	*d.*	
For Coals or Cinders	0	6	per Chaldron.
For Deal Boards or Battens	3	0	per Hundred.
For Poles	1	6	ditto.
For Timber	0	8	per Load or Ton.
For Wheat, Beans, Peas or Rye	1	0	per Last.
For Oats, Barley or Malt	1	0	ditto.
For Bricks and Tiles	0	4	per Thousand.
For Sedge	0	1	per Hundred.
For Stones or Pebbles	0	8	per Ton.
For Turves	0	1	per Thousand.
For Hay	0	4	per Load or 20 Cwt.
For Seeds	1	6	per Last.
For Clay or Sand	0	4	per Ton.
For Salt Fish	0	8	per Cwt.
For Iron or Lead	1	6	per Ton.
For Salt	0	8	ditto.
For Wine or Cider	3	0	per Tun.
For Oil, Vinegar, Pitch, Tar or Soap	0	8	per Ton.
For Butter or Cheese	0	8	ditto.
For Faggots or Billets	0	1	per Hundred.
For Hops	0	4	per Pocket.
For Pales, Barrel or Hogshead Staves	0	1	per Hundred.
For Passage Boats	0	1	each Passenger.
For all other Goods, Wares or Merchandize whatsoever, not herein-before mentioned	0	8	per Ton.
For every Barge, Lighter, Vessel or Boat, either empty or carrying less than a Ton, and whether haled or not..	0	2	each.

Commissioners may borrow money on mortgage of the rates.
From the end of the cut to Littleport, this river is joined by the
Little Ouse at Brandon Bridge, and at Creek Ferry by the Wissey
or Stoke River, and proceeding to Denver Sluice where the New
Bedford River connects with it. Leaving Downham Market to
the east it passes on to Wiggen Hall, where that immense cut
lately finished by Sir Edward Banks, called the Eau Brink Cut,
conducts the waters down to Lynn. The Eau Brink Cut is 300 feet
wide and nearly three miles long ; the ordinary tides rise 15 feet.

Having described the part of this river below Denver Sluice, we now proceed to the upper part, or the

GREAT OUSE RIVER,

WHICH from Denver Sluice to Hermitage Sluice, a distance of twenty miles, in a direct course, is called the New Bedford River. At a further distance of eight miles and three quarters, it reaches St. Ives, and five miles and a half further it arrives at Huntingdon; ten miles from which place it comes to St. Neots; six miles from which place, at Tempsford, is the junction of the Ivel River with it, whence it proceeds eleven miles to Bedford.

The rendering this river navigable may be considered of very ancient date, for as early as the 6th Charles I. the Old Bedford River, twenty-one miles long and 70 feet wide, was cut under authority of the Law for Sewers, for the purpose of conveying the waters of this river, in such manner as to render it a better drainage, and in 1652 the plan of Sir Cornelius Vermuden, for making another cut nearly parallel to the last, was put into execution. In 1649 an act was obtained under the Lord Protector Cromwell, and afterwards confirmed in the 15th Charles II. establishing the Fen Corporation. Under this last act the New Bedford River was completed; both the Old and New Bedford Rivers empty themselves into the Ouse, within a mile of each other, and at about seventeen miles from Lynn; there is also a connection between the Old Bedford River and the River Nen, about twelve miles in length, near Ramsey Mere.

The act of the 11th George IV. authorizes the making of new cuts for the two-fold purpose of navigation and drainage in the north-eastern extremity of the Bedford Level, which is entitled " The North Level Navigation and Drainage."

The part proposed as a navigation and to be called The North Level Main Drain, commences in the Nene Outfall Cut, a short distance below the place where that canal forms a junction with Kinderley's Cut, and at the point where the Shire Drain, separating the counties of Lincoln and Cambridge, falls into the Nene Outfall.

Its course is easterly by Tid Cote and Cross Gate; from whence it proceeds in a straight line, crossing Tid Fen Drain

2 I 2

and by Elloe Bank to Clows Cross, where the navigation is to terminate; but a drainage-cut is to be made from the last-mentioned place in a straight course to the Old Eau Drain at Black Horse Sluice, about two miles south of the town of Crowland. The Navigation Cut is eight miles and three furlongs in length, six miles and a half of which is perfectly straight. The bottom of the canal is to be 2 feet 4 inches above low water in Crab Hole, in the Wash; the sill of the sluice to be 3 feet 4 inches above low water where the neap tides rise 16 feet and springs 23 feet. The bottom of the navigation at the upper end at Clows Cross to be 5 feet above low water at Crab Hole; having therefore, a drainage fall in eight miles and three furlongs, of 2 feet 8 inches. The drain to Black Horse Sluice is seven miles in length and in one straight course, with a fall of 1 foot 10 inches.

The estimate for these works was made by Messrs. Pear and Swanborough, civil engineers, and amounted to £92,517, of which the navigable part was estimated at £54,458.

For the providing of the necessary funds for the executing and maintaining this navigation and drainage, an annual tax of sixpence per acre, for two years is to be levied on all lands comprised in the five districts of the North Level and Great Portsand, with some exceptions not interesting to the general reader; also a further tax of three shillings per acre after the first two years.

Of the before exempted lands, Sutton Common is chargeable with an annual tax of one shilling and sixpence per acre.

The navigation and drainage to be under direction of the North Level Commissioners, who have power to take such tolls on the navigation as they may from time to time, at their meetings, think proper to direct. They are also entitled to bank tolls; but as this does not enter into or form any part of the immediate object of our work, it is purposely omitted.

The act, under authority of which these works are to be executed, was passed on the 29th May, 1830, and entitled, ' *An* ' *Act for improving the Drainage of the Land lying in the North* ' *Level, part of the Great Level of the Fens called Bedford Level,* ' *and in Great Portsand, in the manor of Crowland, and for pro-* ' *viding a Navigation between Clows Cross, and the Nene Outfall* ' *Cut ;*' for which purpose the commissioners may borrow the necessary sums of money on mortgage of the rates and taxes; and when these sums are repaid, the rates and taxes to be reduced; so that the annual amount of receipts be not more than the actual expenditure.

The chief object of the work is to effect a better drainage of these extensive levels; that of the navigation being of minor importance, although it will doubtless materially tend to improve the estates through which it passes, by facilitating the introduction of lime, and by affording a cheaper mode of quitting the surplus agricultural produce of that fertile district.

These rivers, cuts and drainages are so connected together that their advantages are felt in every part of the country through which they pass.

OXFORD CANAL.

9 Geo. III. C. 70, R. A. 21st April, 1769.　　15 Geo. III. C.　9, R. A. 30th Mar. 1775.
26 Geo. III. C. 20, R. A. 11th April, 1786.　　34 Geo. III. C. 103, R. A. 23rd May, 1794.
39 Geo. III. C.　5, R. A. 21st Mar.　1799.　　47 Geo. III. C.　9, R. A. 25th July, 1807.
48 Geo. III. C.　3, R. A. 11th Mar.　1808.　　10 Geo. IV. C.　48, R. A. 14th May, 1829.

THIS is a very extensive and important line of navigation. Commencing in the Coventry Canal at Longford, $315\frac{1}{2}$ feet above the level of the sea, it pursues an easterly course as far as Ansty Hall, which lies on its northern bank; it continues this direction till it crosses a small branch of the Sow River, when it makes a detour and runs southward for some miles; it then turns abruptly to the north, pursuing that track to Casford, and crossing the Swift near Churchover, returns down the valley by Cotton House and Stamford Park, to Clifton. From Clifton the canal follows a southerly course to Hill Morton, leaving Rugby on the west, from Hill Morton to Wolfhampcote, near which place it communicates with the Grand Junction Canal at Braunston Tunnel; here it verges to the west till it opens into the Warwick and Napton Canal, not far from Napton and $332\frac{1}{4}$ feet above the level of the sea. From the junction its direction is to the south; at Marston Wharf it rises to $387\frac{1}{4}$ feet above the level of the sea, and not far from this place is its summit level; passing a tunnel near Fenny Compton it follows the same direction to Banbury, where it crosses a branch of the Churwell; at Nell Bridge it is crossed by the turn-pike-road, and pursuing the same southerly direction, leaving Deddington on the west and Aynhoe on the east, it terminates in the River Thames at the city of Oxford, 192 feet above the level of the sea. Its original line throughout is very winding, but particularly so from its commencement to the summit level. From its commencement in the Coventry Canal at Longford to Hill Morton, a distance of twenty-six miles and a half, it is on a level; in the next half mile there is a rise of 19 feet; it then tra-verses on a level to Napton for about seventeen miles, in which distance it communicates with the Grand Junction and the War-wick and Napton Canals; in the next two miles, the end of the summit at Marston Dobs Wharf, there is a rise of 55 feet 5 inches; for the next ten miles and three quarters is the extent of the sum-mit level; in the next distance of seven miles and a quarter, there is a fall of 77 feet 4 inches to Banbury; from thence to the River Thames at Oxford, where it terminates, is twenty-seven miles and a quarter, with 118 feet fall, making the total length ninety-one miles. The summit level is 55 feet above the northern end of the Grand Junction Canal. It has an aqueduct of twelve arches of 22 feet span each, over the valley at Brinklow, and two others at Casford and Clifton over the Swift and Avon Rivers, which unite in the fork made there by this canal; at Newbold there is a tunnel of a hundred and twenty-five yards in length, passing under the Church Yard and Town's Street; and near Fenny Compton, not far from the summit level, another eleven hundred and eighty-eight yards long. This canal was originally projected by Mr. Brindley, who in 1769 was appointed engineer, and after him Mr. Whitworth. The company in their first act had power to raise £150,000 by shares of £100 each, and if needful a further sum of £50,000. Both these sums, along with £22,300 more, had in 1775 been expended, when the canal was only finished so far as Napton. They again applied to parliament for powers to borrow £70,000; this enabled them in 1778 to complete the canal to Banbury; and again by 26 George III. they obtained parliamen-tary power to borrow a further sum of £60,000, which enabled them to finish the work, and upon the 1st January, 1790, the canal was opened to Oxford.

The first act for this stupendous undertaking was passed in 1769, under the title of ' *An Act for making and maintaining a* ' *navigable Canal, from the Coventry Canal Navigation to the city* ' *of Oxford.*' A second was passed in 1775, entitled, ' *An Act to* ' *amend an Act made in the Ninth of his present Majesty for making* ' *and maintaining a navigable Canal, from the Coventry Canal* ' *Navigation to the city of Oxford.*' A third in 1786, entitled, ' *An Act to amend and render effectual Two Acts of the Ninth and* ' *Fifteenth of his present Majesty, for making and maintaining a* ' *navigable Canal, from the Coventry Canal Navigation to the city* ' *of Oxford.*' A fourth in 1794, entitled, ' *An Act for amending* ' *and altering certain Acts of Parliament for making and maintain-* ' *ing a navigable Canal, from the Coventry Canal Navigation to the* ' *city of Oxford.*' A fifth in 1799, entitled, ' *An Act for explain-* ' *ing, amending and rendering more effectual several Acts, passed in* ' *the Ninth, Fifteenth, Twenty-sixth and Thirty-fourth of his present* ' *Majesty, for making and maintaining a navigable Canal, from the* ' *Coventry Canal Navigation to the city of Oxford.*' A sixth in 1807, entitled, ' *An Act for amending several Acts for making* ' *and maintaining a navigable Canal, from the Coventry Canal* ' *Navigation to the city of Oxford.*' A seventh in 1808, entitled, ' *An Act for amending and enlarging the Powers of the several Acts* ' *relating to the Oxford Canal Navigation;*' and an eighth in 1829, under the title of ' *An Act to consolidate and extend the Powers and* ' *Provisions of the several Acts relating to the Oxford Canal Navi-* ' *gation.*'

As this last act consolidates all the parts of the previous acts, which are not repealed, it will not be necessary to notice them any further than as their clauses and provisions come into this. The company is chartered as " The Company of Proprietors of the " Oxford Canal Navigation," with powers to complete that work from Longford, near the city of Coventry, to the city of Oxford; for accomplishing which they were, by the first and subsequent acts, authorized to raise certain sums of money, amounting in the whole to the sum of £278,648, in shares of £100 each and parts, and to demand certain rates for tonnage, wharfage, and other dues, which it is not requisite to enumerate here, as the regular charges are specified in the consolidated act of George IV. By that act the property of this canal is vested in the company of proprietors, who are to be responsible for all debts formerly, now, or hereafter contracted. The books of accounts and all other documents kept under former acts are to be retained as evidence, and the company has power generally to maintain the canal already made, to make reservoirs for supplying the Warwick and Napton Canal with water, and for rendering navigable the following cuts, which are so numerous and difficult to describe, as to induce us to use the words of the act.

A cut or canal from the Oxford Canal at Five Acres, in Sow, to join the Oxford Canal at Sow Common, to the westward of a bridge called Stone Bridge; also a cut or canal from the Oxford Canal at Colt's Close, in Sow aforesaid, to join the Oxford Canal at Culvert Close, to the south-westward of a bridge called Cater's Bridge; also a cut or canal from the Oxford Canal at Noon Hill, in Ansty in the county of the city of Coventry, to join the Oxford Canal at Topcoal Piece, in Shilton in the county of Warwick; also a cut or canal from the Oxford Canal, opposite to the termination of the last-mentioned cut or canal in Shilton aforesaid, to join the Oxford Canal at a garden in the occupation of Joseph Astell, in Ansty aforesaid; also a cut or canal from the Oxford Canal, at Bottom Mill Field, in Ansty, to the eastward of a bridge called Squire's Bridge, to join the Oxford Canal at Bridge Close, in Ansty aforesaid; also a cut or canal from the Oxford Canal opposite to the termination of the last-described cut or canal in Ansty aforesaid, to join the Oxford Canal at Hill Close, in Ansty aforesaid; also a cut or canal from the Oxford Canal opposite to the termination of the last-described cut or canal in Ansty aforesaid, to join the Oxford Canal at Horse Close, in Combe in the county of Warwick, to the eastward of a bridge called Pridmore's Foot Bridge; also a cut or canal from the Oxford Canal opposite to the termination of the last-described cut or canal in Combe aforesaid, to join the Oxford Canal, at Broad Ground, in Combe aforesaid; also a cut or canal from the Oxford Canal at Broad Ground, in Combe aforesaid, to join the Oxford Canal at Horse Close, in Combe aforesaid; also a cut or canal from the Oxford Canal at House Ground, in Combe aforesaid, to join the Oxford Canal at Combe aforesaid, to the southward of a bridge called

Lord Craven's Bridge; also a cut or canal from the Oxford Canal opposite to the termination of the last-mentioned cut or canal in Combe aforesaid, to join the Oxford Canal at Bridge Close in Stretton under Fosse, in the county of Warwick; also a cut or canal from the Oxford Canal opposite to the termination of the last-mentioned cut or canal in Stretton under Fosse aforesaid, to join the Oxford Canal at River Field, in Stretton under Fosse aforesaid; also a cut or canal from the Oxford Canal at the Hill, in Newbold Revell in the county of Warwick, to join the Oxford Canal at the Cherry Orchard, in Easenhall in the county of Warwick; also a cut or canal from the Oxford Canal opposite to the termination of the last-described cut or canal in Easenhall aforesaid, to join the Oxford Canal at Hall Oaks Close, in Easenhall aforesaid; also a cut or canal from the Oxford Canal opposite to the termination of the last-described cut or canal in Easenhall aforesaid, to join the Oxford Canal at Hall Oaks Wood, in Easenhall aforesaid; also a cut or canal from the Oxford Canal at Crowthorne Close, in Easenhall aforesaid, to join the Oxford Canal at Pierce's Bottom Field, in Little Harborough, in the county of Warwick; also a cut or canal from the Oxford Canal opposite to the termination of the last-described cut or canal in Little Harborough aforesaid, to join the Oxford Canal at Home Close, in Little Harborough aforesaid, to the westward of a bridge called Walton's Bridge; also a cut or canal from the Oxford Canal at Buswell Leys, in Little Harborough aforesaid, to join the Oxford Canal near a bridge called Old Park Bridge, in Little Harborough and Little Lawford aforesaid; also a cut or canal from the Oxford Canal opposite to the termination of the last-mentioned cut or canal in Little Harborough and Little Lawford aforesaid, to join the Oxford Canal at or near the west end of Fall's Turn, in Little Lawford aforesaid; also a cut or canal from the Oxford Canal at Fall's Turn in Newbold upon Avon aforesaid, to join the Oxford Canal at First Cocklands, in Newbold upon Avon aforesaid, to the westward of a bridge called Perkin's Bridge; also a cut or canal from the Oxford Canal at Newbold upon Avon aforesaid, to join the Oxford Canal at Mowlands, in Newbold upon Avon aforesaid; also a cut or canal from the Oxford Canal at Newbold upon Avon aforesaid, to join the Oxford

Canal at Below the Barn, in Newbold upon Avon aforesaid; also
a cut or canal from the Oxford Canal opposite to the termination
of the last-described cut or canal in Newbold upon Avon aforesaid,
to join the Oxford Canal at Penn Close, in Brownsover, to the
westward of a bridge called Master's Bridge; also a cut or canal
from the Oxford Canal at Brownsover, to join the Oxford Canal
at Arnold's Ground, in Clifton upon Dunsmore; also a cut or
canal from the Oxford Canal at Dunsland's Meadow, in Clifton
upon Dunsmore aforesaid, to join the Oxford Canal at Clifton
upon Dunsmore aforesaid; also a cut or canal from the Oxford
Canal at the Heath, to join the Oxford Canal at another place
called the Heath, in Clifton upon Dunsmore aforesaid, to the westward of a bridge called Double Bridge; also a cut or canal from
the Oxford Canal at Clifton upon Dunsmore aforesaid, to the
westward of a draw-bridge, to join the Oxford Canal at Hill
Morton in the county of Warwick, opposite to the lock called
the Lower Lock; also a cut or canal from the Oxford Canal
at Hill Morton Wharf, to join the Oxford Canal to the eastward
of a foot bridge in Hill Morton aforesaid; also a cut or canal
from the Oxford Canal opposite to the termination of the last-
mentioned cut or canal in Hill Morton aforesaid, to join the
Oxford Canal at Kilsby in the county of Northampton; also a cut
or canal from the Oxford Canal at Kilsby aforesaid, to join the
Oxford Canal at Haswell's Meadow, in Barby in the county of
Northampton; also a cut or canal from the Oxford Canal at
Barby Haugh, in Barby aforesaid, to join the Oxford Canal at
Dairy Ground, in Barby aforesaid, northward of a foot bridge;
also a cut or canal from the Oxford Canal at Barby aforesaid, to
the northward of the said foot bridge, to join the Oxford Canal at
Barby aforesaid, to the south-westward of the last-mentioned foot
bridge; also a cut or canal from the Oxford Canal opposite to the
termination of the last-mentioned cut or canal in Barby aforesaid,
to join the Oxford Canal at Wormborough, in Barby aforesaid, to
the north-westward of a bridge; also a cut or canal from the
Oxford Canal opposite to the termination of the last-mentioned cut
or canal in Barby aforesaid, to join the Oxford Canal at Plough
Meadow, in Onley, in the county of Northampton, to the west of
a bridge called Barby Wood Bridge; also a cut or canal from the

Oxford Canal at Rowdyke, in Onley aforesaid, to join the Oxford
Canal at the Meadow, in Willoughby in the county of Warwick;
also a cut or canal from the Oxford Canal, opposite to the termination of the last-mentioned cut or canal in Willoughby aforesaid, to
join the Oxford Canal at Willoughby aforesaid; also a cut or
canal from the Oxford Canal opposite to the termination of the
last-mentioned cut or canal in Willoughby aforesaid, to join the
Oxford Canal at Willoughby aforesaid, to the southward of a foot
bridge called Ellard's Foot Bridge; also a cut or canal from the
Oxford Canal at Two Acre Denny Furlong, in Braunston in the
county of Northampton, to join the Oxford Canal at Kiln Leys, in
Wolfhampcote in the county of Warwick; also a cut or canal
from the Oxford Canal opposite to the termination of the last-
mentioned cut or canal in Wolfhampcote aforesaid, to join the
Oxford Canal at the Eighteens in Wolfhampcote aforesaid.

On the completion of which cuts the following are to be dis-
continued, and if the canal be not completed in five years, the
powers thereof are to cease.

The part of the existing canal which passes from the commencement of the cut or canal herein-before described as commencing at
the Five Acres, in Sow aforesaid, to the termination of the same
cut or canal at Sow Common, in Sow aforesaid, to the westward
of a bridge called Stone Bridge; also the part of the existing
canal which passes from the termination of the cut or canal before
described as terminating at Horse Close, in Combe aforesaid, to
the eastward of a bridge called Pridmore's Foot Bridge, to Sand-
hole Turn, Hopsford Puddle, in Hopsford in the county of
Warwick; also the part of the existing canal which passes from
the termination of the cut or canal before described as terminating
at Bridge Close, in Stretton under Fosse aforesaid, to a wharf
called Stretton Wharf, in Stretton under Fosse aforesaid; also the
part of the existing canal which lies between a bridge called
Thompson's Bridge, in Brinklow in the county of Warwick, and
the commencement of the cut or canal before described as commencing at the Hill, in Newbold Revell aforesaid; also the part
of the existing canal which passes from the Basin in Fennis Field,
in King's Newnham in the county of Warwick, to the termination
of the cut or canal before described as terminating at Pierce's

Bottom Field, in Little Harborough aforesaid; also the part of the existing canal which passes from the commencement of the cut or canal herein-before described as commencing at Buswell Leys, in Little Harborough aforesaid, to the termination of the same cut or canal near a bridge called Old Park Bridge, in Little Harborough and Little Lawford aforesaid; also the part of the existing canal which passes from the limeworks called Mr. Walker's Further Limeworks, in Newbold upon Avon aforesaid, to the commencement of the cut or canal herein-before described as commencing at the east end of Fall's Turn, in Newbold upon Avon aforesaid; also the part of the existing canal which passes from the termination of the cut or canal before-described as terminating at Below the Barn, in Newbold upon Avon aforesaid, to a wharf called Rugby Wharf, in Newbold upon Avon aforesaid, which last-mentioned part of the existing canal lies in the parish or township of Newbold upon Avon aforesaid; also the part of the existing canal which passes from the termination of the cut or canal before described as terminating at Penn Close, in Brownsover aforesaid, to the westward of a bridge called Master's Bridge, to Cosford Puddle, in Cosford in the county of Warwick; also the part of the existing canal which passes from the termination of the cut or canal before described as terminating at Arnold's Ground, in Clifton upon Dunsmore aforesaid, to Clifton Wharf, in Clifton upon Dunsmore aforesaid; also the part of the existing canal which passes from Messieurs Pickford and Company's Offices, in Braunston aforesaid, to the commencement of the cut or canal before described as commencing at Two Acre Denny Furlong, in Braunston aforesaid. The object for making so many new cuts and abandoning certain parts of the old line, has been to shorten the distance, in order to give greater expedition to the trade. The company are authorized to claim the following as

TONNAGE RATES.

	d.	
For all Coal, except on the First Two Miles from the Junction with the Coventry Canal at Longford...................}	1 per Ton, per Mile.	
For all other Goods, Wares and Merchandize................	1¼ ditto.	ditto.

And on the New Cuts the same Charge as if the Canal had been continued the former Length.

The Coventry Canal Company are to take the same Rate for Coal, per Mile, on the Two Miles excepted in the above Scale. And instead of the Rates payable under the former Acts, the following are to be taken.

TONNAGE RATES IN GROSS.

	s.	d.	
For all Coals and Coke which shall pass from the Oxford Canal into the Grand Junction Canal, except such as shall have been previously navigated along the Warwick and Napton Canal........	2	9	per Ton.
For all Goods, Wares, Merchandize and Things, not being Coals, Coke, Lime or Lime-stone, which shall pass from any navigable Canal, except the Warwick and Napton Canal, into the Oxford Canal, and thence into the Grand Junction Canal, or from the Grand Junction Canal into the Oxford Canal, and thence into any other navigable Canal except the Warwick and Napton Canal........	4	4	ditto.
For all Coals and Coke which shall pass from the Warwick and Napton Canal into the Oxford Canal	1	6	ditto.
For all Bar, Pig, Rod, Hoop and Sheet Iron, Castings, and other unmanufactured Iron and unmanufactured Steel, and Warwickshire Sand or Freestone, which shall pass from the Warwick and Napton Canal into the Oxford Canal, or from the Oxford Canal into the Warwick and Napton Canal	1	2	ditto.
For all Grain which shall pass from the Warwick and Napton Canal into the Oxford Canal, or from the Oxford Canal into the Warwick and Napton Canal...	1	6	ditto.
For all Lime and Lime-stone which shall pass from the Warwick and Napton Canal into the Oxford Canal	0	4	ditto.
For all other Goods, Wares, Merchandize and Things which shall pass from the Warwick and Napton Canal into the Oxford Canal, or from the Oxford Canal into the Warwick and Napton Canal....	3	0	ditto.

Such Gross Tonnage to be taken instead of Mileage Rates, for Coal or Coke passing along the said Canal, between the End of the Second Mile from Longford and its Junction with the Warwick and Napton; and for Pig, Bar, Rod, Hoop or Sheet-iron, Castings and all other manufactured and unmanufactured Iron, Steel, Grain, Lime-stone, Lime, Sand, Freestone, and all other Goods, between the Junction with the Warwick and Napton and the Coventry Canal, and *vice versa.*

Warehouses and wharfs may be built and the following demanded as

WAREHOUSING AND WHARFAGE RATES.

	d.	
For all Coals, Metals and other Goods whatever	2	per Ton.
For all Parcels not weighing more than Fifty-six Pounds	2	each.
For all ditto not weighing more than Six Hundred Pounds..............	4	ditto.
For all ditto exceeding One Thousand Pounds	6	per Ton.

If they remain above Twenty-four Hours, One Half-penny per Ton shall be paid for Wharfage and Two-pence per Ton for Warehousing for the first Seven Days, and the same Sums respectively for every further Seven Days.

The company are authorized to raise for the completion of the work, £131,877, on mortgage, at £5 per cent. interest; but they may borrow at a lower rate. It is impossible to describe all the public benefits derived from this important work; but by inspecting our map, it will be seen that the direct line of water communication is through a certain part of this canal, from London to Birmingham, Liverpool, Manchester and the extensive manufacturing districts of the middle and northern parts of the kingdom; and further, it is also the means of conveying an

immense quantity of coal from the coal district in the neighbourhood of Birmingham, to Oxford and other towns situate upon the
banks of the Thames.

OYSTERMOUTH RAILWAY.

44 George III. Cap. 55, Royal Assent 29th June, 1804.

THIS railway commences at the Brewery Bank in the town of
Swansea, where it communicates with the Swansea Canal; it then
travels along the banks of the Swansea Bay in a south-westerly
direction past Sketty, Lelbyputt and Norton Halls, when turning
towards the east it terminates at Oystermouth, not far from Castle
Hill Field ; from Swansea northwards it is continued on the west
side of the Swansea Canal as far as Morriston, communicating with
several mines on the line.

The act for executing this work was passed in the year 1804,
under the title of '*An Act for making and maintaining a Railway
' or Tramroad from the town of Swansea, into the parish of Oys-
' termouth, in the county of Glamorgan.*' By it the proprietors
are incorporated as " The Oystermouth Railway or Tramroad
" Company," with power to raise £8,000, in shares of £100 each;
and in case this should prove inadequate, a further sum of £4,000,
either by subscription amongst themselves, or by the creation of
new shares, or by mortgage of the works. They are also empowered to collect the following

TONNAGE RATES.

	d.	
For all Iron, Goods, Wares and Merchandize, except as below	4 per Ton,	per Mile.
For all Iron Castings	3 ditto.	ditto.
For all Pig-iron	2½ ditto.	ditto.
For all Iron-stone, Calcined Iron-ore, Iron-ore, Rotten stone, ⎫ Coals, Culm, Stone-coal, Coke, Cinders, Charcoal, Timber, ⎬ Stones, Tiles, Bricks and Clay .... ⎭	1½ ditto.	ditto.
For all Lime-stone, Lime, Sand and all Kinds of Manure......	1 ditto.	ditto.

Fractions of a Mile to be paid for as the Quarters therein, and of a Ton, for a Quarter
of a Mile, as a whole Ton.

The Company also have the power of charging according to their discretion for
Parcels not exceeding Five Hundred Weight.

This railroad runs through a district full of mines and minerals,
and affords all the facilities for shipping their produce which works
of this description are intended to supply.

PEAK FOREST CANAL.

34 George III. Cap. 26, Royal Assent 28th March, 1794.
39 & 40 George III. Cap. 38, Royal Assent 30th May, 1800.
45 George III. Cap. 12, Royal Assent 18th March, 1805.

THE Peak Forest Canal commences in the Manchester, Ashton-under-Lyne and Oldham Canal, to the west of the town of Ashton-under-Lyne; at this point it crosses the Tame River, and following a direction nearly parallel to the course of that river, continues for some miles upon the same level; it next branches off by Butter-house Green and Chadkirk to Hyde Bank Tunnel; it then crosses the Mersey a little below Water Meetings, by an aqueduct 90 feet high; passing this aqueduct it arrives at the parish of Marple, where it rises 212 feet by means of sixteen locks to the summit level, which extends to Whaley Bridge and Bugsworth; at the top lock of this summit it is joined by the Macclesfield Canal. At Bugsworth a railway commences, which passing by Chapel Milton and Chapel Townend, where there is an inclined plane six hundred yards long, rising 4 inches per yard, proceeds to Limestone Rock in Peak Forest, a distance of seven miles with a rise of about three-eighths of an inch per yard throughout its whole length, deducting, of course, that part occupied by the inclined plane above-mentioned.

The first act for this work was obtained in 1794, under the title of ' *An Act for making and maintaining a navigable Canal from* ' *and out of the Canal Navigation from Manchester to or near* ' *Ashton-under-Lyne and Oldham, in the county palatine of Lan-* ' *caster, at the intended Aqueduct Bridge in Duckenfield, in the* ' *county of Chester, to or near to Chapel Milton, in the county of* ' *Derby; and a Communication by Railways or Stone Roads from* ' *thence to Load's Knowl, within Peak Forest, in the said county of* ' *Derby; and a Branch from and out of the said intended Canal to* ' *Whaley Bridge, in the said county of Chester.*' By this act the proprietors, who are incorporated as " The Company of Proprie-" tors of the Peak Forest Canal," are empowered to make the canal and railroad, with all necessary works belonging to the same. By the act also Mr. Hodgson is empowered to make tunnels under such parts of the canal as shall pass his estate at Hagg's Bank; mines are reserved to lords of manors, but these are not to be worked to the prejudice of the navigation. For executing this work the proprietors are empowered to raise £90,000, in shares of £100; and in case this should prove insufficient, they may borrow a further sum of £60,000, on mortgage of the rates. For paying interest of capital and other contingencies, they may demand the following

TONNAGE RATES.

		d.	
For all Lime-stone	$1\frac{1}{2}$	per Ton, per Mile.
For all Stone (except Limestone,) Lime, Coal and other Minerals	2	ditto.	ditto.
For all Dung, Clay, Sand and Gravel not passing through a Lock	1	ditto.	ditto.
For all Dung, Clay, Sand and Gravel passing through a Lock	2	ditto.	ditto.
For all Timber, Goods, Wares and other Merchandize, and all other Articles, Matters and Things not herein-before particularized	3	ditto.	ditto.

Fractions of a Mile to pay as a Mile; of a Ton as the Quarters therein, and of a Quarter as a Quarter.

The Sum of Three-pence per Ton is charged for Wharfage for any Time under Ten Days, and the further Sum of One Half-penny per Ton per Day, for any greater length of Time than Ten Days.

No Boat under Fifteen Tons Burthen, when the Water does not, or under Ten Tons when the Water does, flow over the Weirs of any of the Locks, shall pass through any Lock without Consent in Writing, or unless the Owner or Navigator of such Boat shall pay Tonnage equal to Fifteen Tons or Ten Tons respectively as aforesaid.

Proprietors of mines of coal, stone, furnace, or other works are empowered to make branch railways of not more than two thousand yards in length, and branch cuts or canals of not more than four miles in length, to communicate with the said canal or railway, under certain limitations.

Immediately after the act was obtained this work was commenced, but after five years the funds were completely exhausted, and application was therefore made to parliament for a second act, which was granted in 1800, under the title of ' *An Act for altering* ' *and amending an Act passed in the Thirty-fourth Year of his* ' *present Majesty, for making and maintaining the Peak Forest* ' *Canal, and for granting to the Company of Proprietors of the* ' *said Canal further and other Powers.*' By this act it is stated, that of the £90,000 directed to be raised by the first act, £80,600 only had been subscribed, and only part of the subscription paid, whilst of the £60,000 directed to be borrowed, only £36,540 had been obtained, all which had been expended by the proprietors on the work; they are therefore by this act empowered to raise, either by new shares or by promissory notes under the common seal, any sums necessary to complete the undertaking, provided the same shall not in the whole, amount, with the sums already raised, to more than £150,000.

Notwithstanding these enactments, the funds were so unequal to the expenditure, that the debt continued to accumulate, and the proprietors were obliged to apply a third time to parliament; an act was consequently obtained in 1805, entitled, ' *An Act for* ' *enabling the Company of Proprietors of the Peak Forest Canal* ' *more effectually to provide for the Discharge of their Debts, and* ' *to complete the said Canal, and the Cut, Railways and Stone* ' *Roads, and other Works thereof.*' This act having stated that only £69,955 had been raised under the authority of the last act, and that of the whole sum contributed, only £573, 5s. remained unexpended, empowers them to provide a further sum of £60,000 by the creation of new shares, at such prices as to them shall appear most expedient; these new shares having a title to all the benefits secured to the old ones, in proportion to their appointed value.

It will be seen from the commencement of this article, that though the first act directed the canal to be continued as far as Chapel Milton, it only extends to Bugsworth, five furlongs beyond Bottoms Hall, where it crosses the River Goyt; at this point the branch to Whaley Bridge, four furlongs and seventeen poles long, is made under sanction of the first act. The total length of the main line is fourteen miles and seven furlongs; it was executed under the direction of Mr. Benjamin Outram, and opened on the 1st May, 1800.

The work, as originally projected, was designed to supply the country with coal, and limestone for the repair of roads, and with lime for building and manure; but by being connected with the Macclesfield Canal, now in execution, its beneficial effects must be very greatly extended, as thus it becomes one of the lines connecting Manchester with London and the midland counties.

PEAK FOREST, BEARD AND WOODLANDS RAILWAYS.

56 George III. Cap. 29, Royal Assent 21st May, 1816.

THESE railways not having yet been executed, it is only necessary to state that the act for their establishment was obtained in
1816, as ' *An Act for making and maintaining a Railway or*
' *Tramroad from Peak Forest to Beard, and from Peak Forest*
' *aforesaid to or near to Woodlands, all in the county of Derby.*'
The railways are to be executed at the cost of the Duke of Devonshire and Lord George Henry Cavendish.

The estimate for the first road to Beard was made by Mr.
James Meadows, being £1,227 for one mile and about three
quarters; the second was surveyed by Mr. Josias Fairbank, being
a distance of seven miles and three quarters, the execution of
which was estimated by him at £6,637, 15s. 3d.; but as the
time, limited by the act, is expired for making them, it is useless
to remark further upon this article.

PEMBREY HARBOUR, CANAL AND RAILWAY.

6 George IV. Cap. 115, Royal Assent 10th June, 1825.

THIS is not an extensive work; commencing in Pembrey
Harbour, the connecting cut or canal runs directly northward to
the junction with the Kidwelly and Llanelly Canal.

The act for executing this work was obtained in the year 1825,
under the title of ' *An Act for making and constructing a Harbour and*
' *other Works, in the parish of Pembrey, in the county of Carmar-*
' *then, and for making a Canal and Railway from the said Har-*
' *bour to Kidwelly and Llanelly Canal, in the said county;*' by
which certain persons, incorporated as " The New Pembrey Har-
" bour Company," have power to establish a safe and commodious
harbour on the north of Burry River, with a navigable canal,
quays, wharfs, piers and railways, communicating with the Kidwelly and Llanelly Canal; for defraying the expenses attendant

on the same they are to raise £20,000, in shares of £100 each; and should this prove insufficient, they may obtain a further sum of £10,000 by mortgage. They are also empowered to demand as

HARBOUR RATES.

	d.	
For every Ship, Barge, Boat or Vessel, entering or going out of the Harbour	8	per Ton.
For ditto, running into the same by Stress of Weather, and not unloading	6	ditto.
For ditto, staying longer than Seven Days	3	ditto, per Day.

Ships in his Majesty's Service, Custom, Excise and Post-Office Vessels are exempted from these Rates.

Persons using these works are also to pay according to the following schedule for

WHARFAGE RATES.

	s.	d.	
For Coals, Coke, Culm, Ashes, Breeze, and all Sorts of Manure, lying upon or at any Wharf for any Time, not exceeding the Space of Fourteen Days	0	6	per Chaldron, or Ton.
For the same lying longer than Fourteen Days, per Week	0	6	ditto.
For Stone of all Descriptions, for Fourteen Days or less	0	6	per Ton.
For the like, for any Time exceeding Fourteen Days, per Week	0	6	ditto.
For Timber of all Descriptions, for Fourteen Days or less, per Load of Fifty Cubic Feet	1	6	per Load.
For the like, for any Time exceeding Fourteen Days, per Week..	1	6	ditto.
For Iron, Brass, Copper and all other Minerals, for Fourteen Days or less	0	8	per Ton.
For the like, for any Time exceeding Fourteen Days, per Week..	0	6	ditto.
For Hemp, Flax, Pitch, Tar and Rosin, for Fourteen Days or less	1	0	ditto.
For the like, for any Time exceeding Fourteen Days, per Week..	1	0	ditto.
For Grain and Seeds of all Descriptions, for Fourteen Days	0	2	per Quarter.
For the like, for any Time exceeding Fourteen Days, per Week..	0	2	ditto.
For Meal and Flour, for Fourteen Days or less	0	2	per Sack.
For the like, for any Time exceeding Fourteen Days, per Week..	0	2	ditto.
For Bran or Pollard, for Fourteen Days or less	0	1	per Quarter.
For the like, for any Time exceeding Fourteen Days, per Week..	0	1	ditto.
For Hops, Wool and Rags, for Fourteen Days or less	1	6	per Ton.
For the like, for any Time exceeding Fourteen Days, per Week..	1	0	ditto.
For Lime, for Fourteen Days or less	1	0	ditto.
For the like, for any Time exceeding Fourteen Days, per Week..	0	8	ditto.
For Limestone, for Fourteen Days or less	0	6	ditto.
For the like, for any Time exceeding Fourteen Days, per Week..	0	6	ditto.
For all other Goods, Wares and Merchandize, not before enumerated, for Fourteen Days or less	1	6	ditto.
For the like, for any Time exceeding Fourteen Days, per Week..	1	0	ditto.

When the dividends exceed £20 per cent. then these rates are to be reduced. The work was laid down by Mr. James Pinkerton, and the total estimate, including breakwater and harbour, 800 feet by 300 and 24 deep, was £16,449, 9s. 7d.

This is a very useful undertaking; affording great facilities to the shipping of coal and other articles brought down by the canal to the harbour.

PENCLAWDD CANAL.

51 George III. Cap. 106, Royal Assent 21st May, 1811.

THE Penclawdd Canal commences in the River Burry, at Penclawdd, and runs in a crooked course from west to east, to the mines not far from the Paper Mill Lands, with which it is connected by a short railroad; another railroad branches off near its opening into the river, which runs down for a short distance to the south-west. There is a short separate railroad from the river to certain mines on Loughor Common, a little to the north of the main canal.

This work was designed by Messrs. E. Marten and D. Davies, who estimated the canal, from Penclawdd to Kingsbridge, six thousand three hundred and thirty-six yards long, at £3,168, and the railroad, from Travella to Pontllwidda, two thousand eight hundred and eighty yards, at £2,016, making, with sundry collateral branches, &c. a total of £9,934.

The act for forming this work is entitled, ' *An Act for making* ' *and maintaining a navigable Canal, and a Railway or Tramroad,* ' *from the River Burry, at or near the village of Penclawdd, in the* ' *parish of Lanridian, into the township or borough of Loughor,* ' *and divers Branches therefrom, all in the county of Glamorgan.*' By it the proprietors are incorporated as " The Penclawdd Canal " and Railway or Tramroad Company," with the usual powers. They may raise £12,000, in shares of £100 each, and if necessary a further sum of £8,000, on mortgage of the works. The following are ordered to be taken as

TONNAGE RATES.

	d.		
For all Iron, Goods, Wares, Merchandize and other Things....	4	per Ton,	per Mile
For all Iron Castings	3	ditto.	ditto.
For all Pig-iron	$2\frac{1}{3}$	ditto.	ditto.
For all Iron-stone, Calcined Iron-ore, Iron-ore, Rotten-stone, Coals, Culm, Stone-coal, Coke, Cinders, Charcoal, Timber, Stones, Tiles, Bricks and Clay...........................	$1\frac{1}{2}$	ditto.	ditto.
For all Lime-stone, Lime, Sand and all Kinds of Manure	1	ditto.	ditto.

Fractions of a Mile as the Quarters therein, and of a Quarter as a Quarter, except for Lime, Lime-stone and Manure; and of a Ton as the Quarters therein.

The Rates for Parcels not exceeding Five Hundred Weight to be determined by the Proprietors.

Wharfs and warehouses may be built by the company, or private individuals, the rates for using which are to be determined by commissioners, appointed for that purpose.

This is not a very extensive work, but it is one of considerable utility.

PENRHYNMAUR RAILWAY.

52 George III. Cap. 142, Royal Assent 9th June, 1812

THE act for completing this work was obtained in 1812, under the title of ' *An Act for making and maintaining a Railway from* ' *Penrhynmaur, in the parish of Llanfihangel Escelfiog, to Red* ' *Wharf, in the parish of Llanbedrgoch, in the county of Anglesea;* ' *and also a Dock in the parish of Llanbedrgoch;*' whereby certain persons are incorporated as " The Anglesea Railway Company," with power to make railways, a dock, cuts, locks and other necessary works for the same, and to raise the sum of £15,000 for that purpose, in shares of £150 each; and in case this should prove insufficient, they may borrow £8,000 additional, on mortgage of the works.

For paying interest and other contingencies they are authorised to demand the following

TONNAGE AND WHARFAGE RATES

	s.	d.	
For every Vessel entering the Dock, payable by the Master	0	2	per Ton.
For all Goods imported or exported therein	0	2	ditto.
For Horses, Mares, Geldings, Bulls, Oxen, Cows and Heifers imported	2	0	each.
For all Calves, Swine and Sheep imported	0	2	ditto.
For all Dung, Compost, Lime-stone, Manure and Materials for Roads, conveyed on the said Railway	0	2	per Ton, per Mile.
For all Lime, Chalk, Marl, Ashes, Peat, Clay and Bricks............	0	3	ditto.
For all Coal, Cinders, Coke, Culm, Charcoal, Tin, Copper, Lead-ore, Lead in Pigs or Sheets, Iron-stone or Ore, Iron in Pigs, Bar-iron, Tiles, Slates, Flag-stones and other Stones	0	4	ditto.
For all other Goods, Wares and Merchandize whatever	0	6	ditto.

Small Parcels under Five Hundred Weight to be charged according to the Order of the Committee of Proprietors.

Fractions of a Ton to be considered as the Quarters therein, and of a Quarter as a Quarter; Fractions of a Mile as Half a Mile.

They are also empowered to charge for passing on the railway the following rates.

RATES.

	d.
For every Horse, Mare, Gelding, Colt, Mule or Ass, not carrying or drawing any Goods on the Road .... }	2 each.
For all Cows and Horned or Neat Cattle ....,.................	1 ditto.
For all Sheep, Swine and Calves...............................	8 per Score.
For all Carriages and Waggons carrying Persons for Hire........	1 each Passenger.

This is an useful work; commencing at Penrhynmaur Coal Works, it proceeds in a north-easterly direction to Red Wharf Bay, crossing in its course the turnpike-road between Holyhead and Bangor. At Red Wharf Bay it has a branch which follows the shore of the bay for a short distance northwards. The whole length is seven miles and four chains, disposed of in the following inclined planes. From high-water-mark in Red Wharf Bay, there is a rise of 14 feet $7\frac{1}{2}$ inches, in two thousand nine hundred and one yards; in the following length of one thousand seven hundred and forty-six yards, there is a further rise of 38 feet 1 inch; thence to the summit it is five hundred and seventy-two yards, and rises 27 feet $6\frac{1}{2}$ inches; in the next length of one thousand seven hundred and seventy-five yards there is a descent of 27 feet; and the remaining distance of five thousand four hundred and seven yards, to the coal works, is level. Mr. W. W. Bailey surveyed this work in 1812, and his estimate was for a single road, having twenty turns out of sixty yards each in length, £8,797, 8s. 2d. and for a dock or basin at Red Wharf, £1,005, making in the whole £9,802, 8s. 2d. for executing which the Earl of Uxbridge and Holland Griffith, Esq. subscribed £5,000 each.

PLYMOUTH AND DARTMOOR RAILWAY.

59 George III. Cap 115, Royal Assent 2nd July, 1819.
1 George IV. Cap. 54, Royal Assent 8th July, 1820.
1 & 2 George IV. Cap. 125, Royal Assent 2nd July, 1821.

COMMENCING at Bachelor's Hall in the parish of Lydford, at no great distance from the prison erected for the reception of prisoners of war on Dartmoor, the Plymouth and Dartmoor Railway runs in a very circuitous course from north to south by Moortown, Grenofen, Buckland Abbey, Hoo Meavy, and Borringdon to Crabtree in the parish of Egg Buckland, where it crosses the turnpike-road from Plymouth to Exeter, and where the original line terminated; from thence, however, its course was continued, under powers granted by subsequent acts, to the sound at Sutton Pool, a short distance south of Plymouth.

The original line to Crabtree was twenty miles in length, the estimate of which was made by Mr. William Stuart, amounting to £45,000. The original design for communicating with Sutton Pool, and for which authority is given under the act of 1st George IV. was in length two miles and three furlongs, with two branches, one to the limeworks at Catsdown, one mile, two furlongs and eight chains in length, and another diverging from the Sutton Pool Branch, of two furlongs and two chains in length, the estimate for which amounted to the additional sum of £5,677; these, however, have given place to one branch from Crabtree to Catsdown, and from thence to Sutton Pool. The first act for its execution was obtained in 1819, under the title of ' *An Act for making* ' *and maintaining a Railway or Tramroad from Crabtree, in the* ' *parish of Egg Buckland, in the county of Devon, to communicate* ' *with the Prison of War on the Forest of Dartmoor, in the parish* ' *of Lydford, in the said county.*' By this act the company, incorporated as " The Plymouth and Dartmoor Railway Company," has the power of constructing the railway and all necessary works connected with the same. The proprietors are to contribute, for these purposes, the sum of £27,783, in shares of £50 each and parts of shares; but should this prove inadequate for the completion of the work, they may raise, either by subscription, or by the admission of new subscribers, or by mortgage of the works, a further sum of £5,000. For paying the interest of the money advanced and other incidental expenses, the company may charge the following

TONNAGE RATES.

	d.
For all Stone for repairing Roads, and for all Manure	2 per Ton, per Mile.
For all Stone, Cinders, Chalk, Marl, Sand, Lime, Clay, Ashes, Peat, Lime-stone, Iron-stone and other Materials, Building-stone, Pitching and Paving-stone, Bricks, Tiles, Slates, Timber, Lead in Pigs or Sheets, Bar-iron, Waggon-tire and all Gross or Unmanufactured Articles and Building Materials, and for all other Goods, Wares and Things.........	6 ditto. ditto.
For every Horse, Colt, Mule, Ass or other Beast not carrying or drawing Goods	3 each.
For all Cows, Horned or Neat Cattle, driven on the Road	1 ditto.
For all Swine and Sheep	3 per Score.

Small Parcels, not exceeding Fifty-six Pounds in Weight, are to be charged according
to the Determination of the Proprietors of the Road.

Fractions of a Ton and of a Mile to pay for the Quarters therein, and of a Quarter
as a Quarter.

Wharfs and quays may be made either by the proprietors or
the owners of land on the line, for which they are authorized
to demand the following

WHARFAGE RATES.

	d.
For all Coals, Culm, Lime-stone, Clay, Iron, Iron-stone, Lead-ore, or other Ores, Timber, Stone, Bricks, Slates or Gravel .... }	1 per Ton.
For all other Goods, Matters or Things	2 ditto.

If any Articles remain above Twenty-one Days—for the first Ten Days after that Time,
they are to pay an additional Rate of One Penny per Ton ; and One Half-penny
per Ton for every Day afterwards.

The work having been put in execution, it appeared advantageous to the traffic on the line, and to the trade of the town of
Plymouth, that a branch should be made from the lime-works at
Catsdown and Sutton Pool, in the parish of Charles, to communicate with the road at Crabtree; accordingly a second act was
passed in 1820, entitled, ' *An Act for making a Branch Railway,*
' *or Tramroad, from a Place called Crabtree, in the parish of Egg*
' *Buckland, to certain Limeworks at a Place called Catsdown, and*
' *from thence to Sutton Pool in the parish of Charles, all in the*
' *county of Devon, to communicate with the Plymouth and Dart-*
' *moor Railway, at Crabtree aforesaid.*' By this act the company
are authorized to raise for the new branch £7,200, making, with
the former sum granted to be raised, the total of £34,983, which
this act provides shall be raised by shares, or by borrowing of the
Commissioners of Public Works, or by other means; the whole to
be subscribed before the works are commenced.   Tolls to be subject to the same regulations as those of the former act.

Having made considerable progress in the work, the proprietors found that the line might be improved by an alteration in
a certain part thereof, they accordingly applied to parliament for
a third act, entitled, ' *An Act to authorize the Plymouth and*
' *Dartmoor Railway Company to vary the Line of a certain Part*
' *of the said Railway, and to amend the Acts passed for making*
' *the said Railway.*' By this act they are empowered to vary the
line between a place called Jump, in the parish of Bickleigh and
Crabtree, and Leigham Mill, which deviation was nine thousand nine
hundred yards, the estimated cost of which, by Mr. Roger Hopkins,

was £3,379. This estimate included a short tunnel in the land of Addis Archer, Esq. They have also power to raise £5,000 for making these alterations, by subscription or mortgage. It is provided by this act that the mortgage granted to the Commissioners of Exchequer Bills under the former acts shall not be invalidated, and that the execution of any of the acts obtained shall not extend to the altering of the ancient channel of the leat of water flowing to Plymouth for supplying that town, without the consent of the mayor and aldermen of the said town of Plymouth first obtained.

This useful work has proved of great advantage to the country through which it passes.

POCKLINGTON CANAL.

55 George III. Cap. 55, Royal Assent 25th May, 1815.

THE act for executing this work was granted in 1815, under the title of ' *An Act for making and maintaining a navigable* ' *Canal from the River Derwent, at East Cottingwith, in the East* ' *Riding of the county of York, to the Turnpike Road leading from* ' *the city of York to the town of Kingston-upon-Hull, at a certain* ' *Place there called Street Bridge, in the township of Pocklington,* ' *in the said Riding;*' wherein the proprietors are incorporated as " The Pocklington Canal Company," with powers to execute the proposed work, with all necessary tunnels, feeders, aqueducts and channels for the same; for accomplishing which they have authority to raise £32,000, in shares of £100 each, fractional parts of which shares may also be made; and in like manner they may, if it should be necessary, provide an additional sum of £10,000, either by subscription amongst themselves, or by mortgage of the works. For paying interest and other charges they are to demand the following as tonnage rates.

In the annexed Schedule, the Column A, are the Rates to be taken from East Cotting-with to Street Bridge; B, from Street Bridge to East Cottingwith; C, from East Cottingwith to Storthwaite; D, from East Cottingwith to Melbourn and Thornton; E, from East Cottingwith to Beilby; F, from Storthwaite to Melbourn and Thornton; G, from Storthwaite to Beilby; H, from Storthwaite to Street Bridge; I, from Melbourn and Thornton to Beilby; J, from Melbourn and Thornton to Street Bridge; K, from Beilby to Street Bridge; L, from Street Bridge to Beilby; M, from Street Bridge to Melbourn and Thornton; N, from Street Bridge to Storthwaite; O, from Beilby to Melbourn and Thornton; P, from Beilby to Storthwaite; Q, from Beilby to East Cottingwith; R, from Melbourn and Thorn-ton to Storthwaite; S, from Melbourn and Thornton to East Cottingwith; T, from Storthwaite to East Cottingwith.

TONNAGE RATES.

DESCRIPTION OF GOODS.	(A)		(B)		(C)		(D)		(E)		(F)	
	s.	d.	s.	d.	s.	d.	s.	d.	s.	d.	s.	d.
For every Quarter of Wheat, Barley, Beans, Rye, Maslin, Peas, Vetches, Linseed, Mustard and Rapeseed	1	2	1	2	0	4	0	8	1	0	0	4
For every Quarter of Oats and Malt	1	0	1	0	0	3	0	6	0	9	0	3
For every Bag of Flour, Shelling, Pearl Barley, Nuts, Clover, and all other heavy Seeds	0	9	0	9	0	4	0	6	0	8	0	4
For every Chaldron of Lime for Manure	1	6	1	6	1	0	1	2	1	4	1	0
For every Waggon of Coals, Slack and Cinders	6	8	6	8	2	0	4	0	6	0	2	0
For every Ton of Household Furniture	9	0	9	0	4	0	6	0	8	0	4	0
For Bacon, Cheese, Hemp, Flax, Lard, Madder and Tow, per Ton	5	6	5	6	3	0	4	0	5	0	3	0
For every Ton of Brass, Copper, Currants, Nails, Pelts wet, Salt, Shot, Pots, Soap, Sugar and Treacle	7	6	7	6	5	0	6	0	7	0	5	0
For every Ton of Iron, Pig and Bar; Lead, Pig and Sheet	5	6	5	6	3	0	4	0	5	0	3	0
For every Ton of Boxes, Cloth, Coffee, Dying Woods, Dry Goods, Fruit in Chests or Boxes, Glass, Groceries, Hides, Hops, Paint, Parcels, Pitch, Rice, Saltpetre, Spirits, Starch, Sumach, Tar, Tea, Tin, Tobacco, Turpentine, Wines, Welds and Yarn	8	0	8	0	5	0	6	0	7	0	5	0
For every Ton of Oak, Ash and Elm Timber, Forty Feet; Fir Timber, Fifty Feet; Battens, Deals and Pipe Staves	6	8	6	8	2	0	4	0	6	0	2	0
For every Ton of Manure, Gravel and Sand	1	6	1	6	1	0	1	2	1	4	1	0
For every Quarter Roke of Apples, Onions, Pears, Potatoes, Carrots and Turnips	1	2	1	2	0	4	0	8	1	0	0	4
For every Thousand of Bricks	3	0	3	0	1	6	2	0	2	6	1	6
For every Thousand of Tiles	3	6	3	6	1	9	2	3	2	9	1	9
For Hay and other light Seeds, Mill Dust and Bran, per Quarter	1	0	1	0	0	3	0	6	0	9	0	3
For every Firkin of Butter	0	3	0	3	0	1½	0	2	0	2½	0	1½
For every Ton of Bones, Cobbles for paving, and Horns	5	6	5	6	3	0	4	0	5	0	3	0
For every Ton of Alum, Copperas, Fish, Grease, Iron manufactured, Lead ditto, Tallow and Woad	7	6	7	6	5	0	6	0	7	0	5	0
For Chalk, Flags, Flints, Fuller's-earth, Kelp, Ling, Oil Cake, Plaster, Rags, Ropes, Slate, Stone and Whiting, per Ton	5	6	5	6	3	0	4	0	5	0	3	0
For every Ton of Rape Dust, Ashes, Soot and Whale Blubber	4	6	4	6	2	0	3	0	4	0	2	0
For every Bundle of Laths and Willows	0	2½	0	2½	0	1	0	1½	0	2	0	1
For every Pack, Three Hundred and Twelve Pounds, of Dried Pelts, Spetches, and Wool	0	10	0	10	0	5	0	7	0	9	0	5
For every Chaldron of Lime for Building and other Uses	2	0	2	0	1	0	1	5	1	10	1	0
For every Chaldron of Bark	2	3	2	3	1	4	1	8	2	0	1	4

TONNAGE RATES.

(G)		(H)		(I)		(J)		(K)		(L)		(M)		(N)		(O)		(P)		(Q)		(R)		(S)		(T)	
s.	d.	s.	d.	s.	d.	s.	d.	s.	d.	s.	d.	s.	d.	s.	d.	s.	d.	s.	d.	s.	d.	s.	d.	s.	d.	s.	d.
0	8	1	0	0	4	0	8	0	4	0	4	0	8	1	0	0	4	0	8	1	0	0	4	0	8	0	4
0	6	0	9	0	3	0	6	0	3	0	3	0	6	0	9	0	3	0	6	0	9	0	3	0	6	0	3
0	6	0	8	0	4	0	6	0	4	0	4	0	6	0	8	0	4	0	6	0	8	0	4	0	6	0	4
1	2	1	4	1	0	1	2	1	0	1	0	1	2	1	4	1	0	1	2	1	4	1	0	1	2	1	0
4	0	6	0	2	0	4	0	2	0	2	0	4	0	6	0	2	0	4	0	6	0	2	0	4	0	2	0
6	0	8	0	4	0	6	0	4	0	4	0	6	0	8	0	4	0	6	0	8	0	4	0	6	0	4	0
4	0	5	0	3	0	4	0	3	0	3	0	4	0	5	0	3	0	4	0	5	0	3	0	4	0	3	0
6	0	7	0	5	0	6	0	5	0	5	0	6	0	7	0	5	0	6	0	7	0	5	0	6	0	5	0
4	0	5	0	3	0	4	0	3	0	3	0	4	0	5	0	3	0	4	0	5	0	3	0	4	0	3	0
6	0	7	0	5	0	6	0	5	0	5	0	6	0	7	0	5	0	6	0	7	0	5	0	6	0	5	0
4	0	6	0	2	0	4	0	2	0	2	0	4	0	6	0	2	0	4	0	6	0	2	0	4	0	2	0
1	2	1	4	1	0	1	2	1	0	1	0	1	2	1	4	1	0	1	2	1	4	1	0	1	2	1	0
0	8	1	0	0	4	0	8	0	4	0	4	0	8	1	0	0	4	0	8	1	0	0	4	0	8	0	4
2	0	2	6	1	6	2	0	1	6	1	6	2	0	2	6	1	6	2	0	2	6	1	6	2	0	1	6
2	3	2	9	1	9	2	3	1	9	1	9	2	3	2	9	1	9	2	3	2	9	1	9	2	3	1	9
0	6	0	9	0	3	0	6	0	3	0	3	0	6	0	9	0	3	0	6	0	9	0	3	0	6	0	3
0	2	0	2½	0	1½	0	2	0	1½	0	1½	0	2	0	2½	0	1½	0	2	0	2½	0	1½	0	2	0	1½
4	0	5	0	3	0	4	0	3	0	3	0	4	0	5	0	3	0	4	0	5	0	3	0	4	0	3	0
6	0	7	0	5	0	6	0	5	0	5	0	6	0	7	0	5	0	6	0	7	0	5	0	6	0	5	0
4	0	5	0	3	0	4	0	3	0	3	0	4	0	5	0	3	0	4	0	5	0	3	0	4	0	3	0
3	0	4	0	2	0	3	0	2	0	2	0	3	0	4	0	2	0	3	0	4	0	2	0	3	0	2	0
0	1½	0	2	0	1	0	1½	0	1	0	1	0	1½	0	2	0	1	0	1½	0	2	0	1	0	1½	0	1
0	7	0	9	0	5	0	7	0	5	0	5	0	7	0	9	0	5	0	7	0	9	0	5	0	7	0	5
1	5	1	10	1	0	1	5	1	0	1	0	1	5	1	10	1	0	1	5	1	10	1	0	1	5	1	0
1	8	2	0	1	4	1	8	1	4	1	4	1	8	2	0	1	4	1	8	2	0	1	4	1	8	1	4

They may also erect wharfs, warehouses and quays, for the use of which, if goods remain above twenty-four hours, a further rate may be charged at the discretion of the proprietors.

This work commences in the River Derwent at East Cotting-with, not far from Thickit Hall, and running alongside the Pocklington Brook, proceeds for a short distance eastwards, then bending northward by Storthwaite, it takes an easterly course, leaving Melbourn Lodge and Melbourn on the south, till it reaches Beilby, where it turns at a right angle to the north, in which direction it proceeds to Street Bridge, where it terminates at the wharf adjacent to the turnpike-road leading from York to Market Weighton; having traversed a distance of about eight miles and a half, with only four locks.

There is one peculiarity in the execution of this canal, which deserves notice, that the engineer, Mr. George Leather, completed it for a less sum than the original estimate.

The chief objects in making this canal were to obtain coal, and lime for manure to Pocklington and its vicinity, and in return to convey the corn of the neighbourhood to the manufacturing districts; these are fully answered and the concern is likely to pay the adventurers.

POLBROCK CANAL.

37 George III. Cap. 52, Royal Assent 3rd March, 1797.

THOUGH many years have elapsed since the projection of this canal, it will be seen that it has not yet been executed. The act obtained for its completion is entitled, ' *An Act for making and* ' *maintaining a navigable Canal from Guinea Port, in the parish* ' *of Saint Breock, in the county of Cornwall, to Dunmur Bridge,* ' *in the parish of Bodmin, in the said county ; and also a certain* ' *collateral Cut from Cotton Wood to or near to Ruthen Bridge, in* ' *the said parish of Bodmin.*' By it the proprietors were incor-porated as " The Company of Proprietors of the Polbrock Canal," with the power of raising £18,000, in shares of £50 each. The work was projected, under the superintendence of Mr. John

Rennie and Mr. Murray, for supplying the town of Bodmin with coal, and for conveying minerals from the mines in its neighbour-hood. Its direction would have been south-east for about five miles, at a small elevation above the sea, near the north-west coast of Cornwall. Not having been executed, it is unnecessary to quote the proposed tonnage rates.

POLLOC AND GOVAN RAILWAY.

11 George IV. Cap. 62, Royal Assent 29th May, 1830.

THIS railway commences from the River Clyde, at the south quay of the Broomielaw in the city of Glasgow, from whence it crosses the road leading from Paisley to the last-mentioned place, then crosses and runs parallel with the private railway leading from the Govan Colliery to Tradestown; and shortly afterwards it crosses, at right angles, the Glasgow, Paisley and Ardrossan Canal, near its termination at Port Eglinton; thence to Port Eglinton Street, where it terminates after forming a junction with the Govan Railway.

It is in length only one thousand four hundred and eighty-eight yards, with a total rise from the quay of 39 feet 5 inches. There is a branch to Sir John Maxwell's Estate, at Polloc, of three hundred and twelve yards in length, and another near its termination, to the Glasgow, Paisley and Ardrossan Canal, at Port Eglinton, of two hundred and eighty-nine yards in length. The line and branches were designed by Mr. Thomas Grainger, civil engineer, who estimated

The Main Line to cost	£8,000
The Branch to the Canal	950
And the Branch to the Polloc Estate	750
Total.	£9,700

The act authorizing the making of this railway bears date the 29th May, 1830, and is entitled, ' *An Act for making and main-* ' *taining a Railway from the Lands of Polloc and Govan, to the* ' *River Clyde, at the Harbour of Broomielaw, in the county of* ' *Lanark, with a Branch to communicate therefrom.*' The sub-

scribers, consisting of six persons, were incorporated as " The
" Polloc and Govan Railway Company," and empowered to raise
amongst themselves the sum of £10,000 in four hundred shares of
£25 each, and may borrow, if necessary, the further sum of
£5,000 on assignment of the rates as a security.

TONNAGE RATES

	d.	
For Lime-stone, Dung, Compost, Manure and Materials for making or repairing of Roads..	2	per Ton.
For Coal, Coke, Cannel or Gas Coal, Culm, Charcoal, Cinders, Stone, Sand, Bricks, Slates, Lime, Earth, Iron, Lead or others Metals or Minerals Unmanufactured	3	ditto
For Timber, Corn, Flour, Goods, Lead in Sheets, and all other Wares or Commodities	3	ditto.

For the use of any Waggon, Machinery, Engine or Power belonging to the Company,
such additional Sum as they may from Time to Time require.
Fractions to be taken as for a Quarter of a Ton.

The chief object of this railway is to open a better communication between the river of Clyde and the Govan Colliery, and rich
mineral estate of Sir John Maxwell, of Polloc, Bart. A further
advantage will accrue to the inhabitants of Tradestown, by the
conveniences to be constructed at the harbour of Broomielaw, for
the shipping, unshipping and warehousing of every description of
merchandize.

PORTLAND RAILWAY.

6 George IV. Cap. 121, Royal Assent 10th June 1825.

THE act for forming this useful work was passed in the year
1825, and is entitled, ' An Act for making and maintaining a Rail-
' way or Tramroad in the parish of St. George, in the Island
' of Portland, in the county of Dorset;' by which act certain persons are incorporated as " The Portland Railway Company," with
powers to make a railway from the Priory Lands in Portland
Island, to the Stone Piers at Portland Castle; they are also to
raise £5,000, in shares of £50 each, for the payment of expenses
incurred in the execution of the same; and should the above
prove insufficient, they may borrow £2,000 on mortgage of the
works. They are authorized to demand the following tonnage
rates.

TONNAGE RATES.

		_d._		
For all Stone of the best Quality		8	per Ton, per Mile.	
For all Roach Stone, Capping, Ashlars for Building, Limestone and all other inferior Stone, sold at Two-thirds of the Price of the best Portland Stone	}	6	ditto.	ditto.
For all other Goods, Commodities, Wares and Merchandize ..		8	ditto.	ditto.

Fractions of a Ton and of a Mile to be charged as the Quarters therein, and of a Quarter as a Quarter.

These rates the company may from time to time reduce and raise again as occasion may require.

This railroad is not to interfere with or impede the military defence of Portland Castle; and no building is to be erected within two hundred yards of the said castle. If the work is not finished in three years, this act is to be void and of none effect, as far as regards the parts uncompleted. The length is two miles and four chains, and was designed by Mr. James Brown, civil engineer, who estimated the cost at £5,689, 12s.

PORTSMOUTH AND ARUNDEL CANAL.

57 George III. C. 63, R. A. 7th July, 1817. 59 George III. C. 104, R. A. 21st June, 1819.
2 George IV. C. 62, R. A. 28th May, 1821. 9 George IV. C. 57, R. A. 23rd May, 1828.

THIS canal commences from the tideway in the River Arun, at the village of Ford, three miles from the sea at Arundel Harbour, and two miles and three quarters from the town of Arundel, and proceeds westward close to the villages of Yapton, Barnham and Merston, to half a mile from North Mundham, where the Chichester Branch leaves; from thence it proceeds by Donnington to Chichester Harbour, where the principal line of canal terminates, being in length, from the River Arun, eleven miles, seven furlongs and eight chains. Upon this line are four locks. From the bed of the Arun to high water, spring tides, is 15 feet, and a lock of 5 feet above high-water-mark on the bank of the river; one furlong and one chain further on the canal is another lock of 7 feet; from this lock it is level ten miles, five furlongs and three chains, where there is a lock down 7 feet; and at the end of the canal, in Chichester Harbour, is another of 5 feet to high-water-mark, spring tides.

The estimate for this line is £72,270; and for the Chichester
Branch, which is level and one mile, two furlongs and three chains
in length, is £6,500. This canal and branch is supplied from
Chichester Harbour with water, which is lifted by a steam engine
at that end of the canal. The canal is according to section 33
feet at top, 19 feet 6 inches at bottom and 4 feet 6 inches deep.
The channels from the end of the main line of canal in Chichester
Harbour, round Thorney Island and Hayling Island by Thorney
and Langstone Wadeways, and Langstone Harbour, to the end of
the Portsea Canal, is thirteen miles and one furlong. The estimate
for making these wadeways sufficiently deep is £12,914. The
canal from Eastney Lake is two miles, three furlongs and two
chains in length; there are two locks of 5 and 7 feet at the east
end, and a basin at the termination at Portsea. This part is 5
feet deep, and the estimate £18,618; it is supplied with water
by an engine. The distance from the end of the main line of
canal in Chichester Harbour to the canal at Cosham is fifteen
miles and two furlongs, and the length of the canal to Porchester
Lake in Portsmouth Harbour is one mile, two furlongs and four
chains. This branch is 7 feet deep with two sea locks, one at each
end of the canal of 10 feet rise each; the estimate £15,188. The
total estimate is £125,490. The surveys were made by Messrs.
Netlam and Francis Giles, of London; the estimate and execution
of the works by the late Mr. Rennie.

By the first act, entitled, ‘ *An Act for making and maintaining*
‘ *a navigable Canal from the River Arun to Chichester Harbour,*
‘ *and from thence to Langstone and Portsmouth Harbours, with a*
‘ *Cut or Branch fram Hunston Common to or near the city of*
‘ *Chichester, and for improving the Navigation of the Harbour of*
‘ *Langstone, and Channels of Langstone and Thorney,*’ the company
is incorporated under the title of “ The Company of Proprietors
“ of the Portsmouth and Arundel Navigation,” with power to
make a canal from the Arun River, in the parish of Ford and
county of Sussex, to Chichester Harbour, with a branch from the
same at Hunston Common near Chichester to Southgate in the
parish of St. Bartholomew, near the said city, together with
another canal from Langstone Harbour to the harbour at Portsmouth; and to deepen and render navigable the channels of

Thorney and Hayling, as well as the said harbour at Langstone ; and another canal from the said harbour at Milton Common in Portsea, to the Halfway Houses in the same parish and county of Southampton. By this act the proprietors are empowered to raise £126,000, in shares of £50 each, and a further sum of £40,000, if required, on mortgage of the works.

After this first act had been obtained, it was judged expedient to make certain parts of the main line of the canal from the Arun to Chichester Harbour capable of being used by vessels of one hundred tons burthen, and that from Langstone Harbour to Halfway Houses for ships of one hundred and fifty tons, the completion of which works would be materially furthered by an agreement between this company and the proprietors of the Wey and Arun Navigation ; it was therefore determined to apply to parliament for the requisite authority, and a second act was in consequence obtained in 1819, under title of ' *An Act for giving further Powers* ' *to the Company of Proprietors of the Portsmouth and Arundel* ' *Navigation, and to the Company of Proprietors of the Wey and* ' *Arun Junction Canal, and to confirm an Agreement entered into* ' *between the said Companies.*' By this act an agreement between the two companies, for mutual accommodation, was ratified, and the following adjudged, in lieu of former tolls, as the Portsmouth and Arundel Navigation Company's on the part of the main line leading from Hunston Common to Chichester, and on the branch from the same place to Southgate, and from Milton Common to the Halfway Houses.

TONNAGE RATES.

	s.	d.		s.	d.
For all Dung, Ashes, Chalk, Lime, Lime-stone, Marl and Manure	0	3	per Ton, per Mile.	0	2
For all Chalk, Marl, Lime, Lime-stone, except when used for Manure, and for all other Goods, Wares, Merchandize and Things	0	6	ditto. ditto.	0	4
For every Empty Boat, Barge or Vessel passing through any Lock on the said Canals, or either of them	1	6	each, per Lock.	1	6
For every Passenger in the same, not employed as Navigators therein	0	2	ditto, per Mile.	0	2
For every Package not exceeding Two Hundred Weight and addressed to different Persons	0	1½	ditto. ditto.	0	1

Wharfage Rates may also be demanded for Goods shipped or landed in the said Lines, viz. Four-pence per Ton for the first Ten Days, and Three Half-pence per Ton for every subsequent Day they remain

Fractions of a Ton and of a Mile to be taken as the Quarters therein, and of a Quarter as a Quarter.

TONNAGE RATES CONTINUED.

Naval Stores to be exempted from One-sixth of the Rates.

The Company are authorized to demand for all Vessels using Portsbridge Creek, the Tonnage Rates in the Second Column above.

King's Stores are free from the Rates of Portsbridge Creek, and Revenue Boats may enter the Canals Toll Free.

By this act also the agreement between this company and the Wey and Arun is confirmed, whereby the Wey and Arun Company consent to receive for all descriptions of goods conveyed from the port of Portsmouth through their canal into the River Thames, 4s. 6d. per ton, and in proportion for a greater or less quantity than a ton, in times of peace; but in war the rates secured to them by act of parliament, shall be demanded; the Portsmouth and Arundel Company also covenant for themselves that they will only charge 3d. per ton per mile, for all goods conveyed from the port of Portsmouth into and throughout the said Wey and Arun Junction Canal and *vice versa,* but will not extend the said benefit to any goods conveyed out of the Arun Navigation or the port of Arundel, into the said canals, or *vice versa.*

By this act also the Wey and Arun Junction have power to raise £10,000 for completing the necessary alterations, subject to the same regulations as the sum of £99,500 granted by their own private act. This money may, if expedient, be raised on mortgage of the works.

In 1821 another act was obtained as ' *An Act for giving further* ' *Powers to the Company of Proprietors of the River Arun Navi-* ' *gation, and for confirming certain Agreements entered into between* ' *the said Company and the Company of Proprietors of the Ports-* ' *mouth and Arundel Navigation.*' This act recites and confirms two agreements made between the Portsmouth and Arundel Navigation and the Arun Company, whereby certain tolls are respectively to be received and paid by the said companies for goods passing on each respectively, but which it would not be interesting to our readers to quote particularly; it also empowers the Arun Company to complete their works and to receive on them, when finished, 1s. 6d. per ton for all goods, passing on and throughout the Arun Navigation and the Wey and Arun Navigation into the Wey, and *vice versa;* and 1s. per ton for all goods conveyed as before from or to the port of Arundel; and it confirms a power of the first act for enabling the Portsmouth and Arundel Navigation Company to borrow £40,000.

In 1828 a fourth act, entitled, ' *An Act for granting further* ' *Powers to the Company of Proprietors of the Portsmouth and* ' *Arundel Navigation,*' was obtained, whereby the company are empowered to raise an additional sum of £50,000, in £25 shares, each share being entitled for ten years to a dividend of £6 per cent. per annum, the surplus of profits, after paying this amount of dividend to the new subscribers, to be then divided amongst the original shareholders; and if the nett receipts will not pay the said dividend of £6 per cent. per annum to the said new subscribers, the deficiency shall be made up, before any dividend to the old subscribers is declared, and £5 per cent. after the ten years, is to be paid to the new subscribers in preference to the old. The money or any part of it, may be borrowed on mortgage of the works if more advisable.

This is a stupendous work, and from its connexion with others, as seen by the inspection of our map, opens a communication with almost every part of the kingdom; its utility, therefore, is self-evident. By the execution of it, military stores also may be transmitted inland from London to Portsmouth, which would avoid the risks that transports would otherwise incur in time of war, by the necessity of going through the straits of Dover and coastwise.

RAMSDEN'S (SIR JOHN) CANAL.

14 George III. Cap. 13, Royal Assent 9th March, 1774.

THIS canal commences at the River Calder near Cooper's Bridge, and thence runs in a south-westerly direction to the King's Mill, near the town of Huddersfield, in Yorkshire. It was executed under sanction of an act of parliament, entitled, ' *An Act for* ' *enabling Sir John Ramsden, Baronet, to make and maintain a* ' *navigable Canal from the River Calder, between a Bridge called* ' *Cooper's Bridge, and the Mouth of the River Colne to the King's* ' *Mill, near the town of Huddersfield, in the West Riding of the* ' *county of York,*' and is about three miles and three quarters in length, with a rise of 57 feet 4 inches.

This canal, although its length is so short, forms one of the links connecting the two seas, by its communication with the Calder at Cooper's Bridge, and with the Huddersfield Canal at Huddersfield; and has been the chief means of raising Huddersfield to one of the principal markets for woollen goods in the county of York.

The act of parliament empowers the proprietor to take 1s. 6d. per ton on all goods; and he having erected commodious warehouses at Huddersfield, which town is built upon his own estate, the trade there is accommodated upon moderate terms.

REDRUTH AND CHASEWATER RAILWAY.

5 George IV. Cap. 121, Royal Assent 17th June, 1824.

THE act for executing this work was obtained in 1824, under title of ' *An Act for making and maintaining a Railway or Tram-* ' *road from the town of Redruth, in the county of Cornwall, to* ' *Point Quay, in the parish of Feock, in the same county, with* ' *several Branches therefrom ; and also for restoring, improving* ' *and maintaining the Navigation of Restrongett Creek, in the* ' *same county,*' whereby certain persons, incorporated as '' The " Redruth and Chasewater Railway Company," have powers to complete the same, for which purpose they may raise £22,500, in shares of £100 each; and should such sum prove insufficient, they may obtain, in addition to the above, £10,000, either by the creation of new shares, or by subscription amongst themselves. For paying the interest of monies advanced and other contingent expenses, they are authorized to collect the following

TONNAGE RATES.

	d.	
For all Sand, Lime-stone and Lime used as Manure, all Dung, Compost and Manure, and all Materials for Roads........	2 per Ton, per Mile.	
For all Copper, Tin, Lead and other Ores, and all Matters containing Ore, Copper, Tin, Lead, Iron, and other Metals; Timber, Coals, Coke, Culm, Cinders, Stone, Bricks, Earth, Clay, Chalk, Marl, Lime and Sand not used as Manure ..	3 ditto.	ditto.
For Corn, Grain, Flour, and all other Goods and Commodities	4 ditto.	ditto.

Fractions of a Mile and of a Ton to pay as the Quarters therein, and of a Quarter as a Quarter.

Parcels not exceeding Five Hundred Pounds in Weight, to be paid for according to a Rate decided upon by the Proprietors, who may reduce the Rates from Time to Time and raise them again, as Circumstances shall require.

Wharfs, quays and warehouses may be erected by lords of manors or owners of lands on the line, which may be used for goods conveyed on the railroad, subject to the following

WAREHOUSING AND WHARFAGE RATES.

	d.
For all Coals, Culm, Lime, Lime-stone, Clay, Iron, Iron-stone, Copper-ore or other Ores, Timber, Stone, Bricks, Tiles, Slates, Gravel and other Things...	1 per Ton.
For every Package, not weighing more than Fifty-six Pounds.........	2 each
For ditto, not weighing more than Three Hundred Pounds	3 ditto.
For ditto, not weighing more than Six Hundred Pounds	4 ditto.
For ditto, not weighing more than One Ton	6 ditto.
For all Packages above the Weight of One Ton.......................	6 per Ton.

Packages remaining above Forty-eight Hours shall pay in addition for the next Seven Days, a Wharfage Rate of One Penny per Ton; and for Warehousing, a Rate of Two-pence per Ton respectively for the next Seven Days, and for every succeeding Seven Days.

The Company may also erect Wharfs and receive a Wharfage Rate of Four-pence per Ton for all Goods deposited thereon.

The estimate for this work was, as before stated, £22,500, of which £19,500 were subscribed before the passing of the act. The usual powers are granted for that part of the work, which relates to the navigation of Restrongett Creek, and regulations for the mooring of vessels therein, which it is not necessary to enumerate in these pages.

The main line of this railway commences at the extensive tin works on the east side of the town of Redruth, whence it takes a south-easterly course round the mountain of Carn Marth; thence north-easterly by Carrarath to Twelve Heads, whence it takes a south-eastward course by Nangiles and Carnon Gate to Point Quay, situate on an estuary branching out of Carreg Road. Its length is nine miles, two furlongs and four chains; in the first mile and seven chains of which, to Wheel Beauchamp, there is a rise of 103 feet; from thence to its termination it is one gradual inclination with a fall of 555 feet to high-water-mark. From Carnon Gate there is a branch to Narrabo of one mile one furlong; another branch from Nangiles to Wheel Fortune of three furlongs and five chains; another from Twelve Heads to Wheel Bissey, two miles, two furlongs and five chains in length; and another from Wheel Beauchamp to Wheel Buller, of two furlongs four chains in length. The total length of main line and branches is thirteen miles, three furlongs and eight chains, and the estimate, which was made by Mr. Richard Thomas, amounted to £21,900.

The object of this railway is to facilitate the conveyance of the produce of the rich mineral district round Redruth for shipment.

REGENT'S CANAL.

52 Geo. III. C. 195, R. A. 13th July, 1812.   53 Geo. III. Cap. 32, R. A. 15th April, 1813.
56 Geo. III. C. 85, R. A. 2nd July, 1816.   59 Geo. III. Cap. 66, R. A. 14th June, 1819.
2 Geo. IV. C. 43, R. A. 19th April, 1821.

COMMENCING in the Paddington Branch of the Grand Junction Canal near the Harrow Road, and about one-third of a mile from the Edgeware Road, and proceeding to Maida Hill, it passes under the Edgeware Road by a short tunnel; thence crossing Grove Road, it arrives at Park Road, at the west angle of Regent's Park, near Mary-le-bone Chapel, thence passing Grove House and Portland Terrace, it runs eastward parallel to Primrose Hill Road; opposite the Zoological Gardens a branch runs southwards to Cumberland Market, where there is a basin, passing in its course the Horse Barracks and the Jews Harp. Following the main line from Water Meeting Bridge, near the Zoological Gardens, it proceeds eastward, crossing the Pancras Vale Road; then locking down, it again crosses another road called Camden Road, and the new road to Holloway; when passing the King's Road and Randolph's Prebends, it turns towards the south-east to Maiden Lane, whence it proceeds to Horsfall's Basin, a quarter of a mile from which place it enters the tunnel under White Conduit Street and the junction of the streets which communicate with the main and back road to Highgate; it next crosses the New River to Frog Lane, on the east of which is a lock, and also a branch, called the Basin, passing under the City Road; leaving Frog Lane Lock the main line continues its course eastward to the New North Road and Bridport Place. Running parallel with Felton Street, it leaves a second basin on its north bank, not far from Kingsland Road; from Kingsland Road it keeps an easterly course to a third basin, on its south bank, extending to the Imperial Gas Works; from this point it proceeds to the road leading from Margaret Street to London Fields; bending a little to the south, it crosses the Cambridge Heath Road; then diverging a little to the north-east, it arrives at Old Ford Road, whence proceeding nearly south, it crosses Mile End Road; from Mile End Road it proceeds to

Stepney Lane, whence winding to the south-east it passes Salmon Lane, and crossing the Commercial Road, arrives at the basin, from which it locks into the Thames, being a length of above eight miles and a half, with a fall of 90 feet, by twelve locks, exclusive of the tide lock.

This great and arduous undertaking was projected for the purpose of forming a continuous line of canal navigation from the Grand Junction at Paddington Basin, to the River Thames, and the various docks on the east side of the Metropolis; affording thereby an easy mode of conveying merchandize not only from the interior of the kingdom to London, but also to the intermediate parts of the city; and on the other hand to open a line of conveyance to the most distant parts of the country. The first act for this purpose was passed in the year 1812, under the title of ' *An* ' *Act for making and maintaining a navigable Canal from the* ' *Grand Junction Canal, in the parish of Paddington, to the River* ' *Thames, in the parish of Limehouse, with a collateral Cut in the* ' *parish of St. Leonard, Shoreditch, in the county of Middlesex.*' By which act the proprietors were formed into a company styled " The Company of Proprietors of the Regent's Canal," with power to make a canal, to be called the Regent's Canal, from and out of the Grand Junction Canal, in the parish of Paddington in the county of Middlesex, into and through several parishes to communicate with the Thames, in the parish of St. Anne's, Limehouse, and to make a navigable collateral cut from the same in the parish of St. Leonard's, Shoreditch, to Aske Terrace, in the same parish; and to make and maintain all necessary inclined planes, steam-engines, reservoirs, channels, feeders, locks, tunnels, culverts, bridges, &c. &c. that may be required to complete the same. The canal may be supplied with water from all streams on its line and from the Thames, but no water is to be taken from the Thames, when lower than half-flood or ebb tide, nor from such streams as have been previously granted to the Grand Junction Company, nor from the streams, &c. belonging to the New River Company, nor from the Hampstead Water Works. For executing their plans, the proprietors are empowered to raise £300,000, in shares of £100 each; and in case that sum should prove insufficient, they may borrow, on mortgage, or on promissory notes, or by contributions amongst themselves, £100,000 additional. For the payment of interest on sums advanced and other contingent expenses the following are to be charged as

TONNAGE RATES.

	s.	d.	
For all Goods, Wares, Merchandize and other Things, which shall enter the Mouths of the said Canal, either from the Grand Junction Canal or from the River Thames, prior to being navigated or conveyed on the said Canal	0	6	per Ton.
For all Lime, Lime-stone, Chalk, Bricks, Tiles, Slates, Lead, Iron, Brass, Copper, Tin, Platina, Stone and Timber of every Kind, which shall be navigated or conveyed between the Basin next adjoining the Thames and the Turnpike-Road at Mile End, over and above the said Entrance Toll	0	8	ditto
For ditto, between the said Turnpike-Road at Mile End and the Turnpike-Road at Cambridge Heath, ditto......................	0	6	ditto.
For ditto, between the said Turnpike-Road at Cambridge Heath and the Kingsland Turnpike-Road, ditto............................	0	4	ditto.
For ditto, between the said Kingsland Turnpike-Road and the Junction of the said Collateral Cut with the said Canal, ditto	0	4	ditto.
For ditto, between the same Collateral Cut, through the Tunnel at Islington and Maiden Lane, ditto	0	9	ditto.
For ditto, between Maiden Lane aforesaid, and the Turnpike-Road leading from Camden Town to Kentish Town, ditto............	0	4	ditto.
For ditto, between the said last-mentioned Turnpike-Road and the Entrance of the said intended Canal, on the North-east Side of the Crown Land, called Mary-le-Bone Park, ditto	0	4	ditto.
For ditto, between the Entrance of the said Canal into Mary-le-Bone Park aforesaid, through the Tunnel under the Edgeware Road, and the Entrance of the said Canal hereby authorized to be made, into the Grand Junction Canal, ditto...........................	0	9	ditto.

For all other Goods, Wares, Merchandize and Things, (except Coals, Coke or other Minerals and Manure) which shall be respectively navigated or conveyed upon the several Parts or Portions of the said Canal or Collateral Cut herein-before described, a Rate or Sum per Ton equal to One Half in Addition to the respective Rates or Sums per Ton herein-before mentioned and made payable for Lime, Lime-stone, Chalk, Bricks, Tiles, Slates, Lead, Iron, Brass, Copper, Tin, Platina, Stone and Timber.

For all Manure which shall be navigated or conveyed upon the several Parts or Portions of the said Canal and Collateral Cut herein-before described, a Rate or Sum per Ton equal to One Half of the respective Rates or Sums per Ton herein-before mentioned and made payable for Lime, Lime-stone, Chalk, Bricks, Tiles, Slates, Lead, Iron, Brass, Copper, Tin, Platina, Stone and Timber.

	s.	d.	
For all Lime, Lime-stone, Chalk, Bricks, Tiles, Slates, Lead, Iron, Brass, Copper, Tin, Platina, Stone and Timber of every Kind, which shall be navigated or conveyed upon the said Canal the whole Length thereof, including the said Entrance Toll	3	0	per Ton.
For all Lime-stone, Chalk, Bricks, Tiles, Slates, Lead, Iron, Brass, Copper, Tin, Platina, Stone and Timber of every Kind, which shall be navigated or conveyed upon the said Canal, from and out of the said Grand Junction Canal to the said Turnpike-Road at Cambridge Heath aforesaid	2	4	ditto.
For all other Goods, Wares, Merchandize and Things, (except Coals, Coke, or other Minerals and Manure) which shall be navigated or conveyed upon the said Canal from and out of the said Grand Junction Canal to the said Turnpike-Road at Cambridge Heath aforesaid	3	6	ditto.
For all Manure which shall be navigated or conveyed upon the said Canal, from and out of the said Grand Junction Canal, to the said Turnpike-Road at Cambridge Heath aforesaid	1	2	ditto.
For all Coals, Coke, or other Minerals which shall be navigated or conveyed between the River Thames and the said Turnpike-Road at Cambridge Heath	1	0	ditto.

TONNAGE RATES CONTINUED.

	s.	d.	
For ditto, between the said Turnpike-Road at Cambridge Heath, and the Turnpike-Road leading from Camden Town to Kentish Town	0	6	per Ton.
For ditto, between the said Turnpike-Road leading from Camden Town to Kentish Town and the Grand Junction Canal.........	1	0	ditto.
For all other Goods, Wares, Merchandize and Things, (except Coals, Coke, or other Minerals and Manure) which shall be navigated or conveyed upon the said Canal, the whole Length thereof, including the said Entrance Toll	4	6	ditto.
For all Manure which shall be navigated or conveyed upon the said Canal, the whole Length thereof, including the said Entrance Toll	1	6	ditto.
For all Coals, Coke or other Minerals, Lime, Lime-stone, Chalk, Bricks, Tiles, Slates, Lead, Iron, Brass, Copper, Tin, Platina, Stone, Timber, and all other Goods, Wares, Merchandize and Things, which shall be navigated and conveyed upon the Collateral Cut hereby authorized to be made	0	2	ditto.
For every Horse, Mare, Gelding, Mule or Ass, passing on any Towingpath belonging to the Company, (not haling or drawing any Boat, Barge or other Vessel, nor going from Field to Field, or to or from Water or Pasture) before the same shall be permitted to pass through any Bar or Gate, or Bars or Gates (which Bars and Gates the said Company of Proprietors hereby incorporated are hereby empowered to erect, or cause to be erected)..........	0	6	each.

Vessels not passing the whole Length of any of the above Portions of the Line, shall nevertheless pay the full Tolls, except Vessels navigated on the Canal out of the Grand Junction the whole Distance to Cambridge Heath; and all Vessels passing Locks with less than Thirty Tons of heavy Goods, shall pay for Thirty Tons.

Fractions of a Ton to pay for the Quarters therein, but Boats or other Vessels coming out of the Grand Junction shall only pay for their actual Tonnage.

Land-owners on the Line may convey Manure to their Property free of Tolls; they may also use Pleasure-boats on the Canal, provided they do not pass any Lock, in which Case they shall pay the regular Rate.

The tunnel under the New River is to be constructed under the inspection of the surveyor of that company; and all alterations in pipes, &c. to be made with the approbation of the companies to which they belong. Land-owners, lords of manors, or, in case they refuse, the company may make wharfs, warehouses and other conveniences. For these wharfs the following are to be demanded as

WHARFAGE RATES.

	d.	
For all Minerals, Timber and other Goods, lying thereon Twenty-four Hours...	3	per Ton.
For ditto above Twenty-four Hours and not exceeding Thirty Days....	6	ditto.

Coal, Iron and Lime-stone may remain Three Months, paying Sixpence per Ton; but the other Goods after Thirty Days, shall pay One Farthing per Ton additional for every succeeding Day.

An ornamental piece of water is to be made and supplied by the company in Mary-le-bone or Regent's Park, in which park no wharf or towing-path is to be made, except on the north side thereof, and the works in this park are to be finished in one year.

The rights of the corporation of London, as conservators of the Thames, are to be preserved, and the company is to pay them an annuity of £450, as a compensation for the diminution of tolls. A stop or pound lock is to be made for regulating the quantity of water to be taken from the Grand Junction, and to restrain the company from introducing more than a certain quantity of water into the cut at Paddington. This is a very long act, containing a vast number of clauses for protecting the rights of public bodies and private individuals, but we have given above those parts only which are of general interest.

A second act was obtained by the company in 1813, under the title of ' *An Act to amend an Act of the last Session of Parlia-* ' *ment, for making and maintaining a navigable Canal from the* ' *Grand Junction Canal, in the parish of Paddington, to the River* ' *Thames, in the parish of Limehouse, with a collateral Cut, in the* ' *parish of St. Leonard, Shoreditch, in the county of Middlesex ;*' whereby the former act was amended, as far as regarded that part of the work intended to pass through Regent's Park, and an addition thereto towards the south-eastern extremity of the said park is hereby directed to be made, for repaying the extra cost of which, the following is to be demanded from every vessel using this intended cut, as an additional

TONNAGE RATE.

	d.
For all Goods, Wares and Merchandize	3 per Ton.

Fractions of a Ton to pay for the Quarters therein.

A third act was obtained in 1816, entitled, ' *An Act for* ' *altering and amending an Act made in the Fifty-second of his* ' *present Majesty, for making a Canal from the Grand Junction* ' *Canal, in the parish of Paddington, to the River Thames, in the* ' *parish of Limehouse.*' By this act the company is allowed to raise an additional sum of £200,000 for the completion of the works, either by subscription amongst the present subscribers, or by creating new shares and half shares, or by mortgage, or by granting annuities, or by bonds of £100, each bearing interest of £5 per cent. per annum, payable out of the tolls. This act contains a clause to explain which is the proper line through certain grounds belonging William Agar, Esq. at Pancras ; and another authorizing the Bishop of London or his lessee to make docks, basins, wharfs, cranes, warehouses, &c. on the land belonging the Diocese of London; as also another, empowering the company to supply the Grand Junction Canal Company with water from the Thames.

In 1819 a fourth act was obtained under the title of ' *An Act* ' *for altering and amending the several Acts passed for making a* ' *Canal from the Grand Junction Canal, in the parish of Padding-* ' *ton, to the River Thames, in the parish of Limehouse, in the* ' *county of Middlesex;*' whereby the proprietors are empowered to make a collateral cut or canal from that part of the main line which runs through the land of Samuel Pullin, Esq. in St. Mary's, Islington, to pass through and form a dock or basin in the lands of the Prebendary of Wenlock's Barn, and to cross the road from Islington to Finsbury Square, called the city, with all necessary wharfs, warehouses, &c. and to make all requisite cuts and feeders for supplying the same with water from the Thames, and to deepen the basin and channel from the Thames in Limehouse and Stepney, so that the same may admit ships and other vessels. They are also by this act authorized to raise an additional sum of £200,000, in the usual way. The following are granted as additional

TONNAGE RATES.

	s.	d.	
For all Goods, Wares and Merchandize navigated on the intended new Cut	0	6	per Ton.
For all Ships entering the Ship Channel or Basin	6	0	ditto.
For all Boats and Barges ditto	4	0	ditto.

Fractions of a Ton to be paid for according to the Quarters therein.

Water is not to be taken from the Thames, except under certain restrictions mentioned in the act, and the company are to pay to the city of London five guineas per annum, as an acknowledgment for cutting the shore and bed of the Thames below low-water-mark, for the purpose of laying pipes therein; they may also put down two dolphin piles at Limehouse for the haling of vessels into and out of the basin. Several other clauses are inserted for preserving the rights of various parties.

Some doubts having occurred relative to the power of the Commissioners of Exchequer Bills to advance a further sum to this company, another act was obtained in 1821, entitled, ' *An Act to* ' *remove Doubts as to the Power of the Commissioners of Exche-* ' *quer Bills to advance a further Sum of Money to the Regent's* ' *Canal Company, and to amend the Acts for making the said* ' *Canal.*' By this act, which recites the sums already advanced by the commissioners to the company, the said commissioners are empowered to advance a further sum of £200,000 to the said company.

In the year 1827, the Commissioners authorized to issue Exchequer Bills, made an offer to the Regent's Canal Company of a compromise for the whole of the debt due from the canal company, if paid within a certain time, for a much less sum than it amounted to, which offer was complied with; and in order to avail themselves of so advantageous a proposal. a certain number of new shares were created, which produced the money required, and the debt was discharged accordingly.

These shares were taken by the proprietors in proportion to the number of old shares they held, and both kinds of shares now stand in equal value; for notwithstanding shares were selling at the time at £50 each, and the newly created offered at £30, yet as the new shares were offered only to the old shareholders, it had the effect of raising money to pay the debt by calls upon the stock.

Hence the company have now the power of dividing the whole nett proceeds of the work amongst the shareholders; and from its localities, circumscribing, as it does, a great portion of London, together with its other connections, there is the fairest prospect that it will become a very lucrative concern.

To have described the cassoon locks and other mechanical inventions made use of to save the expenditure of water upon this canal, would answer no purpose, as they have been exploded, and the usual and more simple means adopted.

The engineering department of this concern is under the direction of Mr. Morgan.

RIBBLE RIVER.

46 George III. Cap. 121, Royal Assent 12th July, 1806.

THE act for improving the navigation of the Ribble was obtained in 1806, under the title of ' *An Act for improving the* ' *Navigation of the River Ribble, in the county palatine of Lan-* ' *caster ;*' and by it the proprietors were incorporated as " The " Company of Proprietors of the Undertaking, for the Improve- " ment of the Navigation of the River Ribble," with powers to change certain parts of the channel of the same, and to place marks, buoys and signal posts near the obstructions in the same, more particularly at its mouth, beginning the work at Penwortham Bridge near Preston, in Lancashire, and running by Kirkham, in the said county, to the sea. For executing these works the proprietors are empowered to contribute £2,000, in shares of £50 each; but should this sum prove insufficient, they may raise £1,000 in addition, either on security of the works, or by subscription amongst themselves. They are authorized to appoint pilots and to demand according to the following scale as

TONNAGE AND PILOTAGE RATES.

	s.	d.	
For every British Vessel entering or leaving the Port of Preston	2	6	per Ton.
For every Foreign Vessel ditto	3	0	ditto.
For Pilotage from Preston Quay to Naize Point and Frecleton Pool, or *vice versa,* if a British Sloop or Vessel with One Mast	2	6	per Foot of Water drawn.
For ditto with Two or more Masts	3	0	ditto. ditto.
From Naize Point and Frecleton Pool to the furthest or West Buoy next the Sea, or *vice versa,* for every British Vessel	2	0	ditto. ditto.

For every Foreign Ship or Vessel, double the aforesaid Rates.

Government Vessels, Vessels carrying Stones or Merchandize within the Limits of the Port of Preston, Vessels coming from or going to the Leeds and Liverpool Canal and the Douglas Navigation or either of them, through the present or any future Communication made between them and the Ribble, are exempted from the Rates and Duties. Vessels under Fifty Tons may be Piloted by their Masters, and no unlicensed Person is to be fined for assisting Vessels in Distress.

This work commences at Penwortham Bridge, near Preston, and proceeds for a distance of about eleven miles to its mouth in the Irish Sea, in a direction nearly due west; it is crossed not far from its commencement by the railway bridge belonging to the

Lancaster Canal. Its execution was designed to facilitate the transit of goods to and from Preston, and the exportation of such coals as were brought down the Douglas River, which communicates with it near Hesketh.

ROCHDALE CANAL.

34 Geo. III. C. 78, R. A. 4th April, 1794.   40 Geo. III. C. 36, R. A. 30th May, 1800.
44 Geo. III. C. 9, R. A. 23rd Mar. 1804.   46 Geo. III. C. 20, R. A. 21st April, 1806.
47 Geo. III. Cap. 81, R. A. 8th Aug. 1807.

THIS canal commences in the Calder Navigation at Sowerby Bridge Wharf, and runs westward up the vale of Calder, close to that river and the turnpike-road, passing in its course Longbottom, Brearley Mill, Mytholm Royd, May Royd, Hebden Bridge, Mytholm, Underbank, Stoodley and Mill Wood, to the town of Todmorden ; passing Todmorden, and bending southwards, it leaves Scatecliffe Hall on the east; thence it proceeds past Gauxholme and Travis Mill to Warland, at which place the summit level now commences ; it then proceeds to Littleborough, Clegg Hall, Belfield and Lower Place, whence a branch goes off to School Lane near Rochdale; the main line next pursuing a southerly direction, passes Castleton Hall, Royal Earn, Mount Pleasant, Stake Hill, Walk Mill and Slacks, to near Failsworth ; from the last place it bends a little westward of south, passing Newton, Ancoates and Hardwick Green, to the Duke of Bridgewater's Canal, into which it locks at Castlefield, Manchester; previous to its arrival at which place it is joined by the Manchester, Ashton-under-Lyne, and Oldham Canal at Piccadilly Wharf, being rather more than a mile distant from its junction with the Bridgewater Canal, at Castlefield.

According to the levels exhibited in the original design by Rennie, the rise from the Calder and Hebble Navigation at Sowerby Bridge, to the proposed summit near Travis Mill, is 275 feet, in a distance of about eleven miles and a quarter ; and the fall from that point to the Duke of Bridgewater's Canal, at Manchester, is 438 feet 6 inches. It appears, however, from levels recently taken, that it has not been so executed. The rise from Knott Mill, Manchester, to the summit, being now stated to be 533 feet 8 inches, and the fall from thence to Sowerby Bridge 353 feet 7 inches.

This canal is one of the main links in the chain of inland navigation between the east and west seas, being made for vessels of such a size as enables them to navigate in the tideway, and to pass between Liverpool and Hull without the expense of re-shipping their cargoes, thus affording great advantages to the populous towns of Manchester, Rochdale, Halifax, Wakefield, and others on the banks of the intermediate rivers. The Baltic produce can be thus readily conveyed into Lancashire, and the manufactures of Lancashire in return exported through the ports of Goole and Hull, to Hamburgh, Petersburgh, Lubeck, and other continental markets. The stone from Cromwell Bottom and its neighbourhood is hereby also conveyed to Rochdale and Manchester. These connections are likely to make it ultimately an undertaking of considerable profit to the proprietors.

The first act for this undertaking was passed in 1794, under the title of ' *An Act for making and maintaining a navigable Canal,* ' *from the Calder Navigation at or near Sowerby Bridge Wharf,* ' *in the parish of Halifax, in the West Riding of the county of* ' *York, to join the Canal of his Grace the Duke of Bridgewater, in* ' *the parish of Manchester, in the county palatine of Lancaster ; and* ' *also certain Cuts from the said intended Canal;*' whereby certain persons were incorporated as " The Company of Proprietors of " the Rochdale Canal," with the usual powers.

This canal being intended to form a junction with the Duke of Bridgewater's at Manchester, power is granted to him and his heirs to construct on this canal a lock at Castlefield, and to receive for their own exclusive benefit the following

TONNAGE RATES.

	s.	d.	
For all Coal, Stone, Timber and other Goods, Wares, Merchandize and Commodities, except Flags, conveyed from this Canal into the Duke's, and *vice versa*	1	2	per Ton.
For all Flags conveyed in the same Manner	0	2	ditto.

Smaller Quantities to be charged in Proportion.

These Rates are to free the Goods for which they are paid from any further Payment at the Duke's Wharfs, in the Parish of Manchester.

Gauges for regulating the quantity of water taken from the streams and rivulets near to the work, are to be fixed under the inspection of certain commissioners. No water, however, is to be taken from Hebden River or Cowder Beck. Owners of mines and coal works near the line may make collateral cuts or railways thereto, with the consent of the company. The Ashton Canal Company may make a communication between this canal and their own in Piccadilly, Manchester, so that they may at their junction be on the same level, and that no water be taken from the Rochdale to supply the Ashton Canal, but the waste water of both shall be conveyed by a tunnel into the Duke of Bridgewater's Canal.

At the junction between this canal and the Calder and Hebble Navigation, at Sowerby Bridge Wharf, the water of both must be on the same level for two hundred yards from the basin at that place. The Calder and Hebble Company are to build warehouses and wharfs for the Rochdale Company, for depositing goods on which, the latter company shall pay one half-penny per ton per day, except when frost or accidents prevent their removal. On neglect of the Calder and Hebble Company, the Rochdale or lords of manors and owners of land, may build wharfs and warehouses.

For making the canal, feeders, reservoirs and all other works connected with the same, the company may contribute amongst themselves £291,900, in shares of £100 each, interest on which at £5 per cent. is to be paid till the works are finished. And if the above sum should prove insufficient, they may raise £100,000 more by mortgage, or the admission of new subscribers. In consideration of the capital laid out, and providing for interest and other contingencies, they are empowered to demand the following tonnage and wharfage rates.

TONNAGE RATES.

	d.		
For all Lime, Lime-stone, Dung, Manure, Clay, Sand and Gravel, not passing any Lock	$\frac{1}{2}$	per Ton, per Mile.	
For ditto, passing a Lock	1	ditto.	ditto.
For all Coal, Cannel, Stone, except Lime-stone, and other Minerals, not passing a Lock	1	ditto.	ditto.
For ditto, passing a Lock	$1\frac{1}{2}$	ditto.	ditto.
For all Timber, Goods, Wares and other Merchandize, not passing any Lock	$1\frac{1}{2}$	ditto.	ditto.
For ditto, passing a Lock	2	ditto.	ditto.

WHARFAGE

		d.	
Of Coal, Lime, Lime-stone, Clay, Iron, Iron-ore, Timber, Stone, Brick, Tile, Slate and Gravel		1	per Ton.
For all other Goods		3	ditto.

Coal, Iron and Lime-stone may remain Six Weeks ; Timber, Clay, Iron-stone, Lime, Brick, Tile, Stone, Slate or Gravel, Three Weeks; all other Goods, Six Days. One Penny per Ton per Day to be paid in addition for every Day after the respective Times above quoted have expired.

Stone for Roads and Manure, Dung, Soil, Marl, Ashes of Coal and Turf for improving Lands in any Parish on the Line, are free from Tonnage Rates.

Fractions of a Ton and of a Mile to be paid for as the Quarters therein, and of a Quarter as a Quarter.

A second act was applied for and obtained in 1800, under the title of '*An Act for better enabling the Company of Proprietors of* '*the Rochdale Canal to raise Money for completing the said Canal,* '*and to vary the Line of the said Canal, and to alter, explain and* '*amend the Act passed in the Thirty-fourth of his present Majesty,* '*for making the said Canal;*' which, having stated that the company, under the sanction of the former act, had expended the £291,900 they were thereby empowered to raise, and had also incurred considerable debts in the prosecution of the works, goes on to empower the proprietors to increase the rates of tonnage and to raise the sum of £100,000, which the former act empowered them to borrow, in the following manner, viz. to such of the present proprietors as are willing to advance £30 per cent. on their respective shares, promissory notes may be issued payable at the end of eight years, and bearing interest at £5 per cent. per annum, such interest to be paid half yearly; if not paid at the end of eight years, the sums advanced may, if the owners wish, be made capital stock in the undertaking; or the company may borrow money on annuities to be secured on the rates. For meeting the increased expenditure, this act authorizes the demand of the following

ADDITIONAL TONNAGE RATES.

		d.		
For all Stone, Lime, Lime-stone, Dung, Manure, Clay, Sand and Gravel, whether passing or not passing through any Locks		½	per Ton, per Mile.	
For all Timber, Goods, Wares and Merchandize, not passing any Lock		¼	ditto.	ditto.
For ditto, passing a Lock		1	ditto.	ditto.

The Company may fix the Rates for Parcels under One Ton, which Ton is to contain Twenty Hundred of One Hundred and Twelve Pounds each.

The debts of the company continuing to increase on the further progress of the work, and by unforeseen high prices, they applied for a third act in 1804, entitled, ' *An Act for enabling the* ' *Company of Proprietors of the Rochdale Canal, more effectually* ' *to provide for the Discharge of their Debts, and to complete the* ' *whole of the Works to be executed by them, in Pursuance of the* ' *several Acts passed for making and maintaining the said Canal.*' By this act the company had the power of raising £70,000, in addition to the sums before granted, by creating new shares and parts of shares, or by any other means most convenient. This, however, did not answer the end proposed, for in 1806 we have a further act, entitled, ' *An Act for enabling the Company of Pro-* ' *prietors of the Rochdale Canal, more effectually to provide for the* ' *Discharge of their Debts, and to amend the several Acts passed* ' *for making and maintaining the said Canal.*' From this act it appears that the works had already cost £328,900, but were still unfinished, though the canal was partially opened. For the completion of the whole, £143,050 was still required, which sum the present act orders to be raised amongst the shareholders, by calls of not more than £25 on each share of £100; or if this mode should not be approved, the company may issue promissory notes of £25 each, bearing interest at £5 per cent. and when the dividends or clear profits of the company shall amount to £5 per cent. the holders of these notes shall be entitled to an equal division of all the surplus profit. Additional demands for tonnage and wharfage may be made according to the following

SCALE.

	d.	
For all Coal, Lime, Dung, Manure, Marl, Clay, Sand, Gravel and other Minerals, except Stone and Lime-stone, passing or not passing any Lock	½ per Ton, per Mile.	
For all Timber, Goods, Wares and Merchandize, passing any Lock	1 ditto.	ditto.
And in addition to the former Wharfage Rates for all Goods, &c. except Lime-stone	1 ditto.	ditto.

None of the Articles to remain longer than Ten Days.

The last act obtained by this company bears date in 1807, under the title of ' *An Act to alter, amend, explain and enlarge* ' *the Powers of the several Acts passed for making and maintain-* ' *ing the Rochdale Canal Navigation.*' It refers to the mode of rating the company's wharfs, &c. and by which their rates are exempted from parochial rates, and to the amending various clauses in the former acts, which it would not be interesting to our readers to notice. The company, in the year 1818, published an abstract of the bye-laws and penalties, &c. for damaging the works on the line, which particulars are intended for the government of the company's servants and the persons using this navigation.

After the long account we have given of this work, it would be almost superfluous to add that it is of first rate importance. The chief articles of transit are corn, timber, woollen cloth, coals and raw materials for the manufacturing districts and populous neighbourhoods through which it passes; it connects these districts with Hull, Liverpool, London and Bristol, thus opening a communication, if we may so term it, with all parts of the kingdom.

RODON RIVER.

10 George II. Cap. 33, Royal Assent 21st June, 1737.

THE act for making navigable the above river was obtained so long ago as 1737, under the title of ' *An Act for making navigable* ' *the River Rodon, from a little below a Mill, called Barking Mill,* ' *in the county of Essex, to Ilford Bridge, in the said county.*' It is unnecessary to say more on the subject of this article, than that the act was intended to improve the navigation of this tide river, and to enable vessels to pass the bad part of the river and the mill for the length of about two miles. Its use is to convey coals, &c. to Ilford Bridge for the supply of Romford and the neighbourhood.

ROTHER RIVER.

31 George III. Cap. 66, Royal Assent 11th April, 1791.

THIS navigation, which belongs to the Earl of Egremont, commences at the Lower Platt, near the town of Midhurst, Sussex, occupying the course of the River Rother in a great measure the whole length of the navigation. From Midhurst its course is by

Cowley Park, to the village of Ambersham, where it crosses a narrow stripe of Hampshire, a quarter of a mile in breadth; from thence, following the line of the river, it passes within a mile and a half of the town of Petworth; thence by Burton to a little beyond Lower Fittleworth, where there is a cut to the River Arun, near Stopham Bridge, where the navigation terminates. Its entire length is eleven miles.

The act for executing this work was obtained in 1791, under the title of ' *An Act to enable the Earl of Egremont to make and* ' *maintain the River Rother navigable, from the town of Midhurst,* ' *to a certain Meadow called the Railed Pieces, or Stopham Mea-* ' *dow, in the parish of Stopham, and a navigable Cut from the* ' *said River to the River Arun, at or near Stopham Bridge, in the* ' *county of Sussex; and for other Purposes.*' By this act the Earl of Egremont had authority to make the river navigable, and to make, if necessary, a cut or navigable canal from the Rother to Haslingbourn Bridge, as well as to make a navigable communication between the Rother and the Arun Rivers, with all works necessary for the completion of the same. For repaying the money laid out, the Earl is empowered to demand the following

TONNAGE RATES.

	d.	
For all Chalk, Soil or Dung for Manure	1	per Ton, per Mile.
For all Timber, Plank, Coal, Lime, Corn, Grain, Fire-wood and all other Goods and Wares .... }	3	ditto. ditto.

Fractions of a Mile and of a Ton to be charged as the Quarters therein, and of a Quarter as a Quarter.

Owners of lands and lords of manors may erect wharfs, quays and warehouses, and if they refuse so to do, the Earl of Egremont may himself erect the same and charge the following

WHARFAGE RATES.

	d.	
For all Goods, Wares and Merchandize remaining on the Wharfs, &c Three Months .... }	6	per Ton.
For ditto every Week after the said Three Months are expired	3	ditto, each Week.

The principal object is for supplying the interior with coal, and for the export of lead, corn, and that beautiful variegated fossil limestone, well known in London by the name of Petworth Marble.

ROYAL MILITARY OR SHORNCLIFF AND RYE CANAL.

47 George III. Cap. 70, Royal Assent 13th August, 1807.

THE Royal Military Canal and other works therewith connected, were constructed as calculated to stop the progress of the enemy, should the descent threatened by Napoleon ever have been put into execution. Commencing in the tideway at Shorncliff, in the county of Kent, not far from Sandgate Castle, it proceeds from east to west, as far as Hythe, where it makes a very short detour; it then proceeds past the batteries, in a continued westerly direction, leaving Lympne, Bonnington, Ruckinge and Appledore, on its north bank, to the junction with the intended Weald of Kent Canal; it then proceeds to the south, till it unites with the River Rother on the borders of Sussex; in the bed of which river it is continued past Rye, as far as Winchelsea; at this place the river verges to the south-east to its opening into the sea, whilst the canal is continued in a direction due south, from Winchelsea to Cliff End, where it terminates.

The purposes for which it was originally constructed having become no longer necessary, it was deemed expedient by government, that the canal and towing-paths should be turned to some account in a commercial point of view, whilst they were likewise kept in repair, in case they should be wanted as a means of repelling an invading force. An act was accordingly passed in 1807, entitled, ' *An Act for maintaining and preserving a Military* ' *Canal and Road, made from Shorncliff in the county of Kent,* ' *to Cliff End in the county of Sussex; and for regulating the* ' *taking of Rates and Tolls thereon.*' By this act the Speaker of the House of Commons and other principal officers of the State are appointed commissioners for carrying on and maintaining the said canal and road, and to make the necessary orders for regulating the same. They are also empowered to order toll-gates to be erected and rates to be demanded for goods, &c. passing on the canal and towing-path, such rates to be raised or lowered as shall to them appear necessary; tables of these rates to be put up in conspicuous places on the line, and returns of them or any alteration therein to be made to parliament, but no toll-gate is to be erected between the two bridges at Hythe, nor on that part of the road opposite to Appledore, on the towing-path side lying between the River Wall and Appledore Bridge, being the road from Romney to Tenterden. No tolls are to be paid by the owners or occupiers of lands, if they use them only for carrying manure or produce.

The line of this canal is but little elevated above the sea, running near the boundary of Romney Marsh for a considerable distance; the length, from commencement near Hythe to termination near Cliff End, is near thirty miles; it was executed under the direction of government, and is well calculated for the warlike no less than for the commercial purposes of the country.

RUMNEY RAILWAY.

6 George IV. Cap. 62, Royal Assent 20th May, 1825.

THIS railway commences at the Sirhowey Railroad, Pye Corner, in the parish of Bassaleg, and about two miles and a half west from the market town of Newport. It takes a westerly course, running nearly a mile on the western bank of the River Ebbw, thence by the village of Machin to the northern bank of the River Rumney, along which it runs by Bedwas to Trehir, where the river changes for a course directly north, and along the eastern bank of which the railroad runs to Gellyhave Colliery, from whence is a branch railroad communicating with the Sirhowey Railroad to the east, and at the distance only of a mile and a half. From the last-mentioned place it continues to follow the course of the Rumney River by Pont Aberbangoed, near Bedwelty, to Rumney Iron Forges, where it terminates.

The railroad is divided into three planes; the first of which, commencing at Pye Corner, is two miles and three furlongs in length, and rises 114 feet, being but one-third of an inch in the yard; the next plane is ten miles, six furlongs and eight chains in length to Gellyhave Colliery, and rises 209 feet or one-eighth of an inch per yard; the remainder of the railway is eight miles, four furlongs and two chains in length, and rises 133 feet or one-third of an inch per yard. The total length of the railway is twenty-one miles and six furlongs, and the whole rise from Pye Corner is 756 feet. The original estimate was made by Mr. George Overton and Mr. David Davies, and amounted to £47,850, and the whole sum was subscribed for by four individuals, viz.

Sir Charles Morgan, Bart....................£15,950
Joseph Bailey, Esq. 15,950
William Thompson, Esq..................... 7,975
Crawshay Bailey, Esq...................... 7,975
_____
£47,850

The act for the completion of this work was obtained in 1825, and is entitled, ' *An Act for making and maintaining a Railway* ' *or Tramroad from the Northern Extremity of a certain Estate* ' *called Abertyswg, in the parish of Bedwelty, in the county of* ' *Monmouth, to join the Sirhowey Railway, at or near Pye Corner,* ' *in the parish of Bassaleg, in the same county.*' By this act the proprietors are incorporated as " The Rumney Railway Com- " pany," with power to execute the railway and all other neces- sary works, for accomplishing which they are authorized to contribute £47,100, in shares of £100 each; and in case this shall prove insufficient, they may borrow £20,000 in addition, on mortgage of the works. For paying interest, &c. they are to demand as

TONNAGE RATES.

	d.
For all Lime-stone, Lime, Materials for Roads, Dung, Compost and all Sorts of Manure	1 per Ton, per Mile.
For all Coal, Coke, Culm, Cinders, Stone, Marl, Sand, Clay, Iron, Iron-stone, Iron-ore and other Minerals; Building-stone, Pitching and Paving-stone, Bricks, Tiles, Slates, and all Gross and Unmanufactured Articles and Building Materials	1½ ditto. ditto.
For all Manufactured and Unmanufactured Iron	2 ditto. ditto.
For all Lead, Timber, Staves and Deals, and all other Goods, Wares and Merchandize	3 ditto. ditto.

Fractions of a Mile and of a Ton as the Quarters therein, and of a Quarter as a Quarter.

The Proprietors to direct what Rates shall be paid for Parcels not exceeding Five Hundred Pounds.

Wharfs may be erected and the following demanded as wharf- age rates.

WHARFAGE RATES.

	d.
For all Coals, Culm, Lime, Lime-stone, Clay, Iron, Iron-stone, Lead-ore or any other Ores, Timber, Stone, Brick, Tiles, Slates, Gravel or other Things	1 per Ton.
For Parcels not exceeding Fifty-six Pounds	2 each.
For ditto above Three Hundred Pounds and not exceeding Six Hundred Pounds	4 ditto.
For ditto above One Thousand Pounds	6 per Ton.

If the above remain on Wharfs or in Warehouses above Forty-eight Hours, then there shall be paid in addition for the first Seven Days, One Penny per Ton for Wharfage and Two-pence for Warehousing, and the like Sums respectively for every further Seven Days.

Abounding as this country does with such abundance of mineral, the traffic upon this railway will amply repay the spirited proprietors who have embarked so large a capital in the construction of the work.

SAINT COLUMB CANAL.

13 George III. Cap. 93, Royal Assent 1st April, 1773.

THIS canal was executed under the authority of the above act of parliament, which is entitled, ' *An Act for making or con-* ' *tinuing a navigable Cut or Canal from Maugan Porth, through* ' *the several parishes of Maugan, Saint Columb Major, Little* ' *Colan and Saint Columb Minor, to Lower Saint Columb Porth,* ' *in the county of Cornwall,*' and which authorizes John Edyvean, of Saint Austell, in the county of Cornwall, gentleman, and his executors, administrators and assigns to make and complete this canal, and to levy thereon the following

TONNAGE RATES.

	s.	d.	
For all Sand, Dung or other Manure	1	0	per Ton.
For all Coals, Culm or Cinders	3	0	per Chaldron.
For all other Goods, Wares and Merchandize	2	6	per Ton.

It is stated that this canal will afford the means of improving many thousand acres of barren and unprofitable ground within and near the several parishes through which it passes; and it is enacted that it shall be exempted from the payment of any taxes, rates or assessments whatsoever.

For supplying this canal with water, power is given, by the act of parliament, to take all streams within three miles of the same; and also to make reservoirs within the same distance.

The length of this canal is about six miles, and although of short extent is found very beneficial for the exporting minerals and of conveying sand and other manure to the adjoining lands.

SAINT HELEN'S AND RUNCORN GAP RAILWAY.

11 George IV. Cap. 61, Royal Assent 29th May, 1830.

THE main line of railway commences from Cowley Hill Colliery, about two miles north of the town of St. Helen's, from whence its course is southwardly by Gerrard's Bridge Colliery, crossing the Sankey Brook Navigation near St. Helen's; thence by Peaseley Cross, Barton Bank Colliery to Toad Leach, where it crosses the Liverpool and Manchester Railway. Its course hence is by Tibbs Cross, Plumpton Mill, to the River Mersey at Widness Wharf, directly opposite the Old Quay Docks of the Mersey and Irwell Canal; crossing in its course the line of the Sankey Brook Extension near its western termination. Adjoining and communicating with the Mersey, a capacious wet dock, two hundred yards in length with two openings with tide locks, is to be constructed, where ships and other vessels may securely lie while waiting for cargoes.

The length of this railway, embracing the amended line from Runcott Lane towards Cowley Hill Colliery, is eight miles and seven furlongs; and there are thirteen branches which are together in length six miles, five furlongs and eight chains, viz. the branch from near Tibbs Cross, in a north-westwardly direction to the Liverpool and Manchester Railway, at Elton Head Colliery, is one mile, five furlongs and four chains in length; another in a north-westwardly direction, to join and communicate with the Liverpool and Manchester Railway with greater facility, one furlong and five chains in length; and another branch from the same point, communicating with the above railway to the eastward, two furlongs and five chains in length; one from the north side of the Liverpool and Manchester Railway, to communicate with it in a south-westwardly direction, two furlongs and three chains in length, and another branch to the eastward, with the same object, one furlong and five chains in length; from near

Barton Bank Colliery, there is a branch to Broad Oak Colliery, in length seven furlongs and two chains; and from the last-mentioned branch there proceeds two collateral branches, one proceeding northwards to the Sankey Brook Colliery, one furlong and five chains in length, and another from the same point, in an eastwardly direction, to Ashton's Green Colliery, being in length two furlongs and six chains. The branch to Ravenhead Plate Glass Works quits the main line a short distance north of Peaseley Cross, and proceeds in a straight line westwards, across a branch of the Sankey Brook Navigation to the works above-mentioned, and is in length one mile and six chains; from this last-mentioned branch there proceeds three collateral branches, viz. one by Sutton and Burton Head Collieries to Dobson's Wood, which is in length six furlongs; another to the St. Helen's Plate Glass Works, in length one furlong; and another to Messrs. Clare and Haddock's Colliery, in length one furlong and one chain. From near the termination of the main line near Cowley Hill, a branch proceeds in a north-eastwardly direction to Rushy Park Colliery, in length four furlongs and six chains.

The main line, as we have already stated, is eight miles and seven furlongs in length, viz. from the Wet Dock to the Elton Head Colliery Branch, three miles, five furlongs and five chains; thence to the two branches, communicating north-eastwardly and north-westwardly with the Liverpool and Manchester Railway, one mile, five furlongs and four chains; thence to where it crosses the Liverpool and Manchester Railway, one furlong and four chains; from the Liverpool and Manchester Railway to the two branches which communicate with it south-westwardly and south-eastwardly, one furlong and one chain; thence to the Ravenhead Plate Glass Works Branch, one mile and six furlongs; from the last-mentioned branch to where the Rushy Park Colliery Branch leaves the main line, one mile, one furlong and three chains; thence to its termination at Cowley Hill Colliery, two furlongs and three chains, making the total length eight miles and seven furlongs.

From the wet dock the railway is designed to rise gradually 142 feet in nearly one equal plane of four miles in length; and the next four furlongs and a half, terminating at the place called the

Clock Face, is level; from this place there is a descent of 70 feet in one mile and five furlongs by a gradual inclination; and from thence to its termination there is a rise of 18 feet.

The Elton Head Branch rises 44 feet in one inclined plane to the Liverpool and Manchester Railway. The branch to Dobson's Wood has three different inclinations, but altogether the rise from the Ravenhead Branch is 34 feet, and the last-mentioned branch rises 50 feet.

The Broad Oak Colliery Branch is nearly level; and the other remaining branches are of so little moment as scarcely to call for further description.

This work was designed by C. B. Vignoles, Esq. civil engineer, who estimated the cost at £119,980, which includes the sum of £31,620 for the wet dock, and £10,900 for contingencies.

The act authorizing the execution of the above works received the King's assent on the 29th May, 1830, and is entitled, ' *An Act* ' *for making a Railway from the Cowley Hill Colliery, in the parish* ' *of Prescot, to Runcorn Gap, in the same parish, with several* ' *Branches therefrom, all in the county palatine of Lancaster, and* ' *for constructing a Wet Dock at the termination of the said Railway* ' *at Runcorn Gap aforesaid.*'

The subscribers, at the time the bill was in parliament, consisted of forty-one persons, who were incorporated as " The Saint " Helen's and Runcorn Gap Railway Company," with power to raise amongst themselves, the sum of £120,000, (of which, £100,200 was subscribed before the act was obtained) in twelve hundred shares of £100 each; and the whole is directed to be subscribed before the work is commenced. If the above be insufficient, they may raise by mortgage of the undertaking the further sum of £30,000.

The act further directs that the inside edges of the rails shall be 4 feet 8 inches apart, and the outside edges 5 feet 1 inch; and that the railway shall not cross the Liverpool and Manchester Railway on the same level, but either by a tunnel or by a bridge to be constructed under the superintendence of the engineer of the Liverpool and Manchester Railway, and that there shall be not less than three passing places in every mile.

TONNAGE RATES.

	d.	
For Coal, Cannel, Slack and Culm...........................	$2\frac{1}{2}$ per Ton, per Mile.	
For Coke, Charcoal and Cinders............................	2 ditto.	ditto.
For Lime, Lime-stone, Dung, Compost or other Manure and Materials for the Repair of Public Roads	2 ditto.	ditto.
For Stone, Sand, Clay, Building, Pitching and Paving-stones, Flags, Bricks, Tiles and Slates	2 ditto.	ditto.
For Sugar, Corn, Grain, Flour, Dye-woods, Timber, Staves, Deals, Lead, Iron or other Metals and Minerals.........	$3\frac{1}{2}$ ditto.	ditto.
For Cotton and other Wool, Hides, Drugs, Manufactured Goods, and all other Wares and Merchandize	4 ditto.	ditto.

When any Goods are conveyed on this Railway so short a Distance that the Rates do not amount to One Shilling per Ton, the Company are nevertheless empowered to demand that Amount.

TOLLS ON CARRIAGES, &c.

	s.	d.
For every Person passing in or upon any such Carriage any Distance not exceeding Six Miles...	1	0
And any Distance exceeding Six Miles...................................	2	0
For every Horse, Mule, Ass, or other Beast of Draught or Burthen, and for every Ox, Cow, Bull or Neat Cattle, carried in or upon any such Carriage for any Distance not exceeding Six Miles	1	6
And any Distance exceeding Six Miles	3	0
For every Calf, Sheep, Lamb or Pig, for any Distance	0	6

Fractions to be taken as for a Quarter of a Mile and Quarter of a Ton.

When the company carry goods they are allowed the following

TONNAGE RATES.

	s.	d.	
For Coal, Cannel, Culm, Slack, Coke, Charcoal and Cinders (of Sixty-three Cubic Feet)......................	0	3	per Ton, per Mile.
For Lime, Lime-stone and all Sorts of Dung, Compost and Manure, Materials for Roads, Stone, Sand, Clay, Building, Pitching and Paving-stones, Tiles and Slates, Timber, Staves and Deals............................	0	$3\frac{1}{2}$ ditto.	ditto.
For Sugar, Corn, Grain and Flour, Dye-woods, Lead, Iron, and other Metals and Minerals	0	5 ditto.	ditto.
For Cotton and other Wool, Hides, Drugs, Groceries and Manufactured Goods	1	6 ditto.	ditto.
For Wines, Spirits, Vitriols, Glass and other hazardous Goods	1	8 ditto.	ditto.

And for Persons, Cattle and other Animals, such reasonable Charge as shall from Time to Time be determined by the Company.

The Company may charge One Shilling and Nine-pence per Ton for short Distances where the Tonnage does not amount to such a Sum.

TONNAGE ON VESSELS USING THE DOCK.

	d.
For every Ship, Hoy, Bark, Flat or other Vessel, coming into the Dock for the purpose of loading or unloading Goods, and which shall not continue more than Thirty-six Hours, (for Merchandize, &c. which shall be loaded or unloaded)	3 per Ton.
And for every Twelve Hours beyond this period, in addition............	3 ditto.
Vessels coming in Ballast and so leaving the same, and which shall not continue in the Dock more than Twenty-four Hours	3 ditto. burthen.
And for every Twelve Hours beyond such period, in addition	2 ditto.

No Vessel to remain in the Dock more than Seven Days, unless by Permission.

His Majesty's Vessels are exempt from these Tolls.

No Waggon or other Carriage shall be permitted to carry at one Time, including the Weight of such Carriage, more than Four Tons Weight, except in any one Piece of Timber, Block or Stone, Boiler, Cylinder, Bob or single Piece of Machinery, or other single Article which nevertheless shall not exceed Eight Tons, and for which the Company may claim Sixpence per Ton per Mile. And no Piece of Timber, &c. weighing Eight Tons, including the Carriage, shall pass without the special Licence of the Company.

If the works are not completed in seven years, the powers of the act are to cease, except as to such parts as may have been executed.

In this act there is a clause for preserving the rights of his Majesty, of the Mersey and Irwell Navigation Company, of the Liverpool Corporation and Dock Trustees, and of the Liverpool and Manchester Railway Company.

By the execution of this railway, an expeditious mode will be afforded of conveying coals from the extensive coal field of St. Helen's, Wirdle, Parr and Sutton, to the port of Liverpool, and the Cheshire Salt Works; and aided by the dock, quays and other works near Runcorn Gap, will give great facility to the re-shipping of merchandize.

SALISBURY AND SOUTHAMPTON CANAL.

35 George III. Cap. 51, Royal Assent 30th April, 1795.
40 George III. Cap. 108, Royal Assent 9th July, 1800.

THE first act of parliament respecting this undertaking was passed in 1795, and is entitled, ' *An Act for making and maintain-* ' *ing a navigable Canal from the town and county of Southampton,* ' *to the city of New Sarum, in the county of Wilts, with a collateral* ' *Branch to Northam, within the Liberties of the town of South-* ' *ampton.*' This was followed in 1800 by a second act, entitled, ' *An Act for altering and amending an Act made in the Thirty-* ' *fifth Year of the Reign of his present Majesty, entitled, An Act* ' *for making and maintaining a navigable Canal from the town and* ' *county of Southampton, to the city of New Sarum, in the county* ' *of Wilts, with a collateral Branch to Northam, within the liberties* ' *of the town of Southampton.*'

The canal contemplated by these acts of parliament has been in part only made, that portion of it only between Southampton

and Redbridge, where it joins the Andover Canal, being com-
pleted. It was to branch from the Andover Canal at Mitchelmersh,
and passing through the parishes of Mattisfont, Lockerley, West
Dean, East Dean, East Grinstead, West Grinstead, Alderbury,
Peter's Finger, Laverstock and Milford, to proceed to the Avon
River at Salisbury.

That part of the canal between Salisbury and the Andover
Canal was excavated, but in consequence of meeting with an
extensive quick-sand, it would not hold water, and was therefore
abandoned. The projectors of this work contemplated supplying
the interior with fuel at a cheaper rate, and of transmitting, in
return, the agricultural produce of that part of Wiltshire to the
sea coast.

SANKEY BROOK NAVIGATION.

28 George II. Cap. 8, Royal Assent 20th March, 1755.
2 George III. Cap. 56, Royal Assent 8th April, 1762.
11 George IV. Cap. 50, Royal Assent 29th May, 1830.

This canal, which was the first executed in the country, commenced in the River Mersey, at the mouth of Sankey Brook, from
which it derives its name as well as its supply of water; the brook
serving as a feeder to the canal. Running northerly in a circuitous
route and alongside the Sankey Brook, it passes Sankey Bridge;
then bending to the north-west, it passes Winwick Hall, and
leaving Newton Park on the north, proceeds to Gerrard's Bridge
and St. Helen's, where it terminates.

The first act of parliament respecting this navigation was
obtained in 1755, and is entitled, ' *An Act for making navigable*
' *the River or Brook called Sankey Brook, and Three several*
' *Branches thereof from the River Mersey below Sankey Bridges,*
' *up to Boardman's Stone Bridge on the South Branch, to Gerrard's*
' *Bridge on the Middle Branch, and to Penny Bridge on the North*
' *Branch, all in the county palatine of Lancaster.*' By this act
was authorized the collecting of the following

TONNAGE RATE.

	d.
For all Coal, Stone, Slate, Timber and all other Goods and Merchandize	10 per Ton.

Sixty-three Cubic Feet of Coal, Cannel Coal, Charcoal, Coke and Cinders ; Fifty
Cubic Feet of Fir, Poplar, Alder Wood, Withy or Willow ; Forty Cubic Feet of
Oak, Ash or any other Timber, to be rated as a Ton.

A second act of parliament was obtained in 1762, for amending the former, entitled, ' *An Act to amend and render more* ' *effectual, an Act made in the Twenty-eighth Year of the Reign* ' *of his late Majesty King George the Second, for making navigable* ' *Sankey Brook, in the county of Lancaster, and for the extending* ' *and improving the said Navigation;*' which empowered the undertakers to continue the navigation to Fidler's Ferry on the River Mersey, and to take an additional toll of two-pence per ton, making the present

TONNAGE RATE.

	s.	
For all Goods, Merchandize and Commodities whatsoever	1	per Ton.

This act allowed the undertakers till the 29th September, 1768, to complete their works. The length of the canal is about twelve miles, and it has eight single locks of about 6 feet fall each, and two double locks of about 15 feet each, making together about 78 feet fall; the depth is 5 feet 7 inches, and the width sixteen yards, and there are eighteen swivel bridges over it.

An experiment of propelling vessels by steam was tried upon this canal as early as 1797, when a loaded barge was worked up and down by a steam engine on board for a distance of twenty miles; but, singular as it may appear, to this time vessels have continued to be towed upon it by manual labour.

The principal articles carried on this canal are copper-ore, corn and coals; of the latter, one hundred thousand tons annually are conveyed to Liverpool; large quantities to the salt works in Cheshire; to the Anglesea Copper Works, and to the Plate Glass Manufactory near Warrington.

This navigation has three branches running to collieries in its neighbourhood; viz. the South Branch to Boardman's Stone Bridge, near St. Helen's; the Middle Branch to Gerrard's Bridge; and the North Branch to Penny Bridge.

The last act relating to this navigation was obtained chiefly for the purpose of enabling the proprietors to extend their navigation, from above the basin and lock at Fidler's Ferry, where it now enters the tideway of the River Mersey, across Cuerdley and Widness Salt Marshes to Widness Wharf, West Bank, near

Runcorn Gap, and there to terminate at the above-mentioned river. The length of the extension, including the new proposed basin at its termination, is three miles, two furlongs and eight chains, and on one level to the entrance of the basin, where there is to be a double lock, with a fall of 5 feet 6 inches to the level of average spring tide water at Runcorn Gap, which is 19 feet 6 inches above the sill of the Old Dock at Liverpool. The level of average neap tides at Runcorn, above Liverpool Old Dock Sill, is 11 feet 6 inches, and the level of the bottom of the basin and sill of entrance gates is 5 feet above it. The canal is to be 7 feet deep, and a branch is to be made to the west side of the basin terminating near the banks of the Mersey.

Its length is one furlong and seven chains, and level with the basin which is to be two hundred yards in length and fifty in breadth.

This act which received his Majesty's assent on the 29th May, 1830, and is entitled, ' *An Act to consolidate and amend the Acts* ' *relating to the Sankey Brook Navigation, in the county of Lan-* ' *caster; and to make a New Canal from the said Navigation at* ' *Fidler's Ferry, to communicate with the River Mersey at Widness* ' *Wharf, near West Bank, in the township of Widness, in the said* ' *county,*' repeals the former acts of the 28th George II. and 2nd George III. and incorporates the proprietors under the title of " The Company of Proprietors of the Sankey Brook Naviga- " tion."

Previous to the passing of this act the navigation was divided into one hundred and twenty shares; it is now, however, to consist of four hundred and eighty of £200 each, the capital being £96,000; the proprietor, therefore, of one share previous to this enactment, is now entitled to four.

For the purpose of carrying into execution the intent of the act, the company are empowered to borrow, on assignment of the navigation as a security, the sum of £30,000; and for the purpose of creating a sinking fund for repayment of the sum borrowed, the company are required to set apart one-tenth part of the clear profits of the navigation.

As the previous acts are repealed, the following are the ton-nage rates.

TONNAGE RATES.

	d.
For Coal, Cannel Coal, Stone, Slate, Flags, Timber or other Goods, Wares or Merchandize, carried upon the Canal or Branches above Sankey Bridges..	10 per Ton.
For every Description of Goods conveyed upon the Navigation below Sankey Bridges (except such Goods, Wares, &c. as shall be carried upon the said Navigation, and be laden or unladen from or upon any Quay or Wharf in the Rivers Mersey and Irwell above Sankey Brook Mouth, without entering into the said Canal now made or intended to be made) an additional Sum of....................	2 ditto.

EXEMPTION FROM THE ABOVE TOLLS.

Lime-stone, Paving-stones, Gravel, Sand and all other Materials for making or repairing of Roads, Quays and Wharfs, to or upon the Sankey Brook Navigation, and for the private use of the Persons whose Lands shall be cut or made use of for the same; Soapers' Waste, Dung and all Sorts of Manure is also exempted.

As the Land through which the proposed Extension is to be made is the Property of Sir Richard Brooke, Bart. he or his Heirs are permitted to convey any Description of Goods, being his or their own Property or that of his Tenants in Cuerdley, and being *bona fide* the produce of his or their Lands, free of Tolls; and also any Timber, Stone, Bricks or Slates, or other Materials intended to be used for any Building upon any Part of the above Estate in Cuerdley, or for draining the same.

For the better ascertaining the Tonnage of Coal, &c. Sixty-three Feet of Coal, Cannel Coal, Charcoal, Coke and Cinders; Fifty Cubical Feet of Fir, Poplar, Alder Wood, Withy or Willow; and Forty Cubical Feet of Oak, Ash, or other Timber shall be deemed a Ton.

Fractions to be taken as for a Quarter of a Ton.

No Vessels of less Burthen than Thirty-five Tons (except Pleasure Boats) to be permitted to pass a Lock without leave, unless a Tonnage to that Amount is paid.

Lords of manors or owners of land may erect wharfs; but if they refuse, the company may do it, and charge the following

WHARFAGE RATES.

	d.
For Coal, Stone, Lime, Sand or Brick, which shall be loaded from or landed upon any of the Wharfs, Quays or Warehouses, which shall lie more than Six Hours	½ per Ton.
For other Goods, Wares or Merchandize.............................	3 ditto.

For the use of Sir Richard Brooke, Bart. or his tenants in Cuerdley, the company are required to construct three wharfs or landing places, together with a small basin capable of receiving a vessel of eighteen tons burthen.

This act restrains the company from any interference with the rights of the King's Most Excellent Majesty, as regards his Crown or his Duchy of Lancaster; the Mersey and Irwell Company; the Corporation of Liverpool and Trustees of Liverpool Docks; the Liverpool and Manchester Railway Company; and the Owners, Proprietors or Farmers of Sankey Quays.

Mr. John Eyes, of Liverpool, was the original engineer to the undertaking. The Liverpool and Manchester Railway crosses this canal by a stupendous viaduct about a mile from Newton, at the height of 70 feet above the surface water.

2 N

SAUNDERSFOOT RAILWAY.

10 George IV. Cap. 108, Royal Assent 1st June, 1829.

THIS is an act for making a railway from Thomas Chapel, in the parish of Begelly, to Saundersfoot, with two branches therefrom; and a harbour at Saundersfoot, in the county of Pembroke. Messrs. William Bevan and Son, engineers, made an estimate of this work as follows:—

		£.	s.	d.
For the Main Line........ 4¾ miles		6,491	10	0
Ridgeway Branch .... ¾ mile		818	11	10
Wiseman's Bridge Branch 1 mile		2,131	9	8
6½		9,441	11	6
Besides the above, the price of the Land....		525	0	0
Railway Road over the Piers............		240	0	0
Erecting the Breakwater at Saundersfoot ...		7,007	18	10
Making together............£17,214			10	4

Sir Richard Bulkeley Phillips Phillips, Baronet, of Picton Castle, is the only subscriber.

This work was not completed at the time this article was written.

SEVERN RIVER.

19 Hen. VII. C. 18, R. A. ——— 1503.   23 Hen. VIII. C. 12, R. A. ——— 1531—2.
12 Geo. III. C. 109, R. A. 3rd June, 1772.   39 Geo. III. C. 8, R. A. 21st March, 1799.
43 Geo. III. C. 129, R. A. 27th July, 1803.   49 Geo. III. C. 121, R. A. 27th May, 1809.
51 Geo. III. C. 148, R. A. 10th June, 1811.

THE importance which has always attached to this noble river, which without artificial means is navigable to a greater extent than any other in the kingdom, to the incalculable benefit of the country through which it runs, may be estimated by the fact of the first legislative enactment respecting it being at the early period of the reign of Henry VII. entitled, ' *An Act concerning the River* ' *Severn;'* which was followed by another act of his son and successor Henry VIII. entitled, ' *An Act for taking Exactions upon*

' *the Paths of the River Severn.*' In 1772 an act was passed ' *for*
' *making and keeping in Repair a Road or Passage for Horses on*
' *the Banks of the River Severn, between Bewdley Bridge and a*
' *Place called the Meadow Wharf, at Coalbrook Dale, for haling*
' *and drawing Vessels along the said River.*' By this act a number
of persons were appointed trustees for carrying into effect the
provisions of the act, and were empowered to take the following

TOLLS.

	s.
For every Horse passing on the Road, drawing a Barge, Wherry, Boat or other Vessel on the Severn, between the Bridge at Bewdley and the Bridge at Bridgenorth........	7
For every Horse drawing any Vessel between the Bridge at Bridgenorth and Meadow Wharf at Coalbrook Dale	5

Horses drawing Vessels laden with Corn in the Straw, Muck or Lime for Manure, are exempted from all Tolls; as also are Horses which return within Twelve Hours after the Time they have been employed, and for which Tolls have been paid.

The act passed in 1799 states that the trustees had not complied with the provisions of the act of 1772, touching the repairs
of the towing-path, in consequence of which that act was nullified;
but the act of 1799 revives the powers contained in the act of
1772, notwithstanding the commissioners had not held meetings
conformably to the directions of such act.

In 1803 an act of parliament was obtained by a company of
persons who were thereby incorporated by the name of " The
" Company of Proprietors of the River Severn Horse Towing
" Path Extension," which was entitled, ' *An Act for extending*
' *and making the Horse Towing Path or Road, on the Banks of the*
' *River Severn, from Bewdley Bridge, in the county of Worcester,*
' *to the Deep Water at Diglis, below the city of Worcester.*' By
which act the company was empowered to raise amongst themselves, for the purposes of this undertaking, the sum of £5,000, in
one hundred shares of £50 each; and, if necessary, a further sum
of £6,000, either amongst themselves, or by creation of new
shares; and they are authorized to take the following

TOLLS.

	d.
For every Horse or other Beast, passing on any Part of the Towing-path and drawing any Boat, Barge or other Vessel on the River	6 per Mile.
For any less Distance than a Mile	6

Vessels haled by Men pay no Toll.

2 N 2

Another act of parliament, entitled, ' *An Act for making and*
' *keeping in Repair a Road or Passage for Horses on the Banks of*
' *the River Severn, between a certain Place at Coalbrook Dale, to*
' *and above the Welsh Bridge in the town of Shrewsbury, county of*
' *Sa.op, for haling and drawing Vessels along the said River,*' was
passed in 1809, which appointed Lord Ossulston, Lord Barnard,
Sir John Hill, and a number of other persons, trustees for carrying
the purposes of the act into execution, and authorized them to take
the following

TOLLS.

	s.
For every Horse passing along the Towing-path, and drawing a Boat, Barge or other Vessel, between Meadow Wharf at Coalbrook Dale and Mardol and Frankwell Quays above the Welsh Bridge at Shrewsbury...	2 per Mile.

Horses drawing Vessels laden with Corn in the Straw, Muck or Lime for Manure, are
exempted from Tolls, as also are Horses returning within Twelve Hours from the
Time of Paying Toll, and Vessels haled by Men.

The last act of parliament relating to this river was obtained in
1811, by a number of persons, amongst whom were the Earl of
Coventry, the Earl of Essex, Lord Sydney, Lord Somers, Lord
Beauchamp, the Bishop of Worcester and the Bishop of Gloucester,
who were incorporated by the name of " The Company of Pro-
" prietors of the Gloucester and Worcester Horse Towing Path,"
and is entitled, ' *An Act for extending the Horse Towing Path on*
' *the Banks of the River Severn, from Worcester Bridge to a certain*
' *Place below the city of Gloucester called the Lower Parting, situate*
' *at the Corner of Portham Mead, in the county of Gloucester.*' By
this act the company are empowered to raise amongst themselves
the sum of £10,000, in four hundred shares of £25 each; and, if
necessary, a further sum of £5,000, either amongst themselves,
by the creation of new shares, or by assignment of the tolls, &c. as
a security, and they are authorized to receive the following

TOLLS.

	s.
For every Horse or other Beast passing on the Towing-path, and drawing any Boat, Barge or other Vessel on the River	1 per Mile.
For every Distance less than a Mile	1

Vessels haled by Men exempted from Toll.

The immense facilities afforded to the trade of the country by
this river, are too well known to require comment. It has its
source in the Plynlimmon Mountains, which are 2,463 feet above

the level of the sea, in Montgomeryshire, Wales, and after a navigable course of one hundred and seventy-eight miles, with a fall of 225 feet from Welshpool, through the counties of Montgomery, Salop, Worcester and Gloucester, it empties itself into the Bristol Channel.

There is a handsome stone bridge over this river at Worcester; an iron one has lately been erected near Tewkesbury; and the only bridge lower down the river, is a handsome one of stone at Gloucester.

The navigable connections of this river are the Montgomeryshire Canal, which is supplied by it at Newtown; the Shrewsbury Canal at Shrewsbury; the Shropshire Canal at the Hay; the Staffordshire and Worcestershire Canal and the Leominster Canal at Stourport; the Droitwich Canal at Hawford; the Birmingham and Worcester Canal at Diglis, below Worcester; the River Avon at Tewkesbury; the Coombe Hill Canal at Fletcher's Leap; the Hereford and Gloucester (when completed) at Gloucester; the Gloucester and Berkeley Canal at Gloucester, and its outlet at Sharpness Point; the Stroud Canal at Framiload; the Lydney Canal below Lydney; the River Wye at Beachley; the Bristol River Avon at Morgan's Pill; and the Monmouthshire Canal at Newport. In addition to these canals, there are many railways connecting this river with the numerous coal and other mines, which are in its course.

SEVERN AND WYE RAILWAY AND CANAL.

49 Geo. III. C. 159, R. A. 10th June, 1809.   50 Geo. III. C. 215, R. A. 21st June, 1810.
51 Geo. III. C. 193, R. A. 26th June, 1811.   54 Geo. III. C. 42, R. A. 18th May, 1814.
3 Geo. IV. C. 75, R. A. 21st June, 1822.

THIS railway crosses the forest of Dean in a direction nearly from north to south, and connects, as the title implies, the Rivers Severn and Wye. Commencing from the River Wye at a place called Bishop's Wood, and proceeding thirteen miles and a half through the forest, it terminates in a basin at Cross Pill, a little below Lydney, and from thence is connected with the Severn at Nass Point by a canal one mile in length. There are nine branches, amounting together in length to above twelve miles and a quarter, laid from the main line to coal and other mines in the neighbourhood; one from Ridnall's Mill; one other from Park End Bridge to the Birches; one other from Park End Bridge to Scroll's Tump; one other from Park End Bridge to Milk Wall; one other from opposite the Lodge Inclosure up Brookhall Ditches; one other from White Ley to Bixhead Quarries; one other from Cannop Hill, up, through and to the head of Howler Slade; one other from Vallet's Inclosure to Wimblow Slade; and one other from Miery Stock to the summit at Churchway Engine.

The first act of parliament relating to this undertaking was passed in 1809, and is entitled, ' *An Act for making and maintain-* ' *ing a Railway from the River Wye, at or near to a Place called* ' *Lidbrook, in the parish of Ruardean, in the county of Gloucester,* ' *to or near to a Place called the Lower Forge, below Newern, in* ' *the parish of Lydney, in the said county; and for making other* ' *Railways therein mentioned, in the Forest of Dean, in the county* ' *of Gloucester;*' and incorporates the persons who applied for it by the name of " The Lydney and Lidbrook Railway Company." The act states that the undertaking will open an easy communication between the Rivers Severn and Wye and the collieries and quarries in the forest of Dean, and greatly facilitate the conveyance of coal, stone and other productions of the forest to the cities and counties of Hereford and Gloucester.

The proprietors are empowered by the act to raise, amongst themselves, the sum of £35,000, in shares of £50 each, (but of which sum £3,000 is to be reserved for those free miners of the forest of Dean who shall signify their desire to possess shares before the 1st day of August next after the passing of this act, to be divided in shares of £10 each) and if necessary, a further sum of £20,000 may be raised, either amongst themselves, by the creation of new shares, by optional notes, or by mortgage of the undertaking as a security. The act likewise authorizes the company to levy the following

TONNAGE RATES.

	s.	d.	
For all Stone for the Repair of Roads or Highways, and all Manure	0	2	per Ton, per Mile.

TONNAGE RATES CONTINUED.

	s.	d.

For all Coal, Coke, Culm, Stone, Coal Cinders, Chalk, Marl, Sand, Lime, Clay, Ashes, Peat, Lime-stone, Pitching and Paving-stone, Iron-stone, Iron or other Ore, and other Minerals, and Bricks, the Produce of the Forest, from any Place in the Forest to or near to the River Wye at Lidbrook, or to or near to the Lower Forge, or to any Place at a less Distance than the above, where the Goods shall be deposited for Sale, or conveyed farther by other Means than this Railroad, for the whole Distance................................   **3   0 per Ton.**

For all the above Goods, the Produce of the Forest, to the Head of any of the Collateral Branches from the Main Line, to connect with any Road or Railway leading towards Colford or Monmouth, for the whole Distance   **0   6   ditto.**

For all the above Goods, the Produce of the Forest, to any other Place in the Forest, to be there deposited for Sale or conveyed from thence by other Means than this Railroad, excepting those carried to the Heads of the Collateral Branches to connect with any Road or Railway leading towards Colford or Monmouth, for the whole Distance ....   **1   6   ditto.**

For all other Goods and Merchandize, whether the Produce of the Forest or not ....   **0   6   ditto, per Mile.**

EXEMPTION.

A special Exemption is made in favor of the Tenants of the Honourable Charles Bathurst, who are only to pay one-third of the Rate of Tonnage for Coal or Culm carried to or near the Lower Forge; one quarter for that carried to or towards the Middle Forge; and one-fifth for that carried to or towards the Upper Forge.

The forest of Dean belonging to the King, the company are to pay £300 per annum, from the period at which the main line of railway shall be completed, for the ground occupied by it and its branches, and a guinea a week towards defraying the expense of inspectors appointed by his Majesty.

Lords of manors and owners of ground on the railway are empowered, by this act, to erect wharfs and warehouses; and on their refusal so to do, in situations which the company consider desirable, the company of proprietors are authorized, after twelve months' notice having been given to such owners, &c. to do so on their own behalf, and the following wharfage rates may be levied, either by the owners of land or the company, as the case may be.

WHARFAGE RATES.

	d.

For all Coals, Culm, Lime-stone, Clay, Iron, Iron-stone, Lead-ore or any other Ores, Timber, Stones, Bricks, Tiles, Slates, Gravel, Hay, Straw, Corn in the Straw, Manure, for Six Days or less ....   **1 per Ton.**

For ditto for a Month ....   **3   ditto.**

If a longer Period than a Month, for the first Ten Days ....   **1   ditto.**

For every succeeding Day after the expiration of Ten Days............   **1   ditto.**

For all other Goods or Merchandize, for Six Days.....................   **3   ditto.**

For the next Ten Days...   **1   ditto.**

For every succeeding Day after Ten Days ....   **1   ditto.**

The Honourable Charles Bathurst is to allot sufficient land for
wharfs on the Severn, and the company are to guarantee the
wharfage to him from 1st January, 1813, to be not less than
£500 per annum, they making up the deficiency, if any.

The next act of parliament obtained by this company is
entitled, ' *An Act to alter and amend the Lydney and Lidbrook*
' *Railway Act; to vary certain Parts of the said Railway, and to*
' *extend the same from Lydbrook to Bishop's Wood, and from the*
' *Lower Forge to the Cross Pill; and for making a Basin and*
' *Canal to communicate with the River Severn at Nass Point.*'
This act alters the title of the company to that of " The Severn
" and Wye Railway and Canal Company," as it stands in the
heading of this article, and authorizes them to continue the main
line from Lidbrook to Bishop's Wood Furnace on the Wye, and
from the Lower Forge in two branches, one on each side of a
basin to be cut by the company to a creek called Cross Pill; and
they are also to cut a basin at forty yards distance from and above
the creek called Cross Pill, to be two hundred yards in length,
fifty yards in breadth, and 21 feet deep; and a canal of 21 feet
deep, eight yards in width at the bottom and twenty-eight yards
at the top, to extend from the basin to the River Severn at Nass
Point; they are also to make a lock between the canal and outer
harbour, 21 feet wide and 90 feet long, and an outer harbour 28
feet deep, eighty yards long and twenty-six yards wide at the
bottom, with a pair of gates or a lock to open into the Severn with
the tide; they are also required to divert the waters of a creek
called Lidney Pill into this basin and canal, and to stop up the
present course of the creek. The company are authorized to
take the following rates on the canal.

TONNAGE RATES.

	s.	d.
For every Trow or other Vessel passing or entering the Outer Harbour, or going in or coming out of the Canal or Basin to or from the Severn	7	6 each.
For all Goods or Merchandize, which shall be imported or exported into or from the Basin in such Trow or Vessel	0	6 per Ton.

Fractions to be taken as for a Quarter of a Ton.

EXEMPTIONS.

Vessels conveying Coal or other Commodities which have been carried on the Rail-
way, and paid the Tolls authorized to be taken thereon, are exempted from these
Rates; and a special Clause provides that Messrs. Pidcock and Co. the now
Tenants, and any future Tenants, of the Collieries and Iron Works of the Honour-

able Charles Bathurst shall be allowed the Use and Benefit of the Outer Harbour, Basin and Canal, for the conveying of any Coal, Lime-stone, Iron-stone, Iron Metals or any Goods whatever, to and from their Collieries and Iron Works, for the Use thereof or for Sale therefrom, free from all Tolls or Rates; and should there be any obstruction in the Creek or Basin, shall use the Railways by the Sides of the Creek and Basin with like Exemption from Tolls.

Boats of less than Twenty Tons Burthen to pay the same as those of Twenty Tons, except the contrary be allowed by the Company or their principal Agent.

The same Rate of Wharfage to be taken as in former Act.

The rates of the company to be a security to Mr. Bathurst for the £500 per annum guaranteed to him for wharfage rates, and they are also to pay him 10s. per annum for a piece of land of 70 feet in length and forty yards in breadth, on the basin, for a wharf for his tenants, Messrs. Pidcock and Company. The rates for warehouse-room to be the same as those taken upon the Stafford-shire and Worcestershire Canal, at Stourport, in Worcestershire.

In consideration of the company (by consent of the Surveyor General of his Majesty's Woods and Forests) deviating about five hundred yards from their original line, near Daniel Moor Ditches, they are to pay £10 a year, in addition to the £300 per annum provided to be paid in the former act.

The act of parliament obtained by the company in 1811 states that they have expended the £35,000, their original capital, with £15,600, part of the £20,000 which they were empowered to raise in addition thereto by the former act; and authorizes them to raise a further sum of £30,000, either by creation of new shares, or by borrowing it on optional notes. It likewise removes the exemption from tolls of those vessels entering into or going from the canal or basin with coal or other commodities, which have been already carried on and paid the tolls of the railroad, and these vessels are in future to pay the same tolls as others, but it continues the exemption in favor of the tenants of the collieries and iron-works of Mr. Bathurst.

In 1814 the company obtained another act of parliament, authorizing them to raise a further sum of £30,000 in the same manner as in the preceding act.

The last act of parliament respecting this company was passed in 1822, and provides a compensation to Mr. Bathurst, who had built wharfs and warehouses and appropriated land for them, under the authority of the acts of parliament passed herein, but in consequence of the extension of the railway beyond his land to the outer harbour made by the company, he was likely to sustain considerable injury from a diminution of wharfage, by goods being deposited on the wharfs adjoining the outer harbour. The act therefore authorizes the company to pay to Mr. Bathurst, his heirs and assigns for ever, the following

RATES.

d.

For all Coal (not exceeding in the whole, in any one Year, Sixty Thousand Tons) which shall be deposited on any Wharf of the Company, not on Mr. Bathurst's Land, and from thence shipped for any Place Westward of the Holmes Island .... } ½ per Ton.

For all such Coal so deposited and shipped above the Quantity of Sixty Thousand Tons annually .... } 1 ditto.

For all Coal which shall be so deposited and shipped to Bristol or Bridgewater, in the event of a Repeal or Equalization of the present Coastwise Duty on Coal taking place .... } 2 ditto.

And on all Goods landed on the Company's Wharfs (except Coals to be shipped as above, and Materials for Repair of the Company's Works which shall be forwarded within Fourteen Days, or any Goods (not Coal) which shall be landed *in transitu* upon such Wharfs, and shall be transshipped within One Month) the same Wharfage Rate shall be paid to Mr. Bathurst, as would have been, had they been landed on his own Wharfs, and the Tolls of the Company to be a Security for the Payment of these Rates which are in Addition to, and not to affect the £500 per Annum guaranteed to Mr. Bathurst by the former Act.

This railway and canal, by its communication with the Rivers Severn and Wye, opens a channel for the transit of his Majesty's timber in the forest of Dean; and of the coal, stone and iron-ore which abound in the said forest, and which are raised by other parties.

SHEFFIELD CANAL.

55 George III. Cap. 65, Royal Assent 7th June, 1815.

This canal, which connects the town of Sheffield with the River Dunn, commences in the township of Tinsley, in a cut communicating with the River Dunn, and thence passes through the township of Attercliffe, in the parish of Rotherham, and, by an aqueduct, over the road from Worksop to Attercliffe, a distance of a little more than four miles, to Sheffield. There is likewise a side-cut of forty-seven chains in length, running by the side of Car Brook, to the township of Darnal, at the end of which is a reservoir called Darnal Reservoir; there are also two other reservoirs covering in the whole about thirty-two acres and a half.

A very large and commodious warehouse is built at the head of the basin, which basin is two hundred and twenty yards long and forty broad, from which, to the first lock, a distance of nearly three miles, is level; in the next seventeen chains is a fall of 38 feet 5 inches, by six locks; from thence, to a little above Tinsley Wharf, three quarters of a mile, is level; and from thence to the junction with the Tinsley Cut belonging to the River Dunn Company is a fall of 31 feet 8 inches, by five locks, in a distance of seventeen chains and a half, making a total fall of 70 feet 1 inch.

The act of parliament authorizing this canal was obtained in 1815 by a number of persons, amongst whom were Lord Milton and Sir James Graham, who were incorporated by the name of " The Company of Proprietors of the Sheffield Canal," and are empowered to raise, amongst themselves, for the purposes of this act, the sum of £80,000, in shares of £100 each; and, if necessary, a further sum of £20,000, either amongst themselves, by creation of new shares, or by mortgage of the undertaking as a security. They are empowered to charge the following

TONNAGE RATES.

	d.
For all Coal, Coke, Charcoal, Lime-stone, Iron-stone, Slag, Sand, Arsura, Sweep-Washing Waste, Stones, Slates, Pavors, Cord Wood, Cinders, Manure, Bones for Manure, Turnips, Carrots and Potatoes	2 per Ton, per Mile.
For all Pig-lead, Pig-iron, Ballast-iron, Nut or Bushel-iron, Old Cast-iron, Bricks, Old Ropes and Rags, Timber Unbroken, Bones and Hoofs.	3 ditto. ditto.
For all Bar, Rod or Rolled-iron or Steel, Cast-iron Goods, Deals and other Broken Timber, Lime, Onions, Apples, Pears, Peas, Beans, Rape, Line, Cole, Mustard Seed, and all Kinds of Green Groceries, that are not by this Act specially charged by Name	4 ditto. ditto.
For all Dry Groceries of all Descriptions, and all Kinds of Manufactured Goods, Wares and Merchandize in Casks, Hogsheads or other Packages	5 ditto. ditto.
For all Corn, Grain or Malt	1 per Quarter, ditto.
For all other Goods, Matters and Things not specially charged	6 per Ton, ditto

Fractions of a Mile and of a Ton to be charged as the Quarters therein.

Vessels passing any of the Locks of this Canal with less lading than Twenty-five Tons, shall pay a Tonnage Rate for Twenty-five Tons, if there be sufficient Water to pass a Vessel with that Lading; but if the Water in the Lock shall not be sufficient to pass a Vessel with Twenty-five Tons Weight of Lading, they shall then pay for such Lading as the Water would pass.

CRANAGE AND PORTERAGE RATES.

	s.
For every Ton of Goods, Wares or other Merchandize, loaded from or landed upon any of the Wharfs or into the Warehouses of the Company (in consequence of building a Bridge over the River Sheaf)	2

WHARFAGE RATES.

The Column marked thus (*) are the Rates to be taken for above Seventy-two Hours
and not more than Six Days.
The Column marked thus (+) for Six Days but less than One Month.
The Column marked thus (‡) for One Month but less than Six Weeks.
The Column marked thus (₰) for Six Weeks, but less than Two Months.
The Column marked thus (‖) for Two Months but less than Ten Weeks.

DESCRIPTION OF GOODS.	(*)	(+)	(‡)	(₰)	(‖)
	s. d.	s. d.	s. d.	s. d.	s. d
For every Ton of Lead, Iron and Steel of all Kinds, lying on the Wharfs and not Housed	0 4	0 6	0 8	0 10	1 0
For every Ton of Coal, Coke, Charcoal, Lime, Lime-stone, Iron-stone, Sand, Arsura, Sweep-Washing Waste, Stones, Slates, Bricks, Timber, Bones, Hoofs and other Goods and Things whatsoever, lying on the Wharfs and not Housed..........	0 6	0 9	1 0	1 3	1 6
For every Ton of Goods, Wares, Merchandize and other Matters and Things, lying or deposited in the Warehouses or otherwise Housed	1 0	1 6	2 0	2 6	3 0
For every Quarter of Corn, or other Grain and Malt, lying in the Granaries or otherwise Housed...	0 2	0 3	0 4	0 5	0 6

Goods taken away before the expiration of Seventy-two Hours, not to pay any
Wharfage Rate.

The act of parliament provides, that on the completion of the
side-cut, a private railroad of about six hundred yards in length,
running from the Duke of Norfolk's Coal Yard, in the parish of
Handsworth, to the southern termination of the side-cut, should
become public, the company making compensation to the owners
and occupiers of the land through which the railroad passes, and
to all persons who will suffer damage thereby. They are likewise
to keep all the roads in the township of Tinsley in repair, which
had been formerly done by the River Dunn Company.

This canal, by opening a communication between the River
Dunn and Sheffield, is of incalculable benefit to that place, by the
facilities it affords of transmitting articles of its extensive and important manufactories, and also of the coal and iron-stone which
abound in the neighbourhood; and of supplying it with all articles
of domestic consumption.

SHIPLEY COLLIERIES CANAL.
(SEE NUTBROOK OR SHIPLEY CANAL.)

SHREWSBURY CANAL.

33 George III. Cap. 113, Royal Assent 3rd June, 1793.

This canal commences in Castle Foregate Basin, on the east side of Shrewsbury, near the Ellesmere Canal, to which it may be joined by mutual consent, and following the windings of the River Severn, passes Uffington; from thence, having a parallel course with the River Tern, it passes Upton Forge, Withington and Rodington, at which last place it crosses the River Roden; a little further on, it crosses the River Tern by an aqueduct at Long Mill, and runs by Langdon and Eyton, and crossing Ketley Brook, joins the Donnington and Shropshire Canals at Rockwardine Wood, in Shropshire. The proprietors purchased one mile and one hundred and eighty-eight yards of the Ketley Canal, which joins the Shrewsbury Canal at Wombridge, and now forms a part of the line of this work.

The act of parliament, under sanction of which this canal was undertaken, was obtained in 1793, and is entitled, ' *An Act for* ' *making and maintaining a navigable Canal from the North End* ' *of the Shropshire Canal, in the township of Rockwardine Wood,* ' *in the county of Salop, to the town of Shrewsbury, in the said* ' *county.*' It incorporates the company of proprietors by the name of " The Company of Proprietors of the Shrewsbury Canal " Navigation," and authorizes them to raise amongst themselves the sum of £50,000, in shares of £100 each, and, if necessary, a further sum of £20,000 for the purposes of the act, and to take the following

TONNAGE RATES.

	d.
For all Iron, Iron-stone, Coal, Stone, Timber and other Goods, Wares and Merchandize whatever .... }	2 per Ton, per Mile.

And in Proportion for a less Quantity than a Ton or a less Distance than a Mile.
And an addition of One Penny per Ton if passed by Inclined Planes, until the Canal pays a Dividend of Eight per Cent. when this last Rate shall cease.
Boats with less than Eight Tons to pay for that Quantity, except when returning.
All Manure (except Lime) exempt from these Rates.

There is a peculiarity in the construction of the locks on this navigation, which enables a long narrow canal boat, or two or four smaller boats (constructed for passing the inclined planes) to

go through them without unnecessary waste of water. The tunnel near Atcham is also remarkable; it is nine hundred and
seventy yards in length and 10 feet wide, with a towing-path 3
feet wide, constructed of wood, and supported on bearers from the
wall. Mr. Thomas Telford and Mr. William Reynolds were the
engineers for constructing this canal.

The length of the canal is seventeen miles and a half; the first
twelve miles of which, from Shrewsbury to Langdon, is level;
thence to Wombridge, four miles and a quarter, there is a lockage
rise of 79 feet; and from thence to Ketley Canal, another rise of
75 feet by an inclined plane, and thence along the Ketley Canal,
(purchased of Mr. William Reynolds) is level, making, in the
whole distance, a rise of 154 feet, partly by an inclined plane and
partly by locks. The fall from the basin to the Severn at Bagley
Bridge, Shrewsbury, is 22 feet.

This canal traverses a district of country abounding with coal
and iron mines, the proprietors of which, as well as the flourishing
and populous town of Shrewsbury, are greatly benefited by the
facilities of transmission which it affords.

SHROPSHIRE CANAL.

28 George III. Cap. 73, Royal Assent 11th June, 1788.

THE Shropshire Canal commences at the Donnington Wood
Canal, in the parish of Lillishall, and passing by Rockwardine
Wood, Oaken Gates, Hollingswood, Stirchley, and Madeley, pro-
ceeds to the Hay, near which it is united to the River Severn at
Coalport, formerly the Sheep-Wash Meadow, two miles below
Coalbrook Dale. Its length is seven miles and a half; from the
Severn at Calford to the Hay, a distance of three quarters of a
mile, is level; then it rises 207 feet by an inclined plane; it is
then level to Windmill Farm; from which point is a rise of 126
feet by another inclined plane; then level to near Rockwardine
Wood; from thence it falls 120 feet by an inclined plane; and the
remainder of its course to Donnington Wood Canal is level.

The act of parliament authorizing the cutting this canal was
passed in 1788, and is entitled, ' *An Act for making and main-*

' taining a navigable Canal from the Canal at Donnington Wood,
' in the county of Salop, to or near to a Place called Southill Bank,
' and from thence by Two several Branches, to communicate with
' the River Severn, one near Coalbrook Dale and the other near
' Madeley Wood, in the said county; and also certain other colla-
' teral Cuts to join such Canal.' It incorporates the company of
proprietors by the name of " The Company of Proprietors of the
" Shropshire Navigation," and empowers them to collect the
following

TONNAGE RATE.

	d.
For all Iron, Iron-stone, Coal, Stones, Timber, Goods, Wares and Merchandize of every Description .... }	2 per Ton, per Mile.

In addition to which Three-pence is charged for letting loaded Boats down the Inclined Planes.

This canal has assisted, very materially, the trade of its neighbourhood, by its conveyance of the raw materials to the many
large furnaces and works thereabouts, and of their heavy manufactured goods, to the River Severn, thus affording a transit to
both home and distant parts. The collateral cuts are from South-
well Bank, near Stirchley, to Coalbrook Dale; from the iron-
works at Horse Hay is a railway to this canal.

The summit of this canal is 333 feet above the Severn at Coal
Port and Meadow Wharf; and 120 feet above the summit of the
Shrewsbury Canal, to which last it descends by two inclined
planes.

Mr. William Reynolds and Mr. Henry Williams were the engineers, and the work, which was executed for about £47,000,
was opened in the year 1792.

SIRHOWEY TRAMROAD.

42 George III. Cap. 115, Royal Assent 26th June, 1802.

THE act for making this tramroad was obtained by the Monmouthshire Canal Company, and relates principally to their concerns; but as there are a few clauses respecting this tramroad,
not connected with the canal, we shall here extract them.

The act, which is entitled, ' *An Act for making and maintain-*
' *ing certain Railways, to communicate with the Monmouthshire*
' *Canal Navigation; and for enabling the Company of Proprietors*
' *of that Navigation to raise a further Sum of Money to complete*
' *their Undertaking; and for explaining and amending the Acts*
' *passed in the Thirty-second and Thirty-seventh Years of his pre-*
' *sent Majesty's Reign, relating thereto,*' directs that the Monmouthshire Canal Company shall make the tramroad from their
canal, at Newport, for a distance of nine miles, to Tredegar Park;
that for the next mile through the park it shall be made by Sir
Charles Morgan; and that Samuel Homfray, Richard Fothergill,
Matthew Monkhouse, William Thompson and William Forman,
iron masters and intended lessees of the Tredegar Iron Works,
shall complete the railway from the Nine Mile Point to Sirhowey
Furnaces. The act incorporates them by the title of " The
" Sirhowey Tramroad Company," and empowers them to raise
amongst themselves £30,000, in three hundred shares of £100
each; and if necessary a further sum of £15,000, either amongst
themselves, by creation of new shares, or by mortgage of the undertaking as a security; and they, as well as Sir Charles Morgan,
are authorized to take the same tolls and rates on those portions of
the tramroad respectively made by them, as are taken by the
proprietors of the Monmouthshire Canal, and are stated under that
article. This company is to pay the Monmouthshire Canal Company £110 per annum, in consideration of that company making
a mile more in length of the railway than was originally agreed
upon.

SLEAFORD NAVIGATION.

32 George III. Cap. 106, Royal Assent 11th June, 1794.

THE company of proprietors who carried into effect the purposes of this act of parliament, which is entitled, ' *An Act for making*
' *and maintaining a Navigation from Sleaford Castle Causeway,*
' *through the town of Sleaford, in the county of Lincoln, along the*
' *course of Sleaford Mill Stream and Kyme Eau, to the River*
' *Witham, at or near Chappel Hill, in the same county; and for*

' *making necessary Cuts for better effecting the said Navigation,*'
are hereby incorporated by the name of " The Company of Pro-
" prietors of the Sleaford Navigation, in the county of Lincoln."

The act authorizes them to make navigable the Sleaford Mill
Stream and River Kyme Eau, and for that purpose to raise amongst
themselves the sum of £13,000, in one hundred and thirty shares
of £100 each; and, if necessary, a further sum of £6,500, either
amongst themselves, by the creation of new shares, or by mortgage of the tolls. The dividend on these shares is limited to £8
per cent. and should the income in any year be more than
sufficient to pay this dividend, the tonnage rates are to be reduced
in proportion to such excess; a sum of £1,000 having been first
funded to meet any deficiencies. The act of parliament empowers
the company to take the following

TONNAGE RATES.

	s. d.
For all Goods, Wares and Merchandize (except Lime or Lime-stone, Manure of any Kind for Land, or Materials to be used for the Repair of Roads) which shall be conveyed upon any Part of the said Navigation, between Haverholm Mill and Sleaford Castle Causeway, or from above Haverholm Mill to the River Witham, or any less Distance below the said Mill, or from the River Witham, or any less Distance, to any Part of the Navigation above the said Mill..	2　0 per Ton.
From any Part of the Navigation between the said Mill and the second Lock to be erected near Flax Dyke, on the River Witham, or any less Distance below the said second Lock, or from the River Witham, or any less Distance, to any Part of the Navigation between the second Lock and Haverholm Mill	1　6 ditto.
From any Part of the Navigation between the second Lock and a Bridge called Beffrie's Bridge in the Township of South Kyme, to the River Witham, or any less Distance below the said Bridge, or from the River Witham, or any less Distance, to any Part of the Navigation between the said Bridge and the second Lock near Flax Dyke	1　3 ditto.
From any Part of the Navigation between the said Bridge and the first Lock to be erected in Kyme Eau, to the River Witham, or any less Distance below the said Lock, or from the River Witham, or any less Distance, to any Part of the Navigation between the said first Lock to be erected in Kyme Eau and Beffrie's Bridge in the Township of South Kyme................	1　0 ditto.

For every Ton of Lime or Lime-stone, Manure for Land or Materials for Roads, One-half of the several Rates aforesaid, and in proportion for any greater or less Weight than a Ton.

In Consideration of the great increase of Tolls which it is supposed the completion of this Navigation will cause on the River Witham, it is provided by this Act that Boats or Vessels passing through a Lock on this Navigation and paying the Rates thereon, and from thence to the River Witham, shall only pay Half the usual Tonnage Rates levied on that River.

The rates and tolls collected to be free from all taxes and
assessments whatever.

This navigation is about thirteen miles and a half in length, and its elevation very little above the level of the sea. There are two locks; one at Lower Kyme and the other near Flax Dyke, in the parish of Ewerley; and the act requires that locks shall be made at each of the mills on the stream, if required by the owners thereof.

This navigation is principally used for the conveyance of agricultural produce, and for supplying Sleaford with articles of domestic consumption.

SOAR RIVER OR LOUGHBOROUGH NAVIGATION.

6 George III. Cap. 94, Royal Assent 14th May, 1766.
16 George III. Cap. 65, Royal Assent 2nd April, 1776.

THE portion of the River Soar which was intended to be made navigable by the first act of parliament, is that which begins near Loughborough, at a place where Hermitage Brook unites with it, until it falls into the Trent; and by this act, which is entitled, ' *An Act for making the River Soar navigable from the River* ' *Trent, to or near Loughborough, in the county of Leicester; and* ' *for making navigable Cuts or Canals from the said River Soar,* ' *to or near the Rushes, and the Hermitage Pool at Loughborough* ' *aforesaid,*' a number of persons, including the Marquis of Granby and Lord Grey, were appointed trustees for carrying its provisions into effect.

The greater part of the course of the river to be made navigable forms a boundary between the counties of Leicester and Nottingham.

The act of parliament authorizes the trustees to take the following

TONNAGE RATES.

	s.	d.	
For all Stone, Slate or Flags conveyed on the River or Cuts.........	2	0	per Ton.
For all Lime or Lime-stone, Swithland Stone and Slate	2	0	ditto.
For all Coal	2	0	ditto.
For all other Goods, Wares or Merchandize.........................	3	0	ditto.
For every empty Vessel	1	0	each.

Fractions of a Ton in proportion.

EXEMPTIONS.

Stones, Timber, Gravel, Sand or other Materials to be used for making or repairing any Mills within the Limits of the intended Navigation ; Soapers' Waste, Dung or other Manure, unmixt with Lime for Land, other than Lime or Lime-stone.

The tolls and rates to be exempted from all taxes whatever.

In 1776 a second act was passed, entitled, '*An Act for making* '*the River Soar navigable, from the River Trent to Bishop's Mea-* '*dow, within the liberty of Garenton, in the county of Leicester;* '*and for making and maintaining a navigable Cut or Canal from* '*thence, near, or up, and into the Rushes, at Loughborough, in the* '*said county.*' The preamble states, that it being found impracticable to carry into effect the provisions of the former act, in consequence of the frequent floods of the River Soar, a company is incorporated by the name of " The Company of Proprietors of " the Navigation from the River Trent, to the town of Loughbo- " rough," with power to make the river navigable from the Trent to a place called Bishop's Meadow, and from thence to communicate with Loughborough, by a canal through Knight Thorpe and Thorpe Arch, to the Rushes, in that town.

The company are empowered to raise amongst themselves, for the purposes of the act, the sum of £7,000, in seventy shares of £100 each; and, if necessary, a further sum of £3,000, either amongst themselves, by new subscribers, or by mortgage of the navigation, and to take the following

TONNAGE RATES.

	s.	d.	
For all Wheat, Rye, Beans or Peas	0	6	per Quarter.
For Malt	0	4	ditto.
For Barley or other Grain not before enumerated	0	5	ditto.
For all Goods, Wares or Merchandize of all Kinds	2	6	per Ton.

And in proportion for greater or less Quantities.

Lords of manors and land-owners may erect wharfs, &c. on the navigation, and take the following

WHARFAGE RATES.

	d.	
For all Goods, Wares or Merchandize, for Ten Days	6	per Ton.
For every Day after the expiration of Ten Days	½	ditto.

The length of the River Soar, made navigable under authority of these acts of parliament, is seven miles; and the canal, from the river to the town of Loughborough, rather more than a mile and a half. Situated as this canal is, with a fall at one extremity into the Trent Navigation, and into the Leicester at the other, it obtains a communication with the Grand Junction Canal through the Grand Union, and thus becomes a link in the great chain of inland navigation; thereby proving no less profitable to the proprietors than convenient to the public; for this is considered one of the most lucrative concerns of the kind in the kingdom.

SOMERSETSHIRE COAL CANAL.

34 George III. Cap. 86, Royal Assent 17th April, 1794.
36 George III. Cap. 48, Royal Assent 24th March, 1796.
42 George III. Cap. 35, Royal Assent 30th April, 1802.

THIS work commences in the Kennet and Avon Canal at Limpley Stoke, near Bradford, in Wiltshire, and running parallel with Mitford Brook to Mitford Mill, proceeds from thence in a westerly direction by Coombe Hay, Dunkerton, Camerton, High Littleton and Timsbury, to Paulton; a railway branching off from it in the parish of South Stoke, proceeds by Wellow, Foxcote, Writhlington and Radstock, to the collieries at Welton and Clandown, in Somersetshire.

At the commencement of the undertaking, it was designed to have a canal branch to Radstock, running upon one level to within a few hundred yards of the main line between Coombe Hay and Mitford Bridge; but in consequence of their funds being exhausted in completing so much of the canal, the company were unable to carry their lockage down to the level; a short railway was in consequence made on the Radstock Branch, to connect that portion of it, which was completed, with the main line of the canal; but here it may be observed, that above twenty years afterwards, a railway was substituted for the branch canal the whole distance.

To connect the Paulton line of canal with the lower level, the company, in the first instance, made whimsey and jenny roads or inclined planes at Coombe Hay, in lieu of lockage, of 138 feet descent; but after a short time it was found that they did not succeed, and that the company would be obliged to substitute locks for them. To raise funds for this purpose, an act, passed in 1802,

authorized the formation of a separate body called " The Lock
" Fund of the Somerset Coal Canal Company," which body was
to consist of individual proprietors of the Wilts and Berks, Kennet
and Avon, and Somerset Coal Canal Companies, in equal proportions, with powers to raise the sum of £45,000, to erect the requisite lockage and to appoint deputies to manage the same, which
has been carried into execution.

The first act of parliament relating to this undertaking was
passed in 1794, and is entitled, ' *An Act for making and main-*
' *taining a navigable Canal, with certain Railways and Stone*
' *Roads, from several Collieries in the county of Somerset, to com-*
' *municate with the intended Kennet and Avon Canal, in the parish*
' *of Bradford, in the county of Wilts,*' and incorporates a number
of persons therein named by the title of " The Company of Pro-
" prietors of the Somersetshire Coal Canal Navigation," and authorizes them to raise, for the purposes of the act, the sum of
£80,000, in eight hundred shares of £100 each ; and, if necessary, a further sum of £40,000, either amongst themselves or by
mortgage of the tolls as security. This was followed by a second
act of parliament in 1796, entitled, ' *An Act to vary and alter the*
' *Line of a Canal authorized to be made by an Act, passed in the*
' *Thirty-fourth Year of the Reign of his present Majesty, and to*
' *alter and amend the said Act.*' This act authorizes the company
of proprietors to make various alterations and deviations in the
line of the canal and railway.

The last act of parliament relating to this undertaking was
passed in 1802, and is entitled, ' *An Act for enabling the Company*
' *of Proprietors of the Somersetshire Coal Canal Navigation to*
' *vary and alter the Lines of the said Canal and Works, and to*
' *alter and amend the Powers and Provisions of the several Acts*
' *passed for making the said Canal.*' It states that the sums of
£80,000 and £40,000 authorized to be raised under the former
acts respecting this navigation, have been contributed amongst
themselves and expended in the prosecution of the work, and that
the shares have consequently become of the value of £150 each.
The act authorizes a deviation in the original lines, the expense of
which was estimated by Mr. W. Bennett, in 1801, at £33,222,
15s. 2d. and empowers the company to raise a further sum of

£20,000, amongst themselves, by optional notes, or by mortgage of the rates as security; and also the sum of £45,000 for the formation of a fund for erecting the locks required on this navigation, which sum is to be raised and appropriated in the manner stated in a preceding part of this article. The subscribers to the lock fund are not to receive more than £10 per cent. per annum on their subscription, and the surplus to form a sinking fund for paying off the capital; and when that is paid off, the extra tonnage rate for supporting the locks to cease. The act authorizes the company to take the following

TONNAGE RATES.

	d.		
For all Coal, Coke, &c.	2¼	per Ton, per Mile.	
For all Iron, Lead, Ores, Cinders, &c.	4	ditto.	ditto.
For all Stones, Tiles, Bricks, Slate, Timber, &c.	3	ditto.	ditto.
For all Cattle, Sheep, Swine and other Beasts	4	ditto.	ditto.
For all other Goods	4	ditto.	ditto.
For every Horse or Ass Travelling on the Railway	1	each.	
For every Cow or other Neat Cattle ditto	½	ditto.	
For Sheep, Swine and Calves ditto	5	per Score.	

Fractions of a Mile to pay for Half a Mile, and of a Ton as a Quarter of a Ton; Rates for Wharfage to be determined by the Company.

In addition to the above Rates, One Shilling per Ton is paid on all Goods to the Lock Fund, which also receives Three Farthings per Ton from the Coal Canal Company.

This canal is of great importance in the export of coal, with which the neighbourhoods of Paulton and Radstock abound. That useful article is thus forwarded eastward to the Kennet and Avon and Wilts and Berks Canals, by which it is supplied to places on their lines, and also to others on the borders of the River Thames; besides entirely supplying the city of Bath and a part of the neighbourhood of Bristol.

SPITTAL AND KELSO RAILWAY.

51 George III. Cap. 133, Royal Assent 31st May, 1811.

THIS act is entitled, ' *An Act for making and maintaining a* ' *Railway from or near Spittal, in the county of Durham, to or* ' *near Kelso, in the county of Roxburgh; and for erecting and* ' *maintaining a Bridge over the River Tweed, from the parish of* ' *Northam, in the county of Durham, to Coldstream, in the county* ' *of Berwick.*' The part of the county of Durham in which Spittal is situated, is detached from the main body of the county and lying to the northward of the county of Northumberland, and adjoining Berwickshire in Scotland. No steps have yet been taken to carry the provisions of this act into effect.

STAFFORDSHIRE AND WORCESTERSHIRE CANAL.

6 George III. Cap. 97, Royal Assent 14th May, 1766.
30 George III. Cap. 75, Royal Assent 9th June, 1790.

This important branch of inland navigation commences in the River Severn, at Stourport, in Worcestershire, and proceeding in a northerly direction, passes Mitton, Kidderminster, Tittenhall, Penkridge, and Baswich, uniting itself with the Trent and Mersey Navigation, near Haywood, in Staffordshire. In its route it is carried by aqueducts over the Rivers Trent, Sow, Penk, Smester and Stour, and by a tunnel under the town of Kidderminster; there are also two other tunnels, two large reservoirs, and a number of bridges and small aqueducts. At Stourport this canal falls into two basins, and from these, boats descend into the River Severn, by two locks; from this point to the Stourbridge Canal, at Stewponey, there is a rise of 127 feet 6 inches, in a distance of twelve miles and a quarter; from thence to Tittenhall, being eleven miles, is a rise of 166 feet 6 inches; thence to Streetway, ten miles, is level, (and it is joined by the Old Birmingham Canal on this level); and from thence to the Trent and Mersey, at Haywood, is thirteen miles and a half, with a fall of 100 feet 6 inches. Its summit, or highest pound of water is, between the village of Autherly, near Wolverhampton, and the Old Roman Road called Streetway, in the county of Stafford, ten miles in extent, 100 feet 6 inches above the Trent and Mersey Canal, near Stafford; 352 feet above low water at Runcorn; and 294 feet above the Severn at Stourport.

The act of parliament, under sanction of which this canal was executed, was obtained in 1766, and is entitled, ' *An Act for* ' *making and maintaining a navigable Cut, or Canal, from the* ' *River Severn, between Bewdley and Titton Brook, in the county of* ' *Worcester, to cross the River Trent, near Haywood Mill, in the*

' *county of Stafford, and to communicate with a Canal intended to*
' *be made between the said River Trent and the River Mersey.*' It
incorporates a number of persons, therein named, by the style of
" The Company of Proprietors of the Staffordshire and Wor-
" cestershire Canal Navigation," and empowers them to raise
amongst themselves, for the purposes of the act, the sum of
£70,000, in seven hundred shares of £100 each; and, if necessary, a further sum of £30,000. The act also authorizes them
to collect the following

TONNAGE RATES.

		d.	
For all Iron, Iron-stone, Coal, Stone, Timber and other Goods	1½	per Ton, per Mile.	
For all Lime or Lime-stone	½	ditto.	ditto.

Paving-stones, Gravel, Sand, and other Materials for repairing Roads, (Lime-stone
excepted) and Manure for the Grounds of Persons who have had Land taken for the
Canal, shall be exempted from Tonnage Rates, provided such Articles pass through
a Lock only when the Water flows over the Weir.

The works of this undertaking were executed under the direction of the celebrated Mr. James Brindley, who built his first canal
lock on this navigation, at Compton, near the town of Wolverhampton.

A second act of parliament was obtained by this company in
1790, entitled, ' *An Act to enable the Company of Proprietors of*
' *the Staffordshire and Worcestershire Canal Navigation, to im-*
' *prove the Navigation of the River Severn, from Stourport, in the*
' *county of Worcester, to a Place called Diglis, near the city of*
' *Worcester ;*' which states that the company had completed their
canal from the Trent and Mersey Navigation to the River Severn,
but that the river was obstructed in various places by shoals, the
removal of which would be a great benefit to the trade of the river
and this canal, and that the company of proprietors of this navigation were willing to remove such shoals and obstructions at their
own expense; the act, therefore, authorizes them to improve the
navigation of the said river, and empowers them to borrow an
additional sum of £12,000, on mortgage of their tolls and rates.

The trade on this canal is immense, as, from its junction with
the Birmingham Canal at Autherly, a considerable portion of the
hardware manufactures from the counties of Stafford and Warwick, and of coals from the Bilstone and other mines, are carried
on it; great quantities of coal are also brought by the Stourbridge

Canal, which joins it at Stewponey, and with which it supplies, in great part, the counties of Stafford, Worcester and Gloucester ; by the River Severn it communicates with the port of Bristol ; and through the Thames and Severn Canal it has a communication with the city of London ; and by its connection with the Trent and Mersey, communicates with Liverpool, Manchester and Hull.

STAINFORTH AND KEADBY CANAL.

33 George III. Cap. 117, Royal Assent 7th June, 1793.
38 George III. Cap. 47, Royal Assent 1st June, 1798.
49 George III. Cap. 71, Royal Assent 20th May, 1809.

This canal, which is fifteen miles in length, commences at the River Dun Navigation, near Stainforth, in the West Riding of the county of York, whence running in an easterly direction near Thorne and Crowle, and passing to the south of both those places, it communicates with the River Trent at Keadby, in Lincolnshire.

The first act of parliament, authorizing this undertaking, was passed in 1793, and is entitled, ' *An Act for making and main-* ' *taining a navigable Canal from the River Dun Navigation Cut,* ' *at or near Stainforth, in the West Riding of the county of York,* ' *to join and communicate with the River Trent, at or near Keadby,* ' *in the county of Lincoln; and also a collateral Cut from the said* ' *Canal, to join the said River Dun, in the parish of Thorne, in* ' *the said Riding.*' It incorporates the company of proprietors by the name of " The Company of Proprietors of the Stainforth " and Keadby Canal Navigation," and empowers them to raise amongst themselves, for the purposes of this act, the sum of £24,200, in two hundred and forty-two shares of £100 each; and, if necessary, a further sum of £12,100, either amongst themselves or by mortgage of the tolls and rates, and to collect the following

TONNAGE RATES.

		d.	
For all Fir Timber, Fifty Feet to the Ton.....................		1 per Ton, per Mile.	
For all Deals, Twelve Feet Long and Three Inches Thick, to pay as a Ton..	}	1 ditto.	ditto.
For all Ash, Elm and other White Wood of English Growth, Fifty Feet to the Ton......................................	}	1 ditto.	ditto.
For all Oak Timber, Forty Cubic Feet a Ton		1 ditto.	ditto.
For all Coals, Sleck, Cinders, Culm, Charcoal and Lime......		¾ ditto.	ditto.

TONNAGE RATES CONTINUED.

	d.
For Lime-stone...	½ per Ton, per Mile.
For all other Sorts of Stone, Iron-stone, Flags, Paving-stone, Slate, Iron, Pig-iron, Bar-iron, Old-iron, Cast Metal, Bricks and Tiles...	1 ditto. ditto.
For all Wheat, Shelling, Beans, Peas, Vetches and Lentils ; Rape, Line, Cole, and Mustard Seed ; Apples, Pears, Onions and Potatoes ; Eight Winchester Bushels to the Quarter, for the whole Length of the Canal.......................	4 per Quarter.
For Barley, ditto	3 ditto.
For all Malt or Oats, ditto	2 ditto.
For all Groceries, and all Kinds of Linen and Woollen Yarn, Cotton, Flax, Hemp, Manufactured Goods of all Sorts, with every other Kind of Goods, Wares and Merchandize, not before enumerated	1¼ per Ton, per Mile.
For every Boat and Vessel that shall enter the Canal near Stainforth Lock, and turn down the Collateral Cut from Thorne Common to the River Dun at Hangman Hill, or shall navigate from Hangman Hill on the Canal to the River Dun Cut at Stainforth, on all Goods before enumerated ..	6 ditto.

Fractions of a Mile to be taken as a Mile, and of a Ton as the Quarters therein.

EXEMPTIONS.

All Kinds of Dung or other Manure (except Lime) that shall be produced in any Township or Parish through which the Canal passes, and to be carried to some other Township or Parish through which also the Canal passes.

The proprietors may likewise demand the following

CRANAGE AND PORTERAGE RATES.

	d.
For all Goods, Wares and Merchandize (except Corn, Coals, Stone, Lime, Lime-stone, Flint, Clay, English Timber, Bricks, Tiles, Plaster, Soapers' Waste or Ashes and Sandfall, which will not require a Crane, and may be loaded and delivered by the Crew of the Boat or Vessel)	6 per Ton.

WHARFAGE RATES.

The Column marked thus (*) are the Rates to be taken for above Twenty-four Hours and not more than Six Days.
The Column marked thus (+) for Six Days but less than One Month.
The Column marked thus (‡) for One Month but less than Six Weeks.
The Column marked thus (⅔) for Six Weeks but less than Two Months.
The Column marked thus (‖) for Two Months but less than Ten Weeks.

DESCRIPTION OF GOODS.	(*)	(+)	(‡)	(⅔)	(‖)
	s. d.	*s. d.*	*s. d.*	*s. d.*	*s. d.*
For all Goods, Wares and Merchandize (except such as are excepted in the Cranage and Porterage Rates) per Ton......................	0 6	0 9	1 0	1 3	1 6
For all English Timber of all Kinds, and Pig and Bar-iron, per Ton............................	0 3	0 6	0 9	1 0	1 3
For all Coals, Stone, Iron-stone, Lime-stone, Flint, Clay and Sand, per Ton	0 ½	0 1	0 1½	0 2	0 2½
For all Lime, Bricks, Tiles, Plaster and Soapers' Ashes, per Ton..............................	0 1	0 2	0 3	0 4	0 5
For all Corn of all Kinds, Cole, Rape, Line and Mustard Seeds ; Apples, Pears, Onions and Potatoes, per Quarter	0 ½	0 1	0 1½	0 2	0 2½

Lords of manors and owners of land may erect wharfs and warehouses on the canal, and take the above wharfage rates; if they refuse to do so, the company may erect them.

In 1798 a second act of parliament was obtained, entitled, ' *An Act for amending and enlarging the Powers of an Act, passed* ' *in the Thirty-third Year of the Reign of his present Majesty, for* ' *making and maintaining a navigable Canal from the River Dun* ' *Navigation Cut, at or near Stainforth, in the West Riding of the* ' *county of York, to join and communicate with the River Trent,* ' *at or near Keadby, in the county of Lincoln; and also a colla-* ' *teral Cut from the said Canal, to join the said River Dun, in the* ' *parish of Thorne, in the said Riding,*' which repealed that part of the former act authorizing the company to raise the additional sum of £12,100, and empowered the proprietors to raise amongst themselves, in addition to their original capital, the sum of £20,000; and, if necessary, a further sum of £10,000, by mortgage of the tolls, &c.

The last act of parliament relating to this canal was obtained in 1809, and is entitled, ' *An Act to enable the Company of Pro-* ' *prietors of the Stainforth and Keadby Canal Navigation, to raise* ' *a further Sum of Money for the Discharge of their Debts, and to* ' *finish and complete the said Canal Navigation; and for amend-* ' *ing the several Acts passed relative thereto.*' It states that the company of proprietors had raised amongst themselves, nearly the whole of the two sums of £24,200 and £20,000 provided to be raised by the former acts; repeals that clause of the last act authorizing them to raise £10,000 by mortgage of the tolls, &c. and empowers them to raise that sum amongst themselves.

This canal passes through a very flat part of the country, for there is only one lock of 5 feet fall near Thorne, exclusive of the tide-lock where it falls into the Trent at Keadby.

By connecting the Rivers Dun and Trent, it avoids the shoals in the lower part of the former river, and affords a better line of communication with Lincolnshire, the East Riding of York and the port of Hull.

STOCKTON AND DARLINGTON RAILWAY.

1 & 2 Geo. IV. C. 44, R. A. 19th April, 1821.   4 Geo. IV. C. 33, R. A. 23rd May, 1823.
5 Geo. IV. C. 48, R. A. 17th May, 1824.   9 Geo. IV. C. 60, R. A. 23rd May, 1828.

THIS railway commences at the River Tees, near Stockton, in the county of Durham, and thence proceeds in a southerly direction about four miles, to the branch which goes off to Yarm; from thence westerly about eight miles, to the other branch which goes off at Darlington; from thence northerly about three miles and a half, to where the Clarence Railway joins it; and from thence in a north-westerly direction two miles and a half, to the Coundon Branch; thence north-westerly about six miles, to Witton Park Colliery, with five collateral branches; one commencing in the township of Egglescliffe and extending to Yarm Bridge; another commencing at or near Hill House, in Darlington, and terminating near Croft Bridge, in the parish of Hurworth; another commencing at or near Brussleton, and terminating at or near Coundon Turnpike-Gate; another commencing at or near Norlees House, in the township of West Auckland, and terminating at or near Evenlode Bridge; and the other commencing at the Tees, and terminating at or near the south-west end of the town of Stockton-upon-Tees.

By a statement made in September, 1820, by Mr. G. Overton, it appears that the length of

	M.	F.	C.
The Main Line was	26	6	9
The Yarm Bridge Branch	0	6	3
Darlington Branch	0	7	0
Branch to Coundon Turnpike	3	4	0
Branch to Hagger Leases	4	6	0
Branch at Stockton	0	0	7
Total Length of Main Line and Branches	36	6	9

With a rise from the commencement of the railway at Stockton to Escomb Lane, near Witton Park Colliery, of 496 feet 6 inches; the expense of completing the undertaking was also estimated at £84,000.

The first act of parliament was obtained in 1821, by a number of persons who are thereby incorporated by the name of " The Stockton and Darlington Railway Company," and is entitled, ' *An Act for making and maintaining a Railway or Tram-* ' *road, from the River Tees, at Stockton, to Witton Park Colliery,* ' *with several Branches therefrom, all in the county of Durham.*' By this act the company is authorized to raise amongst themselves, the sum of £82,000, in shares of £100 each; and, if necessary, a further sum of £20,000, either amongst themselves, or by the creation of new shares, or they may borrow any portion of the said sums either by optional notes, or by mortgage of the tolls and rates.

The affairs of the company are to be managed by a committee, who are to be under the control of the general assemblies; and the act authorizes them to take the following

TONNAGE RATES.

	s.	d.	
For all Lime-stone, Materials for the Repair of Turnpike-Roads or Highways, and all Dung, Compost and all Sorts of Manure, except Lime	0	4	per Ton, per Mile.
For all Coal, Coke, Culm, Cinders, Stone, Marl, Sand, Lime, Clay, Iron-stone and other Minerals, Building-stone, Pitching and Paving-stone, Bricks, Tiles, Slates and all Gross and Unmanufactured Articles and Building Materials	0	4	ditto. ditto.
For all Lead in Pigs or Sheets, Bar-iron, Waggon-tire, Timber, Staves and Deals, and all other Goods, Wares and Merchandize	0	6	ditto. ditto.
And for all Articles, Matters and Things, above enumerated to pay Tonnage, which shall pass the Inclined Planes upon this Railway	1	0	ditto.
For all Coal which shall be shipped on Board any Vessel in the Port of Stockton-upon-Tees, for the Purpose of Exportation...	0	½	ditto. ditto.

Fractions of a Ton and of a Mile to be taken as the Quarters therein, and of a Quarter as a Quarter.

Owners and occupiers of land, within five miles of the railway, may lay down branches, communicating with the main line ; and lords of manors and owners of land on the line may erect wharfs and warehouses, and take the following

WHARFAGE RATES.

	d.
For all Coals, Culm, Lime, Lime-stone, Clay, Iron, Iron-stone, Lead-ore or any other Ore, Timber, Stone, Bricks, Tiles, Slates, Gravel or other Things, left for Forty-eight Hours	1 per Ton.
For Warehousing any Package not exceeding Fifty-six Pounds	2 each.
For ditto above Three Hundred Pounds and not exceeding Six Hundred	4 ditto.
For ditto exceeding One Thousand Pounds	6 per Ton.

WHARFAGE RATES CONTINUED.

		d.
Wharfage Rate after the expiration of Forty-eight Hours, for next Seven Days	}	1 per Ton.
Warehouse ditto, ditto		2 ditto.
Wharfage for every subsequent Seven Days		1 ditto.
Warehouse ditto, ditto		2 ditto.

If lords of manors, &c. omit to erect wharfs or warehouses, when required so to do, the company may erect them and collect the rates stated above.

The whole money required to be subscribed before the commencement of the work, which is to be completed in five years.

In 1823 the company obtained a second act of parliament, entitled, ' *An Act to enable the Stockton and Darlington Railway* ' *Company to vary and alter the Line of their Railway, and also the* ' *Line or Lines of some of the Branches therefrom, and for altering* ' *and enlarging the Powers of the Act passed for making and main-* ' *taining the said Railway;*' which empowered them to make some alterations in the line of their railway, and an additional branch therefrom, commencing near Hill House in Darlington Bondgate, and terminating at the east end of Croft Bridge, in the parish of Hurworth.

By a plan and estimate made by Mr. George Stevenson, in February, 1823, it appears that the alterations in the line would considerably lessen the distance of the railway, which would be as follows;—

	M.	F.	C.
Main Line from Stockton to Witton Park Colliery	24	5	3
Black Boy Branch to Coundon Lane	2	5	4
Darlington Branch	0	5	2
Croft Branch	3	3	0
Yarm Branch	0	6	3
Total Length of Main Line and Branches	32	1	2

	£
Evenwood Lane or Black Boy Branch and Yarm Branch	3,876
Croft Bridge Branch	7,000
Main Line and other Branches	63,424
Total	£74,300

By this act the company is empowered to erect steam-engines on or near the railway, and also to make and use locomotive engines thereon, and it states that in the former act a tonnage rate of 1*s.* per ton was imposed on all goods passing the inclined planes on the railway, at which time it was intended to have one inclined plane only, but as in consequence of the alteration in the line, which shortens the distance about three miles, a greater number of them will be necessary, the act authorizes the taking 1*s.* per ton on all goods at each; and also empowers the company to take a toll of 6*d.* per mile on every description of carriage, waggon, or cart, which shall be used for the conveyance of passengers or parcels.

The next act of parliament relating to this undertaking was obtained in 1824, and is entitled, ' *An Act to authorize the Com-* ' *pany of Proprietors of the Stockton and Darlington Railway, to* ' *relinquish one of their Branch Railways, and to enable them to* ' *make another Branch Railway in lieu thereof; and to enable the* ' *said Company to raise a further Sum of Money, and to enlarge* ' *the Powers and Provisions of the several Acts relating to the said* ' *Railway.*' The branch railway relinquished by the company, was one leading from Norlees House, in the township of West Auckland, in lieu of which they were authorized to make one from the main line at the north west end of the village of St. Helen's, Auckland, through West Auckland and Evenwood, to Evenwood Bridge, and from thence to Hagger Leases Lane, in the township of Lynesack and Softley.

By an estimate made by Mr. Robert Stevenson, in 1824, the expense of making this branch would be £9,000.

The act empowers the company to raise a further sum of £50,000, by any of the means prescribed in the former acts relating to this railway.

The last act of parliament was passed in 1828, and is entitled, ' *An Act to enable the Company of Proprietors of the Stockton* ' *and Darlington Railway to make a Branch therefrom, in the* ' *counties of Durham and York, and to amend and enlarge the* ' *Powers and Provisions of the several Acts relating thereto.*' The branch authorized by this act of parliament to be made was to commence at the main line, where it crosses Bowesfield Lane, in the township of Stockton, and passing from thence through this township, was to cross the River Tees by a bridge to Carr House Field, in the township of Thomably, in the North Riding of the county of York, and from thence by Stainsby, Stainton, Acklam, Newport, Middlesburgh, Leventhorpe and Ormesby, to terminate in a close adjoining the River Tees, in the township of Leventhorpe or Middlesburgh; and the act directs that one of the arches of the bridge to be erected across the Tees shall be 72 feet wide at the least, and the under keystone of such arch shall not be less than 19 feet in height from the surface of low-water-mark.

An estimate of the expense of this branch was made in January, 1828, by Mr. Thomas Storey, to the following effect:—

	£.	s.	d.
Main Line from the Stockton and Darlington original Line, where it crosses Bowesfield Lane to near Middlesburgh on the River Tees, four miles and nine chains, with an inclined plane near the end, of thirteen chains, together with a suspension bridge across the Tees, 240 feet within the piers	35,786	3	10
Branch from ditto to Cleveland Port, one mile, six furlongs and seven chains, with an inclined plane of fifteen chains at the termination	11,819	9	8
	£47,605	13	6

The underside of the above-named suspension bridge will be 30 feet above low water, and its width 20 feet; and a dock is to be constructed at the ends of the railway 390 feet by 168 feet, into which vessels from the river will have access by a lock 32 feet wide; thereby affording most ample means of putting the coal and other articles on board. In addition to this accommodation, a quay will be formed alongside the river, 600 feet long. The difference between high and low water is 13 feet at Cleveland Port. The act empowers the company to raise an additional sum of £100,000 by any of the means authorized by their former acts, except promissory notes, or they may borrow it on bonds under the common seal of the company; and may take the following rates.

TONNAGE RATES ON THE NEW BRANCH.

d.

For all Coal, Culm, Coke, Cinders, Stone and Lime, which shall be carried on the New Branch, and shipped on Board any Vessel in the River Tees for exportation...... } 1½ per Ton, per Mile.

For all Lime-stone, Materials for the Repairs of Turnpike-Roads, Dung, Compost and all Sorts of Manure .... } 2   ditto.   ditto.

For all Coal, Coke, Culm, Cinders, (which shall not be shipped on Board any Vessel in the River Tees for exportation) Marl, Sand, Lime, Clay, Iron-stone, and other Minerals, Building-stone, Pitching and Paving-stone, Bricks, Tiles, Slates, and all Gross and Unmanufactured Articles and Building Materials, Lead in Pigs or Sheets, Bar-iron, Waggon-tire, Timber, Staves and Deals, and all other Goods, Wares and Merchandize .... } 4   ditto.   ditto.

An additional Toll to be taken on all Goods passing an Inclined Plane, or put into or taken out of any Vessel on the River Tees by means of any Engine belonging to the Company, of .... } 4   ditto.

An additional Toll on Coals, Culm, Cinders, Stone, Lime and Manure whatsoever, carried over the Bridge to be erected across the Tees, of................................... } 2   ditto.

This railway was projected for the purpose of bringing the coal and other minerals, with which this country abounds, to the mouth of the Tees, where the coal is shipped for the supply of London and the eastern coast of the kingdom; and has attracted considerable attention, from locomotive engines being generally and advantageously used upon it.

STORT RIVER.

32 George II Cap. 42, Royal Assent 23rd March, 1759.
6 George III. Cap. 78, Royal Assent 30th April, 1766.

THE first act of parliament relating to this river is entitled, ' *An Act for making the River Stort navigable, in the counties of* ' *Hertford and Essex, from the New Bridge, in the town of Bishop* ' *Stortford, into the River Lea, near a Place called the Rye, in the* ' *county of Hertford,*' and appointed certain persons commissioners for carrying into effect the provisions of the act.

In 1766 a second act was passed, entitled, ' *An Act for making* ' *and continuing navigable the River Stort, in the counties of Hert-* ' *ford and Essex;*' which states, that in consequence of the difficulty experienced by the commissioners appointed under the first act, in raising money for carrying into effect the purposes therein stated, no progress had been made in effecting the said navigation; but that Charles Dingley, George Jackson and William Master-

2 P

man, Esquires, had undertaken to make and continue navigable the said river, provided an act of parliament could be obtained authorizing them to do so, and to collect certain tolls and rates thereon; the act, therefore, empowers them to complete this undertaking, and to collect the following

TONNAGE RATES.

	s.	d.	
For Wheat, Rye, Beans or Peas	0	6	per Quarter.
For Malt or Oats	0	4	ditto.
For Barley, or any other Sort of Grain not before enumerated	0	5	ditto.
For Meal or Flour (Five Bushels to a Sack)	0	4	per Sack.
For Coal, Culm or Cinders	2	6	per Chaldron.
For Lime	2	6	ditto.
For Oil-cakes, Malt-dust, Pigeon Dung or other Manure of any Kind	1	6	per Ton.
For Goods, Wares or Merchandize not before enumerated	2	6	ditto.

And so in proportion for any less Quantity.

Boats returning with a back Lading of Oil-cake, Malt-dust, Pigeon Dung or any other Kind of Manure, which have passed up or down the River immediately before, and paid the Tolls or Rates on their Cargoes, shall be exempted from Tonnage Rate on such Manure.

The tolls, rates and duties on this navigation to be exempted from all taxes and rates whatsoever.

Lords of manors and owners of land on this navigation may build warehouses; and on their refusing to do so, the undertakers may build them. Five years are allowed to the undertakers to complete the navigation.

The part of the river made navigable under authority of these acts, is about ten miles in length, in a southerly and westerly course. It joins the Lea Navigation about a mile and a half from Hoddesden, thus affording a means for the conveyance of corn, malt and other agricultural produce to London.

STOURBRIDGE CANAL.

16 George III. Cap. 28, Royal Assent 2nd April, 1776.
22 George III. Cap. 14, Royal Assent 25th March, 1782.

THIS canal commences at or near Stourbridge, in the county of Worcester, and proceeds parallel with the River Stour to Wordesley Brook, where it crosses the river, and pursues its course to the Staffordshire and Worcestershire Canal, which it joins at a place called Stewponey, near Stourton. It has also two collateral cuts, one from the fens upon Pensnet Chase to its junction, at Wordesley Brook, with the River Stour; and the other from Black Delph to the first branch at the Lays, in the parish of Kingswinford, in Staffordshire.

The first act of parliament sanctioning this undertaking was passed in 1776, and is entitled, ' *An Act for making and main-* ' *taining a navigable Canal, from or near the town of Stourbridge,* ' *in the county of Worcester, to join the Staffordshire and Worces-* ' *tershire Canal at or near Stourton, in the county of Stafford;* ' *and also Two collateral Cuts, one from a Place called the Fens,* ' *upon Pensnet Chase, to communicate with the intended Canal near* ' *the Junction of Wordesley Brook, from the River Stour, and the* ' *other from a Place called Black Delph, upon the said Chase, to* ' *join the first-mentioned collateral Cut, at or near certain Lands,* ' *called the Lays, in the parish of Kingswinford, in the said county* ' *of Stafford;*' and a second act was passed in 1782, for explaining and amending the former act.

The first act of parliament incorporates the proprietors by the name of " The Company of Proprietors of the Stourbridge Navi- " gation," and authorizes them to raise amongst themselves, for the execution of the work, the sum of £30,000, in three hundred shares of £100 each; and by a second act of parliament passed in 1782, they were empowered to raise a further sum of £7,500, making the shares £125 each. They are likewise authorized to collect the following

TONNAGE RATES.

			d.	
For all Coal, Coke, Iron, Iron-stone, Timber and other Goods, which may be conveyed upon the Canal from Stourbridge to Stourton, and passing through any of the Locks at Stourton		}	6	per Ton.
For all Lime or Lime-stone			2	ditto.
For all Coal, Coke, Iron, Iron-stone, Timber and other Goods, passing upon either of the Collateral Cuts and any Lock thereon		}	6	ditto.
Except Coal passing from the Dudley Canal only			3	ditto.
Lime and Lime-stone			2	ditto.

The Staffordshire and Worcestershire Canal Company have power to take Two-pence per Ton per Mile on Coal brought from this Navigation and carried on theirs; and may lessen the Tolls with Consent of the Commissioners.

Goods passing on the Summit of the Canal or Collateral Cut, and which do not pass any Lock, Tonnage free.

Paving-stones, Gravel and other Materials for repairing the Road, (Lime-stone excepted) and also Manure for the Estates of Persons, part of whose Land shall have been taken for this Canal, and not passing through a Lock, are exempted from Toll.

It being supposed that the extension of the Dudley Canal join the Worcester and Birmingham would lessen the profits of this concern, the proprietors of the Dudley Canal are required by the 33rd George III. to make up the annual dividend on the shares in this canal to £12 each, provided not more than £3 is required for that purpose. The width of this canal is 28 feet and the depth 5 feet, and there is a reservoir of twelve acres on Pensnet Chase. From Stewponey, where this canal unites with the Staffordshire and Worcestershire Canal, for about the distance of three-eighths of a mile, there is a rise of 43 feet 3 inches, by four locks; from thence to the Stourbridge Branch, it is level, (and the Stourbridge Branch is also level); thence to the Lays, a distance of one mile and one-eighth, there is a rise of 148 feet, by sixteen locks; and thence to the Dudley Canal, one mile and a half, is level.

This canal is of very great benefit to the town of Stourbridge, and to parts of the counties of Worcester, Gloucester, Hereford and Warwick; the principal articles carried on it are coal, ironstone, glass-house pot clay, glass, nails and other iron goods and manufactures.

STOUR AND SALWERP RIVERS.

14 Charles II. Cap. 13, Royal Assent 19th May, 1662.

The act of parliament respecting these rivers is entitled, '*An 'Act for the making navigable of the Rivers of Stower and Salwerp, 'and the Rivulets and Brooks running into the same, in the coun- 'ties of Worcester and Stafford.*' Under the authority of this act, these rivers were made navigable from the River Severn, at Stourport, to the town of Stourbridge, by means of sluices, weirs and other works; but a sudden and violent flood which soon after occurred destroyed all the works. The Stafford and Worcester and the Stourbridge Canals have since supplied, more effectually, the place of this river navigation.

STOUR RIVER.

4 Anne,   Cap. 15, Royal Assent 16th February, 1705.
21 George III. Cap. 75, Royal Assent 19th June, 1781.

THIS river rises on the borders of the three counties of Cambridge, Suffolk and Essex, and running in an easterly direction, passes Haverhill, Clare and Sudbury, at which place it becomes navigable; and from thence in a south-easterly direction to Bures; and thence easterly by Neyland, Higham, Laugham and Dedham to Manningtree.

An act of parliament respecting this river was passed in 1705, entitled, ' *An Act for making the River Stower navigable from* ' *the town of Manningtree, in the county of Essex, to the town of* ' *Sudbury, in the county of Suffolk.*' In 1781 another act was passed, entitled, ' *An Act for appointing New Commissioners, for* ' *continuing to carry into Execution the Trusts and Powers of an* ' *Act passed in the Fourth and Fifth of Queen Anne, entitled, An* ' *Act for making the River Stower navigable from the town of* ' *Manningtree, in the county of Essex, to the town of Sudbury, in* ' *the county of Suffolk, in the Room and Place of those named in* ' *the said Act, who are since dead; and for explaining and amend-* ' *ing the said Act, and for other Purposes therein mentioned.*'

By this act a considerable number of new commissioners are appointed, any five of whom may carry this and the preceding act into effect.

The said commissioners have power to set out horse towing-paths alongside the said river, upon the proprietors of the navigation paying annual rents to the occupiers or owners of the adjoining lands. The land-owners or tenants are restrained by this act from seizing or taking away any horses on account of damages sustained; but may have their remedy at law. Mill-owners improperly reducing the head of water, are subject to a penalty of £20, and are liable to make good all damages which may arise from their improperly penning the waters, so as to overflow the banks of the river. In this act is a peculiar clause to prevent embezzlement or pilfering any parts of the cargo on board a vessel;

inflicting a penalty of £5 or three months imprisonment to hard labour, on any boatman or other person so offending, by a summary process before a magistrate.

It is not easy now to ascertain the legitimate expense of making this river navigable; but the undertaking consists of forty-eight shares, which of late have sold for £300 per share; and the tolls of the navigation are let for £900 per annum.

TONNAGE RATE.

	s.
For Merchandize and all other Articles, the whole Length of the Navigation	5 per Ton.

STRATFORD-UPON-AVON CANAL.

33 Geo. III. C. 112, R. A. 28th March, 1793.　35 Geo. III. C. 72, R. A. 19th May, 1795.
39 Geo. III. C. 60, R. A. 21st June, 1799.　49 Geo. III. C. 42, R. A. 12th May, 1809.
55 Geo. III. C. 59, R. A. 12th May, 1815.　57 Geo. III. C. 15, R. A. 23rd May, 1817.
2 Geo. IV. C. 631, R. A. 28th May, 1821.

THIS canal commences at King's Norton, in the county of Worcester, about six miles from the town of Birmingham, where it joins the Worcester and Birmingham Canal; and from thence it runs in an easterly direction to Yardley Wood Common, where it takes a southerly course, and passes by Shirley Street, Monkford Street, Lapworth and Preston Bagot, at which place it crosses the River Alne; then proceeding by Wootton, it terminates on the north side of Stratford. The length is about twenty-three miles and a half, and it has four branches; one from near Hockley to Tamworth Quarries, about two miles and a half; one other from near Lapworth to the Warwick and Birmingham Canal, one mile and three quarters; one other from near Wilmcote to Temple Grafton Lime Works, four miles; and a branch from this last cut to Aston Cantlow, one mile.

The first act of parliament sanctioning this undertaking was passed in 1793, and is entitled, ' *An Act for making and maintaining* ' *a navigable Canal from the Worcester and Birmingham Canal* ' *Navigation, in the parish of King's Norton, into the borough of* ' *Stratford-upon-Avon; and also certain collateral Cuts from the* ' *said intended Canal.*' It incorporates the subscribers to the undertaking under the title of " The Company of Proprietors of " the Stratford-upon-Avon Canal Navigation;" empowers them to

raise amongst themselves, for the purposes of the act, the sum of
£120,000, in twelve hundred shares of £100 each, and if that
should be insufficient, a further sum of £60,000, either amongst
themselves or by mortgage of the tolls as security; and authorizes
them to take the following

TONNAGE RATES.

	d.
For all Coal, Coke, Iron, Iron-stone, Timber and other Goods, (except Flag-stone) carried on that Part of the Canal between Salter's Lane in the Parish of Aston Cantlow and Stratford, and upon the Branch to Grafton Field; and except Coal for burning Lime on that Part of the Canal which is between Salter's Lane and Copmass Hill, or upon the Branch to Grafton Field, and except Lime and Lime-stone	1½ per Ton, per Mile.
For all Lime and Lime-stone carried between the Worcester and Birmingham Canal and Salter's Lane, or upon the Cut to Tamworth	1½ ditto. ditto.
For all Lime and Lime-stone carried between Salter's Lane and Stratford, or upon the Branch to Temple Grafton ..	1½ ditto. ditto.
For all Flag-stones, and Coal for the purpose of Burning Lime only carried between Salter's Lane and Copmass Hill, or on the Cut to Temple Grafton	4 ditto.

And so in proportion for less than a Ton, or less than a Mile.

EXEMPTIONS.

Paving-stone, Gravel, Sand and other Materials for making and repairing Roads;
Dung, Soil, Marl, or other Manure (Lime and Lime-stone excepted) for the
Grounds of any Person whose Land shall be taken for the Canal, provided it does
not pass any Lock unless the Water shall flow over the Waste Weir.

A reasonable compensation for Goods remaining on a Wharf more than Twenty-four
Hours to be taken. No Boat of less than Ten Tons to pass any Lock without leave
of the Company or their Agent.

Stop-gates are to be erected on this canal within five hundred
yards of the Worcester and Birmingham; which gates may be
shut if the water is lower in this than the other canal.

Goods carried on this canal and northward on the Worcester
and Birmingham Canal, to pay no higher rates to the latter company, than shall be paid for those carried on this canal between
the junction and Salter's Lane.

The proprietors of the Worcester and Birmingham Canal to
pay to George Perrott, Esq. as a compensation for his dues on the
River Avon, which it is thought will be diminished by this canal,
£400 per annum; and until this canal is made navigable, they
are also to make up to Mr. Perrott the sum of £1,227, which he
now receives for the Lower Navigation of the Avon, if there
should be any falling off in that amount after the passing of this act.

In 1795 the company obtained another act, entitled, ' *An Act* ' *for making a navigable Cut from the Stratford-upon-Avon Canal,* ' *in the parish of Lapworth, unto the Warwick and Birmingham* ' *Canal, in the manor of Kingswood, in the county of Warwick,*' which empowered them to raise a further sum of £10,000, by mortgage of the tolls, &c. and to take on the intended new cut the following

TONNAGE RATES.

	s.	d.	
For all Coal, Coke, Iron, Iron-stone, Stone and other Goods and Things, (except Lime and Lime-stone) which having been carried on any Part of the Warwick and Birmingham Canal, between Birmingham and the Junction with the intended Cut, shall pass along the said Cut into the Stratford-upon-Avon Canal towards the Town of Stratford; or having been carried upon the Stratford Canal between the Town of Stratford and the End of the Cut, shall pass along the said Cut into the Warwick and Birmingham Canal towards the Town of Birmingham........................	1	3	per Ton.
For all other Coal, Coke, Iron, Iron-stone, and other Goods (except Lime, Lime-stone and other Stone)	0	4	ditto.
For all Lime and Lime-stone which has been carried on any Part of the Warwick and Birmingham Canal, and shall pass along the said Cut into the Stratford-upon-Avon Canal	1	2	ditto.
For all other Lime and Lime-stone	0	3	ditto.
For all Flag and other Stone	0	6	ditto.

And so in proportion for a less Quantity than a Ton.

The act provides that the following rates shall be paid to the Warwick and Birmingham Canal Company, over and above the rates allowed them by the act for making their canal, by way of compensation for any injury they may sustain by the intended cut.

TONNAGE RATES.

	s.	d.	
For all Coal, Goods and other Things carried upon any Part of the Stratford-upon-Avon Canal, between the Worcester and Birmingham Canal and the Place where the said Cut is to be made, and along the Cut into the Warwick and Birmingham Canal; and on all Coal, Goods and other Things (Lime and Lime-stone excepted) which shall be carried from the Warwick and Birmingham Canal, along the said Cut into the Stratford-upon-Avon Canal, and along the same towards the Worcester and Birmingham Canal, and also for all Coal which shall be landed upon either Side of the said Cut (not to be used for Burning Lime on either of the Banks of the Cut); and also for all Coal which shall be landed on either Side of the said Cut, within Half a Mile of the Warwick and Birmingham Canal, and used for Burning Lime on either of the Banks of the said Cut	0	11	per Ton.
For all Lime and Lime-stone carried upon the Stratford-upon-Avon Canal, and along the said Cut to and upon the Warwick and Birmingham Canal, towards the Town of Birmingham or towards the Town of Warwick, and landed at any Place upon the Warwick and Birmingham Canal, more than One Hundred Yards from the Town of Warwick..	1	0	ditto.

No higher Rate than Three Half-pence per Ton to be taken by the Proprietors of the Warwick and Birmingham Canal, for passing upon that Canal between the Place where it is to be joined by the intended Cut and the Town of Warwick, on any Coal, Goods or other Things subject to the Payment hereinbefore made payable to that Company, of the Rate of Eleven-pence per Ton.

On all Coal carried from the said Cut on the Warwick and Birmingham Canal towards Birmingham, the same Rate shall be paid to that Company (instead of any other Rates under their or this Act) that would be payable to them on Coal passing from the Town of Birmingham, to the Place where their Canal is to be joined by the intended Cut; and on Coal passing from the said Cut on the Warwick and Birmingham Canal towards Warwick, which shall be unloaded at any Place between the said Cut and the Upper Lock below Hatton Hill, the same Rate shall be paid as would have been had it passed from Birmingham to such Place.

Only Five-pence Half-penny per Ton to be paid to the Worcester and Birmingham Canal Company for any Coal or Coke carried on any Part of their Canal, to the Northward of its Junction with the Stratford-upon-Avon Canal, and which shall pass without being unladen from the Worcester and Birmingham Canal into the Stratford-upon-Avon Canal, to be carried to the Warwick and Birmingham Canal; and Ten-pence Half-penny per Ton only to be paid to the Stratford-upon-Avon Canal Company, for Coal and Coke passing from the Worcester and Birmingham through their Canal to the Warwick and Birmingham Canal.

The next act relating to this canal was passed in 1799, and is entitled, ' *An Act for authorizing the Company of Proprietors of* ' *the Stratford-upon-Avon Canal Navigation, to vary the Course of* ' *certain Parts of the said Canal, directed to be made by an Act,* ' *passed in the Thirty-third Year of the Reign of his present Ma-* ' *jesty; and also to make a Branch out of the said Canal; and also* ' *to vary the Course of a navigable Cut directed to be made from* ' *the said Stratford-upon-Avon Canal, in the parish of Lapworth,* ' *into the Warwick and Birmingham Canal, in the manor of* ' *Kingswood, in the county of Warwick, by another Act passed in* ' *the Thirty-fifth Year of the Reign of his present Majesty; and* ' *for amending the said Acts.*' It authorizes the company to make some alterations in the original line and a branch in the parish of Aston Cantlow; and also to raise a further sum of £35,000, (in addition to £10,000 which they are empowered to raise by the preceding act,) either amongst themselves, by the creation of new shares, or by mortgage of the tolls or granting annuities; if raised by subscription, it is to be divided into twelve hundred quarter shares of £37, 10s. each.

As a compensation to the Warwick and Birmingham Canal for any injury they may sustain by the alteration in the line of the Lapworth Cut, they are to receive $\frac{1}{2}d$. per ton additional on all goods and in all cases in which they are authorized to receive 11d. per ton by the preceding act; and they are to take at the rate of $1\frac{1}{2}d$. per ton per mile on all goods carried on their canal from the place where the intended cut will join it, and where the junction was proposed to be by the former act, which distance is to be taken as a quarter of a mile.

The Stratford-upon-Avon Canal Company not to erect wharfs,
&c. on the intended cut, without leave of the Warwick and Birmingham Canal Company; but Thomas Fetherston may erect
such wharfs, &c. on his land at Lapworth, without such permission; and Mr. Fetherston, or the occupier of his wharfs, are
to pay for the carriage of coal, coke, iron, ironstone and other
goods and things (except limestone) on this canal, $1\frac{1}{2}d$. per ton
per mile; and for limestone $\frac{1}{2}d$. per ton per mile only.

Lords of manors and owners of land may erect wharfs on this
navigation, and on their refusing, the company may do it, and all
coal, merchandize and other things which shall be sold and shipped from such wharfs, between the place where the intended cut
joins the Warwick and Birmingham Canal and Preston Mill (over
and above two hundred tons in each year) shall pay the tonnage rate
of $11\frac{1}{2}d$. per ton to the proprietors of the Warwick and Birmingham Canal, whether it passes on their canal or not.

In 1809 another act was obtained, entitled, ' *An Act to amend*
' *and enlarge the Powers of the several Acts relating to the Strat-*
' *ford-upon-Avon Canal Navigation;*' which, after stating that
the money raised was not sufficient for the purposes of the undertaking, empowers the company to raise a further sum of £90,000,
either amongst themselves or by creation of new shares, the number of such new shares not to exceed three thousand, and to be of
£30 or £40 value, as the company may deem expedient; or the
above sum may be raised by mortgage of the tolls; and should
this amount prove insufficient, they may raise an additional sum of
£30,000 in either of the ways above stated, but the number of
new shares created for raising this £30,000 not to exceed seven
hundred and fifty.

The act of 1815, entitled, ' *An Act to amend several Acts of*
' *his present Majesty, for making the Stratford-upon-Avon Canal*
' *Navigation,*' authorizes the company of proprietors to make reservoirs at Earl's Wood, and (with consent of the owners of land)
to divert streams and use the flood-waters which overflow the
lands at Earl's Wood.

In 1817 the company obtained another act, entitled, ' *An Act*
' *to enable the Company of Proprietors of the Stratford-upon-Avon*
' *Canal Navigation to raise Money, to discharge their Debts, and to*

' *complete the said Canal;*' which states that the company had
raised a great portion of the sums authorized by former acts, but
it had been insufficient for the completion of the undertaking, and
it empowers them to raise an additional sum of £20,000 amongst
themselves, to enable them to pay off their debt and complete the
work; and by the last act of parliament relating to this canal,
passed in 1821, and entitled, ' *An Act to enable the Company of*
' *Proprietors of the Stratford-upon-Avon Canal Navigation, to*
' *subscribe a further Sum of Money, for the Purposes of the said*
' *Navigation,*' they are empowered to raise an additional sum of
£21,882 amongst themselves, to enable them to complete the
navigation.

Upon this work there is a tunnel of three hundred and twenty
yards in length, near Milepole Hill, and several small aqueduct
bridges; from Stratford to Copmass Hill, one mile and a half,
is level; thence to Wilmcote, one mile, is a rise of 86 feet; thence
to Preston Mill, six miles, is level; thence to Preston Green, one
mile and three quarters, is a rise of 76 feet; thence to Lapworth
Hall, one mile, is level; thence to Hockley Heath, two miles and
a quarter, is a rise of 147 feet ; and thence to the Worcester
and Birmingham Canal, ten miles, is level; making a distance of
twenty-three miles and a half, with a rise of 309 feet. The Tamworth Branch is level and connects with the summit pound; the
first two miles and a half of the Temple Grafton Branch is level,
but there is a rise of 20 feet in the next mile and a half.

This work forms a link in the great chain of inland canal communication, and passing through a country abounding with coal
and limestone, affords, by its connection with other canals, the
means of their transit, as well as other commodities, to all parts
of the country.

STRATFORD AND MORETON RAILWAY.

2 George IV. Cap. 63, Royal Assent 28th May, 1821.
6 George IV. Cap. 168, Royal Assent 22nd June, 1825.

THIS railway commences at the Stratford-upon-Avon Canal, in
Old Stratford, Warwickshire, and passes in a southerly direction,

along the side of the turnpike-road leading from Stratford to
Oxford, by Halford Bridge, Clifford Chambers, Atherstone,
Alderminster, Lower Ealington Park, Whitchurch, Armscott,
Tredington, Darlingscote, Stretton-on-the-Fosse and Lemington,
to Moreton-in-Marsh, in Gloucestershire, with a collateral branch
from Stretton-on-the-Fosse, by Ditchford to Shipston-upon-Stour,
in Worcestershire.

The act of parliament under sanction of which this undertaking
was carried into execution, was passed in 1821, and is entitled, ' *An*
' *Act for making and maintaining a Railway or Tramroad from*
' *Stratford-upon-Avon, in the county of Warwick, to Moreton-in-*
' *Marsh, in the county of Gloucester, with a Branch to Shipston-*
' *upon-Stour, in the county of Worcester.*'   By this act a company
of persons, amongst whom were Lord Dudley and Ward and Lord
Redesdale, were incorporated by the name of " The Stratford
" and Moreton Railway Company," with powers to raise amongst
themselves, for the purposes of the act, the sum of £33,500, in
shares of £50 each, and, if necessary, a further sum of £7,000,
either amongst themselves, by creation of new shares or by mortgage of the tolls and rates, and to collect the following

TONNAGE RATES.

	d.
For all Coal, Coke, Culm, Stone, Cinders, Chalk, Marl, Sand, Lime, Clay, Ashes, Peat, Lime-stone, Iron-stone, Building-stone, Pitching and Paving-stone, Bricks, Tiles, Slates, Timber, Lead in Pigs or Sheets, Bar-iron, Waggon-tire, and all Gross and Unmanufactured Articles and Building Materials	3 per Ton, per Mile.
For all other Goods, Wares, Merchandize or Things whatsoever	6 ditto. ditto.

Fractions of a Quarter of a Ton and of a Mile to be considered as Quarters.

Owners of land adjoining the railway may lay collateral
branches on their lands to communicate with this railway; and
may also erect wharfs or warehouses on their land, and on their
refusing to do so when thereto required by the company of proprietors, the act authorizes the company to make such erections,
and empowers them and such lords of manors or owners of land
who shall have erected wharfs, &c. to collect the following wharfage and warehousing rates.

WHARFAGE AND WAREHOUSING RATES.

The Column marked thus (*) are the Rates to be taken for Forty-eight Hours.
The Column marked thus (+)   ditto,   the next Ten Days.
The Column marked thus (‡)   ditto,   every subsequent Day.

DESCRIPTION OF GOODS.	(*)	(+)	(‡)
	s. d.	s. d.	s. d.
For all Coals, Culm, Lime, Lime-stone, Clay, Iron, Iron-stone, Lead-ore or any other Ores, Timber, Stone, Brick, Tiles, Slates, Gravel or other Things, per Ton	0 1	0 1	0 1
For every Package not exceeding Fifty-six Pounds Weight	0 3		
For ditto above Fifty-six Pounds and not exceeding Five Hundred Pounds Weight	0 6		
For all Coals, Culm, Lime, Lime-stone, Clay, Iron, Iron-stone, Lead-ore or any other Ores, Timber, Stone, Bricks, Tiles, Slates, Gravel or other Things	1 0	1 0	0 3

The act directs that the whole sum necessary for making this railway shall be subscribed before the work is commenced, and that it shall be completed in five years.

The management of the company's affairs to be conducted by a committee of five persons, who are to be under the control of the general assemblies of proprietors.

An estimate of the expense of laying down this railway, made in 1821, by Mr. Thomas Baylis, was £33,456, 16s. 8d.

In 1825 a second act of parliament was passed relating to this railway, entitled, ' An Act to amend an Act passed in the First and ' Second Year of the Reign of his present Majesty, entitled, An Act ' for making and maintaining a Railway or Tramroad from Strat- ' ford-upon-Avon, in the county of Warwick, to Moreton-in-Marsh, ' in the county of Gloucester, with a Branch to Shipston-upon- ' Stour, in the county of Worcester; and for making further Pro- ' visions touching the same.'

This act makes some alteration in the line of the branch to Shipston-upon-Stour, and states, that to carry on the work the company had borrowed the sum of £11,300 of different persons, proprietors of shares, and that £36,000 more would be wanted to complete the undertaking, and that Thomas Dudley, Esq. of Shutt End, near Dudley, had agreed to advance them £15,000 as a loan, provided he had a mortgage of the tolls and rates made to him as a security; and that £6,000 more would be raised by the proprietors amongst themselves. The act then authorizes the company to assign the tolls and rates to those proprietors who had advanced the £11,300, as security to them; and to Thomas Dudley, Esq. as a security for the £15,000 to be advanced by him; and although the persons who lent the £11,300 have a prior claim on the tolls and rates to Mr. Dudley, yet in order to induce him to advance the said sum of £15,000, a majority of them, being four-fifths in value, by an agreement dated the 22nd September, 1824, executed by them, agreed that any mortgage of the tolls made to Thomas Dudley, should have priority over any claims which they had or might have on them; and this agreement is confirmed by the act of parliament, which declares that Mr. Dudley shall have preference in payment both of his principal sum and interest, at the rate of £4, 4s. per cent. per annum, over those persons who executed the said agreement and who were creditors of four-fifths of the said sum of £11,300.   And the company are also empowered to raise a further sum of £15,000, in addition to the £15,000 to be advanced by Mr. Dudley, by mortgage of their tolls and rates.

The length of the main line of this railway is about sixteen miles, and the branch to Shipston-upon-Stour two miles and a half; and the rise from the canal at Stratford-upon-Avon to Moreton-in-Marsh is 360 feet.

The principal object of this railway is the conveyance of coal to supply Moreton, Stow and other parts of that country; and, in return, to take stone and agricultural produce.

STROUDWATER NAVIGATION.

3 George II. Cap. 13, Royal Assent 15th May, 1730.
32 George II. Cap. 47, Royal Assent 5th April, 1759.
16 George III. Cap. 21, Royal Assent 25th March, 1776.

This canal commences at the River Severn, near Framiload, in the county of Gloucester, and from thence runs in an easterly direction by Witminster, near which it is crossed by the Gloucester and Berkeley Canal; it thence continues an easterly course, crossing the Stroudwater, by Eastington and Stonehouse, and terminates in the Thames and Severn Canal, at Wallbridge, near Stroud.   The length is rather more than eight miles, with a rise of 102 feet 5 inches.

The first act of parliament relating to this undertaking was
passed in 1730, and is entitled, ' *An Act for making navigable the*
' *River Stroudwater, in the county of Gloucester, from the River*
' *Severn, at or near Framiload, to Wallbridge, near the town of*
' *Stroud, in the same county.*' It appointed certain persons therein
named undertakers for effecting the provisions of the act, and authorized their taking the following

TONNAGE RATES.

	s.	d.	
For all Coals, Corn, Malt, Grain or Meal of any Sort, carried on the Stroudwater between the River Severn at Framiload and Wallbridge, near Stroud...	3	6	per Ton.
For all other Goods, Wares and Merchandize....	5	0	ditto.

And in proportion for a greater or less Weight or Distance.

From the opposition of the millers, arising from the fear of
losing their water, and other causes, this act was not carried into
execution; but in 1759 a second act of parliament, entitled, ' *An*
' *Act to amend and explain an Act made in the Third Year of his*
' *present Majesty's Reign,*' was passed, which authorized John
Kemmett, Arthur Wynde, James Pynock and Thomas Bridge to
carry into effect the provisions of the former act, and giving
them all the powers therein granted to the undertakers, they covenanting to complete the navigation without locks, and consequently without loss of water to the millers. The scheme by
which these gentlemen meant to effect their purpose, was by
shifting the cargoes into boxes, and at every mill to remove them
into other boats by means of cranes; the plan, however, did not
succeed, though it was persevered in to nearly the ruin of the
projectors.

In 1776 another act of parliament was passed, entitled, ' *An*
' *Act to amend an Act, passed in the Third Year of his late Ma-*
' *jesty's Reign, entitled, An Act for making navigable the River*
' *Stroudwater, in the county of Gloucester, from the River Severn,*
' *at or near Framiload, to Wallbridge, near the town of Stroud, in*
' *the same county, and for giving other Powers for the Purpose of*
' *making a Navigation from Framiload to Wallbridge aforesaid.*'
It states that the undertakers appointed by the preceding act had
failed to complete the navigation, and that certain persons had
subscribed £20,000 for that purpose. The act, therefore, incor-

porates these persons by the name of " The Company of Proprie-
" tors of the Stroudwater Navigation," and empowers them to
raise £20,000 amongst themselves, in two hundred shares of £100
each, and, if necessary, a further sum of £10,000, either amongst
themselves, by creation of new shares, or by mortgage of the undertaking, and authorizes them to take the same tolls and rates as
the undertakers under the first act of parliament were empowered
to take, and which are enumerated in a foregoing part of this
article. The tolls and rates to be exempted from all taxes. Fifteen
years allowed to the company to complete the navigation.

No Boat of less than Twenty Tons to pass through the Locks without leave of the
Company, except when the Waste Water runs over the Weir.

The act of parliament, passed in 1783 for making the Thames
and Severn Canal, restrains the Stroudwater Company from taking
more than 2s. 3d. per ton for coal carried on their canal, and passing to the Thames and Severn, and going thereon not more than
one hundred and fifty yards above the high road at Brimscombe,
and 1s. per ton only for coal going more than one hundred and
fifty yards beyond such road.

TONNAGE RATES.

	d.	
For all Flint, Brick, Stone, Clay, Chalk, Salt, Ores, Salt-rock and Lime-stone, passing more than One Hundred and Fifty Yards on the Thames and Severn Canal, above the Road at Brimscombe, and carried on the Stroudwater Canal either up or down	½ per Ton, per Mile.	
For all Timber, Black Glass Bottles and Phials, and Crates of Pottery..	1 ditto.	ditto.
For all Iron, Cast and Wrought, and all other Goods, Wares and Merchandize	1½ ditto.	ditto.

And in proportion for a greater or less Quantity or Distance.

This canal has been of infinite advantage to the town of Stroud,
and the clothing district in the neighbourhood, by furnishing them
with coal at a cheap rate, and conveying their heavy and bulky
goods to various markets; and from its connection with the Thames
and Severn, was the means of forming the first communication by
inland navigation between London and Bristol, and the counties of
Gloucester, Worcester and Hereford.

SURREY (GRAND) CANAL.
(SEE GRAND SURREY CANAL.)

SURREY IRON RAILWAY.

41 George III. Cap. 33, Royal Assent 21st May, 1801.
45 George III. Cap. 5, Royal Assent 12th March, 1805.

THIS railway commences at a basin which connects it with the River Thames at a place called Ram Field, in the parish of Wandsworth, and from thence proceeds in a southerly direction, running parallel with the River Wandle to Mitcham, (where there is a branch from it to Hack Bridge, in the parish of Carshalton;) it proceeds from thence in a south-easterly direction to a place called Pitlake Meadow, in the town of Croydon, where it unites with the Croydon, Merstham and Godstone Railway, already described in this work, and called in our map the southern part. The basin is about a quarter of a mile long, with a lock next the Thames, and is sufficiently spacious to hold thirty barges or more at once. The length of this railway is nearly nine miles, with no where a greater ascent than about 1 inch in 10 feet. It was the first public railway constructed near London, and the expense of its construction, including lock, basin and branch, was estimated by Mr. W. Jessop at £33,000.

The act of parliament authorizing this undertaking was passed in 1801, and is entitled, '*An Act for making and maintaining a* '*Railway from the town of Wandsworth to the town of Croydon, with* '*a collateral Branch into the parish of Carshalton, and a navigable* '*Communication between the River Thames and the said Railway* '*at Wandsworth, all in the county of Surrey.*' It incorporates the subscribers by the name of " The Surrey Iron Railway Company," and empowers them to raise, for the purposes of the undertaking, amongst themselves the sum of £35,000, in three hundred and fifty shares of £100 each, and, if necessary, a further sum of £15,000, either amongst themselves, by creation of new shares or by mortgage of the tolls and rates, and also authorizes them to take the following

TONNAGE RATES.

	d.
For all Goods, Wares and Merchandize whatever, carried into or out of the Dock or Basin	4 per Ton,
For all Dung carried on the Railway	2 ditto, per Mile

2 Q

TONNAGE RATES CONTINUED.

	d.	
For all Lime-stone, Chalk, Lime and all other Manure, (except Dung) Clay, Breeze, Ashes, Sand and Bricks	3 per Ton, per Mile.	
For all Tin, Copper, Lead, Iron-stone, Flints, Coal, Charcoal, Coke, Culm, Fullers' Earth, Corn and Seeds, Flour, Malt and Potatoes......................................	4 ditto.	ditto.
For all other Goods, Wares and Merchandize	6 ditto.	ditto.

Fractions of a Quarter of a Ton to be considered as a Quarter, but all Fractions of a Mile as a Mile.

Lords of manors and owners of land on the railway may erect wharfs and warehouses, and on their refusing to do so when required, the company may erect them, and may receive such reasonable rates and allowance on all goods lying on or in them more than twenty-four hours, as the commissioners appointed under this act shall deem sufficient.

The act provides that nothing contained in it shall prejudice the rights of the Lord Mayor and Corporation of the city of London, as conservators of the River Thames; and that the company shall pay to the said Lord Mayor and Corporation the sum of 21s. as a fine or acknowledgment for opening a communication between the basin and the River Thames, and an annual rent of £10 as a compensation for the diminution of any tolls or rates which may be caused by this undertaking.

A second act of parliament was obtained in 1805 by this company, entitled, ' *An Act to enable the Company of Proprietors of* ' *the Surrey Iron Railway to raise a further Sum of Money, for* ' *completing the said Railway, and the Works thereunto belonging,*' which empowered them to raise an additional sum of £10,000 for the completion of the work, either amongst themselves, by the creation of new shares, or by mortgage of the tolls and rates.

The railway is double throughout, and at the north-west end of Croydon is but about three-eighths of a mile from the Croydon Canal. Its principal object is to facilitate the conveyance of lime, chalk, flint, fullers' earth and agricultural products from its neighbourhood to London; and in return to take from thence coals and manure for the supply of the country through which it passes.

SWALE RIVER.

(SEE OUSE RIVER, YORK.)

SWANSEA CANAL.

34 George III. Cap. 109, Royal Assent 23rd May, 1794.

THIS canal commences in Swansea Harbour, at the mouth of the Tawe River, and running in a direction a little to the eastward of north, and parallel with the River Tawe, passes Landoor, the copper-works of J. Morris, Esq, at Morris Town; afterwards crossing the small River Twrch, it terminates at Pen Tawe, and from whence is continued a railway to the lime-works at Hen-Noyadd, in the parish of Ystradgunlais, in the county of Brecon. There are two railways branching from this canal, each about two miles in length; one near Ynis Tawe, to coal mines, and the other to coal mines and lime-works near Bryan Morgan.

The length of this canal is about seventeen miles, of which a portion, one mile and a half in length, between Landoor Brook and Morris Town, (called Morris's Canal) through the estate of the Duke of Beaufort, was constructed by that nobleman, who receives the tolls thereof. From Swansea to opposite Pont-ar-Tawe, a distance of about eight miles and a quarter, is a rise of 105 feet; from thence to Pont Gwaynclawdd, eight miles further, it rises 237 feet; and there is a rise of 31 feet in the remaining three quarters of a mile, making a rise in the whole distance of 373 feet.

The act of parliament, under authority of which this undertaking was completed, is entitled, '*An Act for making and main-*
'*taining a navigable Canal, from the town of Swansea, in the*
'*county of Glamorgan, into the parish of Ystradgunlais, in the*
'*county of Brecon.*' It incorporates the subscribers by the name of "The Company of Proprietors of the Swansea Canal;" empowers them to raise £60,000 in shares of £100 each, and, if necessary, a further sum of £30,000; and authorizes them to take the following

TONNAGE RATES.

	d.	
For all Iron, Goods, Merchandize, &c. (except Pig-iron, Iron Castings, Calcined Iron-ore, Iron-stone, Iron-ore, Rotten-stone, Charcoal, Coal, Culm, Stone-coal, Coke, Cinders, Timber, Stone, Tiles, Bricks, Clay, Lime-stone, Lime, Sand and all Kinds of Manure	4	per Ton, per Mile.

TONNAGE RATES CONTINUED.

		d.		
For all Iron Castings		3	per Ton,	per Mile
For all Pig-iron..		2¼	ditto.	ditto.
For all Iron-stone, Calcined Iron-ore, Iron-ore, Rotten-stone, Coal, Culm, Stone-coal, Coke, Cinders, Charcoal, Timber, Stone, Tiles, Bricks and Clay	}	3¼	ditto.	ditto.
For all Lime-stone, Lime and all Kinds of Manure		1	ditto.	ditto.
For all Lime, Lime-stone and Manure passing from Swansea to the South Boundary of the Fee of Trewyddfa (about Two Miles)	}	½	ditto.	ditto.

The Tolls taken by the Duke of Beaufort, on that Part of the Canal belonging to him, to be the same as those taken by the Company.

No Boat under Fifteen Tons to pass any Lock when the Water does not flow over the Waste Weir; nor any Boat under Ten Tons to pass when it does so flow, without leave or paying the Tonnage respectively.

Mr. Thomas Sheasby was the engineer employed in this canal, which was completed and opened in October, 1798. The principal objects for which it was executed are the export of coals, ironstone, &c. with which the country abounds, and the conveyance of lime to the intermediate works and country, and of copper and other ores and minerals to the extensive foundries about Swansea.

TAMAR MANURE NAVIGATION.

36 George III. Cap. 67, Royal Assent 26th April, 1796.

THE River Tamar, under authority of this act of parliament, is made navigable from Morwelham Quay, near Calstock, (where the Tavistock Canal begins) up to Boat Pool, from whence a canal has been made, which runs in a course a little to the west of north, by Launceston, Milton Abbott, Bradstone, Lifton, Warrington, Northcott and Tetcott, to Tamerton Bridge, a distance of about twenty-two miles. There is a collateral cut near Poulson Bridge, to Launceston.

The act is entitled, ' *An Act for making and maintaining a* ' *Navigation from Morwelham Quay, in the parish of Tavistock, in* ' *the county of Devon, to Tamerton Bridge, in the parish of North* ' *Tamerton, in the county of Cornwall; and also a certain collateral* ' *Cut from Poulson Bridge, in the parish of Lifton, in the said* ' *county of Devon, to Richgrove Mill, in the parish of St. Stephen,* ' *near to the borough of Launceston, in the said county of Corn-* ' *wall.*' It empowers the company of proprietors to raise amongst themselves, for the purposes of the act, the sum of £121,000, in shares of £50 each, and they are to pay £200 per annum to the Duchy of Cornwall for the liberty of making this navigation. Inclined planes and railways may be substituted in place of locks on this canal.

This canal was designed principally for the supply of coal, seasand and lime as manure, and affords an opening for the export of the agricultural products of the country through which it passes.

TAVISTOCK CANAL.

43 George III. Cap. 130, Royal Assent 27th July, 1803.

This canal commences in the tideway of the Tamar River, (near the commencement of the Tamar Manure Navigation) at Morwelham Quay New Basin, near Calstock, and terminates at the town of Tavistock. Its length is about four miles, in nearly a north-east course, and through Morwelham Down by a tunnel about two thousand six hundred and forty yards long and about 460 feet beneath the highest point of the down above it. It has likewise a branch from Crebar, near the north end of the tunnel, to the slate quarries at Millhill Bridge.

The act of parliament for this canal is entitled, ' *An Act for* ' *making and maintaining a navigable Canal from and out of the* ' *River Tamar, at or near Morwelham Quay, to the town of Tavi-* ' *stock; and also a collateral Cut to lead from the said Canal to* ' *Millhill Bridge, in the county of Devon.*' It empowers the company of proprietors to raise amongst themselves, for the purposes of the act, the sum of £50,000, in shares of £50 each, and to take the following

TONNAGE RATES.

	s.	d.	
For all Lime-stone conveyed through the Tunnel	1	3	per Ton.
For all Building-stone, Slates, Bricks, Tiles, Clay, Sand, Earth, Dung, Ores, Iron and Metals (made marketable) conveyed through the Tunnel..	2	0	ditto.
For all Coal, Coke, Culm, Lime, Timber, Bark, Corn, Grain and all other Goods passing through the Tunnel	3	0	ditto.
For all Building-stone, Slate, &c. as above, carried on any Part of the Canal or its Branches, except in the Tunnel	1	0	ditto.
For all Coals, Coke, &c	1	6	ditto.

Ores may be carried to the Dressing Floor, or the Waste or Rubbish of Mines or Lodes be removed to proper Places on any part of the Canal free of Toll.

Besides the above rates, all goods which pass into or from the Tamar River, and are not loaded at Morwelham Quay, are to pay as below, for reimbursing the owner or occupier thereof, for the loss of wharfage on such goods, viz.

WHARFAGE RATES.

	s.	d.	
For all Slate	0	3	per Ton.
For all Lime-stone	0	6	ditto.
For all Ores, (made marketable) Iron, Bricks, Tiles, Clay, Sand, Earth and Dung	0	6	ditto.
For all other Goods...	1	0	ditto.

In addition to the above, One Penny per Ton is to be paid on all Goods entering the Canal Basin at Morwelham.

By an estimate furnished by Mr. John Taylor and Mr. J. Hitchins, dated in February, 1803, it appeared that the expense of completing the canal, to be 16 feet at top, 8 feet at bottom, and 3 feet deep, and tunnel, would amount to £36,958, 16s.

From the Tamar River, the first one-eighth of a mile is level with high water at Morwelham Quay; thence in a quarter of a mile is a rise of 237 feet; thence about three miles and one-eighth to Tavistock is level; the branch is level to New Quarry about a mile and five-eighths; thence to Millhill Bridge, three-eighths of a mile, is a rise of $19\frac{1}{2}$ feet.

The locks upon this canal are to be calculated for boats of $12\frac{1}{2}$ feet long and 5 feet wide; but the company may erect inclined planes for boats or boxes of goods, instead of locks.

Morwelham Down, through which the tunnel passes, is of hard rock and supposed to be intersected by several fissures or lodes filled with metallic ores. It is the property of the Duke of Bedford, who is the most considerable subscriber to the undertaking, and who has leased to the company the mines which may be found in tunnelling.

The canal crosses the Lumbourn River near Crebar by an aqueduct bridge two hundred yards long and 60 feet above the river. Its principal object is the export of slate, copper-ore and other minerals and agricultural produce; and the import of coals, lime and other articles for the supply of Tavistock and the neighbouring country.

TAY RIVER AND PERTH NAVIGATION.

11 George IV. Cap. 121, Royal Assent 17th June, 1830.

THIS noble river has its source in that romantic district which separates the counties of Perth and Argyle, and but a few miles north of the head of the beautiful Loch Lomond. Its course is eastwardly, embracing Lochs Dochart and Tay; and thence in a southwardly course by the town of Dunkeld and Scone Palace, (the ancient residence of the Scottish Kings) to the city and port of Perth, from which place it gradually widens in a considerable estuary, and falls into the North Sea between Button Ness and Tentmoor Point, about five miles east of the port and harbour of Dundee, and twenty-eight from Perth.

The Tay is navigable at spring tides to the city of Perth, but much obstructed by the floods at one time and the shallows at another, but more in particular by one situate betwixt the quays of Perth and the Friar Town, called the Weel Ford; to remedy which, and to improve the navigation generally, an act was obtained on the 17th June, 1830, entitled, ' *An Act for enlarging,* ' *improving and maintaining the Port and Harbour of Perth; for* ' *improving the Navigation of the River Tay to the said city; and* ' *for other Purposes therewith connected;*' and by which, twenty-six commissioners are appointed to carry the purposes of this act into execution.

The proposed improvements consist chiefly in deepening about fifteen hundred yards in length of the river from the Towns-ford, opposite the Merchant's Pier, on the west side of the river to Friar Town, so as to admit vessels drawing 9 feet 6 inches at neap tides, at that part of the river nearest to Perth, and 14 feet 6 inches at Friar Town Deeps. The quays also are to be rebuilt to the extent of nearly eight hundred yards. Mr. James Jardine was the engineer employed on this business, who estimated the expense at £14,504, the whole of which is to be paid out of the funds of the city of Perth. In consideration of the outlay of this sum, the act empowers the commissioners to demand the following rates.

RATES OF NAVIGATION DUES ACCORDING TO THE TONNAGE.

For every Vessel, Ship, Boat, Bark or Lighter, for every Time it comes to the Port or
Harbour of Perth, and within that Portion of the Precincts of the said Port and
Harbour, lying above the point where the Willowgate Branch of the River falls
into the main Stream below Friar Town the following Dues shall be paid.

		d.
If not Registered at any Port of the United Kingdom (register)........	4½	per Ton.
If Registered at any Port of the United Kingdom	3	ditto.
If only employed in carrying Goods or other Commodities to or from } Dundee, or other Ports in the River Tay.........................	2	ditto.
For every Steam Vessel employed in the River Tay in carrying Passengers and their Luggage exclusively, which shall enter or leave the said Port or Harbour within the Limits set forth as above.	one-third,	ditto.

For every Vessel remaining at the Harbour or Quays of Perth more than Six Months,
one-third more of the above Dues; so remaining One Year, double the above
Dues; and the above Rates for every Six Months it shall so remain beyond One
Year.

For the additional rates and duties leviable upon goods imported and exported, we refer the reader to the Schedule B at the end of the act, as they are far too numerous for our insertion. In addition to these, however, there are the tolls, rates and duties payable to the Lord Provost, Magistrates and Town Council of Perth, comprised under the name of Custom, Anchorage, Sess Boll, Shore Dues and Coal Deacon's Dues; but as these are charges arising from custom and unsanctioned by any parliamentary enactment, we purposely omit them also.

On the credit of the dues, the commissioners may borrow £16,000 sterling for the purposes of the act; and, for further security, the Lord Provost, Magistrates and City Council of Perth are empowered to interpose the security of the common funds of the city, at the same time. Their rights, dues, duties, privileges and jurisdictions are protected by a clause in the act; so also is the right of free port and harbour claimed by the Right Honorable the Earl of Kinnoul, at the Bridge End of Perth, as a part and pertinent of the Barony of Balhousie.

It is provided, by the last clause in the act, that the payment of dues and duties shall not commence until £5,000 of the requisite fund for improving the navigation has been advanced.

The improvement of a navigation, extending nearly thirty miles into one of the most fertile districts of Scotland, cannot fail to be attended with considerable advantage to the trading community of a city where the manufacture of linen cloth and leather, and the processes of bleaching and printing are carried on to a considerable extent.

TEES NAVIGATION.

48 George III. Cap. 48, Royal Assent 27th May, 1808.
9 George IV. Cap. 97, Royal Assent 19th June, 1828.

THE first act for executing this useful work was obtained in 1808, under the title of '.*An Act for making a navigable Cut from* ' *the East Side of the River Tees, near Stockton, into the said River* ' *near Portrack, in the county of Durham; and making various* ' *other Improvements in the Navigation of the said River between* ' *the town of Stockton and the Sea.*' By this act certain persons are incorporated as " The Tees Navigation Company," with power to make a navigable cut from the Tees, from the bridge across that river at Stockton to the junction of the same with the sea at Portrack, and to make the same navigable for ships and other vessels, and to improve, open, dig, widen and cleanse the said river, with its creeks and outlets, in any part between Stockton and the sea ; and also to remove, cut through, or otherwise destroy any rocks, shoals, shallows or other obstructions lying near the bar or mouth of the said river, for stopping the present course of which and for diverting the same, they are also empowered to make embankments, which, however, must be maintained at their own expense. The proprietors have power to enter and use lands for the purposes of this act, proper compensation being made to the owners thereof, for the settlement of which, commissioners are appointed by the act, with authority to fill up vacancies. For completing the works the company may raise £7,000, in shares of £50 each; and, should this prove insufficient, they may raise an additional sum of £5,000, either by the creation of new shares, or by mortgage of the works, or on optional notes.

For paying interest on the capital advanced, borrowed money and other contingencies, they are authorized to demand the following

TONNAGE RATES.

	s.	d.	
For every Ship trading to or from the Tees, from or to any Port in Great Britain	0	6	per Ton.
For ditto, to or from any Foreign Port, except British Vessels laden with Norway Timber only	0	9	ditto.
For every British Vessel laden with Norway Timber only, trading to the Tees	0	6	ditto.

TONNAGE RATES CONTINUED.

	s.	d.
For every Foreign Ship trading to or from the Tees, from or to any Foreign Port, except Foreign Ships laden with Norway Timber only	1	6 per Ton.
For ditto laden with Norway Timber only	1	0 ditto.

Ships of War, Ships in Distress and all Vessels in his Majesty's Service are exempted from these Rates.

The company have also a power to erect light-houses on or near the bar of the Tees, and to charge for them, on every vessel passing the bar, the following

LIGHT-HOUSE RATES.

	s.	d.
For all British Coasting Vessels entering or going out of the River Tees with Goods chargeable to the aforesaid Tonnage Duties at the Rate of Sixpence per Ton, for each Lower Mast	5	0
For all British Vessels from or to Foreign Ports chargeable with the aforesaid Tonnage Duties at the Rate of Sixpence and Nine-pence per Ton, for each Lower Mast	7	6
For all Foreign Vessels chargeable to the aforesaid Tonnage Duties at the Rate of One Shilling and One Shilling and Sixpence per Ton, for each Lower Mast	10	0
For all British Vessels entering only for Anchorage, for each Lower Mast for passing Inwards and Outwards	7	6
For all Foreign Vessels entering only for Anchorage, for each Lower Mast for passing Inwards and Outwards	15	0

In the year 1828 the company obtained a second act, entitled, ' *An Act to enable the Tees Navigation Company to make a navi-* ' *gable Cut from the East Side of the River Tees, near Portrack* ' *in the county of Durham, into the said River near Newport in* ' *the township and parish of Acklam, in the North Riding of the* ' *county of York.*'

By this act the company have the usual powers for making the projected cut, granted to them; they are likewise authorized to raise, for the purposes of this act, £20,000 by the creation of new shares; and they may, if needful, borrow £30,000 in addition to the said £20,000. Dividends of £10 per cent. to be paid annually on shares created under both acts, providing first for the paying off of the regular interest on £3,000 borrowed under power of the former act, and the interest on such sums as shall be borrowed under this act. The proprietors may, from time to time, lessen the rates and again advance them, if requisite; they may also reduce the dues on foreign ships and goods. Owners of land on the north side of the canal may keep a ferry-boat on the same; and the canal is declared to be free from any control of the Commissioners of Sewers. There are other clauses saving the rights of several individuals, of the See of Durham, and of the Corporation of Stockton.

This line of navigation commences in the Tees at Stockton Bridge; it makes a very considerable bend below this point, being indeed almost in a circle; it is also crossed by the Stockton and Darlington Railroad, parallel with which road the new cut is made from near the crossing to its opening into the Tees Mouth.

The work is one of great utility for vessels trading to this part of the country; and since the Darlington Railroad was carried to Stockton, vessels are enabled to take coal from hence for the London market; and when the railway is extended, by the suspension bridge across the Tees, to the proposed docks, this trade will be considerably increased.

THAMES RIVER.

2 Henry VI. C. 9, R. A. —— 1423.	14 Geo. III. C. 91, R. A. 14th June, 1774.
4 Henry VII. C. 15, R. A. —— 1487.	15 Geo. III. C. 11, R. A. 30th Mar. 1775.
23 Henry VIII. C. 18, R. A. —— 1535.	17 Geo. III. C. 18, R. A. 30th April, 1777.
3 James I. C. 20, R. A. —— 1605.	28 Geo. III. C. 51, R. A. 11th June, 1788.
21 James I. C. 32, R. A. —— 1623.	34 Geo. III. C. 65, R. A. 23rd May, 1794.
7 Wm. III. C. 16, R. A 22nd April, 1695.	35 Geo. III. C. 84, R. A. 2nd June, 1795.
11 & 12 Wm. III. C. 21, R. A. 11th Apr. 1700.	35 Geo. III. C. 106, R. A. 22nd June, 1795.
12 Anne, C. 17, R. A. —— 1713	45 Geo. III. C. 63, R. A. 27th June, 1805.
3 Geo. II. C. 11, R. A. 15th May, 1730.	45 Geo III. C. 98, R. A. 10th July, 1805.
7 Geo. II. C. 29, R. A. 13th June, 1733.	47 Geo. III. C. 31, R. A. 1st Aug. 1807.
11 Geo. II. C. 12, R A. 20th May, 1738.	47 Geo. III. C. 70, R. A. 8th Aug. 1807.
18 Geo. II. C. 21, R. A. 2nd May, 1745.	50 Geo. III. C. 204, R. A. 20th June, 1810.
22 Geo. II. C. 46, R. A. 13th June, 1749.	52 Geo. III. C. 46, R. A. 20th April, 1812.
23 Geo. II. C. 26, R. A. 12th April, 1750.	52 Geo. III. C. 47, R. A. 20th April, 1812.
24 Geo. II. C. 8, R. A. 22nd Mar. 1751.	54 Geo. III. C. 223, R. A. 27th July, 1814.
32 Geo. II. C. 16, R. A. 2nd June, 1759.	2 Geo. IV. C. 123, R. A 2nd July, 1821.
4 Geo. III. C. 12, R. A. 5th April, 1764.	5 Geo IV. C. 123, R. A. 17th June, 1824.
11 Geo. III. C. 45, R. A. 29th April, 1771.	8 Geo. IV. C. 75, R. A. 14th June, 1827.
11 Geo. III. C. — R. A. 8th May, 1771.	10 Geo IV. C. 130, R. A. 19th June, 1929.

THIS noble river, the most important in a commercial point of view of any in the world, has one of its sources at a place called The Head of the Isis, or Thames, near the road running from Cirencester to Tetbury, in the county of Gloucester, whence, under the name of the Isis, it flows to Latton, near Cricklade, where it is joined by another branch, whose source is about three miles from Cheltenham; thence passing Cricklade, where it is joined by another branch from the foot of Cleeve Hill, it runs easterly to Lechlade, at which place it becomes navigable, and

where the Thames and Severn Canal locks into it; continuing a
very circuitous course, leaving Faringdon on the south and Bamp-
ton on the north, it proceeds through a part of the grounds of
Blenheim, to Oxford, where the Oxford Canal enters it; proceeding southerly it passes by Nuneham Park to Abingdon, where
the Wilts and Berks Canal joins it; taking a circuitous course,
inclining to the south-east, to near the town of Dorchester, where
it is joined by the Thame, and said to obtain the name of Thames,
from Thame and Isis; it then proceeds in a southerly direction by
Bensington, Wallingford, Streatley, Basilden Park, Maple Durham and Purley Hall, to Caversham Bridge near Reading, where
the Kennet Navigation joins it; passing Caversham Park and
Holme Park, and bending northerly it proceeds by Park Place to
Henley; from thence passing by Fawley Court, Spinfield Lodge
and Bisham Abbey, it runs to Great Marlow; and thence in a
south-easterly course, by Maidenhead, on its way to Windsor;
whence, winding round the Castle Hill, it proceeds, by Datchet,
Staines and Chertsey, to near Woburn Park and Ham; here it is
joined by the River Wey, which connects the Basingstoke Canal
and the Wey and Arun Navigation with it; it now passes Oat-
lands, Ashley Park, Apps Court and Hampton Court Palace, in
an easterly course to Thames Ditton, thence northerly to King-
ston; and thence, in the same direction, by Teddington, Twicken-
ham, and Ham House, to Richmond; it afterwards passes Isleworth and Sion House, to near Brentford, where the Grand
Junction Canal communicates with it at the mouth of the River
Brent; it then continues a winding course, by Kew, Brentford,
Mortlake and Chiswick, to that part of Hammersmith where it is
crossed by the suspension bridge, Putney and Fulham, to Wandsworth, at which latter place the Surrey Railway communicates
with it by means of a basin. A little lower down it is joined by
the Kensington Canal. It pursues its course through London to a
short distance below the tower, where the Saint Katherine Docks
have recently been erected. A little further down are the London Docks; and at Rotherhithe there is a tunnel which has been
cut under and about half-way across the river, but has been
stopped, not only by the water getting through but by want of
funds; it is next joined by the Grand Surrey Canal; and at

Limehouse, on the opposite side of the river, communicates with the Regent's Canal ; as well as with the River Lea, a little further down, by the Limehouse Cut.

Proceeding in an easterly direction, it reaches the Isle of Dogs, round which it makes a winding and circuitous course by Deptford and Greenwich ; but a canal having been cut across the Isle of Dogs, connecting the river and cutting off a large bend, the distance is greatly shortened. It passes the East and West India Docks at Blackwall, and the Commercial Docks on the south side near the Deptford Road, and at Bow Creek receiving the River Lea, continues its course by Woolwich, where a canal is cut up to the Arsenal, a little below which, on the north side, the River Roding falls into it. Passing on to Purfleet, it is joined on its south side by the River Darent ; and about five miles lower down is a short railway to Gray's Thurrock Lime Works; thence it flows on to Gravesend, where the Thames and Medway Canal unites with it ; continuing its course eastward, it reaches Sheerness, where the River Medway and others join it, and where it forms a large estuary, called the mouth of the Thames.

The acts of parliament relating to this river are so numerous, (as will be seen by referring to the head of this article) that we shall only avail ourselves of those parts of them which we consider necessary as a matter of reference, touching the navigation of this river. The first, therefore, from which we shall make any extract is that passed in 1730, and entitled, '*An Act for reviving* '*and amending an Act made in the Sixth and Seventh Years of the* '*Reign of his late Majesty King William the Third, entitled, An* '*Act to prevent Exactions of the Occupiers of Locks and Weirs* '*upon the River of Thames, westward, and for ascertaining the* '*Rates of Water Carriage upon the said River;*' which states that the act of the 7th of King William III. therein referred to, having long since expired, and in consequence of which, the occupiers of locks and weirs on the River Thames, from the city of London, westward, to Cricklade, in the county of Wilts, being in the habit of exacting such exorbitant sums for the passage of barges and other vessels, as greatly to discourage navigation, and increase the rates of water carriage upon the river; and that tolls are now demanded from men haling barges and other vessels on

the river and using the towing-path, which was formerly free to
them ; and that such large sums are demanded by the owners
and occupiers of land through which the towing-path passes, for
horses that are used for haling vessels, as greatly to injure the
trade on the river; for remedy of which, the act appoints commissioners for the counties of Middlesex, Surrey, Berks, Bucks,
Oxon, Gloucester and Wilts, with powers to ascertain and settle
such rates and tolls to be paid by the owners of barges and other
vessels for the use of the towing-path, either by men or horses,
and to the occupiers of all locks, weirs, &c. as they shall consider
fair and reasonable, regard being had to the tonnage of the vessels ; to the rates settled by the act of the 7th of King William
III. and to the expense incurred in the erection of such locks,
weirs, &c. provided, however, that they shall not alter the amount
of any tolls or rates which shall be proved to have been taken for
the preceding thirty-five years or more.

The commissioners are also empowered to fix the rate of carriage to be taken by the owners of barges, &c. and to cleanse and
scour any part of the river they may think necessary; to defray
the expense of which they may impose a rate to be paid by all
barges, &c. passing any place so cleansed and scoured.

The act passed in 1751, entitled, ' *An Act for the better car-*
' *rying on and regulating the Navigation of the Rivers Thames and*
' *Isis, from the city of London, westward, to the town of Cricklade,*
' *in the county of Wilts,*' appoints as commissioners for the counties of Middlesex, Surrey, Berks, Bucks, Oxon, Gloucester and
Wilts, all persons living in such counties who shall be rated to the
land-tax for an estate of £100 a year in value, giving them the
same powers and authority which were given to the commissioners
by the act of 1730, from which we have extracted; which act, as
well as the 7th of King William the Third, is hereby repealed.

The next act of parliament respecting this navigation which
we consider it necessary to refer to, is that passed in 1771, entitled,
' *An Act for improving and completing the Navigation of the*
' *Rivers Thames and Isis, from the city of London, to the town of*
' *Cricklade, in the county of Wilts;*' which states that the act of
1751 (named above) not having vested sufficient powers in the
commissioners therein appointed, for preventing abuses and exac-

tions by the owners of the towing-paths, and of the locks, weirs, &c. and for raising the necessary sums for cleansing and scouring such parts of the river as may require it; and in order to remedy which, the act appoints as commissioners all persons having landed property of the value of £100 per annum, in any of the counties through which the river passes, with the addition of many public functionaries, including the Lord Mayor and Aldermen of London, the Heads of Colleges at Oxford, &c. with powers to fix the rates to be paid by barges or other vessels passing through any lock, provided that such rate be not less than any now taken under authority of any preceding act of parliament, or more than four-pence per ton at any one lock; and also the rate of carriage of all sorts of goods to be taken by the owners of such barges or other vessels.

The act divides the navigation into six districts; the first district from the city of London to Staines Bridge; the second from Staines Bridge to Boulter's Lock; the third from Boulter's Lock to Maple Durham; the fourth from Maple Durham to Shillingford; the fifth from Shillingford to Oxford; and the sixth from Oxford to Cricklade.

The commissioners are authorized to borrow the sum of £50,000 by mortgage of the tolls and rates which they may collect, or by granting annuities; in the latter case the annuity not to exceed £10 per cent. per annum.

The act of 1774, entitled, ' *An Act more effectually to improve* ' *and complete the Navigation of the River Thames, westward of* ' *London Bridge, within the liberties of the city of London, and to* ' *prevent any Vessel or Barge from being moored in Taplow Mill* ' *Stream, in the county of Bucks,*' repeals that portion of the last act which gives the commissioners therein appointed control over the first district of the river, between the city of London and Staines Bridge, and vests in the corporation of London, as conservators of the Thames, the same powers which had been previously given to such commissioners, and empowers the corporation to expend the sum of £10,000 in improving the navigation of that part of the river westward of London Bridge, within the jurisdiction of the city of London, for which they are not to receive any tolls from persons navigating the river.

In 1777 another act was passed, entitled, ' *An Act for enabling* ' *the Mayor, Aldermen, and Commons of the city of London, to* ' *purchase the present Tolls and Duties payable for navigating* ' *upon the River Thames, westward of London Bridge, within the* ' *liberties of the city of London, and for laying a small Toll in lieu* ' *thereof, for the Purpose of more effectually completing the said* ' *Navigation ; and for other Purposes;*' which states that the Mayor, &c. of London, in pursuance of the powers granted to them by the last recited act, had expended the sum of £10,000 in improving the navigation of the river between London and Staines Bridge; that they find, to complete such improvements, an additional sum of nearly £8,000 will be required, which they are willing to expend thereon, provided they are authorized to purchase the old tolls and duties now collected on that part of the river in their jurisdiction, and to collect in lieu thereof a small tonnage rate. The act then empowers the Lord Mayor, &c. to purchase such old tolls and rates, which are then to cease, and in lieu thereof they may take the following

TONNAGE RATES.

	d.	
For all Barges and Vessels navigated on the said River, Westward of London Bridge, to Strand on the Green, or Brentford	½	per Ton.
To Isleworth or Richmond	1	ditto.
To Twickenham or Teddington	1½	ditto.
To Kingston or Hampton Wick	2	ditto.
To Ditton, Hampton Court, Moulsey or Hampton	2½	ditto.
To Sunbury, Walton, Hawford, Shepperton or Weybridge	3	ditto.
To Chertsey or Laleham	3½	ditto.
To Staines and Upwards	4	ditto.

Vessels under Three Tons and all Pleasure Boats are exempted from these Rates.

The corporation are authorized to borrow £15,000 on mortgage, and assign the tolls as security; or by annuity at the following rate. On the lives of persons from the age of forty-five to sixty years, eight per cent. per annum; and on sixty years and upwards, ten per cent. per annum. All writings authorized by this act to be exempted from stamp duty.

The act of 1788, entitled, ' *An Act to explain, amend and* ' *enlarge the Powers of so much of Two Acts, passed in the* ' *Eleventh and Fifteenth Years of the Reign of his present* ' *Majesty, for improving and completing the Navigation of the* ' *Rivers Thames and Isis, from the city of London, to the town*

' of Cricklade, in the county of Wilts, as relates to the Navigation
' of the said Rivers from the Boundary of the Jurisdiction of the
' city of London, near Staines, in the county of Middlesex, to the
' said town of Cricklade,' states that the commissioners had raised
the sum of £38,900, part of £50,000 authorized by former acts
to be raised, which they had expended in improving the navigation
of the river, and empowers them to borrow an additional sum of
£25,000 for the same purposes.

The tolls and rates collected by them to be exempted from all
taxes; and all manure, dung, compost and tillage for land on the
line to be free from all rates or dues.

The act of 1794, entitled, ' An Act for better regulating and
' governing the Watermen, Wherrymen, and Lightermen, upon the
' River of Thames, between Gravesend and Windsor,' authorizes
the Lord Mayor and Aldermen of the city of London to regulate
the fares to be taken by watermen, &c. on the river between
Gravesend and Windsor ; and to make rules and regulations for
their guidance, which are to be approved by one or more of the
judges.

By the act of 1810, entitled, ' An Act for amending, altering
' and enlarging the Powers of Two Acts, passed in the Fourteenth
' and Seventeenth Years of his present Majesty, in relation to the
' Navigation of the River Thames, westward of London Bridge,
' within the liberties of the city of London; and for the further
' Improvement of the said Navigation,' the Corporation of London
are empowered to erect four pound locks, each of which to be 150
feet in length and 20 feet in width in the chamber thereof, with
three pair of gates in each lock, and to be at the following places ;
one near Chertsey Bridge ; another near Shepperton ; another
near Sunbury ; and the other near Teddington.   The act also
authorizes the corporation to borrow a further sum of £40,000 to
carry on the work, by mortgage of the tolls, or by annuities; in
the last case, the rate to be paid on lives from forty-five to sixty,
is ten per cent. per annum ; and on those above sixty, twelve
per cent. per annum.

It also repeals the tolls formerly granted, and in lieu thereof
empowers the collection of the following tonnage rates.

TONNAGE RATES.

	d.	
For all Barges and other Vessels navigated on the River, Westward of London Bridge, to Strand on the Green, Kew or Brentford........ }	1	per Ton.
To Isleworth or Richmond	1½	ditto.
To Twickenham, Ham or Teddington................................	2½	ditto.
To Kingston or Hampton Wick	3	ditto.
To Seething Wells, Ditton, Hampton Court, Moulsey or Hampton	4	ditto.
To Sunbury, Walton, Hawford, Shepperton or Weybridge	4½	ditto.
To Chertsey or Laleham..	5½	ditto.
To Staines and Upwards	6	ditto.

And for passing any of the Locks directed by this Act to be made, an additional Rate of Two-pence per Ton.

Floats or Rafts of Timber to pay the same Rate per Ton as Vessels.

The act passed in 1812, entitled, ' *An Act for altering,* ' *amending and enlarging the Powers of Three Acts of his present* ' *Majesty, for improving the Navigation of the River Thames,* ' *westward of London Bridge, within the liberties of the city of* ' *London; and for further improving the said Navigation,*' authorizes the company to erect another pound lock at East Moulsey; and also to borrow a further sum of £75,000 on such security and in such manner as is directed by the last act of parliament for raising £40,000. The act repeals the tolls granted by the preceding one, and in lieu thereof empowers them to collect the following

TONNAGE RATES.

	d.	
For all Barges and other Vessels, navigated on the River, Westward of London Bridge, to Strand on the Green, Kew or Brentford........ }	1½	per Ton.
To Isleworth or Richmond	2¼	ditto.
To Twickenham, Ham or Teddington................................	3½	ditto.
To Kingston or Hampton Wick	3	ditto.
To Seething Wells, Ditton, Hampton Court, Moulsey or Hampton....	4	ditto.
To Sunbury, Walton, Shepperton or Weybridge.....................	4½	ditto.
To Chertsey or Laleham	5¼	ditto.
To Staines and Upwards	6	ditto.

Another act passed in 1812, entitled, '*An Act to authorize* ' *the Commissioners for improving and completing the Navigation* ' *of the Rivers Thames and Isis, from the Jurisdiction of the city* ' *of London, near Staines, in the county of Middlesex, to the town* ' *of Cricklade, in the county of Wilts, to make a navigable Canal* ' *out of the River Thames, near Milson's Point, in the parish of* ' *Egham, in the county of Surrey, to communicate with the said* ' *River, at or near Bell Weir, in the said parish of Egham; and* ' *to erect Pound Locks in such Cut, with necessary Weirs and other* ' *Works on the said Navigation,*' empowers the commissioners to raise the additional sum of £25,000 by mortgage of the tolls, and to make the cut described in the title of the act.

The act of 1814, entitled, '*An Act for altering, amending*
'*and enlarging the Powers of Four Acts of his present Majesty,*
'*for improving the Navigation of the River Thames, westward*
'*of London Bridge, within the liberties of the city of London;*
'*and for further improving the said Navigation,*' authorizes the
Corporation of London to make a new pound lock at Penton Hook,
in the parish of Staines, and to take on every barge or vessel or
raft or float of timber passing such new lock, an additional rate of
4*d.* per ton. The act also empowers them to raise a further and
additional sum of £70,000 in the same manner as prescribed by
former acts for raising other sums; and to establish a sinking fund
for paying off their debt, for which purpose they are to appropriate £1,000 from the tolls within three months from the passing
of this act, and every subsequent year a sum of £500; which sums
are to be employed, from time to time, as they are received, in
paying off portions of the debt, or to be invested in government
securities until they shall be sufficient in amount to pay off the
whole of the debt. The tolls to be exempt from all rates and taxes.

The act of 1824, entitled, '*An Act to enable the Mayor and*
'*Commonalty and Citizens of the city of London to raise a Sum*
'*of Money, at a reduced Rate of Interest, to pay off the Monies*
'*now charged on the Tolls and Duties payable by virtue of Four*
'*Acts of the Reign of his late Majesty King George the Third, for*
'*improving the Navigation of the River Thames, westward of*
'*London Bridge, within the liberties of the city of London,*' states
that an offer had been made to the Corporation of the city of
London of an advance of a sum of money, on the credit of the
tolls and rates of the river, at an interest of four per cent. per
annum; and as they are now paying five per cent. the act empowers them to raise the sum of £170,000 at four per cent. by
mortgage of the tolls, which sum is to be appropriated to the payment of the existing debt; the present creditors who may be
willing to reduce their rate of interest to four per cent. to remain
creditors at such reduced interest.

In 1827 an act of parliament was passed, entitled, '*An Act*
'*for the better Regulation of the Watermen and Lightermen on*
'*the River Thames, between Yantlet Creek and Windsor,*' which
incorporates the company of watermen, &c. by the name of

" The Master, Wardens and Commonalty of Watermen and Light-
" ermen of the River Thames ;" and among other regulations,
provides that every member of the company should have a licence
for his boat, expressing the number of persons he is allowed to
carry in it, which number, with his name, shall be painted on the
boat; an omission of which subjects the offender to a penalty of
20s. and carrying more than the number expressed in the licence,
to a penalty of 40s. The court of Aldermen of the city of London
to fix the fares to be taken by the members of this company, which
list is to be approved by his Majesty's Privy Council ; and the
penalty for any person taking more than the legal fare is 40s.

We shall here only notice the act of parliament of 1829, entitled, ' *An Act for the Sale of the City Canal, and for other Purposes*
' *relating thereto,*' for the opportunity of remarking, that this canal
was cut by government across the Isle of Dogs, to save the circuitous navigation round that island; and that agreeably to the
purport of this act it was sold to the West India Dock Company,
as will be found stated under the article of " Isle of Dogs Canal."

Since the execution of the Thames and Severn Canal, which
communicates with the River Thames at Lechlade, that very bad
part of the river between Lechlade and Cricklade has been abandoned, and it is now navigated to Lechlade only ; indeed, at this
time, from Oxford to Lechlade is but an indifferent navigation.
The distance of the last-mentioned town from London, by the river,
is one hundred and forty-six miles and a half, and the distances
between the towns on the line as follow :—

	MILES.
From London to Staines Bridge	37½
Thence to ..... Windsor	8
.... Maidenhead	7
.... Marlow	8
.... Henley	9
.... Reading	9
.... Wallingford	18
.... Abingdon	14
.... Oxford	8
.... Lechlade	28
	146½

The total fall from Lechlade to low-water-mark is 258 feet, which upon average is near 21½ inches per mile.

As an account of the receipts and disbursements of the commissioners of the Thames Navigation in the year 1829, was printed during the last session by order of the House of Commons, we take this opportunity of presenting our readers with a copy.

RECEIVED.

	£.	s.	d.
Tolls Collected at Pound Locks	11,834	6	2
Sundries..	143	8	0
	£11,977	14	2

DISBURSED.

	£.	s.	d.
Interest to Bond Holders.........	4,200	0	0
Ditto on Loan from Treasurer	100	0	0
Ditto on Exchequer Loan	338	0	0
One Year's Instalment on Ditto	650	0	0
Salaries to Clerks, Surveyors and Receiver	1,270	0	'0
Rents	209	16	0
Purchases	190	11	0
Surveys and Committees......	289	0	5
Ballasting	130	6	4
Repairs	3,378	14	10
Sundries; viz. Stamps, Printing, Stationery, Lines, Nets, &c.	173	13	5
	£10,930	2	0

NEW WORKS, &c.

	£.	s.	d.
Boulter's Cut and Pound Lock Ferry Houses ,.......................	1,304	2	3
	£12,234	4	3

GEORGE SCOBELL, CHAIRMAN,
EDWARD LAW,
EDWARD MICKLEM,
H. WALTER, } COMMISSIONERS.
JOHN ROLLS,
THOMAS RAYMOND BARKER,
EDWARD GARDINER,

WILLIAM PAYN.

The immense trade of that part of this river which comes within the design of our work, arises principally from having London situated upon its banks, to which great emporium it conveys the produce, not only of the counties through which its winding course proceeds, but of many other parts of the kingdom with which it is connected by other rivers and canals; and on the other hand, it distributes the East and West India and Continental produce, indeed, of nearly all the world; to which may be added, the numerous branches of home manufactures required by the country throughout the whole line of its communication.

THAMES AND MEDWAY CANAL.

39 & 40 Geo. III. C. 23, R. A. 16th May, 1800.   44 Geo. III. C. 46, R. A. 5th June, 1804.
50 Geo. III. C. 76, R. A. 18th May, 1810.   58 Geo. III. C. 18, R. A. 17th Mar. 1818.
5 Geo. IV. C. 119, R. A. 17th June, 1824.

THE first step towards the execution of this work took place in
1799, when Mr. R. Dodd was consulted as to the possibility of
obviating the necessity of the then circuitous passage round the
Nore, from Gravesend to the Medway, at Strood.   He accordingly
proposed a line nine miles and two chains in length, viz. an open
canal six miles, seven furlongs and two chains, and a tunnel two
miles and one furlong, whereby a circuit of no less than forty-
seven miles was to be avoided.   The plan was approved of,
although the estimate was far too low, and an act obtained in
1800, under the title of ' *An Act for making and maintaining a*
' *navigable Canal from the River Thames, near to the town of*
' *Gravesend in the county of Kent, to the River Medway, at a*
' *Place called Nicholson's Ship Yard, in the parish of Frindsbury,*
' *in the said county ; and also a certain collateral Cut from White-*
' *wall, in the said parish, to the said River Medway.*'   By this
act the proprietors were incorporated as " The Company of the
" Thames and Medway Canal," with the usual powers for completing the works ; for defraying the cost of which they were
empowered to raise £40,000, in shares of £100 each; and in
case the said sum should prove insufficient, they may raise, in addition, £20,000 on mortgage of the works or by creation of new
shares.   It is also provided, that tide locks and entrance basins
shall be made at each point of termination in this canal.

Under authority of the above act the work commenced, and
proceeded till that part extending from Gravesend to Denton was
completed, when it was deemed advisable to make a deviation and
other alterations from the original line, which required a new act.
This was obtained in 1804, and is entitled, ' *An Act for enabling*
' *the Company of Proprietors of the Thames and Medway Canal*
' *to vary the Line of the said Canal, and to raise a Sum of Money*
' *for completing the said Canal and the Works thereunto belonging ;*
' *and for altering and enlarging the Powers of an Act made in the*

' *Thirty-ninth and Fortieth of his present Majesty, for making the*
' *said Canal and a collateral Cut thereto.*' The deviation here alluded
to was laid down in 1803 by Mr. Ralph Walker, who proposed a
line nine miles and one chain in length, on a level throughout, and
avoiding the necessity of a tunnel, which was proposed in the
former act.   His estimate for this deviation was £98,147, 10s.

By this act the company had power to undertake the deviation,
and to provide for the expenditure on the same by raising an additional sum for the purpose of completing the work according to
the new scheme.

The line, however, did not yet appear to satisfy the undertakers of the project, for in 1810 we find them obtaining a further
' *Act for enabling the Company of Proprietors of the Thames and*
' *Medway Canal to vary the Line of the said Canal; and for*
' *altering and enlarging the Powers of Two Acts, passed in the*
' *Fortieth and Forty-fourth of his present Majesty, for making the*
' *said Canal and a collateral Cut thereto.*'

In prosecuting the work the company exhausted their resources, and the next act was passed in 1818, under the title of
' *An Act for enabling the Company of Proprietors of the Thames*
' *and Medway Canal to raise a further Sum of Money, for com-*
' *pleting the said Canal and the Works thereto belonging, and for*
' *altering, enlarging, and rendering more effectual, the Powers for*
' *making the said Canal and Works.*'   By this act the company
are empowered to raise a further sum of £100,000 in half shares
of £50 each, or by granting bonds of £100 each, bearing interest
at £5 per cent. to their clerk or treasurer, who are authorized
from time to time to sell the same with the sanction of the said
company; these bonds being secured on the property vested in
the said company.

By the prior acts, the company had authority to demand the
following

TONNAGE RATES.

	d.
For all Goods, Wares and Merchandize landed from any Boat, Barge or other Vessel, having entered any Basin or Pen of Water, or put into any other Boat, Barge or Vessel	2 per Ton.
For every Vessel, Boat or Barge, entering any Basin or Pen of Water, but not passing along the whole Line	4 ditto.

These rates, however, were not considered sufficient, and they were accordingly, by this act, empowered to demand the following in lieu of the former

TONNAGE RATES.

	s.	d.	
For all Goods, Wares, &c. landed from any Vessel, Boat or Barge, and having entered any Basin or Pen of Water, or put into any other Vessel	0	6	per Ton.
For all Vessels entering any Basin or Pen of Water, but not passing along all the Line...	1	0	ditto.

But if the Vessel so paying shall within Forty-eight Hours proceed on the whole Line, then the Rate paid for entering the Basin shall be deducted from the Charge made on that Account.

These rates may be lowered and raised again, as needful.

In 1824 a further extension of the company's powers was obtained by an act, entitled, ' *An Act for enabling the Thames and* ' *Medway Canal Company to raise a further Sum of Money to* ' *discharge their Debts, and to complete the said Canal and the* ' *Works thereunto belonging ; and for altering, enlarging, and* ' *rendering more effectual the Powers for making the said Canal* ' *and Works.*' By this act the company have the power of raising £50,000 by bonds of £1,000 each, bearing £5 per cent. interest, or by promissory notes or bonds under the common seal; and in case the said £50,000 shall not discharge the whole of their debts, they may in like manner raise an additional sum of £25,000, and any part of the sums directed to be raised by the former acts, may be raised by any of the means directed in the present act.

This canal commences in Gravesend Reach, nearly opposite to Tilbury Fort, and at this point, according to the provisions of the act, it has a basin and wharfs. From the wharfs it runs in nearly a straight line from west to east through Gravesend Marshes, a distance of about three miles; then making a detour to the south, it proceeds to join the River Medway nearly opposite Chatham, where a basin is made for the accommodation of vessels using this canal.

This canal, though of so short a length, is one of paramount importance, as to saving distance; an idea of the cost of executing it may be formed from the sums granted for that purpose by the various acts above quoted; and the utility of the work may be estimated from its situation and connection with the populous places on the line; the rates, however, do not appear to have given satisfaction, and the work is consequently not much used.

THAMES AND SEVERN CANAL.

23 Geo. III. C. 38, R. A. 17th April, 1783.   31 Geo. III. C. 67, R. A. 13th May, 1791.
36 Geo. III. C. 34, R. A. 7th March, 1796.   49 Geo. III. C. 112, R. A. 27th May, 1809.
53 Geo. III. C. 182, R. A. 2nd July, 1813.

THIS canal was first projected by Mr. R. Whitworth, in 1782, and after obtaining the sanction of parliament, was afterwards executed by him. It commences in the Stroudwater Canal, at Wallbridge, near Stroud, and thence taking an easterly direction, it runs by Stroud, Chalford and Sapperton; here it is conveyed through the celebrated Tarlton or Sapperton Tunnel, which is the largest in the kingdom; then passing the head of the River Thames or Isis it reaches Siddington St. Mary, at which place a branch about a mile in length runs from it to the town of Cirencester; thence to South Cerney and Latton, where it is joined by a branch of the Wilts and Berks Canal, originally called the North Wilts Canal; then passing Cricklade and Kempsford, it terminates by locking down into the Thames and Isis Navigation at Lechlade.

The act of parliament, under authority of which this undertaking was commenced, is entitled, ' *An Act for making and* ' *maintaining a navigable Canal from the River Thames, or Isis,* ' *at or near Lechlade, to join and communicate with the Stroud-* ' *water Canal at Wallbridge, near the town of Stroud; and also a* ' *collateral Cut from the said Canal at or near Siddington, to or* ' *near the town of Cirencester, in the counties of Gloucester and* ' *Wilts.*' It incorporates a number of persons, who were subscribers to the undertaking, amongst whom are the Earl of Radnor, Lord Dudley and Ward, Sir Edward Littleton, Bart. and Sir Herbert Mackworth, Bart. by the name of " The Company " of Proprietors of the Thames and Severn Canal Navigation," and empowers them to raise amongst themselves, for the purposes of the act, the sum of £130,000, in thirteen hundred shares of £100 each, and, if necessary, a further sum of £60,000, by mortgage of the tolls and rates, and directs that five per cent. per annum shall be paid on the sum so raised during the progress of the work. The act also authorizes the company to take the following tonnage rates.

TONNAGE RATES.

	s.	d.		
For all Coal passing between the Stroud Canal and Sapperton Tunnel	1	3	per Ton.	
Between the West End of Sapperton Tunnel and Cirencester	1	0	ditto.	
Between the Cirencester Branch at Siddington and Lechlade	2	0	ditto.	
For all Iron, Salt, Ores, Salt Rock, Lime-stone, Chalk, Crates of Pottery, Crates of Black Glass, Timber, Flint, Brick, Stone, Clay, Copper, Brass, Tin, Tin Plates, Lead, Spelter, Pot Metal, Window Glass and Plate Glass	0	2	ditto, per Mile.	
For all other Goods and Merchandize whatever	0	3	ditto.	ditto.

And in proportion for any greater or less Distance or Quantity.

Any Goods remaining on any Wharf longer than Twenty-four Hours, to pay such Rate as may be agreed upon with the Parties, and in case of Dispute, to be settled by the Commissioners appointed under the Act.

The act provides that certain rates shall be taken by the company of proprietors of the Stroudwater Navigation, on goods passing from their canal into the Thames and Severn Canal, which rates will be found in our article on the Stroudwater Navigation; and it also directs that on goods passing from the said Stroudwater Navigation into this canal, the company shall take the following

TONNAGE RATES.

	s.	d.	
For all Coal carried from the River Severn through the Stroudwater Navigation, and going on this Canal no further than One Hundred and Fifty Yards above the High Road crossing this Canal at Brimscombe	1	3	per Ton.

For Coal going more than One Hundred and Fifty Yards above the said Road, the usual Tonnage Rates taken on the Canal.

	s.	d.	
All other Goods, Wares and Merchandize passing in like Manner from the Stroudwater Navigation, and no further on this Canal than One Hundred and Fifty Yards above the High Road at Brimscombe	1	0	ditto.

And passing more than One Hundred and Fifty Yards above the said Road the usual Tonnage Rates.

If this Company reduce their Tonnage Rates on Coal to One Penny per Ton per Mile, the Stroudwater Navigation to reduce theirs also to that Sum, on all Coal carried from their Canal to this, and to more than One Hundred and Fifty Yards above the Road at Brimscombe, and all Materials for making or repairing either of these Canals, to pass free on each of them.

Vessels of less than Six Tons to pay a Lock Due of Sixpence at each Lock, for Waste of Water, and in addition to pay for Six Tons of Lading.

In 1791 the company obtained another act of parliament, entitled, ' *An Act to enable the Company of Proprietors of the* ' *Thames and Severn Canal Navigation, to borrow a further* ' *Sum of Money to complete the said Navigation,*' which empowered them to borrow an additional sum of £60,000, by mortgage of the tolls and rates.

The act passed in 1796, entitled, ' *An Act to enable the* ' *Company of Proprietors of the Thames and Severn Canal Na-* ' *vigation, to raise a certain Sum of Money, for discharging* ' *some Arrears of Interest, and other Debts relating thereto,* ' *and to maintain and support the said Navigation,*' empowers the company of proprietors to raise a further sum of £65,000, by the creation of thirteen hundred half shares of £50 each ; and provides that those proprietors of old shares who may wish to take some of the new shares, shall be allowed to subscribe the sum of £37, 10*s.* now due for interest on each original share, as part of the purchase money for a half share, paying the difference of £12, 10*s.* in money.

Another act passed in 1809, entitled, ' *An Act for altering,* ' *amending and enlarging the Powers of several Acts, for making* ' *and maintaining the Thames and Severn Canal Navigation,*' empowers the company to raise a further sum of £200,000, by any of the means prescribed by the former acts of parliament, or by the creation of new shares, in which case the old proprietors are to have the option of taking the same number of new shares as they hold of the original ones, before they are otherwise disposed of.

The last act of parliament relating to this canal was passed in 1813, and is entitled, ' *An Act for altering and amending an* ' *Act made in the Twenty-third Year of the Reign of his present* ' *Majesty, for making and maintaining the Thames and Severn* ' *Canal Navigation.*' It authorizes the company of proprietors to make a dock or basin on their canal at a place called Weymoor Bridge, in the parish of Latton, in Wiltshire, where the North Wilts is proposed to join the Thames and Severn Canal, and empowers them to contribute, as shareholders, the sum of £5,000 towards making the North Wilts Canal.

Goods remaining on any wharf in the basin more than six hours, to pay such rates as may be agreed on.

The length of this canal is thirty miles and seven chains ; from the Stroudwater Canal to Sapperton, a distance of seven miles and three-eighths, with a rise of 243 feet, by twenty-eight locks ; from thence the summit pound continues through the tunnel, which is two miles and three-eighths in length to near Coates, and level; thence to the Thames and Isis Navigation, twenty miles and three-eighths, with a fall of 134 feet by fourteen locks. The first four miles of this canal from Stroud is of the same width and depth as the Stroudwater Navigation, and calculated for the Severn Boats; the remainder of the line is 42 feet wide at top, 30 at bottom, and 5 feet deep, and the locks admit boats of 80 feet in length and 12 feet wide.

The famous tunnel at Sapperton, which was constructed by Mr. R. Whitworth, the engineer employed on this canal, is two miles and three-eighths in length; the arch is 15 feet wide in the clear, and 250 feet beneath the highest point of the hill, which is of hard rock, some of it so solid as to need no arch of masonry to support it; the other parts are arched above and have inverted arches in the bottom. It was first passed on the 20th April, 1789, and on the 19th November following the first vessel passed from the Severn into the Thames.

On the 19th July, 1778, during the execution of this work, his late Majesty King George the Third went to view the tunnel, with which he expressed himself much astonished, and on the construction of which he bestowed the highest praise.

The advantages of forming a communication between the Rivers Thames and Severn, have been always so apparent, that as long ago as the reign of Charles the Second, a bill was introduced into parliament for making the connection by means of the River Avon. It was not however acted upon. At the time the first act was obtained for effecting the junction of these rivers, by means of this canal, the project held out as fair prospects of success and pecuniary advantage to the promoters as any undertaking of the kind in the kingdom.

By connecting London with Bristol, Gloucester and Worcester, and other towns on the banks of the Severn, a safe and easy course to London is opened for not only the trade of Gloucestershire and Worcestershire, but also that of Herefordshire, Monmouthshire and South Wales; to which might be added the trade of the towns on the Thames, which receive their supplies of coal from the mines connected with the Severn. These prospects have not, however, been realized to the extent that was expected, owing, in a great measure, to the inefficient state of the navigation of the upper part of the River Thames, and to the construction of other canals in the neighbourhood, more especially the Kennet and Avon, which affords a much shorter route from Bristol to London.

THANET CANAL.

13 George III. Cap. 47, Royal Assent 10th May, 1773.

THIS canal is the property of the Earl of Thanet, at whose expense it was constructed. It runs from the Leeds and Liverpool Canal, in a direction nearly north, and about one-third of a mile in length, to a little above Skipton Castle.

The act is entitled, ' *An Act to enable the Right Honourable* ' *Sackville, Earl of Thanet, to make a navigable Cut or Canal from* ' *a Place called the Spring, lying near Skipton Castle, in the county* ' *of York, to join and to communicate with the navigable Canal* ' *from Leeds to Liverpool, in a Close called Hebble End Close, in* ' *the township of Skipton, in the said county of York.*'

The whole line through which the canal passes is Lord Thanet's property, with the exception of one close which belongs to the Free Grammar School at Skipton.

Its object is the conveyance of limestone from the quarries about a mile above the castle, to which, railways are laid, which limestone is used at the foundries in the neighbourhood of Bradford, and for making and repairing both turnpike and other roads to a considerable extent beyond Leeds and Wakefield ; besides which, it is burnt into lime for agricultural and building purposes.

TONE RIVER OR TONE AND PARRETT NAVIGATION.

10 & 11 William III. Cap. 8, Royal Assent 24th March, 1699.
6 Anne,   Cap. 9, Royal Assent 11th March, 1707.
44 George III. Cap. 83, Royal Assent 14th July, 1804.

THIS navigation, which is about twenty-seven miles in length, commences in the Grand Western Canal at Taunton, and runs in a direction nearly north, by a bending course, passing Bridgewater, to the tideway in Bridgewater Bay at Start Point, in the Bristol Channel; being, however, joined in its course, at Borough Chapel, by the Parrett River.

It was executed under authority of an act passed in 1699, entitled, ' *An Act for making and keeping the River Tone navigable* ' *from Bridgewater to Taunton, in the county of Somerset,*' and of another in 1707, entitled, ' *An Act for the more effectual making* ' *and keeping the River Tone navigable from Bridgewater to Taun-* ' *ton, in the county of Somerset ;*' and in 1804 a third act was passed, entitled, ' *An Act for explaining and amending Two Acts,* ' *passed in the Tenth and Eleventh Years of the Reign of King* ' *William the Third and the Sixth of Queen Anne, for making and* ' *keeping navigable the River Tone, from Bridgewater to Taunton,* ' *in the county of Somerset.*' These acts appointed certain persons conservators of this river, who were to collect tonnage rates thereon, part of which were to be applied to the maintenance of the navigation, and the remainder for the benefit of the poor of Taunton, and the parishes of Taunton St. Mary Magdalene and Taunton St. James.

In 1811 a number of persons became a company and obtained an act of parliament, authorizing them to make a canal from near Bristol to Taunton ; and as it was supposed that this canal would materially injure the interests derived from the River Tone, the company are directed by the act of parliament to purchase those interests, and to maintain the River Tone out of the tolls arising therefrom, as will be found noticed under the article, " Bridge- " water and Taunton Canal," in this work.

TRENT RIVER.

10 & 11 Wm. III. C. 20, R. A. 4th May, 1699. 10 Geo. III. C. 57, R. A. 16th Mar. 1770. 13 Geo. III. C. 86, R. A. 24th Dec. 1772. 23 Geo. III. C. 41, R. A. 6th May, 1793. 23 Geo. III. C. 48, R. A. 24th June, 1793. 34 Geo. III. C. 95, R. A. 9th May, 1794.

This river rises in the most northern extremity of Staffordshire, near a place called Thursfield, from whence it runs southerly to Handford Bridge, being in its course joined by several other branches ; proceeding through the grounds of the Marquis of Stafford, at Trentham, (where it forms a fine sheet of water) it runs by Stone, and continues in a south-easterly direction by Great Heywood, Wolseley Park, Hagley Park and Rugeley, to Cattor Hall; then, bending north-easterly, it runs by Drakelow Park to Burton-upon-Trent, where it becomes navigable, and is there joined by a short branch from the Trent and Mersey Canal; continuing its course north-easterly by Newton Park to near Swarkestone, where the Derby Canal locks down into it, it proceeds by Donnington Park to Wilden Ferry, there uniting with the Trent and Mersey Canal; thence running easterly a short distance, it is joined by the River Soar or Loughborough Navigation, and on the opposite side by the Erewash Canal; bending a little northerly by Thrumpton and Clifton Halls, where the Beeston Cut, which communicates with the Nottingham Canal, joins it on the north side, it runs down to Nottingham, there receiving the Grantham Canal; proceeding north-easterly it passes East Bridgeford, Stoke Hall, Newark and Marnham Hall, to Torksey Lock, at which place the Foss Dyke Navigation, extending to Lincoln, communicates with it; thence taking a northerly course by Burton Hall, Lea Hall and Gainsborough, it proceeds to West Stockwith, where the Chesterfield Canal locks into it, and where it is also joined by the River Idle; continuing its northerly course by Owston to Keadby Lock, taking the Stainforth and Keadby Canal in its way, it proceeds to the junction with the River Ouse, at a place called Trentfalls, opposite to Flaxfleet, and from the union of these rivers, to the sea, forms the Humber.

The first act of parliament relating to the navigation of the River Trent, was passed in 1699, and is entitled, ' *An Act for* ' *making and keeping the River Trent, in the counties of Leicester,* ' *Derby and Stafford, navigable.*' This act vested the tolls to be taken under its authority in the Earl of Uxbridge, or his lessees, and empowered him or them to take the following

TONNAGE RATE.

	d.
For all Goods carried on any Part of the Navigation	3 per Ton.

It appears that the lessees of the Earl took little pains to improve the navigation, for so many shoals continued to exist, as rendered the river impassable in dry seasons.

In 1770 a second act was passed, entitled, '*An Act for the bet-*
'*ter regulating the Navigation of the River Trent from Wilden*
'*Ferry, otherwise Cavendish Bridge, in the county of Derby, to*
'*Gainsborough, in the county of Lincoln,*' which, after stating that
great irregularities and continual trespasses on the lands adjoining
the river, were committed by the boatmen, provides, that in future
all barges or other vessels going upon the river from Wilden Ferry
to Gainsborough, should be numbered, and have the name and
residence of the owner marked thereon, under a penalty of five
pounds.

Another act of parliament respecting this river, which was
passed in 1772, and entitled, '*An Act for improving and com-*
'*pleting the Navigation of that Branch of the River Trent, which*
'*runs by the town of Newark-upon-Trent, from a Place called*
'*The Upper Weir, in the parish of Averham, in the county of*
'*Nottingham, to a Place called The Crankleys, in the parish of*
'*South Muskham, in the said county,*' appoints commissioners for
improving and completing the navigation of that branch of the
River Trent which runs from The Upper Weir, passing the town
of Newark to The Crankleys; the other branch of the river at
that point passing by Averham, Kelham and South Muskham,
is to unite with that to be made navigable by this act at The
Crankleys.

The act provides that the barges on this branch shall be haled
by men only, and that the commissioners may take the following

TONNAGE RATES.

		d.
For all Coal, Stone, Timber and all other Goods, Wares and Merchandize, which shall be carried on this Branch of the Trent, and landed on any Part of the said Branch......................................	}	4 per Ton.
For ditto carried on this Branch but not landed thereon		2 ditto.

EXEMPTIONS.

Hay and Corn, (not sold but being carried to be laid up in the Yards, &c. of the Owner)
Materials for repairing Roads, (not being Turnpike) and Manure for Lands through
which the Navigation passes, provided the Things, exempted as above pass
through any Lock, at such Times as the Water is flowing over the Waste Weir.

These tolls to be free from all taxes ; and all mortgages,
transfers and other writings connected with this navigation to
be exempt from stamp duty.

The commissioners are empowered to borrow such sum of money as may be necessary for the completion of the work, by mortgage of the tolls, &c.

The next act of parliament, passed in 1783, and entitled, ' *An* ' *Act for empowering Persons navigating Vessels upon the River* ' *Trent, between a Place called Wilden Ferry, in the counties of* ' *Derby and Leicester, or one of them, and the town of Burton-* ' *upon-Trent, in the county of Stafford, to hale the same with* ' *Horses,*' repeals that part of a former act which provides that the barges, &c. on this navigation shall be haled by men only, and allows horses to be used.

This act was followed by another in the same year, entitled, ' *An Act for improving the Navigation of the River Trent, from a* ' *Place called Wilden Ferry, in the counties of Derby and Leices-* ' *ter, or one of them, to Gainsborough, in the county of Lincoln ;* ' *and for empowering Persons navigating Vessels thereon, to hale* ' *the same with Horses ;*' which appointed commissioners to carry the purposes of the act into execution, and who are authorized to take the following

TONNAGE RATES.

	s.	d.
For all Goods from Shardlaw to Gainsborough	1	2 per Ton.
For ditto from Nottingham to Gainsborough	0	10 ditto.

The act also repeals that portion of a former act which limited the haling of barges and other vessels to men only.

The last act of parliament relating to the navigation of this river was passed in 1794, and is entitled, ' *An Act to alter and* ' *amend an Act of the Twenty-third Year of his present Majesty,* ' *for improving the Navigation of the River Trent, and for making* ' *and maintaining a navigable Canal from the said River, in the* ' *parish of Beeston, to join the Nottingham Canal, in the parish of* ' *Lenton, in the county of Nottingham; and also certain Cuts on* ' *the Side of the said River.*'

The canal cut under the authority of this act of parliament, commences in the parish of Beeston, and running northerly joins the Nottingham Canal, in the parish of Lenton.

The act empowers the company to raise amongst themselves, £13,000 in shares of £50 each, and if necessary, a further sum of £10,000, by mortgage of the tolls, &c. and to take the following

TONNAGE RATES.

	d.
For all Goods, Wares, Merchandize, &c. carried from, to or between Wilden Ferry and Gainsborough	9 per Ton.
From Wilden Ferry to Newark-upon-Trent, or the contrary	6 ditto.
From Gainsborough to Nottingham Trent Bridge, or the contrary	6 ditto.
From Wilden Ferry to Nottingham Trent Bridge, or to the Nottingham Canal, or the contrary	3 ditto.
From Gainsborough to Newark, or the contrary	3 ditto.
From Nottingham Trent Bridge to Newark, or the contrary	3 ditto.

And in proportion for a greater or less Quantity or Distance.

Only Half the above Rates to be paid for Coal, Plaster and Lime, upon any Part of this Navigation, except for Vessels navigating between Gainsborough and Dunham Shoal, and navigating no higher up the River.

Only a Half-penny per Ton to be paid on Coal, Plaster, Lime or other Goods, Wares, &c. carried on this River to Dunham Shoal and no further up, and so proportionably in case such Coal, &c. shall not be conveyed the whole Distance from Gainsborough to Dunham Shoal; and no Tonnage of any Kind to be paid for Coal, &c. conveyed down the River from Dunham Shoal to Gainsborough, or from any intermediate Place, and not brought from any Place higher up this River than Dunham Shoal.

The annual rent of £5 paid to this company by the proprietors of the Soar Navigation and Erewash Canal to cease, and in lieu thereof, every laden boat, crossing the Trent at such place, to pay sixpence.

No rates to be taken until the sum of £13,000 be expended for the purposes of the act. The profits on this navigation are not to exceed seven per cent.

The same rates to be taken on the cut as those allowed by former acts on the river.

The length of this river from Burton-upon-Trent, where it becomes navigable, to the Humber, is about one hundred and seventeen miles, and the fall to low-water-mark is 118 feet.

This river, connecting the port of Hull with a wide extent of agricultural, mining and manufacturing country, by means of the various rivers and canals which communicate with it, affords an easy means of export for the manufactures of a large district in Lancashire; the salt from Cheshire; the produce of the potteries in Staffordshire; the coal from Derbyshire; and the agricultural produce of Nottinghamshire, Leicestershire and Lincolnshire. It also opens a communication with the sea by way of Lincoln and Boston; through which channels, as well as the Humber, the articles above enumerated are conveyed ; and in return, the interior of the country is supplied either by Hull and Gainsborough or Boston and Lincoln, with such commodities as are required by an immense population.

TRENT AND MERSEY CANAL.

6 Geo. III. C. 96, R. A. 14th May, 1766.	10 Geo III C. 102, R. A. 12th April, 1770.
15 Geo. III. C 20, R. A. 13th April, 1775.	16 Geo. III. C. 32, R. A. 13th May, 1776.
23 Geo. III. C. 33, R. A. 17th April, 1783.	37 Geo III. C. 36, R. A. 24th Mar. 1797.
37 Geo. III. C. 81, R. A. 6th June, 1797.	42 Geo. III. C. 25, R. A 15th April, 1802.
49 Geo. III. C. 73, R. A. 20th May, 1809.	4 Geo. IV. C. 87, R. A. 17th June, 1823.

8 Geo. IV. C. 81, R. A. 14th June, 1827.

THIS important work commences at a place called Wilden Ferry, in the county of Derby, where the Derwent empties itself into the Trent; thence running in a south-westerly direction, it passes Shardlow, Aston, Weston, Swarkestone (near which it is crossed by the Derby Canal) and Egginton, in the same county; thence continuing to Burton, where it communicates with the River Trent, it proceeds by Wichnor, to its junction with the Coventry and Fazeley Canal at Fradley; from this point, turning to the north-west, it passes by Rugeley to Heywood Mill, where it is joined by the Staffordshire and Worcestershire Canal; then running by Weston to Stone, it there takes a northerly course, passing Trentham to Stoke, where it is joined by the Newcastle-under-Lyne Canal on the south, and the Caldon Branch runs from the north side of it to near Uttoxeter, and a railway branches from it at a place called Frog Hall to the Caldon Lime Works; and there is also a railway leading from the canal to the coal works above Lane End; continuing its northerly course, it passes Etruria and Burslem to the south end of Harecastle Tunnel in Staffordshire; after passing through the tunnel it is joined by the Macclesfield Canal, and then inclines to the north-west, running by Church Lawton, leaving Sandbach on the north-east, to Middlewich, at which place the Middlewich Branch goes from it; from thence it continues a north-west course, passing the salt pits near Northwich, and through Barnton, Saltersford and Preston Tunnels, to Preston Brook, at which place it communicates with the Duke of Bridgewater's Canal, and from thence proceeds in nearly a westerly course to Runcorn Gap, on the River Mersey, in the county of Chester; but this last part has become part of the Duke's Canal.

The first act of parliament, passed in 1766, is entitled, ' *An Act* ' *for making a navigable Cut or Canal from the River Trent, at or* ' *near Wilden Ferry, in the county of Derby, to the River Mersey,* ' *at or near Runcorn Gap;*' it incorporates the subscribers by the name of " The Company of Proprietors of the Navigation from " the Trent to the Mersey," and empowers them to raise amongst themselves, for the purposes of the act, the sum of £130,000, in six hundred and fifty shares of £200 each; and they are authorized, by subsequent acts of parliament, to increase their capital to £334,250. This act likewise allows the company to take the following

TONNAGE RATES.

	d.
For all Coal, Stone, Timber and all Kinds of Goods whatever	$1\frac{1}{2}$ per Ton, per Mile.

Materials for Roads and Manure are exempted from Tolls, provided they pass through the Locks at such Time as the Waste Water flows over the Weir.

Wharfage Rates for Goods remaining more than Twenty-four Hours, as may be agreed.

By a clause in the act of parliament, the Duke of Bridgewater is to complete that portion of the Trent and Mersey Canal running, from its junction with his own at Preston Brook, to Runcorn, such portion to be his property; he is also to receive those tolls and rates thereon, which are mentioned under the article " Bridge- " water Canal."

The acts passed in 1770 and 1775 were for granting further powers to this company, but without any clause which requires extracting.

The act obtained by the company in 1776, is entitled, ' *An* ' *Act to enable the Company of Proprietors of the Navigation from* ' *the Trent to the Mersey, to make a navigable Canal from the said* ' *Navigation, on the South Side of Harecastle, in the county of* ' *Stafford, to Frog Hall; and a Railway from thence to or near* ' *Caldon, in the said county ; and to make other Railways,*' and empowers the company to make that branch canal and railway commencing from Stoke, which we have described in the introduction to this article.

The act of 1783 is merely for amending and comfirming the powers granted by former acts.

That of 1797 is entitled, ‘*An Act to enable the Company of* ‘ *Proprietors of the Navigation from the Trent to the Mersey, to* ‘ *make a navigable Canal from and out of a certain Branch of the* ‘ *said Navigation, called the Caldon Canal, at or near Endon, to* ‘ *or near the town of Leek, in the county of Stafford; and also a* ‘ *Reservoir for supplying the several Canals of the said Company* ‘ *with Water ;*’ and authorizes the company to make such branch from the Caldon Branch to the town of Leek.

The act of parliament of 1802 is entitled, ‘*An Act to enable* ‘ *the Company of Proprietors of the Navigation from the Trent to* ‘ *the Mersey, to make Railways; to alter the Course of the Rail-* ‘ *way from Frog Hall to Caldon, and Part of the Course of the* ‘ *Canal from Frog Hall to Uttoxeter ; and to amend the Trent and* ‘ *Mersey Canal Acts.*’ This act, in addition to authorizing several alterations in the lines of the branches from the canal, empowers the company of proprietors to divide the shares which were originally £200 each, into shares of £100 each.

The act of 1809 amends and enlarges the powers given by former acts, without any particular clauses.

The act of 1823 is entitled, ‘*An Act to enable the Company* ‘ *of Proprietors of the Navigation from the Trent to the Mersey,* ‘ *to make an additional Tunnel through Harecastle Hill, in the* ‘ *county of Stafford, and an additional Reservoir in Knypersley* ‘ *Valley, in the said county; and to amend and enlarge the Powers* ‘ *of the several Acts for making and maintaining the said Naviga-* ‘ *tion, and the several Canals connected therewith.*’ By this act it is provided that all goods, wares and merchandize, using the said intended new cut or canal, shall pay an additional rate of three half-pence per ton per mile, and in proportion for a greater and less distance or weight. For completing the additional works, the proprietors are empowered to borrow £60,000 on mortgage of the works and premises of any or all of their canals. With these powers the company entered upon their new plan, as soon as it had received the sanction of the legislature, and the additional tunnel through Harecastle Hill, and the reservoir in Knypersley Valley, were forthwith completed.

The last act of parliament relating to this navigation was passed in 1827, and is entitled, ' *An Act for enabling the Com-* ' *pany of Proprietors of the Navigation from the Trent to the* ' *Mersey, to make Two Branches or Cuts from and out of the said* ' *Navigation ; and for further amending the Acts of the said Com-* ' *pany.*' By this last act the company are directed to make so much of the line of the Macclesfield Canal as extends from the western part of the regulating pound, in the township of Oddrode, to Hardingswood Lock, in the parish of Audley, and to receive the rates thereon ; and the following are ordered to be collected by them as

TONNAGE RATES.

		d.		
For all Sand, Gravel, Paving-stones, Bricks, Clay, Coal for burning Lime, Lime-stone and Rubble for Roads........	}	1	per Ton, per Mile.	
For all Ashler Stone, Slate, Flag, Spar, Coal except for burning Lime, and other Minerals	}	1½	ditto.	ditto.
For all Timber, Lime, Goods,Wares and all other Merchandize, Articles, Matters and Things............................	}	2	ditto.	ditto.

EXEMPTIONS.

Vessels laden wholly with Dung, Soil, Marl, and Ashes of Coal or Turf for the Improvement of Lands on the Line, are exempted from paying the above Rates, provided they do not pass any Lock, unless the Water is flowing over the Waste Weir of such Lock.

By this act also the company may make a communication with a cut, intended to be made by the Ellesmere and Chester Canal Company at Wardle Green ; and the company shall receive for all goods, conveyed on the said intended cut into or upon the said communication, the following.

TONNAGE RATES.

	d.	
For all Coal, Culm, Coke, Lime-stone and Rock Salt	9	per Ton.
For all Free-stone, Timber, Iron-stone, Slate, Lead-ore, Iron and Lead..	9½	ditto.
For all other Goods, Wares, Merchandize or Things....................	10½	ditto.

By this act also the £200 shares are directed to be divided into shares of £100 each. The company may borrow on mortgage the sum of £20,000, for executing the additional works and for the several other purposes of the act.

It is unnecessary, after what has been said at the commencement of the article, to enter into any minute investigation of the utility of this great national undertaking, whilst to state all the difficulties which occurred in the execution thereof, would extend our remarks beyond an ordinary length; suffice it therefore to say, that the line was projected by Mr. Brindley, and executed by him up to the time of his decease, after that by Mr. Henshall. Besides the extensive one over the Dove, there are no less than one hundred and twenty-six aqueducts and culverts, ninety-one locks and six tunnels. The lockage from Harecastle Summit to the Trent, at Wilden Ferry, is 316 feet; the six locks near Wilden Ferry are 14 feet wide, enabling river boats to come up to Burton; the rest only 7 feet; from the summit to the Duke's Canal at Preston Brook, is a lockage of 326 feet. The famous Harecastle Tunnel, two thousand eight hundred and eighty yards long, is situated upon the summit of this canal. The total length of the canal is ninety-three miles.

ULVERSTONE CANAL.

33 George III. Cap. 105, Royal Assent 8th May, 1793.

The object of this canal is to admit ships to the town of Ulverstone. It commences at Hammerside Hill, in Morecombe Bay, in the Irish Sea, and terminates at the new basin and wharfs at Ulverstone, and is about a mile and a half in length; it is level with high water at ordinary tides, and has a sea lock 112 feet long at its entrance.

The act of parliament authorizing this undertaking, is entitled, ' *An Act for making and maintaining a navigable Cut or Canal* ' *from a Place called Hammerside Hill, in the parish of Ulverstone,* ' *in the county palatine of Lancaster, to a Place called Weint End,* ' *near the town of Ulverstone aforesaid.*' It incorporates the subscribers by the name of " The Company of Proprietors of the " Ulverstone Canal Navigation," and empowers them to raise amongst themselves, for the purposes of the act, the sum of £4,000 in shares of £50 each, and, if necessary, a further sum of £3,000, and to take the following tonnage rates.

TONNAGE RATES.

                                      d.

For all Merchants' Goods, Bar-iron, Pig-iron, Timber, Coal, &c. ....   6 per Ton.
For all Slate, Lime, Iron-stone, Iron-ore and all Kinds of Ores   4   ditto.
For every Vessel continuing in the Basin or Dock more than Four Days after the Cargo is discharged, One Penny per Ton per Week, to be computed from the Register of the Vessel.
For Goods remaining on Wharfs longer than Twenty-four Hours, such Rate as may be agreed on.

A junction may be formed between this and the Lancaster Canal, and coal, culm and cinders carried from the Lancaster into the Ulverstone Canal, are not liable to the sea duty.

Mr. John Rennie was the engineer employed on this canal, which was completed in 1797. It is 65 feet wide at top, 30 feet at bottom, and 15 feet deep; at the lowest neap tides there is a depth of 9 feet water at the gates of the lock, and at spring-tides, of 20 feet. A public swing bridge is erected over the canal at Hammerside.

This canal has fully answered the purposes for which it was undertaken, and is of great benefit to the town of Ulverstone, being most convenient for the iron works established in its neighbourhood.

URE RIVER.

7 George III. Cap. 93, Royal Assent 15th April, 1767.
1 George IV. Cap. 35, Royal Assent 23rd June, 1820.

THE portion of the River Ure made navigable under authority of the above acts of parliament, is that which, commencing at its junction with the Swale, and running in a westerly course, passing Boroughbridge and Newby Hall, terminates at Ripon.

The act of 1767, entitled, ' *An Act for making navigable the* ' *River Ure from its Junction with the River Swale, to the borough* ' *of Ripon, in the county of York,*' appoints certain commissioners to carry into effect the purposes of the act, with powers to borrow such sums of money as they may find necessary for completing the undertaking, upon the credit of the tolls, and to take the following tonnage rates.

TONNAGE RATES.

	s.	d.	
For all Coal, Cinders and Lime (Thirty-two Bushels)	1	6	per Chaldron.
For all Bricks, Tiles, Stone, Slate, Turf and Wood for Fire	1	6	per Ton.
For all Butter, Timber, Marble and other Goods, Wares and Mer-chandize	3	0	ditto.

The act of parliament passed in 1820, entitled, '*An Act for maintaining navigable the River Ure, and its collateral Cuts, from its Junction with the River Swale, to the borough of Ripon, in the county of York,*' states that the commissioners appointed under the former act had greatly improved the navigation of the river, and had made several short cuts connected therewith, and had borrowed several sums of money to enable them to make such improvements, and that such sums, with the interest thereon, now amount to £27,850; and that none of the commissioners now remaining are qualified to act, and that the navigation is falling into decay, certain of the creditors of the navigation are, at their desire, incorporated by the name of " The Company of Proprietors " of the River Ure Navigation to Ripon," and empowered to raise amongst themselves, for the purposes of the act, the sum of £34,000, in two hundred shares of £170 each, and, if necessary, a further sum of £3,400, either amongst themselves, by the creation of new shares, or by mortgage of the tolls; and one hundred and sixty-four of the shares in this navigation are to be reserved for the holders of securities on the navigation, who may take them or remain creditors of the undertaking, at their option. The act also, as heretofore, authorizes the company to take the following

TONNAGE RATES.

	s.	d.	
For all Coal, Cinders and Lime (Thirty-two Bushels a Chaldron)	1	6	per Chaldron.
For all Bricks, Tiles, Stone, Slate, Turf and Wood for Fire	1	6	per Ton.
For all Butter, Timber, Marble and other Goods, Wares and Merchandize	3	0	ditto.

And in proportion for a greater or less Quantity.

Vessels not passing a Lock on the Navigation, to pay no Tolls.

Goods remaining on Wharfs longer than Twenty-four Hours and less than Six Days, to pay Three-pence per Ton, and longer than Six Days, such Rate as may be agreed on.

The act also directs that the company expend £3,000 in repairs of the navigation within five years from the passing of the same.

From Boroughbridge to Ripon are four locks, called Milby Lock, Rhodes's Field Lock, Oxclose Lock and Bell Furrows' Lock. Mr. John Smith was the engineer employed on this work.

The length of this navigation is about eight miles and a half, and its principal object the supply of Boroughbridge, Ripon, and their neighbourhood, with coal and other necessary articles of consumption ; as well as the export of their agricultural products and large quantities of lead, which are carried to Hull by means of its connection with the River Ouse.

As that part of the River Ure below the junction with the Swale has been described in the account of the Ouse River, we refer our readers to that article.

USK TRAMROAD.

54 George III. Cap. 101, Royal Assent 17th June, 1814.

THE act of parliament relating to this tramroad is entitled, ‘ *An Act for making and maintaining a Tramroad or Railway* ‘ *from the parish of Mamhilad, in the county of Monmouth, to or* ‘ *near Usk Bridge, in the said county.*’ It incorporates the com- ‘ pany of proprietors by the name of “ The Usk Tramroad Com- “ pany,” and empowers them to raise amongst themselves, for the purposes of the act, the sum of £6,000, in shares of £50 each, and, if necessary, a further sum of £3,000 either amongst themselves or by the creation of new shares, and to take the following

TONNAGE RATES.

	d.		
For all Coal	3	per Ton, per Mile.	
For all Dung, Compost, Lime-stone and all Sorts of Manure and Materials for repairing Roads...............	2	ditto.	ditto.
For all Lime, Chalk, Marl, Ashes, Peat, Clay, Bricks and Sand	3	ditto.	ditto.
For all Cinders, Coke, Culm and Charcoal, Tin, Copper Lead-ore, Lead in Pigs or Sheets, Iron-stone or Ore, Iron in Pigs, Bar-iron, Tiles, Slates, Flag-stone and other Stone........	4	ditto.	ditto.
For all Timber and other Goods, Wares and Merchandize	6	ditto.	ditto.

Fractions of a Quarter of a Ton or of a Mile to be taken as a Quarter.

The company are also authorized to receive the following tolls.

TOLLS.

	s.	d.
For every Horse, Mare, Gelding, Colt, Mule, Ass or other Beast, (not carrying or drawing any Goods which are liable to a Tonnage Rate) passing through any Toll Gate on the Tramroad..........	0	3 each.
For all Cows, and Horned or Neat Cattle (except Sheep and Swine)..	0	1 ditto.
For all Swine and Sheep	1	0 per Score.
For all Waggons and Carriages, carrying Persons for Hire, for each Passenger	0	1 per Mile.

The act provides that £6,000 shall be subscribed before the
work is commenced, and the railway to be completed in three
years.

The situation and other description of this railway will be
found under the article " Mamhilad Railway," in this work.

WARRINGTON AND NEWTON RAILWAY.

10 George IV. Cap. 37, Royal Assent 14th May, 1829.
11 George IV. Cap. 57, Royal Assent 29th May, 1830.

IN the year 1829 several landed-gentlemen and others interested in the trade of the town of Warrington and its neighbourhood, obtained an act for a railway or tramroad, to join the
Liverpool and Manchester Railway then in a course of execution,
and thereby to afford an easier conveyance than heretofore for
the import and export of goods to and from Warrington and the
adjacent places.   This act is entitled, ' An Act for making and
' maintaining a Railway or Tramroad from the Liverpool and
' Manchester Railway, at or near Wargrave Lane, in Newton-in-
' Mackerfield, to Warrington, in the county palatine of Lancaster,
' and Two collateral Branches to communicate therewith.'

By this act the proprietors are incorporated as " The War-
" rington and Newton Railway Company," with powers to execute the proposed work, and to enter lands, take materials, and
have all other privileges granted on similar occasions. They may
also construct bridges, tunnels, inclined planes, warehouses, wharfs
and all other necessary buildings, including steam engines, none of
which, however, are to be used without consuming their own
smoke. The road is not to pass nearer than twenty yards from
the Sankey Brook Canal, which canal the company is not to obstruct under penalties to be enforced by any two justices of the

peace for the county. The company may also purchase land for wharfs and warehouses on the line, to the extent of ten acres. For putting this act into execution, they are empowered to raise £53,000, in shares of £100 each ; and in case this sum should not prove sufficient for the completion of the work, they may borrow £20,000 additional on mortgage, paying interest half yearly. By this act the following are to be demanded as

TONNAGE RATES.

		d.	
For all Lime, Dung, Earth, Compost and all Sorts of Manure and Materials for Roads, drawn or propelled and carried by and at the Expense of the said Company	}	2	per Ton, per Mile.
For ditto only drawn or propelled by the Company	1¾	ditto.	ditto.
For ditto drawn or propelled and carried by other Persons..	1½	ditto.	ditto.
For all Coal, Coke, Culm, Charcoal, Cinders, Stone, Marl, Sand, Clay, Building, Pitching and Paving-stones, Flags, Bricks, Tiles, Slates, Lime, Earth, Staves, Deals, Lead and Iron in Pigs, or other Metals, drawn or propelled and carried by the Company	} 3	ditto.	ditto.
For ditto only drawn or propelled by ditto	2¼	ditto.	ditto.
For ditto drawn or propelled and carried by others..........	2	ditto.	ditto.
For all Timber, Cotton, Wool, Hides, Drugs, Dye-woods, Sugar, Corn, Grain, Flour, Manufactured Goods, Lead in Sheets, Iron in Bars, and all other Goods, Wares and Merchandize, drawn or propelled and carried by the Company	} 4	ditto.	ditto.
For ditto drawn or propelled by ditto.....................	3½	ditto.	ditto.
For ditto drawn or propelled and carried by others..........	3	ditto.	ditto.
For all other Goods, Wares, and Carriages for conveying Passengers or Cattle which shall pass any Inclined Plane, the Owners shall pay in addition to the above Rates, for every Inclined Plane thus passed over	} 6	ditto.	
For all Persons conveyed in Carriages drawn or propelled, and provided by the Company......................	} 3	each,	ditto.
For ditto not provided by ditto	2¼	ditto.	ditto.
For every Horse, Mule, Ass or other Beast of Draught or Burthen, carried in Carriages drawn or propelled and provided by the Company	} 3	ditto.	ditto.
For ditto not provided by ditto	2	ditto.	ditto.
For every Calf, Sheep, Lamb or Pig, carried in Carriages provided and drawn or propelled by the Company	} 1	ditto.	ditto.
For ditto not provided by ditto	½	ditto.	ditto.

Fractions of a Ton and a Mile to be paid for as the Quarters therein, and of a Quarter as a Quarter.

Carriages and Cattle employed in conveying Materials for Roads and Highways in the Township of Winwick-with-Hulme, or Hay, Straw, Corn in the Straw, Potatoes or other Produce of Land passing to the Barns or Lands of the Owners in the said Township, and other Things used in the said Township, or by the Rector thereof or his Tenants, are exempted from Tolls, provided they are not conveyed in the Carriages or by the Cattle of the Company.

The company may lower the said rates and raise the same again to the amount above quoted; they may also lease to the owners of mines on the line, the tolls of coals, &c. from their own mines, and they may generally let to farm, the tolls.

Small parcels not exceeding five hundred pounds in weight, are to be charged according to rates to be determined by the company. The act also empowers them to charge the following

WHARFAGE, WAREHOUSING AND CRANAGE RATES.

	s.	d.	
For all Coals, Culm, Lime-stone and other Minerals, Timber, Stone, Clay, Bricks, Tiles, Slates, Goods, Merchandize or other Things, landed on the Company's Wharfs and not continuing thereon more than Seventy-two Hours	0	1	per Ton.
For ditto above that Time in addition for Wharfage, for the first Week	0	1	ditto.
For ditto for Warehousing, for the first Week	0	6	ditto.

And for every succeeding Week the same Sums respectively for Wharfage and Warehousing.

	s.	d.	
For Cranage of any Weight not exceeding Two Tons at one Lift....	0	6	ditto.
For Cranage of Two Tons and less than Three Tons at one Lift	1	0	ditto.
For Cranage of three Tons and less than Four Tons at one Lift......	1	6	ditto.

And so on, advancing Sixpence per Ton on each additional Weight of One Ton, raised at one single Lift.

If the railway shall cross the Liverpool and Manchester Railway, the same shall be made under the direction of that company's engineer, and the engines of this company shall by no means interrupt those of the Liverpool and Manchester Railway; and if the Sankey Brook Canal Company shall, under the powers of their own act, determine on making a canal from their present works to Warrington, so as to cross this railway, either under or over, the point and mode of such crossing shall be determined by two engineers appointed, one by each company, whose opinion shall, if necessary, be subject to the decision of a third engineer, appointed umpire between them.

This railway commences on the south side of the railway between Liverpool and Manchester, at Wargrave Lane, in Newton-within-Mackerfield, in the county palatine of Lancaster, and proceeds to Dallum Lane, in Warrington; with a collateral branch, commencing at the intersection of Jockey Lane and Dallum Lane in Warrington, to Cockhedge Field, in the said township of Warrington; and a second collateral branch commencing at the said intersection of Jockey Lane and Dallum Lane, and terminating on the north side of the turnpike-road from Liverpool to Warrington, opposite Bankey or Bank Quay, all in the said county palatine of Lancaster. The length of the main line is about four miles and a quarter, and of the two branches little more than a mile. The line proceeds from Warrington, and is directly north, to Newton.

The act of the 11th George IV. was obtained for the purpose of enabling the proprietors to make a branch from the main line of their railway, where it crosses Newton Brook, to the north side of the Liverpool and Manchester Railway, near Newton Parks, so as to unite with the branch railway intended to be made from the borough of Wigan, where it joins the Liverpool and Manchester Railway.

The branch is one mile and a half in length, with a rise to the Liverpool and Manchester Railway of 49 feet 2 inches, at a point 56 feet 4 inches above the level of the bottom of the plinth course of Newton Viaduct. A deviation line of forty-two chains in length to the above-mentioned viaduct was contemplated, but subsequently abandoned.

Mr. Robert Stephenson is the engineer for this railway, and has estimated the expense of its construction at £7,008, which is to be advanced out of the funds of the original company; the power is here given them to borrow the further sum of £20,000 on mortgage of the undertaking.

The proprietors have taken the opportunity, afforded by the introduction of this bill, to obtain the repeal of a clause in the former act of 10th George IV. by which they were restrained from using locomotive engines on the estates of Thomas Lord Lilford and the Rector of Winwick, in the townships of Burtonwood and Winwick; and this is permitted in consequence of these gentlemen having been satisfied, from recent experiments, that no nuisance or annoyance can arise from their use.

By effecting a junction with the proposed Wigan Branch Railway, a direct communication will be made between the Wigan Great Coal Field and the populous town of Warrington; and it will afford a more expeditious transit for merchandize of every description into the populous districts on the line of this railway.

The work is as likely to answer the expectations of the proprietors as any speculation, of a similar description, lately entered upon.

WARWICK AND BIRMINGHAM CANAL.

33 George III Cap. 38, Royal Assent 6th March, 1793.
36 George III. Cap. 42, Royal Assent 24th March, 1796.

THIS canal commences at Saltisford, in the borough of Warwick, and from thence runs in a north-westerly direction, passing
Budbrook and Bowington, to Kingswood, where it is joined by
the Lapworth Branch of the Stratford-upon-Avon Canal; it then
pursues a northerly course, passing by Knowle and Henwood
Hall to Henwood Wharf, where it again turns off to the north-
west, and passing by Olton End and Kingsford, and crossing a
small part of Worcestershire, near Yardley, it joins the Digbeth
Branch of the Birmingham Canal at the town of Birmingham.

The act of parliament authorizing this undertaking was passed
in 1793, and is entitled, '*An Act for making and maintaining a*
'*navigable Canal from, or nearly from, a Place called The Saltis-*
'*ford, in the parish of Saint Mary, in the borough of Warwick,*
'*unto or near to the parish of Birmingham, in the county of War-*
'*wick, and to terminate at or near to a certain navigable Canal*
'*in or near to the town of Birmingham, called the Digbeth Branch*
'*of the Birmingham and Birmingham and Fazeley Canal Naviga-*
'*tions.*' It incorporates the subscribers by the name of " The
" Company of Proprietors of the Warwick and Birmingham
" Canal Navigation," and empowers them to raise amongst themselves, for the purposes of the act, the sum of £100,000, in one
thousand shares of £100 each, and if necessary, a further sum of
£30,000, and to take the following

TONNAGE RATES.

	s.	d.		
For all Coal, Stone, Iron, Timber and other Goods, conveyed less than Six Miles and passing any Lock	1	0	per Ton.	
For Six Miles and not exceeding Twelve	0	2	ditto, per Mile.	
For Twelve Miles and not exceeding Sixteen, and not passing through the Uppermost Lock at each End of the Upper Summit	2	0	ditto.	
For Sixteen Miles and Upwards, and not passing the said Locks	0	1½	ditto.	ditto.
For passing either of the said Locks	2	3	ditto.	
For passing from Birmingham towards Warwick, and passing the Upper Lock below Hatton Hill	2	9	ditto.	
For any Distance less than a Mile, and not passing a Lock	0	2	ditto.	
For One Mile and less than Six, and not passing any Lock	0	2	ditto.	ditto.

And in proportion for greater or less Quantities.
Lime and Lime-stone are to pay Two-thirds of the above Rates only.
Paving-stones, Gravel, Sand and other Materials for Roads; and Dung, Soil and other
Manure (except Lime and Lime-stone) for the Grounds of Persons whose Lands
have been taken for the Canal, and provided they do not pass any Lock unless the
Water shall flow over the Waste Weir, are exempted from these Rates.
Wharfage on Goods remaining more than Twenty-four Hours, is to be such Sum as the
Parties may agree on.

The act grants to the Birmingham Canal Company certain
tonnages for the permission to join their canal, which will be
found under the head of the " Birmingham Canal Navigations,"
in this work.

The act of parliament obtained by the Stratford-upon-Avon
Canal Company, to connect their canal with the Warwick and
Birmingham Canal, by the Lapworth Cut, also directs certain
rates to be paid by them to the proprietors of the Warwick and
Birmingham Canal, which will be found in the account of the
Stratford-upon-Avon Canal, as the clause is contained in that
canal act.

The length of this canal is twenty-two miles and a half : the
first half mile from its commencement at Saltisford, to near Budbrook, is level; thence to Hatton, two miles and a half, is a rise
of 146 feet by twenty locks; thence to the Stratford Branch, about
four miles, is level; thence to Knowle Common, about four miles
and a quarter, is level; thence to Knowle Wharf, a quarter of a
mile, is a rise of 42 feet by seven locks; thence to near Deritend,
about ten miles, is level; and thence to the Digbeth Branch of the
Birmingham Canal, about a mile, is a fall of 42 feet by five locks.
At the termination at Digbeth a stop-lock is erected, which the
Birmingham and Fazeley Company may fasten up, whenever the
water in this canal is of less depth than 4 feet at this lock.

At Haseley this canal passes through a tunnel of three hundred
yards in length; and there is another tunnel at Rowington ; at
Henwood Wharf it crosses the Blythe River, by an aqueduct;
near Flint Green it passes over the Cole River in the same manner; and there is a third aqueduct over the Rea River near its
termination at Digbeth.

A second act of parliament was obtained by this company in
1796, entitled, ' *An Act for enabling the Company of Proprietors*
' *of the Warwick and Birmingham Canal Navigation, to finish*

' and complete the same; and for amending the Act of Parliament
' passed in the Thirty-third Year of the Reign of his present
' Majesty, for making the said Canal,' which empowers the company to raise a further sum of £50,000 to carry on their work,
by a creation of one thousand half shares of £50 each.

This canal is one of the great lines of communication between
Lancashire and London; by its connection with the Oxford Canal,
through the Warwick and Napton, and thence with the Grand
Junction Canal, near Braunston, it not only opens a communication between London and Birmingham and the neighbouring
commercial towns, but is a means, by its other connections, of
conveying the trade between London, Liverpool and Manchester;
in addition to which, it affords a cheap and plentiful supply of coal
to Warwick, Leamington and the neighbourhood, and therefore
cannot fail to remunerate the proprietors.

WARWICK AND NAPTON CANAL.

34 George III. Cap. 38, Royal Assent 28th March, 1794.
36 George III. Cap. 95, Royal Assent 14th May, 1796.
49 George III. Cap. 72, Royal Assent 20th May, 1809.

THIS canal, commencing at the Warwick and Birmingham
Canal, in the parish of Budbrook, runs in an easterly direction,
leaving the city of Warwick on the south, and passing by
Leamington Prior's, Radford, Long Itchington and Stockton, it
joins the Oxford Canal near Napton-on-the-Hill. In its course,
which is about fourteen miles in length, it crosses the River Avon
near Warwick by an aqueduct bridge, and near Radford and
Long Itchington there are other smaller aqueducts.

The first act of parliament relating to this canal was passed in
1794, and entitled, ' An Act for making and maintaining a navi-
' gable Canal, out of, and from, the Warwick and Birmingham
' Canal now cutting, or intended to be cut, in the parish of Bud-
' brook, in the county of Warwick, into the Oxford Canal, in the
' parish of Braunston, in the county of Northampton.' It incorporates the subscribers to the undertaking, by the name of " The
" Company of Proprietors of the Warwick and Braunston Canal

2 T

" Navigation," and empowers them to raise amongst themselves, for the purposes of the act, the sum of £100,000, in one thousand shares of £100 each, and if necessary, a further sum of £30,000.

The course prescribed by this act was soon found to be inconvenient, the company of proprietors therefore obtained a second act of parliament in 1796, entitled, ' *An Act for authorizing the* ' *Company of Proprietors of the Warwick and Braunston Canal* ' *Navigation to vary the Course of a certain Part of the said* ' *Canal, and for amending and altering the Act made in the Thirty-* ' *fourth Year of the Reign of his present Majesty for making the* ' *said Canal,*' which authorized them to adopt the present line of the canal, and change the name of the company to that of " The " Company of Proprietors of the Warwick and Napton Naviga- " tion ;" and to take the following

TONNAGE RATES.

	s.	d.		
For all Coal and other Goods navigated less than Six Miles, and passing any Lock or Locks	1	0	per Ton.	
From Six and not exceeding Eight Miles................	0	2	ditto,	per Mile.
From Eight and not exceeding Thirteen Miles, for the first Eight Miles	0	2	ditto.	ditto.
After the Eighth Mile	0	1	ditto.	ditto
For all Coal or other Goods navigated along the whole of the Canal or any part thereof more than Thirteen Miles	0	1½	ditto.	ditto.
If such Goods do not pass a Lock	0	1½	ditto.	ditto.

Lime and Lime-stone only half the said Tonnage.

Fractions of a Mile to be taken as a Mile, and of a Quarter of a Ton as a Quarter.

Only Two-pence per Ton per Mile to be taken on Goods carried on this Canal, not exceeding Five Miles from the Warwick and Birmingham Navigation ; nor more than Three Half-pence per Ton per Mile for Free-stone, nor any Tonnage on empty Boats passing for the purpose of fetching Free-stone, or Boats laden with Manure for the Lands of Persons whose Ground has been taken for the Canal.

The first act of parliament contained certain clauses of tonnage rates in favour of the Oxford Canal Company, which by this act are repealed, and in lieu thereof, it is enacted :—

" That the proprietors of the Oxford Canal shall receive, *over and above* the rate of tonnage they are entitled to, on coal, goods, &c. passing on their canal by virtue of any act now in force, the following

RATES.

	s.	d.	
For all Coals navigated out of this Canal into the Oxford Canal (except such as shall be navigated into the Grand Junction Canal)	3	4	per Ton.
For all Goods navigated out of this Canal into the Oxford Canal, or out of the Oxford into this Canal, except such as shall be navigated into or out of the Grand Junction Canal, or from the Coventry Canal, or from any intermediate Place between the said Coventry Canal and this Canal, and also except Lime, Lime-stone and Manure..........	5	2½	ditto.

RATES CONTINUED.

	s.	*d.*	
For all Coal navigated out of this Canal into the Oxford Canal, and along the same into the Grand Junction Canal	2	9	per Ton.
For all Goods (except Coal, Lime, Lime-stone, and Manure) navigated out of this Canal into the Oxford Canal, and along the same into the Grand Junction Canal, or out of the Grand Junction Canal, into the Oxford Canal, and along the same into this Canal	4	4	ditto.

Coal navigated out of this Canal into the Oxford Canal towards Braunston, and laid down on the Banks of such Canal and not carried into the Grand Junction Canal, the usual Tonnage over and above the said Two Shillings and Nine-pence per Ton.

Goods (except Coal, Lime, Lime-stone and Manure) navigated out of this Canal into the Oxford Canal, and along the same towards Braunston, and laid down on the Banks of the said Oxford Canal, and not carried on the Grand Junction Canal, or from any Place on the Oxford Canal, between Braunston and Napton, along the Oxford Canal into this Canal, the usual Tonnage payable for such Goods, Wares and Merchandize (except as aforesaid) on such Canal, over and above the said Four Shillings and Four-pence per Ton.

	s.	*d.*	
Lime and Lime-stone navigated out of this Canal into the Oxford Canal, and whether along the same into the Grand Junction Canal or not...	0	6	per Ton.

This canal is upon the same level with the Warwick and Birmingham Canal at their junction at Budbrook, and is entitled to the waste water of that canal; but from thence to its junction with the Oxford Canal it rises 134¼ feet.

The last act of parliament obtained by this company was passed in 1809, and is entitled, ' *An Act for amending, altering and* ' *enlarging the Powers of the several Acts relating to the Warwick* ' *and Napton Canal Navigation.*' Its principal clause is explaining one in a former act, respecting vessels under twenty tons passing any of the locks, and providing that such vessels may pass them at all times on paying for twenty tons.

By executing this short canal from Warwick to Napton, another and a shorter line of communication is opened between London and Birmingham; besides affording a more direct conveyance for coal to supply the demands of the country connected with the Oxford and Grand Junction Canals, and the River Thames, to the great advantage of many large towns, as well as to the trade carried on between London and Birmingham.

WEALD OF KENT CANAL.

52 George III. Cap. 70, Royal Assent 5th May, 1812.

The act of parliament under sanction of which it was proposed to carry this work into execution, is entitled, ' *An Act for making* ' *and maintaining a navigable Canal from the River Medway,* ' *near Brandbridges, in the parish of East Peckham, in the county* ' *of Kent, to extend to, and unite with, the Royal Military Canal,* ' *in the parish of Appledore, in the said county; and also certain* ' *navigable Branches and Railways from the said intended Canal.*' It incorporates the subscribers by the name of " The Company of " Proprietors of the Weald of Kent Canal," and empowers them to raise amongst themselves, for the purposes of the act, the sum of £320,000, in shares of £100 each, of which sum, £305,800 is to be raised before the work is commenced, and three years is given to them to get this amount of subscription, which must be proved to have been done at the general quarter sessions. The company may raise a further sum of £160,000, if necessary, either amongst themselves, by creation of new shares, or by mortgage of the rates, and also take the following

TONNAGE RATES.

	d.		
For all Chalk, Lime, Marl, Dung, Compost or Manure, which shall pass any Lock......	1½	per Ton,	per Mile.
If not passing through a Lock	1	ditto.	ditto.
For all Coal, Culm and Coke	2	ditto.	ditto.
For all Sea Beach or Shingle......	1	ditto.	ditto.
For all Timber and all other Goods, Wares and Merchandize, passing through any Lock......	3	ditto.	ditto.
If not passing through a Lock	2	ditto.	ditto.

And in proportion for any greater or less Quantity or Distance; but Fractions of a Quarter in both cases to be taken as a Quarter.

The company are also authorized to take the following tolls for passing on the towing-path.

TOLLS.

	d.	
For every Horse, Mule or Ass (not drawing a Vessel) passing through any Toll Gate	1	each.
For every Drove of Oxen or Neat Cattle......	10	per Score.
For every Drove of Swine, Sheep or Lambs	5	ditto.

Vessels in Ballast only or light, to pay Three-pence per Ton per Mile; and all Vessels entering any Basins or Harbours, to pay Three-pence per Ton if they have not passed Ten Miles on the Canal.

Lords of manors or land-owners may erect wharfs, and take the following

RATES.

	d.
For all Coal, Lime, Stone, Clay, Iron, Iron-stone, Lead or any other Ore, Timber, Stone, Bricks, Tiles, Slate, Gravel, Hay, Straw, Corn in the Straw or Manure, for the first Month	1 per Ton.
For all other Goods, Wares and Merchandize, for Fourteen Days	2 ditto.

The act enables the company to make the canal from the River Medway at Brandbridges, through East Peckham, Yalding, Nettlestead, Brenchley, Horsmonden, Goudhurst, Marden, Staplehurst, Cranbrook, Trittenden, Biddenden, Strend Quarter, Holden, Middle Quarter, Tenterden, Ebony and Appledore, there to unite with the Royal Military Canal; also a collateral branch from Middle Quarter to Wye, in the county of Kent, with railways therefrom; and another collateral cut from Goudhurst to Hope Mill; and furthermore to make reservoirs and feeders for supplying the same with water.

This canal would open a communication from the River Thames at Gravesend, by the Thames and Medway Canal, and the River Medway, and by its junction with the Royal Military Canal, to all the places on the coast between Hythe and Winchelsea; thus avoiding the boisterous navigation round the North and South Forelands, as will be seen by reference to our map; but it has not been executed, and probably this delay arises from the restrictive clause which required a large sum to be raised before the work commenced.

WEAR RIVER.

3 Geo. I. C. — R. A. ——— 1716.	13 Geo. I. C. 6, R. A. 24th March, 1726.
20 Geo. II. C. 18, R. A. 17th June, 1747.	32 Geo. II. C. 64, R. A. 2nd June, 1759.
32 Geo. II. C. 65, R. A. 2nd June, 1759.	25 Geo. III. C. 26, R. A. ——— 1785.
49 Geo. III. C. 41, R. A. 12th May, 1809.	59 Geo. III. C. 106, R. A. 21st June, 1819.
11 Geo. IV. C. 49, R· A. 29th May, 1830.	

THIS river is navigable from its mouth to within a short distance of the city of Durham, whence it runs in a northerly direction, passing Finchale Abbey, and Lumley Castle, to Lambton Hall, and from thence turning to the north-east, it empties itself into the sea at Sunderland, being a distance of about eighteen miles.

The first act of parliament relating to this river was passed in 1716, and is entitled, ' *An Act for the Preservation and Improve-* ' *ment of the River Wear and Port and Haven of Sunderland, in* ' *the county of Durham.*' It appointed certain persons, commissioners to execute the powers of the act for a period of twenty-one years, and to take duties as therein specified, to commence from the 24th June, 1717.

In 1726 another act was passed, entitled, ' *An Act for the more* ' *effectual Preservation and Improvement of the Port and Haven of* ' *Sunderland, in the county of Durham,*' which continued the commissioners for a period of twenty-one years, and authorized them to build a pier or quay on the south side and at the mouth of the said river, and to make other improvements thereon.

The act passed in 1747, entitled, ' *An Act for the better Pre-* ' *servation and Improvement of the River Wear and Port and* ' *Haven of Sunderland, in the county of Durham,*' states that the pier authorized by the last act of parliament has been erected, but that it wants additional works ; and that the navigation of the river has become in a bad state, in consequence of the funds, arising from the tolls collected thereon, not being sufficient to keep it in a proper state of order and repair. The act, therefore, appoints new commissioners for a period of twenty-one years, and authorizes them to make the river navigable from Biddick Ford to New Bridge ; and for carrying these works into effect, they are empowered to borrow so much money as may be found necessary, by mortgage of the dues, which are as follow :—

DUES.

	d.
For every Chaldron of Coal or Cinders, to be paid by the Owner	$1\frac{1}{4}$
And to be paid by the Coal Factors or Fitters	$\frac{1}{2}$

The next act of parliament was passed in 1759, and is entitled, ' *An Act for making and completing the Navigation of the* ' *River Wear, from and including South Biddick, or Biddick Ford,* ' *in the county of Durham, to the city of Durham, and for repealing* ' *so much of the Act of the Twentieth Year of this Reign, as relates* ' *to making the said River navigable between the said Two Places* ' *called South Biddick, or Biddick Ford, and New Bridge in the* ' *county of Durham.*' It appoints certain persons therein named, commissioners, with powers to carry the provisions of the act into effect, and to take for the whole distance between Biddick Ford and Durham, the following

TONNAGE RATES.

	s.	d.	
For all Coal or Cinders	1	6	per Chaldron.
For all Lead, Lead-ore, Tar, Lime, Lime-stone, Slate, Flags, or other Stone, Bricks and Pantiles	1	0	per Ton.
For all Corn, Grain and Malt	4	0	per Last.
For Butter..	0	1	per Firkin.
For Manure	0	6	per Ton.
For all Unwrought Iron, Raft Deals, Boards and Timber	2	6	ditto.
For all other Goods, Wares and Merchandize	5	0	ditto.

And in proportion for greater or less Quantities, and for a less Distance.
Iron-stone for the Works of Mr. Cookson, at Whithill, only to pay Two-pence per Chaldron.

The commissioners may borrow money for the purposes of the work, and assign the tolls as security.

Land-owners and lords of manors may erect wharfs and ware-houses, and take such rates as may be agreed on.

Another act was passed at the same time as the one just re-cited, entitled, ' *An Act continuing, amending and rendering more* ' *effectual so much of an Act made in the Twentieth Year of the* ' *Reign of his present Majesty, as relates to the Port and Haven of* ' *Sunderland, and the River Wear, between South Biddick, or Bid-* ' *dick Ford, and the said Port and Haven,*' which appoints com-missioners, in addition to those appointed by the 20th George II. and who may be living, to improve the navigation of the river between Sunderland and Biddick Ford. It also continues the act of the 20th George II. in force for a further period of twenty-one years, and authorizes the commissioners to take the same rates, as are therein directed to be taken.

In 1785 another act was passed, entitled, ' *An Act for the* ' *better Preservation and Improvement of the River Wear and Port* ' *and Harbour of Sunderland,*' which, however, is repealed by an act we shall next notice, which was passed in 1809.

This act, entitled, ' *An Act for repealing an Act passed in the* ' *Twenty-fifth Year of the Reign of his present Majesty for the* ' *Improvement of the River Wear, and Port and Haven of Sunder-* ' *land, in the county of Durham, and for the more effectual Pre-* ' *servation and further Improvement of the same River, Port and* ' *Haven,*' in addition to the preceding act repeals all the foregoing

acts then in force, and after stating that there was a debt of
£5,800 remaining unpaid, authorizes the commissioners, who are
thereby appointed, to take the following

RATES.

	d.	
For all Coal and Cinders, (Seventy-two Winchester Bushels to a Chaldron) to be paid by the Coal Owners	4½	per Chaldron.
And the Fitters or Coal Factors	1½	ditto.

And a Rate of One Penny per Ton on all Vessels entering the Port of Sunderland
except from Stress of Weather.

And to borrow such sum of money as they may consider
necessary, on the credit of the above duties.

The commissioners of this navigation having erected light-
houses, are empowered to charge a rate of $\frac{1}{4}d.$ for every two tons
on vessels entering the port of Sunderland; but on those that take
refuge only in the said port, and do not take a cargo, $1\frac{1}{2}d.$ per
ton, to support the said light-houses.

The next act of parliament relating to this navigation was
passed in 1819, and is entitled, ' *An Act to explain and amend an*
' *Act of the Forty-ninth of his present Majesty, for repealing an*
' *Act of the Twenty-fifth Year of his present Majesty, for the Im-*
' *provement of the River Wear, and Port and Haven of Sunderland,*
' *in the county palatine of Durham; and for the more effectual*
' *Preservation and further Improvement of the same River, Port*
' *and Haven.*' It enables the commissioners to remove all obstructions on the navigation and the port of Sunderland, and to prevent
any future encroachments. The navigation to be surveyed by
Mr. John Rennie, under the authority of the Lords of the Admi-
ralty, and meer stones to be fixed defining its limits, to be called
the Quay Line, between which line and the river, no erection
whatever is to be made.

The celebrated iron bridge was erected over this river near
Sunderland, by R. Burdon, Esq. which is 236 feet span and 100
feet high above high-water-mark.

The act of the 11th George IV. relates chiefly to the river and
port of Sunderland, and is entitled, ' *An Act for the Improvement*
' *and Preservation of the River Wear, and Port and Haven of Sun-*
' *derland, in the county palatine of Durham,*' was obtained chiefly
with a view of remedying the defects of the previous acts, which
are therefore repealed.

The limits of this navigation and haven are from South Biddick or Biddick Ford, including the port and haven of Sunderland, as the same extends from Souter Point, two miles from Sunderland Bar to the north-east, into the sea to five fathoms at low water, and from thence in a supposed direct line till it falls opposite to a point called Ryhope Dean, two miles to the south.

To carry this act into execution, a great number of commissioners are appointed, whose qualification is to consist of real estate of the clear yearly value of £200, or a personal estate of £6,000; they are authorized to deepen and cleanse the said river; to enlarge the channel to the mouth thereof; to contract the entrance; build and repair piers, quays, capsterns, mooring-anchors, posts, landing-places, warehouses, and all other machinery, apparatus and works, for carrying on and maintaining the free navigation of this river; and for these purposes, authority is given to the commissioners to borrow any sum of money required, on security of the following

RATES AND DUTIES.

d.

For all Coals or Cinders brought to this River between South Biddick or Biddick Ford and Sunderland, and from any Staith within the limits of this Act; and for all Coals or Cinders brought to the said River between South Biddick and the City of Durham, every Coal Owner shall pay .... } 4½ per Chaldron of 72 Bushels.

Ditto to be paid by every Fitter or Coal Factor .... 1½   ditto.

EXEMPTION FROM DUTIES.

Cinders burnt from Coals, subject to the previous Duties, are exempt from the Duties hereby imposed for Cinders shipped for exportation or water-borne to any other Place; as also Coals consumed in making Salt, Glass, Glass Bottles, Vitriol, Copperas, Earthenware, Bricks, Tiles, and burning Lime-stone into Lime.

TONNAGE DUTY ON SHIPS USING THE PORT.

d.

For every Ship or Vessel entering the said Port (excepting for safety only and departing without taking any fresh loading) for each Voyage, not exceeding three in the Year .... } 1 per Ton, Register.

LIGHT-HOUSE AND REFUGE DUTY.

s. d.

For every Ship or other Vessel entering the said River or Port of Sunderland (in addition to the above Rates) once in every Voyage .... } 1   0

And for every Two Tons of the Burthen of such Ship or Vessel .... } 0   1¼

For every Ship entering for safety only and departing without taking any fresh loading .... } 0   1½ per Ton, Register.

Owners of Ships in the Lime Trade may compound for their Duties.
King's Ships are exempt.

The rights of the Lord Bishop of Durham to the beacon and anchorage dues of the port and haven of Sunderland, are protected by a clause at the end of the act.

The importance of this navigation arises from the export of coal, which abounds in its neighbourhood, and is conveyed to it by numerous railways, laid down by the proprietors of the different coal-works; the port of London and many large towns situate upon the Thames, as well as all the Eastern Coast, receiving a considerable portion of their supplies from the port of Sunderland.

WEAVER NAVIGATION.

7 Geo. I. C. 10, R. A. 23rd March, 1720.	7 Geo. II. C. 28, R. A. 16th April, 1734.
33 Geo. II. C. 49, R. A. 22nd May, 1760.	47 Geo. III. C. 82, R. A. 8th Aug. 1807.
6 Geo. IV. C. 29, R. A. 2nd May, 1825.	10 Geo. IV. C. 70, R. A. 22nd May, 1829.

The first act for making this river navigable, passed in the 7th George I. entitled, ' *An Act for making the River Weaver navi-* ' *gable from Frodsham Bridge to Winsford Bridge, in the county* ' *of Chester,*' empowering certain undertakers and trustees, and their successors, to execute the works; and when made, to take and receive 1s. 3d. per ton until the charges and expenses of making the same are satisfied, and afterwards only 1s. per ton. Forty bushels of rock salt or white salt, or eight barrels of sugar, each not being more than three hundred pounds weight, or two hogsheads of sugar of not more than one thousand two hundred pounds each, or three hogsheads of tobacco of not more than eight hundred pounds weight each; and that four tierces, each not being more than eight hundred pounds weight, shall be deemed a ton. Sixty-three cubic feet of coal, cannel coal, charcoal, coke and cinders, shall be a ton; that one hundred and twenty pounds weight of clay and flint, shall be taken for one hundred weight, and twenty of such hundred weights of clay to be a ton, and twenty-one of such hundred weights of flint shall be a ton. Fifty feet of round, and 40 feet of square oak, and 50 feet of fir, balk, poplar or other wood, shall be a ton; and one hundred and twenty pounds is rated to the hundred weight.

This act also directs, that after the works are finished and all the expenses paid, the clear produce of the rates shall be employed

in amending and repairing the public bridges and certain highways within the said county, and in such manner as the justices of
the peace at the quarter sessions shall yearly direct; and if there
should be a surplus over and above, such surplus shall, under the
directions of the magistrates, be applied towards the repairs of the
other highways within the county.

The undertakers acting under the 7th George I. having proceeded to carry the work into effect, had incurred a debt of
£20,500, when another act was passed in the 33rd George II.
entitled, ' *An Act to amend an Act passed in the Seventh Year of*
' *the Reign of his late Majesty King George the First, for making*
' *the River Weaver navigable, from Frodsham Bridge to Winsford*
' *Bridge, in the county of Chester, and for the more effectual pre-*
' *serving and improving the Navigation of the said River.*'

This act relieves the undertakers appointed by the 7th George
I. from their liability to the payments of the debt incurred by
them, and directs that all engagements and contracts, and all sums
of money owing, shall be discharged by the trustees appointed by
this act.

This act also directs that all the locks upon the navigation
shall, with all convenient speed, be made of the same dimensions
as the lock at Pickeren's, (they are now constructed 90 feet long
and 18 feet wide;) the act provides that the depth of water-way
shall be 4 feet 6 inches at the least for the whole course of the
navigation; but there is now 6 feet and upwards over the sills
of the different locks.

The navigation of the River Weaver having hitherto been
from the Mersey up the tideway to Frodsham Bridge, it was
found to be very inconvenient and dangerous; to remedy which,
an act was therefore passed in the year 1807, entitled, ' *An Act*
' *to authorize the Trustees of the River Weaver Navigation, to*
' *open a more convenient Communication betwixt the River near*
' *Frodsham Bridge and the River Mersey near Weston Point, in*
' *the township of Weston, in the county of Chester, and to amend*
' *Two Acts relative to the said River.*' A fourth act was passed
in the year 1825, entitled, ' *An Act to repeal certain Parts of, and*
' *to alter and amend an Act passed in the Forty-seventh Year of*
' *the Reign of his late Majesty King George the Third, to authorize*

' the Trustees of the River Weaver Navigation, to open a more
' convenient Communication between the said River near Frodsham
' Bridge and the River Mersey near Weston Point, in the township
' of Weston, in the county of Chester; and to amend Two Acts rela-
' tive to the said River.'

The fifth act was obtained in the 10th year of his present
Majesty, entitled, ' An Act to alter, amend, enlarge and consoli-
' date certain of the Powers and Provisions of the said Acts passed
' relating to the River Weaver Navigation, in the county pala-
' tine of Chester;' in this act, after stating that the trustees under
the power vested in them by the 47th George III. had made and
completed the cut or canal, from the River Weaver to Weston
Point, and that they had also formed, at considerable expense, a
basin, piers, light-house and other works, it is provided that the
said cut or canal, basin, piers, quays, &c. are declared to be a
branch of the River Weaver, but that no rates shall be taken in
respect thereof.

It is provided by the 7th George I. that no tonnage shall be
taken betwixt Frodsham Bridge and a place called Pickeren's
Boat on the River Weaver, except at such times and seasons as the
said river shall not be then navigable without the help of a lock.

The total length of this navigation from Winsford Bridge to
the tideway at Weston Point, is twenty-two miles, five furlongs
and one hundred and sixty-eight yards; there is also a branch
from Witton Brook Lock to Witton Bridge of six furlongs; and
another branch from the canal to a little below Frodsham Bridge
of four furlongs; making the whole length of navigation twenty-
three miles, seven furlongs and one hundred and sixty-eight yards,
with twelve locks, and a total fall of 50 feet from Winsford Bridge
to low water in the tideway at Weston Point.

The general trade upon this navigation is salt, rock salt, coal,
timber, corn, cotton, &c. and lately a considerable trade has been
established in the carriage of flint and clay to the Staffordshire
Potteries.

From the great increase of trade in this part of the country,
the annual receipt for dues on the navigation is said to amount to
upwards of £20,000.

WELLAND RIVER.

13 Elizabeth, Cap. 1, Royal Assent ———— 1571.
12 George III. Cap. 103, Royal Assent 21st May, 1772.
34 George III. Cap. 102, Royal Assent 23rd May, 1794.

THIS river rises about five miles north of Market Harborough, in Leicestershire, and proceeding by Rockingham Castle, winds in a north-easterly course to Stamford, in Lincolnshire, up to which place it is made navigable from the sea; thence it runs in an easterly course to Market Deeping; whence, turning south-easterly, it proceeds, about three miles; then bending to the north-east and passing near Crowland and Spalding, it empties itself into the Wash.

The first act of parliament relating to this river was passed in 1571, and is entitled, ' *An Act for making the River of Welland,* ' *in the county of Lincoln, navigable.*' A second passed in 1772, entitled, ' *An Act for the better Preservation of the Great Bank of* ' *the River Welland, &c.*' the clauses of which it is not necessary here to enumerate, as the principal act, to which we have to refer, was obtained in 1794, under the title of ' *An Act for improving* ' *the Outfall of the River Welland, in the county of Lincoln;* ' *and for the better Drainage of the Fen Lands, Low Grounds and* ' *Marshes, discharging their Waters through the same into the* ' *Sea; and for altering and improving the Navigation of the said* ' *River Welland, by means of a new Cut, to commence below a* ' *certain Place called the Reservoir, and to be carried from thence* ' *through the inclosed Marshes and open Salt Marshes into Wyber-* ' *ton Road, between the Port of Boston and a Place called the* ' *Scalp; and for disposing of the Bore or White Sands adjoining* ' *to the said River; and for building a Bridge over the said Cut.*'

This act appoints three persons therein named, commissioners for executing the purposes of this act, with power to borrow money on the credit of the taxes and pontage, and to take the following

TONNAGE RATES.

	s.	d.	
For all Coal	0	6	per Chaldron.
For all Oats and Malt	1	0	per Last.
For all Wheat, Rye, Barley, Barley Big, Beans, Peas, Cole, Linseed, Hempseed and Mustard-seed	1	0	per Half Last.

TONNAGE RATES CONTINUED.

	s.	d.	
For all Iron, Salt, Lead, Rags, Tobacco, Pipe-clay, Pebbles or Cobbles, Reed, Sedge, Hay, Flax, Hemp or Turves .... }	1	0	per Ton.
For all Currants	1	0	per Butt.
For all Lime and Grindstones	1	0	per Chaldron.
For every Two Pipes, Three Hogsheads or Puncheons, Eight Barrels or Half Hogsheads of Wine or other Liquor .... }	1	0	
For every Eight Packs of Wool; Sixteen Kilderkins, Thirty-two Firkins, Quarter Barrels and Bushels of Sand ; every Five Hundred Pantiles or Paving-Tiles, Five Hundred of Bricks, Twenty Feet of Stone, One Hundred Battens and Half Hundred of Deals .... }	1	0	
For all other Goods, Wares and Merchandize	1	0	per Ton.

The cut contemplated by this act of parliament is to commence at Hooton's Gibbet, and running across the Salt Marshes, to terminate in the Wyberton Road, as near as may be to the Ship Ale-House. It is not to be less than 50 feet wide at the bottom, with a batter of two to one. The south bank is to have 60 feet at the base, 30 feet at the top and 11 feet of perpendicular height ; and the north bank to be 30 feet at the base, 6 feet at the top and 11 feet in height. The threshold of the sea sluice at Wyberton Road is to be laid 1 foot under low-water-mark; the water-way of the sluice 50 feet wide, and adjoining to it there is to be a lock 8 feet wide and 60 feet long, for the use of vessels.

This navigation is highly beneficial for the import of coals, deals, timber, groceries, &c. for the use of the country through which it passes ; and in return it takes the Ketten Freestone, Collyweston White Slates, and malt from Stamford, besides corn and other agricultural products of the country.

WEST LOTHIAN RAILWAY.

6 George IV. Cap. 169, Royal Assent 22nd June, 1825.

This railway commences at the Edinburgh and Glasgow Union Canal, near Ryhall, in the parish of Uphall, and proceeds south-westerly to Houston, where a branch goes off to the Silver Mines ; it is then continued to Howden, where another branch runs off to Balbardie; the main line, passing Whiteburn, proceeds to Shotts, where it terminates.

The act of parliament authorizing this undertaking, is entitled, ' An Act for making and maintaining a Railway from the Edin-

' *burgh and Glasgow Union Canal at or near Ryhall, in the parish*
' *of Uphall, to Whiteburn, and other places, in the counties of Lin-*
' *lithgow and Lanark.*' It incorporates the subscribers by the name
of " The West Lothian Railway Company," and empowers them
to raise amongst themselves, for the purposes of the act, the sum
of £40,700, in shares of £50 each, and, if necessary, a further
sum of £20,000 by mortgage of the tolls, and authorizes them to
take the following

TONNAGE RATES.

	d.
For all Goods, Wares and Merchandize whatever	3 per Ton, per Mile.

Fractions of a Hundred Weight to be taken as a Hundred Weight, of a Ton and a Mile
as the Quarters therein, and of a Quarter as a Quarter.

The company may also establish carriages for the conveyance
of passengers and parcels, and charge the following

FARES AND RATES.

	d.
For each Passenger	2 per Mile.
For Parcels	¼ per Pound, per Mile.

Owners of lands on the line may erect wharfs and warehouses,
and on their refusal the company may do it, and take the following

WHARFAGE RATES.

	d.
For all Coal, Culm, Lime, Lime-stone, Clay, Iron-stone, Stone, Bricks, } Gravel, Hay, Corn in the Straw, Straw or Manure, for Six Months }	½ per Ton.
For all Iron, Lead ore or any other Ore, Tin, Timber, Tiles and Slates	1 ditto.
For any other Goods, Wares and Merchandize	2 ditto.

And for a longer Period than Six Months, a Rate of a Farthing per Ton per Month for
the first Species of Goods enumerated above; a Half-penny per Ton per Month for
the second Species, and a Penny per Ton per Month for the last Species.

The estimate for completing this railway and branches, as
made by Mr. H. Baird, civil engineer, in 1824, is as follows:—

	£.	s.	d.
Basin at Canal, 150 yards by 21........	1,070	0	0
Main Line	35,513	15	4
Silver Mines Branch	9,386	5	0
Balbardie ditto	8,916	0	0
Total...........	54,886	0	4

The length of this railway is about fifteen miles, with a rise of 522 feet; the Silver Mines Branch is four miles and seven chains in length, with a rise of 410 feet; and the Balbardie Branch is four miles and four chains, with a rise of 69 feet.

WESTERN SHIP CANAL.

(SEE GRAND WESTERN CANAL.)

WEY RIVER.

23 Charles II. Cap. 26, Royal Assent 22nd April, 1671.
33 George II. Cap. 45, Royal Assent 15th April, 1760.

This river has its source near Alton, in Hampshire, from whence it runs in a north-easterly course to Farnham; it there turns to a south-easterly direction, passing Waverley Abbey, not far from which it is joined by another branch which rises near Selbourne, and passes by Pierpoint Lodge; thence continuing its course easterly, it reaches Godalming, where it becomes navigable; and thence continuing in a direction a little to the eastward of north, it is joined by the Wey and Arun Canal near Shalford Powder Mills; it afterwards passes by Guildford, Stoke Place, Sutton Place, Wisley, Byfleet and Woburn Park, to its termination in the River Thames; the greater part of the distance from Sutton Place to Byfleet, near which town it is joined by the Basingstoke Canal, is an artificial navigation.

The first act of parliament respecting this river was passed in 1671, and is entitled, ‘ *An Act for settling and preserving the* ‘ *Navigation of the River Wey, in the county of Surrey.*’

In 1760 another act was passed, entitled, ‘ *An Act for extend-* ‘ *ing and continuing the Navigation of the River Wey, otherwise* ‘ *Wye, in the county of Surrey, to the town of Godalming, in the* ‘ *said county,*’ which states that the River Wey is already navigable as far as the town of Guildford, and that great advantages will accrue from its being made navigable as far up as the town of Godalming, and the act appoints commissioners for extending the navigation from the Town-Wharf, below Guildford Bridge, to the said town of Godalming, and authorizes their taking the following tonnage rates.

TONNAGE RATES.

	s.	d.	
For all Timber, Corn, Meal, Flour and other Goods, Wares and Merchandize, (except Chalk, Woollen Rags and other Kinds of Manure) carried upon the Cut from Godalming to Guildford, and lower down than the Wharf at Stone Bridge Brook	1	9	per Ton.
For all Chalk, Woollen Rags or other Kinds of Manure	0	9	ditto.
For all Coal	1	6	per Chaldron.
For the Goods, first mentioned, from Godalming to the Wharf at Stone Bridge Brook	1	6	per Ton.
For all Chalk, Woollen Rags or other Kinds of Manure	0	6	ditto.
For all Coal	1	3	per Chaldron.

The commissioners may borrow such sums as shall be necessary for executing the work, on security of the above tolls.

The length of this river from its junction with the Thames at Godalming, is nearly twenty miles, with a rise to Guildford of $68\frac{1}{2}$ feet; and from Guildford to Godalming $32\frac{1}{2}$ feet.

The keeping of this river navigable is of great service to the towns of Godalming and Guildford, in the conveyance of their chalk, corn and other agricultural products to London, and by furnishing in return supplies of coals, deals, timber and groceries; whilst by its junction with the Wey and Arun and Basingstoke Canals, its connections are extended into Hampshire and Sussex.

WEY AND ARUN JUNCTION CANAL.

53 George III. Cap. 19, Royal Assent 19th April, 1813.

THIS canal commences at the River Wey, near Shalford Powder Mills, between Guildford and Godalming; thence running south, it passes Wonerst Park, Ridinghurst and Lockswood, to New Bridge, where it joins the Arun Navigation, after completing a course of nearly eighteen miles.

This canal was executed under authority of an act of parliament passed in 1813, entitled, ' *An Act for making and maintain-* ' *ing a navigable Canal, to unite the Rivers Wey and Arun, in the* ' *counties of Surrey and Sussex,*' which incorporates the subscribers thereto, by the name of " The Company of Proprietors of " the Wey and Arun Junction Canal," and empowers them to raise amongst themselves, for the purposes of the act, the sum of £90,500, in nine hundred and five shares of £100 each, and, if necessary, a further sum of £9,500, either amongst themselves or by mortgage of the tolls and rates; they are also to demand the following tonnage rates.

2 U

TONNAGE RATES.

	s.	d.	
For all Dung, Ashes, Chalk, Marl, Lime and Lime-stone, intended for Manure, and all Manure..................	0	2	per Ton, per Mile.
For all Chalk, Marl, Lime and Lime-stone and all other Goods and Merchandize	0	4	ditto. ditto.
For all Vessels with not more than Six Tons of Manure, or Four Tons of any other lading, passing through any Locks	1	0	
For all Passengers in Vessels	0	2	per Mile each.
For every Package not exceeding Two Hundred Weight ..	0	1	per Mile.

Fractions of a Ton to pay as the Quarters therein, and of a Quarter as a Quarter; Fractions of a Mile as Half a Mile.

Lords of manors and owners of land on the line may erect wharfs, and on their refusing, the company may erect them and take the following

WHARFAGE RATES.

	d.
For all Coal, Culm, Lime-stone, Clay, Iron, Iron-stone, Lead-ore or any other Ores, Timber, Stones, Bricks, Tiles, Slates, Gravel, Hay, Straw, Corn in the Straw or Manure, not remaining above Twenty-eight Days	3 per Ton.
For all other Goods, Wares and Merchandize, not exceeding Ten Days	2 ditto.
For every Day exceeding the above Times, on any Description of Goods whatever	1 ditto.

The Tolls on the Arun Navigation on Goods passing from Arundel Port through this Canal into the River Wey, to be reduced to One Shilling per Ton.

Ten years are allowed for completing this canal; which, with its towing-path, &c. is to be twenty yards in breadth.

This canal, by connecting the Arun Navigation with the River Wey, which communicates with the Thames, affords an inland line of navigation from London to the sea at Arundel Harbour; and by the execution of the Portsmouth and Arundel Canal, a connection will be opened by the same line to Portsmouth. The benefits to the country through which it passes, and to the great depot at Portsmouth, are so obvious as to require no further remark.

WIGAN BRANCH RAILWAY.

11 George IV. Cap. 56, Royal Assent 29th May, 1830.

THIS railway commences at Wallgate-Street, in the town of Wigan, and pursues a southwardly course across Chapel Lane, the River Douglas, and over the Leeds and Liverpool Canal at the lock No. 21, and thence across the Leigh Branch of the said canal at Dobb's Bridge; thence by Bamforlong, Golborne Smithy, Golborne Park, to its termination at the Liverpool and Manchester Railway, near Parkside Lane Bridge, about a mile and a half east of the town of Newton. The length is six miles, four furlongs and four chains; the first mile and two chains of which from Wigan rises 5 feet; in the next six furlongs and eight chains there is a descent of 11 feet; then a gradual rise of 18 feet in the next distance of two miles, five furlongs and four chains; thence to the Liverpool and Manchester Railway, a fall of 25 feet. A branch is to commence from the main line a mile east of Wigan, which proceeds in a north-easterly direction by Ince Green; thence along the north side of the Lancaster Canal to the road leading from Wigan to Aspull Moor, and near to New Springs or Bark Hill Bridge, where it terminates. Its length is two miles, four furlongs and eight chains, with a rise of 42 feet in the first length of one mile, one furlong and seven chains from the main line; thence to the road leading to Kirklees Engine, which is three quarters of a mile, there is a further rise of 132 feet; and to its termination a further ascent of 15 feet. The line in communicating with the Liverpool and Manchester Railway, opens something like the top of the letter Y, thereby enabling waggons or other carriages the better to communicate with the line of the last-mentioned railway; the part towards Liverpool is forty-two chains in length, while the one towards Manchester is only thirty-three chains. The works designed by Mr. C. B. Vignoles, in 1829, were estimated at £70,000.

The act authorizing the execution of this railway received his late Majesty's assent on the 29th May, 1830, and is entitled, ' *An* ' *Act for making and maintaining a Railway from the borough of* ' *Wigan to the Liverpool and Manchester Railway, in the borough* ' *of Newton, in the county palatine of Lancaster, and collateral* ' *Branches to communicate therewith.*' The subscribers, consisting of nineteen persons only, amongst whom was Sir Robert Holt Leigh, Bart. were incorporated as " The Wigan Branch Railway " Company," with power to raise amongst themselves the sum of £70,000, in seven hundred shares of £100 each, and if necessary, an additional sum of £17,500 on credit of the undertaking. The powers of the act are to cease in seven years, as to the parts then remaining unexecuted. The distance between the inside edges of the rails to be 4 feet 8 inches; the outside 5 feet 1 inch. The communication with the Liverpool and Manchester Railway to be made under the direction of the engineer of that company, and three passing places, at the least, to be on every mile of the proposed railway.

TONNAGE RATES.

	d.	
For all Lime-stone, Dung and all Sorts of Manure, and Coal-slack, drawn or propelled by the Engines or other power, and carried in the Waggons of any Person or body Corporate, other than by the said Company	1	per Ton, per Mile.
For ditto, if only drawn or propelled by and at the expense of the Company, or only carried in their Waggons	1½	ditto. ditto.
For ditto, if drawn or propelled and carried by and at the expense of the Company	2	ditto. ditto.
For all Coal and Lime, and all Materials for making and repairing of Public Roads, drawn or propelled by the Engines or other power, and carried in the Waggons of any Person or body Corporate, other than by the said Company	1¼	ditto. ditto.
For ditto, if only drawn or propelled by and at the expense of the Company, or only carried in their Waggons	1¾	ditto. ditto.
For ditto, if drawn or propelled and carried by and at the expense of the Company	2¼	ditto. ditto.
For all Coke, Charcoal, Cinders, Stones, Sand, Clay, Building, Pitching and Paving-stones, Flags, Bricks, Tiles and Slates, drawn or propelled by the Engines or other power, and carried in the Waggons of any Person or body Corporate, other than by the said Company	2	ditto. ditto.
For ditto, if only drawn or propelled by and at the expense of the Company, or only carried in their Waggons	2½	ditto. ditto.
For ditto, if drawn or propelled and carried by and at the expense of the Company	3	ditto. ditto.
For all Sugar, Corn, Grain, Flour, Dye-woods, Timber, Staves, Deals, Lead, Iron and other Metals, drawn or propelled by the Engines or other power, and carried in the Waggons of any Person or body Corporate, other than by the said Company	2½	ditto. ditto
For ditto, if only drawn or propelled by and at the expense of the Company, or only carried in their Waggons	3	ditto. ditto.
For ditto, if drawn or propelled and carried by and at the expense of the Company	3½	ditto. ditto.
For all Cotton and other Wool, Hides, Drugs, Manufactured Goods and all other Wares, Merchandize and Things whatever, drawn or propelled by the Engines or other power, and carried in the Waggons of any Person or body Corporate, other than by the said Company	3	ditto. ditto.
For ditto, if only drawn or propelled by and at the expense of the Company, or only carried in their Waggons	3½	ditto. ditto.
For ditto, if drawn or propelled and carried by and at the expense of the Company	4	ditto. ditto.

TOLLS FOR COACHES AND OTHER CARRIAGES CARRYING PASSENGERS OR CATTLE.

	s.	d.	
For every Person passing in or upon any such Carriage, not drawn nor propelled nor provided by and at the expense of the Company	1	6	for any Distance.
For every Horse, Mule, Ass or other Beast of Draught or Burthen, and for every Ox, Cow, Bull or other Cattle carried as above	0	4	per Mile.
For every Calf, Sheep, Lamb or Pig conveyed as above	0	9	for any Distance.

TOLLS CONTINUED.

For all Persons, Cattle or other Animals passing in or upon any such Carriage, either drawn or propelled or provided by and at the expense of the said Company, such reasonable Charge as shall from Time to Time be determined by the said Company, who are not compelled to receive less than Sixpence per Ton for short Distances. Fractions to be taken as for a Quarter of a Mile and Quarter of a Ton.

WEIGHTS ALLOWED TO BE CARRIED.

d.

No Waggon or other Carriage to carry at one Time, including the Weight of such Carriage, more than Four Tons Weight, except in any one Piece of Timber, Block or Stone, Boiler, Cylinder, Bob or single Piece of Machinery, or other single Article, which nevertheless shall not exceed Eight Tons, and for which the Company may Claim .... } 4 per Ton, per Mile.

And no Piece of Timber, Stone, &c. weighing Eight Tons, including the Carriage, shall pass at all without the special Licence of the Company.

Lords of manors and owners of ground may erect wharfs, staiths, depots, landing places, cranes, weigh-beams or warehouses, and charge the same rates as the company are entitled to do, which are as follow ;—

WHARFAGE RATES.

s. d.

For all Coals, Culm, Lime, Lime-stone and other Minerals, Timber, Stone, Clay, Bricks, Tiles, Slates, Goods, Merchandize or other Things, loaded, landed or placed in or upon any of the Wharfs, and continuing a longer Space than Two Hours and not exceeding Twenty-four .... } 0 1 per Ton.
If they remain more than Twenty-four Hours, the further Sum per Week for Wharfage of... } 0 3 ditto.
And for the Warehousing for the above Period.................... 1 0 ditto.

And One Shilling per Ton for every further Week such Goods shall remain upon the Wharfs or in the Warehouses.

CRANAGE RATES.

s. d.

For every single Lift of the Crane, being less than Two Tons .... 0 6 per Ton.
Of Two Tons and less than Three .... 1 0 ditto.
Of Three Tons and less than Four .... 1 6 ditto.

And Sixpence on each additional Weight of One Ton, to be raised at one single Lift of the Crane.

The opening of this railway, and its connection with the Liverpool and Manchester and Warrington and Newton Railways, will have a very beneficial effect on the rich mineral district through which it passes; besides providing the public with a cheap and expeditious conveyance for passengers, coal and merchandize, between the populous towns of Wigan, Warrington, Liverpool, Manchester, and various other places.

WILTS AND BERKS CANAL.

35 Geo. III. C. 52, R. A. 30th April, 1795.   41 Geo. III. C. 68, R. A. 20th June, 1801.
50 Geo. III. C. 148, R. A. 2nd June, 1810.   53 Geo. III. C. 68, R. A. 3rd June, 1813.
55 Geo. III. C. 6, R. A. 23rd Mar. 1815.   2 Geo. IV. C. 97, R. A. 8th June, 1821.

This canal, which is of great importance to that part of the country through which it passes, commences in the River Thames, at the south side of the town of Abingdon; thence passing in a south-westerly direction by Drayton and Kingsgrove Commons, to Breach Field, where a short branch proceeds from it to the town of Wantage; thence continuing westward to Challow, passing Sparsholt and Uffington to Longcot Common, where there is another short branch to Longcot Wharf; continuing its course, it passes near Beckett House, Shrivenham, Bourton, Marsden, and Stratton, to the wharf at Swindon; a short distance from which is Eastcott, where the branch, originally called the North Wilts Canal, proceeds from it, and joins the Thames and Severn Canal near Cricklade; the main line, keeping its westerly direction, passes Chaddington, Wootton Bassett, Tockenham Wick, Lyneham and Dauntsey Park; then bending southerly, it passes Foxham, Bencroft, and Stanley House, a little beyond which is a branch to Calne; passing the river by an aqueduct, it then continues its southerly course, leaving Bowood, the Marquis of Lansdowne's Seat, to the left, to Derry Hill, where a branch goes off to Chippenham; pursuing its course it runs by Laycock Abbey and Melksham, to Semington, where it unites with the Kennet and Avon Canal.

The first act of parliament respecting this canal was passed in 1795, and is entitled, ' *An Act for making and maintaining a navi-* ' *gable Canal from the River Thames or Isis, at or near the town* ' *of Abingdon, in the county of Berks, to join and communicate with* ' *the Kennet and Avon Canal, at or near the town of Trowbridge,* ' *in the county of Wilts; and also certain navigable Cuts therein* ' *described.*' It incorporates the subscribers by the name of " The " Company of Proprietors of the Wilts and Berks Canal Naviga- " tion;" empowers them to raise amongst themselves, for the purposes of the act, the sum of £111,900, in eleven hundred and nineteen shares of £100 each, and, if necessary, a further sum of £150,000, either amongst themselves or by mortgage of the tolls and rates; and directs that five per cent. interest shall be paid to the subscribers until the work is completed, and authorizes their taking the following

TONNAGE RATES.

	d.	
For all Hay, Straw, Dung, Peat and Peat Ashes, Chalk, Marl, Clay, Sand, Lime for Manure, and all other Manure and Materials for Roads	$\frac{1}{2}$ per Ton, per Mile.	
For all Coal, Culm, Coke, Cinders, Charcoal, Iron-stone, Pig-iron, Iron-ore, Copper-ore, Lead-ore, Lime, (except for Manure) Lime-stone and other Stone, Bricks and Tiles ..	$1\frac{1}{2}$ ditto.	ditto.
For all Corn and other Grain, Flour, Malt, Meal, Timber, Bar-iron and Lead	2 ditto.	ditto.
For all other Goods, Wares and Merchandize whatever......	$2\frac{1}{2}$ ditto.	ditto.

And in proportion for any greater or less Quantity or Distance; Fractions of a Quarter of a Ton to pay as a Quarter, and any Fraction less than Half a Mile as a Half Mile.

Barges passing any Lock, when the Water does not flow over the Waste Weir, with any of the Goods, first enumerated, on Board, to pay One Penny per Ton per Mile in addition to the Half-penny hereinbefore charged. Goods remaining on Wharfs more than Forty-eight Hours, to pay such Rates as may be agreed on.

Boats under Twenty Tons to pay for Twenty Tons when passing a Lock.

The rates to be exempted from taxes until the annual dividend on shares shall be five per cent.

The canal to be completed in seven years; and if the Kennet and Avon Canal Company obtain an act for bringing their canal to the Wilts and Berks at Semington, then that portion of the Wilts and Berks Canal from Semington to Lady Down, to be transferred to the former company.

In 1801 another act was passed, entitled, '*An Act for enabling* '*the Company of Proprietors of the Wilts and Berks Canal Navi-* '*gation, to raise Money for completing the said Canal, and to* '*alter, explain and amend the Act passed in the Thirty-fifth Year* '*of the Reign of his present Majesty, for making the said Canal,*' which authorizes the company to raise a further sum of £200,000, by creation of new shares and by optional notes.

Another act was obtained in 1810, which contains only a few clauses respecting the application of money; besides repealing that clause of the first act, restricting the conveyance of coal below Reading, and allows it to be conveyed as far as Staines Bridge.

The act of 1813, is entitled '*An Act for explaining and amend-*
'*ing an Act of his present Majesty, for making a navigable Canal*
'*from the River Thames or Isis, near Abingdon, in the county of*
'*Berks, to join the Kennet and Avon Canal, near Trowbridge, in*
'*the county of Wilts, and certain navigable Cuts.*' It merely
makes some regulations respecting the water to be taken at
Beckett.

In 1815 the company obtained another act, entitled, '*An Act to*
'*enable the Company of Proprietors of the Wilts and Berks Canal*
'*Navigation, to raise Money for discharging the Debts of the said*
'*Company,*' which authorized them to raise an additional sum of
£100,000 for the purpose of paying off their debts and making a
reservoir.

The last act of parliament obtained by this company, was
passed in 1821, and is entitled, '*An Act for incorporating the*
'*Company of Proprietors of the North Wilts Canal Navigation*
'*with the Company of Proprietors of the Wilts and Berks Canal*
'*Navigation; and for repealing the several Acts passed for*
'*making and maintaining the said Canals, and for consolidating*
'*the Powers and Provisions thereof in One Act.*' This act states
that the North Wilts Canal was executed under authority of an
act of parliament passed in 1813; that the principal proprietors
in it were also proprietors of the Wilts and Berks Canal, and that
it had been in consequence considered desirable to incorporate
the two canals, which the present act does; it repeals all the
former acts of parliament, and embodies the different clauses,
contained in them, in the present act, without alteration of any,
relating to either the Wilts and Berks or North Wilts Canals; the
tonnage rates and other clauses relating to the latter of which,
will be found in this work under the head of "North Wilts
"Canal."

The number of shares in this canal by different creations now
amounts to twenty thousand; the original subscription was £100
per share; but as money has been wanted to continue the work,
shares have been created at various prices from £60 downwards,
and the last creation was ten thousand at £5 per share.

The length of this canal is fifty-two miles. That part of the
River Thames, where this canal locks into it, is 180⅓ feet above

the level of the sea; from the commencement of the canal to the Wantage River, a distance of seven miles and three quarters, is a rise of $96\frac{1}{2}$ feet; from thence to the east end of the summit level, fifteen miles, is a rise of $71\frac{1}{2}$ feet; the length of the head level is nine miles and three-eighths; from the west end of the head level, near Wootton Bassett, to the branch to Calne, is ten miles and three quarters, with a fall of 130 feet; from thence to the Chippenham Branch one mile and a half with 17 feet fall; and from thence to its junction with the Kennet and Avon Canal at Semington, is seven miles and three-eighths, with a fall of 54 feet. The Wantage Branch is nearly three quarters of a mile in length, and level; the Longcot Branch is nearly half a mile, and level; the branch (heretofore North Wilts Canal) from Eastcote to join the Thames and Severn Canal at Latton, is eight miles and three furlongs, with a fall to Latton, of 58 feet 8 inches; the branch to Calne is three miles and one-eighth long, with a rise of 21 feet; and the branch to Chippenham is nearly two miles, and level.

This canal furnishes coal from the Radstock and Paulton Mines in Somersetshire, which is the means of supplying with fuel the whole district through which it passes, besides affording a good supply of coal to Abingdon and other towns situate on the borders of the Thames; and, on the other hand, enables the agriculturist to export his corn, as well as the cheese for which North Wiltshire is so much celebrated, to both the London and Bristol Markets; it is also the means of conveying building-stone from the quarries in the neighbourhood of Bath to London, and forms one of the lines of communication between London and Bristol; whilst by its junction with the Thames, it is connected with all the midland counties, and by the Severn with Wales and the counties of Gloucester and Worcester; thereby affording an easy and expeditious transit for coal from the Forest of Dean into the counties of Wilts, Berks and Oxford, together with various places on the borders of the Thames. By an inspection of our map, it will be seen that this canal is an important link in the chain of our inland navigations.

Mr. Whitworth was the engineer, under whose direction these works were executed; and that part at first called the North Wilts, was executed for a less sum than the original estimate.

WISBECH CANAL.

34 George III. Cap. 92, Royal Assent 9th May, 1794.

THIS canal commences in the Nene River, at Wisbech, in the county of Cambridge, and after running a short course of about six miles in a south-easterly direction, it terminates in the Old River at Outwell, at the commencement of Well Creek, which connects it with the River Ouse at Salter's Load Sluice.

The act of parliament authorizing this canal, is entitled, ' *An* ' *Act for making and maintaining a navigable Canal from Wisbech* ' *River, at or near a Place called the Old Sluice, in the town of* ' *Wisbech, in the Isle of Ely, and county of Cambridge, to join the* ' *River Nene, in the parish of Outwell, in the said Isle of Ely, and* ' *in the county of Norfolk, and for improving and maintaining the* ' *Navigation of the said River from Outwell Church to Salter's* ' *Load Sluice.*' It incorporates the subscribers by the name of " The Wisbech Canal Company ;" empowers them to raise amongst themselves, for the purposes of the act, the sum of £14,000, in shares of £105 each, and, if necessary, a further sum of £6,000, and to take the following

TONNAGE RATES.

	s.	d.
For every Chaldron of Coal, Lime, Hundred of Battens, Half Hundred of Single Deals, Quarter of Hundred of Double Deals, Load of Fir Timber, Four Packs of Wool, Five Quarters of Oats, Load of Turf, Reed, Sedge, Hay, Flax or Hemp, Five Hundred Pantiles, One Thousand Flat Tiles, Five Hundred Bricks, Twenty Cubic Feet of Stone, Pipe, Butt, Puncheon or Tierce of Wine or Spirituous Liquors, Six Sacks of Flour, Five Barrels of Ale, Beer and Porter	1	0
For every Five Quarters of Wheat, Barley, Mustard-seed, Hemp-seed, Rape-seed, Line-seed, Rye, Peas or Beans......................	1	6
For all other Goods...	1	0 per Ton.

Materials for the Bedford Level or for Roads, to be exempted from Rates.

Goods lying on a Wharf more than Twenty-four Hours, to pay such Rate as may be agreed on.

For Cranage of every Ton of Goods (except Coal) Sixpence.

All Goods passing into or out of this Canal to the Nene River to pay Three-pence per Ton; out of the Produce of which the Commissioners of the Nene Navigation are to have One Hundred Pounds per Annum, and the remainder is to be applied in the Repair and Improvement of Well Creek.

This canal is very little higher than the sea, being embanked through the level fens; there are flood locks at its extremities. It forms a ready connection between the Nene and the Ouse, by which the intercourse between the counties of Lincoln, Cambridge, Norfolk and Suffolk, is rendered more complete and easy.

WISHAW AND COLTNESS RAILWAY.

10 George IV. Cap. 107, Royal Assent 1st June, 1829.

THE Wishaw and Coltness Railway is designed to pass from the collieries of Chapel and Crawfoot, in the parish of Cambusnethan, in the county of Lanark, through Dalziel, Hamilton, Bothwell, Coltness, Overtown, Wishawtown, Motherwell, Burnhouse and Carnbroe, to join the Monkland and Kirkintilloch Railway at Old Monkland; with a branch to Rosehall; a second to the collieries of Stevenson, Carfin and Cleland; and a third from these last places to Law, in the parish of Carluke, in the same county of Lanark.

The act for this work was obtained in 1829, under the designation of ' *An Act for making a Railway from Chapel, in the* ' *parish of Cambusnethan, in the county of Lanark, by Coltness* ' *and Gariongill, to join the Monkland and Kirkintilloch Railway,* ' *where the same passes through the Lands of Coats or Garturk, in* ' *the parish of Old Monkland and county of Lanark.'*

By this act the proprietors are incorporated as " The Wishaw " and Coltness Railway Company," with the usual powers for constructing the same, and for raising £60,000 for the purposes thereof, in shares of £50 each; and in case the said sum shall be found insufficient for the completion of the works, then they are empowered to borrow, on mortgage of the property and rates, a further sum of £20,000. For defraying contingent expenses and paying back the capital subscribed, they are empowered to demand the following

TONNAGE RATES.

	s.	d.	
For all Lime-stone, Dung, Compost, Manure and Materials for Roads	0	2	per Ton, per Mile.
For all Coke, Coal, Kennel or Gas Coal, Culm, Charcoal, Cinders, Stone, Sand, Bricks, Slates, Lime, Earth, Iron, Lead and other Metals or Minerals Unmanufactured ..	0	3	ditto. ditto.
For all Timber, Corn, Flour, Goods, Lead in Sheets and all other Wares, Merchandize, Matters or Things	0	4	ditto. ditto.
For the use of any Waggon, Machinery, Engine or Power belonging the Company, and for all Articles, to pay a Tonnage as hereinafter expressed, passing the Inclined Planes on this Railway, in addition to the Rates	1	0	ditto.

Fractions of a Ton to pay for the Hundred Weights therein, and of a Hundred Weight as a Hundred Weight; of a Mile as the Quarters therein, and of a Quarter as a Quarter.

Proportional Charges are also to be made on Coals, Goods or other Articles, according to the Distances conveyed on the Railway.

The company may provide carriages for the conveyance of passengers, and charge for each person so conveyed a rate of 4*d*. per mile; or they may license carriages for the same purpose, subject to the payment of an annual rent to be agreed upon between the company and the owners thereof. Locomotive engines may be used on the railway, and steam engines may be erected for the inclined planes.

Owners of land may erect wharfs, warehouses and cranes on the line, and if they refuse the company may do so, charging for the use thereof the following

RATES.

		d.	
For all Coal, Culm, Lime, Lime-stone, Clay, Iron-stone, Stone, Bricks, Gravel, Hay, Straw, Corn in the Straw or Manure, for Six Months	}	½	per Ton.
For every Month after		¼	ditto.
For all Iron, Lead or other Ore, Tin, Timber, Tiles and Slates, for Six Months	}	1	ditto.
For every Month after		½	ditto.
For all other Goods, Wares, &c. for Six Months		2	ditto.
For every Month after		1	ditto.

If the work is not finished in five years, then the powers of this act are to cease.

WITHAM RIVER.

22 & 23 Char. II. C. 25, R. A. 22nd April, 1671.   2 Geo. III. C. 32, R. A. 2nd June, 1762.
48 Geo. III. C. 108, R. A. 18th June, 1808.   52 Geo. III. C. 108, R. A 20th May, 1812.
7 Geo. IV. C. 2, R. A. 22nd Mar. 1826.   10 Geo. IV. C. 123, R. A. 4th June, 1829.

THIS river has its source on the confines of Rutlandshire, whence it runs northwardly by Grantham to the city of Lincoln, where, at its junction with the Fossdike Navigation, it becomes navigable. Hence its course is south-easterly by the town of Tattershall, where the Horncastle Navigation effects a junction with it; and three miles further south it is joined by the Sleaford Canal; it then passes through the fens by the town of Boston, five miles below which place it empties itself into The Wash. The length of navigation is about thirty-eight miles, viz. from the city of Lincoln to the Horncastle Navigation, nineteen miles; thence to the Sleaford Canal, three miles; thence to Boston eleven miles; and to the sea a further distance of five miles.

Although the first act of parliament relating to this navigation was passed in the 22nd and 23rd Charles II. A. D. 1671, yet we learn from the preamble that this river had long been used as a navigation. The preamble runs thus—" Whereas there hath been for " some hundred of yeares a good navigacion betwixt the burrough " of Boston and the river of Trent by and through the citty of " Lincolne, and thereby a great trade mannaged to the benefitt " of those parts of Lincolneshire, and some parts of Nottingham- " shire, and Yorkshire, which afforded an honest employment and " livelyhood to great numbers of people. But at present the said " navigacion is much obstructed and in great decay by reason " that the rivers or auntient channells of Witham and Fosdyke, " which runn betwixt Boston and Trent are much silted and landed " up and thereby not passable with boats and lyters as formerly, " to the great decay of the trade and intercourse of the said citty " and all market and other towns neare any of the said rivers, " which hath producet in them much poverty and depopulation. " For remedy whereof and for improvement of the said naviga- " cion, may it please your most excellent Majestie that it may " bee enacted, &c."

It has been thought that the Witham, previous to the Norman Conquest, was a tideway navigation for ships to Lincoln; and that it was navigable at a very early period, may be inferred from the circumstance that the Fossdike Canal, ' an ancient Roman Work,' was scoured out by Henry I. in the year 1121, for the purpose of opening a navigable communication between the Trent and the Witham at the city of Lincoln, so that that place, which was then in a very flourishing state and enjoying an extensive Foreign trade, might reap all the advantages of a more ready communication with the interior.

The precise period at which the channel of the Witham ceased to be useful for navigation purposes is uncertain; but we learn that in the 9th of Edward III. a commission issued, directed to Adam de Lymberg, Geffery de Edenham, and others, to enquire into the state of the navigation, &c. who effected some improvements. In the 39th of the same reign, parliament was petitioned by the merchants and tradesmen of Lincoln, complaining of the total insufficiency of the navigation. Up to the 49th of

Edward III. the navigation appears to have been supported by a
drainage rate; but in Michaelmas Term of this year, a present-
ment to the Court of King's Bench, having for its object the im-
posing of this burthen for ever on the owners of the adjacent lands,
was unsuccessful, and it was then abandoned.   Other commissions
have, from time to time, been issued for improving the river;
one in the 8th of Richard II. directed to John Duke of Lancaster,
and others of the nobility; but it does not appear that much was
done betwixt this period and the passing of the act of 23rd Charles
II. entitled, ' *An Act for improveing the Navigacion betweene the*
' *towne of Boston and the River Trent;*' and by which act, the
necessary powers were granted to the Mayor and Corporation of
Lincoln, who were authorized, for this purpose, to receive certain
tolls upon the Witham and Fossdike, but restrained from laying
out monies derived from the navigation of the Fossdike on the
improvement of the Witham, and *vice versa.*   Notwithstanding
this act, the corporation confined their operations to the restoring
of the Fossdike only.

The act of the 2nd George III. is entitled, ' *An Act for drain-*
' *ing and preserving certain Low Lands called The Fens, lying on*
' *both sides of the River Witham, in the county of Lincoln; and*
' *for restoring and maintaining the Navigation of the said River,*
' *from the High Bridge, in the city of Lincoln, through the borough*
' *of Boston, to the Sea;*' in the preamble of which act it is stated,
that by the sand and silt brought in by the tide, the outfal to the
sea had for many years last past been greatly obstructed, and that
the navigation had in consequence been lost, or nearly so.   The
act appointed commissioners for the purpose of carrying its provisions into execution; and for defraying the necessary expenses
of the navigation, they were empowered to collect, for every
description of goods, wares, merchandize, or other commodities,
passing up or down the river, the sum of 1*s.* 6*d.* per ton.

In 1808 another act was obtained, entitled, ' *An Act for ren-*
' *dering more effectual an Act of his present Majesty, for draining*
' *certain Low Lands lying on both sides of the River Witham, in*
' *the county of Lincoln; and for restoring the Navigation of the*
' *said River, from the High Bridge, in the city of Lincoln, to the*
' *Sea,*' by which the commissioners are authorized to build a lock

in the parish of Washingborough, 80 feet long and 16 feet 6 inches in width, and to remove the locks at Barlings Kirkstead and Stamp End, and to do other works, with the double object of improving the navigation and effecting a better drainage for the extensive fens which border on the Witham. The former tonnage being repealed by this act, the following were granted.

TONNAGE RATES.

	s.	d.
For all Goods, Wares, Merchandize or Commodities, carried or conveyed from any Place within One Mile of Lincoln High Bridge, to within the like Distance of the Grand Sluice near to Boston, or from any Place within One Mile of the said Grand Sluice to within the like Distance of Lincoln High Bridge	3	0 per Ton.
For any Distance upon the said Navigation, not exceeding Twelve Miles, as and for a Gross Tonnage thereon......	.1	6 ditto.
For all Goods, Wares, Merchandize or Commodities carried or conveyed any greater Distance than Twelve Miles upon the said Navigation, and not being subject to the payment of Three Shillings per Ton	0	1½ ditto, per Mile.

Fractions as for a Quarter of a Ton and Quarter of a Mile.

All Goods, Wares, Merchandize and Commodities on which a Toll or Duty shall become due or payable under the Authority of this Act shall, for the Purpose of ascertaining such Toll or Duty, be estimated and taken to be of the several Weights following, and be paid for accordingly.

QUALITY.	QUANTITY.	WT. T. C.	QUALITY.	QUANTITY.	WT. T. C.
Coals	One Chaldron..	1 3	Five Feet and Half Posts	Ninety........	1 0
Coke	100 Strike	1 0	Single Deals........	Half Hundred..	1 0
Oats, Malt or Bark..	10 Quarters....	1 0	Double Deals	Quarter Hund.	1 0
Barley and Rape....	7 Quarters	1 0	Battens	100............	1 0
Wheat, Beans & Peas	5 Quarters	1 0	Thatch Reed	500 Bunches ..	1 0
Whole Lime........	1½ Chaldron ..	1 0	Groceries	2 Hogsheads ..	1 0
Slacked Lime	2 Chaldrons ...	1 0	Woad..............	1 ditto	¾ 0
Potatoes	130 Pecks	1 0	Spetches	8 Packs........	1 0
Timber, Oak, Ash or Elm	40 Feet........	1 0	Squares at Nine Inches	250............	1 0
Fir Timber	50 Feet........	1 0	Sheep	20	1 0
Bricks..............	500............	1 0	Porter	6 Barrels......	1 0
Flat Tiles	1,000	1 0	Flour	8 Sacks........	1 0
Pan Tiles	500............	1 0	Seeds	10 Quarters....	1 0
Oil Cakes	6 Pounds and a Half a Pair 1,000	1 0	Glass	12 whole Crates	1 0
			Hemp Seed	40 Strike	1 0
Other ditto in Proportion.			Posts 4½ Feet	120............	1 0
			Pavement Bricks ...	300............	1 0
Wine	2 Pipes........	1 0	Stone	16 Cubic Feet.	1 0
Felloes	120............	1 0	Paving Stone	10 Super. Yards	1 0
Seven Feet Posts....	60	1 0	Pots..............	6 Crates	1 0

All other Goods, Wares, Merchandize and Commodities, to be estimated and paid for after the Rate of Two Thousand Two Hundred and Forty Pounds per Ton.

No Toll or Duty shall be paid, taken, or demanded, for any Goods, Wares, Merchandize or Commodities, carried or conveyed from Brayford Meer through the High Bridge in the City of Lincoln, and which shall not pass upon or through any Part of the said River Witham lying Eastward of the Place where the Old Stamp End Lock formerly stood, nor for any Goods, Wares, Merchandize or Commodities, carried or conveyed through or upon any part of the said River Witham above the said Place where the said Old Stamp End Lock formerly stood, through the High Bridge into Brayford Meer, nor shall any greater Toll or Duty be due or payable on the said Navigation upon Goods, Wares, Merchandize or Commodities imported from the Baltic immediately into the Port of Boston, and which shall pass from thence into the said River Witham, nor for any Flint, Stone, Pig-iron or Lime-stone, carried or conveyed on the said River Witham than the Proportion of Two-thirds of the Toll due and payable under the Authority of this Act.

For the purposes of this act, the commissioners are authorized to borrow, on security of the rates and tolls, the sum of £30,000 for drainage purposes; and a further sum of £70,000 on the credit of the navigation tolls.

In 1812 another act was obtained, entitled, ' *An Act for ren-* ' *dering more effectual an Act of his present Majesty, for draining* ' *certain Low Lands lying on both sides of the River Witham, in* ' *the county of Lincoln; and for restoring the Navigation of the* ' *said River; and for repealing another Act of his present Majesty* ' *in relation to the said Drainage and Navigation.*'

By which act the proprietors are incorporated as " The Company of Proprietors of the Witham Navigation," with powers to deepen, widen and embank the old course of the said river, from the Grand Sluice, in the borough of Boston, to a certain lock to be erected in a certain new cut to be made near Hasley Deeps, and to make a cut from the said Hasley Deeps, through Branston to The Woadhouses in Fiskerton, and from thence to the High Bridge in the city of Lincoln; the company are also authorized to build a new lock in the said new cut, and a weir in the east bank of the river at Bargate Drain, in the parish of St. Botolph, Lincoln; with various other works near the said place: for completing the purposes of the act, they are to raise £120,000, in shares of £100; and in case of deficiency, a further sum of £60,000, by creating new shares or by mortgage; they have also an acre-tax amounting to £1,400 per annum, granted on the lands, adjoining the Witham, becoming payable on the passing of the act; together with another acre-tax of the same amount, payable in proportion to the distance from time to time completed; they are also empowered to receive the following rates.

TONNAGE AND OTHER RATES.

                                                                              *. d.

For all Goods, Wares, Merchandize or Commodities, carried or con-
    veyed from any Place within One Mile of Lincoln High Bridge,
    to within the like Distance of the Grand Sluice near to Boston, or ⎬ 3 0 per Ton.
    from any Place within One Mile of the said Grand Sluice, to within
    the like Distance of Lincoln High Bridge ....

And for any Distance upon the said Navigation, not exceeding ⎬ 1 6 ditto.
    Twelve Miles..

For any Goods carried or conveyed any greater Distance than Twelve Miles upon the
    said Navigation, and not being subject to the payment of the said Gross Tonnage
    of Three Shillings per Ton, nor to the payment of any Toll or Duty upon either
    of the said Navigations from the River Witham to Horncastle and Sleaford, One
    Penny Half-penny per Ton per Mile; provided the aggregate Toll or Duty, after
    the Rate aforesaid, shall not exceed the said Gross Tonnage of Three Shillings per
    Ton.

Goods, Wares or Merchandize liable to pay Toll on the Horncastle and Sleaford
    Canals, are subject to a Toll of Nine-pence per Ton if carried upon any Part of the
    Witham Navigation; and an additional Toll of One-half the Amount of Toll pay-
    able for navigating the River.

The next act obtained, was passed in 1826, under title of
' *An Act for enabling the Company of Proprietors of the Witham*
' *Navigation to complete the Drainage and Navigation by the River*
' *Witham, and to raise a further Sum of Money for that Purpose.*'

By this act the proprietors are empowered to raise an additional sum of £60,000 for the completion of the works, in shares
of £100 each, or by mortgage of the tolls and rates. Debentures,
bearing interest at £5 per cent. are also to be given to the proprietors of old shares, as security for the payment of arrears due
to them. Several other clauses, chiefly reserving the rights of
various persons and public bodies, as in former acts, are inserted
in this, but are not necessary to be quoted here.

The last act relating to this useful navigation received the
royal assent on the 4th June, 1829, and is entitled, ' *An Act to*
' *authorize the raising a further Sum of Money for completing the*
' *Drainage and Navigation by the River Witham, and for amending*
' *the Acts relating thereto ;*' which, after reciting the works which
the act of 52nd George III. empowered them to do, and what
had been already executed, it states that the company of proprietors had, under authority of that act, contributed amongst themselves, in shares of £100 each, the sum of £156,800, and had
raised by mortgage of the tolls and duties the further sum of
£23,200, and which sums had been expended; and that by the
act of 7th George IV. the proprietors had raised amongst themselves, in shares of £100 each, the sum of £52,100, and by mort-

2 x

gage £7,900, which sums have been also expended in carrying into execution the works authorized by the 52nd George III. but the navigation was yet imperfect; the proprietors were by the last recited act, authorized to raise a further sum of £50,000 on mortgage of the navigation, and a further sum of £20,000, if necessary.

The chief advantages derived from this navigation, are the facilities it affords of communicating with the rich agricultural district of the interior of the county of Lincoln, further augmented by the manner in which the Sleaford and Horncastle Navigation diverges from it. By the local position of this river and its connexion with the Trent, and the numerous canals which emanate from it by means of the Fossdike, an inland communication is established with all parts of the kingdom, and, of consequence, an additional degree of importance will necessarily attach to it.

WORCESTER AND BIRMINGHAM CANAL.

31 Geo. III. C. 59, R. A. 10th June, 1791.   38 Geo. III. C. 31, R. A. 26th May, 1798.
44 Geo. III. C. 35, R. A. 23rd Mar. 1804.   48 Geo. III. C. 49, R. A. 27th May, 1808.
55 Geo. III. C. 66, R. A. 7th June, 1815.

THIS canal commences at the junction of the Birmingham and Birmingham and Fazeley Canals, at Farmer's Bridge, at the upper end of the town of Birmingham, and thence runs in a south-westerly direction to its junction with the Dudley Canal, at Selly Oak; thence it takes a south-easterly course to King's Norton, where the Stratford-upon-Avon Canal unites with it; and thence by a course nearly south-west the whole distance, and passing by West Heath, Oswald, Alvechurch, Tardebig, Stoke Prior, Hewell Park, Hadzor, Hanbury Park, Oddingley and Iplip Hall, and a short distance to the eastward of the towns of Droitwich and Bromsgrove, it joins the River Severn at Diglis, a little below Worcester.

It was made under the sanction of an act of parliament passed in 1791, and entitled, ' *An Act for making and maintaining a* ' *navigable Canal from, or from near to, the town of Birmingham,* ' *in the county of Warwick, to communicate with the River Severn,* ' *near to the city of Worcester,*' which incorporates a number of persons therein named, who were subscribers to the undertaking, by the name of " The Company of Proprietors of the Worcester " and Birmingham Canal Navigation," and empowers them to raise amongst themselves, for the execution of the work, the sum of £180,000, in eighteen hundred shares of £100 each, and if that should be insufficient, a further sum of £70,000, either amongst themselves or by mortgage of the tolls and rates, and authorizes them to take the following

TONNAGE RATES.

	s.	d.	
For all Coal, Iron, Iron-stone, Stone, Timber and other Goods and Things (except Lime and Lime-stone) carried on any Part of the Canal	2	6	per Ton.
For the same Goods if carried any Distance less than Ten Miles from the Head of the Canal	0	3	ditto, per Mile.
For all Lime and Lime-stone on any Part of the Canal	0	10	ditto.
Except it be carried the First Ten Miles from the Head of the Canal	0	1	ditto. ditto.
For all Coal, Iron, Iron-stone, Stone, Timber and all other Goods and Things whatever, carried into or out of the River Severn, into or out of the Basin near Worcester	0	1	ditto.

For Goods remaining longer than Twenty-four Hours on Wharfs, such Rates as the Parties may agree upon; and in case of Dispute, the Commissioners named under the Act to decide.

EXEMPTIONS.

Materials for Roads and Manure for Grounds of Persons whose Land has been taken for the Canal, provided they do not pass any Lock except when the Water flows over the Waste Weir.

No Barge or other Vessel under Thirty-five Tons to pass through any Lock without Leave of the Company or their Agent.

Lords of manors and owners of land on the line may erect wharfs and warehouses, and on their refusing to do so when required, the company may erect them.

The act restricts the company from making the canal nearer than 7 feet to the Birmingham and Birmingham and Fazeley Canals, without leave of the proprietors of those canals; and it also provides that the company shall, as compensation to the Droitwich Canal Company, in case they should sustain any diminution of profits from this work, make up the profits of that company to £5 per cent. on each share; the shares to be considered as of the value of £160, at which price the Worcester and Birmingham Canal Company are to purchase them, when thereto required by any of the proprietors. They are also to make up the dividends of the Stourbridge Canal Company £9 per share; and to make compensation to the Dudley Canal if their profits are decreased. This last clause was repealed by the act of parliament for extending the Dudley Canal to this navigation. The company is also to pay £40 per annum to the Corporation of Worcester, in lieu of the water-bailiff's tolls.

By the Stratford-upon-Avon and Dudley Extension Acts, the proprietors of this canal are allowed the following

TONNAGE RATES.

	s.	d.	
For all Goods and other Things (except Coal and Coke) passing from Birmingham on any Part of this Canal, and along the Stratford Canal and the Cut, into the Warwick Canal	0	1½	per Ton, per Mile.
For all Goods and other Things (except Lime and Lime-stone) passing out of the Stratford Canal, and from the Junction towards Worcester, upon the First Ten Miles from the Head of the Canal at Birmingham	0	3	ditto. ditto.
For all Lime and Lime-stone passing out of the Stratford Canal, and from the Junction towards Worcester, upon the first Ten Miles from the Head of the Canal at Birmingham	0	1	ditto. ditto.
For all Goods and other Things (except Lime and Lime-stone) passing out of the Stratford Canal, and from the Junction towards Worcester, upon any Part of the Canal, except the First Ten Miles from the Head of the Canal at Birmingham	2	6	ditto.
For all Lime and Lime-stone passing out of the Stratford Canal, and from the Junction towards Worcester, upon any Part of the Canal, except the first Ten Miles from the Head at Birmingham	0	10	ditto.
For all Goods and other Things (except Lime and Lime-stone) passing from Birmingham to the Junction with the Stratford Canal, and from thence along the Stratford Canal towards Stratford, and from the Stratford Canal towards Birmingham	0	1½	ditto. ditto.
For all Lime and Lime-stone passing as above	0	½	ditto. ditto.
For all Coal and Coke upon any Part of the Worcester and Birmingham Canal, and along the Stratford Canal and Junction into the Warwick Canal	0	5½	ditto.
For all Coals, Goods, Merchandize and other Things, which shall pass from the Dudley Extension Canal, and along the Worcester and Birmingham to or towards Birmingham	0	2	ditto.
For all Coals, Goods, Merchandize and other Things, which shall pass from the Dudley Extension and along the Worcester and Birmingham Canal, to the Junction of the Stratford-upon-Avon Canal, and along the same to or towards the Town of Stratford only, the same Tonnage as though the same had passed from the Head of the Canal at Birmingham, reckoning as from Birmingham	0	1½	ditto. ditto.

For all Goods (except Coal and Coke) passing from the Dudley Extension, along the Worcester and Birmingham Canal towards Worcester, and not passing into the Stratford-upon-Avon Canal, the same Tonnage per Mile, according to the Distance the same passes on the Worcester and Birmingham Canal, as is payable for such Goods passing from the Town of Birmingham, and upon the same Part only of the said Canal.

Some of the rates allowed by the above acts are also mentioned in the Stratford-upon-Avon and Dudley Canal Articles; but as there are some omissions, the whole have been repeated here.

The next act of parliament relating to this navigation was passed in 1798, and is entitled, ' *An Act for amending and* ' *enlarging the Powers of an Act passed in the Thirty-first Year of* ' *the Reign of his present Majesty,*' and it empowers the company to raise the additional sum of £149,929, 1s. 1½d. either amongst themselves, by the creation of new shares, in number twelve hundred and fifty-nine, to be called half shares, and to be of the value of £69, 8s. 10½d. each, by granting annuities or by mortgage of the tolls and rates, and to take the following additional

TONNAGE RATES.

	s.	d.
For all Coals, Iron, Iron-stone, Stone, Timber and other Goods and Things (except Lime and Lime-stone) upon any Part of the Canal, (except the first Fourteen Miles from Birmingham) the additional Sum of Three-pence per Ton per Mile, not exceeding in the whole..............................	1	0
For all Lime and Lime-stone upon any Part of the Canal, (except as above) the additional Sum of One Penny per Ton per Mile, not exceeding in the whole	0	4

And the additional Sum of One Penny per Ton to be taken on Goods and other Things carried to and from the River Severn, into or out of the Basin intended to be made in or near the City of Worcester, and not passing on any other Part of the said Canal; but nothing in this Act to affect the Rates granted to this Company by the Dudley and Stratford Canal Acts, except such Goods and Merchandize as shall pass from the Dudley Canal, and not pass from out of the Stratford Canal.

This was followed by an act which the company obtained in 1804, entitled, ' *An Act for enabling the Company of Proprietors* ' *of the Worcester and Birmingham Canal Navigation to raise* ' *Money to discharge their Debts, and to complete the said Canal* ' *Navigation; and for amending the several Acts passed for making* ' *the said Canal Navigation,*' which states that the company had not been able to raise the money authorized by the last act of parliament, and empowers them to raise the sum of £49,680 amongst themselves, by a contribution of £27, 12s. on each share.

In 1808 another act was obtained, entitled, ' *An Act to amend* ' *and enlarge the Powers of the several Acts relating to the Wor-* ' *cester and Birmingham Canal Navigation,*' which empowers the company to raise the further sum of £168,000, by the creation of four thousand two hundred new shares of £40 each, or by granting annuities or mortgage of the tolls and rates; and, if necessary, an additional sum of £40,000, by the creation of one thousand new shares of £40 each; and it repeals that part of the act of 1798 authorizing money to be raised by the creation of half shares.

The last act of parliament respecting this canal was passed in 1815, and is entitled, '*An Act for enabling the Company of Pro-*
'*prietors of the Worcester and Birmingham Canal Navigation to*
'*complete and extend their Works, and for better supplying the*
'*said Canal with Water; and also for vesting in Trustees for the*
'*said Company of Proprietors, his Majesty's Rights and Interest*
'*in certain Lands and Hereditaments in the parishes of King's*
'*Norton and Northfield, in the county of Worcester, forfeited to*
'*the Crown.*'

After several clauses prescribing the mode of making reservoirs, &c. the act states that the company having purchased some lands for reservoirs, which they were not empowered by the acts of parliament to do, they had become forfeited to the Crown, but that his Majesty had remitted the forfeiture, and the act authorizes the company to re-sell such lands, provided, however, that if the debt of £27,096, 10s. 4d. due from the company to their late treasurers, be not paid on or before the 29th day of September next after the passing of this act, the lands above-mentioned to be sold, and the above debt to be discharged from the proceeds.

The intention of making a basin at Lowesmore being abandoned, and one in lieu thereof being made at Diglis, that part, of the former act which authorizes a tonnage rate of two-pence per ton on all barges or other vessels passing from the Severn into any basin belonging to the company, is repealed, but they are allowed to take the following additional

TONNAGE RATES.

	d.
For all Coal, Iron, Iron-stone, Stone, Timber or other Goods or Things which shall be conveyed on this Canal from the River Severn to any Part of the Canal between Sidbury Bridge and Lowesmore Bridge, or from those Points to the Severn, and not passing any other Part of the Canal	6 per Ton.
For ditto from the Severn to the Basin to be made at Diglis, or any Part of the Canal between the Severn and Sidbury Bridge	4 ditto.

The act also empowers the company to raise a further sum of £90,000, either amongst themselves, by the creation of two thousand two hundred and fifty additional shares of £40 each, or by granting annuities or mortgage of the tolls and rates.

The length of this canal is twenty-nine miles; its breadth at top 42 feet and depth of water 6 feet; and it passes through five tunnels in its course. That at West Heath is two thousand seven hundred yards long, 18 feet high and 18½ feet wide within the arch, and the depth of water therein is 7½ feet; at Tardebig is another of five hundred yards in length; that at Shortwood is four hundred yards long; at Oddingley is one of a hundred and twenty yards; and at Edgbaston one a hundred and ten yards in length.

From the Birmingham Canal, the first fourteen miles is level; and in the remaining fifteen miles there is a fall of 428 feet by seventy-one locks, which are 15 feet wide and 81 feet long each, to the River Severn.

Where the summit pound of this canal connects with the Birmingham and the Dudley and Stratford Canals, stop-locks are erected, which the several companies may shut and lock up when the supplies of this or the other canals fail.

The Worcester and Birmingham Canal is the direct communication between the River Severn and the town of Birmingham, and by that means forms a connection with the Rivers Trent and Mersey, and all the great trading towns in the north of England; and by its junction with the Stratford-upon-Avon Canal, it communicates with all the principal towns in the eastern part of the kingdom; it is also the channel for supplying Worcester and the borders of the Severn down to Tewkesbury and Gloucester, with coal; and in return, conveys the hops and cider of that part of the country northward, and more particularly affords a ready means for the export of the Birmingham Manufactures, through the port of Bristol, to any part of the world.

WORSLEY BROOK.

(SEE BRIDGEWATER'S CANAL.)

WREAK AND EYE RIVERS OR LEICESTER AND MELTON MOWBRAY NAVIGATION.

31 George III. Cap. 77, Royal Assent 6th June, 1791.
40 George III. Cap. 55, Royal Assent 20th June, 1800.

THE first act for rendering navigable the Rivers Wreak and Eye, was obtained with a view to complete the communication between Leicester and Melton Mowbray, into the navigation from which former place the present work opens in Turnwater Meadow. This act bears date in 1791, and is entitled, '*An Act for making 'navigable the Rivers Wreak and Eye, from the Junction of the 'said River Wreak with the Leicester Navigation at Turnwater 'Meadow, to Mill Close Homestead, in the parish of Melton Mow- 'bray, in the county of Leicester.*' By it the proprietors are incorporated, with the usual powers for making and maintaining the navigation, and for cutting new channels, &c. where required. For defraying expenses, they are empowered to raise £25,000 in shares of £100 each; and should this prove insufficient, they may raise a further sum of £5,000 by the creation of new shares or on mortgage of the rates, which are directed to be as under:

TONNAGE RATES.

	s.	d.		
For all Coal navigated from the Leicester Navigation to Eye Kettleby, Sysonby or Melton	2	6	per Ton.	
For ditto any shorter Distance	0	2¼	ditto,	per Mile.
For all Iron, Timber, &c. navigated to ditto	4	0	ditto.	
For ditto any shorter Distance	0	4	ditto.	ditto.

Dung, Materials for Roads, Lime and other Kinds of Manure are exempted from Rates and Tolls, under the same restrictions as the Leicester Navigation Act requires.

The company having proceeded in the execution of their plan, had occasion again to apply to parliament for authority to collect additional funds, and in consequence obtained a second act in 1800, under the title of '*An Act for enabling the Company 'of Proprietors of the Navigation, from Leicester to Melton 'Mowbray, in the county of Leicester, to complete their Naviga- 'tion, and to discharge the Debts contracted by them in the making 'thereof, and for amending the Act passed in the Thirty-first Year 'of the Reign of his present Majesty, for making and maintaining 'the said Navigation.*'

By this act it is recited, that in the progress of their undertaking, the commissioners have not only expended the two several sums of £25,000 and £5,000 which they were empowered to borrow, but also the whole of their receipts for tolls and duties since the opening of the said navigation, amounting to £7,000, and have contracted debts to the sum of £4,000, some part of their works still being incomplete; they are, therefore, empowered to raise the sum of £10,000 in shares or by mortgage of the rates, and to take the following tonnage rates.

TONNAGE RATES.

	s.	d.	
For all Coal navigated from the Leicester Navigation to Eye Kettleby, Sysonby or Melton Mowbray, and not so far as the Fifth Lock on the Oakham Canal	1	0	per Ton.
For all Coal navigated from the Leicester Navigation to the said Fifth Lock on the Oakham Canal	0	6	ditto.
For ditto navigated upon any Part of the said Navigation, and not navigated so far as Eye Kettleby, Sysonby or Melton Mowbray	0	1	ditto, per Mile.
For all Iron, Timber and other Goods, Wares and Merchandize (except as hereinafter is excepted) navigated from the Leicester Navigation to Eye Kettleby, Sysonby or Melton Mowbray and not carried so far as the said Fifth Lock on the Oakham Canal	1	6	ditto.
For ditto (except as hereinafter excepted) navigated from the Oakham Canal, Melton Mowbray, Sysonby or Eye Kettleby, to the Leicester Navigation	1	6	ditto.
For ditto (except as hereinafter excepted) navigated more than Five Miles upon the said Navigation, and afterwards carried to the said Fifth Lock on the Oakham Canal...	0	9	ditto.
For ditto (except as hereinafter excepted) navigated upon any Part of the said Navigation, and not carried so far as from the Leicester Navigation to Eye Kettleby, Sysonby or Melton Mowbray, or not so far as from the Oakham Canal, Melton Mowbray, Sysonby or Eye Kettleby, to the Leicester Navigation	0	1½ ditto.	ditto.

For all Lime, Lime-stone and Stones to be used for Building, and Materials for paving and repairing Roads, Half of the Rates, Tolls and Duties hereinbefore authorized to be taken on Coals.

EXEMPTIONS.

No additional Tonnage Rates or Duties whatever shall be taken on any Goods, Wares or Merchandize, which shall pass from the Oakham Canal and shall be carried no further than the Public Basin at Melton Mowbray, nor on any Timber, Stone, Lime or other Material for the use of the Oakham Canal.

The length of this navigation, from its junction with the Leicester in Turnwater Meadow, to Melton, is eleven miles, in a north-west direction; the design of executing it is the same which induced the proprietors of the Leicester Navigation to undertake that work, and the benefits accruing to the various districts on the line of the work itself, and its communications, are of very considerable importance.

WYE AND LUGG RIVERS.

14 Char. II. C. 14, R. A. 19th May, 1662.   7 & 8 Wil. III. C. 14, R. A. 7th March, 1695.
13 Geo. I. C. 34, R. A. 15th May, 1727.   49 Geo. III. C. 78, R. A. 20th May, 1809.

THIS delightful river has, like the Severn, its source in the mountains of Plynlimmon, which are at an elevation of 2,463 feet above the level of the sea, and separate the counties of Cardigan and Montgomery. Its course is in a south-eastwardly direction, west of the town of Rhayader, in the county of Radnor, from whence it becomes the boundary between that county and Brecknockshire; it thence passes by Builth to the town of Hay, situate on the borders of Herefordshire, and where the Wye first becomes navigable. Its course hence lies northwardly to Whitney Bridge, where it is crossed by the Hay Railway. Hence its course is very circuitous by Moccas to the city of Hereford; thence to near Mordiford, where the River Lugg, which is navigable for a short distance, falls into it. Its course hence is southwardly by Fownhope, the town of Ross, and Welsh Bicknor, where it enters Monmouthshire; hence it takes a south-westerly course by Lidbrook to Monmouth, where it is considerably augmented by the waters of the Munnow, and half a mile further by the River Trothy. Its course from Monmouth is directly south, and forming the division between Gloucester and Monmouthshire; passing Chepstow and its romantic castle, to the estuary of the Severn, into which it enters three miles south of the last-mentioned town, and eight miles north of King's Road, at the mouth of the Avon.

The navigable part of this river from Hay to the Severn is ninety-nine miles and a half, viz, from Hay to Hereford, thirty miles; from Hereford to the mouth of the River Lugg, seven miles and a half; from thence to the town of Ross, twenty-one miles and a half; from thence to Lidbrook, eight miles; thence to Monmouth, twelve miles; and thence to the Severn, twenty miles and a half.

Four several acts of parliament have been obtained relating to this river, the first of which was passed in the 14th Charles II. entitled, ' *An Act for the making navigable the Rivers Wye and Lugg,* ' *and the Rivers and Brooks running into the same, in the counties* ' *of Hereford, Gloucester and Monmouth.*' The second act was obtained in the 7th and 8th years of King William III. and entitled, ' *An Act for making navigable the Rivers of Wye and Lugg, in the* ' *county of Hereford.*' And in the 13th of George I. another act for amending the last recited act was passed, which is entitled, '*An* ' *Act for explaining and amending an Act passed in the Seventh* ' *and Eighth Years of the Reign of his late Majesty King William*

' the Third, entitled, *An Act for making navigable the Rivers* ' *Wye and Lugg, in the county of Hereford, and for making the* ' *same more effectual.*' But as it appeared the powers vested in the trustees by these acts, were insufficient for carrying into execution the respective provisions, another act was applied for in 1809, and which received the royal assent on the 20th May, in that year; it is entitled, ' *An Act for amending several Acts for* ' *making navigable the Rivers Wye and Lugg, in the county of* ' *Hereford, and for making a Horse Towing-Path on certain Parts* ' *of the Banks of the said River Wye.*' By this act Sir George Cornewall and Sir John Geers Cotterell, Baronets, and thirty-one other gentlemen, together with the trustees appointed in pursuance of the above-recited acts, were incorporated by the name of " The " Company of Proprietors of the Rivers Wye and Lugg Naviga- " tion and Horse Towing-Path," with power to contribute amongst themselves the sum of £6,000, in one hundred and twenty shares of £50 each, and a further sum of £3,000 if necessary. The act authorizes the company to make a horse towing-path between Hereford and Lidbrook, a distance of thirty-seven miles, and on which part of the river only, they are entitled to the following tolls.

HORSE TOWING-PATH TOLLS.

	d.
For every Horse or other Beast passing on any Part of the Path, and drawing any Vessel navigating the River	6 per Mile.
For any less Distance than a Mile	6

Vessels haled by Men are free of Toll.

By reason of the Wye extending nearly one hundred miles into the interior of Wales, and through the rich agricultural districts of the county of Hereford, it is found exceedingly useful, from the facility it affords of shipping the extra produce to the more populous mineral districts of Glamorganshire, as well as Bristol and its neighbourhood. The navigation, however, of the lower part of this river is, during spring tides and when the wind blows fresh from the south-west, attended with no inconsiderable risk, as the tide, at its confluence with the Severn, sometimes reaches the extraordinary perpendicular elevation of 60 feet, which necessarily causes a tremendous and overpowering rush of water up the narrow channel of the Wye.

WYRLEY AND ESSINGTON CANAL.

32 George III. Cap. 81, Royal Assent 30th April, 1792.
34 George III. Cap. 25, Royal Assent 28th March, 1794.

THIS canal, under authority of the first act of parliament passed respecting it, commenced at Wyrley Bank, in the county of Stafford; and from thence, running at first in a southerly course over Essington Wood and Snead Common, and thence south-easterly by Bloxwich, it proceeded to near Birch Hill, in the parish of Walsall; near Snead Common a cut was made from it, which taking a westerly course, and passing by Wednesfield, joined the Birmingham Canal near Wolverhampton. By the act obtained in 1794 for extending this canal, another cut was made, which, commencing at Birch Hill, took a northerly direction as far as Pelsall Wood, and from thence passing in an easterly course by Brown Hills, Cats Hill, a little to the south of Lichfield, and by Treford, it connects with the Coventry Canal near Huddlesford; there are also two branches; one from near Cats Hill to Hay Head Lime Works, and the other from near Pelsall Wood to Lords Hay; besides a small branch to a colliery on the south side of Essington Wood.

The act of 1792 is entitled, ' *An Act for making and main-* ' *taining a navigable Canal from, or from near, Wyrley Bank, in* ' *the county of Stafford, to communicate with the Birmingham and* ' *Birmingham and Fazeley Canal, at or near the town of Wolver-* ' *hampton, in the said county; and also certain collateral Cuts* ' *therein described from the said intended Canal.*' It incorporates the subscribers to the undertaking by the name of " The Company " of Proprietors of the Wyrley and Essington Navigation," and empowers them to raise amongst themselves, for the purposes of the act, the sum of £25,000, in two hundred shares of £125 each, and, if necessary, a further sum of £20,000, either amongst themselves or by mortgage of the tolls and rates, and to take the following tonnage rates.

TONNAGE RATES.

			d.
For all Corn and other Grain, Hops, Timber and other Things, (except Coal, Coke, Iron, Iron-stone, Lime, Lime-stone, Rock-stone and other Minerals)	}	2 per Ton, per Mile.
For the above excepted Articles		9 ditto.

Boats of less than Twenty Tons passing any Lock to pay for Twenty Tons.

No Vessels to pass to or from this Canal into the Birmingham and Fazeley Canal, unless the Water in this Canal shall be at least Six Inches higher than that in the Birmingham and Fazeley, at the Junction of the Canals, and all surplus Water is to pass into the Birmingham Canal, the Proprietors of which may take the Water used in Lockage upon certain Parts of this Canal.

The proprietors of the Birmingham Canal may take, for all goods which are carried from this into their canal, the following

TONNAGE RATES.

		d.
For all Goods which shall be landed within One Mile of the First Lock leading towards Autherly	}	2 per Ton.
For ditto carried towards the Staffordshire and Worcestershire Canal, and which shall pass through any Lock	}	6 ditto.

The act passed in 1794, entitled, ' *An Act for extending the* ' *Wyrley and Essington Canal,*' empowers the company to raise amongst themselves, for the purpose of extending this canal as stated in the first part of this article, the sum of £75,000, and, if necessary, the further sum of £40,000, to be divided into shares of the same value as those in the first act, and authorizes their taking the following

TONNAGE RATES.

		s.	*d.*	
For all Coal, (except Slack or Coal used for burning Lime-stone or Bricks) Iron and other Minerals, and except such Coal as has passed on the Wyrley and Essington Canal, and has paid Nine-pence per Ton, and shall not pass through any Lock	}	0	9	per Ton.
For such of the above Goods as shall have paid Nine-pence upon the Wyrley and Essington Canal or upon this Canal, and shall afterwards pass through the Lock at Cats Hill	}	1	3	ditto.
For such of the above Goods as shall be produced from Ground situated below the Lock near Cats Hill, and shall be conveyed between Cats Hill and Huddlesford	}	2	0	ditto.
For all Slack or inferior Coal for burning Lime-stone and Brick, Lime-stone and Lime, not passing a Lock....	}	0	6	ditto.
For such as shall have passed on the Wyrley and Essington Canal, and shall pass a Lock	}	0	9	ditto.

The act directs that the company shall purchase the shares of such proprietors as shall not be satisfied with the extension.

Mr. W. Pitt was the engineer employed on this canal, which is twenty-four miles in length from the Coventry Canal to its junction with the Birmingham Canal. In the first eight miles of this distance to the reservoir at Cannock Heath is a rise of 270 feet, by thirty locks; and the remaining sixteen miles to the Birmingham Canal is level. In the first half mile of the Wyrley Branch, from its leaving the main line, is a rise of about 36 feet by six locks; and the remaining three miles is level. The branch to the Essington Colliery, which is about a mile in length, has a rise of about 24 feet by four locks. The branches—to Hay Head Lime Works, five miles and a half in length; to Lords Hay Coal Pits, two miles and a half; and to near Walsall, half a mile long, are all on the same level with the Long Pound.

This canal is of great service in conveying the produce of the mines which abound in its vicinity to the manufactories of Wolverhampton and its populous neighbourhood; and by its connection, through the Coventry Canal, with the Trent and Mersey Canal to the north and the Oxford Canal to the south, a communication is opened with the Rivers Trent and Mersey, and also with the River Thames.

INDEX.

INDEX.

RICHARD NICHOLS, TYPOGRAPHER, WAKEFIELD.

The material originally positioned here is too large for reproduction in this reissue. A PDF can be downloaded from the web address given on page iv of this book, by clicking on 'Resources Available'.

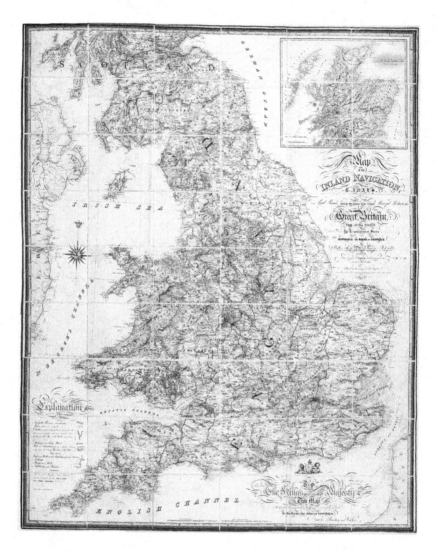

The material originally positioned here is too large for reproduction in this reissue. A PDF can be downloaded from the web address given on page iv of this book, by clicking on 'Resources Available'.

Printed in the United States
by P.J. Bookmasters

Printed in the United States
By Bookmasters